WINDOWS 98

IN A NUTSHELL

A Desktop Quick Reference

WINDOWS 98
IN A NUTSHELL

A Desktop Quick Reference

Tim O'Reilly, Troy Mott & Walter Glenn

O'REILLY®

Beijing • Cambridge • Farnham • Köln • Paris • Sebastopol • Taipei • Tokyo

Windows 98 in a Nutshell

by Tim O'Reilly, Troy Mott, and Walter Glenn

Published by O'Reilly & Associates, Inc., 101 Morris Street, Sebastopol, CA 95472.

Editor: Tim O'Reilly

Production Editor: Ellie Fountain Maden

Printing History:

August 1999:   First Edition.

ISBN: 1-56592-486-X

Table of Contents

Part II: Alphabetical Reference

Chapter 8—Hidden Gems on the Windows 98 CD-ROM ... *396*

Part III: Under the Hood

Part IV: Appendixes

Preface

It's easy to get started with Windows 98. The user interface is fairly intuitive, especially for today's more sophisticated user, who has been working with computers for years. But getting really proficient with the system is pretty hard, especially since Microsoft has apparently decided that the graphical interface and online help make good documentation redundant.

Windows 98 is a complex system. There are a lot of ways to do things. It's hard to remember the location of the specific user interface element you need to accomplish a particular task, and there are many features that are completely hidden if you rely on the graphical interface alone.

There are many books on Windows 98, but most of them suffer from a step-by-step tutorial organization that makes you wade through too many words to find what you need. That's where this book comes in. It provides a condensed but thorough reference to Windows 98, with an organization that helps you get right to the information you need.

We don't document every element of the graphical interface, but we tell you how to get to each important dialog box, and what you need to know about it that isn't obvious from the labels and instructions embedded in the interface. We do document hidden programs, and provide a wealth of useful tips. Think of this book as a cross between *Windows 98 for Non-Dummies*, *The Windows 98 Resource Kit*, and *Windows 98 Secrets*, boiled down to the essence, and you have the general idea. Despite the relatively small size of this book, we guarantee you that it contains more information about Windows 98 than any other book on the market.

Our focus is on user applications, though, not on system or network administration. While we give you a basic understanding of these deeper levels and what's available, specific installation details and detailed configuration information for system and network administrators are largely beyond the scope of the book. Especially with networked systems, there are also settings that are dependent on decisions made by your network administrator or Internet Service Provider. Whenever possible, we give you the information you need, but at times, all we can tell you is where to go for additional information.

We have tried to speak universal truths about Windows 98 itself, but sometimes we have inevitably fallen into describing Windows 98 as it happens to be installed on our particular machines. Microsoft gives so many configuration options that the truth is, for better or worse, that each user's machine represents a slightly different installation of Windows 98. Of all the code and data Microsoft ships on the Windows 98 CD-ROM, only about half is used in any particular user's configuration. So what we say about Windows 98 may or may not be quite true about Windows 98 as it's installed on your system.

Also, for all the statements (from Microsoft and others) that Windows 98 is "integrated" and "seamless," the fact is that the system is actually amazingly modular, customizable, and "seamy." This is a good thing, not a bad thing. This book shows a lot of different ways to modify Windows 98 to suit your needs; also check out the book *Windows 98 Annoyances*, by David Karp (O'Reilly & Associates). But this almost infinite customizability and modularity of Windows 98 also means that many of our statements about the product—such as, for example, that the Control Panel includes a Multimedia applet, or that the Desktop corresponds to the \ *Windows\Desktop* directory, or that Windows 98 even *has* a Desktop—are, strictly speaking, false, or at least serious oversimplifications.

Basically, Windows 98 is a platform and set of capabilities, not a single stable product with a fixed set of features. In this book, we give you the information you need to tap into all of Windows 98's capabilities, not just those that come configured out of the box.

Organization of the Book

This book is broken into four parts.

Part I, *The Lay of the Land*

This part of the book is designed to give you the big picture. It consists of three chapters:

Chapter 1, *Using Windows 98*, gives a brief review of the Windows 98 Graphical User Interface (GUI) and other elements of the system, aimed mainly at people who are new to Win 98.

Chapter 2, *What's New in Windows 98*, gives a quick summary of new features for people who are already familiar with Windows 95, and just want to know what's different. It also gives a summary of what's new in Windows 98 Second Edition.

Chapter 3, *Task Index*, helps you find things. One of the big problems with graphical user interfaces is remembering where some vital control can be found. Where was that dialog box you stumbled across last month that let you change the default window background? This chapter gives you shorthand instructions for how to do many common tasks in both the GUI and the command line.

Part II, *Alphabetical Reference*

This part of the book contains alphabetically organized reference pages for each major element of Windows 98. Once you're at a given point in the system, what can you do there?

For GUI-based applications, we don't document every menu, button, and dialog box—the GUI is often self-evident. Instead, we focus on non-obvious features, and provide helpful hints about power user features and things that will make your life easier.

For command-line–based programs, we cover every option, since these programs are not as obviously self-documenting (though many do support the conventional /? command-line option for help).

This part is divided into five chapters:

Chapter 4, *The Windows 98 User Interface*, provides a detailed reference page for each major element you'll see on the Win 98 Desktop. It describes elements of both Web View and Classic View interfaces.

Chapter 5, *The Control Panel*, provides a detailed reference page for every Control Panel dialog box.

Chapter 6, *Start Menu Programs and Other Graphical Applications*, covers all of the major GUI applications that are either installed with a typical installation or can easily be installed from the Add/Remove Programs Control Panel applet and launched from the Start Menu.

Chapter 7, *DOS and Other Command-Line Utilities*, covers all the command-line utilities in the Win 98 GUI. Some applications covered in Chapter 6 have command-line equivalents, and these are also documented in this chapter. All of these commands documented here can be run from the MS-DOS command line, the Run prompt, or the Address Toolbar.

Chapter 8, *Hidden Gems on the Windows 98 CD-ROM*, describes some of the major ways you can customize Windows 98, various add-ons that are hidden on the installation CD-ROM, upgrades available online via Windows Update, and other information that influences how Windows 98 will look and act.

Part III, *Under the Hood*

This section describes some of the underlying mechanisms in Windows 98. It is strongly suggested reading for anyone who really wants to understand how the system works. "Give a man a fish and he will eat for a day. Teach him how to fish, and he will eat for a lifetime."

Chapter 9, *Web Integration*, describes the new Win 98 features for integrating web content with the desktop and in folders.

Chapter 10, *The Windows Script Host*, describes Windows Script Host (WSH), the new framework that allows you to use various scripting languages to automate common tasks.

Chapter 11, *The Batch Language*, covers the commands used to create batch files —an older automation mechanism held over from DOS—that can still be used under Windows 98.

Chapter 12, *Windows Startup*, outlines the Windows 98 startup process and discusses the various points at which you might want to intervene. It also describes the format and contents of important system configuration files, and documents several commands that can be issued only from within these files.

Chapter 13, *The Registry*, describes the organization of the Registry, the central Windows 98 configuration database, and lists some of the most interesting entries it contains. It also describes how to use *regedit*, the Registry Editor.

Part IV, *Appendixes*

This section includes various handy quick reference lists.

Appendix A, *Keyboard Accelerators*, gives a list of keyboard accelerators (also known as hotkeys and keyboard shortcuts).

Appendix B, *Filename Extensions*, gives a list of standard filename extensions and associated programs.

Appendix C, *System File and Directory Organization*, gives an annotated listing of standard system files and directories. A more extensive description of some of the most important files and directories is given in Chapters 9 and 10.

Appendix D, *Special/Reserved Characters*, gives a list of the characters that have special meaning in Windows 98.

Conventions Used in This Book

The following typographical conventions are used in this book:

Constant width
> is used to indicate command-line computer output, code examples, Registry keys, and keyboard accelerators (see "Keyboard Accelerators" later in this section).

Constant width italic
> is used to indicate variables in examples and in Registry keys. It is also used to indicate variables or user-defined elements within italic text (such as path names or filenames). For instance, in the path \ *Windows\username*, replace *username* with your username.

Constant width bold
> is used to indicate user input in examples.

Italic
> is used to introduce new terms and to indicate URLs, variables in text, user-defined files and directories, commands, file extensions, filenames, directory or folder names, and UNC pathnames.

This symbol indicates a tip.

 This symbol indicates a warning.

Path Notation

Rather than using procedural steps to tell you how to reach a given Windows 98 user interface element or application, we use a shorthand path notation.

So we don't say, "Click on the Start menu, then click on Find, then Files or Folders. You'll see a dialog box that allows you to specify what you want to look for. Enter a filename in the Named: field." We simply say: Start → Find → Files or Folders → Named. We generally don't distinguish between menus, dialog boxes, buttons, checkboxes and so on, unless it's not clear from the context. Just look for a GUI element whose label matches an element in the path.

The path notation is relative to the Desktop or some other well-known location. For example, the following path:

Start → Programs → Windows Explorer

means "Open the Start menu (on the Desktop), then choose Programs, then choose Windows Explorer." But rather than saying:

Start → Settings → Control Panel → Display → Appearance

we just say:

Control Panel → Display → Appearance

since Control Panel is a "well-known location" and the path can therefore be made less cumbersome. If the item in question is visible on the Desktop, no path is shown, but we may show keyboard accelerators that can be used to open or activate it.

Paths will typically consist of clickable user interface elements, but they may include text typed in from the keyboard, as in:

Start → Run → `telnet`

or:

`Ctrl-Alt-Del` → Shut Down

There is often more than one way to reach a given location in the user interface. We often list multiple paths to reach the same location, even though some are longer than others, because it can be helpful to see how multiple paths lead to the same destination.

The following well-known locations are used as starting points for user interface paths:

Control Panel
> Start → Settings → Control Panel

Context menu
> Right-click on an item to display this context-specific menu

Explorer
> The two-pane Explorer file view; Start → Programs → Windows Explorer

My Computer
> The My Computer icon on the Desktop

Network Neighborhood
> The Network Neighborhood icon on the Desktop

Properties
> Object under discussion → Context menu → Properties

Recycle Bin
> The Recycle Bin icon on the Desktop

Start
> The Start button on the Desktop Taskbar

xxxx menu
> Menu *xxxx* on a window's menubar (e.g., File, Edit)

Keyboard Accelerators

When keyboard accelerators are shown (such as Ctrl-Alt-Del), a hyphen means that the keys must be held down simultaneously, while a plus means that the keys should be pressed sequentially. For example, pressing Ctrl and Esc simultaneously (Ctrl-Esc) pops up the Start menu, but you then pick an item by typing the underlined letter in its name. So, for example, the sequence to reach the Control Panel using a keyboard accelerator (Start → Settings → Control Panel) would be represented as Ctrl-Esc+S+C.

Even though we show an accelerator character (such as the C in Ctrl-C) as uppercase, you don't need to type the Shift key. In fact, in some cases, the accelerator will have a different meaning if Shift is held down at the same time, so we'll always mention it explicitly if it's needed.

Command-Line Syntax

The conventions used for representing command-line options and arguments are described in the introduction to Chapter 7.

We'd Like to Hear from You

We have tested and verified all of the information in this book to the best of our ability, but you may find that features have changed (or that we have made mistakes). Please let O'Reilly know about any errors you find by writing:

O'Reilly & Associates, Inc.
101 Morris Street
Sebastopol, CA 95472
800-998-9938 (in U.S. or Canada)
707-829-0515 (international/local)
707-829-0104 (fax)

You can also send us messages electronically. To be put on the mailing list or request a catalog, send email to:

nuts@oreilly.com

To ask technical questions or comment on the book, send email to:

bookquestions@oreilly.com

Windows 98 Resource Links

For your convenience, we are maintaining a web page on the O'Reilly site that contains a list of all the URLs from this book, organized by chapter. It is our hope to keep the links on this site up-to-date.

Please visit us at:

http://www.oreilly.com/catalog/win98nut/

and click on "Win98 Resource Links."

Acknowledgments

For the Windows 95 Edition

Andrew Schulman was instrumental in helping get the first edition of this book off the ground. He taught both of us most of what we know about Windows, and his sensibility informs much of this book. It was Andrew who insisted on the importance of the command line. He convinced us by showing the magic he could make happen in the user interface by typing a few seemingly arcane incantations at the DOS prompt.

Andrew also did much of the detailed research for the first edition, providing not only important technical direction but also many of the web references we point you to for additional information.

That being said, any mistakes that remain are our own. Andrew's role was largely advisory, and he did not have the time to review everything we wrote or repair any inaccuracies that we introduced.

David Karp, the author of *Windows 98 Annoyances* (O'Reilly & Associates), also made major contributions to the book. Eric Sloan did a superb job as a technical reviewer, and so did Eric Pearce.

We are also indebted to the generosity of hundreds of Windows 95 and Windows 98 users who've created web sites to share tips, insights, and detailed documentation on particular aspects of the system they've uncovered. We refer to some of these sites in the book, but there are many others that also contributed to our understanding of Windows, taught us useful tips, or corrected our assumptions.

Thanks also go to Sheryl Avruch, for managing the production team, Nancy Kotary, the production editor, Rhon Porter and Robert Romano, who created the illustrations. Thanks also to Bob Herbstman, Katie Gardner, and Tara McGoldrick for all their help with the formatting of the manuscript and making all those last-minute changes.

Troy adds: I would especially like to thank my wife, Lisa, who gave me a tremendous amount of support and encouragement and tolerated my absence for the *many* nights and weekends I spent working on the book.

Tim adds: It's been a long time since I've written a book, and I'd almost forgotten how all-consuming it can be. I'd like to thank my wife Christina, since, like Lisa, she put up with a terminally distracted husband for many months. I'd also like to thank the many people I work with at O'Reilly & Associates, who kept the company running smoothly while I had my head down writing the book.

For the Windows 98 Edition

Most of the same cast of characters who worked on *Windows 95 in a Nutshell* put in a repeat performance for the Windows 98 edition. However, there were several people new to the project:

Special thanks to Walter Glenn for the tremendous amount of work he did on the book over the last couple of months. Without his effort, it's doubtful that this version of the book would have made it onto the bookshelves.

Thanks to John Fronckowiak for writing an early draft of the Windows Scripting Host chapter. Stein Borge wrote the final version of this chapter, taking time out from his upcoming book on WSH to give us a hand. Ron Petrusha lent his expertise on this chapter as well.

PART I

The Lay of the Land

CHAPTER 1

Using Windows 98

This chapter provides a quick overview of the features of the Windows 98 user interface, which should be sufficient to help you get oriented and make the most of the system fairly quickly. If you're already familiar with Windows 98, you can probably skip this chapter, but you may be surprised by how much you can still learn. You might find the section entitled "The Command Line" particularly illuminating. Even if you're familiar with other Desktop GUIs, such as the Macintosh, Windows 3.1, Windows 95, or the X Window System, you should at least skim this chapter to find out what is different.

If you're a complete computer novice, you may want to pick up a Windows 98 tutorial. Even though this chapter is more introductory than the rest of the book, it still moves pretty quickly. Still, if you just take your time, and try a few things as you go along, maybe you'll find you don't need step-by-step instructions after all.

The Desktop

Like the Macintosh and other versions of Windows before it, Windows 98 uses the metaphor of a Desktop with windows and file folders laid out on it. This Desktop metaphor is provided by a program called Windows Explorer (*explorer.exe*). Windows 98 is set up to run this program automatically every time you start Windows 98.

Figure 1-1 shows the main features of the Windows 98 Desktop. The callouts in the figure highlight some of the special-purpose icons and buttons that appear on the Desktop. Each of these is described further in Chapter 4, *The Windows 98 User Interface*.

Point and Click Operations

Windows 98 offers two different ways in which you can use your desktop:

*   Classic Style, which is very similar to Windows 95.

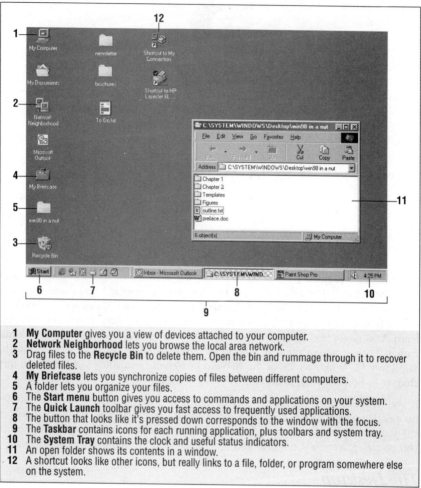

1 **My Computer** gives you a view of devices attached to your computer.
2 **Network Neighborhood** lets you browse the local area network.
3 Drag files to the **Recycle Bin** to delete them. Open the bin and rummage through it to recover deleted files.
4 **My Briefcase** lets you synchronize copies of files between different computers.
5 A folder lets you organize your files.
6 The **Start menu** button gives you access to commands and applications on your system.
7 The **Quick Launch** toolbar gives you fast access to frequently used applications.
8 The button that looks like it's pressed down corresponds to the window with the focus.
9 The **Taskbar** contains icons for each running application, plus toolbars and system tray.
10 The **System Tray** contains the clock and useful status indicators.
11 An open folder shows its contents in a window.
12 A shortcut looks like other icons, but really links to a file, folder, or program somewhere else on the system.

Figure 1-1: Windows 98 Desktop features

- Web Style, which lets you interact with desktop and folder items as you would elements of a web page.

You can also create a custom style that incorporates elements of both the Classic and Web styles. You can select whether to use Classic, Web, or Custom style via `any open folder` → View → Folder Options → General. Note that the style you choose defines how you interact with items on your system, not whether your desktop or any given folder is viewed as a web page.

If you are one of the few computer users who haven't used a graphical user interface before, here are some things you need to know:

- PCs usually come with a two-button mouse (unlike the one-button mouse used with the Macintosh). Some PCs come with three-button mice, as well as touchpads, trackballs, and other input devices.

- To *click* an object means to move the pointer to the desired screen object and click once with the button on the left. *Double-click* means to click twice in rapid succession with the button on the left. (Clicking twice slowly doesn't accomplish the same thing.) *Right-click* means to click with the button on the right. If your mouse has three buttons, you should just use the buttons on the left and the right, and read your computer's manual to find out how to use the button in the middle. (You can often configure the middle button to take over functions like double-clicking, cut and paste, and so on.)

Classic Style

In Classic style, you interact with desktop items in much the same way as on a Macintosh or in previous versions of Windows. Classic style is the default choice in Windows 98. Here is a brief run-down:

- Double-click on any icon on the Desktop to open it. If the icon represents a program, the program is launched (i.e., opened). If the icon represents a data file, the file is opened by the associated program. (The associations between files and programs are controlled by the filename extension (e.g., *.xls* for an Excel file, *.doc* for a Word file, *.htm* or *.html* for an HTML file, *.txt* for a text file, and so on.) By default, the extensions don't show up on the Desktop, but they are part of the underlying file system, and can be viewed either with the Windows Explorer application or in a DOS window.) If the icon represents a folder, a window opens, and the contents of the folder are shown as icons within the window, just as in Windows 95 or on the Macintosh.

- Single-click on an icon to select it. Click again (but not so quickly as to suggest a double-click) on the text, and the name of the icon will be highlighted, with a text insertion cursor showing. Type new text to rename the object represented by the icon, or click yet again to place the cursor and edit the name. In either view, you can also rename an icon by selecting it and pressing F2, or by right-clicking on it and choosing Rename.

- Click the right mouse button on any icon to pop up a menu of other actions that can be performed on the object. The contents of this menu vary depending on which object you click, so it is typically called the *context menu*. The context menu for a file includes functions such as Open, Print, Delete, Rename, Create Shortcut, and so on. The context menu for the Desktop itself includes functions such as Arrange Icons or New (to create new empty files or folders). See Chapter 4 for additional details.

- Click and hold down the mouse button over an icon while moving the mouse to *drag* the object. Drag a file icon onto a folder icon to move the file into the folder. Drag a file icon onto a program icon to open the file with that program. Drag it onto another file icon to rearrange the order of icons on the Desktop. Drag an open window by its titlebar to move it around the Desktop. To copy a file rather than move it, press Ctrl while you drag the file to a new folder.

- By dragging a file with the right mouse button instead of the left, you can easily control whether you want to copy, move, or create a shortcut with the file. With the release of the button, a small menu will pop up providing you with a set of options (Move Here, Copy Here, Create Shortcut(s) Here) to choose from.

- Hold down the Ctrl key while clicking to select an additional item. Anything already selected remains selected. You can select a group of files to delete, for instance, then drag them all to the Recycle Bin at one time. Hold down Shift while clicking to select a whole group of items at one time. Think of the first selection as an one endpoint, and the second selection (the Shift-click) as the other. Everything in between will be selected. The actual result depends a bit on the arrangement of items to be selected. If the items are in a linear list, the result is obvious, as is the case if they are in a neat rectangle, but if they are in some other geometric layout, you may need to experiment to get a feel for exactly what may be selected. For example, in Figure 1-2, clicking on My Briefcase and then Shift-clicking on the Win 98 folder selected *outfile* and the *Notes in a Nut* folder, but not the file *andrew. txt*. (You can tell which items are selected because their icons are rendered in gray rather than white.) Once you have selected a group of items, you can Ctrl-click on individual items in the group to deselect them.

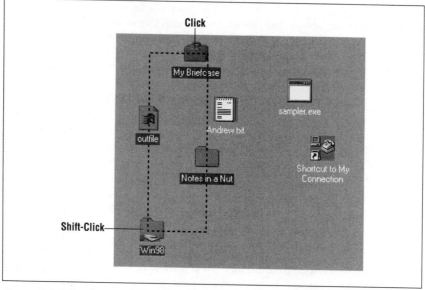

Figure 1-2: File selection with Shift-click

- You can also select a group of icons or other graphical elements by starting a drag on the background of the window (rather than on a particular item). A rectangular *rubber band* outline will stretch from where you started holding down the mouse button to the point where you released it, and anything touching the rectangle will be selected.

- Ctrl-A will select everything in the folder (or on the Desktop, if that's where the focus is). This corresponds to Edit → Select All. (See "Windows and Menus" later in this chapter if you don't know what we mean by the term *focus*.)

Web Style

When using Web style, you interact with desktop objects in much the same way as when using a web page. The main visible difference in Web style is that icons appear underlined, just like links on a web page (see Figure 1-3). Most functions in Web style work the same as in Classic style. Here are the differences:

- In Web View, double-clicking doesn't work. Instead, each Desktop or folder icon is underlined, just like a link in a web page. Moving the pointer over an object selects it, and single-clicking activates it.

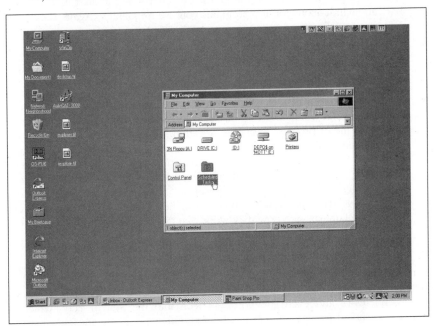

Figure 1-3: Desktop with Web style activated

- To rename an item, you must use the Rename command or press F2. A click will activate the file.
- You can still select multiple items using the Shift and Ctrl keys. However, instead of using Shift-click or Ctrl-click, hold the Shift or Ctrl key down while moving the pointer over the desired item.

Starting Up Applications

Windows 98 has more ways to launch a program than just about any other operating system. You can:

- Double-click on a program icon in Explorer, on the Desktop, or in a folder window in Classic View; or single-click on it in Web View.
- Pick the name of a program from the Start menu. (See "Start Menu" in Chapter 4 for details.)

- Type the name of a program in the Address Toolbar, which can be displayed as part of the Taskbar. This same Address Toolbar is now part of every folder window, so you can now type a command name at virtually any point on the screen to launch a new command. (See "Windows and Menus" later in this chapter, and "Toolbars" in Chapter 4 for details.)

- Type the name of a program in the Run dialog launched from the Start menu, or keep a DOS window open and type the name of the program at the DOS prompt. (Start → Run → command will open a DOS window.)

- Click on a program's icon in the Quick Launch Toolbar to start it. This Toolbar can include icons for any programs you use frequently. (Again, see "Toolbars" in Chapter 4 for details.)

- In Classic View, double-click on a file associated with an application to launch that application and open the file. In Web View, single-click on a file.

- Right-click on a file, executable, or application icon and choose Open.

- Create shortcuts to files or applications (including DOS commands). A shortcut is a kind of pointer or link—a small file and associated icon that simply point to a file or program in another location. You can put these shortcuts on the Desktop, in the Start menu, and in many other "active locations." Double-click on a shortcut to launch the program. To launch programs automatically at startup, just place a shortcut in the startup directory (\Windows\Start Menu\Programs\StartUp). Shortcuts are one of the really nice things about Windows 98. They are a key to much of its flexibility, so you should be sure to become familiar with how they work. See "Shortcuts" in Chapter 4 for more details.

- Select an icon and press enter.

Some programs are really "in your face." For example, if you install AOL 4.0, it puts an icon on the Desktop, in the Office Shortcut Bar, on the Start menu (in two places, no less!), and even shoehorns an icon into the System Tray, which is normally reserved for system status indicators. Other programs are fairly hard to find. Without this book, you might spend hours poking around in the Explorer trying to find a particular program.

Chapter 6, *Start Menu Programs and Other Graphical Applications*, and Chapter 7, *DOS and Other Command-Line Utilities*, solve that problem. They include a complete alphabetical list of almost every application and command that comes with Windows 98. The introductions to those chapters give a bit more background about each of Win 98's ways to launch programs, and a few hints about the best way to customize them for your use.

Windows and Menus

Any open window contains a frame with a series of standard decorations, as shown in Figure 1-4.

If multiple windows are open, only one has what is called the *focus*. The window with the focus is the one that will respond to keystrokes, mouse clicks, and so on. The window with the focus will usually be on top and will have its titlebar high-

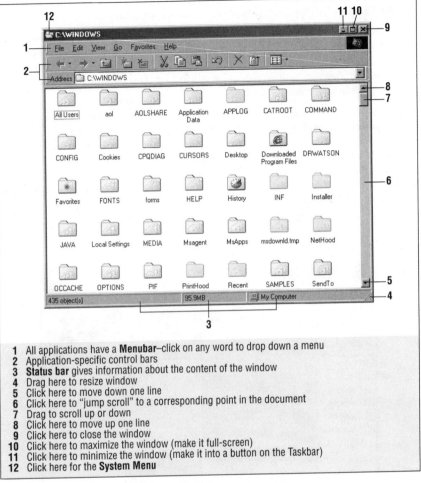

Figure 1-4: Window controls—standard decorations

1 All applications have a **Menubar**–click on any word to drop down a menu
2 Application-specific control bars
3 **Status bar** gives information about the content of the window
4 Drag here to resize window
5 Click here to move down one line
6 Click here to "jump scroll" to a corresponding point in the document
7 Drag to scroll up or down
8 Click here to move up one line
9 Click here to close the window
10 Click here to maximize the window (make it full-screen)
11 Click here to minimize the window (make it into a button on the Taskbar)
12 Click here for the **System Menu**

lighted or colored in some way. To give a window the focus, just click on any visible portion of it, and it will pop to the front. Be careful where you click on the intended window, however. For some windows, clicking on a button or file will activate it, even though the window does not already have focus. Also, within a given window, only a single control has the focus—shown on buttons by an outlined focus rectangle, or in edit boxes with a blinking insertion point.

In addition, a window gets the focus any time you pop it up from the Taskbar. (More on that later.)

Often, new users are confused when they try to type into a window and nothing happens. It might be in front but still not have the focus, or the wrong control has the focus. (For example, a click on the Desktop might have moved the focus there.) Check to see that the desired window's titlebar is highlighted: for example, the focus window's titlebar might be bright blue rather than light gray. Like many other elements of Windows 98, the colors here can be specified by the user. See Control Panel → Display → Appearance → Inactive Title Bar.

Some windows can be set to have the property Always on Top. This means that when you drag another window into the same space, the one set to be Always on Top will slide on top of the other window, hiding part of its contents. For example, the Taskbar is often set to be Always on Top. Note that a window can be on top without having the focus.

Almost every window has a few standard drop-down menus (File, Edit, and Help), as well as any application-specific menus. Click on the menu title to drop it down. Click on an item in the menu to execute it. Any menu item whose name ends with "..." pops up a dialog box that asks you for more information. Any menu item with a right-pointing arrow leads to a cascading menu with more options, as shown in Figure 1-5. Note that, depending on the screen layout, the menu may cascade to the left instead of the right, even though the arrow points to the right. If you decide not to execute any item on the menu, click anywhere else in the window to make the menu disappear.

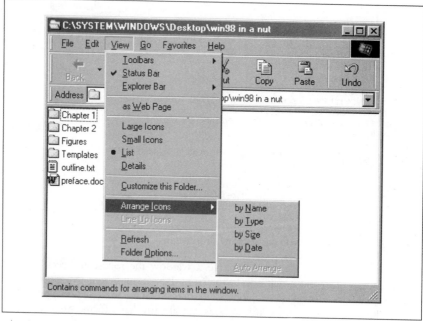

Figure 1-5: A cascading menu

You can also use keyboard accelerators to execute almost any menu item. See "Keyboard Accelerators" later in this chapter for details.

One thing that is often perplexing to new Windows 98 users is the dynamic nature of its menus.

As on the Macintosh, menu items that are grayed out are temporarily disabled. (For example, you can't delete or rename a file from a folder's File menu if no file is selected.) But Windows 98 goes one step further. Depending on what is selected in a window, you may see completely different items on the menu. See "Network Neighborhood" in Chapter 4 for an example.

Each window also has a "system menu" hidden behind the little icon on the left corner of the titlebar (see item 12 in Figure 1-4). Clicking on the icon opens the menu. You can also pop down the System menu by pressing Alt-space. The System menu duplicates the function of the maximize, minimize, and close buttons at the right end of the titlebar, but it also lets you move or resize the window without the mouse. (See "Keyboard Accelerators," the next section, for details.) There's also a Restore menu item, which is used to restore a maximized window to its normal open view on the Desktop. The System menu can also be accessed by right-clicking on a minimized window on the Taskbar, and the Restore menu item can be used to restore a minimized window to its normal open view. Sometimes the System menu adds other interesting functions. (For example, the system menu for non-graphical programs, such as the MS-DOS prompt or *xcopy32.exe*, provides Edit, Toolbar, and Properties menu items.) Every program you start is represented by a button on the Taskbar. Right-clicking a program's Taskbar button will also pop open the system menu, even when the window is not visible.

The scrollbar sometimes appearing on the right of windows contains a rectangle called the *slider*. If you drag the slider up and down, the contents of the window move in the opposite direction. The arrows at the top and bottom of the scrollbar move the contents a line (or some similar increment) at a time. Clicking once in the empty area of the scrollbar causes the screen to scroll one screenful; clicking and holding scrolls until the slider reaches that point.

When you open a folder in a window, the default behavior is to open it in the current window. This is convenient in keeping desktop clutter down. You can change this default behavior by choosing View → Folder Options → Custom → Settings → Open each folder in its own window. This setting opens a new window every time you open a folder. This is a global change that affects all folders. Whichever option you choose, you can override it on a per-use basis by holding down the Ctrl key when you open a folder. For example, if the default action is to open a folder in the same window, you can open it in a separate window by holding the Ctrl key.

Keyboard Accelerators

While the Explorer and many other Windows 98 applications provide graphical controls for most common operations, these programs also support an extensive array of *keyboard accelerators*. (We prefer this term to *keyboard shortcuts*, the term

Microsoft uses, since they also use the word "shortcuts" for the ubiquitous link files that allow programs to be accessible from many different points in the system. Keyboard accelerators are sometimes also called *hotkeys*.) Some of these keyboard accelerators (such as F1 for help, or Ctrl-C to copy and Ctrl-V to paste) date back to the days of DOS; others are specific to Windows 98.

Appendix A, *Keyboard Accelerators*, gives a complete list of keyboard accelerators. Some of the most important ones are described below:

Menu navigation

When the focus is on a window, press Alt, followed by the underlined character in any menu title, followed by the underlined character in any menu item, to activate that menu and menu item. For example, Alt-F+O (that is, pressing Alt and F together, followed by an O) will select Open from the File menu, if the application has one. The underlined character will usually be the first character in the menu or menu item name, unless there is more than one item with the same name, in which case the program's author will have chosen some other letter. The menu pops up as you type the menu's accelerator, so you can see the item accelerators. You don't need to remember anything.

There are two exceptions to Alt as an initial character. Use Ctrl-Esc to pop up the Start menu, and right-click on an item to pop up its context menu. Once a menu is visible, typing any of the underlined characters will choose the corresponding item. In the Start menu, most items don't have underlined accelerators; just use the first letter. Most new keyboards also sport two new useful keys. The Windows key (it has the Windows logo on it) will open the Start menu no matter where in the system you are (unless Windows isn't running). The Context key (it has a menu and mouse pointer on it) will open the context menu for any selected item that has a context menu.

Note that once a menu is visible, you can mix pointer clicks and keystrokes. For example, you could pop up the Start menu with the mouse, then type S for settings, then click on Control Panel. Or you could type Ctrl-Esc, click on Settings, and type C for Control Panel.

If there is a conflict, and multiple items on a menu have the same accelerator key, pressing the key repeatedly will cycle through the options. You must press Enter when the correct menu item is highlighted to actually make the selection.

In addition, pressing Alt or F10 will select the first item on an application's menubar. Use the right and left arrows to move along the menubar and the up and down arrows to move to a specific menu item. Press Enter to execute the selected item.

Window manipulation without the mouse

Alt-space will open the system menu. The menu items all have individual accelerators. Accordingly, Alt-space+N will minimize a window; Alt-space+X will maximize it; Alt-space+R will restore a maximized window to its normal view, and Alt-space+C will close it. Alt-space+M will move a window, and Alt-space+S will (re)size it using the arrow keys rather than the mouse. In either of the latter cases, the cursor will change to a little four-pointed arrow. Use the arrow keys to move or resize the window in the desired direction, and press Enter when you're happy with the result. Press Esc to cancel the operation. Note that some windows can't be resized.

Editing

In most applications, Ctrl-X will cut a selected item to an invisible storage area called the Clipboard, Ctrl-C will copy it to the Clipboard, and Ctrl-V will paste it into a new location. Delete will delete the selection without saving it to the Clipboard. There is a single system-wide clipboard shared by all applications. This lets you copy something from a document in one program and paste it into another document in another program. You can paste the same data repeatedly until it's replaced on the Clipboard by new data. (An optional application called the Clipboard Viewer lets you save a selection in the clipboard to use at a later date. See Chapter 6 for details.)

While you probably think of cut and paste operations as something you do with selected text or graphics in an application, the same keys can be used for file operations. For example, select a file on the Desktop, type Ctrl-C, move to another folder, type Ctrl-V, and you will have made a copy of the entire file, not of just its icon.

Ctrl-Alt-Del

Pops up a Close Program dialog box that allows you to interrupt a program that is "frozen" (not responding to its normal controls) or reboot the system.

Alt-Tab and Alt-Esc

Let you switch to another application that is running or folder that is open. Alt-Tab pops up a little window with icons representing the open programs, so that you are in effect choosing from the open applications or folders; Alt-Esc cycles directly among the programs themselves. (More specifically, it drops the active window to the bottom of the pile.)

Tab and arrow keys

Within a window, Tab will move the focus between fields. Use Shift-Tab to move backwards. A field may be an individual data item or a list. For example, in a folder window, Tab will switch between the drop-down list in the toolbar and the file display area. Use arrow keys in either area to make a new selection without moving the focus. Sometimes a dialog box will have one or more regions, indicated by a rectangular box within the dialog box. The arrow keys will cycle through buttons or fields only within the current regions. Tab will cross region boundaries and cycle through all the buttons or fields in the dialog box.

Common Controls

Many application and system windows use a common set of controls in addition to the ubiquitous titlebar, menubar, system menu, and scrollbars. This section describes a few of these common controls.

Figure 1-6 shows some of the common controls in Control Panel → Display → Screen Saver and the additional dialog box that pops up from its Settings button.

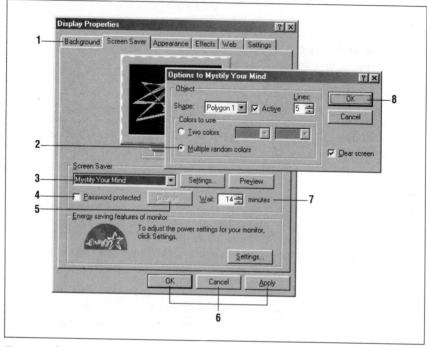

Figure 1-6: Common controls in Windows applications and dialogs

Some of these controls are as follows:

1. Tabbed dialogs

   Settings may be grouped into separate tabbed dialog pages. For example, see Control Panel → System or Control Panel → Display. Click on any tab to bring that page to the front.

2. Radio buttons

   Radio buttons are used for mutually exclusive settings. Clicking on one causes any other that has been pressed to pop up, just like on an old-time car radio. The button with the dot in the middle is the one that has been selected. Sometimes you'll see more than one group of buttons, with a separate outline around each group. In this case, you can select one radio button from each group.

3. Drop-down lists

   Any time you see a downward-pointing arrow next to a text field, click on the arrow to drop down a list of other values. Often, a drop-down list contains a history of previous entries you've made into a text entry field. Pressing the first letter will often jump to that place in the list, as long as the list has the focus. The down arrow (or F4) will also drop down the currently selected list.

The arrow keys will scroll through the stored entries, even if the list is not already dropped down. Microsoft sometimes calls these lists "Look In Lists." For an example, see Start → Find Files or Folders → Name & Location.

4. Checkboxes

   Checkboxes are generally used for on/off settings. A checkmark means the setting is on; an empty box means it's off. Click on the box to turn the labeled setting on or off.

5. Grayed-out (inactive) controls

   Any control like this one that is grayed out is disabled because the under-lying operation is not currently available. In the dialog box shown in Figure 1-6, you need to click the "Password protected" checkbox before you can use the Change button.

6. OK, Cancel, Apply

   Most dialogs will have at least an OK and a Cancel button. Some also have Apply. The difference is that OK accepts the settings and quits the dialog, and Apply accepts the changes, but doesn't quit. (This is useful in a dialog with multiple tabs, so that you can apply changes before moving to the next tab.) Cancel quits without making any changes. If you click Cancel after clicking Apply, your changes will probably already have been applied, and will not revert to their original settings. But don't be surprised if some applications respond differently! Microsoft has never been clear with application developers about the expected behavior of these buttons.

7. Counters

   You can either select the number and type in a new value, or click on the up or down arrow to increase or decrease the value.

8. The default button

   When a set of buttons is displayed, the default button (the one that will be activated by pressing the Enter key) has a bold border around it. The button or other area in the dialog box that has the additional dashed outline has the focus. You can move the focus by clicking with the mouse, typing the under-lined accelerator character in a button or field label, or pressing the Tab or arrow keys.

   In some dialog boxes, the default button (the button the Enter key presses) is *hardcoded*—it will always be the same. But in others, the default button follows the focus from button to button. For example, right-click on the Taskbar and select Properties. The Taskbar Options tab (see Figure 1-7) has the OK button hardcoded as the default. Note that the bold border will stay on this button even when you move the focus among the checkboxes. The Start Menu Programs tab (see Figure 1-8) does not have a hardcoded default button. As you move the focus between buttons, the default button highlight moves with it. In Figure 1-8, the Add button currently has the focus and is accordingly the button that will be activated by pressing Enter.

   Regardless of which button is the default, pressing Esc always has the same effect as clicking the Cancel button: it cancels the dialog box.

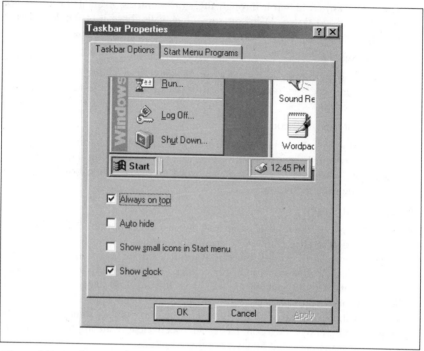

Figure 1-7: A tab containing a hardcoded default button

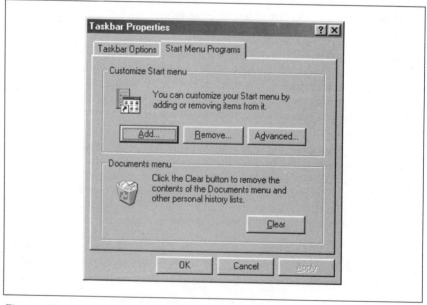

Figure 1-8: A tab without a hardcoded default button

Two more common controls not shown in Figure 1-6 are:

Expand/collapse tree buttons

Hierarchical lists are often presented with small plus sign (+) buttons (see Figure 1-11). Clicking on the + expands an item to show one additional level of detail. Clicking a – sign collapses (hides) all subsidiary details. For example, see "Editing the Registry" in Chapter 13, *The Registry*, or Control Panel → System → Device Manager.

Column headers

Sometimes Windows 98 presents ledger-like lists of items with multiple columns; each column has a header. For example, use Start → Find → Files or Folders to search for something like *.doc* (all files with a *.doc* extension). The returned list uses the column heads format, with headers such as Name, In Folder, Size, and so on (if you can't see them all, maximize the window with Alt-Space-x). Clicking on a column heading makes that column the basis for sorting the list; clicking again in the same column reverses the sort order. If icons are displayed in the list, the items are *active*; that is, you can click, double-click, or right-click on them to open them or perform some other action. Drag the lines dividing the headers to resize the width of columns or drag the headers to rearrange them. Double-click on column header separators to size columns automatically to the widest contents.

Views of Folders

The contents of a folder can be shown using large icons, using small icons, in a list, or in a list with details. Which view will be the default for a given window depends to some extent on the application. For folders, the default view is using large icons, but you can almost always use the View menu to change the viewing preferences. Also, Windows 98 will remember the view setting for each folder by default and will display it the same way the next time the folder is opened. You can change this option via View → Folder Options → View → Remember each folder's view settings.

You can also elect to view a folder as a web page. The default web page view for a folder simply creates a section to the left of the file listing that shows the details for any selected file. If a picture file is selected (*.bmp*, *.jpg*, etc.), the actual picture is shown in this section. This view for Standard folders is generated by *folder.htt* in the *Windows**Web* directory. Special folders, such as the Control Panel folder, have a Web view generated by a separate *.htt* file. You can also build custom Web views for folders; this is discussed in Chapter 9, *Web Integration*.

If you want more information about files than their names, the most useful view is the Details view, which will show you not only the name of each file the folder contains but also its size, type, and the last date and time it was modified. The List view is the default choice for the Explorer, My Briefcase, and many other programs that list detailed information about files or system characteristics. Figure 1-9 shows the Details view of a folder.

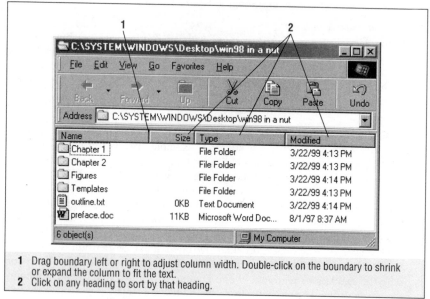

1 Drag boundary left or right to adjust column width. Double-click on the boundary to shrink or expand the column to fit the text.
2 Click on any heading to sort by that heading.

Figure 1-9: The Details view

Toolbar and Status Bar

By default, every folder has a visible Status bar at the bottom, which shows the number of items in the folder and the amount of disk space they occupy. The status bar will also show information regarding any selected file or files. Click View → Status bar to disable this display.

You can also turn on a Toolbar using View → Toolbar. The Toolbar gives you all kinds of nifty navigation and data manipulation tools. These all duplicate functionality you get from various menus and keyboard accelerators, but they are arranged in a handy palette.

Figure 1-10 shows the buttons on the Toolbar for a folder.

The Command Line

Many beginning Windows 98 users think they have left the command line behind. Advanced users realize that the command line is often the quickest and most powerful way to get what they want. To create a *cdsample* directory on your *C:* drive and copy the necessary files from the Win 98 CD-ROM to run the CD samples, for example, it is quicker to type:

```
C:\>mkdir \cdsample
C:\>copy d:\cdsample\*.* \cdsample
```

than to click on My Computer; then click on the icon for your CD-ROM drive (containing the Windows 98 CD-ROM); then navigate to the folder \cdsample; select all the files; then click File → Copy (or Ctrl-C); then navigate to a new

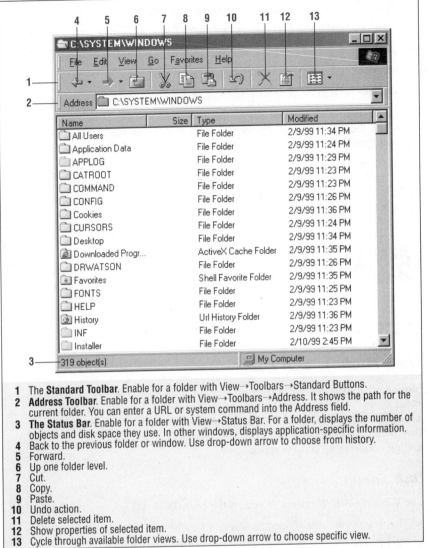

1 The **Standard Toolbar**. Enable for a folder with View→Toolbars→Standard Buttons.
2 **Address Toolbar**. Enable for a folder with View→Toolbars→Address. It shows the path for the current folder. You can enter a URL or system command into the Address field.
3 **The Status Bar**. Enable for a folder with View→Status Bar. For a folder, displays the number of objects and disk space they use. In other windows, displays application-specific information.
4 Back to the previous folder or window. Use drop-down arrow to choose from history.
5 Forward.
6 Up one folder level.
7 Cut.
8 Copy.
9 Paste.
10 Undo action.
11 Delete selected item.
12 Show properties of selected item.
13 Cycle through available folder views. Use drop-down arrow to choose specific view.

Figure 1-10: Toolbar and Status bar on a folder window

location—either on the Desktop, or via the Explorer or My Computer, or some other folder on your hard disk; then right-click to get the context menu; then click New → Folder; then type the folder name; then open the folder; and then click Edit → Paste (or Ctrl-V) to copy in the files. That's a heck of a sentence, and a heck of a lot of steps for what ought to be an easy task.

Once you learn the real name of a program rather than its Start menu shortcut name (see Chapter 6), it's almost always quicker to start it from the Run prompt or the Address Toolbar (see below) than it is to navigate the Start menu hierarchy. Which is really easier? Clicking your way through five menus:

> Start → Programs → Accessories → System Tools → Backup

or typing:

> backup

into the Run prompt or Address Toolbar?

Typing a command is much faster than carefully dragging the mouse through cascading menus, where a slip of the mouse can get you somewhere entirely different than you planned.

Finally, there are many useful programs that don't appear on any menu. Once you know what you're doing, you can put shortcuts to them on the Start menu of the Desktop—but once you know what you're doing, you might just find it easier to type the program name!

 Windows 98 provides an incredibly convenient way of entering commands. Most windows sport an Address Toolbar into which you can type URLs or system commands. The Windows 98 Taskbar itself also has an Address Toolbar that you can activate using Taskbar → right-click → Toolbars → Address.

Files, Folders, and Disks

Files are the basic unit of long-term storage on a computer. Files are organized into folders, which are stored on disks. (Under DOS, Windows 3.1, and Unix, folders were more often referred to as *directories*, and both terms are still used.) This section reviews fundamental filesystem concepts, including file and disk naming conventions and file types.

Disk Names

Like Windows 3.1, Windows 98 retains the basic DOS disk naming conventions:

A: Represents the first "floppy" (usually 3.5-inch) disk drive on the system

B: Represents the second floppy disk drive, if present

C: Represents the first hard disk drive

D: Often represents a CD-ROM drive, but can represent an additional hard disk drive or other removable drive

E:–Z:

Represent additional hard disk drives or removable cartridges such as Zip or Jaz drives

In addition, shared items on other networked systems can be mapped to drive letters so that they appear as local drives when using this syntax. See "Network

---

Neighborhood" in Chapter 3 for details. Networked drive letters aren't always consecutive.

Pathnames

Files are stored hierarchically on a disk, in folders (directories) that can be nested to any arbitrary level.

The file system on any disk begins with the root (top-level) directory, represented as a backslash. Thus *C:* represents the root directory on the *C:* drive. Each additional nested directory can be represented as another element in the path, with a backslash used to separate each one. *C:\Windows\System\Color* means that the *Color* folder is in the *System* folder in the *Windows* folder on the *C:* drive.

Each running program has its own current drive and current directory. Pathnames can be absolute (starting with the root) or relative (starting with the current directory). For example, if the focus is on the Desktop and you create a new directory (using the Desktop context menu → New → Folder), the pathname to that directory will be something like *\Windows\Desktop\New Folder*.

In many places in Windows 98 (including—but not limited to—the command line in Start → Run or the MS-DOS prompt), the special names . and .. refer to the current directory and the parent of that directory, respectively (the parent is the directory one up from the current directory); the directory name ... refers to the grandparent (two levels up), ... the great-grandparent, and so on.

The Explorer gives a tree-structured view of the file system. See Chapter 4 for details. In addition, in many cases when you open, save, or find a file within an application, you will see a Browse button, which typically leads to a mini-Explorer view of the file system. Figure 1-11 shows a Browse dialog box.

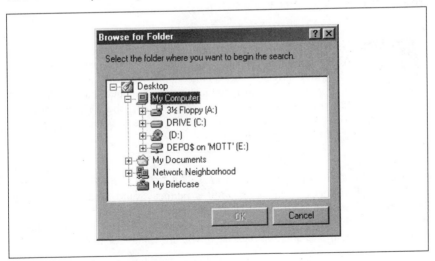

Figure 1-11: A Browse dialog box

Network Pathnames

Files on any shared network can be referred to via a UNC (Universal Naming Convention) pathname. The first element of a UNC pathname is a system name, prefixed by a double backslash. The second element is the remote file, folder, or device's share name. A remote system that makes a resource available for sharing will define this name as well as any password required to access it.

For example, the UNC path *printsrv1**othello* refers to a printer named *othello* attached to a machine named *printsrv1*, and the UNC path *troy**nutshell**win95* refers to the *win95* folder in the *nutshell* folder on a machine named *troy*.

For more information on UNC pathnames, see "Network Neighborhood" in Chapter 4.

Short Names and Long Names

DOS and Windows 3.1 supported filenames with a maximum of eight characters, plus a three-character file type extension separated from the name by a period (e.g., *myfile.txt*). The maximum length of a pathname was 80 characters.

Legal characters included any combination of letters and numbers, extended ASCII characters with values greater than 127, and the following punctuation characters:

```
$ % ^ ' ` - _ @ ~ ! ( ) # &
```

Windows 98 supports long filenames (up to 260 characters), which can include the additional punctuation characters:

```
+ , ; = [ ] .
```

(Appendix D, *Special/Reserved Characters*, lists the characters you can't use, and explains their special meaning to the system.)

Windows 98 supports pathnames up to MAX_PATH characters long. The MAX_PATH value can vary depending on the file system (e.g., FAT is 255 and VFAT is 260 characters). Even if the MAX_PATH value is 255 characters, an individual application may have restrictions that prevent the pathname from reaching the 255-character mark. This is why you can't necessarily create a filename in the Explorer that is 255 characters long.

For example, a file could be named *Sales Report 3-5-97*. Extensions are no longer limited to 3 characters; for example, *.html* is perfectly valid (and separate from *.htm*). Note, however, that *really* long filenames are impractical, since the maximum length of a pathname is 260 characters, including backslashes, depending on the application and file system you are using (see note).

You can use embedded spaces in names, but since whitespace is often used to separate arguments to commands, you must place quotes around any name that includes spaces when using the command line.

Windows 98's file system is case-preserving, but also case-insensitive. For example, "FooBar" will be preserved with the capital F and B. However, searches for "foobar", "FOOBAR", and so on would all find this same file, and attempting to create a file named "FOOBAR" will fail if "FooBar" already exists.

Long filenames can be used in the version of DOS that comes with Windows 98. However, some of the older utilities that come with the system don't recognize long filenames, or use an old-style filename and extension to recognize the file type.

As a result, Windows 98 always keeps two names for each file: its long name (if one exists) and its short name and extension. The short name consists of the first six letters of the long name, a tilde, a number from 1 to 9 (the number is incremented for each long filename that would otherwise map to the same short name—after ~9, those six characters are reduced to five), and the file type extension, if any. (If an extension is longer than three characters, the first three characters will be used as the DOS extension.) Any spaces in the first six characters are removed.

For example, use the DOS *dir* command on the directory *C:\Windows\Desktop*, and you'll see that My Briefcase has become *MYBRIE~1*. (See Figure 1-12.) As another example, *\Program Files* becomes *\PROGRA~1*.

Using older DOS disk utilities (such as backup programs, defragmenters, etc.) that don't understand long filenames could result in the loss of long filename information and file corruption.

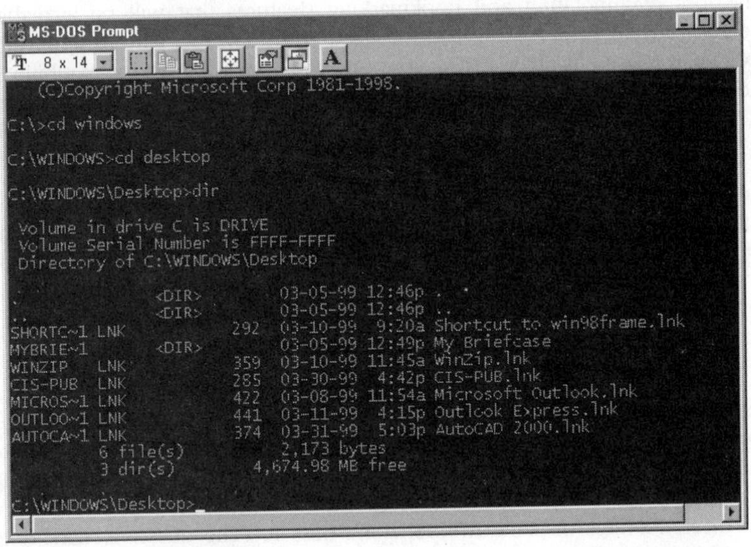
MS-DOS Prompt
8 x 14
A
(C)Copyright Microsoft Corp 1981-1998.
C:\>cd windows
C:\WINDOWS>cd desktop
C:\WINDOWS\Desktop>dir
Volume in drive C is DRIVE
Volume Serial Number is FFFF-FFFF
Directory of C:\WINDOWS\Desktop
. <DIR> 03-05-99 12:46p .
.. <DIR> 03-05-99 12:46p ..
SHORTC~1 LNK 292 03-10-99 9:20a Shortcut to win98frame.lnk
MYBRIE~1 <DIR> 03-05-99 12:49p My Briefcase
WINZIP LNK 359 03-10-99 11:45a WinZip.lnk
CIS-PUB LNK 285 03-30-99 4:42p CIS-PUB.lnk
MICROS~1 LNK 422 03-08-99 11:54a Microsoft Outlook.lnk
OUTLOO~1 LNK 441 03-11-99 4:15p Outlook Express.lnk
AUTOCA~1 LNK 374 03-31-99 5:03p AutoCAD 2000.lnk
6 file(s) 2,173 bytes
3 dir(s) 4,674.98 MB free
C:\WINDOWS\Desktop>

Figure 1-12: The dir command in a DOS box

File Types and Extensions

The extension of a DOS-style filename represents the type of the file, and is used by Windows 98 and many Windows applications to identify the application that will be used to open that file. Even though file extensions are not a reliable guide to a file's type, Windows 98 relies heavily on them.

Some filename extensions and their application associations are:

.doc
>A Word document

.xls
>An Excel spreadsheet

.txt
>A text file, to be opened with Notepad

Appendix B, *Filename Extensions*, gives a list of the most common extensions and their associated applications. If you click on a file of an unknown type, the Open With dialog will pop up. See "File Types" in Chapter 4 for details.

Extensions that are associated with a known program are hidden by Windows 98 by default. This is a very bad idea, since extensions are still used by the system to identify file types. Change this in the Explorer by selecting View → Folder Options → View and unchecking "Hide file extensions for known file types."

Online Help

Windows 98 comes with a new Help standard called HTML Help. Although this is a big change for Help developers (HTML is used instead of RTF), the user won't notice too much difference between HTML Help and the older WinHelp, except for the loss of annotating and bookmarking (features that will be available in future HTML Help files). HTML Help is used with the new Win 98 applications, but WinHelp is used in older applications and also for backward compatibility (see "Windows Help and Windows HTML Help Viewer" in Chapter 6 for more information). When you select Start → Help, the *windows.chm* file is automatically launched, and you will be using HTML Help.

Most windows have a Help menu, which you can pull down with the mouse or by typing Alt-H. In addition, press F1 at almost any time to launch an online index to help topics or context help for the current dialog box. The Index tab is often the most useful. Just type a few words that relate to what you're interested in, and if they match a help topic heading, you'll go right to the appropriate point in the index.

In addition, some applications (and many system property sheets and dialog boxes) include a question mark icon on the titlebar. Click on the question mark; the cursor will change to a question mark and an arrow. Move it to some item in the window that you're confused about and click. A small window that explains the purpose of the button or other user interface element will pop up. This is one of the nicest features of Windows 98: don't miss it. (The question mark help is often very useful and there's no searching involved.) However, both forms of help can be unhelpful—sometimes they'll tell you just what you need to know, but more often they'll simply repeat the obvious.

Furthermore, if you hold the pointer over many screen objects (such as items on the Taskbar or a window's toolbar), additional information will pop up in a little "tooltips" bubble that stays up until you move the pointer. This feature is usually limited to toolbars and other main controls—you'll rarely see tooltips in dialogs. In most cases, this will give a phrase describing the operation of the object. In others, it might provide additional functionality. For example, placing the pointer on the system clock pops up the date.

In some applications, even those without the question mark icon on the titlebar, right-clicking a user interface item will pop up a little "What's This?" tooltips bubble. Click on the bubble for an expanded explanation.

At the command line, you can get help on the available command-line options by typing:

```
commandname /?
```

Finally, Windows 98 includes a number of readme files, which typically contain *release notes*—information about special handling required for specific applications or hardware devices. The file *C:\Windows\readme.txt* contains a list of all the other readme files on the system. Or you can just look in the \ *Windows* directory for any file with the extension *.txt*. Use Notepad or any other ASCII text editor or word processor to read them.

Shutting Down

You shouldn't just turn off the power to a Windows 98 machine, since it caches a lot of data in memory and needs to write it out before shutting down. See "Shut Down" in Chapter 4 for additional details.

CHAPTER 2

What's New in Windows 98

This chapter is designed as a quick-start summary for users who have used Windows 95 and just want to know the key changes in Windows 98, and also for Windows 98 users who want to know what is new in Windows 98 Second Edition. This chapter doesn't explain the new features in detail. It just highlights them and points to the sections in the book where they are covered in more detail.

The treatment is idiosyncratic. We tell you the features we think are important and useful, not necessarily the ones that Microsoft is hyping. The summary starts with the really useful new features, then follows with those that are not so useful, and then discusses some under-the-hood changes.

Useful New User Interface Features

Here are some of the most useful new user-interface features:

The Address Toolbar

> We're big fans of using the command line to extend the power of the point-and-click interface. The new Address Toolbar that you can display in the Taskbar (Taskbar → right-click → Toolbars → Address) or detach and anchor anywhere else on the desktop is the most convenient method yet for having a command line available at all times. You can type URLs into this command line to pop a new web page up into your browser, or you can type a system command name, just like you can with the Run prompt. See "Toolbars" in Chapter 4, *The Windows 98 User Interface*, for details. The Address Toolbar can also be displayed as part of any folder window.

HTML View

> This is the most hyped new feature of Windows 98—the "integration" of Internet Explorer into the desktop. You can view folders, or your entire Desktop, using the new View → As Web Page option. The default result is a slightly more verbose view of folders that shows some additional descriptive information and properties to the left of the file display in the folder. You can

also replace the HyperText Template (*.htt*) that is used to format the view. This allows you to create useful special-purpose web pages within your folders. You can also create special areas on the Desktop that are web-aware and contain output from web pages. This is especially useful if you are connected full-time to the Internet (rather than on a dialup link). See Chapter 9, *Web Integration*, for details.

Other folder view options
Folder titlebars now include a new web-like set of toolbars, including forward and back buttons.

The Quick Launch Toolbar
This is another toolbar you can display in the Taskbar or detach and anchor elsewhere on the desktop. It lets you install buttons for frequently-accessed applications. See "The Quick Launch Toolbar" in Chapter 4 for details.

Other toolbars
You can display the contents of the Desktop in a toolbar, or a set of favorite web page links. You can also create a custom toolbar showing the contents of any other folder or URL. See "Toolbars" in Chapter 4 for details.

Scheduled tasks
You now have the ability to schedule programs (such as backup or virus scanning) at predetermined times. The Scheduled Tasks facility was formerly available only in Microsoft Plus. It is now a standard part of the system. See "Scheduled Tasks" in Chapter 4 for details.

Microsoft Plus! 98

The following is a list of the main Plus! 98 programs:

Games
Contains Golf Lite, Lose Your Marbles, Spider Solitaire

McAfee VirusScan
Fully-functioning version of VirusScan

Deluxe CD Player
Main feature that surpasses *cdplayer.exe* in the downloading of play lists from the Web

Desktop Themes & Organic Art Screensaver
Additional backgrounds and screensavers

Disk Cleanup & Maintenance Wizard
Slight additional feature for programs that already come with Windows 98

Picture It! Express
Image editor with limited functionality

Easier customization of the Start menu

You can now add new shortcuts to the Start menu by dragging them onto the menu (rather than having to open an Explorer window to modify the folder whose contents are used to generate the menu). Similarly, you can take items off the Start menu by dragging them out of the menu, and you can drag items into a new order. You can also right-click on items in the Start menu to get at their shortcut properties. For more information, see "Start Menu" in Chapter 4.

Easier setup of online services

There is now an online services folder on the desktop, which includes icons for AOL, Compuserve, Prodigy, and ATT Worldnet. (Of course, the corresponding icon for the Microsoft Network appears directly on the desktop, making it more visible and easier to access.) These icons are actually short-cuts to setup programs, and require you to insert the Windows 98 CD-ROM to actually install the software that will let you access the online service. See "Online Services Folder" in Chapter 4 for details.

TweakUI

The TweakUI utility allows you to customize the Windows 98 interface. It used to be available only by download from Microsoft's site as part of the PowerToys collection of unsupported utilities, but is now on the Windows 98 CD-ROM. It is still not installed by default, but at least it is now a standard installable part of the system. See "TweakUI" in Chapter 8, *Hidden Gems on the Windows 98 CD-ROM*, for details.

Better backup

Windows 98 includes a much better backup utility than Windows 95. See "Backup" in Chapter 6, *Start Menu Programs and Other Graphical Applications*, for details.

Other new utilities and accessories

Windows 98 also includes many other useful new utilities, including NetMeeting, Outlook Express, FrontPage Express, Microsoft Chat, Personal Web Server, Registry Checker, System Information Utility, and System File Checker. See Chapter 6 for details.

Windows Update

Windows Update is a web site extension for Windows 98. It provides registered users access to the latest updates, features, and drivers for Windows 98. See Chapter 4 for details.

Windows Script Host

Finally, there's support for automation of repetitive tasks. Combine WSH with scheduled tasks, and you start to have the rudiments of a useful system for power users. See Chapter 10, *The Windows Script Host*, for details.

HTML Help

Windows 98 HTML Help, which uses compiled HTML, now comes with an HTML Help engine, but Win 98 also still contains the older Winhelp engine, *winhlp32.exe*, that uses compiled RTF files. Although new Win 98 applications (including Start → Help) are supported with HTML Help, many of the older applications still use Winhelp. See "Windows Help and Windows HTML Help Viewer" in Chapter 6 for more details.

Power management

Windows 98 includes built-in support for the Advanced Configuration and Power Interface (ACPI), which provides features such as hard disk spin down, shut down to standby or full power off, and power management schemes.

Multiple monitor support

You can now attach more than one monitor to the same system. This is great for some demanding applications, such as publishing or certain types of games, where you may want to be able to look at more than one screen side by side. Configuring multiple monitors is discussed in the "Display" section of Chapter 5, *The Control Panel.*

Bogus Features

Here are some of the more useless new features, and some pre-existing features that have been set back by intended improvements that are buggy or ill-conceived:

The Channel Bar

When you first start Windows 98, you wonder what to do with this monstrosity, a space-hogging opportunity for Microsoft to push various online sites who've paid them money to be in your face. See "Channel Bar" in Chapter 4 for information on how to turn it off!

Animated menus

Is it you, or do you remember cascading pop-up menus being faster in Windows 95? Sure enough, Microsoft's "animated" menus are considerably slower, at least if you have real work to do. See "TweakUI" in Chapter 8 for information on how to turn off this feature.

The contents of the Quick Launch Toolbar

While the toolbar itself is actually a nifty new feature, the fact that it's on by default, and prepopulated with buttons for Microsoft applications only, means that Microsoft has given themselves one more opportunity to put their own applications in a preferred position. See "Toolbars" in Chapter 4 for information on how to put the programs you use most often in this toolbar.

Dial-up networking is now more inconvenient for laptop users

If you frequently dial from more than one location, you can no longer change locations on the fly in implicit Dial-Up Networking connections. You have to start the connection explicitly in order to change the location, since the location no longer appears in the dialog that goes with implicit connections. See "Dial-Up Networking" in Chapter 4 for details. For those of you with Windows 98 Second Edition (or IE5), you will have the ability to change locations on the fly in implicit DUN connections.

Under the Hood

Now we're back to improvements.

FAT 32

The File Allocation Table (FAT) maps file contents to physical sectors on the disk. The old 16-bit FAT16 file system was limited to partitions no larger than 2 gigabytes, while the 32-bit FAT32 system can handle partitions of virtually any size, but the cluster size depends on the partition size. Perhaps more importantly, the FAT32 file system is more efficient in its use of space, since it allocates space in 4K chunks vs. the 32K chunks used by FAT16. (Under FAT16, even a 1K file would use up 32K of disk space behind the scenes, and a 33K file would use up to 64K.) However, disks are not automatically converted if you upgrade, and even some new systems don't automatically use FAT32. See "Drive Converter" in Chapter 6 for a discussion of the issues in converting disks to use FAT32.

More device driver support

Windows 98 includes many more drivers for the latest hardware add-ons, including Universal Serial Bus (USB) devices, firewire (IEEE 1394) devices, DVD players and encoders, infrared devices, and MMX processors.

Performance improvements

Windows 98 uses an algorithm similar to that used by the Norton SpeedStart utility (part of Symantec Norton Utilities 3.0) to speed up application launches. Supposedly, applications will start up to three times faster. In fact, new versions of Norton Utilities use the application data provided by Windows 98 instead of SpeedStart.

Improved Registry backup

Windows automatically runs the Registry Checker (*scanregw.exe*) at startup. The Registry Checker makes a backup of the Registry files, checks for errors, and so forth. By default, the last five backups are saved, so if you've screwed up royally, you can revert to more than just the most recent backup. See Chapter 13, *The Registry*, and "Registry Checker" in Chapter 6 for details.

Windows 98 Second Edition

Windows 98 Second Edition is essentially a maintenance release that contains updated components, more hardware support, and a few new features. If you bought a new computer or a shrinkwrapped copy of Win 98 after June of 1999, then you've likely got the second edition. You can tell which edition is installed by checking out Control Panel → System → General.

Although there are a number of small interface changes, patches, and updates in the second edition, following are a few of the more important additions:

Updated components

Many of the components available in Win 98 have been updated since the original release. Such components include Internet Explorer 5.0, Outlook Express 5.0, FrontPage Express, NetMeeting, DirectX 6.1, Windows Media Player, and Chat 2.5. The updated versions are available through Windows Update for free download (see Chapter 4 for more information) if you have the original version. We cover all of the features from these new updates in the applicable entries in Chapter 6.

For details about DirectX technology, see *http://www.microsoft.com/ directx/*.

Networking

The big addition here is Internet Connection Sharing, which allows Windows 98 computers on a small peer network to share a single Internet connection (dial-up or direct). The computer providing the connection automatically supplies other computers on the network with private IP addresses using a simplified version of the Dynamic Host Configuration Protocol (DHCP). Network address translation maps these private addresses to a set of public addresses, allowing all of the computers on the network equivalent Internet access. See Chapter 5 for details on the new ICS.

Hardware support

Win 98 Second Edition provides support for new hardware made available since the original Win 98 release. This includes USB Type 2 devices and IEEE 1394a storage devices, xDSL and cable modem support, and added support for the Intel Pentium III processor.

TweakUI, FrontPage Express, and Real Player have been left out of the Second Edition of Windows 98

For details on obtaining TweakUI, see "TweakUI" in Chapter 8. Details on acquiring FrontPage Express and Real Player are described in their respective sections in Chapter 6.

CHAPTER 3

Task Index

A lot of tasks that ought to be easy in Windows 98 aren't, because the complexity of the interface means that the controls you need are buried somewhere out of sight. This chapter contains shorthand instructions to get to the right part of the Windows 98 interface for over 100 common tasks.

Each task is presented as the answer to a "How do I..." question (e.g., How do I change the color depth of my display?), followed by the shorthand way to execute the answer (e.g., Desktop → right-click → Properties → Settings), and the location in the book where you can find a detailed discussion of the task (e.g., Chapter 5, *The Control Panel*, "Display" on page 129). We've divided the tasks into the following eight categories:

> Files and Folders
> Getting Information About the System
> Customizing the Desktop
> Other Customizations
> Internet, Web, Email
> Start Menu Programs
> Dial-Up Networking, Networking
> Maintenance, Troubleshooting
> Advanced Customization/The Registry

If you're new to Windows 98, or if you just want to jog your memory when you can't quite remember where a particular setting is located to tweak something, then this is the place to start.

Files and Folders

1. Create a new folder?

   Inside any folder (or on Desktop) → right-click → New → Folder

   Chapter 1, *Using Windows 98*, on page 5

2. Rename a file?

any file → right-click → Rename

Chapter 1, *Using Windows 98*, "Classic Style" on page 5

3. Automatically clear my documents folder each time Windows shuts down?

Control Panel → TweakUI → IE4 → Clear document ... on exit

Chapter 8, *Hidden Gems on the Windows 98 CD-ROM*, "TweakUI" on page 419

4. Change the target folder for My Documents?

My Documents → right-click → Properties → Target

Chapter 4, *The Windows 98 User Interface*, "Shortcut Properties" on page 89

5. Find a file when I don't know its name?

Start → Find → Files or Folders → Name & Location → Containing text

Chapter 4, *The Windows 98 User Interface*, on page 68

6. Copy a file to the desktop instead of moving it or creating a shortcut?

File → right-drag → release → Copy Here

Chapter 1, *Using Windows 98*, on page 5

7. Change the program associated with a particular extension?

Start → Settings → Folder Options → File Types → *any file type* → Edit

Chapter 4, *The Windows 98 User Interface*, "File Types" on page 63

8. Open a file with a different program than its default association?

any file → Shift-right-click → Open with

Chapter 4, *The Windows 98 User Interface*, "File Types" on page 63

9. Display the contents of a shared folder on another machine in my network?

`C:\>dir \\`*machine*`\`*folder*

Chapter 7, *DOS and Other Command-Line Utilities*, "dir" on page 319

10. Customize an individual folder?

Folder → View → Customize folder

Chapter 9, *Web Integration*, "Windows Web Explorer" on page 446

11. Quickly delete an entire directory (and its subdirectories) without sending it to the Recycle Bin?

`C:\>deltree` *directory*

Chapter 7, *DOS and Other Command-Line Utilities*, "deltree" on page 317

12. List all files on your local drive, sorted by size?

`C:\>dir \ /s /os`

Chapter 7, *DOS and Other Command-Line Utilities*, "dir" on page 317

13. Quickly create a set of numbered directories (such as for chapters in a book)?

    `C:\>for %x in (1 2 3 4 5) do md ch0%x`

    Chapter 7, *DOS and Other Command-Line Utilities*, "for" on page 335

14. View the contents of a file without launching the associated program?

    Right-click on the file → Quick View

    Chapter 6, *Start Menu Programs and Other Graphical Applications*, "Quick View" on page 260

15. Drag a file to a folder in Windows Explorer without having to open the folder first?

    Drag the file over a folder and hold for two seconds to "pop open" the folder

    Chapter 4, *The Windows 98 User Interface*, "Windows Explorer" on page 108

16. Delete a file without sending it to the Recycle Bin?

    Hold down Shift while dragging the file to the Recycle Bin or pressing Del

    Chapter 4, *The Windows 98 User Interface*, "Recycle Bin" on page 80

17. Synchronize files between two computers?

    Desktop → Briefcase

    Chapter 4, *The Windows 98 User Interface*, "Briefcase" on page 49

18. Make the recycle bin stop asking if I'm sure I want to delete every file?

    Recycle Bin → right-click → Properties → Global → Display delete confirmation...

    Chapter 4, *The Windows 98 User Interface*, "Recycle Bin" on page 80

Getting Information About the System

1. Make sure my modem is working?

    Control Panel → Modems → Diagnostics → *any modem* → More Info

    Chapter 5, *The Control Panel*, "Modems" on page 148

2. Find out how much disk space I have left?

    My Computer → *any drive* → right-click → Properties → General

    Chapter 4, *The Windows 98 User Interface*, "My Computer" on page 72

3. Find out how much memory I have?

    My Computer → right-click → Properties → General → Computer

    Chapter 4, *The Windows 98 User Interface*, "My Computer" on page 72

4. Find out what version of Windows 98 I have?

    My Computer → right-click → Properties → General → System

    Chapter 4, *The Windows 98 User Interface*, "My Computer" on page 72

5. Find out whether a drive is formatted with FAT32?

   My Computer → *any drive* → right-click → Properties → General

   Chapter 4, *The Windows 98 User Interface*, "My Computer" on page 72

6. Find out what programs (or processes) are running?

   `Ctl-Alt-Del`

   Chapter 4, *The Windows 98 User Interface*, "Shut Down" on page 95

7. Display the status of the computer's used and free memory?

   `C:\>mem`

   Chapter 7, *DOS and Other Command-Line Utilities*, "mem" on page 348

8. Quickly check the status of system resources?

   Start → Run → `rsrcmtr`

   Chapter 6, *Start Menu Programs and Other Graphical Applications*, "Resource Meter" on page 267

9. Monitor memory functions and disk cache settings?

   Start → Run → `sysmon`

   Chapter 6, *Start Menu Programs and Other Graphical Applications*, "System Monitor" on page 277

10. Find out what IRQs my hardware is using?

    Control Panel → System → Device Manager → Computer → Properties → View Resources → Interrupt Request

    Chapter 5, *The Control Panel*, "System" on page 167

11. Determine how much free space I gain in converting a FAT drive to FAT32?

    Address → `fat32win`

    Chapter 8, *Hidden Gems on the Windows 98 CD-ROM*, "FAT32 Conversion Information Tool" on page 403

Customizing the Desktop

1. Add an item to my Start menu?

   Left-drag item to the Start menu and place it in any folder to create shortcut

   Chapter 4, *The Windows 98 User Interface*, "Start Menu" on page 96

2. Change my desktop size/resolution?

   Desktop → right-click → Properties → Settings

   Chapter 5, *The Control Panel*, "Display" on page 128

3. Change the color depth of my display?

   Desktop → right-click → Properties → Settings

   Chapter 5, *The Control Panel*, "Display" on page 129

4. Control which "special" icons appear on my desktop?

   Control Panel → TweakUI → Desktop

   Chapter 8, *Hidden Gems on the Windows 98 CD-ROM*, "TweakUI" on page 419

5. Get rid of the animated "Click to begin" on my taskbar?

   Control Panel → TweakUI → Explorer → Animated 'Click here to begin'...

   Chapter 8, *Hidden Gems on the Windows 98 CD-ROM*, "TweakUI" on page 418

6. Toggle the Active Desktop on and off?

   Desktop → right-click → Active Desktop → View as Web Page

   Chapter 4, *The Windows 98 User Interface*, "The Active Desktop" on page 48

7. Hide desktop icons when Active Desktop is on?

   Desktop → right-click → Properties → Effects → Hide icons when the desktop is viewed as a web page

   Chapter 9, *Web Integration*, "The Active Desktop" on page 437

8. Turn an HTML file into Active Desktop wallpaper?

   Control Panel → Display → Background → Wallpaper

   Chapter 9, *Web Integration*, "Wallpaper" on page 443

Other Customizations

1. Associate a sound with a system event?

   Control Panel → Sounds → *any event* → select sound

   Chapter 5, *The Control Panel*, "Sounds" on page 165

2. Make my monitor turn itself off when not being used?

   Control Panel → Power Management → Turn off monitor

   Chapter 5, *The Control Panel*, "Power Management" on page 161

3. Change the double-click speed of my mouse?

   Control Panel → Mouse → Double-click speed

   Chapter 5, *The Control Panel*, "Mouse" on page 149

4. Change how close together (in pixels) two clicks must be to be considered a double-click?

   Control Panel → TweakUI → Mouse → Double-click

   Chapter 8, *Hidden Gems on the Windows 98 CD-ROM*, "TweakUI" on page 418

5. Change my logon password?

   Control Panel → Passwords → Change Password → Change Windows Password

   Chapter 5, *The Control Panel*, "Passwords" on page 159

6. Convert a drive from FAT to FAT32?

   Start → Run → **cvt1**

   Chapter 6, *Start Menu Programs and Other Graphical Applications*, "Drive Converter" on page 194

7. Change the date/time?

   System Tray Clock → double-click → Date & Time

   Chapter 4, *The Windows 98 User Interface*, "System Tray" on page 98

8. Change the name of my computer?

   Control Panel → Network → Identification → Computer name

   Chapter 5, *The Control Panel*, "Network" on page 155

9. Restart Windows without rebooting my computer?

   Start → Shut Down → Shut Down → **Shift-OK**

   Chapter 12, *Windows Startup*, "Restart the computer" on page 509

10. Make Windows 98 remember my window settings?

    Control Panel → TweakUI → Explorer → Save Explorer window settings

    Chapter 8, *Hidden Gems on the Windows 98 CD-ROM*, "TweakUI" on page 418

11. Keep windows from autoplaying audio and/or data CDs?

    Control Panel → TweakUI → Paranoia → Things that happen behind your back

    Chapter 8, *Hidden Gems on the Windows 98 CD-ROM*, "TweakUI" on page 422

12. Capture a screenshot of my desktop?

    Press **PrintScrn** and paste as *.bmp* into any graphics program (e.g., MS Paint)

    Appendix A, *Keyboard Accelerators*, on page 571

13. Capture a screenshot of an active window?

    Press **Alt-PrintScrn** and paste as *.bmp* into any graphics program (e.g., MS Paint)

    Appendix A, *Keyboard Accelerators*, on page 571

14. Add items to my Send To menu?

    Place shortcuts in \ *Windows\Sendto*

    Chapter 4, *The Windows 98 User Interface*, "Send To" on page 87

15. Make sure Windows 98 is "Y2K-ready?"

    Start → Windows Update → install Windows 98 Year 2000 fix

    Chapter 4, *The Windows 98 User Interface*, "Windows Update" on page 111

16. Make a program run automatically when Windows starts?

    Place a shortcut for it in \ *Windows\Start Menu\Programs\Start Up*

    Chapter 4, *The Windows 98 User Interface*, "Startup Folder" on page 98

Internet, Web, Email

1. Get Outlook Express to check my email automatically?

   Tools → Options → General → Check for new messages every...

   Chapter 6, *Start Menu Programs and Other Graphical Applications*, "Outlook Express" on page 244

2. Send a picture with an email message in Outlook Express?

   New Message window → Insert → File Attachment

   Chapter 6, *Start Menu Programs and Other Graphical Applications*, "Outlook Express" on page 246

3. Find out a person's email address?

   Start → Find → People → Look In

   Chapter 4, *The Windows 98 User Interface*, "Find Files and Folders" on page 69

4. Change my home page in Internet Explorer?

   View → Internet Options → General → Home Page

   Chapter 6, *Start Menu Programs and Other Graphical Applications*, "Internet Explorer" on page 211

5. Protect my child from offensive Internet sites?

   Control Panel → Internet → Content → Content Advisor → Enable

   Chapter 5, *The Control Panel*, "Internet" on page 136

6. Make Internet Explorer stop notifying me when downloads are complete?

   Control Panel → Internet → Advanced → Notify when downloads complete

   Chapter 5, *The Control Panel*, "Internet" on page 141

7. Configure how much space is taken on my drive by temporary Internet files?

   Control Panel → Internet → General → Settings → Amount of disk space to use

   Chapter 5, *The Control Panel*, "Internet" on page 135

8. Make Internet Explorer stop disconnecting automatically?

   Control Panel → Internet → Connection → Settings → Disconnect if idle...

   Chapter 5, *The Control Panel*, "Internet" on page 139

9. Change the search engine used when I type ? *keyword* in the IE address bar?

   Control Panel → TweakUI → General → Search Engine

   Chapter 8, *Hidden Gems on the Windows 98 CD-ROM*, "TweakUI" on page 418

10. Create an Active Desktop item from IE ?

    right-drag a link from IE → Create Active Desktop Items Here

    Chapter 9, *Web Integration*, "Embedding Actively" on page 441

11. Read cached web pages offline?

    IE → File → Work Offline → click History button

    Chapter 6, *Start Menu Programs and Other Graphical Applications*, "Internet Explorer" on page 213

12. Save entries I've typed into web forms at my favorite sites using IE5?

    Tools → Internet Options → Content → AutoComplete

    Chapter 6, *Start Menu Programs and Other Graphical Applications*, "Internet Explorer" on page 214

13. Launch the Radio Toolbar in IE5?

    View → Toolbars → Radio

    Chapter 6, *Start Menu Programs and Other Graphical Applications*, "Internet Explorer" on page 218

14. Share Outlook Express 5 with multiple users and accounts?

    File → Identities → Add New Identity

    Chapter 6, *Start Menu Programs and Other Graphical Applications*, "Outlook Express" on page 246

15. Create Mail Rules and filter message using Outlook Express 5?

    Message → Create Rule from Message

    Chapter 6, *Start Menu Programs and Other Graphical Applications*, "Outlook Express" on page 247

16. Send a fax using Windows 98?

    Address → `awsnto32`

    Chapter 8, *Hidden Gems on the Windows 98 CD-ROM*, "Microsoft Fax" on page 406

17. Host a web site on my local system?

    Add/Remove Programs → Install → *Win 98 CD\add-ons\pws\setup.exe*

    Chapter 6, *Start Menu Programs and Other Graphical Applications*, "Personal Web Server" on page 257

18. Copy local files to my web site on my ISP?

    Start → Programs → Internet Explorer → Web Publishing Wizard

    Chapter 6, *Start Menu Programs and Other Graphical Applications*, "Web Publishing Wizard" on page 286

19. Create web pages if I don't know HTML?

    Start → Programs → Internet Explorer → FrontPage Express

    Chapter 6, *Start Menu Programs and Other Graphical Applications*, "FrontPage Express" on page 200

Task Index

20. Watch TV on my computer?

Quick Launch Bar → Launch Web TV for Windows (with a compatible tuner card)

Chapter 6, *Start Menu Programs and Other Graphical Applications*, "Web TV for Windows" on page 287

Start Menu Programs

1. Record a sound?

Start → Programs → Accessories → Entertainment → Sound Recorder

Chapter 6, *Start Menu Programs and Other Graphical Applications*, "Sound Recorder" on page 272

2. Perform statistical calculations?

Address → calc → View → Scientific

Chapter 6, *Start Menu Programs and Other Graphical Applications*, "Calculator" on page 180

3. Connect to a chat server?

Address → cchat → File → New Connection

Chapter 6, *Start Menu Programs and Other Graphical Applications*, "Microsoft Chat" on page 228

4. Temporarily disable autoplay or autorun of a CD?

Hold the Shift key down when inserting the CD

Chapter 6, *Start Menu Programs and Other Graphical Applications*, "CD Player" on page 183

5. Quickly access the MS-DOS command line?

Address → command

Chapter 7, *DOS and Other Command-Line Utilities*, "command" on page 307

6. Quickly access the Windows Setup tab in the Add/Remove Programs applet?

Address → control appwiz.cpl ,2

Chapter 7, *DOS and Other Command-Line Utilities*, "control" on page 309

7. Make telephone calls using the computer?

Address → dialer

Chapter 6, *Start Menu Programs and Other Graphical Applications*, "Phone Dialer" on page 259

8. Make a Win3.1 program compatible with Windows 98?

Address → mkcompat

Chapter 6, *Start Menu Programs and Other Graphical Applications*, "Make Compatible" on page 226

9. Back up files from my hard drive to a tape or diskette?

   Address → `msbackup`

   Chapter 6, *Start Menu Programs and Other Graphical Applications*, "Backup" on page 175

10. View all users connected to a shared directory?

    Address → `netwatch`

    Chapter 6, *Start Menu Programs and Other Graphical Applications*, "Net Watcher" on page 236

Dial-Up Networking, Networking

1. Disable call waiting when I use a dial-up connection?

   Control Panel → Telephony → To disable call waiting...

   Chapter 5, *The Control Panel*, "Telephony" on page 169

2. Create new locations for dial-up networking?

   Control Panel → Telephony → My Locations

   Chapter 5, *The Control Panel*, "Telephony" on page 169

3. Find a computer on the network without browsing Network Neighborhood?

   Start → Find → Computer

   Address → `\\computername`

   Chapter 4, *The Windows 98 User Interface*, "Find" on page 69

4. Share a folder on a network?

   Folder → right-click → Sharing... → Shared As

   Chapter 4, *The Windows 98 User Interface*, "Network Neighborhood" on page 74

5. Make Win 98 stop asking if I want to use a dial-up connection when it can't find a computer on my network?

   Dial-Up Networking → Connections → Settings → Don't prompt to use Dial-Up Networking

   Chapter 4, *The Windows 98 User Interface*, "Dial-Up Networking" on page 63

6. Synchronize my clock with the clock on another computer?

   Address → `net time \\computername /set`

   Chapter 7, *DOS and Other Command-Line Utilities*, "net time" on page 360

7. Find out what's taking a site so long to respond?

   `C:\>ping hostname`

   Chapter 7, *DOS and Other Command-Line Utilities*, "ping" on page 367

8. Look under the hood and trace the route taken to connect to a web page?

   `C:\>tracert hostname`

   Chapter 7, *DOS and Other Command-Line Utilities*, "tracert" on page 389

9. Start Windows 98 in safe mode with networking support?

Press F6 at startup

Chapter 12, *Windows Startup*, on page 510

Maintenance, Troubleshooting

1. Run *defrag* without having it restart so many times while running?

    Win 98 *CD\Tools\mtsutil\defrag.inf* → right-click → Install → Restart your system

    Chapter 8, *Hidden Gems on the Windows 98 CD-ROM*, "MTS Utilities" on page 408

2. Troubleshoot problems during Windows startup?

    Address → msconfig

    Chapter 12, *Windows Startup*, "System Configuration Utility" on page 514

3. Restore my hardware and software system settings from a backup without having to reinstall all my applications?

    Boot Computer with CD support → Win 98 *CD\Tools\sysrec\pcrestor.bat*

    Chapter 8, *Hidden Gems on the Windows 98 CD-ROM*, "System Recovery" on page 414

4. Schedule my system to run *defrag*, *scandisk*, and compression agent automatically?

    Address → tuneup

    Chapter 6, *Start Menu Programs and Other Graphical Applications*, "Maintenance Wizard" on page 226

5. Verify system files and replace those that are corrupted?

    Address → sfc

    Chapter 6, *Start Menu Programs and Other Graphical Applications*, "System File Checker" on page 274

6. Free disk space by removing unneccesary files from the system?

    Address → cleanmgr

    Chapter 6, *Start Menu Programs and Other Graphical Applications*, "Disk Cleanup" on page 190

Advanced Customization/The Registry

1. View and modify the Registy?

    Address → regedit

    Chapter 6, *Start Menu Programs and Other Graphical Applications*, "Registry Editor" on page 265

2. Verify and repair the Windows 98 Registry?

    Address → `scanregw`

    Chapter 6, *Start Menu Programs and Other Graphical Applications*, "Registry Checker" on page 264

3. Make IE's AutoComplete more efficient?

    `HKLM\SOFTWARE\Microsoft\Internet Explorer\Main\UrlTemplate`

    Chapter 13, *The Registry*, "Ten cool things you can do in your registry" on page 564

4. Change your default search engine for IE?

    `HKCU\Software\Microsoft\Internet Explorer\Main key`

    Chapter 13, *The Registry*, "Ten cool things you can do in your registry" on page 564

5. Get rid of Start → Documents?

    `HKCU\Software\Microsoft\Windows\CurrentVersion\Policies\Explorer`

    Chapter 13, *The Registry*, "Ten cool things you can do in your registry" on page 564

6. Get rid of Start → Favorites?

    `HKCU\Software\Microsoft\Windows\CurrentVersion\Policies\Explorer`

    Chapter 13, *The Registry*, "Ten cool things you can do in your registry" on page 565

7. Disable the Shut Down command?

    `HKCU\Software\Microsoft\Windows\CurrentVersion\Policies\Explorer`

    Chapter 13, *The Registry*, "Ten cool things you can do in your registry" on page 565

8. Change the size of my desktop icons?

    `HKCU\Control Panel\Desktop\WindowMetrics`

    Chapter 13, *The Registry*, "Ten cool things you can do in your registry" on page 565

9. Change the registered user and company names for Win 98?

    `HKLM\Software\Microsoft\Windows\CurrentVersion`

    Chapter 13, *The Registry*, "Ten cool things you can do in your registry" on page 565

10. Change my default Win 98 installation path?

    `HKLM\Software\Microsoft\Windows\CurrentVersion\Setup`

    Chapter 13, *The Registry*, "Ten cool things you can do in your registry" on page 565

PART II

Alphabetical Reference

CHAPTER 4

The Windows 98 User Interface

This chapter provides an alphabetical reference to many of the major user interface elements in the Windows 98 Desktop.

The Control Panel (used by facilities such as the Microsoft Network, Internet Explorer, and Dial-Up Networking) is covered in a separate chapter, since it's a complex environment in its own right. Many of the utilities and accessories on the Start menu are covered in Chapter 6, *Start Menu Programs and Other Graphical Applications*, and DOS and command-line utilities are covered in Chapter 7, *DOS and Other Command-Line Utilities*.

The alphabetical reference entries are as follows:

Active Desktop	*Online Services Folder*
Briefcase	*Printers*
Channel Bar	*Properties*
Clipboard	*Recycle Bin*
Context Menus	*Run*
Desktop	*Scheduled Tasks*
Dial-Up Networking	*Send To*
File Types	*Shortcuts*
Find Files and Folders	*Shut Down*
Folder Options	*Start Menu*
Icons	*Startup Folder*
Inbox	*System Tray*
Internet	*Taskbar*
Login	*Toolbars*
My Computer	*Windows Explorer*
Network Neighborhood	*Windows Update*

Note that because of the variety of Windows 98 installation options, not every system will have each of these features on its Desktop. Note also that while most of these items are visible on the Desktop, some are contained within folders or menus. In addition, a few (context menus, File Types, and Properties) refer to context-specific menus or dialogs that can be popped up from many different objects, and will be different for each object.

Each entry contains a brief description, a shorthand path showing how to get to the item, a figure (if some aspect of the user interface is sufficiently complex to require it), and a set of notes focusing on features that are buried in the user interface, not obvious, or undocumented.

Almost all of these user-interface elements are provided by the Windows 98 Explorer. If a user interface element has a corresponding file or folder (as well as being an element of the Explorer), that is shown on the far right of the title line:

Entry Name \pathname
Brief description.

The path notation we use to show how to reach each user interface element is described in the Preface. If there is more than one way to reach a given user interface element, multiple paths are shown. For example:

> My Computer → Printers
> Start → Settings → Printers

Active Desktop

Integrate web functionality with your desktop.

> Desktop → right-click → Active Desktop → View As Web Page
> Control Panel → Display → Web → View my Active Desktop as a web page

Description

Active Desktop can do two related, but separate, things. It allows you to use an *.html* document as your desktop wallpaper using Control Panel → Display → Background → Wallpaper. Chapter 5, *The Control Panel*, and Chapter 9, *Web Integration*, contain information on activating and using this feature.

Active Desktop also allows you to use Active Desktop items, which are essentially web pages embedded in your desktop. Any URL can be used as an Active Desktop item. You can enable desktop items using Control Panel → Display → Web. Clicking New allows you to manually enter a URL or visit the Microsoft Active Desktop Gallery.

Notes

- If the dialog offering gallery access has been disabled, you can go there directly at *http://www.microsoft.com/windows/ie/ie40/gallery/* (as long as you use IE as your browser).

- Once you embed an item in your desktop, you can use the item by moving your mouse over it. Move your mouse to the top edge of the item to open a toolbar that lets you move and close the item and sometimes access additional properties.

See Also

"Display" in Chapter 5

Chapter 9

Briefcase

\ *Windows\Desktop\My Briefcase*

Synchronize files between two computers.

Desktop → My Briefcase

Desktop → context menu → New → Briefcase

Description

Before going on a trip, you might want to copy a set of files on your Desktop to the Briefcase, then move the Briefcase to the laptop (or to a floppy disk). You can edit either the original files or the ones in the Briefcase. Then, when you return, copy the Briefcase back to the original machine and use Briefcase menu → Update to synchronize the Briefcase and original copies of the files. If the machines are networked, you can synchronize files without having to copy the Briefcase back and forth. Synchronization will work with UNC paths to networked files or folders.

To put a file in the Briefcase, you can drag its icon to the Briefcase folder, or you can use the Send To menu, which lists My Briefcase as an option. Figure 4-1 shows the Details view of the contents of a Briefcase.

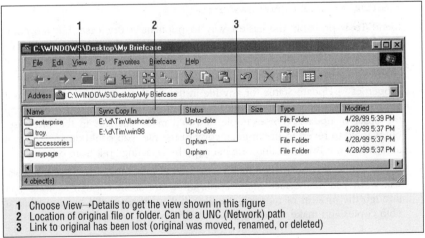

1 Choose View→Details to get the view shown in this figure
2 Location of original file or folder. Can be a UNC (Network) path
3 Link to original has been lost (original was moved, renamed, or deleted)

Figure 4-1: My Briefcase with several synced and orphaned folders

Notes

- You can initiate an update from either the Briefcase menu or the File menu. The Briefcase menu gives you an Update All option, and the File menu allows the update of only selected files (though you can of course Select All).

- When you update the contents of the Briefcase, Windows displays several details, including the modification date of each file and the direction in which

---

the Briefcase intends to make the update. You can right-click on the directional arrow to change the direction or skip the update.

- The Briefcase mechanism uses the date and time of update to determine which of the two copies of the file is the most up-to-date, so be sure that the clocks on both machines are synchronized.

- My Briefcase is automatically created on the Desktop if you choose Portable setup when installing Windows 98, or if you choose it as part of a Custom installation. To install it later, use:

  Control Panel → Add/Remove Programs → Windows Setup → Accessories → Details → Briefcase

- Create a Briefcase on a floppy if you frequently work on the same set of files at work and at home. You can then synchronize (Briefcase → Update All) at the beginning and end of each day to make sure you have the latest copy on both machines.

- You will need multiple Briefcases if you are using floppy disks for the transport mechanism and you have more files than will fit on a single disk. By default, Send To will recognize only My Briefcase, but you can drag and drop to any Briefcase. (See "Send To" later in this chapter for a discussion of how to add additional items—such as other Briefcases—to the Send To menu.)

  You can create multiple Briefcases by right-clicking on the Desktop and choosing New → Briefcase, or by using the following command line:

  ```
  rundll32 syncui.dll,Briefcase.Create
  ```

  (Send To is probably the easiest way to populate a Briefcase, but the command line could be useful if, for instance, you wanted to create a batch file that created a new Briefcase and then copied the contents of the current folder to it.)

- Properties → Update Status for any file in the Briefcase will give details about which version is considered more up-to-date, and gives options for changing the order of update. (For example, if you'd made changes in the Briefcase, but wanted to revert to the original copy of the file, you could do so. You can also unlink the Briefcase and original copy by selecting Split from original.)

- If you screw up and make changes to both copies of the file, the Briefcase will warn you of the fact. Some applications are smart enough to walk you through the process of merging the files, but for most, you'll have to look at both copies and make the changes manually.

 Visto Corp (*http://www.visto.com/*) has a new twist on the Briefcase. You can keep a Visto Briefcase on their web site, and have access to it from wherever you are. The Visto Assistant synchronizes the web-based Briefcase with the one on your disk. It also synchronizes with contact managers, including Microsoft Outlook, Lotus Organizer, and Starfish Sidekick.

Channel Bar

View a predefined collection of web sites.

> Control Panel → Display → Web → Internet Explorer Channel Bar
> *any open IE window* → Channels button
> Favorites → Channels

Though it has been hyped as a way of delivering cool active content right to your desktop, the Channel Bar is really nothing more than a specialized favorites folder. It contains a collection of URLs that you can visit with the click of a button. By default, the channel bar active desktop item is displayed when you start Windows 98, as shown in Figure 4-2. Clicking a channel launches that web site in a full-screen browsing window. You can also display the channel bar in any open Internet Explorer window by clicking the Channel button on the toolbar.

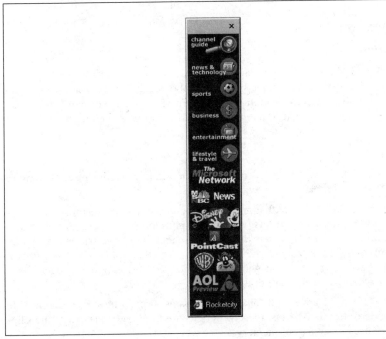

Figure 4-2: The Channel Bar

Many of the URLs in the Channel Bar are configured using Channel Definition Format, which basically means that the web site provider has configured a file that specifies when and how content should be delivered automatically to your desktop. The Channel Bar can also contain URLs for standard web pages.

By default, the Channel Bar only contains the web sites of a group of content providers who've signed up with Microsoft to be "in your face." For most users, therefore, the Channel Bar is simply an annoying feature of Windows 98. It duplicates functionality found elsewhere, and the desktop item consumes valuable screen real estate. You can fill it with your own URLs, but you'll likely find that the regular Favorites folder or the Quick Links toolbar suits you better. You can turn off the Channel Bar desktop item by simply closing it. You will be asked whether you wish to launch it automatically the next time you start windows. You can also turn it off using Control Panel → Display → Web → Internet Explorer Channel Bar.

The Channel Bar does have some beneficial uses. Many network administrators find it useful to define portions of their intranet using Channel Definition Format and then include those portions on the Channel Bar of users' desktops. This allows users easy access to up-to-date company information.

Clipboard

A shared, system-wide storage area for holding and moving data.

> Edit → Cut (Ctrl-X)
> Edit → Copy (Ctrl-C)
> Edit → Paste (Ctrl-V)

Description

The Clipboard is an invisible storage area, unless you've installed the Clipboard Viewer. Data can be cut or copied to the Clipboard, then pasted in a new location, in either the same application or a different application. You must first select the data to be cut or copied. Data in the Clipboard can be pasted again and again, until it is replaced by new data.

Notes

- The Clipboard holds only one item at a time. Cutting or copying something to the Clipboard replaces its previous contents.

- You can paste only data that an application is prepared to receive. For example, you cannot paste an image into an application (such as DOS) that recognizes only text. (DOS can't *really* even paste text, but Windows simulates it by typing out the contents of the Clipboard.) Note that applications like Photoshop have their own non-Windows clipboards, and export the data *sometimes* when you switch applications.

- The Clipboard Viewer and Clip Tray programs display the otherwise-invisible Clipboard. In other words, these programs are Clipboard "viewers." The Clipboard itself is an area of memory.

- In a DOS window, you must use the buttons on the taskbar to make selections, copy, and paste.

- Some older (Windows 3.0) applications instead recognize the keyboard accelerators Ctrl-Insert for copy and Shift-Insert for Paste.

See Also

"Clipboard Viewer" in Chapter 6
"Clip Tray" in Chapter 8, *Hidden Gems on the Windows 98 CD-ROM*

Context Menus

Right-clicking on many windows, icons, or user interface items will pop up a menu with various special operations. The menu's contents will vary depending on which item you've right-clicked, so it is normally called the context menu.

To view the context menu for an object:

Right-click
Shift-F10 when the object is selected
The context menu button on some keyboards

Description

Figure 4-3 shows the context menu for a folder. Context menus for other types of objects are discussed in the entry for each object.

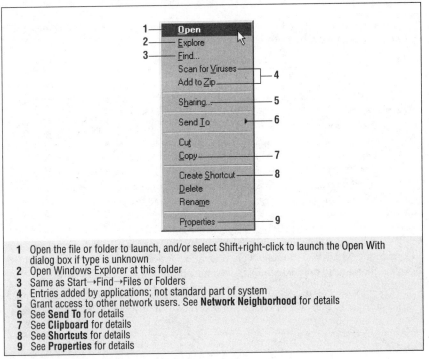

1 Open the file or folder to launch, and/or select Shift+right-click to launch the Open With dialog box if type is unknown
2 Open Windows Explorer at this folder
3 Same as Start→Find→Files or Folders
4 Entries added by applications; not standard part of system
5 Grant access to other network users. See **Network Neighborhood** for details
6 See **Send To** for details
7 See **Clipboard** for details
8 See **Shortcuts** for details
9 See **Properties** for details

Figure 4-3: Context menu for a folder

Notes

• Context menus exist for all of the major interface elements—files, folders (including system folders like My Computer, Network Neighborhood, Recycle Bin, and My Briefcase), the Desktop, the Taskbar, the System Tray, and so on—but they often also exist for elements within an application window or dialog.

At the least, individual buttons or other user interface elements often have a context menu consisting of the single entry "What's This?", which gives a short description of what that element is used for. However, in some cases, the context menu is more extensive. For example, right-clicking in the results window of a Find search yields a View menu that allows you to customize the way the results are displayed.

If you're ever stuck, try right-clicking on a user-interface element and see if anything helpful pops up.

- Right-clicking on the titlebar of a window gives you the context menu for the window. (This is typically the same system menu that you will get by clicking on the icon in the leftmost corner of the titlebar.) Right-clicking in the body of the window gives you the context menu for the application, or the selected element within the application, if one exists. Note that this is different from the context menu that you get by clicking on the program's icon when it is not running.

- The context menu for the Desktop includes a New entry, which allows you to create a new Folder, Shortcut, or empty file.

 Any program or command line on the system can be made into a new "verb" on a context menu using View → Options → File Types → Edit from any folder or Explorer window. See "File Types" later in this chapter. (To create new verbs directly in the Registry, see *Windows 98 Annoyances*, by David Karp, O'Reilly & Associates. Note that customizing the context menu for HKEY_CLASSES_ROOT*\ shell lets you create verbs for all files; normally they'll apply to particular file types, based in turn on file extensions; objects—drive, folder, unknown, etc.; or URL prefixes—http, ftp, etc.)

- The bold item (usually, but not always, at the top) is the default action, carried out when you double-click. View → Options → File Types → Edit lets you change the default action as well as letting you add new actions.

- Most new keyboards also include a context key (looks like a menu with a pointer on it) that will open the context menu of any selected item.

Desktop

\Windows\Desktop
\Windows\Profiles\username\Desktop

The most visible element of the Explorer user interface. Supports icons, windows, and drag-and-drop functionality.

An overview of the Desktop is provided in Chapter 1, *Using Windows 98*. This section mainly consists of a few implementation notes and useful tips.

Notes

- The Desktop is a folder, and can contain files and other folders. When you put something on the Desktop, you are really putting it in the folder \ *Windows\Desktop* (or \ *Windows\Profiles*username*\Desktop* if multiple user profiles are in use). Similarly, any changes you make to that folder—even from the DOS prompt—will result in immediate changes on the Desktop. Rename, copy, or delete files in \ *Windows\Desktop* using the command line or the Explorer, and the Desktop will change accordingly.

- The Desktop is created and maintained by Windows Explorer (*explorer.exe*). The Explorer creates the Desktop only when it is run during startup, using the shell= setting in the file \ *Windows\system.ini*. Subsequent invocations of the Explorer present the normal paned view. If shell= is given some other command (e.g., *command.com*), the Desktop, the Start menu, and the Taskbar will not be shown.

- Some icons on the Desktop (such as My Computer, Recycle Bin, and Network Neighborhood) aren't files or folders, but system objects. They act like folders but have some special characteristics—including additional menus.

- Desktop → right-click → New allows you to create new folders, shortcuts, or empty files of various types.

- Desktop → right-click → Properties (also on the context menu) is the same as Start → Settings → Control Panel → Display.

- Icons can be arranged on the Desktop by type (system facilities, folders, and files, in that order), alphabetically by name, by date (with the most recent first), and by size (with the smallest first). Select AutoArrange if you want the icons to automatically go into neat rows; unselect it if you want to be able to drag them anywhere on the Desktop. When the Desktop gets full, auto-arrange stops working.

- You can specify that the Active Desktop be viewed as a web page, thereby making it customizable with HTML, JavaScript, animated GIF files, and so on.

- The Quick Launch toolbar includes a Show Desktop button that instantly hides all open windows, thus allowing access to your desktop. If you click the button a second time without opening any new items, all windows are restored to their original state.

Dial-Up Networking

Configure a dial-up connection to a remote network.

> My Computer → Dial-Up Networking
> Start → Programs → Accessories → Communications → Dial-Up Networking

Description

Dial-Up Networking (DUN) allows you to dial into an Internet service provider (or to a Windows NT or NetWare server) and, once the connection is made, to use the same kind of networking facilities you can use on a local area network. On a Windows NT network, this means using normal networking services, such as file and printer sharing and email. On the Internet, this means the Web, email, and so on.

Configuring the connection itself is not too difficult. However, there are some things you will need to do before you can configure a connection to a remote network:

1. If Dial-Up Networking is not already installed (you'll know because the folder won't be there), you can install it using Control Panel → Add/Remove Programs → Windows Setup, as discussed in Chapter 5. DUN is a sub-component of the Communications category.

2. Configure a modem using Control Panel → Modems, as discussed in Chapter 5. Properties you configure using Control Panel → Modem are global properties that represent the default behavior of the modem itself. These properties can be overridden for individual DUN connections.

3. Configure a location using Control Panel → Telephony, as discussed in Chapter 5. A location defines information about where you are calling from, including area codes, call waiting, and calling cards. You will probably be given the chance to configure a location automatically when you configure a modem. Also, if you haven't configured a location by the time you are ready to set up your first DUN connection, you'll be given the chance to do so then. Control Panel → Telephony just offers a little more control, plus the ability to set up multiple locations. For each DUN connection, you will be able to select the location you are dialing from each time you dial the connection.

4. Optionally, configure networking using Control Panel → Network, as discussed in Chapter 5. For the most part, this information is configured for you when you install DUN. An adapter named Dial-Up Adapter is installed. The TCP/IP protocol is also installed and it (along with any other installed protocols) is bound to the Dial-Up Adapter. Since you will be able to individually configure protocol properties for each connection, you should really just leave Control Panel → Network alone, unless the administrator of the remote network tells you otherwise.

Once these criteria are met, you can create a DUN connection. Double-clicking "Make New Connection" in the DUN folder launches a wizard that lets you name the connection, choose the modem you wish to use, and enter the phone number for the remote server. Once created, an icon for the new connection shows up in the DUN folder.

To access the connection from a more convenient location, you can make either a .dun file copy or a shortcut to it. You can create a .dun file of a DUN connection by left-dragging (or right-dragging using copy) a DUN connection to another location. This isn't a shortcut, but an actual copy of the DUN parameters, so any changes you make to the original DUN connection won't be updated in the copy. This .dun file can be copied to other computers for use. To make a shortcut (.lnk) of a DUN connection, right-drag the icon to a location and choose "Create Shortcut(s) Here." The shortcut will launch the original DUN connection, so any changes made to the orginal DUN connection via the shortcut will be updated.

You will now need to define some properties specific to your connection using *any connection* → right-click → Properties. The properties sheet for a connection has four tabs: General, Server Types, Scripting, and Multilink.

General

Lets you change the area code, phone number, and country code for a connection and also specify whether the area code and dialing properties should be used for this particular connection.

The General tab also lets you specify a modem to be used for the connection. The Configure button pops open a tabbed dialog that lets you set modem options for the connection. See Control Panel → Modem for a discussion of the options. The settings are the same; however, any values set here will override the Control Panel settings for this particular connection.

The modem property sheet accessed here has one additional tab that is not accessible from the Control Panel. The Options tab lets you specify things like operator-assisted dialing, but more importantly, in the context of modem settings, it lets you specify "Bring up terminal window before dialing." Use this option if you want to issue AT commands directly to your modem.

Server Types

Lets you configure the type of server you are dialing into, as well as advanced options governing the connection to the server and the protocols the connection can use (see Figure 4-4). Many of the advanced options and allowed network protocols are enabled or disabled based on the type of server you choose.

Types of servers include:

PPP: Internet, Windows NT Server, Windows 98
> PPP stands for Point-to-Point Protocol, a flexible dial-up protocol that supports TCP/IP over dial-up, as well as NetBEUI and IPX/SPX. PPP is the server type of choice for most Internet connections, as well as for dialing into Windows NT or Windows 98 dial-up servers.
>
> For an Internet connection, you typically should turn off all of the advanced options, unless otherwise instructed by your ISP. Only the TCP/IP protocol should be enabled, and the others should be off.
>
> If the PPP server is actually a front end to an NT or NetWare-based network, then "Log on to network," "Enable software compression," and "Require encrypted password" should probably be turned on, and any protocols used by your network should be turned on. Many NT networks support all three protocols.

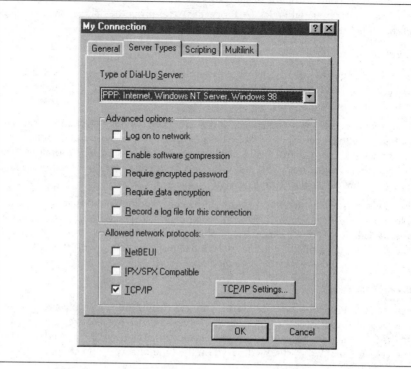

Figure 4-4: Setting server types

 Of the three supported protocols, you can only configure additional settings for TCP/IP. Most modern ISPs and corporate networks use something called Dynamic Host Configuration Protocol (DHCP) to assign IP addresses, DNS and WINS server addresses, and default gateway addresses to client computers automatically. This means that you will likely not need to configure any additional TCP/IP settings, as the remote network should do all the work for you. If, however, you do need to enter IP or name server addresses (the administrator of the remote network will let you know), do it here. Settings you make here will override global protocol settings made with Control Panel → Network → Configuration → *any protocol* → Properties.

SLIP: Unix Connection

Serial Line Internet Protocol is a predecessor to PPP that has fallen out of wide use. If you connect to a SLIP server, you can only use TCP/IP as a network protocol. NetBEUI and IPX/SPX are not supported over SLIP. If you are connecting to the Internet, you should usually turn off "Log on to network."

NRN: NetWare Connect

When connecting to a NetWare server via dial-up networking, you will have a unique IPX address for each session.

CSLIP: Unix Connection with IP header Compression

CSLIP is simply a form of SLIP server that supports IP header compression, also known as Van Jacobson header compression.

Windows for Workgroups and Windows NT 3.1

When connecting to a peer network running Windows for Workgroups or a Windows NT Server 3.1 network.

Scripting

If you are using PPP to connect to a modern ISP or a corporate or peer network, authentication on that network is usually handled automatically using one of two authentication protocols: PAP (Password Authentication Protocol) or CHAP (Challenge Authentication Protocol). However, if you are using SLIP to connect to a Unix host, or are connecting via older terminal servers, you may need to build an explicit login script for your connection. A login script is simply a series of commands issued to the remote server to authenticate you on the network and possibly perform additional commands as well.

The Scripting tab lets you choose your login script and also edit it using Notepad. Windows 98 includes four sample scripts in the *Program Files\Accessories* folder that you can customize for your login:

Cis.scp

Script file that demonstrates how to establish a PPP connection with CompuServe, which requires changing the port settings to log in.

Pppmenu.scp

Script file that demonstrates how to establish a PPP connection with a host that uses a menu system.

Slip.scp

Script file that demonstrates how to establish a SLIP connection with a host.

Slipmenu.scp

Script file that demonstrates how to establish a SLIP connection with a host that uses a menu system.

Script files have the extension *.scp*; they describe the various prompts and responses of the login process using a simple language. For example, the following script (which is very similar to the *generic.scp* script that comes with the scripting package) waits for a login prompt (a string ending with the characters "ogin:"), and then sends the username from the Connecting To dialog box. It sends an explicit carriage return (<cr>), waits for a prompt ending with the characters "ssword:", sends the password from the Connecting To dialog box, followed by another carriage return:

```
proc main
waitfor "ogin:"
transmit $USERID
transmit <cr>
waitfor "ssword:"
```

```
transmit $PASSWORD
transmit <cr>
endproc
```

It's typical to search for only the end of a string ("ogin" rather than "Login" or "ssword" rather than "Password") because that insulates you from variations in the case of the prompt's first letter. This is particularly important when debugging new scripts—small differences in the prompt and the string you wait for can cause the script to keep waiting until the login attempt finally times out.

The best way to build a script is to log in manually by setting Connection → Properties → Options → Bring up terminal window after dialing, and then fire up the connection. Write down exactly what prompts appear and how you respond, then build that into the script. If you can't get a script to work reliably, you can even leave this option set and do the login manually every time you connect. Just hit F7 or click Continue after the login process is complete.

Windows 98 also includes a document that explains how to write and modify logon scripts. The file is called *Script.doc* and is located in your Windows directory.

Some Tips and Gotchas

- PCs and Unix systems use different conventions for ending lines. PCs use a carriage return and a line feed; Unix systems use only a line feed. You may need to specify an explicit return or line feed to proceed to the next step in the script.

- You need match only the end of a prompt string. The last five or six characters are sufficient. Keeping the matching string short helps avoid problems such as not matching case or spaces exactly.

- If you're having trouble with your script, check a`ny connection` → Properties → Scripting → Step through script, and watch its progress during the connection, so you can see where it gets hung up.

- Don't confuse the connection's login with any network login required after the PPP session is started. Connection → Properties → Server Type → Log on to network controls whether your system will log on to the remote Netware or NT network once the lower-level PPP login has taken place. See "Passwords" in Chapter 5 for additional details.

Multilink

Multilink is a subcomponent of the PPP protocol that allows you to combine connections using two or more modems into a single logical connection. Thus, you could use two 56k modems to achieve a virtual 128k connection. Multilink must also be supported by the remote server you are dialing in to as well as the hardware drivers. To enable multilink, simply add the device (modem) and supply a phone number. Note that many ISPs will use a separate phone number for multilink connections than for regular connections. Also, many ISPs charge extra for additional simultaneous connections to their network. When you dial your connection, a connection will be made with the primary device (the one configured the connection) and then with any additional devices specified on the Multilink tab.

Launching a Connection

Once you have configured the properties for a dial-up connection, you can launch that connection in one of two ways: explicitly or implicitly. To use a connection explicitly, double-click on its icon to open the Connect To dialog box shown in Figure 4-5. If you change the phone number on this dialog, you will change it for this use only. The number will not be remembered. Strangely enough, a drop-down list is provided to select area codes, but multiple phone numbers are not supported. This means that if, for instance, you are calling into a site with multiple phone numbers, you must create a separate DUN connection for each one or enter the number manually.

You can also select any location to dial from and open the Dial Properties dialog, which opens a dialog that is essentially identical to Control Panel → Telephony → My Locations, with this addition: you can specify that the call be dialed as a long-distance call. Settings made in this dialog are reflected on Control Panel → Telephony → My Locations. Once you click Connect, the connection is dialed and you can then open tools such as IE, if connected to the Internet, or Network Neighborhood, if connected to a Windows network.

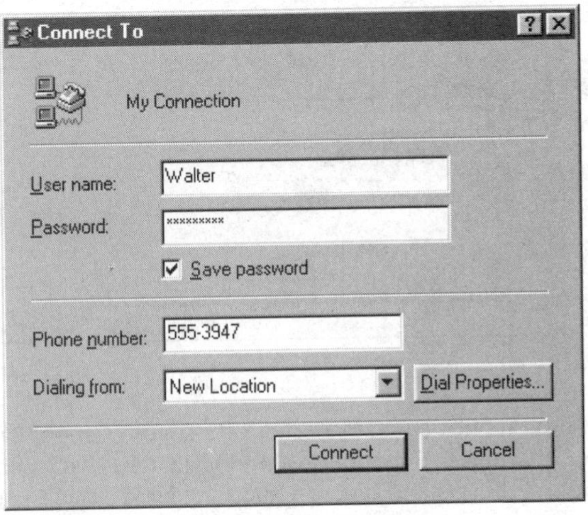

Figure 4-5: An explicit connection

To use a connection implicitly, just start up any Internet-aware application. Applications such as Internet Explorer can be configured to dial a connection automatically if they are not already connected to a network. When the application tries to connect, it brings up the Dial-up Connection dialog shown in Figure 4-6. If you choose to connect automatically, this dialog will not be shown for subsequent connections. If you do not wish to connect, you can choose to work offline, in which case you will only have access to cached information. Settings pops up the modem information for the connection, which is the same as *any connection* → Properties → General → Configure.

One big thing missing from implicit connections (something that was available in previous versions of Windows) is the ability to choose different locations when making an implicit connection. This was quite handy for travelling users who connect to the Internet from multiple locations. In Windows 98, the only way to change locations is to first make an explicit connection and then launch your Internet application. This feature has been added to the Win 98 Second Edition. See "Internet Explorer" in Chapter 6 for details.

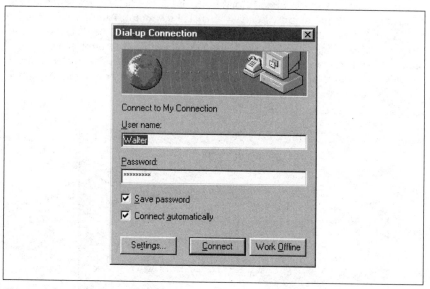

Figure 4-6: An implicit connection

To set up details for implicit DUN connections for IE, use Control Panel → Internet → Connection → Settings. This opens a dialog that lets you choose the DUN connection you wish to use and lets you specify certain dialing parameters, such as the number of times to attempt a connection and how long to wait between connections. You can also enter your authentication information for the remote network. Consult "Internet" in Chapter 5 for more information.

Notes

- The implicit connection dialog in IE5 still does not allow you to change locations, but does allow you to specify a DUN connection to use. Thus, you could configure a separate DUN connection for each location you may dial from.

- Strictly speaking, the facilities for establishing networking links with remote computers are referred to as Remote Network Access, or RNA. You'll see evidence of this in the names of the underlying DLLs used to provide the networking services—such as *rnasetup.dll* or *rnaui.dll*. On NT servers, the related facilities are referred to as Remote Access Services, or RAS. Dial-Up Networking is just the most visible RNA application, and there are some differences in the way applications use RNA functionality.

- You may often find yourself scratching your head wondering why you can't change a value in a certain dialog or just why Microsoft decided to do things the way they did. The main reason is that Connection information is stored in the Registry, but for backward compatibility with older applications, some location information is stored in the file \ *Windows\telephon.ini*.

As a result, information that is set in the connection (such as the phone number) is presented as a read-only field in the location. What makes things even more complicated is that other dial-up applications that are not Internet-related and don't use Dial-Up Networking, such as HyperTerm, make their own connection-like objects, and even use the common pool of locations stored in *telephon.ini*. Locations are stored at:

```
HKCU\Software\Microsoft\Windows\CurrentVersion\Telephony\Locations
```

- By default, a dialog box pops up after a connection is made informing you that, indeed, a connection has been made. Once you make a connection, a status icon that looks like two PCs connected together is also placed on the System Tray. You can disable both of these settings using Dial-Up Networking → Connections menu → Settings. This menu also allows you to specify how numbers should be redialed and whether you should be prompted to make a dial-up networking connection if a normal network connection fails.

- Dial-Up Networking → Connections → Dial-Up Server allows you to configure Windows 98 to receive calls from other computers. This can be extremely useful for retreiving information from your system when you are away. Simply designate the modem you wish to receive calls on, select Allow caller access, and provide a password if you want one. If the Dial-Up Server option does not appear on the Settings menu, you need to install it using Control Panel → Add/Remove Programs → Windows Setup.

File Types

Open a file of an unknown type, or associate file types with a different application.

any folder → View → Folder Options → File Types

If you try to open a file of an unknown type (by double-clicking or using right-click → Open, or using the File → Open command from within an application), you will get a dialog that asks you to identify which program you want to use to open the file (see Figure 4-7).

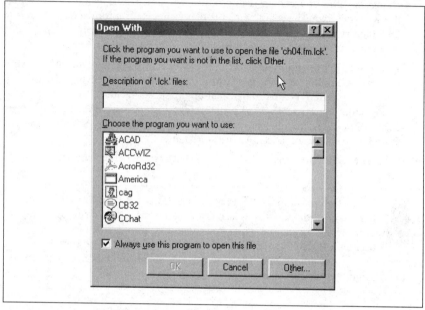

Figure 4-7: The Open With dialog box

If you want to force a new association (for example, because you want *.htm* and *.html* files to be opened by Netscape rather than by Internet Explorer), or just want to open a file with another application than the one that opens it by default, select the file (click once), then hold the Shift key down and right-click on the file, choosing Open With from the context menu.

Or go to View → Folder Options → File Types in any folder Explorer window. Scroll through the list of file types, then click Edit to change any particular association. You can also change associations for objects such as drive, folder, and unknown—see "Context Menus" earlier in this chapter. Click New to create a new file/program association. Figure 4-8 shows a sample Edit dialog box for the Text Document (*.txt*) file type.

For an existing file type, you will typically see one or two actions, such as Open or Print. The one that is in bold type is the default action—the one that will be invoked when you double-click on a file of the specified type.

Other actions can be placed on the file's context menu. Note that you can have more than one open action (although only one can be the default). For example, a text file could have an Open with Notepad action and an Open with Word action, or it could use any other program that allows you to edit text files (such as the DOS *edit* command, or a third-party editor such as *emacs* or *vi* from the MKS Toolkit).

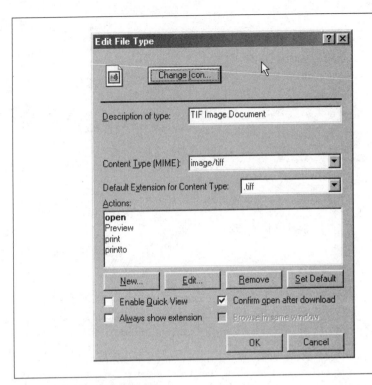

Figure 4-8: The Edit dialog box

Click New or Edit to create a new action or edit an existing one. The resulting dialog lets you specify the command line to be used. For example, to print using Notepad, use the command `C:\Windows\notepad.exe /p`. (Command-line options for all standard Windows 98 commands are given in Chapter 6. For third-party applications, these may be hard to find.)

Not all programs give access to their internal functions via command-line options, though. For example, look at the open action for the content type *.tif* image in Figure 4-9.

Sure enough, there's a command line. But "Use DDE" is also checked. DDE stands for Dynamic Data Exchange; it is an ostensibly defunct technology (supposedly replaced by OLE, COM, ActiveX, and who knows what else) that actually plays an important part in Windows 98. For example, both the Explorer and Netscape Navigator can be "driven" with DDE. While command lines specify options given to a program just before it starts, DDE commands can be sent to an already running program. If you're interested in one widely used DDE interface (it's supported by Microsoft as well as Netscape), see "Netscape's DDE Implementation" at either of the following locations:

> *http://developer.netscape.com/docs/manuals/communicator/DDE/abtdde.htm*
> *http://www.spyglass.com/products/smosaic/sdi/sdi_spec.html*

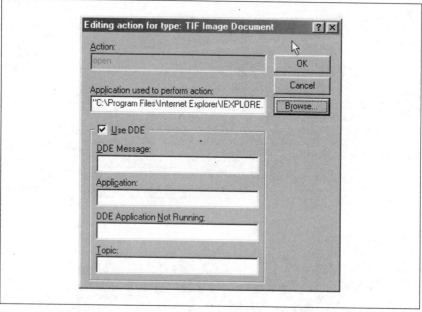

Figure 4-9: Dynamic Data Exchange in an open action dialog box

Note that you can have more than one extension for a content type. For example, if you have Netscape Navigator installed, the type Netscape Hypertext Document corresponds to the extensions *.htm*, *.html*, *.xbm*, and *.shtml*. Files with any of these extensions will be opened by Netscape Navigator. See Chapter 13, *The Registry*, for an explanation of this behavior.

Notes

- Clicking "Always use this program to open this file" on the Open With dialog box will create a permanent association between the file type (as defined by its extension), rather than performing one-time transient operations for this specific file.

- The list of file type-program associations is kept in the Registry at HKEY_ CLASSES_ROOT. See Chapter 13 for a detailed explanation.

- Sometimes you want to get the Open With dialog for a file whose type is already registered, so that you can use a different application to open it. As noted previously, select the file, then Shift-right-click on it to get a context menu including Open With.

- Alternatively, you can create a batch file (and then put a shortcut to it on the Desktop, the Start menu, or the Send To folder) containing the following command line:

```
rundll32 shell32.dll,OpenAs_RunDLL %1
```

Find Files and Folders

Quickly locate any file on the system, using either the filename, the date and time the file was created or modified, text contained in the file, or some combination of these criteria. A list of files matching the criteria will appear in the lower window.

Start → Find → Files or Folders
Explorer → Tools → Find → Files or Folders
any folder → right-click → Find
F3 while focus is on the Desktop
Right-click in Explorer left pane
Ctrl-F or F3 in any folder

Search Criteria

Information entered on all three tabs works together to define the criteria for the search. For example, you can search for a file with a specific name, or leave the filename blank and search for all files created since a specific date, or construct a complex search using multiple criteria. Find remembers search criteria, so you can refine a search by defining additional criteria and repeating the search. See Figure 4-10.

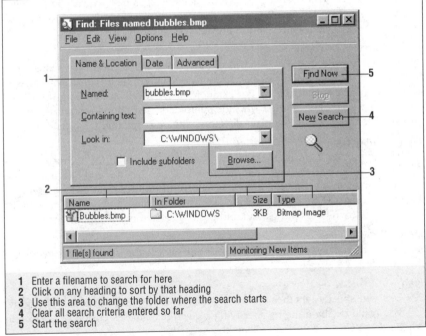

1 Enter a filename to search for here
2 Click on any heading to sort by that heading
3 Use this area to change the folder where the search starts
4 Clear all search criteria entered so far
5 Start the search

Figure 4-10: The Find Files and Folders dialog box

Because the search results area in Find is "active," you can perform any action you like on the files or folders that appear there. You can copy them, rename them, move them, make shortcuts to them—even delete them. This makes Find a workable alternative to the Desktop or the two-paned Explorer view as a primary interface for working with files and folders. One particularly powerful feature is that once you've found a group of files with some common characteristics (such as file type/extension, modification date, or contents), you can select all and then act on them as a group.

Find → Name & Location → Named

Enter any part of the desired filename(s). Find does a substring search; unless you're used to wildcards, you don't have to use them. For example, the string "exec" would return *autoexec.dos, autoexec.bat,* and *jobexec.dll.* However, *find* also recognizes the standard file-naming wildcards (? and *). For more information on the rules of using these wildcards, see "Wildcards, Pipes, and Redirection" in Chapter 7. You can enter multiple filenames by separating them with a comma (e.g., **.txt, *.bat*).

Find also keeps a history of previous filename searches, which you can view by clicking on the down arrow to the right of the field. (This history is preserved even when you clear the previous search using New Search.)

Find → Name & Location → Look in

Can be given a drive (and optional folder) in which to make the search. You can specify multiple drives or folders by separating their names with a semi-colon (and optional space). For example: *C:\; D:* will search both the *C:* and *D:* drives. By checking the "Include subfolders" box, Windows will search all subdirectories within the main directory you are searching.

Find → Name & Location → Containing text

Lets you enter a string of up to 128 characters to search for. Carriage returns are not allowed—they will start the search. $ matches the end of a line in text files, and can be used to "anchor" a search, to find text that ends a line. Find will locate ASCII strings in non-text (binary) files, but it will not locate Unicode (two-byte) strings. Cut and paste accelerators are supported.

Find → Date

Lets you specify a range of dates during which the desired files were last changed.

Find → Advanced → Of type

Lets you specify whether to search for files of only a given type. Obviously, you could do the same by specifying a given filename extension (e.g., *.exe*) in Find → Name & Location → Named.

Find → Advanced → Size is

Lets you specify a specific size for a file or a minimum (At least) or maximum (At most) size.

If you're like me, you may find yourself leaving files of a particular type (e.g., Excel worksheets or Word files) strewn all over your file system. A good way to gather them up into one place is to search for all files of a given extension (e.g., *.xls*), then Select All in the Find Results window, and then Shift-right-click. Choose Create Shortcut from the context menu, and put the shortcuts into a single folder. This way, you can organize your files both by type and by project or other subject-oriented category. Rebuild your "file type" folders periodically using the Date Modified tab of Find → Files & Folders to find your latest work.

Find Dialog Menus

- File menu → Open Containing Folder: opens not the file that has been selected in the Find results window, but the folder that contains it. This can be handy if you want to work on a set of related files. Find one, and go to the folder that contains them all.

- File menu → Save Search: saves the search criteria in a file on the Desktop. If Options → Save Results is checked, the results of the search (and not just the criteria) are saved in the file. Unfortunately, the results can't be read in another application, only read back into the Find window.

  The save filename depends on the search criteria. If the search was for a named file, the name searched for will be part of the saved filename. Otherwise, it will be called All Files (with a number in parentheses if you save multiple searches).

Notes

- Start → Find → Computer is a separate Find function that looks for a named computer on your network. This is handy if you have a very large Network Neighborhood. Enter any character(s) contained in the destination computer name to get a list of UNC pathnames containing those characters. Case is not significant. The list in the output window is active, so once you've found your target computer, you can click on its icon to open a window onto its contents, just like in Network Neighborhood.

- Start → Find → On the Internet launches your web browser with the default search page.

- Start → Find → People launches the find utility for the Windows Address Book, which is discussed in the "Outlook Express" section in Chapter 6.

See Also

"dir" and "find" in Chapter 7

Icons

It's easy to take icons for granted. They are a ubiquitous and seemingly immutable feature of the Windows 98 interface, but in fact, you have a degree of control over what icons are used for various types of files. In particular, you can use any icon you like for any shortcut you create, using Properties → Shortcut → Change Icon.

By default, the Change Icon dialog box for a shortcut usually points to \Windows\System\shell32.dll, which contains about 70 different icons, including the standard icons for folders, disks and so on. A browse button lets you search for other sources of icons. But where do you browse?

- \Windows\System\pifmgr.dll contains almost 40 additional icons. Except for the MS-DOS prompt icon, you've probably never seen many of these icons. A lot of them are fun and original.

- \Windows\moricons.dll contains about 100 icons, including icons for many non-Microsoft applications.

- \Windows\System\rnaui.dll contains seven icons with telephone imagery. (This is the default icon set for Dial-Up Networking shortcuts.)

- \Windows\Progman.exe contains about 40 icons, including pointing hands, arrows, a safe, a mailbox, doors, interoffice mail envelopes, and many more.

- \Windows\System\user.exe contains the MS Windows icon, a triangular warning icon, a question mark bubble icon, and so forth.

- Any file on your disk with the .ico extension is fair game. Unfortunately, the browse button doesn't make them easy to find. Use Find → Files or Folders and look for *.ico; a small copy of each icon will appear in the Find display next to its name and location. If you see something you like, navigate to it with Change Icon → Browse. (Unfortunately, you can't just copy the path from the Find dialog box and paste it in.)

- Any executable (.exe) file with a unique icon may contain its icon (or icons) within it. For example, drivespace.exe contains eight icons, most with a disk or hardware theme, plus one incongruous yellow smiley face; \Windows\mplayer.exe has multimedia-related icons; and \Windows\regedit.exe has a number of building-block–type icons. Pick any .exe file from the Browse dialog box; if it contains no icon, you'll get a message to that effect, but otherwise, the icon will be extracted and can be applied to your shortcut.

- Any bitmap (.bmp) file can serve as an icon, although most large bitmap files will lose too much detail at icon size. Simply copy the .bmp file, and change the .bmp extension to .ico. (Again, use Find → Files or Folders to search for .bmp files on your disk—or look at the many graphics file archives on the Net.) To see what the icon looks like, you can just copy or move it to the Desktop. Any file with the .ico extension will appear there with itself as the icon.

Inbox

Launch Windows Messaging, if installed. Windows Messaging is a older utility that shipped with Windows 95 to support email and fax. It has largely been replaced with Outlook and Outlook Express.

Notes

- If the Inbox icon isn't on your Desktop, then Windows Messaging has probably not been installed. Windows Messaging is no longer included as part of the Windows setup, but it is included on the Windows 98 disk in *tools* *oldwin95\message*.

- Fax messages appear in Microsoft Exchange, but you must install both Windows Messaging and Microsoft Fax to send and receive fax messages. Without the Inbox icon on the Desktop, you won't be able to use Windows Messaging or Microsoft Fax services.

See Also

"Windows Messaging" and "Microsoft Fax" in Chapter 8

Internet

Start Internet Explorer to browse the World Wide Web.

> Desktop → Internet
> Start → Programs → Internet Explorer
> Start → Run → `iexplore`

Internet Explorer is a complex program that is pretty much integrated in Windows 98. For more information on IE, see Chapter 9 and "Internet Explorer" in Chapter 6.

Notes

Internet → Properties is the same as Control Panel → Internet. This property sheet controls Internet settings that affect any Internet applications that use Microsoft's wininet API (including third-party applications). See Chapter 5 for details.

See Also

Internet in a Nutshell by Valerie Quercia (O'Reilly & Associates)

Log Off User

Close all programs and log on to Windows 98 again.

> Start Menu → Log Off *username*

Notes

Logging off and back on as the same user is a great way to do a quick reboot of Windows 98. This is occasionally sufficient to release any frozen programs. It's also a great way to force Win 98 to save any Explorer settings, such as the positions of the icons on the Desktop.

Logon

Depending on your configuration, you may be asked to log on when your system boots up. There are three reasons you may need a login name and password:

- Windows 98 is multiuser—that is, more than one person can use the same machine, with a somewhat separate Desktop layout, Start menu, and so on. See "Passwords" in Chapter 5 for more information.

- If your machine is connected to a local area network, your logon name is required to access any network services.

- If you want the system to be able to remember passwords automatically for applications like Dial-Up Networking or Internet access, you must enter an initial logon user name.

- Windows 98 provides three different types of logins, which you can select at Control Panel → Network → Configuration → Primary Network Logon. Client for Microsoft Networks is the primary logon used for accessing networks. Windows Logon is used for logging on to the local system only. Microsoft Family Logon is used in conjunction with user profiles to present a list of users that can log on to the local system. If any of these logons are not available, you can install them using Control Panel → Network → Configuration → Add → Client → Microsoft.

In any of these cases, you should choose a password when you receive your system. You can later change this (using Control Panel → Passwords). See Chapter 5 for additional information.

Notes

If you are the only user of your computer, but need a login so passwords will be remembered, TweakUI (see Chapter 8) lets you configure the system to automatically supply your username and password.

My Computer

In addition to the Explorer view and the DOS view, you can still use the hierarchical folder-in-folder view of the Desktop by clicking My Computer → Drive (C:).

Notes

- My Computer also gives you access to all drives on the system (fixed, removable, CD, network, etc.), as well as the Control Panel, Printers, Scheduled Tasks, and Dial-Up Networking.

- Shift-double-click on My Computer to start up the double-pane Explorer window view, with the same starting point.

- Choose Explore from the context menu of any folder to launch Windows Explorer at that starting point.

- My Computer → Properties is the same as Control Panel → System.

- My Computer → Drive (C:) → Properties gives useful statistics on the amount of disk space used and free, access to disk utilities, and to sharing. This is true for additional disks on your system as well.

- My Computer → View → "as Web Page" and single-click on any drive to view statistics on the amount of disk space available in the left pane of the folder.

Network Neighborhood

Access the local network.

> Desktop → Network Neighborhood
> Explorer → Network Neighborhood

Description

The Network Neighborhood (see Figure 4-11) provides a quick way to reach other systems on a local or wide area network. When the system is connected, other systems on the same network are displayed as icons in the *Network Neighborhood* folder on the Desktop. Click on any icon to connect to that system.

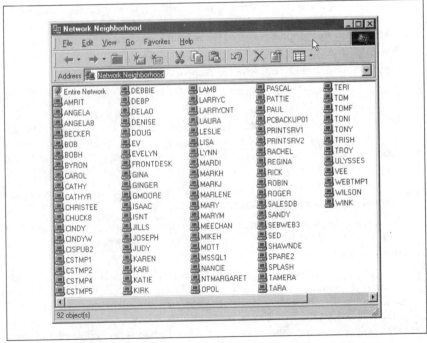

Figure 4-11: Network Neighborhood folder

Other systems might include print or file servers or other user's client machines. Often a network is divided into workgroups. If so, only the local workgroup will be shown. Click on Entire Network to step up a level and see the other workgroups.

 If you are connected to a local area network and the Network Neighborhood icon is not displayed, go to Control Panel → Network → Configuration → Add → Client → Client for Microsoft Networks.

Any user can designate folders on his or her machine for sharing with other users. You will usually be asked for a password before you can access Shared resources, if passwords were configured.

Notes

- If you have access to a file or folder on a remote machine, you can create a shortcut to it on your own Desktop or in your own folders, just as you can with a local file.

- On the command line or in the Explorer, you can refer to a resource on a remote system by a UNC (Universal Naming Convention) pathname. A UNC path consists of the name of the remote system followed by the name of the shared resource. For example, the UNC path \\tim\c\inanut refers to the folder called *inanut* on the shared C drive on a machine called *tim*.

- To view or change the name of your own system, as shown in the Network Neighborhood, use Control Panel → Network → Identification.

- Network Neighborhood → Properties is the same as Control Panel → Network.

- To share a folder on your machine, go to the folder's context menu → Sharing. If "Sharing..." does not appear on the context menu, sharing is not enabled. Go to Control Panel → Network → Configuration → File and Print sharing and click on "I want to be able to give others access to my files."

The Sharing dialog box (see Figure 4-12) lets you specify the name and access permissions for a shared folder or printer.

By default, the folder or printer will be set to Not Shared. Click Shared As if you want it to be shared. By default, the Share Name will be the same as the name of the folder.

You can grant read-only access (the default), which will allow others to view or copy the contents of any files in the folder. Full access will allow them to read and write any files. Click Read-Only or Full and specify the password that will be required to access the folder. If you want some users to have read-only access and others full access, click Depends on Password and specify two different passwords.

For a printer, full access will allow others to delete jobs from the print queue. You may want to grant full access to printers only to the system or network administrator.

If you leave the password field blank, no password will be required.

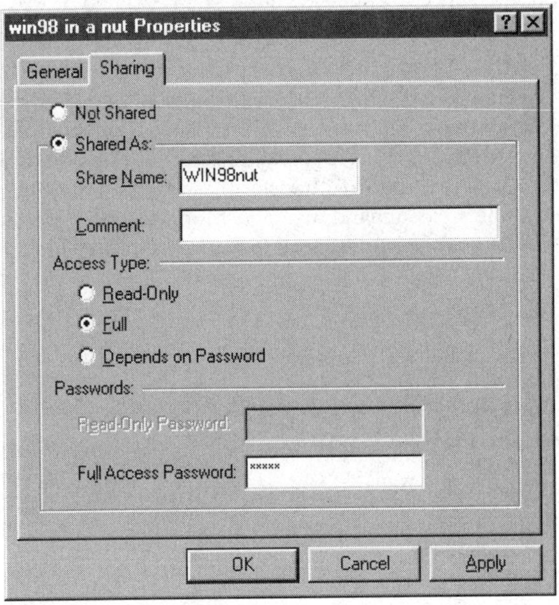

![win98 in a nut Properties dialog box showing the Sharing tab with Shared As selected, Share Name WIN98nut, Access Type Full selected, and a Full Access Password field filled with asterisks.]

Figure 4-12: Folder properties → Sharing

The icon for any folder that is shared will change from the standard folder icon to one of a hand holding a folder.

If you are using TCP/IP on both your local area network and the Internet, you need to be careful with File and Printer Sharing. You should either make sure that all your shares are password-protected or make sure that File and Print Sharing is not bound to TCP/IP → Dial-Up Adapter. Otherwise, your shared folders will be accessible to anyone out there on the Net.

You can check whether your shares are password-protected using Net Watcher (*netwatch.exe*). Use View → By Shared Folder, then use Administer → Shared Folder Properties for each share.

- You can map a networked disk or folder to a drive letter using the Map Network Drive button on a folder toolbar or in the Explorer at Tools → Map Network Drive. This corresponds to the net use command, and is especially useful for making network access easily available to older DOS-based programs. You can similarly map network printers to local printer ports (LPT1 and so on) by selecting the printer in the Network Neighborhood window and then using File → Capture Printer Port.

- If you experience network problems, an application that attempts to access the network may appear to freeze your system. Wait 20 or 30 seconds and the system will respond again. Most network programs have a built-in timeout, and will give up after that timeout period.

- Network Neighborhood works only with other Microsoft systems. For example, even though you might be using a TCP/IP network (either on a LAN or via Dial-Up Networking), any Unix systems on the network won't show up in the Network Neighborhood. To transfer files to or from a Unix system on the network, use the *ftp* command; use *telnet* for "terminal" access to such a system. A very cool program called Samba can be used to mount a TCP/IP system on Network Neighborhood. See *Windows 98 Annoyances* for details.

See Also

"ftp," "net," and "telnet" in Chapter 7

Online Services Folder

Program Files/Online Services

Install software for major online services, including AOL, AT&T, CompuServe, MSN, and Prodigy.

    Desktop → Online Services
    Program Files → Online Services

If you do not see this folder on your desktop or in the Program Files folder, chances are Online Services has not been installed. You can install it using Control Panel → Add/Remove Programs → Windows Setup.

Description

The Online Services folder on the desktop really just provides shortcuts to executable files found in Program Files → Online Services. These executable files install the software used to connect to each of the major online services. Usually, you will be asked to supply the Windows 98 CD to load the actual executable files for the online service. Once installed, shortcuts for launching the service will be provided in the Start → Programs folder and likely on your desktop, as well.

Notes

The versions of the software that come with Windows 98 are not necessarily the most recent versions that a particular online service has to offer. You can often find the most recent versions available for download on the Internet. If you need to install the online service software to get on the Internet in the first place, you should use the version on the CD-ROM. Once you're online, you will be able to find a more recent version through the online service itself.

When you install the software for most online services, setup will automatically configure a Dial-Up Networking connection for you. You can then use this connection in any of the ways described in the "Dial-Up Networking" section of this chapter. This means, for example, that you can set IE to implicitly dial a connection to your online service provider without having to first log on to the provider using their proprietary software. If setup does not create a DUN connec-

---

tion for you (some use their own interface), you can often find instructions for setting one up yourself through the online service.

Printers

The Printers folder contains an Add Printer icon plus icons for any installed printers. Once a printer is installed, you can print from within your applications, drag items to the printer icons to print them, or click on the printer icon to see or change the status of current print jobs.

> Start → Settings → Printers
> Control Panel → Printers
> My Computer → Printers

Like Fonts (see Chapter 5), Printers is a "virtual folder" rather than a normal Control Panel entry. The folder should include an icon for each printer that is installed on your system.

Add Printer is a wizard that helps you select the appropriate printer driver for a local or network printer. See "Printers" in Chapter 5 for details.

The context menu for any printer allows you to select that printer as the default printer and specify whether print spooling ("offline printing") should be enabled for it. Note that if offline printing is selected, you can print to a network printer even when you aren't connected, or to a local printer when it is turned off; when the printer becomes available, you will be asked whether to print any files in the queue. See "Printers" in Chapter 5 for a description of printer properties.

File → Print is the standard way to print for most applications. Right-clicking on a file, then selecting Print from its context menu allows you to send a file to the printer without opening it first. You can also create a shortcut to a printer on the Desktop and then drag and drop a file on the printer icon.

 If you drag more than one file to a printer icon, the system will open a separate copy of the application for each file. This may be okay for text files and a small application like Notepad, but drag a group of Word or Excel files to the printer and you'll bring the system to its knees.

Double-click on any printer icon for a view of the printer's job queue. You'll see the document name, status (printing, paused, and so on), the owner of the job, progress (in number of pages printed), and when the job was started. You can drag your own jobs up and down to change their priority. Use the Printer menu to pause the printer or purge all print jobs. Use the Document menu to pause or cancel printing for any selected document(s). For a shared network printer, you can only pause, change the priority of, or delete your own jobs.

Properties

Right-click on many objects, then select Properties from the context menu for configuration controls and information about the object.

> *many objects* → right-click → Properties
> Alt-double-click
> Alt-Enter if the item is already selected

Description

Almost every context menu includes a Properties entry. These vary greatly depending on what kind of item has been selected. For example, some of the Control Panel functions such as Display and Date/Time are also available via Properties.

This section describes file and folder properties. Other types of property sheets are described as appropriate elsewhere in the book.

At minimum, a property sheet for a file, folder, or shortcut will have a General tab (see Figure 4-13).

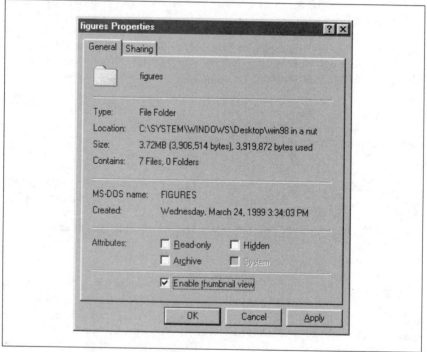

Figure 4-13: A property sheet for a folder

Most of the information on the first page is fairly self-explanatory. A few things need a bit of explanation:

MS-DOS name

The eight-character "short filename" plus three-character extension. If the file has only a short name, this will be the same name that shows up in the Explorer. But if the file has a long name, you will see only the first six characters of the long name, followed by a tilde (~), a digit, and the extension.

Attributes

Check Read-only to prevent a file from being modified by yourself or others. (Obviously, someone else could pop up the property sheet and change the attribute, but it prevents inadvertent modification.)

Check Archive if you want the file to be backed up when a backup program is next run. This attribute is automatically set whenever you modify a file, and is sometimes cleared by the same backup programs when the file is copied. By default, hidden files do not show up in the Explorer or via the DOS *dir* command. See "attrib" in Chapter 7 for more information about file attributes.

Enable thumbnail view

Creates thumbnail graphics of the files in a folder if the file format allows. Once you enable thumbnail view using a folder's properties, you can activate the thumbnail view using that folder's View → Thumbnails command.

Notes

- Folders, printers, and disk drives have a second property tab called Sharing. See "Network Neighborhood" earlier in this chapter for details. Shortcuts to MS-DOS programs have five separate property tabs. See "Shortcuts" later in this chapter for details.

- To see the amount of disk space used by a group of files, select them, then view the Properties entry for the selected list. On the first tab, you'll see the size of the whole group. Change any of the attributes, and the change will be applied to all of the files in the selected group. (Unfortunately, if any of the files in the selected group has a different attribute from other files in the group, the checkbox for that attribute will be grayed out, so this does not work in all cases. This seems like rather poor user interface design.)

- Files of certain types, such as Microsoft Word files, will have additional property pages that are generated by the application that created them. Word files, for example, have pages that let you summarize and view the statistics for documents.

Recycle Bin   \Recycled

Move files to temporary storage, pending true deletion.

    Recycle Bin
    File → Delete
    Del key

Description

Drag any item from the Desktop to the Recycle Bin icon to delete it. File → Delete on the menubar of a folder also moves items to the Recycle Bin, as does selecting

---

the item and then pressing the Delete key. By default, files are not deleted immediately, but are stored until the Recycle Bin runs out of space, at which point they are deleted, oldest first, to make space. Until that time, they can be retrieved by double-clicking on the Recycle Bin icon, browsing through the contents of the Recycle Bin window, and dragging or sending the file elsewhere.

 Files dragged to the Recycle Bin (or otherwise deleted) from floppies, network drives, or other external drives such as Zip drives will not be stored in the Recycle Bin. They are simply deleted.

Properties

- A slider allows you to specify how much of each drive can be allocated to the Recycle Bin. The default is 10%. You can specify the same value for all drives or set a separate value for each drive. Keep in mind that on today's huge drives, 10% can be a lot: 10% of a 1 gigabyte disk is 100 megabytes of stored junk. The amount of space actually used by the files in the Recycle Bin is displayed in the Bin's status bar when you open it.

- A checkbox allows you to specify that deleted files are not to be stored in the Recycle Bin but removed immediately from the disk. Check this box only if you want to live dangerously.

- A checkbox asks if you want to display a delete confirmation dialog. If the delete confirmation is enabled, the confirmation dialog is displayed regardless of how you send files to the recycle bin (drag, Del key, Send To menu). If confirmation is disabled, this dialog is never shown. Regardless of the setting, a confirmation is always shown when you empty the recycle bin.

 To delete a file without sending it to the Recycle Bin, use Shift +Delete or the *del* command on the command line.

Another way to send files to the Recycle Bin is to add a Recycle Bin shortcut to the Send To folder. Then you can send something out for recycling by clicking Send To → Recycle Bin.

Notes

- With the Details view (the default), you can sort the contents of the Recycle Bin by name, by original location (useful in case you want to put something back where it was!), by Date deleted, by type, or by size. Click on any of the headings to sort contents by that heading. Click again on the same heading to reverse the order of the sort.

- You can delete the entire contents of a floppy disk by dragging the disk icon to the Recycle Bin. You will be prompted for confirmation. You cannot drag the image of a hard disk (such as *C:*) to the Recycle Bin (since the Recycle Bin itself is contained on that disk), nor can you drag key components of the user interface, such as the My Computer, Network Neighborhood, Control Panel, Dial-Up Networking, Printers, and Fonts folders to the Recycle Bin. (Well, you can drag them there, but they won't go in!)

- Some of these Desktop items can be deleted by right-clicking and selecting delete. So if something won't go, try again this way. Some of these items can be removed from the Desktop using TweakUI (see Chapter 8). If you still can't get rid of it, see *Windows 98 Annoyances* (O'Reilly & Associates).

- You can also manipulate the contents of the Recycle Bin from the command line or the Explorer by working in the *Recycled* folder.

Run

Start programs by typing in a command line.

> Start → Run

The Start menu lists many common Windows 98 applications and accessories, plus any third-party applications you've installed, but it is far from complete, and navigating to the program you want is often fairly tedious.

Ironically, the increasing complexity of the system pushes even the most graphically oriented user back in the direction of the command line. Just about the quickest way to run any program that isn't already on your Desktop is to type the name of the program at the command line. Windows 98 offers three different command lines: the Address Toolbar, the Run dialog, and a DOS window.

Address Toolbar or Run Dialog versus DOS window

If you keep an Address Toolbar visible at all times (see "Toolbars" later in this chapter), it is far and away the most convenient of the three command lines. The Run Dialog is a close second. However, if you are a heavy user of command-line utilities, you may still find a DOS window most useful. The Address Toolbar and Run Dialog have the advantage of keeping a command history, so you can click on the little down arrow to the right of the text entry area (or use the up and down arrow keys) and re-execute previous commands. (On the other hand, you can duplicate this functionality in a DOS window using the *doskey* command.) More significantly (and this is a big advantage), you can type the name of a file, folder, URL, or UNC path, and it will be automatically opened by the appropriate application (if one is registered). Doing this in a DOS window will get you the message "Bad command or file name." (However, see "start" in Chapter 7 for an easy way to run filenames, URLs, and so on from the DOS prompt or a batch file.)

A DOS window has an advantage in that it can always be left open and that it provides useful file management commands (internal to *command.com*) such as *dir, del, copy*, and so on. To open a DOS window:

> Start → Programs → MS-DOS Prompt

or:

> Address → command

or:

Start → Run → command

One important difference between the one-line prompts (Address or Run) and a DOS window is the context in which commands run. A command interpreter, or shell, always has a particular context, or environment, in which it runs. This environment can create significant differences in the results when you type a command name.

A significant example of this is the search path, the sequence of directories that will be searched to find an executable file with a name matching the command you type. In DOS, the search path is stored in a variable called PATH, which is typically set in the file *C:\autoexec.bat*, a startup file that is automatically executed (if present) when the system is booted. (See "path" and "set" in Chapter 7 for more information on the content on the search path; see Chapter 11, *The Batch Language*, for more information on *autoexec.bat*.) A typical PATH setting might look like this:

```
set PATH=C:\;C:\WINDOWS;C:\WINDOWS\COMMAND
```

which says to look in the three directories *C:*, *C:\Windows*, and *C:\Windows\ Command*. If there is a file with the same name in any of these directories, the one that is found first (i.e., in the directory that occurs earlier in the search path) will be executed first.

The search path followed by the Run prompt and the Address Toolbar is:

1. \Windows\Desktop

2. \Windows\System

3. \Windows

4. The contents of the variable PATH, if found. (It's a good idea to put \Windows\Command in your path.)

5. The App Paths registry key

At either the Run prompt or in a DOS window, you will get an error message if you type the name of a command that is not in any search path. If you do this in the address toolbar, the system will treat the command as a URL, prefix it with *http://*, and try to find it on the Internet.

When you install applications, they sometimes (but not always) update the search path setting in *autoexec.bat* or the Registry settings that control the Run prompt or Address Toolbar path. Many more recent applications (including those in Microsoft Office) don't rely on the directory search path at all, but instead store the individual application's path in the Registry, under the key HKLM\SOFTWARE\ Microsoft\Windows\CurrentVersion\App Paths. So, for example, if you've installed Microsoft Office and you type winword at the Run prompt, Word will quite predictably execute. But type it at the DOS prompt, and you'll get the message "Bad command or file name." If you want to be able to run Word from the DOS prompt, you need to add the directory *C:\Program Files\Microsoft Office\ office* to your search path, or type the complete pathname of the command. Neither of these options may be acceptable, especially if you use a lot of applications with this behavior. Fortunately, the *start* program (see Chapter 7) is aware of the App Paths Registry key. So the surest way to run *winword* or any similar application from the DOS prompt is simply to type start winword. You can also give start the name of any file and it will open the file using the associated application.

A further consequence of the environment concept is that commands typed into a DOS window or the Run prompt or Address Toolbar sometimes have a scope that is local only to that window. For example, the DOS *break* command, which controls the frequency with which the system checks for Ctrl-C interrupting a program, sets that condition for only the window from which it was issued. It therefore doesn't make any sense to type that command at the Run prompt or Address Toolbar. If you do, it creates what you can think of as a tiny bubble of execution context in which it holds true, and then exits without a trace.

In addition, there are a number of commands you can issue at the DOS prompt that are built in to the DOS command interpreter, *command.com*. These built-in commands are labeled as such in Chapter 7. They cannot be issued from the Run prompt or Address Toolbar.

For the most part, though, you can use the three command lines interchangeably. If you type the name of a Windows GUI application, it will launch in its own window. If you type the name of a text-based program (for example, *ping*) it will display its output in the current DOS window, or, if issued from the Address

Toolbar or Run dialog, will launch its own DOS window, which will last only as long as the command itself is executing.

See Also

For more information on the DOS command interpreter, see Chapter 7. For more information on the Address Toolbar, see "Toolbars" later in this chapter.

Scheduled Tasks

Set a time when a program will be automatically executed.

My Computer → Scheduled Tasks- → Add Scheduled Task

Description

Why run *scandisk* or a backup while you sit at your computer? Windows 98 includes the Scheduled Tasks feature that was formerly a part of Microsoft Plus! The wizard lets you pick a program to run and a time to run it. Each scheduled task appears as a separate file in the Scheduled Tasks folder.

The interface is a little clunky. The wizard makes you pick the program name from a listbox (it would be nice just to be able to type it). You then choose whether to schedule the task daily, weekly, monthly, one time only, when you boot your computer, or when you log in. If you pick one of the regular time-based options (say monthly), you're given a chance to set the time and which day to run on.

The last dialog in the wizard confirms the task you've scheduled, as shown in Figure 4-14.

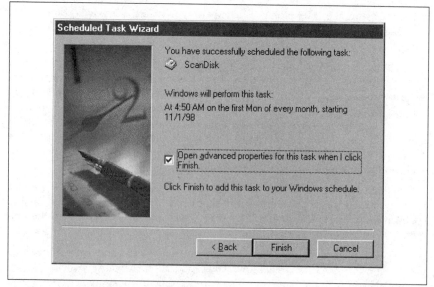

Figure 4-14: Confirming the scheduled task

If you check "Open advanced properties for this task when I click Finish.", you'll get to the Properties dialog for the scheduled task. You can bring up this same dialog at any time by either double-clicking or right-clicking on the icon for the task that is created in the Scheduled Tasks folder when you finish with the wizard.

If you look at this three-tabbed dialog, you can see that it gives a much more compact and powerful user interface for controlling and scheduling a job. Figure 4-15 shows the first tab.

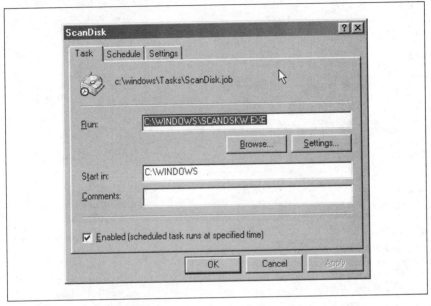

Figure 4-15: Choosing the task to run

From this dialog, you can see several things:

- Each task is stored in a file in the folder \ *Windows\Tasks*, and has the extension *.job.*

- You can see the command line to be run, and can modify it by typing in additional options. If the command has a settings dialog of its own, a Settings button will appear below the command line.

- The task can be enabled or disabled via a checkbox in the dialog. This means that if you temporarily want to disable the task, you can do so without having to start all over when you want to re-enable it.

The second tab, Schedule, gives you easy, fine-grained control over the task schedule. Figure 4-16 shows the Schedule tab.

There are three particularly useful functions that may not be immediately obvious:

- The drop-down list under Schedule Task includes an option not available via the wizard: "When Idle." That is, you can schedule a task to run whenever the computer has been idle for a specified period of time.

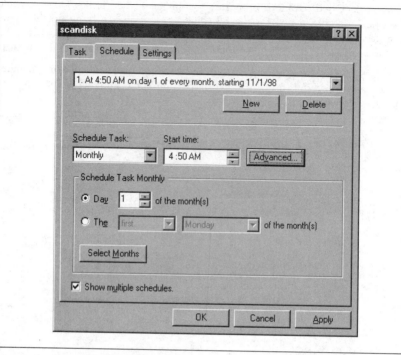

Figure 4-16: Modifying the schedule

- If you check the box Show Multiple Schedules, the informational area at the top of the dialog changes to a drop-down list, and you can schedule the same task for multiple different times.

- The Advanced button pops up yet another dialog, shown in Figure 4-17, which lets you set a date after which the task will stop running, or an interval during which the task will be repeated.

The Settings tab gives you additional control over your task. You can:

- Set a scheduled task to stop after it has run for a certain length of time.

- Only start the task if the computer is idle.

- Stop the task if the computer is active.

- Not run the task if a portable computer is running on batteries, or stop the task if the computer starts running on batteries.

- Wake the computer up from standby in order to run the task.

Given the amount of power that is given by the Properties dialog, power users will most likely think of this as the primary interface. Rather than working through the wizard to create a new scheduled task, you might find it easier to simply copy an existing *.job* file and then modify it. First copy a *.job* file from the *Windows\Tasks* directory, paste it into the same directory, rename the copy, and finally open the properties dialog for the new job.

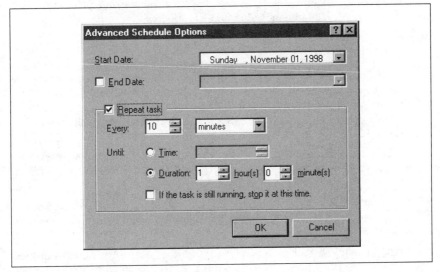

Figure 4-17: Advanced schedule properties

Notes

- The Details view of the Scheduled Tasks folder shows the schedule for the task as well as the next time it will be run, and the last time it was run. This gives you a good overview of what you've got scheduled.

- Be careful not to schedule two tasks at the same time. This will slow down both tasks and they may interfere with each other.

- The Advanced menu on the Scheduled Tasks folder lets you start and stop (or simply pause) the scheduler, the program that is running behind the scenes to start up any scheduled tasks. (If the scheduler is stopped, no scheduled tasks can be run.) If you don't have any tasks scheduled, you probably do want to stop the scheduler, since otherwise it's one more process running on your computer and slowing it down.

  The Advanced menu also lets you ask to be notified whenever a task is skipped (for example, because you've set the task to be run only when the computer is idle, and it is active at the scheduled time).

- You can also view the log recording information about scheduled tasks. This is a text file stored in \ *Windows\SchedLog.txt.*

Send To

Send a selected item to a program, disk drive, or folder.

     context menu → Send To

Right-click on any file or folder and select Send To to copy quickly to My Briefcase, a floppy disk in the *A:* drive, an Internet mail client, or any other application or folder that shows up in Send To menu. The result is the same as if the file was dragged into that program: if it's sent to an Explorer component (such as My Brief-case or drive *A:*), it might be moved or copied—otherwise, it's opened.

Notes

- The options that appear in the Send To menu are determined by the contents of the *Windows\SendTo* folder. To add another Send To recipient, place a shortcut to the desired program into that folder. For example, if you put a shortcut to *winword.exe* into that folder, you could "send" a text file to Word to open it there rather than using Notepad (which would normally be used to open a file with a *.txt* extension).

  Or add a shortcut to Notepad if you want to be able to easily open text files that don't have the right extension (**.txt*) for Notepad to recognize them auto-matically. That way you can just select Send To Notepad.

- If you place a shortcut to the Send To folder itself in *Windows\SendTo*, you can create new Send To destinations simply by sending them to the Send To folder!

- Place shortcuts to folders in Send To for an easy way to organize your files. You can work on files on the Desktop then use Send To to move them to their storage location when you're done. You can even create shortcuts to shared folders on other machines.

- If you want to have a lot of Send To locations, you can create subfolders in *Windows\SendTo*. They will show up as cascading submenus on the Send To menu.

 Send To works a bit differently depending on the destination. Send-ing to a folder (including the Recycle Bin) actually moves the file there or copies if the source and destination are on different drives; sending to a program simply opens the file. You can use Send To on shortcuts with impunity, but when you use it on an original file, remember that you may actually be moving the file.

Shortcuts

A link to a program, file, system object, printer, URL, or part of a document.

> *any file or folder* → context menu → Create Shortcut
> Desktop → context menu → New → Shortcut

You'll notice that some of the items on the Desktop may be labeled "Shortcut to...". A shortcut is also sometimes called a *link*. It is a small file (with the exten-sion *.lnk*) that points to another file, and, if it is a shortcut to a program, contains instructions for executing it. The icon for a shortcut has a small arrow in its lower-left corner by default.

When you create a new shortcut, it will always have the filename "Shortcut to..." plus whatever the original filename was. You can "train" Windows 98 to change

---

this default behavior by creating and renaming three shortcuts in a row. Do this by right-dragging a file from an Explorer two-pane window onto the Desktop and immediately renaming it to remove the "Shortcut to..." prefix; repeat twice for a total of three times. This trick works only for shortcuts dragged from an Explorer window, not those created in a normal folder view. If you have TweakUI installed, you can toggle this behavior with Control Panel → TweakUI → Explorer.

Creating Shortcuts

While you can start a program or open a folder by double-clicking on its icon on the Desktop, very few programs are actually stored on the Desktop, unless you yourself put them there.

If you find that there's a program you use often, and you want it on the Desktop, use the Explorer to navigate to the directory where the program's executable is stored. (The location is given along with the description of each program in the alphabetical program listings in Chapter 6.) You could move the original program icon to the Desktop, but that's often not wise, since the program may have various supporting files that belong with it in the directory in which it was originally installed. Instead, create a shortcut. When you drag an *.exe* file in Explorer, it automatically makes a shortcut. This won't work if you have other types of files selected as well when you drag, or you are are dragging to a removable or floppy drive.

The best way to create a shortcut is to right-drag an item and select "Create Shortcut(s) Here."

You can also put shortcuts in the Start menu folder, the Send To folder, or many other locations. Many system menus such as these are built dynamically from shortcuts stored in a particular folder, so to add a new menu item, all you need to do is put a shortcut in the right place.

You can also create shortcuts to DOS programs. This is a handy alternative to typing at the command line, and lets you put the DOS programs on the Desktop, the Start menu, and the Office Shortcut Bar. See "Shortcut Properties of DOS Programs" later in this section for more information.

You can also create a shortcut to a local or network printer. Dragging a file onto the shortcut sends that file to the printer without forcing you to open the associated program. Putting printer shortcuts in your Send To menu lets you conveniently send files to printers other than your default printer.

You can also create a shortcut to a URL, which is called an Internet shortcut, and has the extension *.url*. You can do this using the Desktop → right-click → New → Shortcut menu and typing in the URL yourself. You can also right-click any page in IE and choose Create Shortcut to point a shortcut to the current page. An even better way to do this is to drag the icon next to the URL in the Address Toolbar to the location where you wish to create the shortcut.

Shortcut Properties

To get more information about a shortcut, go to its property sheet. Figure 4-18 shows an example of the second page of a shortcut's properties.

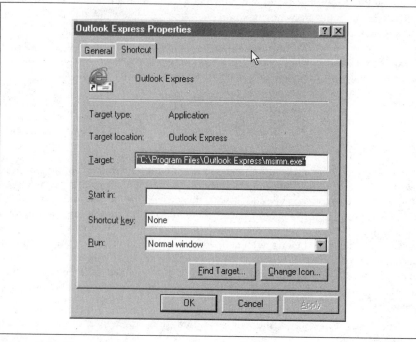

Figure 4-18: Shortcut properties

Target

    If the shortcut is to an executable with a command-line equivalent (including, but by no means limited to, DOS programs), you can specify any command-line options or arguments here. For example, if I want a shortcut to telnet to a Unix system, *foo.oreilly.com*, I would change the target from *C:\Windows\ telnet.exe* to *C:\Windows\telnet.exe foo.oreilly.com*. Note that if you type the name of a shortcut at the Run or command prompt, any parameters or options supplied there will override options set on the Target line.

Start in

    If the shortcut is to a program, this option specifies the working folder in which the program will first look for files to open or save.

Shortcut key

    You can map a key sequence to open or execute the shortcut. Press any key on the keyboard here and you will see Ctrl+Alt+*key* appear as the shortcut key sequence. Type that sequence to launch the shortcut without clicking on it. You should check Appendix A, *Keyboard Accelerators*, to make sure you aren't creating conflicts with any existing keyboard accelerator.

If you delete a shortcut with a keyboard accelerator configured, Windows *won't* release the accelerator. It will warn you when you try to create another accelerator that duplicates a previous one, whether or not it's been deleted. If you've defined a keyboard accelerator, clear it before deleting the shortcut.

Run
A drop-down list allows you to specify whether the target application should run in its normal window, maximized, or minimized.

Find Target
Click this button to open the folder containing the original file to which this shortcut is a link. The original file will be selected in the folder window.

Change Icon
You can select from hundreds of available icons. See "Icons" earlier in this chapter for details.

Shortcut Properties of DOS Programs

Since DOS programs weren't originally designed to function in a Windows environment, they've been retrofitted using a construct called Program Information Files (*.pif* files). Notice that the MS-DOS name on the General tab for any shortcut to a DOS program ends with the *.pif* extension. (Actually, these *.pif* files apply not so much to DOS programs as to character-mode programs. Besides DOS programs, Windows 98 also supports character-mode 32-bit Windows programs, called *console* applications, such as *xcopy32.exe*, *start.exe*, and *rundll32.exe*.)

The *.pif* file contains the information required for the character-mode program to function in the Windows environment. The property sheet is the interface for editing the *.pif* file.

A *.pif* file's properties have the following five tabs in addition to the General tab: Program, Font, Memory, Screen, and Misc.

Program
This tab is similar to the Shortcut tab of a normal shortcut (as shown in Figure 4-18). It lists the command line associated with the shortcut, with information such as the working directory, a keyboard accelerator (the Shortcut key), if one exists, and whether the program should run in a normal window, minimized, or maximized. There's a "close on exit" checkbox; removing the check is useful for programs whose output you need to see after the program has exited (*mem.exe*, for example).

The Advanced button lets you specify how the program will interact with Windows. Some older programs (especially games and other programs that are accustomed to having full control over the hardware) have difficulty cooperating with Windows. There are two workarounds: prevent Windows from answering "yes" to any "is Windows running?" calls the program might make (this is similar to faking the DOS version number with *setver.exe*; see Chapter 12, *Windows Startup*), and closing Windows before running the program (MS-DOS mode). The default is "Suggest MS-DOS mode as necessary." If this box is checked, when you click on the shortcut, Windows does its best to determine whether the program needs MS-DOS mode and puts up a dialog asking if you want to enter MS-DOS mode. See Figure 4-19.

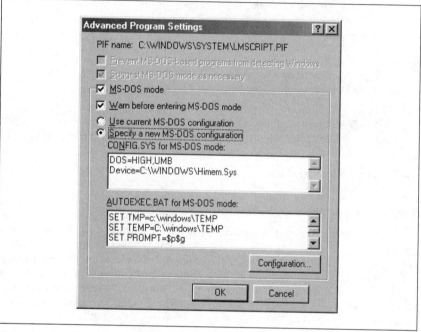

Figure 4-19: Advanced program settings

If you check MS-DOS mode, clicking on the shortcut will close all Windows programs and shut down Windows before running, and will restart Windows when it is done. You can then choose from two radio buttons: "Use current MS-DOS configuration" and "Specify a new MS-DOS configuration." If you choose the former, MS-DOS mode will use your existing *config.sys* and *autoexec.bat* files (if present). If you choose the latter, MS-DOS mode will construct and load temporary versions of those files containing the commands listed on the dialog box shown in Figure 4-20. Type in additional commands or click Configuration for a wizard that will help you build additional entries for these files, but you shouldn't use this unless a particular program requires it.

Font

Lets you choose the display font size for the DOS window (see Figure 4-20). Fonts are identified by a width and height in pixels (e.g., 7 × 12).

Memory

Lets you specify any specific memory or extended memory settings required by the program. In particular, you can set the size of the DOS environment space.

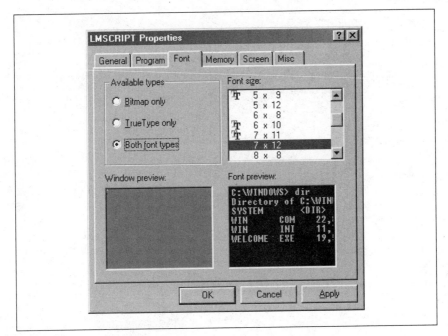

Figure 4-20: The Font tab

Screen

This tab has several useful options. You can specify whether the program will run full size or in a window, and the initial size of the window in lines.

If you choose "Display toolbar," the DOS window will include a useful toolbar that gives you access to the Clipboard, the properties, the font, and a button to switch into full-screen mode. (To return from full-screen mode to window mode, press Alt-Enter.)

"Restore settings on startup" means that if you change the font or size, they will be remembered the next time you start up this program.

Misc

The Misc tab is shown in Figure 4-21.

Allow screen saver

Unless this box is checked, an open DOS program window will not give up control of the screen to a screen saver, effectively disabling the screen saver. However, if it is checked, performance may suffer, so you may not want to choose this setting while running games or other performance-intensive programs.

Always suspend

Keeps the program from using any system resources when it is invisible. Select this for programs that don't do anything useful when running in the "background." (Communications programs should never leave "Always suspend" checked, or they will likely hang up if you switch to another window.) The Idle sensitivity slider controls how long the

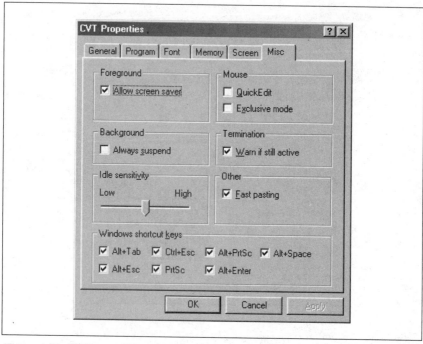

Figure 4-21: The Misc tab

program will need to go without any keyboard input before it is considered inactive and has its CPU utilization reduced.

QuickEdit

Enable the mouse for selections and cut and paste in the DOS window if this is checked. Otherwise, you must click the Mark button on the toolbar before you can make selections. Note that QuickEdit will not work with all programs (which is why the Mark button is provided on the toolbar).

Exclusive mode

Reserve the mouse for use by this program. It can't be used outside this program's window. Set this only if the program absolutely requires it.

Warn if still active

Many DOS programs don't have the nice Windows feature of asking you to save your files if you haven't done so when you exit. Checking this box tells Windows to warn you if you try to close this program's window while it is still running.

Windows shortcut keys

If the program uses some of the keyboard accelerators that are normally used by Windows, you can disable them here. Clear the checkbox for a key sequence if you want Windows to ignore it when the program is in use.

Shut Down

Shut down the system.

> Start → Shut Down
> Ctrl-Alt-Del → Shut Down

A Windows 98 machine should never be simply turned off, because the system caches data in memory and needs time to write it out to disk before it is turned off. Use Shut Down before you turn off the power.

Notes

- Start → Shut Down pops up a dialog box from which you can choose to stand by, shut down, restart, or restart in MS-DOS mode. The old Ctrl-Alt-Del "three-finger salute" is no longer a system-wide "Vulcan nerve pinch." Instead, it brings up a Close Program dialog box from which you can end a specific task or shut down the system. Ctrl-Alt-Del will also show you the list of all currently running prorgrams or processes. If you choose Shut Down from this dialog box, shutdown will begin immediately. You don't have the same options as you get with Start → Shut Down. If you hit Ctrl-Alt-Del a second time within the Close Program dialog, the system will immediately restart without first attempting to close any programs

- Some programs cannot be closed automatically by the shutdown process. If one of these programs is running, you will be given an opportunity to close the program and continue with shutdown (click OK) or to cancel (click Cancel) the shutdown operation.

- To restart Windows without rebooting the hardware, hold down the Shift key while clicking OK in the Shut Down dialog box.

See Chapter 12 for a more detailed description of system startup and shutdown.

Start Menu

A quick way to get to many of the most common system functions.

> Desktop → Start
> Ctrl-Esc
> Press the Windows logo key on Win95/98 keyboards

The Start menu is one of Windows 98's answers to the growing size and complexity of the operating system. There's just not enough room on the Desktop for every program or file that a user wants to keep handy.

The Start menu includes a few important system commands, followed by cascading menus labeled Settings, Documents, and Programs (see Figure 4-22).

One of the fastest ways to use the Start menu is to press Ctrl-Esc or the Windows key, then use underlined letters or arrow keys to pick items from the menu. For example, Ctrl-Esc+R will pop up the Run prompt.

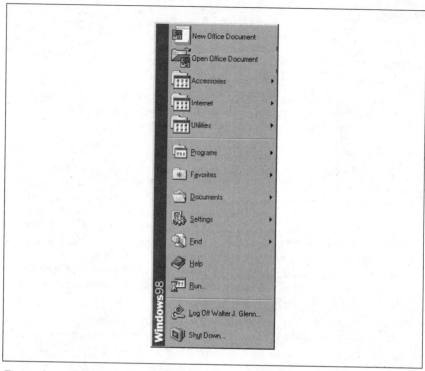

Figure 4-22: The Start menu

Notes

- Any file or folder stored in the folder \ *Windows\Start Menu* will show up on the Start menu. Not all the entries are created this way, however. Some of the menu items are built into the Explorer, and others are stored in other folders.

- To add a program to Start → Programs, just put a shortcut to the program into \ *Windows\Start Menu\Programs.* You could add a shortcut to any other frequently used folder or document as well. Folders can be nested; each level of nesting will result in another level of cascading menu. Feel free to reorganize Start → Programs any way you like.

  Since everything in that directory is a shortcut, you can delete things without fear. You can also rename them or put them in subdirectories so that they appear in a different order. And, of course, you can make new programs appear on the Start menu by putting shortcuts to them into that directory.

  Start → Programs can also be customized using Taskbar → Properties → Start menu Programs. The Advanced button launches an Explorer window with its root at the \ *Windows\Start Menu\Programs* folder; you can reorganize using the Explorer. You can also right-click on the Start menu button and select Explore or Open.

- You can also add programs and folders to the top level of the Start menu by dragging and dropping their icons onto the Start button. This will place a shortcut directly into the *Windows\Start Menu* folder rather than *Windows\Start Menu\Programs*; the icon for the program will appear in alphabetical order in a section at the top of the Start menu. You should do this only for programs that you use fairly often. Good programs to add there might be the Explorer and DOS. Adding folders at this level is a great way of organizing all of your programs into categories. Once you have created new folders, you can move the program shortcuts from the Start Menu → Programs folders into your own folders and leave all those other shortcuts (uninstalls, readmes, etc.) behind.

Start Menu Customization Tips

If you like keyboard accelerators, you might consider adding some numbered items to the top of your Start menu. Pick your nine favorite programs, and create shortcuts whose names begin with a number. For example 1 Solitaire, 2 Hover... :) Then you only have to type `Ctrl-Esc 1` to start the first program, `Ctrl-Esc 2` for the second, and so on.

- Start → Programs can get fairly cluttered, since most programs add shortcuts to this menu as part of their installation process. As a result, you might not notice a couple of important subfolders:

  - Start → Programs → StartUp contains shortcuts to any programs that will be started automatically when the system boots up. Put shortcuts to programs into the folder *C:\Windows\Start Menu\Programs\StartUp* to have them run automatically. See "Startup Folder" later in this chapter for additional details.

  - Start → Programs → Accessories contains many of the bundled Windows 98 utilities, including system tools and games.

- Start → Documents contains a cache of shortcuts to any files recently opened from Explorer. The cascading menu off this item reflects the contents of the folder *Windows\Recent*, and any file operations performed on that folder will be reflected in this menu. You can also clear the cache (i.e., remove all the shortcuts from this folder) using Taskbar → Properties → Start Menu Programs → Documents Menu → Clear. But if you want to clear some of the entries but not others, you need to go to the folder with the Explorer or the DOS prompt and do the dirty work there.

- In addition to rearranging the contents of your Start Menu using Taskbar → Properties → Start Menu Programs, Windows 98 allows you to rearrange program and folder shortcuts on the Start Menu simply by dragging them. Click Start, then click and drag the item you wish to move to any other location on the Start Menu. You can also add a shortcut for any item to the Start menu by dragging the item to the Start button, holding the cursor there for two seconds, then placing the item where you wish.

See Also

Chapter 5 for a discussion of Start → Settings
Other entries in this chapter for a discussion of other menu items
Chapter 6 for a complete information on all programs accessible from Start →
Programs.

Startup Folder   *\Windows\Start Menu\Programs\StartUp*

If you want a program to start up automatically when you reboot the system, put a
shortcut to it into the directory *C:\Windows\Start Menu\Programs\Start Up*. If you
want it to start up minimized (in which case it will simply appear in the Taskbar),
set the shortcut's Properties → Program → Run to Minimized.

Notes

- If you want programs in the Startup folder to run in a particular order, instead
  of putting in shortcuts to each program, create a single DOS batch file, containing lines of the form:

  ```
  start programname
  ```

  The programs will start in the order in which they are listed in the batch file.
  If you want a program to complete before the next one starts, use start /w.

- Another way to have the programs in the Startup folder run in a particular
  order is to rename the shortcuts in the folder by adding a number in front of
  the name in the order you want them to run in. For example, you could do
  the following: 1Virusscan, 2SystemCheck, etc.

- To bypass the programs in the Startup folder, hold down the Shift key while
  the system is booting. Keep holding it down until the Desktop is complete
  with pointer. Obviously, this won't work if you have to log in as part of the
  startup process.

- In addition to the startup folder contents, the Registry settings HKEY_LOCAL_
  MACHINE\Microsoft\Windows\CurrentVersion\Run and \CurrentVer-
  sion\RunServices specify a list of programs to run, as does the Run= entry
  in the *win.ini* file. (See Chapter 9 for details.) See also \CurrentVersion\
  RunOnce, \CurrentVersion\RunOnceEx, and \CurrentVersion\Run-
  ServicesOnce.

- You can also selectively disable startup items from the *StartUp* folder, *config.
  sys*, *autoexec.bat*, and *win.ini* using the System Configuration Utility. See
  Chapter 12 for more.

System Tray

A part of the Taskbar is used for displaying various system status indicators,
including the system clock. If no status indicators have been selected, the System
Tray will not be displayed. The clock is displayed by default on most systems.
Some of these icons are "active"—but they are extremely inconsistent in this
behavior: some respond to a right-click, some to a left-click, some to a double-
click, and some don't respond at all.

Table 4-1 summarizes the indicators that can be put into the System Tray with the location of the checkbox that controls whether the item is to be displayed.

Table 4-1: System Tray Indicators

Item	Control Location
Audio volume	Control Panel → Multimedia → Audio → Show volume control
Clock	Taskbar → Properties → Taskbar Options → Show Clock
Desktop color palette, resolution and font size	Control Panel → Display → Settings → Advanced → Show settings
Dial-Up connection	Dial-Up Networking → Connections menu → Settings → Show an icon on Taskbar after connected
FilterKeys	Control Panel → Accessibility Options → Keyboard → Filter Keys → Settings
Language	Control Panel → Keyboard → Language → Enable Indicator
MouseKeys	Control Panel → Accessibility Options → Mouse
Power status	Control Panel → Power Management → Advanced → Show Power Meter
PCMCIA card	Control Panel → PC Card → Socket Status → Show Control
StickyKeys	Control Panel → Accessibility Options → Keyboard → StickyKeys → Settings

User Interface

Notes

- Leave the pointer over the clock for a few seconds to display the date in a Tooltips bubble.

  Right-click or double-click on the clock when it is displayed to adjust the system date or time. (You can also do this with the Date and Time commands or Control Panel → Date/Time.) The tabbed dialog that appears also allows you to set the time zone and have the system automatically adjust the clock for daylight savings time changes.

- The System Tray is available to any application that chooses to use it—or misuse it. For example, AOL 4.0 installs a startup icon in the System Tray (as well as just about anywhere else it can put one)—a clear abuse of the intended purpose.

- The language indicator is useful only if multiple keyboard layouts are enabled. Click on the indicator to display a popup menu that lets you switch between available keyboard layouts.

- The power status indicator is generally useful only on laptops. It shows a plug when the system is connected to AC power, and a battery when the system is running on the battery. The height of the color in the battery gives a rough idea of how much power is left; to get a more precise estimate, hold the pointer over the indicator until a Tooltips bubble pops up showing the percentage charge remaining.

- The PC card indicator gives you a quick way to get to the Control Panel → PC Card property sheet. This is useful if you are going to be taking PC cards in and out of your system frequently, since the system prefers to be notified before you do so.

Taskbar

The Taskbar contains buttons for each open window on the Desktop (see Figure 4-23). The button corresponding to the window that has the focus appears depressed. To bring a window to the front, click on its Taskbar button. When a window is minimized, its icon appears on the Taskbar rather than on the Desktop itself (as in Windows 3.1).

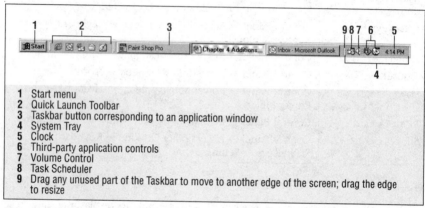

1 Start menu
2 Quick Launch Toolbar
3 Taskbar button corresponding to an application window
4 System Tray
5 Clock
6 Third-party application controls
7 Volume Control
8 Task Scheduler
9 Drag any unused part of the Taskbar to move to another edge of the screen; drag the edge to resize

Figure 4-23: The Taskbar

Notes

- By default, the Explorer displays the Taskbar at the bottom of the screen. You can drag it to the top or either side using any empty space on the bar as the drag handle.

- As you open more windows, the Taskbar buttons become smaller, displaying less and less text. If you have so many open windows that only the 16 × 16 icon for each one is showing on the Taskbar, no more will be displayed. A small "spin control" will be displayed so that you can rotate which icons are visible.

  However, you may want to modify the size of the Taskbar by dragging the edge up or down (or sideways, if you've moved it to the right or left side of the screen).

- If the focus is on the Taskbar, you can use the arrow keys to move between the buttons for open programs. Ctrl-Esc will open the Start menu.

- By default, windows are scattered around the Desktop as left by the user. The context menu for the Taskbar lets you cascade all open windows or tile them horizontally or vertically. You can also use the context menu to minimize all windows at once (reduce them to the Taskbar) or to move them to the Desktop.

Properties

- Enable Taskbar → Properties → Taskbar Options → Always on top (see Figure 4-24) to specify that the Taskbar can't be covered by open windows as you move them around the Desktop. Note that the working Desktop space is decreased with this option—maximized windows stop above the Taskbar.

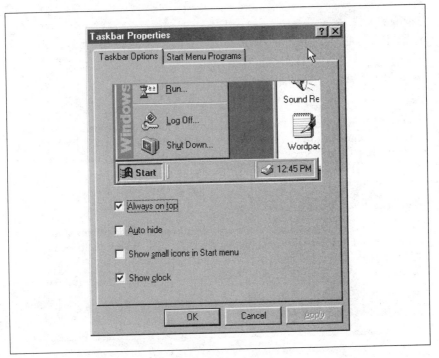

Figure 4-24: The Taskbar Options tab

- If Taskbar → Properties → Taskbar Options → Auto hide is enabled, the Taskbar will be invisible until you move the pointer to the edge of the screen where it is hidden. It will then slide up into view. This gives you a bit more Desktop real estate, but can be a little disconcerting. Even if Auto Hide is on, if you give the Taskbar the focus, it will stay visible until you give the focus to another window.

- Enable Taskbar → Properties → Taskbar Options → Show small icons in Start menu shrinks the size of the Start Menu icons so that the menu is not so obtrusive when it pops up.

- Enable Taskbar → Properties → Taskbar Options → Show Clock to display the time in the System Tray if it's not already visible.

- Taskbar → Properties → Start menu can be used to add or remove programs from the Start menu. The Add... button prompts you for the name of a program command line; a wizard will add a shortcut to the *Windows\Start Menu\Programs* folder. The Advanced... button launches an Explorer view of the Start menu folder hierarchy. See "Start Menu" earlier in this chapter for an easier way to customize the Start menu.

- Another button on the same property sheet lets you clear the contents of the Documents menu. (You can do the same thing from the command line or the Explorer by deleting all the shortcuts from the folder *Windows\Recent.*)

Toolbars

Dockable toolbars for launching applications or web pages.

> Taskbar → right-click → Toolbars
> Folder → View → Toolbars

Description

Windows 98 expands the TaskBar with up to four new Toolbars, the Address Toolbar, the Quick Launch Toolbar, the Links Toolbar, and the Desktop Toolbar. Just right-click on any empty portion of the Taskbar to pop up the context menu for the Taskbar, and then choose your toolbar(s). The Address Toolbar and the Links Toolbar can also be displayed as part of any folder window.

Arranging and Resizing Toolbars

You can drag any of the toolbars out of the Taskbar and dock them at any point on the screen, but I prefer to keep the Address and Quick Link toolbars as part of my Taskbar, as shown in Figure 4-25.

Figure 4-25: The Taskbar containing Address and Quick Link Toolbars

Note that before enabling the Toolbars, I resized my Taskbar to be double height, so that there's room for everything.

Each toolbar has a vertical bar that acts as a drag handle on the left. When you position the pointer over the drag handle, the pointer changes to a horizontal two-headed arrow (<->), and then to <-||-> when you hold down the mouse button. Moving the toolbars around seems intuitive at first, but you can get into trouble pretty quickly. You can drag the handle sideways to adjust the length of the toolbar, or double-click on the drag handle to quickly expand or contract the toolbar. But if you drag it vertically (while the taskbar is horizontal), you can end up with odd-shaped toolbars that then seem difficult to reposition. For example, Figure 4-26 shows the kind of configuration you can end up with.

The problem is that it isn't completely obvious how you got into this state or what to do about it. The trick is to drag the handle vertically again rather than horizon-

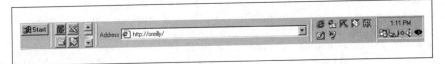

Figure 4-26: An unhappy arrangement of toolbars

tally. When you let go, the toolbars will snap into a new arrangement, even though there isn't any visual feedback while you're dragging.

You can completely rearrange the position of the toolbars by dragging any one of them completely over another. The two will flip positions when you let go of the mouse button.

To drag any of the toolbars to some other point on the screen, just drag it right off the Taskbar and position it where you want it on the Desktop. Note that you can't have an application in full screen mode covering the Desktop when you do this. The toolbar will change to a square window; you'll need to resize it by dragging one of the corners in order to get it back into rectangular toolbar shape. If you drag it to an unoccupied side of the screen, it will dock there. If you close a toolbar, you will have to re-enable it using Taskbar → Toolbars.

In order to get a Toolbar back onto the Taskbar, drag it over the Taskbar and hold it there until you get a silhouette of the Toolbar over the Taskbar. When you let go of the mouse button, the toolbar will drop back into the Taskbar. This is all pretty ugly and unpredictable, but if you play around, you can get a feel for it.

The Address Toolbar

The Address Toolbar is just about my favorite new feature in Windows 98. While its main purpose is to make it easy to type in a web address and point your browser at that address, it also can be used to type in a command name, just like the Run prompt! (See "Run," earlier in this chapter, for details.) This means that you can easily choose between point and click and command-line operations, whichever is easier for launching a given command. Because I keep the Address Toolbar visible in the Taskbar all the time as well as in each open folder window, it's become my primary command-line interface. I almost never use the Run prompt or a DOS window any more.

One major difference between the Run prompt and the Address Toolbar is how they treat an unknown address or command. The Address Toolbar assumes that any unknown text string is a web address. So, for example, typing `oreilly` in the Address Toolbar will launch your browser and start looking for *www.oreilly.com*. If you type the same string at the Run prompt, you'll get the message "Cannot find the file 'oreilly' (or one of its components). Make sure the path and filename are correct and that all required libraries are available." While the Run prompt will recognize a line beginning with *http://* or *www.* as a web address and launch the browser, it will assume that any other string is the name of a command.

Like the Run prompt, the Address Toolbar features a drop-down list containing the history of all recently-entered URLs and command-lines. Pick an item from the drop-down list to re-execute the command or revisit the specified web site.

Although useful for issuing commands, the Address Toolbar does have one drawback when used in this fashion. When you issue a command, the command is opened in a new window. Once the command has finished, that window closes instantly. If you are issuing a command for which you need to see a response (like *ping* or *dir*), you'll have to have very fast eyes. For these types of commands, you are better off using the MS-DOS Prompt.

The Desktop Toolbar

The Desktop Toolbar was intended as a handy way of getting at the contents of your Desktop when it's covered with open windows. It contains an icon for every file, folder, or shortcut on the Desktop. You can set the Toolbar to be Always on Top so you can easily bring anything to the front. Of course, if you have a lot of things on your Desktop, this toolbar can itself get pretty unwieldy, so I don't find it too useful. Your mileage may vary. Of course, you can also just use the Show Desktop button in the Quick Links Toolbar (see below) for quick desktop access.

The Links Toolbar

The Links Toolbar is the same as the Links Toolbar in Internet Explorer. By default, it contains icons for various Microsoft web pages. (Even the Link "Customize Links" takes you to a page on the Microsoft site, which simply gives information on how to modify the Toolbar.) If you don't want to make the visit, here's what you'll learn:

- To add a link to the toolbar, just drag a web link from your web browser or from the Address Toolbar and drop it on the Links Toolbar.

- To delete a link, right-click on it and select Delete from the context menu.

- To modify one of the existing links, right-click on it, and select Properties from the context menu. You can change the icon. You can also keep the link but change the target URL. For instance, you could change the Internet Start link from Microsoft's home page to another site, such as *www.yahoo.com*.

- To rearrange the links in the toolbar, just drag and drop them to a new position.

As with many Windows 98 user interface features, you can also use either Explorer or the DOS command line to work directly in the folder containing the shortcuts used to generate the toolbar. In this case, the relevant folder is *C:\WINDOWS\ favorites\links*. Create or delete shortcuts in this folder and they will show up on the Links Toolbar.

In addition, the context menu for each toolbar includes an Open command, which opens a folder window containing the shortcuts used to generate the toolbar. Once you've opened the window, you can delete, rename, or drag and drop files and shortcuts here, just like you can with any other folder window.

If you've modified the contents of a toolbar folder, Toolbar → right-click → Refresh will refresh the view of the Toolbar.

The Quick Launch Toolbar

The Quick Launch Toolbar contains icons for frequently-accessed applications. By default, it contains shortcuts for Microsoft Internet Explorer, Outlook Express, the

Channel Bar, and the Desktop. As with the Links Toolbar, you can rearrange the shortcuts used to generate the Toolbar. In this case, the relevant folder is *C:\ WINDOWS\Application Data\Microsoft\Internet Explorer\Quick Launch*. You can also add and rearrange items on the Quick Launch Toolbar by simply dragging them where you wish them to go. It's helpful to drop shortcuts into the toolbar for your most-frequently used applications.

 One of the niftiest icons on the Quick Launch Toolbar is the Show Desktop icon: ✍. Don't delete this one! Click on this to bring the Desktop to the front. I find this far superior to displaying the Desktop Toolbar. In order to make sure that this icon is always visible, you might want to drag it to the front of the list of icons.

Custom Toolbars

You can also create custom toolbars using Taskbar → right-click → Toolbars → New Toolbar. You'll get a dialog similar to the one in Figure 4-27. Simply pick a folder or URL whose contents you want made into a toolbar (such as Control Panel or Dial-Up Networking) and click OK. If you want to create a completely new folder, you'll have to create the target folder first, since you can only pick existing folders.

You can also create a custom toolbar out of any Internet address. Instead of entering the name of a folder (as in Figure 4-27), just type the URL. This will create a toolbar that actually displays the web page you indicate. This type of toolbar is most useful when it is not docked to the Taskbar, but free-floating. This essentially gives you a floating browser window with no controls or menus cluttering things up. Clicking a link in the toolbar opens a new, full IE window. If you don't wish to use Active Desktop items, you can still achieve much the same effect using custom toolbars with Internet addresses.

There is one bad thing about custom toolbars. When you close one, you essentially have to start over and recreate it to get it back. You cannot simply enable it, as you can with the preconfigured toolbars.

Toolbar Context Menus

Each toolbar has its own context menu, which allows you to modify the appearance of the toolbar:

- View. Allows you to display either large or small icons. (Small is the default value, and you probably don't want to change it.)

- Show Text. Uses a label as well as an icon for each toolbar item. This is useful if you have a toolbar containing a bunch of icons of the same type. It's the default setting for the Links toolbar, but not for the Quick Launch toolbar.

- Refresh. Rebuilds the toolbar if you've changed the underlying folder and shortcuts used to generate it.

- Open. Opens a window on the folder containing the shortcuts used to generate the toolbar.

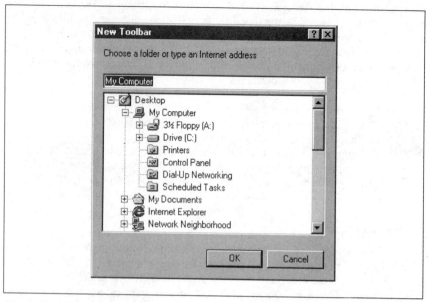

Figure 4-27: The New Toolbar dialog

- Show Title. Shows the name of the toolbar. A waste of space for the standard toolbars, but perhaps useful if you set up a lot of custom toolbars.

- Toolbars. This is the same as Taskbar → right-click → Toolbars. It lets you enable or disable the various toolbars, or create a custom toolbar.

- Close. Closes the toolbar.

When the toolbar is on the Desktop (but not in the Taskbar), the context menu also includes these items:

- Always on Top. The toolbar floats on top of any window that would otherwise cover it.

- Auto Hide. Just like the Taskbar, a toolbar docked to an edge of the screen can be set to disappear when not in use. Move the pointer to the edge of the screen where it is docked and the toolbar will rise into view. This item is visible but grayed out if the toolbar is on the Desktop but not anchored to a screen edge.

Windows Explorer   *\Windows\Explorer.exe*

View all the folders and files on your computer.

> Start → Run → explorer
> Start → Programs → Windows Explorer
> Context menu → Explore
> Shift-double-click on any folder

Many users think of the Desktop interface as "Windows 98" and the Explorer as an application within it, but in fact, the Explorer is the program that creates and maintains the Desktop and many of the other visible features of Windows 98. However, when you run the Explorer as a separate application, it provides a useful two-pane view of files and folders that allows you to navigate the file system easily. (See Figure 4-28.) It is that view of the Explorer that is discussed here.

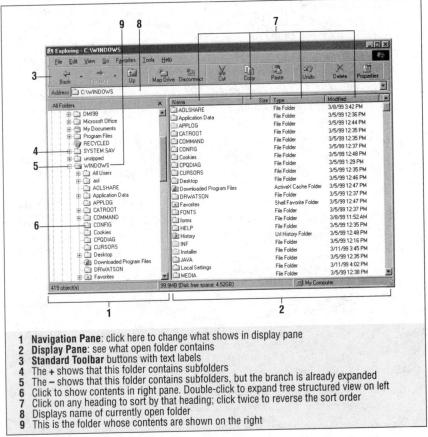

1 **Navigation Pane**: click here to change what shows in display pane
2 **Display Pane**: see what open folder contains
3 **Standard Toolbar** buttons with text labels
4 The + shows that this folder contains subfolders
5 The – shows that this folder contains subfolders, but the branch is already expanded
6 Click to show contents in right pane. Double-click to expand tree structured view on left
7 Click on any heading to sort by that heading; click twice to reverse the sort order
8 Displays name of currently open folder
9 This is the folder whose contents are shown on the right

Figure 4-28: The double-pane Explorer window

Unlike the Windows 3.1 interface, in which you end up with dozens of open windows if you want to navigate somewhere deep in the file system, the Explorer maintains a tree-structured view of the file system in the left pane and opens only a single target folder in the right pane. This behavior applies only to folders, however. If you double-click on a file or program icon in the right pane, a separate application window will open, just as it does on the Desktop.

It may help to think of the left pane as the "navigation pane"—actions here control what will be displayed on the right pane. The right, or "display pane," shows the results. Think of this pane as equivalent to any other window, such as a folder open on the Desktop. (This will become very clear to you if you select an alternative view such as View → Large Icons. The right pane will then resemble a normal folder view.)

- Click on any folder in the left pane to show its contents in the pane on the right.

- A plus sign (+) by any folder indicates that it contains subfolders. Click on the plus sign (or double-click on the folder itself) to show the subfolders as part of the tree-structured view in the left pane. The plus sign will change to a minus sign. Click on the minus sign (or double-click on the open folder) to collapse that branch of the filesystem tree.

- You can perform the same actions on folders or files shown in either of the Explorer panes that you can perform on them in any open window:

  - Double-click on any file or folder in the right pane to open it. A folder will open in the right Explorer pane; a file will open its associated application.

  - Drag a file or folder from the Explorer pane onto the Desktop or into any other folder. If you drag a file onto another folder in the navigation pane of Explorer and hold the cursor over the plus sign of a collapsed folder for about two seconds, that folder will expand. If you hold the file(s) over the top or bottom edge of the navigation pane, the view will scroll.

  - Pop up the context menu for any file or folder in either pane and use it to create Shortcuts, Send To, Rename, Delete, or any other operation you can perform on files.

Everything that works on the Desktop works in the Explorer, because the Desktop is just part of the Explorer. Each additional instance of the Explorer that you start up is actually just a separate thread of execution in the same program that also creates and maintains the Desktop.

Notes

- The portion of the file system that is initially displayed in the Explorer depends on how you invoke the program.

  Start → *Programs* → *Windows Explorer*
  Starts at root of Windows drive; usually *C:*

  any folder → *context menu* → *Explore*
  Starts at selected folder

  Start → *Run* → explorer *pathname*
  Give *pathname* as argument, or *C:* by default

- The Explorer has many command-line options. See "Windows Explorer" in Chapter 6 for details.

- The amount of free space left on your disk is shown in the Explorer status bar when you select a disk icon.

- You can undo most actions that you perform in Explorer by choosing Edit → Undo or pressing Ctrl-Z.

Quick Navigation Tips

Scrolling around full Explorer windows can take a long time. Typing the first letter of any file or folder will jump right to the first matching file or folder. Press the letter again to go to the next matching file or folder. This behavior applies only to folders that are already expanded (i.e., visible in the left pane).

Backspace will take you back up one level in the folder hierarchy. When the focus is in the left pane, the left arrow will do the same, but will also close the open branch. The right arrow will expand branches (any folder with a + next to it); the up and down arrows will move through the expanded branches in a linear fashion, but will not expand any branch that is not already open. Press Enter to expand or open the currently selected folder. Left and right arrow keys on the keyboard can expand and contract branches.

Cut, copy, and paste keys (Ctrl-X, Ctrl-C, and Ctrl-V) can be used in the right pane to move or copy files from one location to another. This can be easier than drag and drop when the files are in folders that aren't close together. Ctrl-A selects all.

To get a two-pane Explorer view of any folder, press Shift while you double-click on the folder.

User Interface

- If you prefer the Windows 3.1 File Manager, use Start → Run → winfile. You can start the Windows 3.1 Program Manager with Start → Run → progman. Keep in mind that you can't view long filenames in *winfile*.

 The Explorer is smart enough to figure out when a floppy disk is full. So you can safely go to a large folder, Select All, copy, and paste to a floppy. When the disk is full, you'll be prompted to insert a new disk.

Windows Update   *http://windowsupdate.microsoft.com/*

An online service that provides updates and add-ons for Windows 98.

To Launch
    Start → Windows Update
    Start → Programs → Accessories → System Tools → Windows Update
    http://windowsupdate.microsoft.com/

Description

Windows Update is a web site (see Figure 4-29) on which Microsoft has made updates and certain add-ons available for Windows 98. These includes updates to Win 98 components available in Win 98 setup, security fixes, the Win 98 Y2K fix, bug patches, and additional components. When you first log on to the site, the Product Updates link is where you'll find all the goodies. A message will pop up asking whether you would like your computer checked for currently installed products and their versions. Microsoft promises that no information will be sent to them. If you select yes, your system is scanned and the list of product updates is tailored to display only those not already installed on your system. Select no and all available components are displayed. Components are presented as a checklist, so you can download and install them in batch.

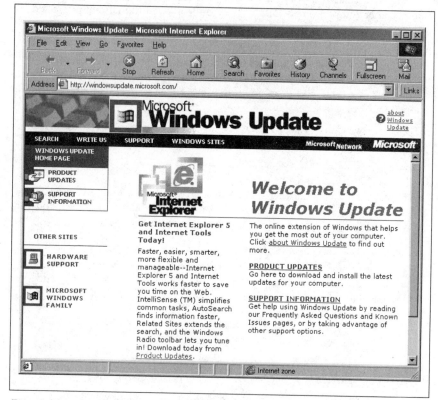

Figure 4-29: Windows Update

It would be useless to try to include an up-to-date list of what's on the site. However, following is a list of some of the more important (and fun) items you can find there. If you have Windows 98 Second Edition, you already have many of these fixes installed.

Windows 98 Year 2000 Update

Fixes potential Y2K conflicts in Win 98. Though Microsoft claims these problems only affect a few users, this download is a must-have.

Internet Explorer Security Fixes

Fixes security holes found in Internet Explorer. Each of these items is downloaded and installed as a separate patch. Examples of fixes include:

Internet Explorer "Window.External.Jscript" Security Update

This update resolves an issue that can cause Internet Explorer to close unexpectedly when browsing a web page that contains malicious JScript script.

Internet Explorer "Frame Spoof" Security Fix

This patch corrects a vulnerability in Internet Explorer 4 that could allow a malicious web site operator to create a bogus window that imitates a window on a legitimate web site. The threat posed by this vulnerability is that the false window could collect information from you and send it back to the malicious site.

Internet Explorer 5 and Internet Tools

The latest version of Microsoft's browser. IE5 includes a number of under-the-hood fixes meant to increase speed, stability, and compatibility with the latest Internet standards. Other improvements include a searchable URL history, support for multiple DUN connections, and an expanded AutoComplete feature. Also included with the browser are updated versions of Outlook Express, MS Chat, and NetMeeting. See "Internet Explorer" in Chapter 6 for details on the new IE5 features.

Windows Critical Update Notification

A background applet that scans the Windows Update site whenever you log on to the Internet and pops up a message if a new critical update is available. This one is pretty useful if you don't care to check in on the site yourself, but still wish to be aware when security and bug patches are released.

Newest Versions of Windows Components

As optional components of Windows 98, such as Front Page Express, DirectX, and Accessibility Options are released, they are made available here.

Driver Updates

Launches an applet that scans your system for currently installed drivers and checks them against a database of current drivers available from Microsoft. If new versions are found, you will be able to install them directly from the site.

Desktop Themes

Includes many additional desktop themes not available on the Win 98 CD-ROM.

Windows Update also allows you to uninstall updates, patches, and drivers using a Restore page. Replaced files will be restored during the process. If you are unable to connect to Windows Update for some reason (or if you just don't want to), you can also use the Update Wizard Uninstall utility (*upwizun.exe*) included with Windows 98. Run it from the Tools menu of System information (*msinfo32.exe*) or just enter *upwizun* at the Run prompt. The utility will present a list of updates you can uninstall.

Notes

Here are a few alternate URLs for accessing some of the downloads available from the Windows Update site.

- Many of the security patches for Internet Explorer and Outlook Express are available at the following location: *http://www.microsoft.com/windows/ie/security/*.

- The DirectX patch is available at the DirectX Home Page: *http://www.microsoft.com/directx/*.

- The latest version of the Windows Media Player is available at: *http://www.microsoft.com/windows/mediaplayer/*.

CHAPTER 5

The Control Panel

The Control Panel provides a point-and-click environment for configuration of many Windows 98 features. The Control Panel also demonstrates just how inconsistent the Windows 98 interface can be.

When you choose Start → Settings → Control Panel, you get to a folder containing various icons (or control panel applets) representing system features. (See Figure 5-1.)

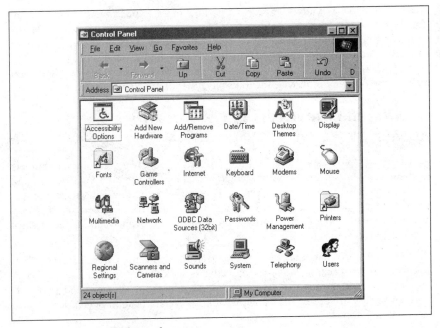

Figure 5-1: The Control Panel

Double-clicking on most of these icons pops up a tabbed property sheet controlling the associated system features (such as Date/Time, Display, and so on). These are often the same property sheets you can get to by right-clicking on some other item on the Desktop and then choosing Properties. (For example, Control Panel → Display is the same as Desktop → Properties, and Control Panel → Date/Time is the same as the Property sheet you get when you right-click or double-click on the clock in the System Tray.)

However, double-clicking other icons (such as Add New Hardware) spawns a wizard that walks you through the process of configuring a new device.

Still others, such as Fonts, are shortcuts to virtual or system folders. Inside the Control Panel → Fonts folder, which is just a shortcut to \Windows\Fonts, you'll find all of the font files used on the system. Double-clicking on any one of the font files will launch a program (fontview.exe) that allows you to see what that font looks like. But if you want to add a new font, for instance, use the File menu of the Fonts folder window, or just drag a font file into the folder: hardly what you'd expect, given the user interface to the rest of the Control Panel icons.

Even the majority of the Control Panel icons, those that use the property sheet approach, can be confusing, since very similar property sheets can show up at different points in the system. For example, the property sheets at My Computer → Dial-Up Networking → connection → Properties → Configure seem almost identical to those at Control Panel → Modems → modem → Properties. As it turns out, though, in this case the Control Panel sets defaults that individual connection properties can override. What's even more confusing is that one setting, the Extra Settings in the Advanced Connection Settings window, is not overridden.

The lesson: while Windows 98 makes a good attempt to put an easy-to-use graphical front end on system configuration, it's impossible to completely hide the underlying complexity and inconsistency of the system. As a result, we sometimes go a little deeper "under the hood" than you might find in other books. However, time spent understanding how things are connected underneath can help you make sense of many otherwise inexplicable system behaviors.

Command-Line Access to Control Panel Applets

As it turns out, you can also access the property sheet style control panel applets (and some of the wizards) from the command line, using the control.exe program. This is really just a shell for another program called rundll.exe, but it has a much simpler syntax. With control.exe, you can create batch files or shortcuts that pop up the relevant control panel applet, in some cases even opening the control panel applet to a specific tab.

Most of the control panel applets are stored in files with the extension .cpl. When you start up the Control Panel, it populates its window by searching \Windows\ System for any files with this extension. (Some others are incorporated into software and hardware drivers.) This allows third-party application developers to add control panel applets.

The command-line syntax (hardly something that you'd want to type on a regular basis, but good for embedding in batch files, or shortcuts on the Desktop or in the Start menu) is as follows:

```
control filename.cpl {,applet_name} {,property_tab}
```

For example:

```
control timedate.cpl ,Date/Time ,1
```

Note the placement of the commas. This is not accidental. The comma immediately precedes the command-line argument (with no space), rather than following the preceding argument, as you might expect. Get the commas wrong, and the command line won't work at all.

In practice, you don't usually need to include the applet name, and can just specify the property tab. For example:

```
control sysdm.cpl ,1
```

will pop up the Device Manager. If you regularly add or configure devices, embedding this command line in a shortcut is a lot easier than going to Control Panel → System and then clicking on the second tab.

In documenting each of the control panel applets in this chapter, we've generally omitted the applet name, choosing the shorter format except in those cases (such as Add New Hardware and Keyboard) where the applet name must be specified, because more than one control panel applet shares a single .cpl file. Keep in mind that every applet on a user's system may not be documented here, since they're extensible and defined by an open specification. For example, if you've installed TweakUI on your system, you will have a TweakUI icon in your Control Panel.

Finally, to cement the "quirky syntax" prize, not all tabbed control panel applets recognize the property tab arguments from the command line. It's not up to control.exe to recognize this syntax, but rather the .cpl applet itself, and not all do.

Control panel applets sometimes reside within .dll files; these can be loaded via the [MMCPL] section of \Windows\control.ini, with a statement such as "ScanSet=Lpscnmgr.dll." The [don't load] section of control.ini excludes cpls that would otherwise normally be loaded. For example, the setting "sticpl.cpl=no" excludes the Scanners and Cameras applet. Also, TweakUI can be used to exclude any control panel applet. See "TweakUI" in Chapter 8, *Hidden Gems on the Windows 98 CD-ROM*, for more information about TweakUI.

If a third-party application has added a control panel applet and you want to temporarily keep it from appearing in the Control Panel, simply give the .cpl file another extension or move it to another folder than \Windows\System.

Accessibility Options

\Windows\System\access.cpl

Manage features to make Windows 98 more usable by people with disabilities.

To Launch

Control Panel → Accessibility Options

Command Line

```
control access.cpl [,property-tab]
```

Property Tabs

,0 Keyboard

,1 Keyboard

,2 Sound

,3 Display

,4 Mouse

,5 General

Each Accessibility Options property tab consists of a series of checkboxes to enable various options, along with a settings button to configure that option. The following sections outline the options and associated settings for each tab. Many of the accessibility options also have an associated keyboard accelerator (a bit of a misnomer, since most are quite complex!) that allows you to toggle it on and off. The accelerators are not enabled by default.

Keyboard

StickyKeys lets you type the individual keys that make up keyboard accelerators one after another rather than all together. For example, with StickyKeys enabled, typing Ctrl, then Alt, then Del one after another would have the effect of Ctrl-Alt-Del. StickyKeys are useful if you have trouble holding down multiple keys at once. Keyboard accelerator: press Shift five times.

FilterKeys lets you configure Windows 98's behavior when a key is held down. FilterKeys → Settings lets you control how long a key must be held down before it starts to repeat and how fast it repeats once it starts. Similar functions are available at Control Panel → Keyboard → Speed. However, FilterKeys also lets you disable keyboard repeat completely. Keyboard accelerator: hold down the right Shift key for eight seconds.

ToggleKeys causes the keyboard to beep whenever you press Caps Lock, Num Lock, or Scroll Lock. Keyboard accelerator: hold down Num Lock for five seconds.

Sounds

SoundSentry lets you substitute visual warnings (e.g., flashing the titlebar or the entire screen) for sounds normally made for the system. Keyboard accelerator: none.

ShowSounds lets you substitute captions for sounds in programs that support this feature. Not many do. Keyboard accelerator: none.

Display

High Contrast lets you pick white on black, black on white, or a custom Desktop scheme. (This is the same list as available at Control Panel → Display; look for schemes with large or extra large in the scheme name for appropriate entries.) To create your own scheme (and add it to the Custom list), go to Control Panel → Display. Keyboard accelerator: left Alt+left Shift+Print Screen.

If you have trouble seeing the display, you may also want to use large pointers or enable Mouse Trails (which leaves a ghost track when you move the pointer). These are settable at Control Panel → Mouse → Pointers and Control Panel → Mouse → Motion, respectively.

Mouse

MouseKeys lets you use keys on the numeric keypad to move the pointer around the screen (see Figure 5-2).

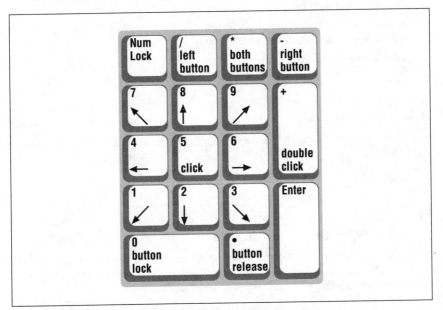

Figure 5-2: The numeric keypad with MouseKeys

Move the pointer to an object and press Ins to start dragging. Press Del to end the drag.

Press the – key to switch "clicking" to the right button. That is, – then 5 to right-click or – then + to right–double-click. "Right-click" mode remains enabled until you press / to switch back to left-clicking.

Hold down Shift while using the arrow keys to move the pointer pixel by pixel; hold down Ctrl to move in big jumps.

The Settings dialog box lets you control how fast the pointer moves and how quickly it speeds up when you hold down a key:

Top speed

We recommend a high speed, but try different settings for yourself.

Acceleration

For maximum control, we recommend a slow acceleration.

Use MouseKeys when Num Lock is [on/off]

Toggle this checkbox if you plan to use the numeric keypad for numbers as well as MouseKeys. Show MouseKey status on screen. We like having the icon in the System Tray, especially since MouseKeys occasionally turns itself off for no obvious reason. Keyboard accelerator: `left Alt+left Shift+Num Lock`.

General

Automatic Reset lets you choose whether to apply the chosen Accessibility Options to the current session only rather than leaving them in place, and also lets you set a timeout to turn them off after the system has been idle for a set number of minutes.

Notification lets you specify whether messages or sounds should be used to let you know when an accessibility option is turned on or off.

SerialKey devices enables the use of special alternative input devices attached to a serial port.

Add New Hardware

\ *Windows\System\sysdm.cpl*

Run a wizard that will autodetect newly installed hardware and install the appropriate drivers.

To Launch

Control Panel → Add New Hardware

Command Line

```
control sysdm.cpl Add New Hardware
```

Generally, Windows 98 will detect new hardware and use the appropriate drivers automatically (this is called "Plug and Play"). However, you may sometimes need to intervene manually (this is called "Plug and Pray").

The wizard will first search for plug-and-play devices on your system. You must go through this process even if the device you are adding is not plug and play. If any plug-and-play devices are found, you will get the chance to add or configure them. Once the plug and play configuration phase is over, you can have the wizard autodetect non–plug-and-play devices, or you can specify one manually.

If you ask the wizard to autodetect new hardware, it will look for any hardware devices for which it does not have associated drivers and ask you for configuration only for that device. If you want to add a specific device by name, specify No and step through the wizard to pick the general type of the device, then the specific manufacturer and model. If your model is not listed or you have a specific driver installation disk you want to load, click the Have Disk... button. The disk must include an *.inf* file provided by the manufacturer.

Notes

- The "Add New Hardware" argument is necessary on the command line because *sysdm.cpl* contains multiple control panel dialog boxes. Running `control sysdm.cpl` by itself launches the System Properties dialog box (Control Panel → System).

- You should have the Windows 98 CD-ROM handy when using this wizard, or the wizard will eventually stall. Fortunately, it recovers more gracefully than many Windows programs.

- You can modify information for existing hardware devices using Control Panel → System → Device Manager.

- Windows will often ask to insert CD-ROM for drivers already on your Hard Disk. You can point to *C:\Windows* and *\Windows\System* to use them.

Add/Remove Programs   *\Windows\System\appwiz.cpl*

Add or remove programs from the system, set up various system options, and create startup disks.

To Launch

Control Panel → Add/Remove Programs

Command Line

```
control appwiz.cpl [,property-tab]
```

Property Tabs

,0   Install/Uninstall

,1   Install/Uninstall

,2   Windows Setup

,3   Startup Disk

Install/Uninstall

Lets you install a new program from a floppy disk or CD-ROM, and offers a scrollable list of all programs that can be uninstalled by Windows. This list includes Microsoft applications and all well-behaved third-party applications, but in most cases does not include system components. (That's the next tab.)

Windows Setup

Lets you install and remove various Windows 98 system features, including Accessibility Options, Accessories, Communications, Multilanguage Support, Multimedia, System Tools, and Online Services. Components that have already been installed will be checked.

Note that the first-level checkbox is usually only the top level, and each component may have additional subcomponents visible via the Details button. At the bottom of the Description area, you'll see a message like "7 of 8 components selected." This refers to the subcomponents that are available by clicking on the Details button. Figure 5-3 shows the Communications component, and the eight subcomponents can be seen in Figure 5-4. In other words, if you're trying to figure out what's installed, don't look at just the first dialog box.

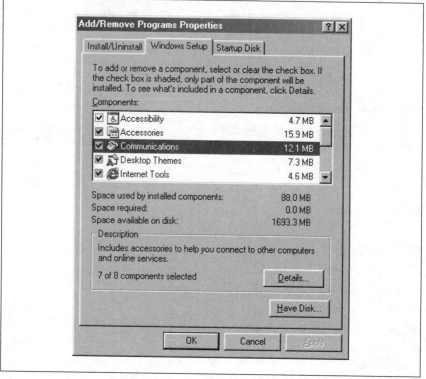

Figure 5-3: The Communications component

Table 5-1 lists the components found on the Windows Setup tab, and the various details for each component, which can be viewed by selecting the component and pressing the Details button. Keep in mind that the details may vary slightly depending on what version of Windows 98 you're running, the hardware you're running it on, and other factors. You will typically need to have the Windows 98 CD handy to install any element that hasn't already been installed.

Select any item to see a brief explanation of its contents and how much disk space it takes up.

Startup Disk

Lets you store essential system files onto a floppy. This startup disk can be used to boot your system if you are having problems booting from your hard drive. A boot menu allows you to load real-mode CD-ROM drivers, perform a clean boot without CD, or view a help file on using the startup disk to solve routine startup problems. In addition, a RAM drive is created in your system memory during startup that can be accessed like a regular fixed drive. The

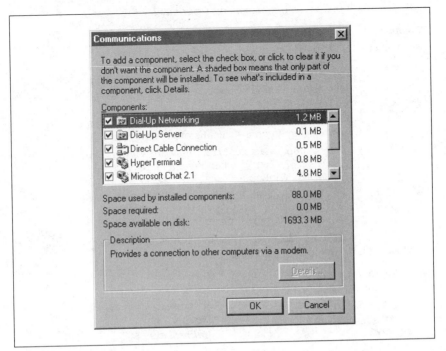

Figure 5-4: Details of the Communications component

Table 5-1: The Windows Setup Components

Components	Details
Accessibility	Accessibility Options, Accessibility Tools
Accessories	Calculator, Desktop Wallpaper, Document Templates, Games, Imaging, Mouse Pointers, Paint, Quick View, Screen Savers, Windows Scripting Host, Word Pad
Communications	Dial-Up Networking, Dial-Up Server, Direct Cable Connection, HyperTerminal, Microsoft Chat 2.1, Microsoft NetMeeting, Phone Dialer, Virtual Private Networking
Desktop Themes	Baseball, Dangerous Creatures, Desktop Themes Support, Inside your Computer, Jungle, Leonardo da Vinci, More Windows, Mystery, Nature, Science, Space, Sports, The 60's USA, The Golden Era, Travel, Underwater, Windows 98
Internet Tools	Microsoft FrontPage Express, Microsoft VRML 2.0 Viewer, Microsoft Wallet, Personal Web Server, Real Audio Player 4.0, Web Publishing Wizard, Web-Based Enterprise Management
Microsoft Outlook Express	Microsoft Outlook Express
Multilanguage Support	Baltic, Central European, Cyrillic, Greek, Turkish

Table 5-1: The Windows Setup Components (continued)

Components	Details
Multimedia	Audio Compression, CD Player, Macromedia Shockwave Director, Macromedia Shockwave Flash, Media Player, Microsoft NetShow Player 2.0, Multimedia Sound Schemes, Sample Sounds, Sound Recorder, Video Compression, Volume Control
Online Services	America Online, AT&T Worldnet Service, CompuServe, Prodigy Internet, The Microsoft Network
System Tools	Backup, Character Map, Clipboard Viewer, Drive Converter (FAT 32), Net Watcher, System Monitor, System Resource Meter, WinPopup
Web TV for Windows	WaveTop Data Broadcasting, Web TV for Windows

compressed *Edb.cab* file on the startup disk is used to populate the RAM drive with handy utilities, including:

Attrib.exe	*Format.com*
Chkdsk.exe	*Mscdex.exe*
Debug.exe	*Scandisk.exe*
Edit.com	*Sys.com*
Ext.exe	*Uninstal.exe*

You can learn about many of these commands in Chapter 7, *DOS and Other Command-Line Utilities*. You can also add your own favorite commands to the *Edb.cab* file using most standard compression utilities.

If you want to boot automatically into the Win 98 GUI, then you also need an *autoexec.bat* with at least one line:

```
c:\windows\win.com
```

You will also need to copy the *msdos.sys* file from *C:* to the startup disk in order for this to work.

See Chapter 12, *Windows Startup*, for more information on each of these files.

Notes

- Add/Remove Programs → Windows Setup installs everything that has been checked in the Components list, but it also removes everything that has been unchecked, so be careful not to unintentionally remove some existing component when installing something new.

- If your system doesn't match the contents of this book (e.g., if you can't find a program we describe), look in Add/Remove Programs to see if a relevant component is installed. (It could also be something that Microsoft added in a later version.)

- TweakUI (see Chapter 8, *Hidden Gems on the Windows 98 CD-ROM*) can be used to add, remove, or edit items in the Add/Remove Programs list. After all, once you've removed a program, you may never want to see it again!

Date/Time

Set the date, time, or time zone.

To Launch

Control Panel → Date/Time
Double-click on clock in System Tray

Command Line

```
control timedate.cpl [,property-tab]
```

Property Tabs

,0   Date & Time

,1   Time Zone

Date & Time

.Gives you a graphical, self-explanatory control panel for setting the system date and time. Since this is the only built-in calendar in the system, it's also useful if you want to figure out if a date next March is a Tuesday or a Wednesday—as long as you remember to set the calendar back to the current date before you exit, or choose Cancel rather than OK when closing the dialog.

Time Zone

Use the list box at the top, which contains a complete listing of the world's time zones, to pick the appropriate zone for where you are located. Each zone is accompanied by the number of hours it varies (+ or −) from Greenwich Mean Time (GMT).

A checkbox on this tab also allows you to specify whether the system should adjust automatically for daylight savings changes.

Notes

- Even if you don't need to change the time zone, the Time Zone tab can be very handy, since it lists the variance from GMT for most major locations worldwide. If you need to figure out what time it is in Tokyo, you can do so, using your system clock and some simple addition or subtraction.

- Time Zone names and other data are stored in the Registry. To add new Zone names, use *tzedit.*

See Also

"date" and "time" in Chapter 7
"Time Zone Editor" in Chapter 8

Desktop Themes

Personalize your Desktop with additional wallpaper, screen savers, sounds, and pointers.

Command Line

```
control themes.cpl
```

Choose a theme from the drop-down box (see Figure 5-5) and a sample will be displayed. Although these settings can be configured from individual tabs in the Display, Mouse, and Sounds applets in the Control Panel, Desktop Themes combines all of the options into one place, allowing you to easily pick and choose a screen saver, sound event, pointer, wallpaper, and so on, in coordinated "themes."

Another nice thing about Desktop themes is that you can sample different themes and options without committing to any changes on your system. This is similar to the ability to view different screen savers in the Display applet before you commit to them.

Microsoft Plus! 98 contains many, many more wallpapers, cursors and screen savers than the standard distribution.

Figure 5-5: The Desktop Themes dialog box

Display

\Windows\System\desk.cpl

View or modify settings for video adapter and monitor, and for Windows 98 background, screen saver, web desktop, and general appearance.

To Launch

Control Panel → Display
Desktop → right-click → Properties

Command Line

```
control desk.cpl [,property-tab]
```

Property Tabs

,0 Background

,1 Screen Saver

,2 Appearance

,3 Settings (video adapter and monitor)

,@web

,@effects

Most modern video adapter drivers will add additional tabs for special features and settings.

Background

Select the wallpaper for your desktop. Any bitmap (*.bmp*) file can be used as wallpaper. The default list of bitmaps shows *.bmp* files stored in the *Windows* directory, but a Browse button lets you look for other bitmaps on the disk or on the network. Large bitmaps can be centered, while small ones with repeating patterns are usually better tiled. You can also stretch a bitmap to fit the screen, but long stretches distort the image.

In addition to *.bmp* files, you can use *.rle* (Run Length Encoded) files. These are bitmap files that have been compressed by encoding repeating pixel values into a more compact format. Bitmaps can be saved in *.rle* format by many graphics programs. If you want to use one of these, just type **.rle* in the browse dialog box and navigate to the folder where the file is stored.

You can also use any HTML document as your wallpaper, but this requires that you turn on the Active Desktop. Selecting a link on your desktop will open a new browser window. For more on using HTML documents on your desktop, see Chapter 9, *Web Integration*.

A pattern is a very small bitmap file that is tiled across your entire screen. You can only set a pattern if your wallpaper is set to none. However, once you set a pattern, you can then set any bitmap wallpaper you like. The pattern will fill any leftover space around the wallpaper.

If you are using multiple monitors, backgrounds can behave a bit strangely. Patterns work as you would expect, tiling across all of your monitors. The same is true if you tile a wallpaper bitmap. If you center or stretch a wallpaper bitmap, the image is shown on each monitor, centered or stretched. If you use an HTML document wallpaper, the entire document is displayed on your main monitor and the background pattern for the document is displayed on additional monitors.

Screen Saver

Specify whether a screen saver will become active if you leave your machine unattended. In addition to choosing a screen saver, you can specify whether a password is required to regain access to the screen. If you don't click the

Change button to set a screen saver–specific password, your password will be the same as the one you use to log on to Windows 98.

Many individual screen savers have their own control panel dialog boxes, accessible by selecting the screen saver and clicking Settings.

Figure 5-6 shows the controls for the Mystify Your Mind screen saver.

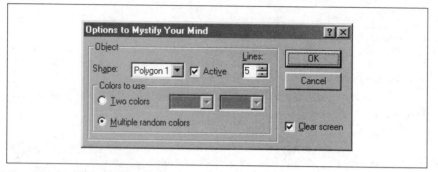

Figure 5-6: Screen saver controls

 Screen saver *.scr* files (usually stored in \ *Windows\System*) are really just Windows executables with a different file extension. They can even be executed from the command line.

The Screen Saver tab in Control Panel → Display also provides a handy yet misplaced shortcut for opening the Power Management Control Panel applet, which can be used to control energy-saving features of your monitor.

Appearance

Offers a large selection of schemes that govern the appearance of Windows 98 GUI elements: the size and color of titlebars, windows, menus, icons, and so on. Among the most useful schemes are Windows Standard, Windows Standard (Large), and Windows Standard (Extra Large). You can also set the size and color of about 20 different user-interface elements individually.

If you decide to modify the individual elements, you should save them as a new scheme using the Save As button. The scheme is saved in the Registry. If you don't save your changes as a named scheme, they will be lost when you switch to another scheme.

The Desktop Themes Control Panel applet offers an expanded version of schemes referred to as Desktop Themes, which combine schemes with sounds, wallpapers, and so on. For more information, see "Desktop Themes" earlier in this chapter.

If you click the down arrow by Display Properties → Appearance → Color, you get a palette of available colors. Clicking the Other button at the bottom of the Palette gets you into a wonderful little color editor. Dragging the mouse pointer through a rainbow-hued color space lets you explore the full range of possible colors on your monitor. You can save any you like to a custom color palette. As an added geek thrill, you can see the Hue and Saturation values (as well as the RGB color values) change as you move through the color space. A slider on the left controls the luminosity. You can see how, regardless of the hue, as the luminosity goes up, the color washes out to white, and as the luminosity goes down, it fades into black. A neat, hands-on exposure to color theory at work.

(Incidentally, this dialog box is a standard part of Windows, not tied in particular to the Display control panel applet. For example, in MS Paint, see Colors → Edit Colors → Define Custom Colors.)

Figure 5-7 shows this hidden gem. The black-and-white figure doesn't do it justice. It's fun to play with even if all you want to do is understand how colors work.

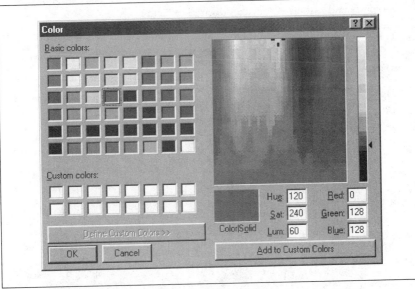

Figure 5-7: Color options in the Display dialog box

Effects

Controls how desktop icons are displayed. You can change the icon associated with various desktop items, such as My Computer and the Recycle Bin. You can also specify whether icons are visible when the desktop is viewed as a web page. As you'll see in Chapter 9, a web desktop can be a powerful customization tool and can incorporate much of the functionality of desktop icons. The Effects tab is also used to configure various visual effects for the desktop. Disabling certain of these effects, such as window animation and showing window contents while dragging, can help improve the display performance on slower systems. Other effects are primarily cosmetic.

Web

Used to turn the Active desktop on and off and to select Active Desktop items that should be displayed. This is not the same as using an HTML document for your wallpaper, as you can do on the Background tab. Desktop items are HTML documents that are essentially embedded into your desktop. By default, the Internet Explorer Channel Bar is the only available desktop item. You can add new items by visiting the Microsoft Active Desktop Gallery or by specifying a URL. Many web sites also offer the ability to automatically place items on your desktop.

The Web tab also provides a handy shortcut to the Folder Options window that is typically accessed from the View menu of any open folder.

Settings

Controls the Windows 98 monitor arrangement, Desktop resolution, and the size of the font in the Windows 98 user interface. Also lets you choose your monitors and associated device drivers. See Figure 5-8.

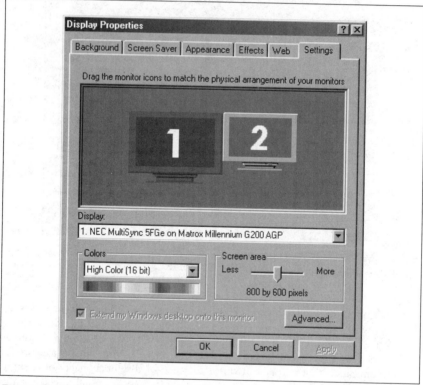

Figure 5-8: The Settings tab in Display Properties

Monitor Arrangement Window

Contains an icon for each monitor configured on your system. Drag the monitor icons to reorder your monitors and to match the vertical placement. Clicking an icon selects that monitor. Any settings made on the

Settings tab are made to the selected monitor. You can also select a monitor using the drop-down Display menu. Double-clicking an icon opens that monitor's properties—the same window opened using the Advanced button. Holding down the mouse button pops up a large identification number on the selected monitor. This is useful if you use a number of identical monitors. Both of these commands are also available by right-clicking the icon for a monitor.

Extend my Windows desktop onto this monitor

Specifies whether the selected monitor should be included as part of the Windows desktop. When you first install Win 98, only the primary monitor is included. You must select others to include.

Colors

Lets you choose from up to seven color settings, depending on your display adapter: 2 colors, 4 colors, 16 colors, 256 colors, High Color (16 bit), True Color (24 bit), and True Color (32 bit). You can choose a different color depth and screen area combination for each monitor. The 256-color setting is generally adequate for the standard Windows 98 Desktop and applications, but higher color depth is necessary if you want to display photographs or other images with lots of color gradations.

One thing many users find confusing is the way that the number of colors seems linked to the resolution or screen area: you can't always have lots of colors and a high resolution at the same time. The color depth and resolution are in fact closely related to the amount of video RAM. This isn't the amount of system RAM, but the memory installed on your video card.

Here's how it works. A system looks up colors from a color table using a value for each individual pixel on the screen. An 8-bit value for each pixel can point to 2^8, or 256 colors. A 16-bit value can point to 2^{16}, or 65,536 colors, and a 24-bit value can point to 16 million unique colors. If you use a larger number of bits per pixel, you need more video RAM. Similarly, you need more RAM for higher resolution, because higher resolution means that the screen display is made up of more pixels.

The horizontal and vertical dimensions (in pixels) are multiplied to find the total number of pixels on the screen. Then that number is multiplied by the amount of memory required by each pixel to get the total memory required by a particular setting. For example, to find out how much video RAM is required by 1024 × 768 in RGB mode (24-bit, or 16 million colors), use the following formula:

$$\frac{1024 \text{ pixels} \times 768 \text{ pixels} \times 24 \text{ bits/pixel}}{8 \text{ bits/byte}} = 2,359,296 \text{ bytes (2.4 MB)}$$

If you have only 2 MB of video RAM (a common amount), you won't be able to set your display to this mode. However, you'll be able to use a resolution of 800 × 600 with this color depth, since that will require only 1.4 MB of video RAM. To use a higher resolution, you'd have to drop your color depth to 16-bit mode (65,536 colors), which would require only 1.6 MB.

Advanced Properties

Leads to a separate dialog box with five tabs: General, Adapter, Monitor, Performance, and Color Management.

The General tab lets you configure the size of fonts displayed on the system and whether a control that brings up the Settings tab should be placed in the system tray. The control also lets you choose popular color depth/resolution combinations even without opening the Settings tab. The General tab also lets you specify whether or not the system needs to be restarted to activate new display settings (most commonly made on the settings tab).

The Adapter tab allows you to change the current video driver (although the manufacturer of your video hardware may require a different method), and to change the refresh rate of the display. Set the refresh rate to Optimal, unless you encounter a problem—in that case, set it to the highest setting that will work with your hardware.

The Monitor tab lets you specify your monitor hardware—a good idea if Windows can't do it automatically. Windows uses this setting to determine the maximum resolution, color depth, and refresh rate of your monitor, which are all reflected in the settings. If you know that your monitor (or video card) supports something that Windows isn't letting you do (such as a higher refresh rate or resolution), odds are that it's not configured properly.

Check the "Monitor is Energy Star compliant" option to allow Windows to shut the monitor off after a period of inactivity. (Further settings are inconveniently located in the Power Management Control Panel applet.) Only check this box if your monitor supports this feature.

The Performance tab lets you control hardware graphics acceleration. This tab is the place to come if you are experiencing any display-related problems.

The Color Management tab lets you associate standard color profiles with a monitor, providing you with an accurate color display. Windows 98 includes basic profiles for many monitors. Certain high-end graphics software may include additional color profiles for some monitors.

Notes

There may be additional system-specific tabs, especially on laptop machines, as well as tabs added by applications. For example, McAfee VShield (virus-detection software) installs a ScreenScan tab.

Fonts

\Windows\Fonts

View available fonts on the system, and install new fonts.

To Launch

Control Panel → Fonts
Start → Run → \windows\fonts

Unlike most of the other items in the Control Panel window, Fonts is not a control panel applet (.cpl file) but a shortcut to a system folder.

The folder contains a file for each font available on the system. Double-click on any font to view it using the *fontview* program, or right-click on any font and select Properties to see more information about the font.

Menus

All of the control panel–like functionality is provided by the menubar of the font folder:

File → Install New Font

Allows you to copy a new font from another folder, disk, or network drive to the Fonts directory. You can also drag and drop a font file from the Explorer.

View → List Fonts by Similarity

Lets you choose a font and then list other fonts by their relationship to the selected font. (The relationship is based on the PANOSE type-matching system; see *http://www.fonts.com/hp/panose/*.) This can be handy if you're trying to find a replacement font that is close to one you're currently using.

View → Details

Gives filenames and sizes for each font.

View → Hide Variations

Shortens the list of fonts by eliminating bold and italic forms of each font from the listing.

Notes

- Fonts can be either bitmapped (some older screen fonts, which have the *.fon* extension) or scalable (used in word processors and graphics applications). TrueType fonts are the most common scalable fonts on Windows machines, and have the *.ttf* extension. TrueType fonts often emulate equivalent Adobe PostScript fonts, although not exactly (since Microsoft didn't want to license the original font designs). Times New Roman is roughly equivalent to Times Roman, and Arial is roughly equivalent to Helvetica. Small differences between the fonts can make major differences in printing, so if absolute fidelity is required, you should install additional fonts to match those stored in your output device.

  You can use Adobe Type 1 fonts with Windows 98, but you need Adobe Type Manager. See *http://www.adobe.com/*.

- The *charmap* program (Start → Programs → Accessories → Character Map) is perhaps more useful than *fontview*. You can't get as good a look at what the font looks like, but you can see what characters are contained in it and what key will generate each character. (This is especially useful with symbol fonts.) You can select non-keyboard characters for pasting into other applications. Figure 5-9 shows the Wingdings font as it appears in *charmap*. See "Character Map" in Chapter 6, *Start Menu Programs and Other Graphical Applications*, for further details.

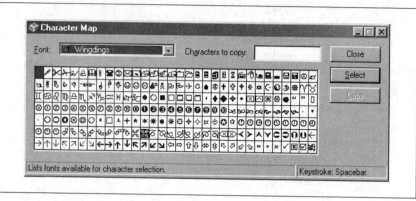

Figure 5-9: Wingdings in charmap

- There is not always a one-to-one mapping between font name (e.g., in a drop-down list for font selection) and font file. For example, the *Vgasys.fon* and *Vgaoem.fon* files contain several of the fonts used in DOS windows. Still others are found in the *Dosapp.fon* and *8514oem.fon* files.

- The *Marlett.ttf* font is used for constructing user interface elements such as the minimize, maximize, and close buttons on the Windows titlebar, the checkmark that appears when you click on a checkbox, the arrows that appear in scrollbars and drop-down lists, and so on. As a kind of security measure, this file actually doesn't show up in the Control Panel; if you were to delete it, Windows 98 wouldn't work properly, so it's marked as a hidden file. It won't show up in the Explorer either, even if you tell the Explorer to display hidden files! However, you can view it from the command line (`fontview \Windows\Fonts\marlett.ttf`), or from the drop-down font list in Character Map (*charmap*).

- Other useful special-purpose fonts that feature symbols (often called dingbats by typesetters) include *Wingdings.ttf*, *Mapsym.ttf* (map symbols), Symbol (*symbol.ttf* and *symbole.fon*), and the various math fonts.

- See *http://www.oreilly.com/homepages/comp.fonts/ifa/* (the Internet Font Archives) for more information about fonts.

 Normally, only valid font files can be moved or copied to the Fonts folder. However, if the Fonts folder has lost its "magic," other types of files may be placed inside. If these other files are still in the Fonts folder when it is repaired (spontaneously or with TweakUI), the non-font files won't be visible, even to the Explorer or Start → Find → Files or Folders. The only way to see them and get them out is from the DOS prompt (using *dir* and *move*) or the old Windows 3.1 File Manager (*winfile*).

Game Controllers

Select the models of joystick, gamepad, pedals, or other game controllers connected to your system and optionally test or calibrate them.

To Launch
Control Panel → Game Controllers

Command Line
`control joy.cpl`

There are two tabs for this applet: General and Advanced. These tabs are not individually accessible from the comand line.

General
Lets you select, test, and calibrate game devices. You can add a controller to the list once the device is physically connected to your system. Plug and Play game controllers should be configured automatically. Viewing the properties of a controller opens a separate dialog box with two tabs: Settings and Test.

The Settings tab lets you calibrate your controller. This sets the range of motion for the device. If your controller has extra features, such as a rudder or point-of-view (POV) hat, you also can calibrate these features.

The Rudders/Pedals checkbox enables the use of rudder controls on supported devices. If this checkbox is unavailable, either you don't have a rudder control, or you specified a four-axis joystick. It is often necessary to disable the rudder controls on joysticks if you are also using pedals as your rudder controls.

The Test tab lets you test the range of motion, triggers, and other supported features of your controller using a convenient graphic interface.

Advanced
Lets you assign a controller to a specific controller ID. Some games may not support the extra features found on some controllers or may not support the controller itself. Assigning a different controller ID lets you fake games into thinking that a different type of controller is actually being used. The Advanced tab also lets you specify different port drivers for your gameport, if your controller requires it.

Infrared   *Windows\System\infrared.cpl*

Configure the infrared device attached to your computer.

To Launch
Control Panel → Infrared
System Tray Icon

Command Line
`control infrared.cpl`

The Infrared Control Panel icon is only visible if you have an infrared device installed on your system. Infrared devices typically install automatically using Plug and Play, but you can also install them using the Add New Hardware Control Panel icon.

There are four property tabs for the Infrared Control Panel: Status, Options, Preferences, and Identification. These tabs are not individually addressable from the command line.

Status

Shows you the current status of your device (enabled or disabled) and any error messages regarding your device. The Status tab also displays information about current infrared connections.

Options

Lets you configure a number of options concerning your infrared hardware. You can enable and disable infrared communication, specify whether and how often the device should search for other devices in range, limit connection speed, and choose whether software should be automatically installed for any Plug and Play devices that are found within range.

Preferences

Lets you configure infrared software settings. You can display an Infrared monitor icon in the system tray, specify whether the Control Panel is automatically opened should infrared communication be interrupted, and specify whether a sound should be played during certain events.

Identification

Lets you provide a computer name and description that identifies your system to other infrared devices and to other computers on your network. If no name is visible here, you must enter one in order to communicate with other infrared devices on a network.

 The information you configure at Control Panel → Infrared → Identification is the same as the information you configure at Control Panel → Network → Identification. Be careful changing your computer name, especially if your system is connected to a network, as you could potentially disrupt network services.

Notes

- When you install an infrared device, an infrared adapter and the fast infrared protocol are added to your Network profile, which can be viewed at Control Panel → Network → Configuration. Your specific infrared device may have additional configuration options accessible here.

- When you install an infrared device, a folder named Infrared Recipient is added to My Computer and a shortcut to that folder is added to the Send To menu. Both of these allow you to transfer files over the infrared connection.

Internet

Configure Internet settings used by Internet Explorer (IE) and any other applications that use Microsoft's WinInet API.

To Launch

Control Panel → Internet
Internet Explorer → View → Options

Command Line

```
control inetcpl.cpl [,property-tab]
```

Property Tabs

,0 General

,2 Connection

,3 Navigation

,4 Programs

,5 Security

,6 Advanced

General

Lets you configure the URL for your home page, what color to use for windows and links, what fonts should be displayed, your language preference, and certain accessibility options (see Figure 5-10). Accessibility options generally govern how fonts and styles are displayed in IE. Note that these Internet settings are just for IE; Netscape Navigator and Communicator do not use them. The General tab also lets you configure Temporary Internet Files and History.

Temporary Internet Files

Internet sites don't necessarily change all that often. Since an .html file must be downloaded temporarily to your machine in order for you to view it, it's possible to keep these downloaded files around for quick access in case you want to go back to the same page again. Settings control what percentage of your disk should be used for these temporary (cached) files and how often IE should check to make sure that it has the most current versions.

History

IE keeps a history of Internet sites you have already visited so that finding a site again is more convenient. This history is arranged by day and week. You can set the number of days for which you wish IE to keep track.

Security

Lets you specify the security settings for different predefined zones of Internet content. There are four basic zones: Internet, intranet, Trusted, and Restricted (see Figure 5-11). By default, all sites are placed into one of the first two zones. All sites found on your local network are placed into the intranet zone. All other sites are placed into the Internet Zone. You can manually add sites

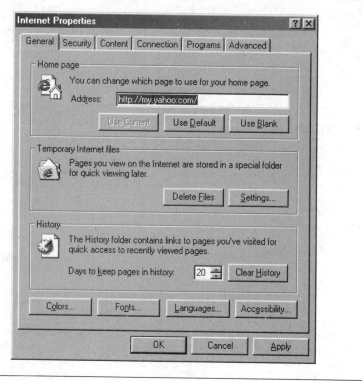

Figure 5-10: The General tab for IE configuration

to the Trusted and Restricted zones. Security settings for each zone are preset, but you can change these settings if you wish. For each zone, you can specify High, Medium, Low, or Custom security settings. Security settings govern such things as how ActiveX controls and Java applets are used, how files are downloaded, and how user authentication takes place.

Content

Contains a number of functions that allow you to control what can and can't be viewed by IE (see Figure 5-12). Many of the features here are not widely used and still have a few kinks to be worked out.

Content Advisor

Lets you use an Internet ratings service to screen out potentially offensive content. The first time you use this function, you will be asked to define a supervisor-level password that will later be used to change any of the content ratings.

By default, the only content advisor installed is RSACi (the Recreational Software Advisory Council Internet advisor; see Figure 5-13). RSACi depends on voluntary ratings by sites as to the amount of violence, nudity, sex, and profanity they contain. While this may seem silly, sites

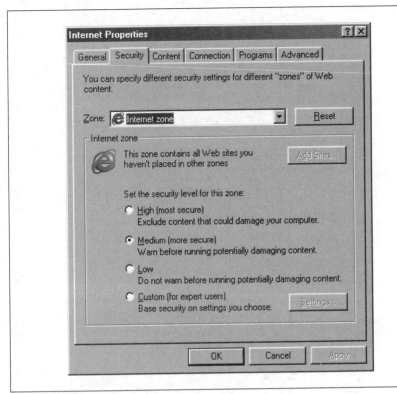

Figure 5-11: The Security tab

with potentially objectionable content (such as porn sites) are embracing such "self-regulation" to forestall more stringent government regulation.

The rating system is fairly self-explanatory—you choose one of four levels for each of four types of "objectionable" content (Language, Nudity, Sex, Violence); by default, every slider is set to the lowest level. One problem with this system is that the browser expects a rating from every site and requires a password to access sites with no ratings. Since few sites have RSACi ratings, this can become quite a hassle.

Ratings services publish their ratings in files of type *.rat*. A source for additional rating service files is *http://www.classify.org/pics.htm*. Download the *.rat* file for a given service, save it in *\Windows\System*, then go to the Advanced tab → Ratings Systems button to add the ratings file to the Content Advisor → Ratings tab.

Certificates

It's fairly easy for one site to masquerade as another. Digital certificates, which use cryptography to create unique identifiers that can't be forged, can be used by sites that want to prove their identity to you. Here, you can identify which certificate authorities (certificate issuers) you want to trust. Unfortunately, you can't add new certificate authorities, and if IE

Control Panel

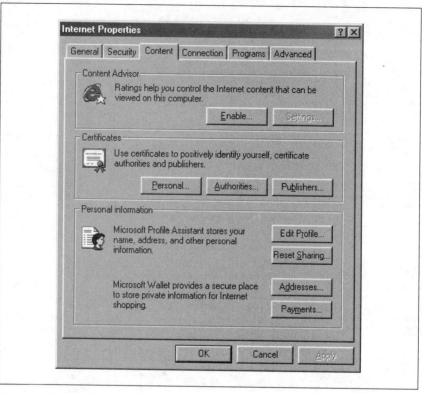

Figure 5-12: The Content tab

receives a certificate by an authority it doesn't know about, it will not display the associated web page. Especially in an intranet context, companies sometimes self-certify their pages. You can view pages that have no certificate at all, but an unknown certificate will block display of the page: hardly a desired feature.

Personal Information

Lets you configure personal and financial information about yourself using Microsoft Profile Assistant and Microsoft Wallet.

Microsoft Profile Assistant is used to store personal information, such as your name and email address, that is often required by forms on web sites. Web sites that support the use of the Profile Assistant can automatically draw this information from the assistant.

Microsoft Wallet is similar to the Profile Assistant, except that Wallet stores private financial information, such as credit card numbers and expiration dates. The information you store in Wallet is encrypted and can only be viewed by you. Wallet supports many industry-standard payment methods, including Secure Sockets Layer (SSL) and Secure Electronic Transaction (SET), and supports many add-on payment methods, such as digital cash and electronic checks.

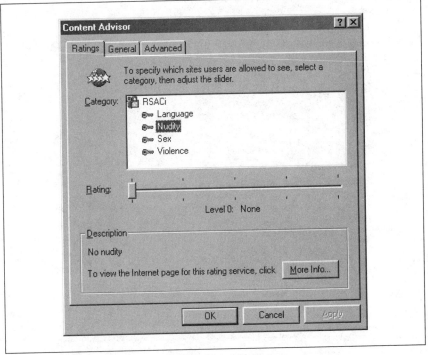

Figure 5-13: RSACi, the default IE content advisor

Right now, very few sites make full use of the functionality provided by either Profile Assistant or Wallet. This may change in the future, but for now these tools can still be useful as just a convenient location to store these types of information, but due to privacy concerns, you may understandably not feel comfortable doing this.

Connection
Describes your connection to the Internet (see Figure 5-14). You have the option of running the Internet Connection Wizard, which is the same wizard run the first time you launch Internet Explorer, or configuring the connection yourself. The wizard is basically an oversimplified set of questions that in the end achieves the same thing as manual configuration. Windows 98 also supports the automatic configuration of connection settings by a remote server. You can enter the URL for such a server using the Configure button.

If you use a dial-up connection, check Connect to the Internet using a modem. Settings brings up a separate dialog box (see Figure 5-15) that allows you to choose the Dial-Up Networking Connection you wish to use, how many times a connection should be attempted before IE gives up, and your username and password for logging on. You can also configure IE to disconnect after a certain number of idle minutes, connect automatically when IE subscriptions need to be updated, and perform a security check before dialing. The security check basically checks to make sure that Windows File

Control Panel

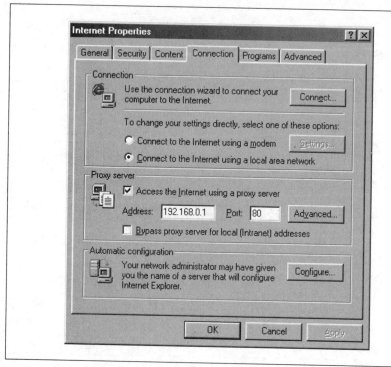

Figure 5-14: The Connection tab

and Printer Sharing is not enabled over the dial-up connection. This is highly recommended.

 It's a bit dangerous to use the automatic idle disconnect feature if you are using Internet applications other than IE, since IE doesn't recognize activity in other applications (such as Telnet). This can cause unexpected hangups.

If your computer is connected to the Internet via an actual network (this includes when you are using a proxy server), check Connect to the Internet using a local area network.

If you are using a firewall or proxy server for caching information or for sharing an Internet conection, you will also need to enter the IP address (or computer name) of the proxy server and the port that IE should use. Typically, the port used by HTTP for web documents is 80. You can also use the Advanced button to separate proxy servers and/or port numbers for each Internet application and to specify individual site addresses that are allowed to bypass the proxy server. The exception list can contain hostnames, domain names, or port numbers. Port numbers should be preceded by a colon. Each entry is separated by a semicolon. For example, the following exception

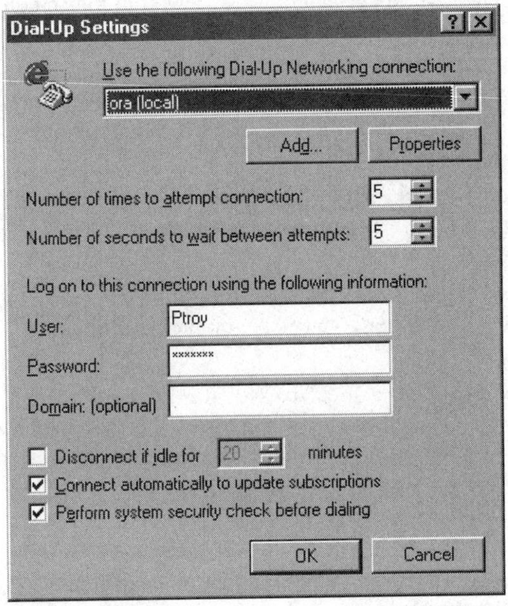

Figure 5-15: Dial-Up Settings

would allow direct connections to any host within the *foo.com* domain, to the specific host *magic.foobar.com,* and to port 80 on any other host:

```
foo.com;magic.foobar.com;:80
```

Programs

Lets you choose what programs to use for sending mail, reading Internet news, placing Internet calls, viewing calendar scheduling, and viewing contact information. If the "Internet Explorer should check to see whether it is the default browser" box is checked, any time you start up IE (as long as it isn't already your default browser), it will ask you whether you want to make it your default browser. So this setting is really just a shortcut to change a bunch of file/program associations; see the Explorer View → Options → File Types. For a utility that makes this process a little easier, see *http://www.annoyances. org/win98/software/* . Unless you're fond of what has come to be called "nagware," we recommend leaving this box unchecked.

Advanced

Contains additional security settings in a hierarchical tree. Many of these settings are rarely used and most are self-explanatory. Useful settings include:

Notify when downloads complete

Normally, a message pops up when a download is complete, interrupting whatever you are doing. Disabling this feature is particularly helpful when you perform multiple downloads at once.

Launch browser in full screen window

Specifies that web pages are always viewed in full-screen mode.

Use AutoComplete

By default, IE automatically tries to complete addresses as you enter them. Many users find this distracting. Also, many blind-access utilities read the suggestions as they appear, which can be quite annoying.

Use Smooth Scrolling

Specifies whether a page slides gradually when you click the scrollbar, a feature than can be distracting to many users.

Underline Links

Specifies whether links on pages should be underlined always, never, or only when you hover your mouse pointer over them.

Multimedia

Multimedia can be a great part of the web experience, but it can also slow down the delivery of web pages. The multimedia section lets you control whether certain multimedia elements, such as pictures, videos, and sounds, are downloaded for dispay.

Printing

Enables or disables the printing of background colors and images when you print a web page. Print speed can be increased considerably with this option disabled.

Internet Connection Sharing   *\Program Files\ Win98RK\ batchs.exe*

Share a Dial-Up Networking Internet connection with networked computers.

To Install

Add/Remove Programs → Windows Setup → Internet Tools → Internet Connection Sharing

To Launch

Address → icssetup
Start → Run → icssetup
Control Panel → Internet → Connections → Sharing

Description

Internet Connection Sharing allows you to share a Dial-Up Networking Internet connection with other users on a network. Configuring ICS will happen in three phases. First, your computers will need to be networked. Second, you will set up the computer that will share its Internet connection. Finally, you will set up the other computers on the network (the clients) to connect to the Internet through the Connection Sharing computer.

Configuring Your Network

If you don't already have your computers networked, Windows 98 makes it pretty easy to do so. The first thing you'll have to do is physically network the computers together. This requires installing a network interface card (NIC) in each computer

---

and running networking cable between the computers. The type of network cable you run will depend on the type of NIC you buy. There are two basic types of setups to consider for a small network:

- Twisted pair cable is similar to that used for telephones. With twisted pair, you can wire two computers directly together, but networking three or more computers requires a central hub.

- BNC networking cable is a coaxial cable similar to that used for cable television. It is also referred to as thin ethernet cable. With BNC, computers are "chained" together and no hub is required.

Whatever type of network you choose to build, you can usually find pretty good instructions on installing the cable in the documentation that comes with your network interface cards.

Once your network is physically installed, you will need to configure each computer. When you install most modern networking cards, Win 98 will automatically recognize the card and will install several items for you, including the drivers for the NIC, the Client for Microsoft Networks, and the TCP/IP protocol. These items are available for further configuration at Control Panel → Network → Configuration. In the following sections on setting up the Connection Sharing computer and on setting up the client computers, I'll cover the configuration of these items. You can find more details about general network configuration in Chapter 4, *The Windows 98 User Interface*.

Configuring the Conection Sharing Computer

The Connection Sharing computer is the one which will share its Internet connection with the other computers on the network. Your first task will be to configure its Internet connection. For this, Dial-Up Networking must be installed. You can install DUN using Add/Remove Programs → Windows Setup → Communications → Dial-Up Networking. You can find out more about configuring a Dial-Up Networking Connection in Chapter 4.

Once the Internet connection is configured, you are ready to install ICS on the Connection Sharing computer. You can do this using Add/Remove Programs → Windows Setup → Internet Tools → Internet Connection Sharing. When ICS is first installed, Win 98 will launch an ICS setup wizard that walks you through the configuration. Be careful here. For some reason, if you cancel this wizard, ICS will be completely uninstalled and you'll have to reinstall it using Windows Setup.

The ICS wizard really only does two things for you. The first is to ask whether you will be sharing a dial-up connection (like a typical modem or ISDN connection) or a high-speed connection (like ADSL or a cable modem). This information is presumably used to optimize your network settings. The second thing the ICS wizard will do is create a client setup disk that can be used to automatically set up a client browser to connect to the Internet through the Connection Sharing computer. You'll see more about this in the next section.

Once ICS is set up, you can configure it further using Control Panel → Internet → Connection → Sharing or by entering icssetup.exe at the Run prompt. Either of these actions brings up the Internet Connection Sharing dialog box shown in Figure 5-16. Here, you can enable or disable ICS, elect to show an ICS icon in the taskbar (this icon flashes to let you know when ICS is being used), change which connection is used to access the Internet, and change which NIC is used to access your home network.

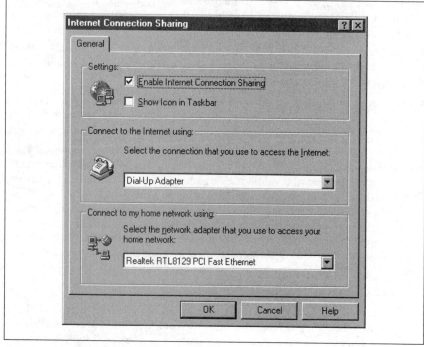

Figure 5-16: Configuring ICS (icssetup.exe)

Behind the scenes, you should also know that ICS makes some changes to the network setup of the Connection Sharing computer. First, an Internet Connection Sharing adapter and protocol are added to Control Panel → Network → Configuration and are bound to the various other protocols there. There's not much configuration for you to worry about here, but don't be surprised when you see all the new items. Second, the IP address of the Connection Sharing computer is set to 192.168.0.1, which is a reserved IP address not used on the Internet.

Configuring the Client Computers

Once you have configured the Connection Sharing computer, it is time to configure the client computers. A client computer can be any system running Windows 95 or Windows 98. Note that a client does not have to be running Win 98 Second Edition.

The first thing you will do is configure the client with the appropriate TCP/IP settings. To do this, go to Control Panel → Network → Configuration. You'll see a protocol listed named TCP/IP → *name_of_your_NIC*. Open the properties for this item and configure the information on the following tabs:

IP Address tab

ICS includes a version of the Dynamic Host Configuration Protocol (DHCP) that lets the connection sharing computer automatically assign TCP/IP addressing information to client computers. This is the easiest way to use ICS. Just select the "Obtain an IP Address automatically" option on this tab. Alternately, you can specify a static IP address in the 192.168.0.2 through 192.168. 0.254 range.

WINS Configuration tab

If you are using DHCP, select the "Use DHCP for WINS Resolution" option on this tab. If you chose to assign static IP addresses, you will need to set the WINS server address as 192.168.0.1.

Gateway

Remove any installed gateways that are listed on this tab. If you are using DHCP, leave this tab blank. If you are using static IP addressed, set the gateway as 192.168.0.1.

DNS Configuration

Select the "Disable DNS" option.

You'll need to restart your computer after configuring these TCP/IP settings. Once that is done, you are ready to configure your client to access the Internet using the Connection Sharing computer. To use ICS, you will need to be running Internet Explorer 3.0 or later or Netscape Navigator 3.0 or later. The easiest way to set up the client is to use the *icsclset.exe* program on the client configuration disk that was made while running the ICS wizard. This program configures your browser to connect to the Internet using your network adapter. Of course, it's not too difficult to do this manually, either. With IE4, just go to Control Panel → Internet → Connection and choose the "Connect to the Internet using a local area network" option. You will also want to make sure that you are not set to use a proxy server.

Notes

- When a computer on your network sends a request to the Internet, its private IP address is transmitted to the Connection Sharing computer. The Connection Sharing computer translates that private IP address to the IP address of the Connection Sharing computer, and then sends it on to the Internet. When the results are returned, the Connection Sharing computer translates the IP address back again and routes it to the correct computer on your network. This means that the only computer on the network visible to the Internet is the Connection Sharing computer.

- ICS maintains a log of its activities in *Windows**icslog.txt*.

- If you are using ICS and you install Netscape Navigator 4, Navigator may require that you configure a Dial-Up Networking connection. This may happen even if the computer does not have a modem. To get Navigator to work, you will have to install a "dummy" modem and DUN connection. The dummy modem can be any standard modem type and no actual modem needs to be installed in the computer.

See Also

> "Dial-Up Networking" in Chapter 4
> "Internet" and "Modems"

Keyboard

\Windows\System\main.cpl

Control the speed of key repetition, the cursor blink rate, the keyboard language and layout, and the keyboard hardware that is attached to the system.

To Launch

> Control Panel → Keyboard

Command Line

```
control main.cpl Keyboard [,property tab]
```

(You must specify "Keyboard," because by default, *main.cpl* launches the Mouse control panel applet.)

Property Tabs

,0 Speed

,1 Language

Speed

Controls the speed of character repeat and cursor blinking. Sliders allow you to specify how long a key must be held down before it starts to repeat, and how fast it will repeat once it starts. A test box lets you check out your settings before you OK them. Another slider lets you set the blink rate of the text cursor.

Language

Lets you specify the keyboard layout. Use Language → Properties to switch to a foreign-language keyboard layout or an alternative English-language layout such as Dvorak.

If multiple languages are enabled, you can also choose the keyboard accelerator that will be used to switch between languages (left Alt+Shift or Ctrl+Shift).

The Enable indicator on Taskbar checkbox has meaning only if multiple languages are enabled. If the indicator is displayed, you can click on it to display a popup menu of available keyboard layouts.

Modems

\Windows\System\modem.cpl

Configure any modems used with your system.

To Launch

> Control Panel → Modems

Command Line

```
control modem.cpl
```

If you have not already installed a modem, this command will run the Install New Modems wizard; otherwise, it will bring up Modems Properties with a list of available modems.

This configuration involves a fairly complicated tree of interconnected dialog boxes and property sheets, many of them with very similar names. Configuration is further complicated by the fact that applications that use the modem, such as Dial-Up Networking, create individual dial-up connection records, which often use dialog boxes very similar to those in the Modems icon.

The settings made in Properties and Dialing Properties for any modem are the global defaults, but they can be changed in any specific dial-up connection. What's more, changes here will not propagate to any existing connections. Furthermore, the property sheet for a given connection has a Configure button that gives additional options not available in Control Panel → Modems. (See "Dial-Up Networking" in Chapter 4 for additional details.)

The hierarchy of property tabs, buttons, and dialog boxes under Control Panel → Modems looks like this:

```
General → Add
        → Remove
            → any modem → Properties → General
                        → Properties → Connection
                        → Properties → Connection → Port Settings
                        → Properties → Connection → Advanced → Dialing
                                    Properties → My Locations
                            → Properties → Distinctive Ring
                            → Properties → Forwarding
Diagnostics → Driver
            → More Info
```

General → Add

An entry point to the Install New Modems wizard (part of Add New Hardware). General → Remove lets you remove an installed modem from the list.

General → any modem → Properties → General

Set the port, speaker volume, and maximum line speed for connections using the modem. The maximum speed may be greater than the actual line speed of your connection, since your modem may do data compression, and, if so, will be able to accept data from the system faster than it actually sends it over the phone. If your communications applications are experiencing errors, you may want to reduce the maximum value.

Modems normally try to connect first at their highest rated speed. If the remote modem cannot match that speed, or the line quality is poor, they cycle down to the next available speed. Check "Only connect at this speed" if you don't want to use a lower speed when the connection is poor.

General → any modem → Properties → Connection → Connection preferences

Set the number of data bits, the parity, and the number of stop bits. These days, the correct answers are almost always 8, none, and 1. Serial connections send each byte of data in a frame consisting of a start bit, 7 or 8 data bits, an optional parity (error-checking) bit, and one or two stop bits. In the past, various operating systems used different combinations of data, parity, and stop bits; nowadays, you shouldn't need to change the defaults unless you're communicating with an older system or online service.

General → any modem → Properties → Connection → Call preferences
If you travel internationally, you need to uncheck "Wait for dial tone before dialing," since Windows 98 won't recognize the dial tone offered by most foreign phone networks. You can also set the timeout for how long to wait before hanging up if a connection is not completed (i.e., when you hear the modems screaming at each other, but not finding a mutually satisfactory tone). You can also set how long a connection should be left idle before hanging up.

General → any modem → Properties → Connection → Port Settings
Set the sizes of the data buffers in the modem. You shouldn't need to change this unless you're having problems.

General → any modem → Properties → Connection → Advanced
"Use error control" and "Compress data" will be appropriate for only certain combinations of modem and online service. The compression specified here is hardware compression. If you are using a compressed protocol, the two may conflict, and you should disable hardware compression.

"Extra settings" are Hayes-compatible modem command strings to be sent to the modem on initialization. (Don't type the AT prefix to get the modem's attention, since the extra settings will be tagged on to the end of the existing initialization string. For example, for dial-pulse, whose Hayes command is ATDP, you would just put DP.) A list of these AT commands is available at *http://www.compaq.com/athome/presariohelp/us/modems/modatcr.html.*

The option to "Record a log file" logs debugging information in the file *\Windows\modemlog.txt.*

General → any modem → Properties → Distinctive Ring
In some areas, you can have multiple phone numbers assigned to a single phone line. Each number rings with a distinctive ring. The Distinctive Ring tab lets you specify the type of call (data, voice, fax) according to the ring pattern.

General → any modem → Properties → Forwarding
Lets you configure the activation and deactivation codes if your telephone line supports call forwarding.

General → Dialing Properties
Provides access to the My Locations dialog box. See "Dial-Up Networking" in Chapter 4 and "Telephony," later in this chapter, for details.

Diagnostics
Provides information about the modem installed on each COM port. More Info actually sends various information requests to the modem and returns the result. You can interrogate the modem directly if you set Connection → Properties → Configure → Options → Bring up terminal window before dialing.

- Additional information about the modem can be found via the Device Manager (Control Panel → System → Device Manager).

- For more information on Dial-Up Networking connections, see Chapter 4.

Mouse

Control pointer cursors and mouse movement parameters.

To Launch

Control Panel → Mouse

Command Line

`control main.cpl`

There are three property tabs, but the [,property-tab] syntax does not work for this control panel. The tabs are as follows:

Buttons
Specify a right- or left-handed mouse. If you select left-handed, the meaning of click and right-click are reversed from the standard usage specified in this book. You can also specify how close together two clicks must occur to be considered a double-click.

Pointers
Pick from several schemes, each of which determines the shape and size of pointer icons (arrow, hourglass, text insert, and so on). Click Browse to look at possible cursor icons in \Windows\Cursors to substitute another cursor for any of those shown. Plus! includes many additional schemes and individual cursors.

Motion
Specify the speed with which the pointer moves in response to mouse movements, and whether the pointer should leave a "ghost trail" showing its path (useful for laptops or where the visibility of the pointer is problematic).

Multimedia

Control sound volume, video playback, and other multimedia features.

To Launch

Control Panel → Multimedia

Command Line

`control mmsys.cpl [,property-tab]`

Property Tab

See Figure 5-17 for a display of the Property tab.

,0   Audio

,1   Video

,2 MIDI

,3 CD Music

,4 Devices

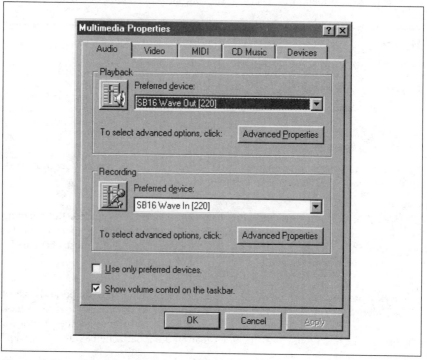

Figure 5-17: Multimedia Properties dialog box

Audio

Lets you change the preferred devices for playback and recording of *.wav*
files (such as those used for system sounds), and lets you configure properties of those devices. A checkbox also lets you display the volume control
icon in the system tray. The preferred device drop-down menus in both the
playback and recording sections of the Audio tab let you select from a list of
all available audio hardware on your system. The Advanced Properties
buttons open separate dialog boxes that allow you to configure sample rate
conversion, hardware acceleration, and speaker configuration. Large icon
buttons beside the drop-down menus open the system-wide Volume Control
(*sndvol32.exe*) and Recording Control (*sndrec32.exe*) utilities, which are
discussed in detail in Chapter 6.

Video

Choose whether a video file will be displayed in a window or on the full
screen. The window can be the original size (as defined in the video source
file), scaled to double the original size, to $\frac{1}{16}$, $\frac{1}{4}$, or $\frac{1}{2}$ of the screen size, or
in a maximized window.

MIDI

Configure MIDI output from the PC. MIDI is the Musical Instrument Digital Interface, a standard for mixing computers and musical instruments (usually synthesizers). See *http://www.midi.com/*.

CD Music

Select the drive to be used for CD music applications like *cdplayer.exe*, and control the volume.

Devices

Lets you browse an Explorer-like expandable/collapsible tree view of available multimedia devices (audio devices, MIDI instruments, mixers, line input devices, video and audio compression codecs, and so on), and display or change properties for each one.

Notes

Control Panel → System → Device Manager may be helpful for reconfiguring multimedia hardware.

See Also

"CD Player," "Sound Recorder," and "Volume Control" in Chapter 6

Network

Configure your system for use on a network.

To Launch

Control Panel → Network
Network Neighborhood → Properties

Command Line

```
control netcpl.cpl
```

The Network control panel applet lets you configure both Microsoft and non-Microsoft networks, assuming you have the appropriate network devices and drivers installed. There are three property tabs: Configuration, Identification, and Access Control (see Figure 5-18). They are not individually accessible from the command line.

You will usually have to reboot your system after changing any of the settings in this control panel applet. You may also need to have the Windows 98 CD handy.

Configuration

Lets you configure the components needed to network your system, choose the type of logon you wish to use, and enable File and Printer Sharing.

There are four types of components: clients, adapters, protocols, and services. Each has a distinctive icon. Click Add for a description of each icon if they are not obvious to you.

Client

A client is the software that allows your computer to connect to other computers. Clients are available for many types of networks, including

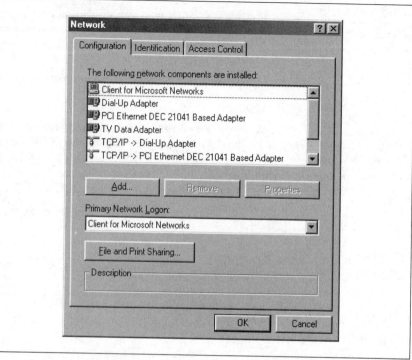

Figure 5-18: Network dialog box

Microsoft, Banyan (VINES), Novell (NetWare), Sunsoft (PC NFS), and others.

By far, the most common client used is the Client for Microsoft Networks, which allows access to Windows 98 peer networks, Windows NT networks, and the Internet. Client for Microsoft Networks → Properties allows you to specify whether your system should log onto a Windows NT domain. A domain is a group of computers sharing a common security policy and account database. The combination of domain name and computer name uniquely identifies the computer on the network. The NT domain name has nothing to do with the DNS domain name used by TCP/IP networks.

Client for Microsoft Networks → Properties also allows you to choose whether to reconnect all network drives whenever you log on, or to wait until you actually use those drives to connect. The "Quick logon" option will decrease the time it takes to log on, but will increase the time it takes the first time you try to access a given network drive.

Adapter

An adapter is the hardware device, such as an Ethernet Adapter, that makes the physical connection to a network. Some software, such as Dial-Up Networking, also requires that an adapter be installed even though the adapter does not represent an actual physical device. To add a new adapter, click Add → Adapter, select the appropriate adapter from the manufacturer/model list, and have your Windows 98 CD handy. The Properties page for each adapter generally contains hardware-specific settings, which are not discussed here.

Protocol

A protocol is a set of standards that establish how computers communicate over a network. When an adapter is configured to use a given protocol, the protocol is said to be bound to that adapter. Protocol bindings are actually represented in the component list, meaning that a single protocol may be on the list more than once. For example, you might see TCP/IP → Dial-Up Adapter and TCP/IP → 10 Mbps Ethernet Adapter. This means the TCP/IP protocol is bound to both of those adapters.

TCP/IP is the standard protocol used on the Internet and is quickly becoming the standard protocol used on many other types of networks as well. We thought it appropriate, therefore, to include a brief discussion of TCP/IP configuration. Choosing Properties for any bound instance of the TCP/IP protocol opens a separate dialog box with seven tabs: IP Address, WINS Configuration, Gateway, DNS Configuration, NetBIOS, Advanced, and Bindings.

The IP Address tab uniquely identifies your computer to other computers on the network (see Figure 5-19).

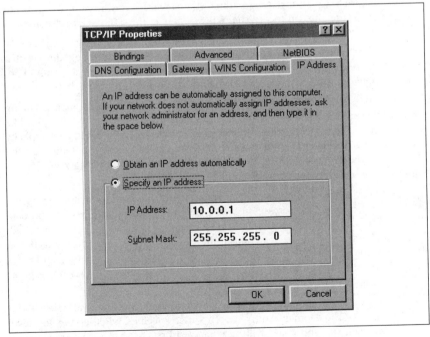

Figure 5-19: IP Address tab in TCP/IP Properties

An IP address is a 32-bit number, typically written as four decimal numbers from 0 to 255, separated by dots. For example, the IP address of the machine that hosts *john.doe.com* is 10.0.0.1.

Some TCP/IP networks support a protocol called DHCP (Dynamic Host Configuration Protocol), which automatically assigns IP addresses from an available pool. You will almost always choose "Obtain an IP address automatically" when dialing in to an Internet service provider, although this option is also used with many local area networks. If DHCP is used, all of the address fields will be filled in automatically.

If you explicitly specify the IP address, you must get the correct address for your machine and for any DNS or WINS servers from your network administrator.

The subnet mask is used to tell the system which part of the IP address is the network address and which part is the host address. The subnet mask to be used depends on the size of your network and whether the network administrator has divided it up into subnetworks. A common subnet mask is 255.255.255.0; however, this is not something you can guess. Ask your network administrator or ISP for the correct value.

The WINS Configuration tab is used to configure the Windows Internet Naming Service (WINS), which allows you to use programs that require Microsoft's older NetBIOS protocol over a TCP/IP network. See Figure 5-20. Your network administrator will let you know if you need to configure this protocol. The WINS server is the TCP/IP-based computer that will perform the mapping between the two protocols.

The Gateway tab lets you configure a router or other device that connects two otherwise incompatible networks. Check with your network administrator about whether you need to fill in this tab.

The DNS Configuration tab lets you configure the Domain Naming System (DNS), which is the Internet facility for mapping IP addresses like 10.0.0.1 into names like *john.doe.com* and vice versa. You must specify your computer's name and the DNS domain to which it belongs, as well as the IP addresses of two or more computers that will act as domain name servers for your system. (See Figure 5-21.)

Your network administrator or Internet service provider will give you the appropriate IP addresses to enter here. Type the IP address in the data entry area containing four subfields separated by dots, then click Add. The servers will be searched in the order in which you add them. If you want to change the search order, you must remove existing addresses and add them back in the correct order. The dialog box does not support drag or move operations.

Note that if you are in a large network, there may be multiple subdomains. The Domain suffix search order specifies whether the top-level domain or subdomain will be contacted first. As with DNS server search order, you must enter them in the right order, and re-enter them to change the order.

The NetBIOS tab lets you enable NetBIOS over TCP/IP.

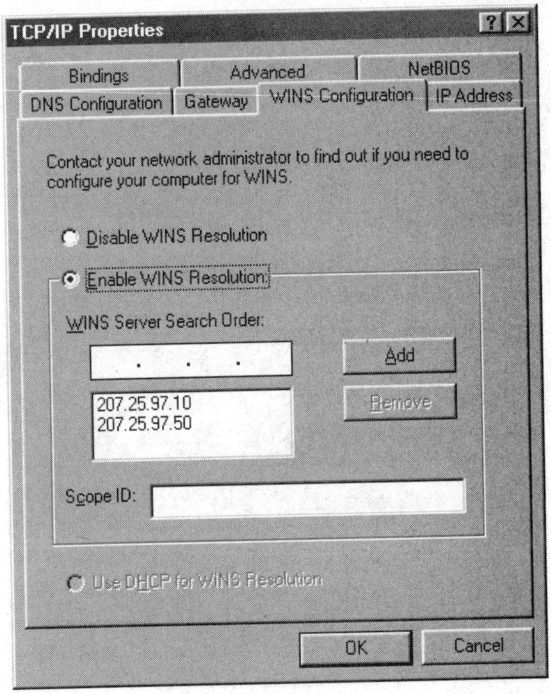

Figure 5-20: WINS Configuration tab

The Advanced tab doesn't really let you configure anything for the TCP/IP protocol.

The Bindings tab lets you specify which services will communicate using this protocol. The components on the available list will depend on what network services are installed on your system.

Service

A service is a program that allows your system to provide services to other systems. File and Print sharing, for example, allows you to share folders, files, and printers on your system with other systems on the network. File and Printer Sharing for Microsoft Networks → Properties allows you to specify your system as the Browse Master or LM announce for a network. This means that your system will maintain the list of available resources (folders and printers) for the network or workgroup. On most local area networks, an NT server will provide these functions.

Identification

In order to participate in a network, each computer must have a name that is unique on its segment of the network. The name can have up to fifteen characters, and cannot include spaces. It will be the first component of any UNC pathname referring to files on your computer. For example, entering bob as

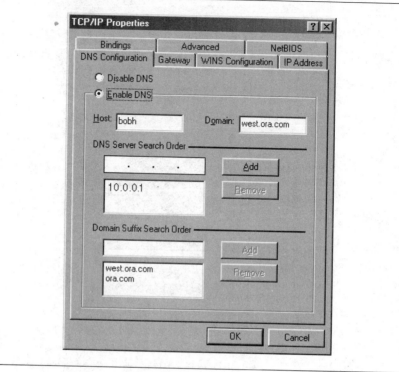

Figure 5-21: DNS Configuration tab

the name of your computer will mean that any shared resources on your computer, such as printer1, will be known as \\bob\printer1.

Computers can be organized into workgroups for purposes of resource sharing. You can enter a new name of up to fifteen characters into the workgroup field, but you shouldn't do so without the cooperation of your network administrator, since workgroup naming must be coordinated with that on other computers.

The description field is optional, but it's wise to put in a comment giving more information about the computer, such as the name of the user or the resources that are available for sharing on that computer. Two or more computers must have the same workgroup name to show up side by side in Network Neighborhood. Otherwise, connected machines will show up in "Entire Network" in the Network Neighborhood.

Access Control

There are two options for access control: share level and user level. Share-level access means that any time you designate a resource for sharing (folder → Properties → Sharing or Printers → selected printer → File → Sharing), you must specify a password that other users must type in before they can access the shared folder or printer. User-level access control allows a master list of users and/or workgroups to be granted access to shared resources without having to supply a password. The master list is kept not on your computer, but on the network server, so you shouldn't specify user-level access control without the cooperation of your network administrator.

Virtual Private Networking

Lets you securely connect to a private network, such as a LAN, over a public network, such as the Internet.

To Install
Add/Remove Programs → Windows Setup → Communications → Virtual Private Networking

Description

Virtual Private Networks (VPNs) use the Point-to-Point Tunneling Protocol (PPTP) to establish a connection between your system and a remote network over a TCP/IP-based network such as the Internet. Once that connection is established, the VPN can encapsulate data packets generated by other network protocols (such as IPX/SPX or NetBEUI), encrypt that data, and send it securely over the public network using a process called tunneling.

When you install VPN using Windows Setup, several networking components are added to Control Panel → Network → Configuration, including:

- Microsoft Virtual Private Networking Adapter

- A Dial-Up Adapter with VPN support

- The NDISWAN protocol

In addition, the TCP/IP protocol is bound to the new dial-up adapter. None of these components are really configurable, but it is important to know what they are there for should you come across them. For more information on using Control Panel → Internet, see the section earlier in this chapter.

Once VPN is installed, you can connect to a PPTP-enabled server by simply creating a dial-up networking connection to it (see Figure 5-22). You can learn more about creating a DUN connection in Chapter 4. Following are a few things specific to setting up a connection to use with VPN:

- On the Server Types tab of the connection's property sheet (*connection* → right-click → Properties → Server Types), you need to select "Require encrypted password" and "Require data encryption." Both of these options are added to the Server Types tab when VPN is installed.

- When you run the new connection, you are given a number of additional details about the authentication process. This is a good way to be sure that VPN is actually working.

Notes
- PPTP comes in two versions: 40-bit and 128-bit encryption. Win 98 ships with the 40-bit version, but you can download the more secure 128-bit version from *http://mssecure.www.conexion.com/cgi-bin/ntitar.pl.*

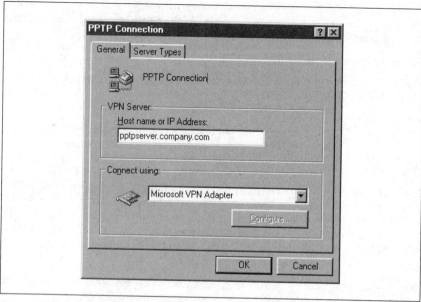

Figure 5-22: Property sheet for the VPN connection in the DUN folder

- When connecting to the PPTP server, you will actually run two DUN connections. The first connects you to your ISP and establishes a connection to the Internet. The second connects to the PPTP server over the first connection.

ODBC/32-bit ODBC

To Launch

Control Panel → ODBC

Command Line

```
control odbccp32.cpl
```

ODBC (Open Database Connectivity) is a standard for connecting applications to compliant databases. The ODBC control panel lets you associate an ODBC driver with a data source name. These are closely tied to any MS Office applications that are installed. When Access is installed, for example, it installs several database drivers, all of which are shown here. This applet is useful primarily to people developing database applications.

Passwords

Change passwords and enable remote administration or user profiles.

To Launch

Control Panel → Passwords

Command Line

```
control password.cpl
```

The Passwords control panel has three tabs: Change Passwords, Remote Administration, and User Profiles. They are not individually addressable from the command line.

Change Passwords

Changes the Windows password as well as passwords for other password-protected devices. (For example, if you've enabled a screen saver with a password, you can change that password here.)

Remote Administration

Allows your system to be administered from a remote computer. It includes remote Registry administration, remote policy administration (System Policy Editor), and possibly other settings.

User Profiles

Specifies whether user profiles are enabled, or whether all users of the machine use the same settings. Profiles allow users to customize the Desktop and other preferences.

Notes

- If user profiles are enabled at Control Panel → Passwords → User Profiles, two things happen:

  - The user branch of the Registry (*user.dat*) will keep track of all information that is different from user to user. The user branch of the Registry is stored in two files: the system default *user.dat* and the individual user's *user.dat*.

  - If individual Desktops and Start menus are enabled via checkboxes on Control Panel → Passwords → User Profiles, the system folders \ *Windows\Desktop* and \ *Windows\Start Menu* will be replaced by \ *Windows\Profiles\ username\ Desktop* and \ *Windows\Profiles\ username\ Start Menu*.

- A good way to pick a password that is easy for you to remember but hard for others to guess is to use the initials of a phrase that is meaningful only to you. For example, "I Like My Dog Spot Quite A Lot!" might become ILMDSQAL! While the character sequence might not stick in your mind, you can always remember the phrase to reconstruct it, and over time it will become easy to use. A minimum of six characters, with punctuation, numbers, and a combination of upper- and lowercase characters, makes for a password that is harder to crack.

- The exact password requirements for your system may be set by a system administrator using the System Policy Editor. The administrator can set the minimum password length, whether or not a password must include numbers as well as letters, and whether passwords can be cached (remembered) by applications. It is even possible to disable the Password control panel so that users can't change the passwords that are assigned to them. System policies are typically implemented only on corporate networks, and are set on a logon server, not on the Windows 98 client.

The use of passwords can lead you to believe that Windows 98 provides some level of security for user files. In fact, any user can gain access to your machine at the initial login prompt without knowing your password. All they have to do is hit Esc to log in as the "default" user. Or they can type in a new login name (and optional password). This will create a new user profile with the same settings as those of the default user. As one wag put it, Microsoft offers two security options: Windows NT wears a chastity belt, and Windows 95 and 98 wear a fig leaf.

- Many users on single-user machines don't like being asked for a login name and password when they boot up, so they leave the login name field blank. On subsequent reboots, you will not be prompted for a username or password. However, this can cause problems for subsystems such as Dial-Up Networking. Even though Dial-Up Networking uses a different password than the initial login, the system's ability to remember passwords is enabled only if you use a login name to begin with. However, if you install TweakUI from the Win 98 CD-ROM (see Chapter 8), you can fool the system into logging in for you automatically.

- Use Control Panel → Display → Screen Saver → Password protected to require a password to regain access to the system after a screen saver has kicked in.

PC Card (PCMCIA)

Stop a PCMCIA card before removing it from its slot. This is visible only if the computer has a PCMCIA slot.

To Launch

Control Panel → PC Card (PCMCIA)

Command Line

```
control main.cpl,PC Card (PCMCIA)
```

There are two tabs: Socket Status and Global Settings. They are not individually addressable from the command line.

Socket Status

Select a PC card from the list, and click Stop before removing it from the slot. If you swap PC cards often, specify a Stop control for each specific PC card on the Taskbar. "Display warning if card is removed before it is stopped" can be unchecked only if a control is displayed on the Taskbar.

Global Settings

Specifies memory allocation for the selected card. Use Automatic selection unless you know what you're doing. You can also disable PC card sound effects here.

Notes

If you omit the comma and the "PC Card (PCMCIA)" argument on the command line, you will get the Mouse control panel instead. There are several control panels within *main.cpl*, and Mouse happens to be the first.

Power Management

Control power management features of the computer.

To Launch

Control Panel → Power Management
Control Panel → Display → Screen Saver → Settings...

Command Line

control main.cpl ,Power

Power management refers to the ability of a computer to step down its power usage gradually when left unattended, eventually going all the way to shutdown.

Windows 98 will give you access to power-management features only if your computer supports them and they are enabled in the computer's BIOS (Basic Input/Output System). To enter your computer's BIOS setup screen, see your user's manual. (That being said, it's usually accessible by pressing the Del key just after your computer is first turned on.) Look for a setting called APM (for advanced power management), and make sure that power management is enabled.

There are four tabs: Power Schemes, Alarms, Power Meter, and Advanced. Two of these tabs, Alarms and Power Meter, are only visible if you are using a Notebook computer. The remaining tabs also change a bit if you are using a notebook.

Power Schemes
Lets you choose and configure a power scheme for your system. A power scheme is a set of preconfigured power options. Options you can configure include how many idle minutes before your system goes into standby, before your monitor turns off, and before your hard disks spin down. If you are using a notebook computer, you can set these options separately for when your computer is plugged in or using the battery.

Alarms
Lets you sound alarms or display pop-up messages when the battery level gets low and when the battery level gets critically low. You can also force the computer to go to standby mode or shut down when these events occur.

Power Meter
Shows you the current source of power (outlet or batteries) and the percentage of power remaining for all batteries in your computer.

Advanced
Lets you configure several advanced power options. Click to show a power meter on the taskbar to graphically display remaining battery levels at all times. You can also specify that a password be required for access to the computer when it comes off standby mode. If you are using a notebook, you

can specify separately whether it should shut down or go to standby when you use the power button or shut the lid.

Notes

- Most laptops have power-management subsystems of their own, which are usually more sophisticated than the generic Windows power management features.

- If you omit the ,Power argument on the command line, you will get the Mouse control panel instead. There are several control panels within *main. cpl*, and Mouse happens to be the first.

- APM support in Win 98 is unstable, so use it with caution.

Printers

Add a new printer, or get and set information about existing printers.

To Launch

Control Panel → Printers
Start → Settings → Printers
My Computer → Printers

Command Line

control main.cpl,Printers *(launches the Add Printer wizard)*

Control Panel → Printers is a virtual folder showing one icon for every configured printer. Control Panel → Printers → Add Printer is a wizard that steps you through the process of configuring a new printer. If you choose Add Printer → Next → Local, you will see a list of printer manufacturers and models to choose from. If your printer is not listed, and you have an installation disk containing drivers for your printer, click "Have Disk."

LPT1: is the standard parallel printer port for the PC, but a printer can also be connected to either of the two standard serial ports, COM1: or COM2: as well as LPT2:–LPT4:. Choose FILE: to create a pseudo-printer that will copy the output destined for a printer to a disk file instead. This is useful if you want to save the PostScript that would be generated for printing into a file, or if you don't have a printer attached to your system, but have access to one in some form elsewhere.

By default, the name given to the printer will be its model name, but you can give it any name you like. In an installation with multiple printers, it's often nice to come up with a suite of related names—constellations, Shakespearean characters, or what have you.

If you choose Add Printer → Network, the system will look through the Network Neighborhood for existing printers. What you are really doing is creating a shortcut to that existing printer. If you already know the printer name, type its UNC pathname (see "Network," earlier in this chapter) or browse until you find it. You need not give it the same name as it has at its destination, but it would probably be wise.

Printer Properties

Use the Properties sheet for any selected printer to get detailed configuration information about the printer and change any of its settings. With the exception of Properties → Paper, you probably don't need to change any of the settings, and it is better to set this in your applications.

Properties → Details → Capture Printer Port can be used to link a network printer to a logical printer port name. This can be useful for older DOS programs that require a DOS-style printer port name such as LPT1:; you fool DOS programs into thinking there's an LPT1!

Notes

- If you are browsing the Network Neighborhood and come across a printer, you can easily install it by dragging the printer icon to your printers Folder. Depending upon how the printer is set up on the network server, you may need to have the Windows 98 CD or the printer driver disk to complete the installation. You can also drag the icon to your desktop to create a shortcut to the printer. You can then print files by dragging them onto that shortcut.

- You can double-click a printer icon in the Printers folder to open a list of pending print jobs for that printer. You can reorder or even delete jobs that are queued (see Chapter 4 for details).

Regional Settings

Control the display of country-specific information such as numbers, currency, time, or dates in Windows and in applications (such as MS Office) that support regional settings.

To Launch

Control Panel → Regional Settings

Command Line

```
control intl.cpl [, property-tab]
```

Property Tabs

,0 Regional Settings

,1 Number

,2 Currency

,3 Time

,4 Date

Regional Settings

This is the master tab. Select a location here, and the other tabs will show the standard representation for numbers, currency, and so forth in that location.

Number

Shows the default treatment of numbers in that region. This includes things like the decimal point, the number of digits shown after a decimal, how digits are grouped and how the groups are separated, and so on. For example, the number represented in the U.S. as 123,456,789.00 will be represented as 123 456 789,00 in France.

Currency

Shows the default representation of currency, including the currency symbol for the region and its placement before or after the numbers.

Time

Shows the treatment of time, as demonstrated by the system clock in the System Tray. While there is less variation in time representation than in the other categories, there are variations in whether A.M./P.M. indicators are used, whether leading zeros are shown for hours before 10, and whether a 12- or 24-hour clock is used.

Date

Shows the treatment of dates, in both short form (12/24/98) and long form (December 24, 1998).

Notes

- After changing the location and either clicking Apply or trying to switch to another tab, you will be told that the settings will not take effect until you restart the machine. This does not appear to be the case. For instance, if you have a clock displayed in the System Tray, you can see it change to the new format as soon as you click Apply or go to another tab. Excel and Word also appear to recognize the new regional setting immediately.

- Even if you are not changing regions, this control panel can be a useful resource for finding out the standard representations in other countries.

- Although you can modify any of the settings without changing the region itself, there really isn't a good reason to do this, since they accurately reflect local custom.

- Not all applications pay attention to these settings.

Scanners and Cameras   \Windows\System\sticpl.cpl

Configure scanners, cameras, and other still-image devices.

To Launch

Control Panel → Scanners and Cameras

Command Line

```
control sticpl.cpl
```

This Control Panel icon is only visible if you have previously installed a still-image device. You can do this using the Add New Hardware wizard if Plug and Play does not automatically detect the device.

The Scanners and Cameras Control Panel applet has two tabs: Devices and Logging Settings. These tabs are not individually accessible from the command line.

Devices

Shows a list of still-image devices configured on your system. Typically, these devices are Plug and Play and are added automatically. Add launches a wizard that lets you specify the manufacturer/model of your device and what port that device is connected to. Properties launches a separate dialog that lets you view information about and test your device. Certain device models also include additional configuration parameters.

Logging Settings

Lets you log messages and warnings that have to do with the still-image device. You can independently log trace messages, warnings, and errors. Logging can be useful in helping support personnel troubleshoot problems with your device.

Notes

The Scanners and Cameras Control Panel is not compatible with all devices; it can crash if the device not supported.

Sounds

Control the sound schemes used by Windows and Windows applications to signal various system events.

To Launch

Control Panel → Sounds

Command Line

```
control mmsys.cpl,Sounds
```

The Sounds control panel (see Figure 5-23) lets you associate specific sounds with various Windows events. Additional sound associations can be installed by various applications. This is the place to change or remove all those annoying noises that Windows makes when it starts up, shuts down, or wants to let you know that you've made a mistake.

Under each application, you'll see a list of events (such as Exit Windows or Maximize). Any event that has an associated sound will be accompanied by a speaker icon. Select the event, and see the name of the associated sound file. Use the drop-down list under Sound Name to change the sound associated with the selected event. Change the sound to "(None)" if you don't want to hear a sound for that event. To hear a preview of a given sound, click the arrow in the Preview box.

Sounds are stored as .*wav* files in the *Windows**Media* directory. You can use the Browse button to add sound files stored elsewhere on your disk. See *http://www.yahoo.com/Computers_and_Internet/Multimedia/Sound/Archives/WAV/* for more sounds.

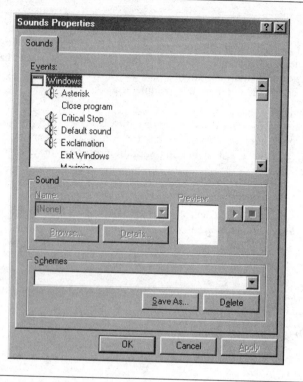

Figure 5-23: The Sounds control panel applet

 If your system has a microphone, you can use the Sound Recorder (*sndrec32*) to record your own sounds and attach them to Windows events. You can also use *sndrec32* to edit the existing sound files— creating various special effects, or just changing the volume.

Sounds are grouped into Schemes, just like Desktop patterns and window borders. Change the scheme, and all of the sound associations change. Try some of the different schemes, and preview the various sounds until you find one you like.

Notes

- If you omit ,Sounds on the command line, you will get the Multimedia control panel instead. Sounds is really the sixth tab of the Multimedia control panel.

- If you change any of the specific sound/event associations, use the Save As button to save them as a new scheme. (You can also modify the existing schemes by saving your custom scheme with one of the existing names.) Note that you don't need to save a scheme for any individual changes to be remembered when you exit the control, but be aware that they will be lost if you ever switch to another scheme.

- The sound volume is controlled by Multimedia → Audio → Volume (*sndvol32. exe*). You'd expect to find it here or as an icon in the Control Panel, but you'd be wrong.

- The only way to disable the system beep is with TweakUI. If you remove the sound event for errors, the built-in computer speaker will still beep when an error occurs.

System

Manage hardware and device drivers.

To Launch

Control Panel → System
My Computer → Properties

Command Line

```
control sysdm.cpl [,property-tab]
```

Property Tabs

,0 General

,1 Device Manager

,2 Hardware Profiles

,3 Performance

General
Gives information about the manufacturer and the registered user: not very useful, except to learn which build of Windows you're running (4.10.1998, 1111, etc.).

Device Manager
Gives you an Explorer-like expandable/collapsible tree view of the hardware devices known to your system. Select a device and click Properties to get information about the device. (Double-clicking on the device name will also open the Property sheet.) Note that the properties for generic device types (like Keyboard or Modem) won't contain much information. You have to expand the view to see and select specific devices first.

The data available here is not the same as the properties available from other parts of the Control Panel. For example, Device Manager → Modems → *any modem* will not give you the same properties as Control Panel → Modems. The information here is of a lower level; you should not change these settings manually, since it will interfere with your system's automatic plug-and-play configuration. Discussion of this material is beyond the scope of this book. (See *Windows 98 Annoyances* from O'Reilly & Associates.)

Possibly more interesting than specific devices are the properties under the first heading, Computer (see Figure 5-24). You can use this dialog box to view information such as the IRQ (Interrupt Request) for each device, I/O addresses, and reserved memory. Using this summary view is easier than going to the properties for each individual device.

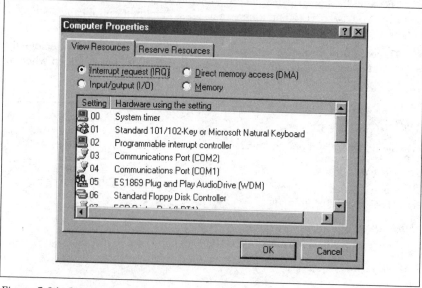

Figure 5-24: Computer Properties in the Device Manager tab

Use the Print... button to print out and store a complete record of settings. This is especially useful if you plan to make any changes.

If you actually want to change the resource for any device, you must go back to the main Device Manager list and open the Property sheet for the desired device.

Hardware Profiles

Hardware profiles provide a way of optimizing the drivers that are loaded for a computer that can be used in more than one configuration. For example, you might have different profiles for a portable computer when it is docked and undocked. Profiles can also provide a way to use certain devices that might otherwise conflict.

Performance

Contains some useful information about your system, such as the amount of memory and whether disk compression is installed. Advanced settings should be modified only by system administrators or knowledgeable users.

Telephony

\Windows\System\telephon.cpl

Configure system-wide dialing properties and view installed telephony drivers.

To Launch

Control Panel → Telephony
Control Panel → Modems → Dialing Properties

Command Line

```
control telephon.cpl
```

The telephony Control Panel applet has two tabs: My Locations and Telephony Drivers. These tabs are not individually accessible from the command line.

My Locations

Used to establish different locations you may dial from. For each location, you can define a unique set of dialing parameters.

Country and Area Code

Specify the country and area code you will be dialing from. Area Code Rules lets you set special rules for dialing other numbers within your area code. You can set it to always dial the area code, or you can configure it based on telephone prefixes.

Access an Outside Line

Specify the code that should be dialed, if any, to establish access to an outside line for both local and international calls. You may also need to use a comma after the code to specify that your modem should wait for two seconds before continuing to dial the number. This is necessary if the application using the modem must hear a dial tone before dialing.

Call Waiting

If a location has call waiting, you should disable it before making data connections, as some modems will drop the line in response to a call-waiting signal. Even if your modem can handle it, it is polite to disable call waiting so that the party dialing in does not just hear the phone ring with no answer; with call waiting disabled, they will get a busy signal.

Check "To disable call waiting, dial" and enter the appropriate code. The most typical U.S. code is *70, but some regions use other codes. Any code you enter will be remembered in the drop-down list.

Call waiting is disabled only for the duration of the present call, and is re-enabled when you close the connection.

Trying to disable call waiting on a line that has no call waiting will make it impossible to place a call. Use multiple locations if you call from lines with call waiting and without.

Calling Card

If you are dialing from a location where you need to use a calling card to pay for the call, check "For long distance calls, use this calling card" and select the appropriate card from the drop-down list. The Calling Card button opens a separate dialog that lets you enter details about the rules for using calling cards. For example, if you were using an AT&T Direct Dial card, you would select this choice from the drop-down menu list, and the access codes for both Long Distance and International calls automatically drop into the fields below it. Additionally, the dialing sequence is automatically configured for this calling card option. You can view the sequence by clicking on the Long Distance Calls or the International Calls buttons below. If your particular card is not available from the drop-down list, you can manually enter the access codes and the dialing sequence as well. Select the New button to create a new calling card profile.

Telephony Drivers

Lets you configure the drivers used for telephony. Clicking Configure for most drivers simply opens the Modems Control Panel applet.

Users

Add, configure, and delete multiple users.

To Launch

Control Panel → Users

Command Line

```
control inetcpl.cpl,Users
```

This applet is present only if your system is configured for multiple users (see Figure 5-25).

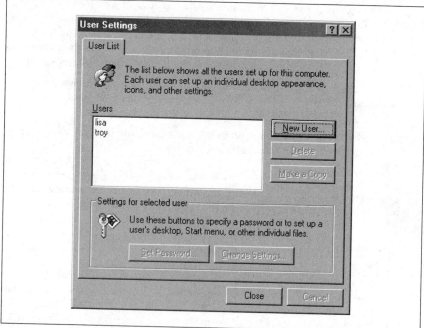

Figure 5-25: The Users applet

The first time you click this icon, it will launch a wizard that steps you through the creation of your first user. This wizard is the same one used when you add a new user, as described below. This control panel contains only one property tab: User List.

Use the New User button to add a new username. An applet will pop up and walk you through lists of dialog boxes with checkboxes to enable or disable options on the Desktop, the Start menu, the Favorites folder, and so on.

The Delete button deletes the selected user. Interestingly enough, you don't need a password to delete a user.

To change the password of a user, select a user and click Set Password.

To change individual settings of a user (the same settings that are available when pressing the New User button), select a user and click Change Settings.

Control Panel

CHAPTER 6

Start Menu Programs and Other Graphical Applications

This chapter provides alphabetical reference entries for the 70 or so graphical accessories, games, and system utilities that are either installed as part of a typical Windows 98 system, or can be added easily using Control Panel → Add/Remove Programs. See Chapter 7, *DOS and Other Command-Line Utilities*, for DOS commands and other command-line utilities and Chapter 8, *Hidden Gems on the Windows 98 CD-ROM*, for additional programs hidden on the CD-ROM.

Note that while the programs in this chapter typically appear on the Start Menu, or can be run from a menu item in another graphical program, they can also be run from any of the system command lines (DOS window, Run prompt, or Address Toolbar) by typing the filename of the actual executable program. See the introduction to Chapter 7 for more information on running programs from the command line.

We've arranged the applications in this chapter by common name, which we've derived from the shortcut names in the Start menu for those applications that have one, and from the dialog name of the application for those that don't. Table 6-1 provides an easy cross-reference between the common name and the executable filename of an application. The Typical column defines the applications that are available with the typical installation, and the Start column lists whether or not an application has a shortcut in the Start menu once it's installed.

Table 6-1: Executable Filenames of Graphical Applications

Common Application Name	Executable Filename	Typical	Start
Automatic Skip Driver Agent	*asd*		
Backup	*msbackup*		✓
Calculator	*calc*	✓	✓
CD Player	*cdplayer*	✓	✓
Character Map	*charmap*		✓

Table 6-1: Executable Filenames of Graphical Applications (continued)

Common Application Name	Executable Filename	Typical	Start
Clipboard Viewer	*clipbrd*		✓
Connection Wizard	*icwconn1*		✓
Control Panel	*control*	✓	✓
Direct Cable Connection	*directcc*		✓
Disk Cleanup	*cleanmgr*	✓	✓
Disk Defragmenter	*defrag*	✓	✓
Dr. Watson	*drwatson*	✓	
Drive Converter	*cvt1*	✓	✓
DriveSpace 3	*drvspace*	✓	
File Manager	*winfile*	✓	
Font Viewer	*fontview*	✓	
FreeCell	*freecell*		✓
Frontpage Express	*fpxpress*	✓	✓
Hearts	*mshearts*		✓
HyperTerminal	*hypertrm*		✓
Imaging	*kodakimg*	✓	✓
Internet Explorer	*iexplore*	✓	✓
IP Configuration	*winipcfg*	✓	
Maintenance Wizard	*tuneup*	✓	✓
Make Compatible	*mkcompat*	✓	
Media Player	*mplayer*	✓	✓
Microsoft Chat	*cchat*		✓
Microsoft Netmeeting	*conf*	✓	✓
Minesweeper	*winmine*		✓
Net Watcher	*netwatch*		✓
Netshow Player 2.0	*nsplayer*		✓
Notepad	*notepad*	✓	✓
Object Packager	*packager*	✓	
Outlook Express	*msimn*	✓	✓
Paint	*mspaint*	✓	✓
Personal Web Server	*pws*	✓	
Phone Dialer	*dialer*	✓	✓
Program Manager	*progman*	✓	
Quick View	*quikview*	✓	
RealPlayer	*rvplayer*		
Registry Checker	*scanregw*	✓	✓
Registry Editor	*regedit*	✓	
Resource Meter	*rsrcmtr*		✓

Start Menu Programs

Table 6-1: Executable Filenames of Graphical Applications (continued)

Common Application Name	Executable Filename	Typical	Start
ScanDisk	*scandskw*	✓	✓
Signature Verification Tool	*sigverif*	✓	✓
Solitaire	*sol*		✓
Sound Recorder	*sndrec32*	✓	✓
System Configuration Editor	*sysedit*	✓	
System File Checker	*sfc*	✓	✓
System Information	*msinfo32*	✓	✓
System Monitor	*sysmon*		✓
Task Manager	*taskman*	✓	
Telnet	*telnet*	✓	
Update Information Tool	*qfecheck*	✓	
Version Conflict Manager	*vcmui*	✓	✓
Volume Control	*sndvol32*	✓	✓
Wavetop Data Broadcasting	*wavetop*		
Web Publishing Wizard	*wpwiz*		✓
WebTV for Windows	*tvx*		✓
Windows Explorer	*explorer*	✓	✓
Windows Help	*winhlp32*	✓	
Windows Report Tool	*winrep*	✓	✓
WinPopup	*winpopup*	✓	
WordPad	*wordpad*	✓	✓

Format of Each Entry

Each entry starts with the name, the location of the executable file, and a brief description. For instance:

Solitaire   \ *Windows\sol.exe*

The popular Microsoft Solitaire game that comes with Windows 98.

This is followed by instructions on how to launch the program. If there is more than one way to do it, we generally list the most convenient one first. For example:

    Address → sol
    Start → Run → sol
    Start → Programs → Accessories → Games → Solitaire

We then give a brief description of the program. We don't document every obvious feature of the graphical user interface (if one exists), but we do highlight important features.

Where appropriate, we also provide interesting side notes, as well as references to sources of additional information, including useful web sites.

Automatic Skip Driver Agent   \Windows\asd.exe

Remove or re-enable disabled drivers or operations that fail during startup.

To Launch

> Address → asd
> Start → Run → asd
> Start → Programs → Accessories → System Tools → System Information →
>   Tools menu → Automatic Skip Driver Agent

Description

If a driver or operation fails on two consecutive Win 98 startups, Win 98 automatically marks that driver or operation as disabled so that it can be skipped during the next startup. Operations that *asd* monitors include starting a device, mapping an address space, setting power states, and calling various BIOS. You can run *asd* to get details on the failed component and to attempt to restart it. Details usually include a recommendation for fixing the problem (usually updating the driver).

Notes

If a driver or operation failed and has been disabled by *asd*, it is flagged with a yellow exclamation point in Device Manager and you will likely get an error message as well. Opening the properties of the failed component in Device Manager will give you much the same information that asd → Details does. In addition, the property sheet in Device Manager lets you re-enable the component and provides a shortcut to the Driver Update wizard.

Backup   \Program Files\Accessories\Backup\msbackup.exe

Copy (back up) files from your hard drive to a floppy disk or tape.

To Launch

> Address → msbackup
> Start → Run → msbackup
> Start → Programs → Accessories → System Tools → Backup

Description

Microsoft Backup (see Figure 6-1) works by creating a backup set, or a set of selected files to be backed up to a floppy disk or tape. This backup set, along with all the selected options available in *msbackup* (e.g., data compression, password protection, error report listing, etc.) are saved in a backup job. Create the backup set using an Explorer-like two-pane view to select the files you want backed up. Click on any folder icon to open it and navigate through the file system. Click on the checkbox next to a file or folder to select it for backup.

The first time you run *msbackup*, it runs a wizard that creates a backup set called *MyBackup.qic*, which includes every file in the system. If you have a tape drive,

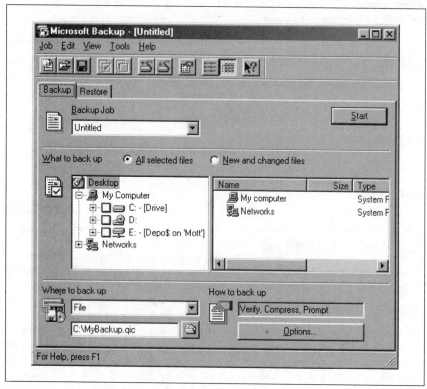

Figure 6-1: The Microsoft Backup utility dialog box (msbackup.exe)

Jaz drive, Zip drive, or other high-volume backup medium, you might actually want to back up this job. If you have only floppies, you probably want to navigate to a particular folder or folders and define a smaller backup job! To define a new backup job, select Job → New or click the New Backup Job button on the toolbar (notice how "Untitled" is listed in the Backup Job scrollbar). Select a particular set of files and folders to be backed up, plus a destination for the backup (a disk or tape drive), and then choose Job → Save As, type the name of the job, and select the Save button. If you modify any of the options (Job → Options or the Options button), be sure to save them since they will apply only to the current job. Once the job is saved, you can begin the backup process by clicking the Start button.

 Backup doesn't check the archive file attribute (see "attrib" in Chapter 7), but instead relies on its own internal records in the backup set. You must load a specific backup set to do an incremental backup of files that have changed since that backup set was last run.

To restore files, select the Restore tab and then load a particular backup job by choosing the Restore From device and location. You then need to select the files you want to restore in the Explorer-like two-pane view, and select the Start button.

Notes

- To do another backup of the same set of files, load the desired backup job. Obviously, if you want to create a new backup job, it may be easier to open an existing backup job and modify it than to start from scratch. Be sure to save the new backup job if you want to use it again.

- The "All Selected Files" and "New and Changed Files" radio buttons on the main *msbackup* dialog let you select a full backup (all selected files in the set are backed up) or an incremental backup (only selected files in the set that have changed and are new are backed up). You can also specify whether to verify the backup, whether to use compression, and whether to erase the current contents of the backup medium before copying the new files onto it. Verification does a compare operation between the backup and the original when the backup is finished. It's always wise to be safe and use this option. Compression, on the other hand, should be done with caution, and should not be done with hardware compression. Compressing data that has already been compressed causes the data to occupy more media space in some instances.

- View menu → Selection is useful for determining the number and size of files selected in a backup set before a backup is initiated.

- Restore tab → Options button allows you to choose whether the restored file will overwrite an existing file, overwrite an existing file only if it's older than the backed up file, or prompt you before overwriting.

- When backing up or restoring files, *msbackup* has an option to back up or restore the Registry.

- Options → Exclude lets you exclude files with registered and custom type extensions.

- You can also do backups with *xcopy32*, or even (for smaller filesets) with the Explorer. For example, use Find → Files or Folders to select files by name or date, then Select All, copy, and drop onto a floppy disk. The Explorer is smart enough to ask for another floppy if needed. What you lose is the fine-grained control that *msbackup* gives you over exactly which files to restore and how, along with support for tape drives. You have to keep track of that manually. But there are certainly cases where that is entirely adequate.

- There are wizards for performing a backup and restore: Tools → Backup Wizard and Tools → Restore Wizard respectively.

- To toggle the welcome dialog on or off that pops up when you open *msbackup*: Tools → Preferences → check/uncheck the "Show startup dialog when Microsoft Backup is started" box.

- The Options → Report tab contains many variations for creating different types of reports, including errors, warnings, and unattended messages generated from backing up and restoring files. The option to perform an unattended backup is also useful and available on this tab. Reports are saved as

.txt files (same name as the job) at \ *Program Files\ Accessories\ Backup\ Reports.*

See Also

"xcopy32" in Chapter 7

http://www.seagatesoftware.com—A scaled-down version of Seagate Backup. It is not compatible with '95 Backup, which was based on HP Backup.

Calculator
\ *Windows\ calc.exe*

Windows 98 calculator.

To Launch

Address → calc
Start → Run → calc
Start → Programs → Accessories → Calculator

Description

By default, the Calculator starts in standard mode, but a scientific mode is also available (View → Scientific) for performing complicated calculations (see Figure 6-2).

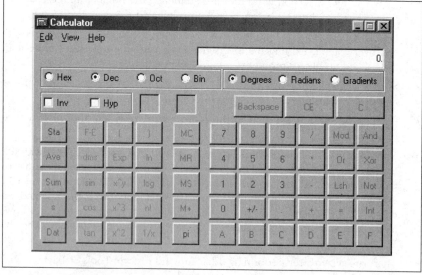

Figure 6-2: Calculator in scientific mode

If you select the scientific mode and close the Calculator, the next time you open the Calculator it will be in scientific mode. (The mode is saved in the Registry.)

The following description focuses on the more complex scientific calculator; those functions that are available in the standard calculator are identical there.

Entering Data and Performing Calculations

Data can be entered by clicking the buttons, or from the keyboard. All keys have keyboard equivalents. Non-obvious equivalents are documented as appropriate in the following sections. The +/- key changes the sign of the entered number (keyboard equivalent = F9). The Int key displays only the integer part of a decimal number. To see only the fractional part, use Inv + Int (keyboard equivalent = ;).

Click MS to store a number in memory. To recall it, click MR. To clear the memory, click MC. To add the displayed number to the number already in memory, click M+. When a number is stored in memory, an M appears in the box above the memory buttons. Only one number can be stored in memory at a time. The keyboard equivalents are listed in Table 6-2.

Table 6-2: Calculations and Keyboard Equivalents

Calc Button	Keyboard Key	Action
C	Esc	Clear all calculations
CE	Del	Clear last entry
Back	Backspace	Clear last digit
MC	Ctrl-L	Memory clear
MR	Ctrl-R	Memory recall
MS	Ctrl-M	Memory store
M+	Ctrl-P	Memory add

Number System

By default, the number system is decimal. Click the radio buttons to switch. Or use keyboard equivalents (see Table 6-3).

Table 6-3: Number Systems and Keyboard Equivalents

Keyboard Key	Action
F5	Hexadecimal
F6	Decimal
F7	Octal
F8	Binary

Hexadecimal values A–F can be entered from the keyboard or using the A–F buttons on the calculator. When in binary mode, selecting Dword, Word, or Byte will display 32-, 16-, or 8-bit values, respectively; 16- or 8-bit values are the low-order bits of a 32-bit number (see Table 6-4 for keyboard equivalents).

Table 6-4: Binary Mode Keyboard Equivalents

Keyboard Key	Action
F2	Dword
F3	Word
F4	Byte

Bitwise operations buttons and keyboard equivalents are listed in Table 6-5.

Table 6-5: Bitwise Buttons and Keyboard Equivalents

Calc Button	Keyboard Key	Action
Mod	%	Modulus
And	&	Bitwise AND
Or	|	Bitwise OR
Xor	^	Bitwise exclusive OR
Lsh	<	Left shift (right shift via Inv + Lsh, or >)
Not	~	Bitwise inverse

If you convert a fractional decimal number to another number system, only the integer part will be used.

When in Decimal mode, the Deg, Rad, and Grad radio buttons switch between degrees, radians, and gradients (see Table 6-6).

Table 6-6: Decimal Mode Keyboard Equivalents

Keyboard Key	Action
F2	Deg
F3	Rad
F4	Grad

Statistical Functions

To perform a statistical calculation, you must enter the first data, then click the Sta button (this opens the Statistics Box; see Figure 6-3), click the Dat button (displays the data in the Statistics Box), and then continue entering the data, clicking Dat after each entry. When you've finished entering all the numbers, click the statistical button you want to use (Ave, Sum, or S). The buttons available in the Statistics Box are listed in Table 6-7.

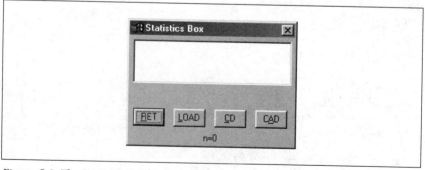

Figure 6-3: The Statistics Box

Table 6-7: Statistics Box Buttons

Calc Button	Action
RET	Returns the focus to the calculator
LOAD	Displays the selected number in the Statistics Box in the Calculator display area
CD	Clears the selected number (data)
CAD	Clears all numbers (data) in the Statistics Box

Scientific Calculations

The Inv and Hyp checkboxes modify the function keys listed in Table 6-8.

Table 6-8: Scientific Calculations Buttons and Keyboard Equivalents

Calc Button	Keyboard Key	Action
Inv	i	Sets the inverse function for sin, cos, tan, Pl, x^y, x^2, x^3, Ln, log, sum, and s.
Hyp	h	Sets the hyperbolic function for sin, cos, and tan.
F-E	v	Turns scientific notation on and off. Can only be used with decimal numbers. Numbers larger than 10^{15} are always displayed with exponents.
( )	( )	Starts and ends a new level of parentheses. The maximum number of nested parentheses is 25. The current number of levels appears in the box above the) button.
dms	m	If the displayed number is in degrees, convert to degree-minute-second format. Use Inv + dms to reverse the operation.
Exp	x	The next digit(s) entered constitute the exponent. The exponent cannot be larger than 289. Decimal only.
Ln	n	Natural (base e) logarithm. Inv + Ln calculates e raised to the nth power, where n is the current number.
sin	s	Sine of the displayed number. Inv + sin gives arc sine. Hyp + sin gives hyperbolic sine. Inv + Hyp + sin gives arc hyperbolic sine.
x^y	y	x to the yth power. Inv + x^y calculates the yth root of x.
Log	l	The common (base 10) logarithm. Inv + log yields 10 to the xth power, where x is the displayed number.
Cos	o	Cosine of the displayed number. Inv + cosin gives arc cosine. Hyp + cosin gives hyperbolic cosine. Inv + Hyp + cosin gives arc hyperbolic cosine.
x^3	#	Cubes the displayed number. Inv + x^3 gives the cube root.
n!	!	Factorial of the displayed number.

Calc Button	Keyboard Key	Action
tan	t	Tangent of the displayed number. Inv + tan gives arc tan. Hyp + tan gives hyperbolic tan. Inv + Hyp + tan gives arc hyperbolic tan.
x^2	@	Squares the displayed number. Inv + x^2 gives the square root.
1/x	r	Reciprocal of displayed number.
Pi	p	The value of *pi* (3.1415...). Inv + Pi gives 2 × pi.

Notes

By right-clicking on any button on the calculator, you can choose the "What's This?" option for information about the selected button.

See Also

There are many different types of calculators available on the Web. For an extensive list:

> *http://www-sci.lib.uci.edu/HSG/RefCalculators.html*

For a good example of a calculator created with JavaScript:

> *http://www.sonic.net/~undoc/WebCalc.html*

CD Player

\Windows\cdplayer.exe

Play audio CDs in the CD-ROM drive.

To Launch

> Address → cdplayer
> Start → Run → cdplayer
> Start → Programs → Accessories → Multimedia → CD Player

Description

By default, *cdplayer* should start automatically once an audio CD is inserted into the CD-ROM drive, but it can also be run from the DOS prompt, the Run prompt, or the Start menu.

You can control the volume in several ways. From the *cdplayer* interface (see Figure 6-4), choose View → Volume Control. You can also click or double-click the volume icon on the Taskbar, if you have checked the "Show Volume Control on the Taskbar" box in the Multimedia control panel applet (Control Panel → Multimedia → Audio). Another option is to type sndvol32 at the Run prompt.

Configurable playlists (Disk → Edit Play List) store information from CDs, including the title, the artist, and the names of each track on the CD. With *cdplayer*, you can select individual tracks, and even skip to locations within a track.

Figure 6-4: CD Player in action (cdplayer.exe)

cdplayer stores several hundred bytes of information about each CD in *cdplayer. ini*, and *.ini* files (including *cdplayer.ini*) are limited to 64K in size, so if you have a substantial collection of CDs, 64K may not be enough space.

It is possible to create a batch file to run *cdplayer* and maintain multiple playlists in *.ini* files. The batch file temporarily copies one of the *.ini* files over *cdplayer. ini*, and then copies any changes back to the source file. You will need to insert start /w in front of the batch line that launches *cdplayer.exe* to prevent the batch file from continuing on to the next instruction in the batch file. See Chapter 11, *The Batch Language*, for an example.

Associated Files

> *cdplayer.ini*
> *sndvol32.exe*

Notes

- Insert an audio CD, select your CD drive in the Explorer, and find the tracks (*.cda* files). Here are some things to try:

  - Right-click Control Panel → System on a track and choose "Play," or double-click on a track and it will play automatically.

  - Drag a track onto your Desktop. Create a shortcut, and rename the shortcut after the song. Whenever you have the CD in the drive, you can double-click on the shortcut to play the song. You can drag tracks to your hard drive and put them in your Start menu, or create a directory with CD tracks in it.

- To disable AutoPlay temporarily, press the Shift key when inserting an audio CD.

- You can turn off the AutoPlay feature by doing the following:

  1. Right-click on the My Computer icon.

  2. Choose the Device Manager tab.

  3. Open the CD-ROM branch, and select the entry for your CD-ROM drive.

4. Click Properties, and then choose the Settings tab.

5. Turn off the "Auto insert notification" option.

6. Click OK, and then OK again.

See Also

Download Pro Audio CD Player, which provides more options than *cdplayer.exe*:

> *http://www.aldridge.com/cdplayer.html*

For detailed information on the format of *cdplayer.ini, .cda* files, and so on:

> *http://www.binzen.de/cdplayer/*

Microsoft Plus! 98 comes with a Deluxe CD Player that contains options such as the ability to download tracklists from the Internet and advanced audio control.

Character Map

\ *Windows\charmap.exe*

Display symbols and special characters from specified fonts.

To Install

Control Panel → Add/Remove Programs → Windows Setup → System Tools → Character Map

To Launch

Address → charmap
Start → Run → charmap
Start → Programs → Accessories → System Tools → Character Map

Description

charmap lets you copy symbols and characters from specified fonts to the Clipboard for pasting into Windows documents (see Figure 6-5).

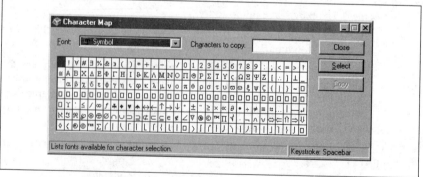

Figure 6-5: Character Map (charmap.exe)

To use Character Map:

1. Select a font from the Font drop-down list.

---

2. Double-click each character you want (or click once and then click the Select button). Each character will appear in the "Characters to copy" box. (To magnify a character, click it and hold down the mouse button.) See Figure 6-5.

3. Click Copy to copy the character(s) to the Windows clipboard.

4. Switch to your other application, click where you want the character(s) to appear, and paste (using either the Edit menu or Ctrl-V).

5. Select the newly inserted character(s), and then change them to the same font you used in Character Map. (This step is crucial!)

Notes

- Although Microsoft's documentation says that *charmap* works only with Windows-based programs, this isn't necessarily true. It is true, however, that *charmap* may not be effective with programs such as Notepad where fonts can't be specified. The key is that except for the more common "special" characters, the target program must be able to select fonts. Otherwise, select the target program's hard-coded font in *charmap*.

- *charmap* is helpful not only for selecting non-English characters, but also for "dingbats" (see the two "Wingdings" fonts); Greek characters (see the "Symbol" font); fractions (see the "MS Reference" font); and so on. For more information on Win 98 fonts, see the "Fonts" section in Chapter 5, *The Control Panel*.

- *charmap* is useful for finding out what key combination will produce a non-standard character in any given font. Select a character in any cell, and see the corresponding keystrokes on the status bar. All characters can be generated by the Alt-key combinations.

- It is useful to save *charmap* characters with *cliptray.exe* for easy access over time. See Chapter 8 for details about using *cliptray*.

chat

See "Microsoft Chat."

Clipboard Viewer   \Windows\clipbrd.exe

View the contents of the Clipboard.

To Install

Control Panel → Add/Remove Programs → Windows Setup → System Tools → Clipboard Viewer

To Launch

Address → clipbrd
Start → Run → clipbrd
Start → Programs → Accessories → System Tools → Clipboard Viewer

Associated Files

clipbrd.ini

Description

clipbrd.exe is a Clipboard viewer (see Figure 6-6). Typically, the Clipboard is accessed with the Cut, Copy, and Paste commands available in most programs, but *clipbrd* lets you preview the contents of the Windows Clipboard and save it to a file. This is useful if you have blocks of repetitious text you'd like to paste into programs at different times.

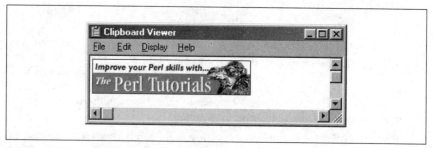

Figure 6-6: The Clipboard Viewer (clipbrd.exe)

Notes

- Supported Clipboard formats include text, bitmap, DIB bitmap, picture, SYLK, TIFF, OEM text, palette, Pen Data, RIFF, and Wave Audio. Applications may also provide their own clipboard viewers so they can display some custom format. This is called "owner display."

- *clipbrd*'s File → Save menu item saves the Clipboard contents as a *.clp* file; it can then be restored at a later time with File → Open.

- Chapter 8 contains information about the Clip Tray, a program that places an icon in the system tray and allows you to create, edit and quickly paste into the Clipboard any saved ClipTray text entries. This is much easier than loading *clipbrd* to open individual *.clp* files from a directory.

Connection Wizard

\Program Files\Internet Explorer\ Connection Wizard\icwconn1.exe

Connect your system to the Internet with a wizard.

To Launch

Address → `icwconn1`
Start → Run → `icwconn1`
Start → Programs → Internet Explorer → Connection Wizard
Desktop → Connection Wizard

Description

The Internet Connection Wizard steps you through setting up IE4 to connect to the Internet using either a dial-up or LAN connection. The wizard is installed in a typical Windows setup and is run automatically the first time you run IE4 or one of its related components, such as Outlook Express. Using the wizard, you have three options for configuring your Internet connection: sign up for a new ISP account, set up your system to use an existing account, or tell the wizard to go away because you're already set up.

If you choose to sign up for a new account, the wizard will use your modem to contact the Microsoft Referral Service and download a list of ISPs in your area. It is then up to you to contact the ISP of your choice and set up an account.

If you choose to have the wizard help you set up an existing account, you'll be given two more choices: whether to connect using an online service (like AOL) or to connect using an ISP account or LAN. If you choose an online service, the wizard will refer you to the Online Services folder found on your desktop to install and configure software for the service of your choice. If you choose an ISP, the wizard will actually run the DUN Connection wizard to set up a new dial-up-networking connection, as discussed in Chapter 4, *The Windows 98 User Interface*. If you choose a LAN connection, you will need to know whether your LAN uses a proxy server or whether it is directly connected to the Internet. Either way, the wizard really just walks you through setting up the same connection settings that you can find at Control Panel → Internet → Connection.

For the most part, we recommend that you configure your connection yourself using the methods we have discussed in the "Dial-Up Networking" section of Chapter 4 and the "Internet" section of Chapter 5 instead of using the Connection Wizard. The reason for this is that it will give you a better sense of how your system is set up in case you need to change settings or troubleshoot later. And, as you'll see when you try it, it's really no easier to use the wizard.

Notes

- We have found the Microsoft Referral Service to be extremely unreliable. At last attempt, the number that is provided with the original release of Win 98 is no longer in service. Even when it was, the ISP list was rarely up-to-date.

- In Windows 98 Second Edition, this Start Menu shortcut is called Internet Connection Wizard and is found at Start → Programs → Accessories → Internet Tools → Internet Connection Wizard. It is used in setting up IE5, which is installed with Windows 98 Second Edition.

Control Panel   \Windows\control.exe

Display the Control Panel, which contains most of the configuration applets for Windows 98.

To Launch

Address → control
Start → Run → control
Start → Settings → Control Panel

Description

control launches the Control Panel folder, which contains many applets used to configure everything from Accessibility Options to Sounds. Many of the applets in *control* are also accessed from a context menu (e.g., right-click on the Desktop for the Display applet) or the System Tray (e.g., double-click on the time for the Date/Time applet). Chances are, if you need to configure something in Windows 98, this is the place to look. See Figure 6-7.

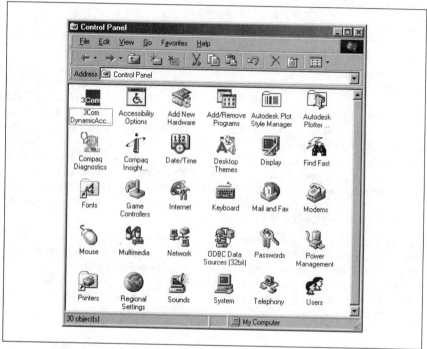

Figure 6-7: The Control Panel (control.exe)

See Also

"rundll32" and "control" in Chapter 7
Chapter 5

Direct Cable Connection

\ *Windows*\ *directcc.exe*

Establish a direct serial/parallel cable connection between two computers.

To Install

Control Panel → Add/Remove Programs → Windows Setup →
    Communications → Details → Direct Cable Connection

To Launch

Address → `directcc`
Start → Run → `directcc`
Start → Programs → Accessories → Communications → Direct Cable
    Connection

Description

By running *directcc*, you can establish a direct serial or parallel cable connection between two computers in order to share the resources of the computer designated as the host. *directcc* must be running on both computers, since it requires a client and a server. If the host is connected to a network, the guest computer can also access the network. For example, if you have a portable computer, you can use a cable to connect it to your work computer and network. To establish a local connection between two computers, you need a compatible serial or null-modem parallel cable. Parallel cables transmit data simultaneously over multiple lines, making it the faster of the two connection methods. Serial cables transmit data sequentially over one pair of wires, and are slower than parallel cables. Use a serial cable only if a parallel port is unavailable.

The first time you run *directcc*, you will be asked if the computer you are using will act as the host or the guest. The host listens on the designated port for contact from the guest. On subsequent invocations, you will be asked on the host to check your settings, then click Listen to start up the connection.

Notes

- To have the guest connect automatically upon startup, change the shortcut in the Start menu to "directcc.exe connect." To do this, use the Explorer to navigate to the shortcut (\ *Windows\Start Menu\Programs\Accessories\ Communications*) or navigate the Start Menu (Start → Programs → Accessories → Communications). Right-click on the Direct Cable Connection shortcut, choose Properties, click the Shortcut tab and add connect in the Target line after *C:\Windows\directcc.exe*. (See Figure 6-8.)

- You can also have the guest connect automatically by typing `directcc` connect from the DOS or Run prompt.

- Both the guest and host computer must be running *directcc*, and must use the same type of port. You should start *directcc* on the host first.

- Direct Cable Connect and Dial-Up Networking can operate at the same time.

See Also

The two sites below were written for Windows 95, but the information is relevant to *directcc* in Windows 98 as well.

For detailed information on using *directcc.exe*:

    http://www.tecno.demon.co.uk/dcc.html

For information on *directcc* troubleshooting:

    http://www.cs.purdue.edu/homes/kime/directcc/faq95.htm

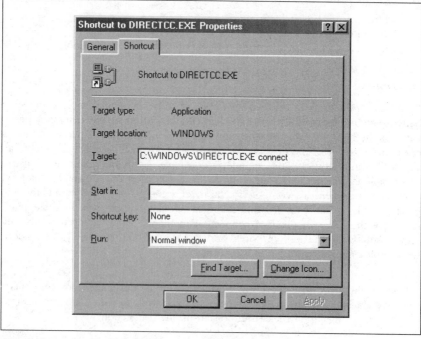

Figure 6-8: Automatically connecting to Direct Cable Connection (directcc.exe)

Disk Cleanup

\Windows\cleanmgr.exe

Remove unused files from your drive.

To Launch

Address → cleanmgr
Start → Run → cleanmgr
Start → Programs → Accessories → System Tools → Disk Cleanup
My Computer → *any drive* → right-click → Properties → Tools → Disk Cleanup

Description

When you first run Disk Cleanup (*cleanmgr*), you must select a drive to clean. *Cleanmgr* lets you automatically remove all files from certain locations, including:

- Temporary Internet Files (*Windows**Temporary Internet Files*). Also, you can set the maximum size of this folder using Control Panel → Internet → General → Settings → Amount of disk space to use. Note that copies of cookie files (regularly stored in *Windows**Cookies*\) for IE4 are also stored in this folder, but are not deleted along with other Internet files.

- Temporary Setup Files. Some programs create temporary folders in the *Windows* folder during installation and then don't clean up after themselves.

- Downloaded Program Files (*Windows**Downloaded Program Files*). This folder contains mostly ActiveX and Java applets downloaded from the Internet. Note that if you clean out this folder, these controls will have to be downloaded again when you revisit the site that uses them.

- Recycle Bin (*Recycled*).

- Temporary Files (*Windows**TEMP*). This actually deletes all files in the *TEMP* folder that have not been modified in over a week.

Notes

- The More Options tab provides shortcuts to Add/Remove Programs → Install/Uninstall, Add/Remove Programs → Windows Setup, and FAT32 Converter (*cvt1.exe*).

- The Settings tab lets you specify that *cleanmgr* be run automatically whenever the currently selected drive runs low on disk space.

Disk Defragmenter
*Windows**defrag.exe*

Reorganize the files on a disk to optimize disk performance.

To Launch

Address → defrag
Start → Run → defrag
StartStart → Programs → Accessories → System Tools → Disk Defragmenter

Description

A heavily fragmented disk (one in which the data that make up files are no longer stored contiguously on the disk) affects machine performance, because it takes longer to find and piece together fragmented files. Running *defrag* makes it easy to monitor and maintain system performance so that you can identify problem issues and remove them. If system performance starts to drop off, run *defrag* to see if it helps.

defrag includes a graphical user interface (see Figure 6-9), but it can be run from Windows or MS-DOS. Figure 6-10 displays the meaning of all the graphical cluster boxes that are visible when running *defrag*. Select the Legend button to pop up the Defrag Legend dialog. If you use *defrag* from the command line, you can use options to control the behavior of the program without having to configure settings in the user interface. If you type *defrag* at the command line without options, you will launch the *defrag* dialog, which contains the user interface for configuring settings. That being said, defragging a large disk can take the better part of an hour, so ideally you should do this when you have the time or can walk away (see "Scheduled Tasks" in Chapter 4).

Notes

- My Computer → disk drive → Properties → Tools → Defragmentation status tells you how long it has been since *defrag* was used on the drive, and gives you the option to Defragment Now.

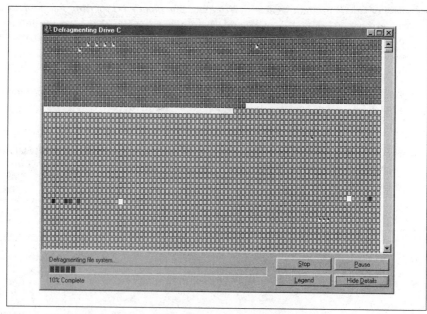

Figure 6-9: defrag in action—the Details view (defrag.exe)

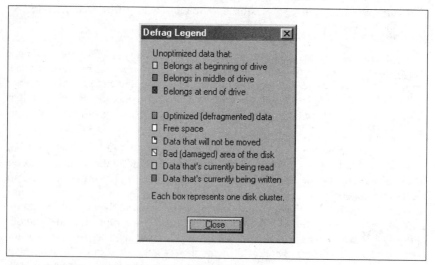

Figure 6-10: Meaning of the defrag Details view

 Defrag will suggest you don't need to continue at levels that really would improve performance. You should run *defrag* regularly, and tell it to continue whenever fragmentation is over 2 or 3%.

- You can run other programs while *defrag* runs in the background, but this is not recommended as it can cause other programs and *defrag* to run slowly: *defrag* has to restart as other programs touch the disk. Keep in mind that even a screen saver is a running program that will slow down *defrag*. Turn off any screen savers for best performance. Also, you may want to turn off the Task Scheduler (see "Scheduled Tasks" in Chapter 4) and even the Office Shortcut Bar, if you have that running.

- With Scheduled Tasks, you can run *defrag* when you're away from your system (for example, on Sunday nights). Note that *defrag* will stop if it finds disk or file errors, so it's a good idea to run *scandisk* just before *defrag*, either from a batch file or by setting *mstask* to run these programs in sequence.

See Also

"ScanDisk"
"Scheduled Tasks" in Chapter 4
"defrag" in Chapter 7

Dr. Watson
\Windows\drwatson.exe

Provides system error information when a GPF occurs.

To Launch

Address → drwatson

The Dr. Watson application is automatically installed with the typical Windows 98 installation. *drwatson* should be started whenever Windows is started. One way to do this is to edit the [windows] section of the *win.ini* file as follows:

```
load=drwatson.exe
```

Another way to start *drwatson* automatically is to create a shortcut for the utility and place it in the *\Windows\Start Menu\Programs\StartUp* directory. When Dr. Watison is running, you'll notice the program icon in the system tray.

Description

Dr. Watson is a diagnostic tool that provides information on the internal state of Windows when a system error (General Protection Fault, or GPF) occurs. It collects information such as system details, running applications, startup applications, kernel drivers, user drivers, MS-DOS drivers, and 16-bit modules. Dr. Watson can usually diagnose any system problems you may be having, and can be used by Microsoft to help evaluate the problem (if you use Microsoft Tech Support).

Dr. Watson remains inactive until a GPF error occurs, unless you right-click on the Dr. Watson icon in the system tray and select the Dr. Watson command. When either action occurs, a dialog box will appear asking for comments on the activities prior to the error. The comments you input will be added to a file as long as you select File → Save or File → Save As from the dialog. You have two ways of saving a Log file when selecting File → Save As: a Dr. Watson log file (*.wlg*) or a text file (*.txt*). The default for File → Save is a *.wlg* file and is recommended if you want to use the Dr. Watson application to view a GUI version of the information.

If, however, you want to use a text editor such as Notepad to view the information, save the file as a *.txt* file—the same information is displayed in a textual single-column format.

Sometimes Dr. Watson detects a fault that might not be fatal, and you have the opportunity to ignore the fault or close the application. If you choose to ignore the fault, Windows continues without performing the faulting instruction. You might be able to save your work in a new file at this point, but you should then restart Windows.

Notes

- By right-clicking on the Dr. Watson icon and selecting Options, you can configure the number of Log files you want to keep (50 maximum), and the directory you want to save them in. You can also select the "Open new windows in Advance view" radio button if you want to automatically view all Dr. Watson Log files in Advance view, which is recommended since it provides tabs of all the various information collected.

- Once you've opened a Log file (*.wlg*), View → Options is the same Options dialog you can select from the Dr. Watson icon without loading a Log file or running the Dr. Watson command.

- It is possible to print a *.wlg* file from within Dr. Watson with the File → Print command.

Drive Converter

\ Windows\cvt1.exe

Convert a drive formatted with FAT or FAT16 to FAT32.

To Launch

> Address → cvt1
> Start → Run → cvt1
> Start → Applications → Accessories → System Tools → Drive Converter

Description

Windows 98 includes support for a new version (FAT32) of the File Allocation Table (FAT) file system, which is used to structure your drive and to map the locations of files. FAT32 is more efficient than its predecessors (FAT and FAT16).

With FAT and FAT16, hard drives are formatted into clusters ranging from 4K to 32K, depending on the size of the disk. A cluster is a logical, rather than a physical, unit of storage on a hard disk that is managed by the operating system. On larger drives, this 4K to 32K range causes a great waste of space, as every file on the drive takes up a minimum space equal to the cluster size. Thus, even 2K files might take up 32K of space. Also, FAT and FAT16 do not support partitions larger than 2 gigabytes.

FAT32 improves on earlier versions by creating clusters of 4K regardless of drive size. In addition, FAT32 supports drives well over the 2 GB limit. While FAT32 seems just wonderful (and it really is), there is a catch. Computers running FAT or FAT16 (such as Windows 3.x, Windows NT 4.0 and earlier, and pre-OSR2 versions

---

of Windows 95) won't recognize drives formatted with FAT32. This means you won't be able to dual-boot with another operating system. In addition, older disk utilities and compression programs designed to work with FAT and FAT16 usually won't work with FAT32. If you format a removable disk with FAT32, other operating systems will not be able to see the files on the disk. One last warning: once you have made the conversion to FAT32, there is no way to return to your old file system. If these concerns don't apply to you, then go for it. You have nothing but speed and disk space to gain.

 There are several different versions of Windows 95. You can tell which version you have by right-clicking on the My Computer icon and choosing Properties from the context menu that appears. The revision code is displayed to the right of the Windows logo. If it says Windows 95 4.00.950, you have the the original release version; if it says Windows 95 4.00.950 A, you have Service Release 1 (SR1); if it says Windows 95 4.00.950 B, you have OSR2; and if it says Windows 95 4.00.950 C, you have OSR2.5.

If you already have a disk formatted with FAT or FAT16, you can use Drive Converter (*cvt1.exe*) to convert it to FAT32 while preserving the data on the disk. *cvt1* launches a straightforward wizard that lets you choose which drive you want to convert. Once you make the selection, *cvt1* scans your system for known applications that may not work with FAT32. The list of known applications is stored in the Registry at:

```
HKEY_LOCAL_MACHINE\SYSTEM\CurrentControlSet\Control\SessionManager\
CheckBadApps400.
```

Once the application scan is done, you'll be given the opportunity to back up your drive using *backup.exe*. The system will then need to restart in MS-DOS mode to finish the conversion. Once done, the system will restart again.

Notes

- Computers on a network that run FAT or FAT16 will still be able to access your files over the network even if you convert to FAT32.

- FAT32 will not work with some compression software. If your drive is compressed with this software, *cvt1* will not let you convert it.

- Partition Magic is also handy for converting, creating, and resizing FAT32 drives. You can also combine partitions that were too big for FAT16.

Drive Space 3   \ *Windows\drvspace.exe*

Compress and uncompress data on floppy disks or hard disk drives.

To Launch

    Address → drvspace
    Start → Run → drvspace
    Start → Programs → Accessories → System Tools → DriveSpace

Description

DriveSpace 3 can compress and uncompress data on floppy disks, removable media, or hard disk drives, and can be used from the command line or from its graphical interface. The first time you use DriveSpace 3 to compress data or space on a drive, the disk will have 50 to 100 percent more free space than it did before. You can use a compressed drive just as before compressing it. When you run DriveSpace 3 without command-line arguments (see "drvspace" in Chapter 7 for command-line arguments), the DriveSpace Manager appears, with menu commands for selecting the operations to perform. See Figure 6-11.

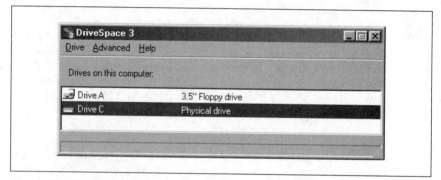

Figure 6-11: DriveSpace 3 launched from command line without arguments

DriveSpace 3 creates a new uncompressed drive, called the host drive, where it stores the compressed volume file (.cvf). If the host drive contains any free space in addition to the .cvf, you can also use it to store files that must remain uncompressed.

Notes

- Before you use DriveSpace 3 to compress a drive, you should back up the files the drive contains.

- To compress the startup hard disk drive, a drive must contain at least 2 MB of free space. Other hard disk drives and floppy disks must have at least 768K of free space.

- If a drive-letter conflict occurs, DriveSpace 3 resolves the conflict by reassigning its drive letters.

- DriveSpace 3 can create a compressed drive of up to 2 GB.

- When mounting a compressed drive, you must assign a drive letter to the compressed volume file.

- To mount a compressed disk that wasn't present when you started your computer (for example, a floppy disk), you need to mount it using Advanced → Mount.

- If any files on the drive are open, DriveSpace 3 will prompt you to close them before it compresses the drive. For drives that always have files opened (such as the drive containing Windows 98), DriveSpace 3 will restart the computer and use a limited version of Windows in place of Windows 98 while it com-

---

presses the drive. To do this, a directory named *failsave.drv* is created that contains the system files required for this operation. After compression, your computer will restart again, this time with Windows 98. When the compression is completed, DriveSpace 3 shows how much free space is available on the drive.

File Manager

\ *Windows\winfile.exe*

The Windows 3.1–style File Manager.

To Launch

> Address → `winfile`
> Start → Run → `winfile`

Description

If you're accustomed to Windows 3.1, you may want to use *winfile* instead of the Explorer, although there are some drawbacks. *winfile* (see Figure 6-12) lets you rename file extensions and delete files without being prompted.

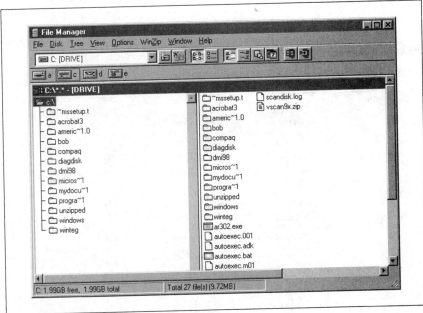

Figure 6-12: Windows 3.1–style file manager (winfile.exe)

Notes

- *winfile* does have limitations that the Explorer doesn't. The most obvious ones are that *winfile* lacks support for long filenames and doesn't support context menus (right-click).

- Although you can select the "Indicate Expandable Branches" option, you can't use the plus and minus sign, as you can in the Explorer.

See Also

"explorer" in Chapter 7

Font Viewer

View TrueType fonts.

To Launch

Address → `fontview [/p]` `<filename.extension>`
Control Panel → Fonts
Double-click on any *.fon* or *.ttf* file

Description

fontview is normally invoked automatically by double-clicking on a font file. If run from the command line, the complete filename of the font, including its extension (such as *.fon* or *.ttf*), must be typed. To print the font information, use the `/p` option.

Examples

View the Times New Roman font (see Figure 6-13):

```
C:\>fontview \windows\fonts\times.ttf
```

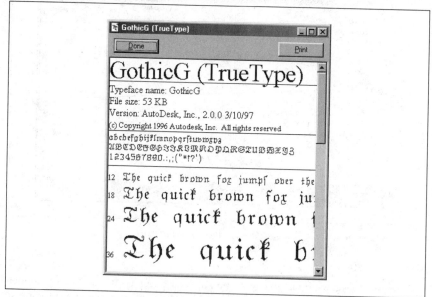

Figure 6-13: TrueType font viewer (fontview.exe)

Notes

- Windows 98 keeps most font files in *Windows**Fonts*.

- *fontview* does not display every character in the font; it only shows some basic information such as the font's copyright notice, the file size, the version, and "The quick brown fox jumps over the lazy dog. 1234567890" in sizes from 12 to 72 points.

- *fontview* is not helpful for special characters. See "Character Map" for a full display of all characters.

See Also

Control Panel → Fonts

FreeCell

\Windows\freecell.exe

A solitaire card game.

To Launch

Address → `freecell`
Start → Run → `freecell`
Start → Programs → Accessories → Games → FreeCell

Description

freecell is a Windows 98 solitaire card game (see Figure 6-14). The object of the game is to move all the cards to the home cells, using the free cells. It feels like a cross between Solitaire and the Towers of Hanoi computer science problem.

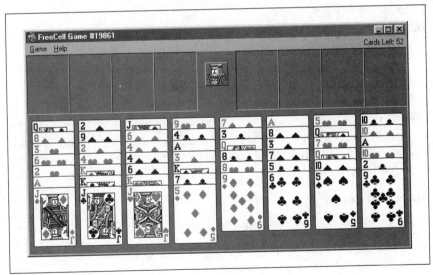

Figure 6-14: FreeCell solitaire game (freecell.exe)

Notes

- In *freecell*, there are 32,000 different instances of the game. *freecell* is unlike *sol* in that, according to the help, "It is believed (although not proven) that every game is winnable." In fact, it has been proven that one game, #11982, is not winnable.

- Another variation of *freecell* is Spider, a classic solitaire game played with two decks of cards. Spider is available with Microsoft Plus! 98.

See also

"Solitaire"

There is an incredibly active FreeCell community on the Web at:

http://www.yahoo.com/Recreation/Games/Computer_ Games/Titles/Strategy/Freecell/

For a catalog of *freecell* solutions:

http://members.aol.com/wgreview/freecell.htm

For FreeCell Plus, which has many more options than *freecell*:

http://www.goodsol.com/freeplus.html

For a web version of FreeCell written in Java:

http://www.cool.com/way/cool/cell/

FrontPage Express   *\Program Files\FrontPage Express\bin\fpxpress.exe*

Create or edit web pages.

To Launch

Address → fpxpress
Start → Run → fpxpress
Start → Programs → Internet Explorer → FrontPage Express
any *.htm* or *.html* file → right-click → Edit (if IE is the default browser)

Description

FrontPage Express (*fpxpress.exe*) lets you create web pages either using a What-You-See-Is-What-You-Get (WYSIWYG) graphical environment or by editing the actual HTML.

WYSIWYG Editing

In the default graphical environment (see Figure 6-15), you can enter content directly onto the page and actually see in real time what the web page will look like when it is viewed in a browser. Figure 6-15 shows the makeup of the "Hotspots" page of the *inkspot.com* web site. A background image provides the split black and white page. Nested tables (represented by dashed lines) help position elements on the page. Text and graphics make up the actual content.

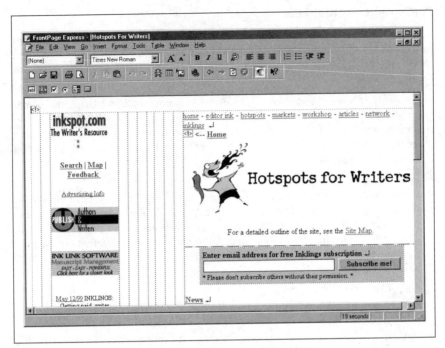

Figure 6-15: File Open results of the inkspot.com "Hotspots" page

FrontPage Express is a feature-packed product and it would be impossible to completely describe it here. However, the next several sections should clue you in to some of the things you can do with FrontPage Express.

Creating, Opening, and Publishing Web Pages

You can create web pages in FrontPage Express starting with either a blank page or with pre-fashioned templates by selecting File → New. Templates are included for creating a survey form and for creating a confirmation page (used to confirm the submission of a form). A form page wizard and a home page wizard are also included. You can open existing web pages in FrontPage Express from your local system or directly from the Internet using File → Open. When you save a new page using FrontPage Express, you can choose to save the page as a file or publish the page to a web server. If you choose to publish, the Web Publishing Wizard (*wpwiz.exe*) walks you through the submission of the page to a web server.

To select *fpexpress* as your default HTML editor even if you use Netscape Navigator as your default browser, use the File Types dialog (see "File Types" in Chapter 4) to change the Edit action for the file type Netscape Hypertext Document to the command `fpexpress.exe %1`.

Putting Stuff on Your Page

You can begin typing text directly onto your page, just as you would with a word processor. Editing the text is just as easy. Highlight the text you wish to edit and choose the font, size, style, color, and justification using the Format toolbar or the Format menu.

You can insert other objects into your web page at any point by placing the cursor there and choosing what you wish to insert using the Insert menu or the corresponding buttons on the toolbar. Use this method to insert pictures, videos, and other types of files and components into your page. Here are some of the things you can insert using this menu:

Insert → Break
> The break dialog contains four options: Normal line break, Clear left margin, Clear right margin, Clear both margins. By default these options apply different attributes of the HTML <br> tag, which insert line breaks into a text flow. If you are interested in changing the <br> tag to a different tag, use the Extended button. For a good HTML reference, see *HTML: The Definitive Guide.*

Insert → Horizontal Line
> Insert a simple horizontal line running the width of the page or table cell.

Insert → Symbol
> Open a dialog from which you can choose any symbol available in the current font.

Insert → Comment
> Let you insert a comment into the HTML code for the page. Comments will not show up in the browser window.

Insert → Image
> Insert an image by specifying a file location or URL. The Image dialog box also includes a Clip Art tab that is apparently a non-functioning hold-over from the full version of FrontPage 97, which ships with web clip art.

Insert → Video
> Insert a video (*.avi* file) by specifying a file location or URL.

Insert → Background Sound
> Insert a sound to play (Wave, MIDI, AIFF, or AU sounds) when the page loads by specifying a file location or URL.

Insert → File
> Insert a file, such as a *.txt* file or another *.htm* file, into your web page.

Insert → WebBot Component
> Insert an automatic component into your page. WebBot components are discussed later in this section.

Insert → Other Components
> Insert components such as ActiveX controls and Java applets. Most of these types of controls will have their own detailed instructions for setting things up.

Insert → Form Field
> Insert Form components. Forms are discussed later in the section.

Insert → Marquee
> Insert a text marquee that scrolls horizontally across the page.

Insert → HTML Markup
> Insert HTML code into the web page. FrontPage Express "massages" the HTML for your page, even if you enter it directly using View → HTML. If you have a snippet of code that needs to remain unchanged, insert it as HTML markup.

Insert → Script
> Insert a JavaScript or VBScript applet into your page. For good reference books on these topics, see *JavaScript: The Definitive Guide* or *Learning VBScript*.

To create a hyperlink (a link to another web page), highlight the text you wish to use as a link (you can also select an image) and choose Insert → Hyperlink. You can also click the Create or Edit Hyperlink button from the Standard toolbar. A dialog box (shown in Figure 6-16) lets you choose an open page to link to, enter a URL, or even create a new page to serve as the link.

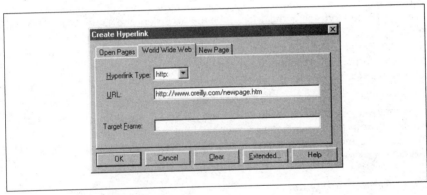

Figure 6-16: Creating a hyperlink

If you enter a URL, you can choose from several different link formats, including:

`http`
> The standard format used to link to another web page.

`https`
> Used to link to a secure web page.

`file`
> File used to link to a file or folder on the local system.

`mailto`
> Used to link to an Internet email address.

If the page you are using is part of a frameset (a web page broken into several frames), you can use the Target Frame field to indicate the name of the frame in which the linked-to page should be loaded.

Modifying the Properties of a Page

View → Page Properties lets you change the basic elements of a page. These elements include such things as the title of the page, a background sound that plays when the page is loaded, a color or image to serve as the background, and page margins. Page Properties → Custom lets you add system and user variables to your page.

Using Tables

Tables are often used in web pages to give you control over page layout that regular HTML just doesn't provide. In the example in Figure 6-15, a large table with two columns provides the main layout for the page. A narrow left column keeps navigation items on the black bar. The wider right column keeps the rest of the page's content on the white background. Additional tables are created within the cell on the right (this is called nesting) to provide the two-column layout of the page.

You can easily create tables using Table → Insert Table. A dialog box opens (see Figure 6-17) that allows you to specify the number of columns and rows you want. When using the Table toolbar button, hold down the button and select the number of rows and columns by dragging the cursor over the squares shown in Figure 6-18 and releasing the mouse button to insert the table. You can also specify other parameters, such as how the table should be aligned on the page (left, center, right), the size of the borders between table cells (0 means no visible border), and the cell padding and spacing. You can also specify the width of the table as a percentage of the width of the whole page or in actual pixels.

Once you define a table, you can modify the properties of individual cells, rows, or columns by right-clicking the area and choosing the appropriate properties command from the pop-up context menu. Along with providing control over the physical placement of items, these Properties pages allow you to assign background colors to cells, rows, columns, or an entire table.

Using WebBot Components

WebBot components provide some automatic functionality that you can include in a web page using Insert → WebBot Component. FrontPage Express comes with three WebBot components:

- The Include component lets you insert the body of another web page into the current page. This feature is great for including elements you want shown on every page of a site, such as a copyright footer, for example. You could create one footer page and use the Include component to include it on other pages in your site. You would then need to make changes only to that single footer page instead of modifying all of your pages.

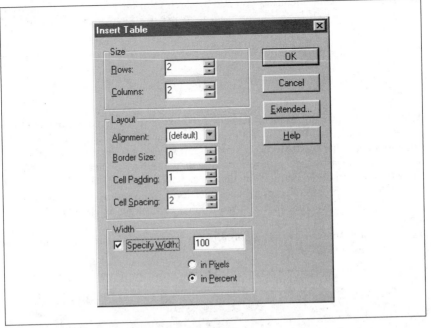

Figure 6-17: Creating a table in FrontPage Express

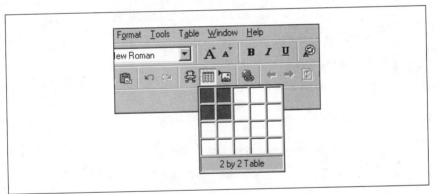

Figure 6-18: Creating a two-row, two-column table using the Table toolbar button

 The Include WebBot component will only work with servers that support FrontPage extensions (e.g., Microsoft IIS). When attempting to use WebBots with servers that don't have the extensions, you will get the following message: "getting URL from Server..." but it will fail to retrieve the page.

- The Search component lets you add a search form for your site to the current page. The search form can be used to search for keywords on all pages of your site.

- The Time Stamp component automatically inserts the time and date that a page was last modified.

Using Forms

A form is usually comprised of several text boxes, check boxes, radio buttons, drop-down menus, and or lists for entering information and buttons for submitting or clearing that information. In FrontPage Express, a form shows up as a box formed with a dashed line (longer dashes than used for indicating a table), as shown in Figure 6-19. Form elements (text boxes, buttons, etc.) are grouped within the form box. You can create a new form by inserting any form element into your web page using Insert → Form Field or clicking an item on the Form toolbar. Once the form is created, you can then add new fields to it in the same manner. You can also create a form using the Form Wizard available when creating a new document.

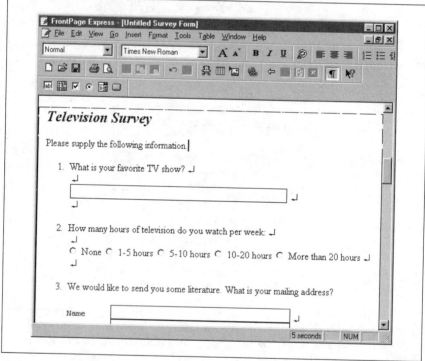

Figure 6-19: Creating forms in FrontPage Express

When users fill in and submit a form using a browser, the information can be submitted to a text file, a database, a custom program, or even emailed to someone. You can make these settings by right-clicking anywhere inside the form box and choosing Form Properties from the context menu. Choose the appropriate form handler (what the information should be submitted to) and make any settings specific to that handler. To save a form submission to a file, for example, you would choose the WebBot Save Results Component as your form handler. Settings for that handler include the location, name, and type of the file to which to save results. Other settings include additional information (such as time and date) to include with the user-entered information and the address of a confirmation page to which a user should be sent after the submission.

In addition to getting properties of the form in general, you can also access properties for particular form fields by right-clicking them and choosing Form Field Properties from the context menu. Settings you can make are usually the name of the field and any initial values the field might contain.

When learning about forms (or any other sort of web design for that matter), one of my favorite techniques is to use FrontPage Express to open a page from the Internet on which someone has already done what I would like to do. I then take a tour through the properties pages of the various form elements to see how that author set things up. This is also a great way of "borrowing" forms from sites to use on your own custom pages. For example, I've set up my own search page that includes the search forms for most of the major search engines all in one handy location.

HTML Editing

FrontPage Express also allows you to directly modify the HTML of a web page, as shown in Figure 6-20. To view and edit the HTML for a page, just select View → HTML.

If you are used to creating your own HTML using a text editor like Notepad, you might consider switching to FrontPage Express for two very good reasons. The first is that when editing HTML, FrontPage Express adds color-coding, indents, and other formats to the HTML to make it easier to work with. HTML tags appear in purple, variables in red, values in blue, and text in black.

The second reason for using FrontPage Express to create your HTML is that you can keep both the HTML view and graphic view open at the same time. Changes you make to the HTML are immediately reflected in the graphical representation. This means no more saving your file and refreshing it in your browser each time you want to see what your changes look like.

 The HTML produced by FrontPage Express (and any other Microsoft applications, such as Word, which allows you to save as HTML) is actually not compliant with the HTML specification, and can cause problems when viewed with non-Microsoft browsers.

Notes

- FrontPage Express has been left out of Windows 98 Second Edition, but you can install it by running Windows Update, which is covered in Chapter 4.

Figure 6-20: Editing HTML directly in FrontPage Express

- FrontPage Express is basically identical to the FrontPage Editor that was part of FrontPage 97. FrontPage 97 (and its successors) includes the additional ability to manage framesets, create image maps, and support Active Server pages. In addition, FP97 adds web site management features and additional WebBot components.

- You can open any page from the Web in FrontPage Express by clicking the Edit button in IE4 or by supplying a URL in the Open dialog of FrontPage Express itself.

- Right-click a hyperlink and choose Follow Hyperlink from the context menu to open the linked-to page in FrontPage Express.

Hearts
\Windows\mshearts.exe

Card game that can played over the network with other Win 98 users.

To Launch

Address → mshearts
Start → Run → mshearts
Start → Programs → Accessories → Games → Hearts

Description

The object of Hearts (see Figure 6-21) is to have the lowest score at the end of the game. Unlike the other games that come with Windows 98, it is designed to be played with other players on a network (although it can also be played as a solitaire game). The online help tells you how to play the game, and provides strategy and tips.

mshearts uses the Network Dynamic Data Exchange (*netdde.exe*) program to share data in memory over a network. Under Windows 98, *netdde* is not automatically started. If you play Hearts over the network on a regular basis, you should create a *netdde.exe* (*\Windows\netdde.exe*) shortcut and place it in the *StartUp* directory (*\Windows\Start Menu\Programs\Startup*) to make Windows 98 start it every time the system boots.

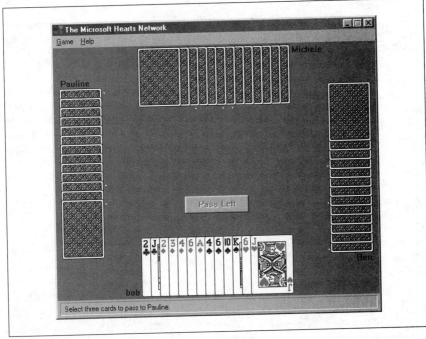

Figure 6-21: Hearts card game (mshearts.exe)

Notes

- To play against the computer (virtual players Pauline, Michele, and Ben), select "I want to be dealer," then press F2 to "begin with current players" rather than "wait for others to join." The game will provide basic directions on how to play.

- Network player versions must be compatible with the dealer's version.

- Microsoft's Internet Gaming Zone web site (*http://www.zone.com/*) has ongoing Hearts games.

See Also

> *http://www.yahoo.com/Recreation/Games/Card_Games/Hearts/*
> *http://www.ccnet.com/~paulp/software/hearts/hearts.htm*

Hyper Terminal   *Program Files\Accessories\Hyper Terminal\hypertrm.exe*

Terminal access to remote computers.

To Launch

> Address → `hypertrm`
> Start → Run → `hypertrm`
> Start → Programs → Accessories → Communication → HyperTerminal

Description

With HyperTerminal and a modem, you can connect to a remote computer that supports terminal access, send and receive files, and so on. This is useful for connecting to computer bulletin boards; however, dial-up terminal access has largely been replaced by the Internet.

HyperTerminal uses connection files and locations similar to those used by Dial-Up Networking. HyperTerminal comes with a number of predefined connections for services such as MCI Mail, CompuServe, and AT&T Mail. You can open one of these existing connections or create a new one. Connections are stored in *.ht* files in the directory *\Program Files\Accessories\HyperTerminal*. HyperTerminal uses the locations and credit card information stored in the *telephon.ini* file, but the actual connections are distinct from those used by Dial-Up Networking. See "Dial-Up Networking" in Chapter 4 for additional details on locations.

Notes

- You'll notice the HyperTerminal folder is opened when navigating through the Start menu and selecting HyperTerminal. This allows you to select and launch preconfigured *.ht* files, thus saving you the trouble of launching *hypertrm.exe* and then opening the *.ht* files you frequently use from within the application.

- To use HyperTerminal with Minitel service, you must install the two Arial Alternative fonts that can be found on the Win 98 CD at: *\tools\reskit\ desktop\minitel*.

- You can get a version of HyperTerminal newer than the default Win 98 version from *http://www.hilgraeve.com/*.

- Network managers use HyperTerminal frequently for connecting to network devices using VT100 emulation (Unix machines, routers, hubs, switches, CSU/ DSUs, etc.).

Imaging   *\Windows\kodakimg.exe*

Read or import different types of image file formats, and scan and store images.

To Launch

> Address → kodakimg
> Start → Run → kodakimg
> Start → Programs → Accessories → Imaging

Description

With *kodakimg.exe*, you can transform any paper or fax-based information into an electronic image document that can be stored, filed, retrieved, edited, printed, faxed, and shared. *kodakimg.exe* can read or import several different types of image file formats, including *.awd* (Microsoft FAX), *.bmp, .dcx, .gif, .jpg, .pcx, .tif, .wif* and *.xif.* Imaging allows you to open and read fax images, but if you need to convert this image to a text file, you will need additional third-party Optical Character Recognition (OCR) software.

You can not only view an image, you can zoom in and out, view certain portions, and even mark up the image with the Annotation Toolbox. The imaging software supports standard black and white, grayscale, and color image documents. The viewing and readability of black and white documents can be significantly enhanced by using the product's scale-to-gray technology (View → Scale to Gray). If you have a scanner, you can use *kodakimg.exe* to create, append, and edit scanned images.

Notes

- If you have a scanner plugged into your computer, you can use Imaging to recognize a scanned image, but more than likely your scanner will have come with third-party software containing greater functionality that can also do this. Before you can scan for the first time, you must specify a scanner with File → Select Scanner. Once you've selected a scanner, you can scan a new document by doing the following:

  1. File → Scan New
  2. Follow the instructions on the screen. See your scanner's help or documentation for more information

  With a new scanned document or an active document on your screen, you can send it as a fax or email by selecting File → Send.

Start Menu Programs

Internet Explorer *\Program Files\Internet Explorer\iexplore.exe*

The Microsoft browser used to access resources on the Web and the local drive. This section describes both IE4 and IE5, plus the IE plugins for Macromedia Shockwave and Flash, Microsoft Wallet, and the VRML Views plugin.

To launch Internet Exporer 4 or 5:

> Address → iexplore
> Start → Run → iexplore
> Start → Programs → Internet Explorer → Internet Explorer
> Click IE Icon in Quick Launch toolbar

Internet Explorer 4

Description

Internet Explorer (IE) 4 is a full-featured browser that can be used to view the Web as well as your local drive. IE recognizes the standard protocol types like *http*, *ftp*, *telnet*, and also the *file* protocol. You can select your mail and news applications at View → Internet Options → Programs, which gives you access to these programs from within IE. Figure 6-22 shows the O'Reilly home page in an Internet Explorer window.

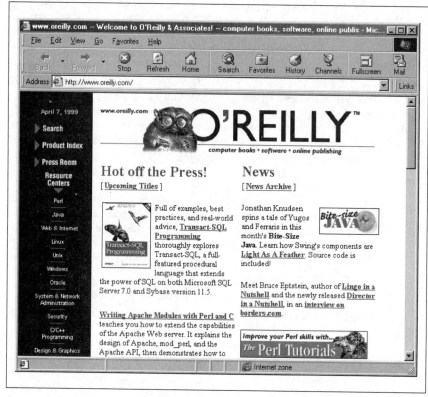

Figure 6-22: The O'Reilly home page viewed with Internet Explorer (iexplore.exe)

In this section, you will find some of the non-obvious highlights about IE 4.

The following syntax can be used from the command line:

```
iexplore [-nohome] [url]
```

−nohome

Starts IE without loading the home page. You can also specify any URL (e.g., *altavista.digital.com*), and it will be loaded instead of the home page.

Notes

- View → Internet Options provides a lot of configurable options for IE and gives you direct access to the Control Panel Internet applet. For instance, it allows you to access the Microsoft Wallet application for storing and receiving your own personal credit card information. See "Internet" in Chapter 5 for details.

- The History Folder stores URLs for up to 20 days. The number of stored days can be altered in View → Internet Options → General, where you can also view or clear the History Folder. Click the History button on the toolbar to place the folder in the left pane of IE.

- The Favorites menu item allows you to store shortcuts, or bookmarks, to your favorite external sites or local drive folders. You can also manage your subscriptions using the Favorites menu. Click the Favorites button on the toolbar to place the folder in the left pane of IE. You can even enable the thumbnail view from the properties sheet of the Favorites folder if you want to view a snapshot of your favorite sites.

- The Forward and Back buttons have a drop-down list feature that lets you quickly move forward or backward, skipping over sites you don't want to load.

- By using the File → Send command, you can send an HTML page or a link by email. Your default mail software will automatically be launched and the information will fill a blank email page. You just have to select the email address and send it on its way.

- The Edit → Page command automatically launches FrontPage Express and loads the HTML source of the page you are browsing.

- IE has an autocompletion feature, which allows you to leave off *http://* and even *www* in your URLs, and the site will still be found and loaded, as long as the site is in the *.com*, *.edu*, or *.org* domain. IE also stores a Most Recently Used (MRU) list of previous sites you've typed in the address bar, and possible matches will show up when typing a similar URL.

- You can view the contents of your hard drive in the IE window and even launch applications. For instance, if you type in \windows, everything in the \Windows directory will be shown.

- You can enter UNC network pathnames into the IE Address line to view any shared folders.

See Also

Chapter 4

For the latest and greatest regarding Internet Explorer:

http://www.microsoft.com/ie/

Additional Internet Explorer 5 Features

The following features are new in Internet Explorer 5 (IE5), which is automatically installed as part of Windows 98 Second Edition. If you are running the first edition of Windows 98, you can upgrade to IE5 (free of charge) by running

Windows Update and choosing the IE5 upgrade, or by downloading it from Microsoft's site at: *http://www.microsoft.com/windows/ie/*.

AutoComplete

Although AutoComplete in IE4 helped finish any URLs you typed from the Address bar, in IE5 there is a new feature that saves previous URLs typed in the Address bar, along with any entries you've typed into web forms, including password entries. When you type information into these fields, AutoComplete suggests matches. Figure 6-23 shows a list of URLs being suggested from the Address bar in IE5.

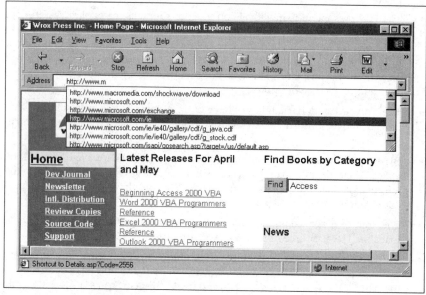

Figure 6-23: The AutoComplete feature in action

The more characters you type in the Address bar, the narrower the list of suggestions will be, until the list disappears. To choose a URL from the list, just use the arrow keys on your keyboard and press enter, or use your mouse.

The AutoComplete options can be configured at Tools → Internet Options → Content → AutoComplete, as shown in Figure 6-24.

In the AutoComplete Settings dialog you can toggle the AutoComplete feature on and off for web addresses, forms, usernames on forms, and passwords. You can also clear the AutoComplete history for forms and passwords using the buttons on this dialog, and you can clear the web address history with a button on the Internet Options → General tab. All of this information is encrypted, so web sites have no way of gaining access to it from your machine.

AutoSearch

In IE4 when you typed a word (e.g., "fool") in the Address bar, the AutoCompletion feature would treat the word as part of a URL and in this example would load

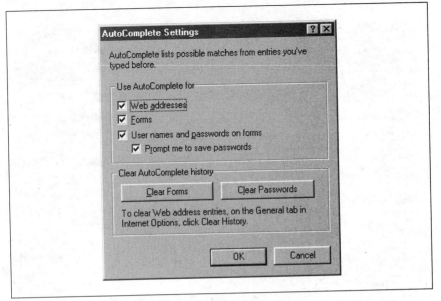

Figure 6-24: AutoComplete settings dialog

http://www.fool.com/. If you switch on the AutoSearch feature in IE5, typing "fool" in the Address Bar will launch the search engine provider selected, return the results in the main window and initiate the Search Bar, as shown in Figure 6-25. So, in essence, using AutoSearch turns the Address Bar into a search engine rather than an autocompletion engine.

There are four different AutoSearch options (see Figure 6-26) that can be configured at Tools → Internet Options → Advanced → Search From The Address Bar:

1. "Display results, and go to the most likely site"

   This option is only available if you select MSN as the search provider. Even if you select the "Display results, and go to the most likely site" option in the Advanced tab of Internet Properties, it won't work unless you've selected MSN as the search provider using the Customize button on the Search bar (see below for details).

   It takes the keywords entered in the Address Bar (in this case "fool"), loads them into the MSN search engine, returns the most likely site in the window, and places a list of URLs of the other likely sites in the Search bar (see Figure 6-23).

2. "Do not search from the Address bar"

   Prevent autosearching from running in the Address Bar.

3. "Just display the results in the main window"

   This option will work with any of the AutoSearch providers.

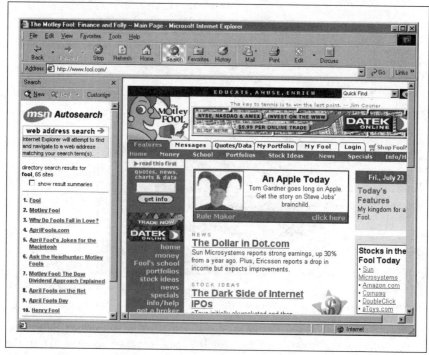

Figure 6-25: The actived Search bar returning the autosearch of "fool"

It returns the results of the keywords typed at the Address bar in the main window (this saves a couple of steps, since normally you'd have to go to the search provider web site and then type in your keywords.)

4. "Just go to the most likely site"

This option only works with MSN configured as the default search provider.

It displays the most likely web page (if one keyword, it usually loads a site with that word in the domain name), but doesn't put any of the links in the Search bar.

The Search bar shown in Figure 6-23 is automatically launched when using Auto-Search from the Address bar. If you click on the Customize button, you are given two main options: "use the search assistant for smart searching" and "use one search service for all searches." These options (shown in Figure 6-26) alter the view of the Search bar. By default, the search assistant option is selected and you can go through the various checkboxes and determine (from the available services) the search engines you'd like to run when looking for URLs, email addresses, businesses, etc. from the Search bar. If you select the one search service option, you will be given a drop-down list of search engines to choose from when using autosearch in the Address Bar. The Next button appears once you've used search engines in the search bar and offers quick access to any other services checked in the customize search settings dialog.

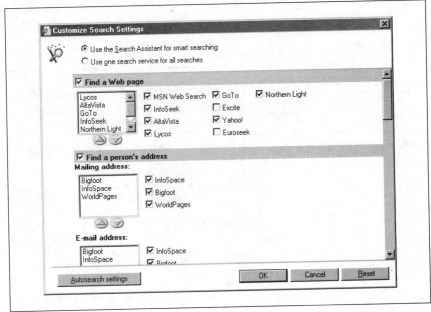

Figure 6-26: Customize Search Settings dialog for the Search bar view

The AutoSearch Settings button launches the Customize Autosearch Settings dialog shown in Figure 6-27. As mentioned, the search provider must be set on MSN in order for Autosearch to really work. Without this setting, you can disable Autosearch or just display the results in the main window. It is still useful to use other search engines with Autosearch and just display the results in the window, since it saves you the time of navigating to those search provider sites and entering a search from their web page.

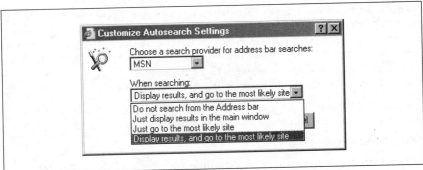

Figure 6-27: Autosearch options when MSN is chosen as the search provider

Related Links

From any web page, you can select the Tools → Show Related Links option. This will open the Search bar filled with a list of related links based on the web page in the window (see Figure 6-28). The Alexa service is generating these links based on contact information received from official Internet Registration organizations around the world. For more information about Alexa, see their web site: *http://www.alexa.com/*.

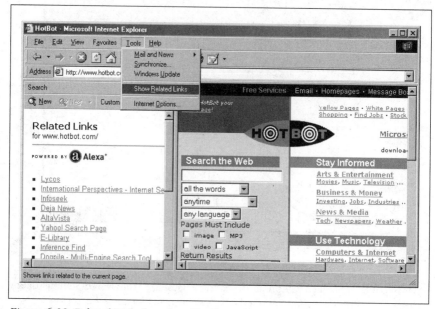

Figure 6-28: Related Links based on HotBot web page in main window

Windows Radio Toolbar

The Radio toolbar is available as long as the Windows Media Player is installed. To launch the Radio toolbar, select View → Toolbars → Radio.

By selecting the Radio Stations drop-down list, you can choose the Radio Station Guide option (see Figure 6-29). This opens the station guide, which has the following URL: *http://webevents.microsoft.com/radio/*. From this station guide, you can enter a zip code that will choose station buttons based on the location. Selecting a button will open the web site for the station, run the audio, and place a shortcut to the station in the Radio Stations drop-down list.

You can add any selected station to the Radio subfolder in the Favorites folder by selecting the "Add Favorites to Station" option in the Radio Stations drop-down list.

Offline Synchronization

You can make any web page shortcut in the Favorites folder available offline by right-clicking on it and choosing the "Make available offline" option. This launches a wizard that walks you through the following options:

1. Make other linked pages available offline. If yes, choose between 1 and 3 links deep, but be careful because this can take up a lot of disk space.

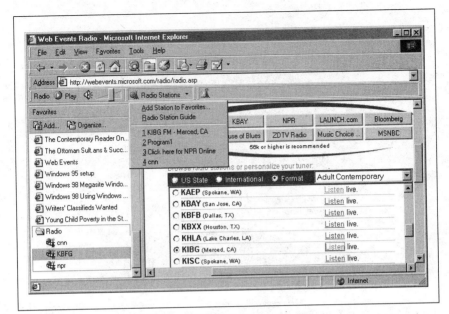

Figure 6-29: Radio Stations drop-down list

2. Select synchronization options. The default option is to only allow synchronization when chosen from the Tools menu. You can create your own schedule, which will take you to a dialog where you can set the synchronization between 1 and 99 days, set the time, and be given the option to automatically connect if you aren't connected to the Internet.

3. Set a password for synchronization or not.

You can require a password to be given before the site can be viewed offline by entering a username and password.

You can configure any of these options from the Properties sheet of the item in the Favorites folder that you've run this wizard on.

Before going offline, you can select Tools → Synchronize, which allows you to set up and synchronize all items on which you've used the offline wizard as well as any CDF items you may have downloaded to the Active Desktop (see Figure 6-30). This will ensure that all of your offline pages are current.

When you're ready to work offline, select File → Work Offline. You can then view any of your offline pages from the Favorites folder (they have the red dot on the corner of the icon, as shown in Figure 6-30). In order to work online again, just select File → Work Offline again.

History Bar

Although IE4 has a History bar that can be toggled on by selecting the History button on the standard toolbar, in IE5 a couple of new features have been added. You can now sort by four different views (Date, Site, Most Visited, and Order

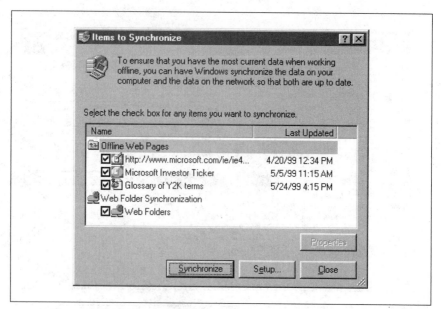

Figure 6-30: Synchronizing data with the Offline Wizard

Visited Today) using the View drop-down list, and you can search for words by selecting the Search button (see Figure 6-31).

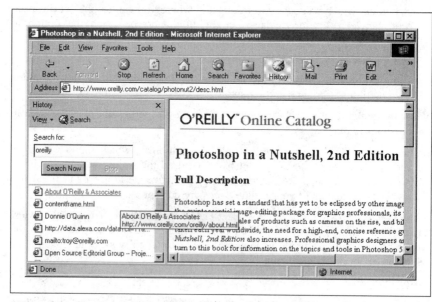

Figure 6-31: The View and Search features in the History bar

Multiple DUN Connections

If you are using dial-up networking to connect to the Internet, launching IE5 without being connected pops up the dial-up connection dialog shown in Figure 6-32. From this dialog you can select an individual connection, which is great if you have multiple locations or numbers that you use dial-up networking with. You can also select the Settings button, which launches the Internet Options Control Panel applet, allowing you to configure the settings of any of your multiple connections. See Chapter 5 for more details on the Internet Options applet.

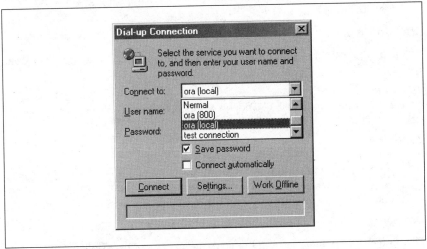

Figure 6-32: Multiple connections for dial-up networking

Macromedia Shockwave Director and Flash Plugins

Play content created with Macromedia Shockwave Flash and Director within Internet Explorer.

To Install
> Add/Remove Programs → Windows Setup → Multimedia → Macromedia Shockwave Director
> Add/Remove Programs → Windows Setup → Multimedia → Macromedia Shockwave Flash

To Launch
> Visit a web site that uses Flash or Director content.

Description

Macromedia Director is an application used to combine graphics, sound, animation, text, and video into interactive presentations. Macromedia Flash is used to create interactive vector-based graphics and animations for the Web. The Shockwave players (both for Director and Flash) can be installed individually with Win 98 setup and are used to play back content created with Director and Flash from within Internet Explorer. You cannot run either as a stand-alone application; they are launched automatically whenever you visit a web page that includes Director or Flash content.

Notes

- Newer versions of the Shockwave players than the one that ships with Win 98 are available for free download both through Windows Update and from *http://www.macromedia.com/*.

- Right-click an embedded Shockwave presentation to open a context menu that provides controls such as rewinding and fast-forwarding, zooming in and out, looping the presentation, and disabling high-quality graphics for faster downloading.

Microsoft Wallet

Lets you automatically submit credit card and addressing information to supported web sites.

To Install
> Add/Remove Programs → Windows Setup → Internet Tools → Microsoft Wallet

To Launch
> Start → Run → `control inetcpl.cpl ,2`
> Visit a supported web site
> IE4 → View → Internet Options → Content → Payments
> Control Panel → Internet → Content → Payments

Description

Microsoft Wallet is similar to the Profile Assistant, except that Wallet stores private financial information, such as credit card numbers and expiration dates. Few sites make full use of the functionality provided by either Profile Assistant or Wallet. This may change in the future, but for now these tools can still be useful just as a convenient location to store these types of information.

See Also
> "Internet" in Chapter 5

VRML 2.0 Viewer

View virtual reality web sites within Internet Explorer.

> Add/Remove Programs → Windows Setup → Internet Tools → Microsoft VRML 2.0 Viewer

To Launch
> Visit a web site that uses VRML.

Description

VRML 2.0 Viewer is used by certain web sites and 3-D chat engines to let you move around and interact with objects in a 3-D environment. VRML viewer cannot be run as a stand-alone app. It is a plug-in that is activated when you visit a web page using VRML, such as shown in Figure 6-33.

Figure 6-33: Moving around in VRML

Controls used for moving around are built into VRML, yet may change for some sites you visit. The VRML navigation device shows up as the blue borders on the left side and bottom of the world shown in Figure 6-33. On the left border are navigation modes. Hover your mouse over any letter to see what it does. Click the letter to enter that mode. Each mode affects the function of the mouse and arrow keys. Modes include:

W   Walk. Move forward/backward and left/right.

P   Pan left/right and up/down without moving.

T   Turn left/right and forward/backward (usually used only for flying).

R   Roll to the left or right (usually used only for flying).

G   Go to the point you click on with the mouse.

S   Study an object that you click on with the mouse.

There are also several controls along the bottom border, including:

Z   Zoom out from the scene.

Up   Straighten up the scene.

V   Click to choose a View to jump to from a pop-up menu. Use left and right arrows to go back and forward through views.

R   Restore the scene.

You can also access the control menu for VRML by right-clicking anywhere within the scene. Context menu items allow you to choose viewpoints and modes (as you would with the navigation controls), select the speed of movement, and select the quality of the graphic display. Lower quality means better performance and higher quality means worse performance.

Use the options command on the context menu to specify advanced options, including whether to use hardware acceleration, whether to load textures for objects (not doing so decreases download times), and how objects should be shaded both when you are and are not moving. Use Options → Worlds → Prevent collisions to prevent bumping into others in worlds that support multiple users.

Notes

- If your cursor turns into a hand when you hover it over a certain object, then clicking on that object will link you another HTML location, VRML file, or viewpoint in the current VRML file.

- A number of VRML environments have been crafted and you can find a number of them through *http://www.microsoft.com/vrml/offworld/*. You can also do a search on "VRML" on your favorite search engine to turn up all kinds of worlds.

- Downloading and manuevering in VRML worlds can really bog down over slow Internet connections, especially in multi-user worlds. You'll likely end up frustrated if you have anything less than a 56K connection to the Internet.

IP Configuration   \Windows\winipcfg.exe

Display the current TCP/IP settings on your computer.

To Launch

    Address → winipcfg
    Start → Run → winipcfg

Description

winipcfg displays TCP/IP configuration information from your computer (see Figure 6-35). It also allows you to release or renew a dynamically allocated IP address. With no arguments, *winipcfg* displays the dialox box shown in Figure 6-34. New to Windows 98 is the command-line equivalent, *ipconfig*. The same command-line options available in *ipconfig* are also available in *winipcfg*. Rather than duplicating those here, you can find a complete listing in Chapter 7.

Notes

- *winipcfg* is useful if you have two different ways of connecting to a network. For example, you might have two different kinds of modems (e.g., one ISDN or cable) for connecting to two different kinds of networks, or you might dial in on your laptop, and then connect it directly at the office. After you've used one, you need to clear the cache of network info in order to use the other without rebooting Windows. This is done by clicking "Release All" and then "Renew All."

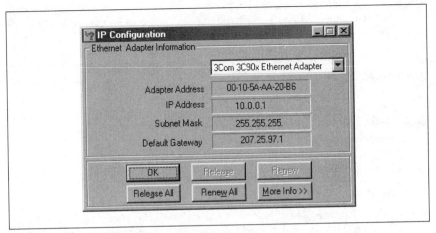

Figure 6-34: IP Configuration (winipcfg.exe)

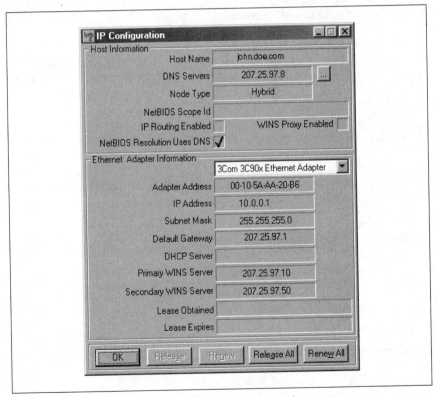

Figure 6-35: IP Configuration with More Info>> selected

- For more information on IP configuration values, see "Network" in Chapter 5. The Lease Obtained and Lease Expired fields will contain data only if you are using DHCP.

Maintenance Wizard   \ *Windows\tuneup.exe*

Lets you schedule maintenance tasks on your system.

To Launch

> Address → tuneup
> Start → Run → tuneup
> Start → Programs → Accessories → System Tools → Maintenance Wizard

Description

Maintenance Wizard is basically a convenient way of scheduling four tasks: defrag, scandisk, disk cleanup, and compression agent. The wizard steps you through setting up the times at which each task should be run and specifying options for running each task. The options you can set are the same as the options available when running the utilities manually.

Notes

- In addition to scheduling these tasks, *tuneup.exe* also lets you specify which programs in your startup folder should be run each time you start up. A better way of doing this, however, is with the System Configuration Utility, which is discussed in Chapter 12, *Windows Startup*.

- Once you have set up your programs, subsequent launchings of *tuneup.exe* will let you either adjust your current settings using the wizard or run all of the tasks right now.

- You can start and run all scheduled tasks in succession using Start → Run → tuneup /autorun. This also can be done using a batch file in the *C:\ Windows\Start Menu\Programs\Startup* directly (see Chapter 11 for details on creating batch files).

See Also

> "ScanDisk"
> "Disk Defragmenter"
> "Disk Cleanup"

Make Compatible   \ *Windows\System\mkcompat.exe*

Change settings to make a Win 3.1 program compatible with Win 98.

To Launch

> Address → mkcompat
> Start → Run → mkcompat

Description

mkcompat.exe lets you change settings to try to make a poorly behaving Win 3.1 program compatible with Windows 98. When run, it will display a list of five checkboxes corresponding to common problems with Windows 3.1 programs. *mkcompat* uses these options to activate switches in the Win 3.1 program (after you save the option(s)) to trick Windows 98 into running the program.

To use *mkcompat* when the *mkcompat* window is displayed:

1. Select File → Choose Program, and navigate to the application you want to affect.

2. Check any of the following options that seem applicable to the Win 3.1 problem you're having:

   – Don't spool to enhanced meta files

   – Give application more stack space

   – Lie about printer device mode size

   – Lie about Windows version number

   – Win 3.1–style controls

3. Select File → Save

4. Try running the modified file. If none of the options seems to work, you can load the application in *mkcompat* again and select File → Advanced Options. This will provide you with a lot more options (see Figure 6-36).

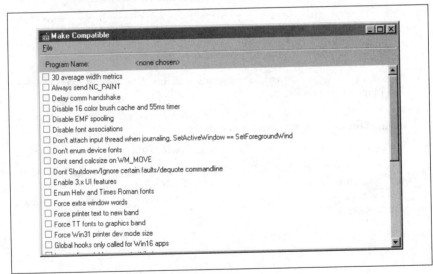

Figure 6-36: Some advanced options for mkcompat.exe

Note

Use with caution!

Media Player

Windows\mplayer.exe

Windows 98 multimedia player.

To Launch

> Address → mplayer
> Start → Run → mplayer
> Start → Programs → Accessories → Entertainment → Media Player

Description

mplayer is the default media player (version 4) that comes with Windows 98 (see Figure 6-37). With *mplayer* you can play the following types of files: ActiveMovie, *.avi* (Video for Windows), *.wav* (sound), *.mid* or *.rmi* (MIDI, or Musical Instruments Digital Interface), and *.cda* (audio CDs). You can launch *mplayer* and then open any of these types of files, or by default Media Player will be launched when you double-click on them.

Figure 6-37: The Windows 98 multimedia player (mplayer.exe)

Notes

- All sorts of songs recorded as *.mid* files can be downloaded from the Web and played by *mplayer*.

- Any files playable by *mplayer* can be inserted as objects into a WordPad document, and then run from within WordPad.

- With Edit → Options, you can set the auto-rewind and auto-repeat features.

- The newest version, Media Player 6.0, also plays the following file types: *.asf*, *.ra*, *.rm*, *.mp3*, *.mov*, and *.vod*, and contains a Favorites menu. Use Windows Update or download from *http://www.microsoft.com/windows/windowsmedia/*.

See Also

> *wordpad*

Microsoft Chat

Windows\cchat.exe

Conduct chat sessions over the Internet.

To Install

Control Panel → Add/Remove Programs → Windows Setup →
Communications → Microsoft Chat

To Launch

Address → cchat
Start → Run → cchat
Start → Programs → Internet Explorer → Microsoft Chat

Description

Microsoft Chat is a graphical client that allows you to conduct chat sessions with
other users over the Internet using IRC (Internet Relay Chat) servers. *cchat* uses a
unique "comic strip" style to show the chat, as shown in Figure 6-38. When you
launch *cchat*, by default the File → New Connection dialog box appears and you
can either choose Microsoft Chat Server from the list or type in another known
comic chat server address. It's possible to chat with members on different plat-
forms connected to the Internet who aren't using Microsoft Chat. Be sure to click
the "Don't Send Microsoft Chat Specific Information" checkbox on the View →
Options → Settings tab if this is the case before connecting to the chat server so
you don't send them comic-specific messages.

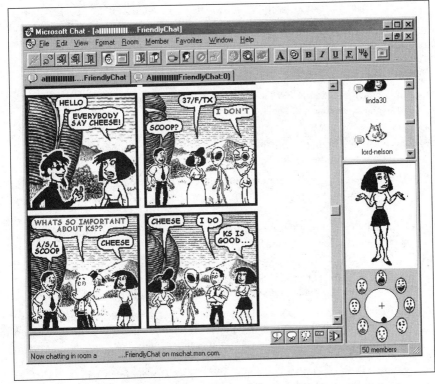

Figure 6-38: cchat's unique comic-strip style of chat

Before connecting to a chat server, you should select your character if you plan to chat in a comic strip. To choose a character, click the View → Options → Character tab and select a character from the list. You can choose an emotion at this time, or you can select different emotions while you chat to better convey your intended meaning. To chat in a comic strip rather than in text, select View → Comic Strip. You will then have the options to say, think, whisper, or play a sound when chatting and have this displayed in a comic strip rather than just straight text. If you select another character in a live comic chat before you "say" something, your character will appear in the comic strip talking directly to that character.

To begin a chat session, select File → New Connection and choose one of the default Microsoft chat servers (e.g., *mschat.msn.com*) or enter a known chat server address. Note how you can change your Personal Info, Character, and Background information in the tabs on the connection dialog before you connect to a chat server. Keep in mind that this information will be available to other chat users once you begin a chat session. Once you are connected to the server, you can enter, leave, or even create your own rooms using the following commands respectively: Room → Enter Room, Room → Leave Room, or Room → Create Room. If you add a room to your Favorites directory, it will then be available on the connection dialog.

Microsoft Chat 2.1 comes with Windows 98, but Windows 98 Second Edition contains the newer 2.5 version. You can, however, use Windows Update to upgrade to the 2.5 version if you are running Windows 98. See some of the Notes later in this section for details about the new 2.5 features.

Notes

- In Windows 98 Second Edition, the Start Menu shortcut is Start → Programs → Accessories → Internet Tools → Microsoft Chat.

- The View → Options → Comics View tab allows you to change the number of comic strip panels to horizontally display in the chat window. The default is two panes, and the maximum is four.

- The View → Options → Setttings tab allows you to set the directory you want sound files to be available from when chatting. The default directory is \ *Windows\Media*, and the sound must be a *.wav* file.

- You can chat in more than one room at a time by launching extra instances of Microsoft Chat for each room.

- You can create macros to pre-set text for messages in the View → Options → Automation tab. Set a key combination (e.g., Alt+T) so you can "call" the message during a chat session.

- Microsoft Chat 2.5 supports a large number of IRC and IRCX commands and surpasses version 2.1 with new features like automation rules, private sound and action, and login notification capabilities (see *http://support.microsoft. com/support/kb/articles/q187/9/91.asp* for access to these new commands and features). You can upgrade using the Windows Update feature in Windows 98 (*http://windowsupdate.microsoft.com/*) or connect directly to the chat site listed in the See Also section.

- Using Chat 2.5, you can download new characters from any room you chat in. To automatically download all new characters, select the View → Options → Comics View → "Automatically download characters you don't have" checkbox.

- With Chat 2.5, you can find out who is in a chat room before you join by selecting Room → Room List → *select a room* → List Members button.

- Chat 2.5 allows you to privately send a message to a specific person, rather than the entire chat room. Select the person you want to "whisper" to by clicking on their character, the select Member → Whisper Box and type your message.

See Also

For V-Chat 3D online interactive chatting:

http://www.microsoft.com/windows/ie/chat/

Microsoft NetMeeting
\Program Files\NetMeeting\conf.exe

Let users collaborate and share information in real time over a network or the Internet.

To Launch

    Address → conf
    Start → Run → conf
    Start → Programs → Internet Explorer → Microsoft NetMeeting

Description

NetMeeting allows multiple users to collaborate and share information by connecting to an Internet Locator Server (such as *ils.microsoft.com*) or by connecting directly to another user's IP address.

Internet Locator Server is a directory server designed by Microsoft that allows users to host meetings and allows other users to view a directory of all the users on the server, similar to the way a chat server works. You can browse the directory of users and join any meetings they are hosting. ILS 2.0 is part of Microsoft Site Server and is also available for free download from *http://www.microsoft.com/ downloads/*, if you are interested in running your own server on the Internet or a local network. When you first run NetMeeting, you can choose from a list of popular ILSs to which to connect (most are run by Microsoft). Once connected, the NetMeeting directory view (shown in Figure 6-39) lists users that are hosting meetings on the server.

You can also use NetMeeting without connecting to an ILS. One person must host a meeting and multiple other users can then join the meeting by manually entering the hosting member's IP address.

Regardless of whether you connect using an ILS or directly using IP addresses, one user hosts a meeting and others join. Members can then talk (with audio and video), transfer data, chat, collaborate over a whiteboard, and even share an application. Audio levels are configured with a wizard the first time you start

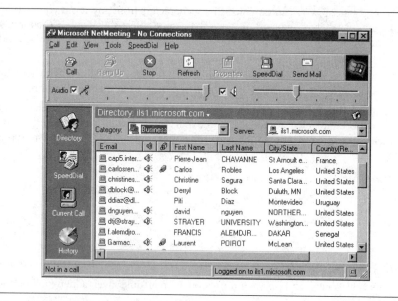

Figure 6-39: ILS directory view

NetMeeting. Any microphone set up correctly in Win 98 is fine. You can adjust levels later using Tools → Audio Tuning Wizard. Video devices are detected automatically if they are set up in Win 98. You can choose an available video device in NetMeeting using Tools → Options → Video.

From the main window, you can host a new meeting using Call → Host Meeting. You can join a meeting in progress either by selecting a user from the directory view (shown in Figure 6-39) or by using Call → New Call, which opens a separate dialog that lets you enter the IP address or name of the computer you wish to call. If you are connecting over a LAN, the computer name should work fine. If you are connecting over the Internet, you will need to use the IP address of the person hosting the call. The host can find out the IP address using *winipcfg* or *ipconfig*.

Whether you host or join a call, the call window then becomes active, as shown in Figure 6-40.

Application Sharing

While in the call window, any member can share a running application using Tools → Share Application → any_running_application. Other members can then see the application and any actions the sharing user takes within that application. The sharing member can also pass control of the application to other members. Any member with control of the application can paste information into the app from their local clipboard. Best of all, only the user sharing the application needs to have it actually installed on his or her system.

Whiteboard

An area where users can share information graphically (see Figure 6-41). The whiteboard looks much like a standard graphics program and allows users to

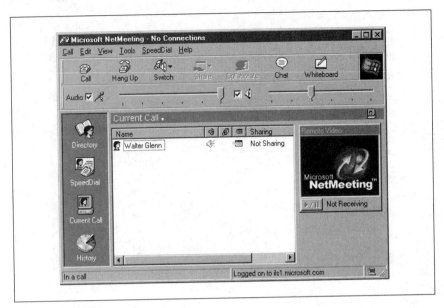

Figure 6-40: Call view

collaborate by drawing or creating predefined objects. Users can also paste areas or whole windows from other apps into the whiteboard as a basis for collaboration. There is one difference between the whiteboard and regular graphics applications, however. The whiteboard is object-based instead of pixel-based, meaning that once graphic objects are created, members can then drag them to new locations, if desired.

File Transfer

Allows a user to send files to other members in a meeting. You can send a file using Tools → File Transfer → Send File. A dialog opens that allows you to specify the file and the members who should receive it. You can also send a file to all members by simply dragging the file into the call window. Once a file is sent, other members can individually accept or decline the transfer.

Chat

Lets users communicate by typing messages in a traditional chat client. This is useful if you do not have audio support. Chat can also be a great way to dynamically record meetings. One user can enter meeting notes into the chat window (which is separate from the main NetMeeting window) and have those notes sent to each member, who can then review at any time what has already been discussed. Once the meeting is over, you can save the chat record as a standard .txt file.

Notes

- In Windows 98 Second Edition, the shortcut is Start → Programs → Accessories → Internet Tools → NetMeeting.

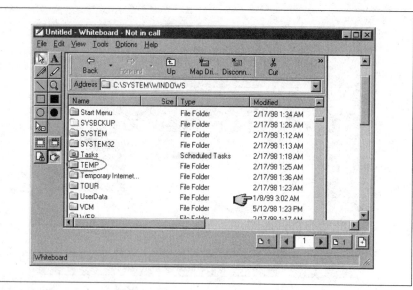

Figure 6-41: NetMeeting Whiteboard

- NetMeeting sets up your audio levels the first time you run it, so it's best to have your microphone ready to go before you install it. You can also adjust these levels later using Tools → Audio Tuning Wizard.

- If you want NetMeeting to run automatically when you start Windows, select Tools → Options → General → Run when Windows starts. This will also set NetMeeting to alert you of incoming calls. The other thing you will need to do is set NetMeeting to automatically log onto an ILS server using Tools → Options → Calling → Log onto directory server when NetMeeting starts.

- When you are in a meeting where multiple members use audio and/or video, you can switch to the specific member you want to hear or see using Tools → Switch Audio and Video → *any connection*.

- Windows 98 Second Edition comes with NetMeeting 3.0, which has the following new features:

  - Use local and remote address books to find and call people

  - Send and receive encrypted data and protect a meeting with a password

  - Share the desktop remotely, and share one document among several meeting participants

  You can use Windows Update to upgrade to NetMeeting 3.0 if you are using Windows 98.

See Also

"Internet" in Chapter 5
"Network" in Chapter 5
"Windows Update" in Chapter 4
"setup" in Chapter 7

Minesweeper

Minesweeper game.

To Install

Minesweeper should be installed by default, but if not:

Add/Remove Programs → Windows Setup → Accessories → Games

To Launch

Address → winmine
Start → Run → winmine
Start → Programs → Accessories → Games → Minesweeper

Description

The object of Minesweeper (Figure 6-42) is to uncover "safe" areas on a playing field, without stepping on any landmines.

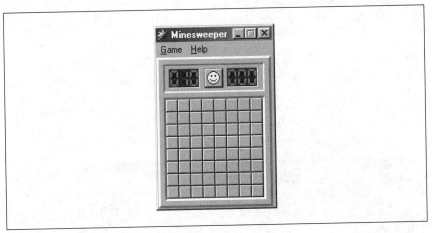

Figure 6-42: Minesweeper game (winmine.exe)

Use the left mouse button to uncover squares. Use the right mouse button to mark squares.

Associated Files

\Windows\winmine.ini

Notes

- The beginner game uses an 8 × 8 grid with 10 mines; intermediate uses a 16 × 16 grid with 40 mines; expert uses a 30 × 16 grid with 99 mines. You can also create custom games, such as an easy 30 × 30 grid with only 10 mines, or a difficult 8 × 8 grid with 60 mines.

- If a number appears on a square, it specifies how many mines are in the eight squares that surround the numbered square.

See Also

See the Yahoo! Minesweeper page:

> *http://www.yahoo.com/Recreation/Games/Computer_Games/Titles/
> Strategy/Minesweeper/*

A web-based Java version is available at:

> *http://www-mtl.mit.edu/~aarong/java/Minesweeper.html*

Net Watcher   *\Windows\netwatch.exe*

View users connected to your shared directories.

To Install

Add/Remove Programs → Windows Setup → System Tools → Net Watcher

To Launch

Address → `netwatch`
Start → Run → `netwatch`
Start → Programs → Accessories → System Tools → Net Watcher

Description

netwatch is a very useful tool if you have shared directories that are being
accessed. By running Net Watcher, you won't have to guess about who is
connected to your shared drives. You will be given this information automatically,
along with lots of other details (see Figure 6-43).

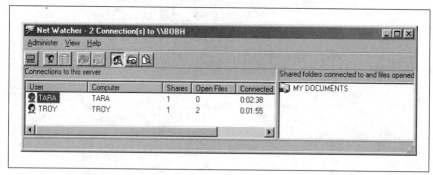

Figure 6-43: Net Watcher list of connected users (netwatch.exe)

There are three different view options in *netwatch*:

1. By connections

   Displays the username, computer name, number of shared directories, open
   files, connected time, and idle time. You can disconnect a user when in this
   view.

2. By shared folders

Displays the folder name, "shared as" name, access type (full, depends on password, etc.), and comment. You can add a shared folder when in this view.

3. By open files

Displays the open filename, the name of the directory being shared, the username that is accessing the file, and the open mode (e.g., Read/Write). You can close a selected file when in this view.

Note

If there is a server to which you have access that you'd like to administer with Net Watcher, select Administer → Select Server, and provide the information.

NetShow Player 2.0 \Program Files\Microsoft NetShow\Player\nsplayer.exe

View streaming multimedia content over a network or the Internet.

To Install

Add/Remove Programs → Windows Setup → Multimedia → Microsoft NetShow Player 2.0

To Launch

Address → nsplayer
Start → Run → nsplayer
Visit a URL with embedded NetShow content
Start → Programs → Internet Explorer → NetShow Player

Description

NetShow Player is the client side of the NetShow platform, which is used for streaming multimedia content (formatted in Advanced Streaming Format, or ASF) over networks. NetShow Player can be used in two ways. The first way is as a stand-alone application (see Figure 6-44), in which you can play local *.asf* files or designate a URL for a remote *.asf* file.

The second way NetShow Player is used is as an embedded application in a web page. In this case, NetShow Player actually runs within the IE4 browser window whenever you visit a URL with NetShow content. Most of the same controls are available in the browser window as in the stand-alone NetShow application.

Notes

- Since the release of Win 98, NetShow Player has been largely replaced by the new Windows Media Player, which you can download for free using Windows Update. Media Player includes support for *.asf* files and many other media formats, such as WAV, AVI, MPEG, and QuickTime.

- If you are using Netscape Navigator, you will not be able to view embedded NetShow content using the NetShow Player that comes with Windows 98. Instead, you will need to download the latest version of NetShow from Win-

Figure 6-44: Viewing streaming media with NetShow Player (nsplayer.exe)

dows Update (Start → Windows Update) or from *http://www.microsoft.com/netshow/*.

- If you are experiencing poor-quality playback using NetShow, you can try increasing the buffer by using File → Properties → Advanced → Buffer *x* seconds of data. Try increasing the value from the default 3 seconds to around 10 seconds.

- If vertical marks appear under the slider bar for a particular *.asf* file, it means that markers have been set in the file that allow you to jump to a specified point in the presentation. Hover your mouse over a marker to see a pop-up description of it.

Notepad

\Windows\notepad.exe

Edit ASCII text files.

To Launch

Address → notepad [/p] [*filename*]
Start → Run → notepad [/p] [*filename*]
Start → Program → Accessories → Notepad

Description

By default, Win 98 is set up so that double-clicking on a *.txt* file runs Notepad (see Figure 6-45). Notepad is also launched by default with other files such as *.bat* and *.inf.*

Notepad handles files only up to 57K. If you try to use it to open a larger file, the following message will appear: "This file is too large for Notepad to open. Would you like to use WordPad to read this file?" Press the Yes button to launch w*ordpad.*

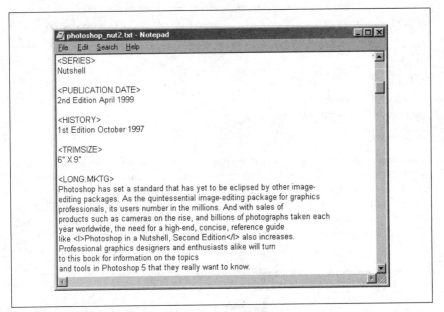

<SERIES>
Nutshell

<PUBLICATION.DATE>
2nd Edition April 1999

<HISTORY>
1st Edition October 1997

<TRIMSIZE>
6" X 9"

<LONG.MKTG>
Photoshop has set a standard that has yet to be eclipsed by other image-
editing packages. As the quintessential image-editing package for graphics
professionals, its users number in the millions. And with sales of
products such as cameras on the rise, and billions of photographs taken each
year worldwide, the need for a high-end, concise, reference guide
like <I>Photoshop in a Nutshell, Second Edition</I> also increases.
Professional graphics designers and enthusiasts alike will turn
to this book for information on the topics
and tools in Photoshop 5 that they really want to know.

Figure 6-45: Notepad ASCII text editor (notepad.exe)

notepad accepts the following option:

/p   Prints the file without opening an editing window. This option is used to
create the print action on the context menu for many file types, such as *.txt*,
.bat, and *.inf*.

Notes

- Notepad is a very small program, so it loads faster than WordPad or Word.

- F5 places a date/time stamp at the current cursor location. This makes Notepad handy for keeping logs of telephone calls (start, stop time).

- The Word Wrap feature (Edit → Word Wrap) will reformat long lines so that
they are visible in the Notepad window without horizontal scrolling. Unfortunately, this option must be reset each time you use Notepad.

- If you type *.LOG* (must be uppercase) as the first line in a text file, Notepad
will put the time and date at the bottom of the file (with the cursor right
below it) every time you open that file.

See Also

"edit" in Chapter 7
"WordPad"

For a good third-party editor, try UltraEdit-32:

http://www.ultraedit.com/

Object Packager

Create "packages" for insertion into documents via object linking or embedding
(OLE).

To Launch

Address → packager
Start → Run → packager

Description

A package displays as an icon that represents a file, part of a file, or an executable command. This makes it possible to create "executable menu" documents
containing icons that, when clicked, run various commands. Most of the functionality provided by Object Packager is available without explicitly running the
program. For example, in WordPad, you can insert various types of objects into a
document by dragging and dropping or with Insert → Object (see Figure 6-46).

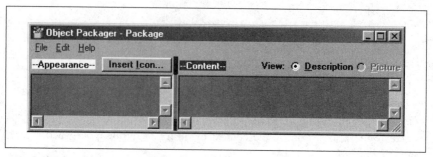

Figure 6-46: OLE package creation (packager.exe)

In particular, you can insert links to executable files into documents, so that when
the reader double-clicks on an icon representing the link, Windows 98 runs the
executable file. Such executable menu documents can be created from within any
OLE-enabled program, including WordPad.

However, some programs allow you to insert a file, but don't provide any place
for you to specify a command line to that file. You could insert an object representing *command.com*, for example, but not command.com /c dir, or *control.
exe* but not control.exe timedate.cpl ,1.

This is one area in which *packager* is essential. If you right-click on a newly
inserted object and select Package Object → Edit Package from the context menu,
Windows 98 will run *packager*. You can then select Object Packager's Edit →
Command Line menu item, and give the object a full command line, including
options such as /c dir.

Notes

- If you run *packager* explicitly after assembling a package, you can then select
  Edit → Copy Package to copy the package to the Windows 98 clipboard. You
  can then switch to another application and insert the package via Paste
  (Ctrl-V). The Object Packager window is split into two panes: the Appear-

ance window displays the icon that will represent the package you insert, and the Content window displays the name of the document that contains the information you want to insert.

- To create a package, copy the contents of the Appearance and Content windows and paste the information into a document. The package appears in the document as an icon.

- If the package contains a sound or animation file, the sound or animation will play. If the package contains a picture, text, or spreadsheet, the program associated with that file type will open, displaying the information. For example, if the package contains a bitmap, *mspaint* opens (default setting), displaying the picture.

See Also

"Paint" and "WordPad"

Outlook Express   *\Program Files\Outlook Express\msimn.exe*

An Internet mail client and newsreader.

To Install

Add/Remove Programs → Windows Setup → Outlook Express

To Launch

Address → `msimn`
Start → Run → `msimn`
Double-click the Outlook Express icon on the Desktop
Quick Launch Bar → "Launch Outlook Express"
Start → Programs → Internet Explorer → Outlook Express

Description

Outlook Express (*msimn.exe*) is the default email client installed with Windows 98 (see Figure 6-47). It uses either the Post Office Protocol 3 (POP3) or the Internet Message Access Protocol 4 (IMAP4) Internet mail protocols to receive mail and the Simple Mail Transfer Protocol (SMTP) to send mail. Most Internet Service Providers (like AOL, Netcom, and even local ISPs) use POP3 and SMTP for mail transfer. Outlook Express also functions as a newsreader for participating in Internet newsgroups.

Outlook Express installs automatically with Windows 98. The first time you run it, you'll be asked where you wish to store mail and news data. If your system is set up to run with a single user, the default data path is *\Windows\Application Data\Microsoft\Outlook Express*. If your system is set up for multiple users, the default path is *\Windows\Profiles\user_name\Application Data\Microsoft\Outlook Express*.

Since it would require more space than we have here to cover Outlook Express in detail (and since much of its use is fairly intuitive, anyway), this section shows you some of the general locations within the Program that will be useful to you.

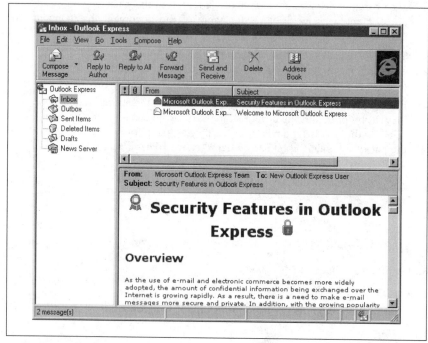

Figure 6-47: Outlook Express (msimn.exe)

Tools → Accounts

The first time you run Outlook Express, the Internet Connection Wizard will also automatically run to step you through setting up your first mail account. Outlook Express supports the use of multiple mail and news accounts. Once the program starts, you can set up additional accounts using Tools → Accounts → Add → Mail to run the wizard again. Choosing Tools → Accounts → Add → News runs a wizard that lets you configure a news account. Once your accounts are set up, you can configure them at any time using Tools → Accounts, as shown in Figure 6-48.

You can access the properties for any account by double-clicking it. Account properties let you set things like your name and email address, server information, what Dial-Up or networking connection to use, advanced security, and some other advanced features. Figure 6-49 shows the Servers tab of a mail account's properties.

Tools → Address Book

The Address Book is great for storing names and information for those people you send email to on a regular basis. You can create aliases, store phone numbers in the Business tab so they can be viewed from the Address Book list, and, when creating a new message, you can select the To, Cc, or Bc button to launch the Address Book.

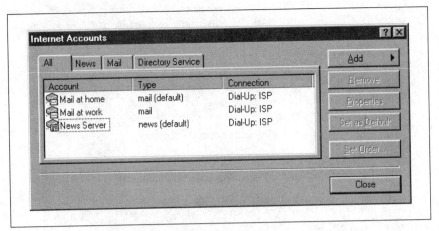

Figure 6-48: Managing Outlook Express accounts

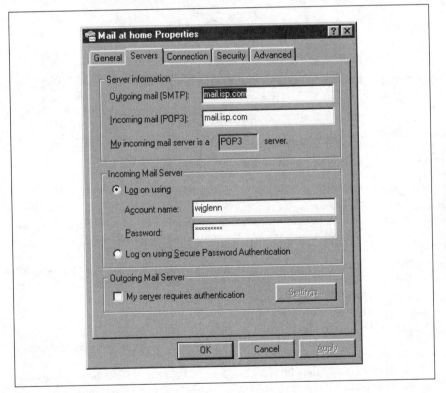

Figure 6-49: Viewing account properties

Tools → Inbox Assistant

The Inbox Assistant is used to apply a certain set of actions to incoming messages that meet specified criteria. The example shown in Figure 6-50 causes Inbox Assistant to move all messages whose subject line contains the words "get," "rich," and "quick" directly to the Deleted Items folder as soon as they are downloaded.

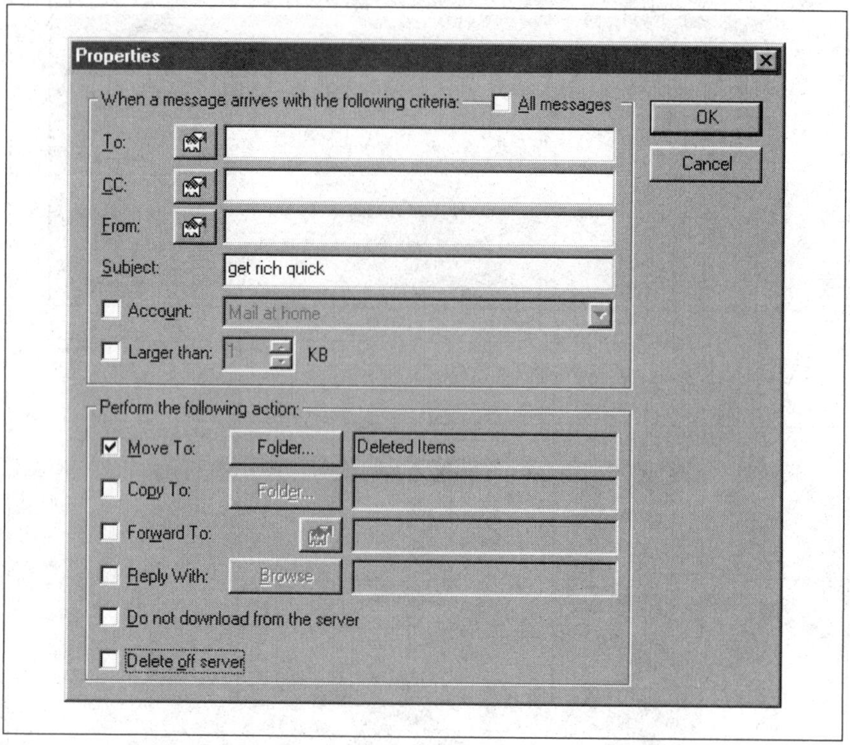

Figure 6-50: Creating inbox rules

Tools → Newsgroup Filters

It can sometimes be annoying wading through the thousands of messages that can exist in a single newsgroup. Newsgroup filters let you weed out some of the extraneous messages. You can specify that postings not be displayed if they are from certain people (in Usenet parlance, this is referred to as a "bozo filter"), contain certain words in the subject, are over a certain length, or are over a certain age.

Tools → Options

Specify options that govern the behavior of Outlook Express and apply to all mail and news accounts (see Figure 6-51). This is where you control things like how often Outlook Express checks for mail when it's running and whether it is the default email program. The Dial Up tab lets you specify whether a connection is dialed automatically when you start Outlook Express, whether it should hang up after getting your messages, and whether it should dial automatically when you do a Send and Receive.

The name *msimn.exe* gives a taste of the history of this program. Originally called Microsoft Internet Mail and News, it was renamed Outlook Express to position it

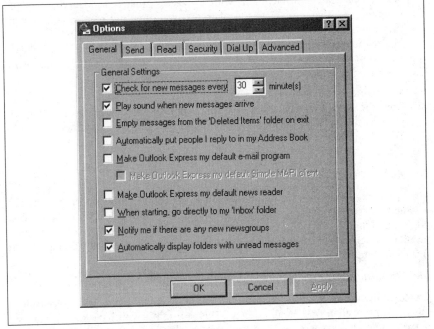

Figure 6-51: Configuring Outlook Express options

as the "lite" version of Microsoft's Outlook application. In fact, the two programs share nothing but the name.

Notes

- By default, Outlook Express automatically compacts your mail and news files when it detects that 20% of your storage space is being wasted. You can adjust this percentage using Tools → Options → Advanced → "Compact files when...". You can also click Clean Up Now to perform the compression whenever you want.

- Outlook Express is not a MAPI-compatible application and therefore will not support extra services such as Microsoft Fax. For that, you will need to use Windows Messaging (see Chapter 4) or the full version of Outlook.

- If you access the same account from two computers, you may wish to set one computer up to download messages, but not delete them from the server. Set up your other system to delete messages after downloading them. This way, one system always has a complete set of messages. Do this using Tools → Accounts → *any account* → Properties → Advanced → Leave a copy of messages on server.

- If you have multiple accounts set up and do not want one included when you click Send and Receive, go to Tools → Accounts → *any account* → Properties → General and deselect "Include this account when doing a full Send and Receive."

- When you send an attachment with a message that is formatted in HTML, recipients who view messages in plain text will often not receive your attachments intact. If you are having this problem, use Tools → Options → Send → Mail Sending Format → Plain Text to specify that messages be sent in plain text format. You can also change the format for an individual message using that message window's Format menu.

- To include a file attachment with a message, use Insert → File Attachment from the New Message window when composing a new message. You can also do this by right-clicking a file in Windows Explorer and choosing Send To → Mail Recipient from the file's context menu. This launches a blank New Message window with the file attachment included.

Outlook Express 5 Features

The following features are new to Outlook Express 5, which is automatically installed as part of the Windows 98 Second Edition. If you are running the first edition of Windows 98, you can upgrade to Outlook Express 5 (free of charge) by installing Internet Explorer 5. (Outlook Express 5 is automatically installed with IE5.) See "Internet Explorer" for details.

Identity Management

Create numerous individual accounts or create multiple accounts for yourself if you have more than one email address. This is useful if you have more than one person using Outlook Express 5 on the same machine.

Multiple identities are also a good way to foil spammers. Use one mail account to communicate with friends and business associates, and another for use on mailing lists or anywhere that the address might be harvested by spammers.

To add a new identity, select File → Identities → Add New Identity (see Figure 6-52). You can then enter the name of the new user and select a password if you want to. To later change identity settings, select File → Identities → Manage Identities (see Figure 6-53). Use the Properties button to change your identity name or password. You can change the startup identity by selecting an identity in the "Start up using" drop-down list. To switch identities at any time, select File → Switch Identity. The first time you switch to the new identity, a wizard will prompt you to configure Internet setup information.

To share contacts in your Address Book between identities, open the Address Book and select View → Folders and groups. To make a contact available to other identities, place it in the Shared Contacts folder (shown in Figure 6-54). You may want to copy a contact to the Shared Contacts folder, but any changes made to the original contact won't be updated in the Shared Contacts folder. In other words, the contacts will be separated and no synching will occur between them.

Improved Sorting and Filtering

Automatically move, delete, color-code, or flag messages, create rules for messages, and block certain senders' mail from reaching the Inbox. The following commands are found in the Message menu and provide you with sorting and filtering capabilities.

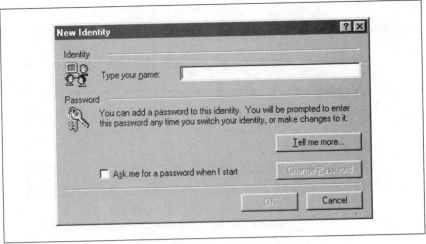

Figure 6-52: The Add New Identity dialog of Outlook Express 5

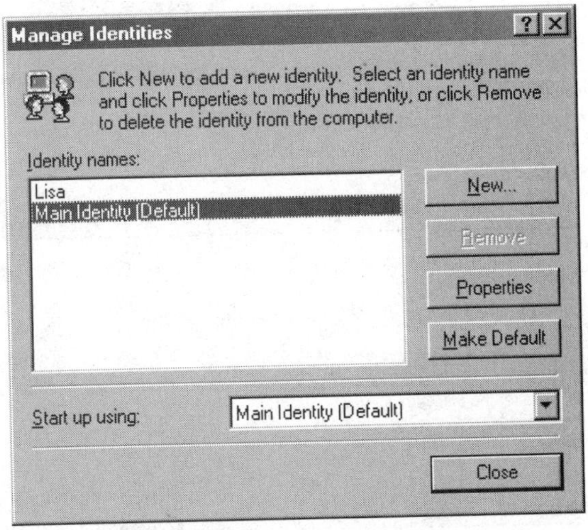

Figure 6-53: The Manage Identities dialog of Outlook Express 5

Message → Create Rule from Message

This is the main command for sorting and filtering messages in Outlook Express 5. This command pops up the New Mail Rule dialog when used as shown in Figure 6-55 (only a single message must be selected). There are four parts or windows to this dialog:

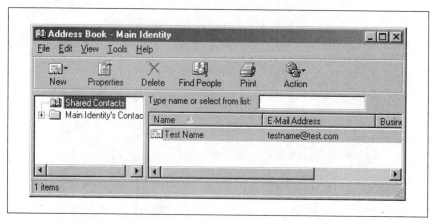

Figure 6-54: The Shared Contacts folder accessed through the Address Book

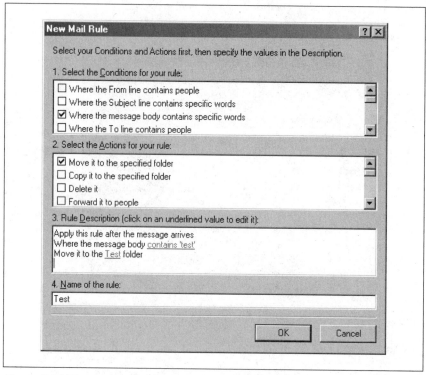

Figure 6-55: The New Mail Rule dialog

Be careful to create only the minimal necessary set of filtering rules, especially if you are on an intermittent dialup connection. It takes time to process the rules and act on the messages, and a complex set of rules can bring your mailer to its knees. This is why a lot of users prefer host-based mail filters using a program like Procmail. (See *http://www.ii.com/internet/robots/procmail/.*)

1. Select the conditions for your rule

   There are many conditions you can set that are very straightforward. An example is the "Where the To line contains people" condition. By checking this condition, the line is placed in the Description window with a hyperlink over the word "people." Select the hyperlink to pop up a dialog that will allow you to add the names of people from your Address Book or any email addresses you'd like to simply type in.

   You can select multiple conditions (the "and" value is applied to each condition), but be sure the conditions make sense. For instance, if you check the "For all messages" condition, make sure you really want to apply the rule to all your messages.

2. Select the Actions for your rule

   The actions are also very straightforward. An example is the "Forward it to people" action. By checking this action, the line is placed in the Description window and the "people" will have a hyperlink over it. Click the hyperlink to pop up a dialog for adding the people.

   Like conditions, you can select multiple actions (the "and" value is applied to each action), but you also need to make sure the action makes sense. For instance, you may want to use the "Do not download it from the server" action for one or several senders (this can be useful if you are using multiple machines), but it may not make sense to choose this for all senders.

3. Rule Description

   This window holds the descriptions of all the conditions or actions that have been selected. As mentioned, hyperlinks are present in the descriptions, allowing you to configure the conditions and actions. This window is crucial for creating rules.

4. Name of the Rule

   The name you define in this window will be used to define both mail and news rules, and you can rename the rule or reconfigure it at: Tools → Message Rules → Mail.

   To set rules for mail or news messages without selecting a single message, go to Tools → Message Rules → Mail. Once there, you can move to the Mail Rules, News Rules, or even the Blocked Senders tab, as shown in Figure 6-56.

Message → Block Sender

Moves the selected message sender to the Blocked Senders List, which automatically sends any messages from this sender to the Deleted Items folder,

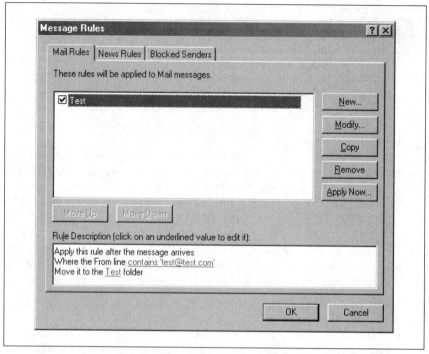

Figure 6-56: The Message Rules dialog

rather than to the Inbox (if the Inbox is set as your default folder for receiving messages). To view the Blocked Senders List (in case you want to add or remove any senders directly), go to Tools → Message Rules → Blocked Senders (see Figure 6-56). Once you add, remove, or modify any senders from this tab, be sure to select the OK button or all modifications will be lost.

Be sure to read the message that pops up right after you add a sender to the Blocked Senders List. Selecting the Yes button will automatically move every message in any folder from this sender into the Deleted Items folder. This is especially dangerous (if you select Yes by mistake) if you've checked the Tools → Options → Maintenance → "Empty messages from the Deleted Items folder on exit" box.

Message → Flag Message

This does exactly what it sounds like. Select one or several messages and click the Flag Message command to add a little flag in a column (as long as the column is activated at View → Columns) near the message to remind yourself that the message needs a follow-up. You can also just click in the flag column to add a flag to a message. To remove the flag, select the message(s) and click the command again, or just click on the flag itself (see

Figure 6-57). You can sort the messages by this column to group all the flagged messages for later review.

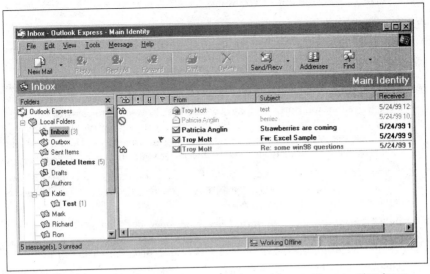

Figure 6-57: Offline use of Flag Message, Watch, and Ignore Conversation icons

Message → Watch Conversation

Watch a conversation that is of interest to you by clicking the Message → Watch Conversation command, or by clicking in the Show/Hide column (as long as the column is activated at View → Columns). This adds the glasses icon shown in Figure 6-57 in the Show/Hide column. You can customize the color of watched messages by going to Tools → Options → Read. If you select View → Current View → "Group messages by conversation," all original conversations will have a + sign next to them, and any replies or forwards to this same conversation will be nested underneath the original.

Message → Ignore Conversation

This is similar to the Watch Conversation command, except you mark messages with Ignore Conversation when you aren't interested in them. In fact, if you click on the glasses icon in the Show/Hide column, it will change to the Ignore Conversation icon shown in Figure 6-57. To hide all ignored messages, select View → Current View → "Hide read or ignored messages." You can alter this to hide only ignored messages by first selecting the "Hide read or ignored messages" view, then going to View → Current View → Customize current view. Or, if you'd like to create any custom view, go to View → Current View → Define Views.

Online/Offline Synchronization

If you want to prevent Outlook Express from attempting an Internet connection so you can work offline (see Figure 6-57) to read and respond to email messages (makes the most sense with a dial-up connection), then select File → Work Offline. If you are using a dial-up connection, you may even want to reduce online time by configuring Outlook Express to hang up after sending and receiving messages. To do this, check the Tools → Options → Connection → "Hang up after sending and receiving" box. You can reconnect at Tools → Send and Receive → select the option you want.

Multiple Signatures

The following three categories are most important when using multiple signatures:

Create a default signature to appear on all messages using an account

To create a signature, click the Tools → Options → Signature → New button (see Figure 6-58) and then either enter text in the Edit Signature box or click the File button and enter the path (or use the Browse button) where the text or HTML file is located that you'd like to use as your signature. Make sure you then click the "Add signatures to all outgoing messages" checkbox, and the signature will be automatically attached to all of your outgoing messages.

If you only want signatures attached to new messages, and not to any messages you reply to or forward, then click the "Don't add signatures to Replies and Forwards" checkbox.

Create multiple signatures to insert into email messages

To use a signature(s) on individual messages only, rather than having one default signature attached to outgoing messages, make sure to clear the "Add signatures to all outgoing messages" checkbox on the Tools → Options → Signature tab (see Figure 6-58).

To add a signature to an email message, select Insert → Signature and choose a signature. To create multiple signatures that are available when using Insert → Signature, go to Tools → Options → Signatures → New and type a signature into the Edit Signature box, or choose a text or HTML file. To name the signature, use the Rename button (these names will show up for you to choose from when inserting a signature into a message).

Create multiple default signatures for separate accounts

To assign different signatures to different accounts, select the signature in the Signatures window, click the Advanced button, shown in Figure 6-58, and then select the account you want to use the signature with. This, of course, is only useful if you have more than one email account.

Hotmail

If you want to use Microsoft's HTTP email program Hotmail, use the wizard in Outlook Express to install it. Go to Tools → New Account Signup → Hotmail, and the wizard will walk you through the installation. The information you'll need can be obtained from your Internet Service Provider or system administrator.

Paint   \Program Files\Accessories\mspaint.exe

Create, modify, or view image files.

To Launch

Address → mspaint
Start → Run → mspaint
Start → Programs → Accessories → Paint

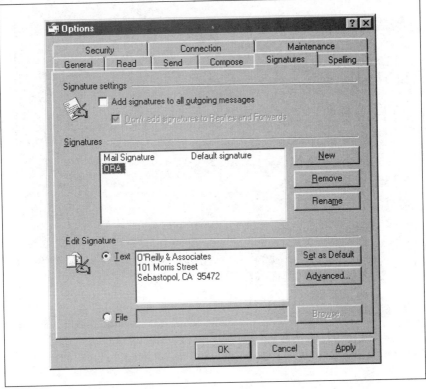

Figure 6-58: The Tools → Options → Signature tab

Description

mspaint is a graphics program that comes with Windows 98, allowing you to create, modify, or view image files (see Figure 6-59).

mspaint deals primarily with bitmap files (*.bmp*). With MSPaint, you can create or open monochrome bitmap files, as well as 16-color, 256-color, and 24-bit *.bmp* files (you can create 256-color icons with *mspaint*, since they're really just 32×32 *.bmp* files). You can also create or open *.pcx* files (PC Paintbrush), which store images from 1 to 24 bits in pixel depth, and are recognized by most still-image graphics programs. With this version of MSPaint, you can even create and open *.gif* and *.jpeg* files.

Some of the tasks you can perform with images in MSPaint are:

File → Set as Wallpaper (Tiled or Centered)
    Set *.bmp* files as wallpaper for your Desktop

View → Zoom → Show Grid
    Show a grid (Ctrl+G)

View → Zoom → Show Thumbnail
    Show a thumbnail

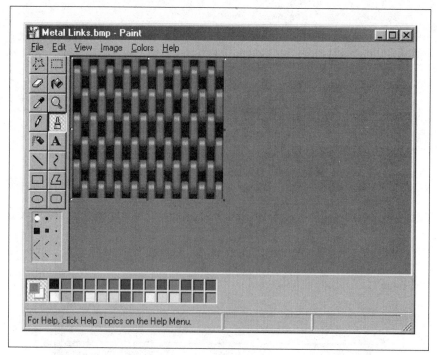

Figure 6-59: Paint graphics program (mspaint.exe)

Image → Flip/Rotate
Flip/Rotate (Ctrl+R)

Image → Stretch/Skew
Stretch/Skew (Ctrl+W)

Image → Invert Colors
Invert colors (Ctrl+I)

Colors → Edit Colors
Edit colors

Image → Attributes
Alter width or height

File → Send
Send an image by mail or fax

Notes

- If you convert an image to black and white (Image → Attributes → Black and White), you'll lose all of the color information, and the action can't be undone.

- You must save a newly created file before choosing it as wallpaper.

- If you paste an image into MSPaint that is larger than the bitmap you currently have open, you are prompted and can choose to have the bitmap enlarged.

- MSPaint doesn't allow editing of text that's been created, because the text on the screen is actually a graphic. To change the text, you must erase it with the Eraser button, and recreate it with the Text button on the toolbar.

- If you'd like the Explorer to show miniature previews (icons) of *.bmp* files in the Explorer, make the following change to the Registry:

  a. Navigate to `HKEY_CLASSES_ROOT\Paint.Picture\DefaultIcon`

  b. Select the Default value

  c. Modify the value data to `%1`

  To change it back so that the MSPaint icon shows instead:

  a. Navigate to `HKEY_CLASSES_ROOT\Paint.Picture\DefaultIcon`

  b. Select the Default value

  c. Modify the value data to `c:\progra~1\access~1\mspaint.exe,1`

  These directions assume that your *mspaint.exe* file is in the default directory (*\Program Files\Accessories*). You may need to reboot your machine for this to take effect.

See Also

For a more advanced image editing tool, download the shareware version of Paint Shop Pro:

> *http://www.jasc.com/*

Personal Web Server   *\Windows\System\inetsrv\pws.exe*

Lets you host a web site on your Windows 98 system.

To Install

> Control Panel → Add/Remove Programs → Install → *Win 98 CD\add-ons\ pws\setup.exe*

To Launch

> Address → **pws**
> Start → Run → **pws**
> System Tray Icon → right-click → Properties

Description

Personal Web Server is a limited-feature version of Internet Information Server 4.0 that allows you to host and manage a web site on your Windows 98 system. It features support for Active Server Pages and drag-and-drop publishing,

Personal Web Server looks like it is one of the components you can install simply by using Add/Remove Programs → Windows Setup → Internet Tools, but it is not. Specifying this component here only installs a help file that tells you how to install

PWS from the Win 98 CD. Furthermore, the help file is buried in the Windows help system, meaning that you have to search the main Windows help or open \Windows\Help\pws.chm.

You actually install PWS using a setup program found on the Win 98 CD (\add-ons\pws\setup.exe). During installation, you need to specify the location for your web server files to be stored (the default is \webshare\wwwroot) and a location for Microsoft Transaction Server (default \Program Files\mts) to be installed.

Once PWS is installed, users with network access to your computer (and you, of course) can browse to the web server with the URL *http://computer_name*. You can modify this home page (\inetpuc\wwwroot\default.asp) using any HTML editor you wish or using the Home Page Wizard that is part of PWS.

You can manage PWS by right-clicking the System Tray icon and choosing Properties or by running *pws.exe* from the \Windows\System\inetpub directory. Either of these actions opens the Personal Web Manager (see Figure 6-60), which provides a central management area for controlling your web site.

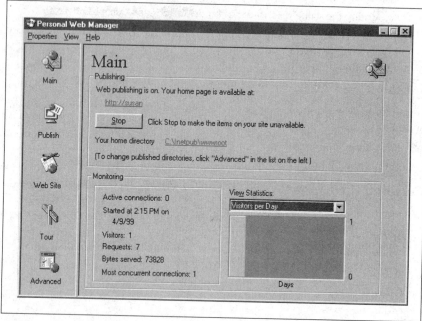

Figure 6-60: Personal Web Manager (pws.exe)

Main

Lets you stop and start the WWW service and view access statistics about your server (refer to Figure 6-60).

Publish

Launches the Web Publishing Wizard (discussed elsewhere in this chapter), which allows you to publish files on your computer or network. Whenever you publish a file, that file is copied to the \inetpub\webpub directory. A link named "View my published documents" is added to your home page that lets users open published files in the file's original format.

Once you've published your first files, clicking the Publish icon lets you add and remove files to and from the published list. You can also refresh all published files. This recopies the files from their original location. If the files were moved from their original location, you'll have to remove the files and add them again.

Web Site

Launches the Home Page Wizard, which walks you through the creation of a simple home page for your site. Using the wizard, you can enter personal information and favorite links, create a guest book where people can leave public messages, and create a drop box where people can leave private messages for you. Once you have created the page, clicking the Web Site icon in PWS allows you to edit the page or view your guest book and drop box.

Though the wizard can be useful for people who really just want to get some sort of page up quickly, you're going to be much better off using something like Notepad or Front Page Express if you want to do any real web page creation.

Tour

Launches a simple HTML tour of some of the features of PWS.

Advanced

Lets you examine, create, and edit virtual directories, as well as set certain site-wide parameters, as shown in Figure 6-61.

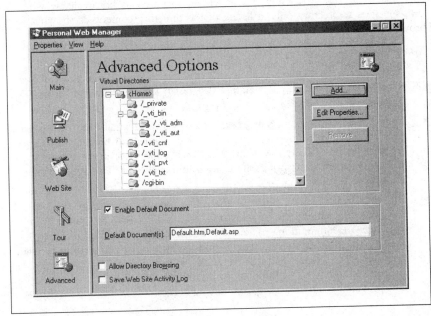

Figure 6-61: Advanced PWS properties

Virtual directories are representations within your web site of actual directories on your drive or network. The primary virtual directory is the Home directory, which corresponds to the location you specified during setup (*inetpub\wwwroot* by default). You can create a new virtual directory out of any folder on your local system or a system on your network. The alias you give to a new directory forms the URL used to browse it. For example, if you create a new virtual directory with the alias "recipes," the URL to access that directory would be *http://computer_ name/recipes*. For each virtual directory, you can also set three permissions:

Read

>   This allows anonymous users to open and view documents (web pages) in a directory. This is the standard permission given to all virtual directories.

Execute

>   This allows any application to be executed from a virtual directory. Typically, you would not put both read and execute permissions on the same directory, as it might let people read your executables.

Scripts

>   This allows script engines to run from within the folder without having to enable the Execute permission. Scripts is used to let trusted applications and web pages run scripts.

The Advanced page also lets you designate the default documents for your site. These are documents that are loaded automatically when a user enters a URL that specifies only a directory and not an actual filename. If a file by any of the default document names exists in the directory, it will be loaded. Multiple default documents may be entered and are given preference according to their listed order. If you enable directory browsing and a default document is not available when a URL specifies a directory only, a listing of the directory contents is shown in the browser.

Notes

- In Windows 98 Second Edition, the following Start Menu shortcut loads Microsoft's online help page: Start → Programs → Accessories → Internet Tools → Personal Web Server.

- In addition to making a pretty good web server for a small LAN, PWS is good for developing web sites that you intend to publish to bigger web servers, such as IIS or O'Reilly's Website Pro. Once you've got a site the way you want it, you can publish it easily using a tool such as Front Page or the Web Publishing Wizard.

- File and Printer Sharing must be enabled on your computer in order to run PWS. We recommend you do this prior to installing PWS at Control Panel → Network → Configuration → File and Printer Sharing. By default this will share all files and printers over all connections, which can be a security problem. You can go to Control Panel → Network → Configuration → TCP/IP--Dial-Up Adapter → Properties → Bindings to disable file sharing for that connection, thus preventing Internet users from having access.

- When you install PWS, a Publish icon is placed on your desktop. Dragging files onto the icon opens PWS, launches the Publish wizard, and automatically fills in the path for you.

- If you are operating behind a firewall or proxy and wish to use PWS, you must make sure that requests for local (or intranet) URLs are not sent to the proxy server. If they are, you will not be able to access your web site or run the PWS wizards. To set this option, select Control Panel → Internet → Connection → Bypass proxy server for local (intranet) addresses.

- If you are interested in learning about programming Active Server Pages, around 60 MB of ASP documentation comes with PWS. However, it is not part of the typical installation. To install it, rerun setup and choose Add/Remove.

Phone Dialer

\Windows\dialer.exe

Dial voice telephone calls.

To Install

Control Panel → Add/Remove Programs → Windows Setup →
    Communications → Details → Phone Dialer

To Launch

Address → `dialer`
Start → Run → `dialer`
Start → Programs → Accessories → Communications → Phone Dialer

Description

Dials voice telephone calls, acts as a proxy for applications making simple voice telephony requests, and maintains a phone-call log (see Figure 6-62).

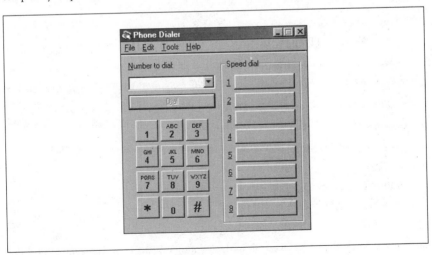

Figure 6-62: Using Phone Dialer (dialer.exe)

Associated Files

\Windows\dialer.ini, \Windows\calllog.txt

Notes

- *dialer* can log incoming as well as outgoing calls (Tools → Show Log → Log → Options).

- Even though there is no option to save the call log to a file, it is automatically saved as \Windows\calllog.txt. The call log window can also be cut and pasted to a different file.

- "Speed dial" numbers and the last twenty dialed numbers are kept in *dialer. ini.*

- *dialer* has about twenty built-in calling-card options (AT&T, British Telecom, MCI, US Sprint, etc.), and the ability to add new calling cards.

- To use *dialer* to handle voice-call requests from other programs, see Tools → Connect Using.

See Also

"Modems" in Chapter 5
"Dial-Up Networking" in Chapter 4

Progam Manager   \Windows\progman.exe

The Windows 3.1 Program Manager, which was replaced by the Explorer in Win 95.

As of Windows 98, the groups have been removed from the Program Manager, so there isn't much use for the program unless you go to the trouble of creating your own groups in *progman.ini.*

See Also

"explorer" in Chapter 7

Quick View   \Windows\System\VIEWERS\xd5 uikview.exe

View the contents of a file without launching the associated application.

To Install

Add/Remove Programs → Windows Setup → Accessories → Quick View

To Launch

Address → `quickview`
right-click on a file → Quick View

Description

quikview (Quick View) lets you view the contents of a file without launching the associated application, if the file has a Quick View–registered extension (see Figure 6-63).

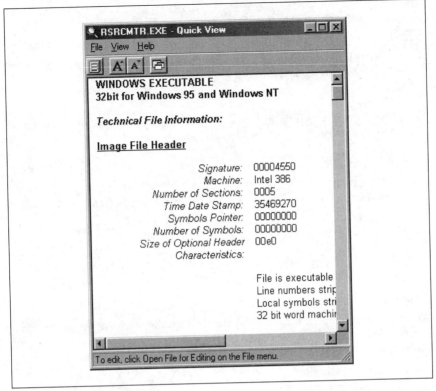

Figure 6-63: Quick View

Notes

There are several ways of registering Quick View with most of your applications, as listed here:

- Alter the Registry (see Chapter 13, *The Registry*, for details about the Registry) to enable Quick View with most files:

  a. Start → Run → `regedit`

  b. Expand the branches to `HKEY_CLASSES_ROOT`

  c. Look for a key that reads *

  d. Under this key, add a new key, and call it QuickView

  e. Set the value of (default) to * and close *regedit*

  You should now be able to use Quick View for all types of files, except those that Quick View doesn't understand, such as *.pcx* files.

- Use the Send To menu with Quick View:

  a. Create a shortcut to *quickview.exe* (in *Windows**System**Viewers*) in your *Windows**SendTo* directory.

  b. Now when you right-click on a file, you can "Send To" Quick View.

- Use the Desktop:

  a. Create a shortcut to *quickview.exe* on your Desktop.

  b. You can now drag any files you want to be viewed onto the shortcut.

  c. Good for opening questionable Word files, because it doesn't run macros. No threat of viruses!

See Also

Try Quick View Plus, which gives you the power to view, copy, and print almost any file or attachment:

> *http://www.jasc.com/*

Real Player

\Program Files\Real\Player\rvplayer.exe

Real-time audio and video delivery system for the Web (RealPlayer).

To Install

Add/Remove Programs → Windows Setup → Internet Tools → Real Audio Player 4.0

To Launch

When you click on a Real Audio or Video link on the web, the *.ra* or *.rm* file is downloaded to the \ *Windows\ Temporary Internet File* directory and then played. To launch the program manually:

Address → `rvplayer`
Start → Run → `rvplayer`

Description

With *rvplayer*, you can enjoy live and pre-recorded audio and video clips on the Web.

Notes

- RealPlayer has been left out of Windows 98 Second Edition. It can be downloaded from *http://www.real.com/*.

- Using the RealPlayer is straightforward. It should be quite obvious how to use the stop, pause, play, and volume controls if you've ever played a tape or CD (see Figure 6-64).

- You can adjust Audio Quality versus CPU Usage with a sliding bar in View → Preferences → Advanced. If you notice a decrease in performance while playing a RealAudio file, just slide the bar. Experiment to discover the best setting for your machine and Internet connection.

- In order to use the Custom Destinations and Daily Briefings features, you'll need to upgrade to RealPlayer G2. By pressing any of the buttons, you will be taken to the download site.

Figure 6-64: RealPlayer (rvplayer.exe)

- To change the number of files stored in File → Open Recent navigate to View → Preferences → General and enter the number (15 maximum) in the Recent Clips box.

- If the audio sounds too fast or slow, scratchy, or distorted, navigate to: View → Preferences → Advanced. Click either the "Disable 16-bit sound" or "Disable custom sampling rates" checkbox to modify the way your player and sound card work together.

- If you are experiencing rebuffering (receiving data at a slower bandwidth than the required bandwidth for the clip), but you aren't experiencing any packet loss, you may have a slow connection speed. Select View → Statistics → Details to view connection speed and the required clip rate. There are several possible rebuffering solutions:

  - Set the connection bandwidth higher than the actual bandwidth: View → Preferences → Connection → set the Bandwith pull-down menu to a level higher than your actual connection (e.g., if you have a 28.8K modem, set it to 56K).

  - Configure *rvplayer* to buffer the entire clip prior to playback: View → Preferences → General → select the "Buffer entire clip up to available memory" button.

  - If you don't have enough memory to buffer the entire clip, change the buffer setting: View → Preferences → General → select the "Buffer at least 60 seconds before playing" button. The higher you set this number, the more memory is needed, but if the number surpasses the memory, *rvplayer* will still buffer as much as possible.

- To play clips consecutively, create a *.ram* (RealAudio metafile) file, which is a text file with each line of text containing a *.ra* (RealAudio) address. The format for the line of text is as follows:

```
pnm://ra file name
```

`pnm://` refers to a RealAudio server, but you can use the `http://` protocol instead as long as the remote server is configured properly. You can also create a *.ram* file that accesses local files by using the File protocol. The following example illustrates the use of the http and File protocols:

```
File:c:\download\dejavoodoo.ra
File:c:\download\tlies.ra
http://www.kwsband.com/Real%20Audio/sride.ra
http://www.kwsband.com/Real%20Audio/sss.ra
```

- In View → Preferences → Transport, you'll find the Network Transport and UDP Port sections. By default, *rvplayer* receives data packets using UDP (User Datagram Protocol). If you are behind a packet-filtering firewall, you probably won't be able to receive UDP packets, so you should select the TCP (Transmission Control Protocol) instead. Keep in mind if you use TCP with a modem, you may experience gaps in the audio stream. Most versions of the Player automatically detect if you can't receive data via UDP and switch to TCP.

- If you're on a local area network (LAN), and your firewall is preventing the RealAudio stream from reaching you, it is possible to receive the audio stream without exposing your company's network to security risks. For more information, see:

  http://service.real.com/firewall/index.html

See Also

  http://service.real.com/kb/
  http://service.real.com/help/errors/

Registry Checker   \ *Windows*\ *Command*\ *scanregw.exe*

Find and fix problems in the Registry.

To Launch

  Address → `scanregw`
  Start → Run → `scanregw`
  Start → Programs → Accessories → System Tools → System Information →
      Tools menu → System File Checker

Description

Registry Checker (*scanregw.exe*) runs automatically each time you start your system and scans the Registry for inconsistencies. If no problem is found on the first time it runs during a given day, a backup of the Registry is made. These backups actually include the *User.dat* and *System.dat* files, as well as the *Win.ini* and *System.ini* configuration files. Backups are stored as *.cab* files in the \ *Windows*\ *sysbckup* folder. Backups are given the name *Rbxxx.cab*, where *xxx* is a unique number assigned by *scanreg*. Five good backups are maintained at any given time. When a sixth backup is formed, the oldest backup is deleted.

If a problem is found during a scan of the Registry, *scanregw* can restore the Registry from a known good backup. If no backup exists, *scanregw* can also

---

attempt to fix the registry. In addition, *scanregw* optimizes the performance of the Registry each time it runs by removing unused space in the *User.dat* and *System.dat* files.

Registry Checker is actually two executable files: *scanregw.exe*, which is the protected-mode Windows executable, and *scanreg.exe*, which is the MS-DOS real-mode executable. *scanregw* is the file that actually runs each time you start Windows and when you run Registry Checker from the System Information utility (*msinfo32.exe*). If *scanregw* finds a problem and needs to restore or fix the registry, it will prompt you to restart the computer. On restart, *scanreg* will run in MS-DOS mode to perform the actual restoration or fix.

You can also run *scanreg* from the command prompt in MS-DOS real mode (not Windows) manually, if you wish. This might be useful, for example, if Registry problems are preventing you from even starting the Windows GUI. The syntax for running *scanreg* is:

```
scanreg [/option]
```

scanreg accepts the following options:

backup
> Back up the registry and related system configuration files.

restore
> Choose a backup to restore.

fix Repair the registry.

comment="comment"
> Adds *comment* to the CAB file while backing up.

Notes

- If *scanregw* has already backed up the Registry for the day but you wish to back it up again, just run *scanregw* manually. After checking the Registry, it will ask you whether you wish to perform another backup.

- You can keep *scanregw* from running each time you start Windows using Start → Run → msconfig → Startup → disable Scan Registry option. If you do this, be sure that you regularly back up your registry manually or automatically using something like Task Scheduler.

- More information can be found in *Windows 98 Annoyances* from O'Reilly & Associates.

Registry Editor   *\Windows\regedit.exe*

View and modify the contents of the Registry.

To Launch

> Address → regedit
> Start → Run → regedit

Description

regedit allows you to view and modify the contents of the Registry, the master file that stores configuration settings for Windows 98 and many of the applications on your computer. The Registry is described in detail in Chapter 13, which also provides a tutorial on using *regedit*. *regedit* gives a two-pane view of the Registry, somewhat similar to the one in the Explorer, except that in this case, you're looking at the Registry database rather than files and folders. (See Figure 6-65.)

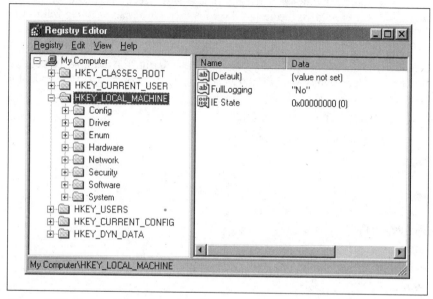

Figure 6-65: Registry Editor (regedit.exe)

Notes

- You can import all or part of the Registry using the Registry → Import Registry File command in *regedit*. To export all or any selected part of the Registry, you can use the Registry → Export Registry File command. Exported Registry files have the extension *.reg*.

- *.reg* files are straight ASCII text (with the signature "REGEDIT4" as their first line). They can be viewed and modified with any text editor or word processor that can read and save plain text files. If modifying a *.reg* file with Word-Pad or Word, remember to save it as plain text.

- A new feature in the Windows 98 version of *regedit* is the Edit → Copy Key Name menu command. This feature copies a key name from the Registry into the Clipboard, along with its entire Registry path.

- By default, Windows 98 associates *.reg* files with *regedit*: double-clicking on a *.reg* file's icon in the Explorer imports the *.reg* file's contents into the Registry. Since any modifications to the Registry can alter your system, a dialog box pops up when you double-click on a *.reg* file asking if you are sure you want to add this information to the Registry. If you proceed, another dialog box will pop up telling you whether or not the action was successful.

- *regedit* can be used to view and modify the Registry on other machines. See Registry → Connect Network Registry.

- Use of *regedit* can be disabled with *poledit*.

See Also

"System Policy Editor" in Chapter 8
"regedit" in Chapter 7
Chapter 13

Resource Meter   *\Windows\rsrcmtr.exe*

Monitor the system resources programs are using.

To Install

> Add/Remove Programs → Windows Setup → System Tools → Details →
> System Resource Meter

To Launch

> Address → `rsrcmtr`
> Start → Run → `rsrcmtr`
> Start → Programs → Accessories → System Tools → Resource Meter

Description

When running, the Resource Meter places a small icon in the System Tray. The Resource Meter monitors the resources for the following three areas of your running computer: system resources, user resources, and GDI (Graphics Device Interface) resources.

The percentage of each of these resources that is free is represented by the green lines on the icon in the System Tray. If resources drop dangerously low, the line turns yellow. If you see red lines, then your situation is near-critical.

For exact free resource amounts, hold your cursor over the icon for a moment, and a small ToolTip will appear with exact percentage free figures for System, GDI, and User resources.

You can obtain an even clearer display by double-clicking the icon (or right-clicking, and selecting Details). When you do this, a window will appear (see Figure 6-66). When any of the three graphs drops below 50 percent, you should close some programs to free resources.

Note

To load the Resource Meter automatically when you run Win 98, place a shortcut to *rsrcmtr* in the startup folder (*\Windows\Start Menu\Programs\StartUp*).

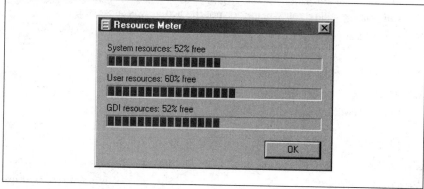

Figure 6-66: Resource Meter (rsrcmtr.exe)

ScanDisk

\ *Windows\scandskw.exe*

Check the disk surface for errors.

To Launch

Address → **scandskw**
Start → Run → **scandskw**
Start → Programs → Accessories → System Tools → ScanDisk

Description

ScanDisk checks the disk surface, files, and folders of your computer for lost clusters (and other things), correcting them if they exist, thus freeing disk space by getting rid of unusable information. There are two separate versions of ScanDisk. The executable for one version is called *scandskw*, which is run from within Windows. The executable for the other version is called *scandisk* (\ *Windows\ Command\scandisk.exe*), which is run from the real-mode command line (before Windows is launched during setup). Typing *scandisk* from the command line in Windows actually runs *scandskw* by quickly loading a DOS box that launches ScanDisk and then closes the DOS box. In Windows, then, running *scandisk* or *scandskw* from the command line using the *scandskw* options will give you the same end result. See Chapter 7 for the command-line options.

Don't confuse running *scandskw* from the command line with running *scandisk* from the MS-DOS real-mode command line. There is one set of command-line options for *scandskw* run from Windows, and another set of options for *scandisk* run from real-mode DOS. Both of these sets of options are covered in Chapter 7.

When run from Windows, ScanDisk provides two processes to choose from:

Standard

Checks your file allocation table, folders, and files for errors such as cross-linked files, lost file fragments, invalid file dates, and invalid file names. You also have the option to have ScanDisk automatically fix any problems. It's a good idea to run the Normal scan once a day. This can be accomplished by putting a *scandskw* shortcut in the *StartUp* directory, or by configuring this in the Task Scheduler (*mstask.exe*).

Thorough

Does everything discussed under "Standard," plus it checks the integrity of the hard drive surface. The Surface Scan finds potential bad sectors on your hard drive. The process then marks bad areas to prevent those sectors from being used. If data is saved to a bad area, you run the risk of losing that information.

The surface scan can also give you the warning signs of hard drive failure by marking bad sectors on the drive. You might consider running the Thorough Scan about once a month.

Windows ScanDisk (*scandskw.exe*) can be run from a batch file or as a shortcut from the Target box of ScanDisk.

The following steps illustrate how to run *scandskw* when Windows starts:

1. Copy a shortcut to *scandskw* from the \ *Windows* directory to your startup directory (\ *Windows\Start Menu\Programs\StartUp*) and right-click the icon.

2. Click Properties → Shortcut (see the dialog box in Figure 6-67).

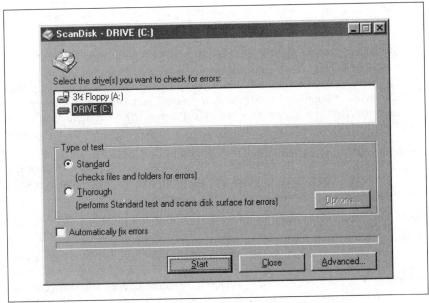

Figure 6-67: Windows ScanDisk properties (scandskw.exe)

3. After the text in the Target box (*C:\Windows\scandskw.exe*), specify one or more of the command-line options described later in this section.

4. Click OK, and the next time you start Windows, *scandisk* will automatically run in whatever fashion you've specified.

Notes

- The DOS version of ScanDisk can also check unmounted drives compressed with DoubleSpace or DriveSpace, but it can't check for long filename integrity. As a rule, you should use the Windows version of ScanDisk first and then the MS-DOS version if you need to correct other problems.

- You have the option to replace, append, or disable a log file that's created once ScanDisk has run. The name of the file is *scandisk.log*, stored in the root drive. *scandisk.log* will report all of the ScanDisk results.

See Also

"scandskw" in Chapter 7

Signature Verification Tool
\Windows\sigverif.exe

Lets you verify digital signatures on device drivers from Microsoft.

To Launch

Address → `sigverif`
Start → Run → `sigverif`
Start → Programs → Accessories → System Tools → System Information → Tools menu → Signature Verification Tool

Description

Microsoft digitally signs device drivers shipped with Win 98 so that you can verify that they have not been modified since testing. Drivers developed by third-party manufacturers are submitted to Microsoft for testing and, once those drivers pass the hardware standards testing, they are signed as well. The Signature Verification Tool (*sigverif.exe*) lets you verify that drivers have not been modified in any way since testing.

sigverif works much like Start → Find → Files and Folders. Choose whether you want to search for signed or unsigned files, specify the directory to search, and let it go to work.

Notes

Windows 98 also includes a feature called Signature Checking that allows Win 98 to inspect driver files for signatures whenever they are installed. You can set this using System Policy Editor → Open Local Registry → Local Computer → Windows 98 System → Install Device Drivers → Digital Signature Check. You can configure the policy to allow installation of all drivers, block installation of all unsigned drivers, or warn of but allow installation of unsigned drivers.

Solitaire
\Windows\sol.exe

The popular Microsoft Solitaire game.

To Launch

Address → sol
Start → Run → sol
Start → Programs → Accessories → Games → Solitaire

Description

The following are some options available when playing *sol* (see Figure 6-68 for a sample game):

- Draw one card at a time
- Draw three cards at a time
- Enable scoring
- Play Las Vegas–style, in which each card costs $1 ($52 per game); each card scored earns $5 (11 cards scored wins $3)
- Time the game
- Undo the last action only
- Choose a new deck back

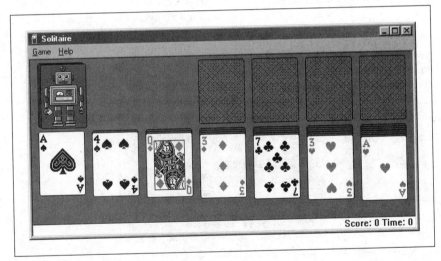

Figure 6-68: Solitaire (sol.exe)

 If you start a game drawing three cards at a time, trying to switch to Game → Options → Draw One will start a new game. Press Ctrl-Alt-Shift while you draw to draw a single card in a Draw-3 game.

Notes

You don't have to be limited by the deck back options available to you in *sol*. You can download many others from the URLs in the "See Also" section.

See Also

"FreeCell" (the deterministic version of Solitaire)

For add-ons and downloadable Solitaire versions:

> *http://www.solitairecity.com/*
> *http://www.solitairecentral.com/*
> *http://www.goodsol.com/*

Sound Recorder   \ *Windows\sndrec32.exe*

Record and play sound files with a *.wav* extension.

To Launch

> Address → sndrec32
> Start → Run → sndrec32 [play] [/close] [*filename.wav*]
> Start → Programs → Accessories → Entertainment → Sound Recorder

Description

sndrec32 lets you control recording and playback of sound files. It pops up a window with controls that should be familiar to anyone who has ever used a cassette tape recorder. The buttons across the bottom (see Figure 6-69) represent (from left to right) reverse, fast forward, play, stop, and record. The slider lets you postition the "playback head" anywhere within the sound file, with an immediate readout of the total length of the sound file in seconds and your position in the file. A waveform display gives a visual readout of the sound as it plays.

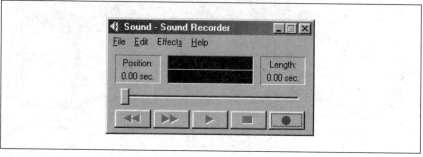

Figure 6-69: Record and play .wav files (sndrec32.exe)

When running *sndrec32* from the command line, you can use the following options:

/play
> Play the specified file (*filename.wav*). Without this option, the file will be loaded but not played.

/close
> Close when finished playing. (The default is to remain open.)

The following are some of the tasks and options you can perform with *sndrec32*:

- File → New allows you to create a new, blank sound file (*.wav*). If your computer has a microphone, you can use these blank files to record your own sounds. Or just record a sound and then choose Save As. Note that *sndrec32* is unlike many Windows applications in that Save doesn't automatically call Save As if the filename isn't already known. The Save As dialog includes a Change button that lets you change the format of the saved data. You can get to this same format selection from File → Properties.

- The Effects → Increase Volume and Effects → Decrease Volume options work by increasing or decreasing the amplitude of the recorded sound wave data. When you decrease the volume level of the recorded wave, you risk losing signal clarity, thus giving less audio detail and creating distortion. Increasing the volume of an ordinary speech file shouldn't affect the quality, but music files are less forgiving due to their wider dynamic range.

- The Effects → Increase Speed and Effects → Decrease Speed options are similar to the volume options, except that you are dealing with the speed in which the sound is being played, rather than the volume at which it's being played.

- The Effects → Reverse option reverses the order in which the *.wav* samples contained in the file are played.

- The Effects → Add Echo is fun to use, but the only way to remove the echo is to select Revert before you save the file.

- To mix sound files, move the slider to the place you want to overlay the second sound file, use Edit → Mix With File, and select the *.wav* file you want to mix.

Notes

- Really big *.wav* files take a long time to open in *sndrec32*, since it must read in the whole file before playing it. If this becomes a problem, use View → Options → File Types on any folder to change the default Play action for *.wav* files to Media Player (*mplayer.exe*), which "streams" the audio so it can start playing while the file is still loading. Alternatively, there is a Preview tab on the Properties dialog box for *.wav* files that lets you do a "quick listen."

- Note that there are two context menu actions for *.wav* files, Play and Open. Open loads the file but does not play it until you click the Play control. The Play action typically uses the /play and /close options to play the sound file and then exit. (Be sure to include these options if you change the play program to *mplayer*.)

- When editing a *.wav* file, you can return the file to its original condition (if you haven't saved it) by selecting File → Revert.

- You can mix only an uncompressed sound file. If you don't see a green line in the waveform area of the window, the file is compressed and you can't modify it.

- You can open up as many copies of *sndrec32* as you like, up to the limits of your computer's memory. This comes in handy when editing many different *.wav* files.

You can record from your system's CD drive or from any external device you can hook up to "live in" on a multimedia sound card by turning off the system microphone and turning on the other input device using the volume control (*sndvol32* → Options → Properties → Recording). See "Volume Control" for details.

See Also

For details on mixing, inserting audio files and *sndrec32* audio properties and sound formats:

> *http://www.skwc.com/WebClass/Task-Sound1.html*

(The site mentions Windows 95, but the information is applicable to Windows 98.)

System Configuration Editor \ *Windows* \ *System* \ *sysedit.exe*

Edit system intialization files.

To Launch
>   Address → sysedit
>   Start → Run → sysedit

Description

sysedit (shown in Figure 6-70) opens the following files simultaneously in overlapping windows: *autoexec.bat*, *config.sys*, *system.ini*, *win.ini*, *protocol.ini*, and *msmail.ini*, using a Notepad-style text editor.

By automatically loading these system setting files, *sysedit* makes it quick and easy to view or make changes to them. If you select one of the files and make changes to it, make sure that you save it before closing the editor.

Notes

- The Window → Tile option neatly arranges the system files into six equal subwindows, making it easier to navigate among the files.

- See "System Configuration Utility" in Chapter 12 for a console application containing all of the startup files and options.

System File Checker \ *Windows* \ *sfc.exe*

Verify the integrity of your system files.

To Launch
>   Start → Run → sfc
>   Start → Programs → Accessories → System Tools → System Information →
>   Tools menu → System File Checker

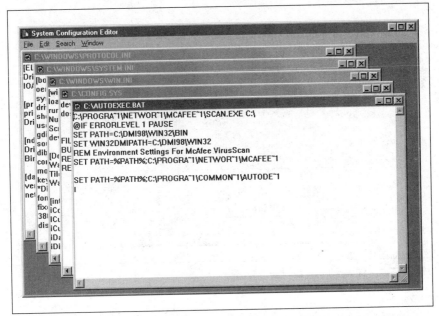

Figure 6-70: System Editor (sysedit.exe)

Description

System File Checker (*sfc.exe*) scans your system for corrupt, changed, or missing files (see Figure 6-71). By default, *sfc* only checks for corrupted files, but you can specify that it check for missing and changed files by choosing Settings → Settings → Check for changed/deleted files. If *sfc* finds problems with a file during a scan, it will prompt you to restore the original file from the Win 98 CD.

Change in a file is determined by comparing files on your system with a baseline contained in a database named *Default.sfc*, which is stored in your \Windows\ folder. If a changed file is found, you are given one of three options:

- You can update *Default.sfc* to reflect the change in the file. Choose this option only if you are sure that the file is not corrupt. It is also wise to backup *default.sfc* before doing this. You can also create a new baseline file for your system by going to Settings → Advanced → Create and specifying a new .sfc file. You can then run the scan and update the verification information to create a baseline for your system.

- You can restore the original *sfc* settings and any changes you may have made up to that point by choosing a source location for the file (like the Win 98 CD) and optionally backing up the replaced file to \Windows\Helpdesk\SFC.

- You can ignore the problem.

As you can see from Figure 6-71, *sfc.exe* can also be used to extract a single file from your Win 98 CD that you would like to restore. This can be useful if you are getting errors reported for a single file. Often, restoring the original can fix the problem.

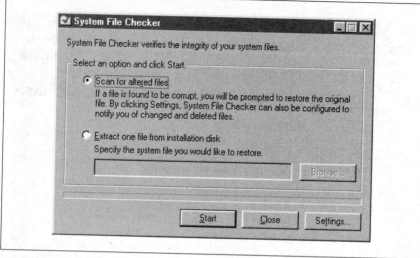

Figure 6-71: System File Checker (sfc.exe)

Notes

- You can change the search criteria used by *sfc* using Settings → Search Criteria. This tab allows you to select the folders and file types you want *sfc* to check. If you make changes on this tab, those changes will be saved in the .*sfc* file specified on Settings → Advanced. Therefore, it is best to create your own .*sfc* file before changing search criteria.

- If you do change your original *Default.sfc* file, you can restore the original using Settings → Advanced → Restore Defaults.

System Information

Program Files\Common Files\Microsoft Shared
msinfo\msinfo32.exe

Display system information.

To Launch

Address → msinfo32
Start → Programs → Accessories → System Tools → System Information
Start → Run → msinfo32

Description

System Information (*msinfo32*) collects and displays various configuration information from your system. Information is presented in a dual-pane interface with components on the left and reports of those components on the right. Components are broken down into four broad categories:

Hardware Resources

Displays common resources used by hardware, such as IRQ, DMA, and I/O addresses. Though useful, this same information is available more easily using Control Panel → System → Device Manager.

Components

Displays information about your actual hardware components, such as display, modem, and port information. Again, most of the information useful for common purposes can be found in Device Manager.

Software Environment

Displays information regarding software currently loaded into memory. This is the place to go to find out exactly what is running on your system right now.

Applications

Displays information on installed applications. Right now, only new software from Microsoft is reported in this category.

Notes

- *msinfo32* can also be used to view reports made by other utilities, such as Dr. Watson (*.wlg* files), Windows Report Tool (*.cab* files), and even *.txt* files.

- You can print a report from *msinfo32*, but you can only print the entire system information collection, which usually comes out to more than 75 pages. If you want to print only sections of the system information, copy it to Notepad and print it from there.

- If information is being about a component is being improperly reported (or not reported at all), try View → Refresh (F5).

- The Tools menu of *msinfo32* provides a convenient way to launch a number of other utilities, including: DirectX Diagnostic Tool, Windows Report Tool, Update Wizard Uninstall, System File Checker, Signature Verification Tool, Registry Checker, Automatic Skip Driver Agent, Dr. Watson, System Configuration Utility, ScanDisk, and Version Conflict Manager. You can find more on some of these tools in their entries in this chapter.

System Monitor   \Windows\sysmon.exe

Monitor memory functions and disk cache settings.

To Launch

Address → sysmon
Start → Run → sysmon
Start → Programs → Accessories → System Tools → System Monitor

Description

Using *sysmon*, you can monitor many functions and settings, such as current virtual memory and disk cache size, and max/min settings for virtual memory and disk cache (see Figure 6-72). For virtual memory, you'll see the actual virtual memory size go up as you open more applications.

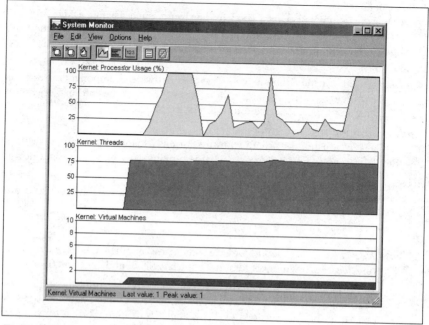

Figure 6-72: System Monitor (sysmon.exe)

When you first start the System Monitor, the display is blank. Click the first box on the toolbar, or Edit → Add Item; then, in the Category list, select the feature you want to monitor (e.g., File System). In the Item list, select the item or items you want to monitor (e.g., Bytes read/second or Bytes written/second).

You can display the same output in any of three formats: Line, Bar, or Numeric Charts. Select the view with the last three toolbar buttons or the View menu.

Notes

- To create a log of your current *sysmon* session, use File → Start Logging and File → Stop Logging. By default you can save a *sysmon.log* file at the root, but since it pops up a Save As dialog, you can save the log file in any location with any name.

- Options → Chart allows you to modify the update interval—every second is the fastest setting, and every hour is the slowest.

- File → Connect lets you monitor a remote computer.

- The Explain button on the Add Item dialog gives an explanation of what each possible value means.

Task Manager

\Windows\taskman.exe

Display currently running programs.

To Launch

Address → `taskman`
Start → Run → `taskman`

Description

With *taskman* (see Figure 6-73), you can start new programs and shut down individual programs or Windows itself. In the Options menu, you can select several different ways for the programs to be viewed in *taskman*. For example, you can select Always on Top, Text in Buttons, and Small Icons, to name a few.

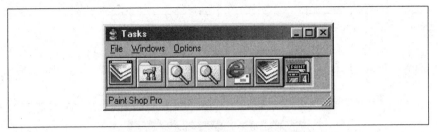

Figure 6-73: The Task Manager (taskman.exe)

Notes

* *taskman* also has options to arrange ("tile" and "cascade") the windows of your currently running programs, thus bringing a bit of Windows 3.1 functionality back to the Windows 98 Desktop.

* Because *taskman* can start new programs (see the File → Run Application menu item), it could be used as a minimalist alternative to the Explorer by putting `shell=taskman.exe` instead of `shell=Explorer.exe` in the [boot] section of *system.ini*.

Telnet   \ *Windows\telnet.exe*

Create an interactive session on a remote computer using TCP/IP.

To Launch

Address → `telnet`
Start → Run → `telnet`

Description

telnet (shown in Figure 6-74) is a Windows Sockets–based application that simplifies TCP/IP terminal emulation with Windows 98. Your host computer uses the TCP/IP protocol to run the Client Telnet, negotiating a session with the other computer (the remote host or Server Telnet). Once the terminal settings are determined and set, you can log in to the other computer and access files. Each instance of the *telnet* application is limited to one connection. However, the application itself can be launched multiple times to create simultaneous connections to a single host or multiple hosts.

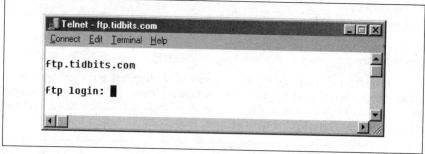

Figure 6-74: Sample telnet session (telnet.exe)

telnet is useful for connecting with a Unix shell account. In addition, there are many useful library catalogs and other services provided via *telnet*. See Figure 6-75.

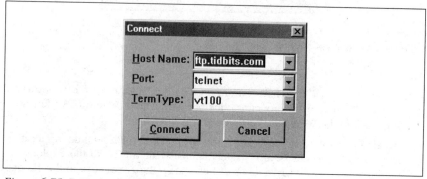

Figure 6-75: Initiating a telnet connection (telnet.exe)

Notes

- Local Echo causes everything you type to be displayed in the *telnet* window.

- The Blinking Cursor option makes it easier for you to keep track of the cursor location in the window.

- The VT-100/ANSI setting will serve your purposes in most cases, unless the remote host instructs you differently when you log in.

- The Buffer Size setting (default: 25) specifies the number of lines of text the *telnet* window will maintain in its line buffer. Increasing this number allows you to scroll further back in the session to review previously displayed data.

- Start Logging allows you to save all data displayed in the *telnet* window to a file. You can review this file with a text editor.

- *telnet* provides Edit → Copy and Edit → Paste, but doesn't support the usual Ctrl-C and Ctrl-V keyboard accelerators.

- Adding "http 80/tcp" to the port number list in the *Windows**Services* file enables you to type http instead of 80 as the port when connecting to a web server.

- Various *telnet* settings (i.e., WinPosTop, Machine1, Rows, etc.) are stored in the Registry at:

  `My Computer\HKEY_USERS\Default\Software\Microsoft\Telnet`

For more information on using *telnet* for email:

  http://faq.total.net/other/telnet/telnet.html

(The site mentions Windows 95, but the information is applicable to Windows 98.)

To download a shareware program that locates the appropriate address, login name, and port for libraries and *telnet* resources all around the world:

  http://www.lights.com/hytelnet/

For a more sophisticated *telnet* program, try downloading Tera Term (Pro), a free software terminal emulator for MS-Windows:

  http://spock.vector.co.jp/authors/VA002416/teraterm.html

Update Information Tool

\Windows\qfecheck.exe

Check versions of system files.

To Launch

    Address → qfecheck
    Start → Run → qfecheck

Description

The Win 98 Update Information Tool (*qfecheck*) allows you to find out which versions of updated system files are installed on your computer. You can also check to see whether the versions installed match the versions listed in your Registry.

There are two tabs in the *qfecheck* program: Registered Updates and Updated Files Found (see Figure 6-76):

Registered Updates
    Displays the system file updates that are found in your Registry. If a file or component is designated as Invalid, the version of the file on your drive doesn't match the version in the Registry. If a file or component is designated as Not Found, either the file is not installed on your drive or *qfecheck* can't find the file on your computer.

Updated Files Found
    To search for all system update files, whether or not they're in the Registry, click the Search Files button and specify the path you want to search. If a file appears on this list that does not appear on the Registered Updates list, it's probably because you installed an update without using the installation program or installed one of the early update releases.

Notes

- Once you've used the Search Files option in the Updated Files Found tab, you can right-click on any of the returned files and choose the Explore option.

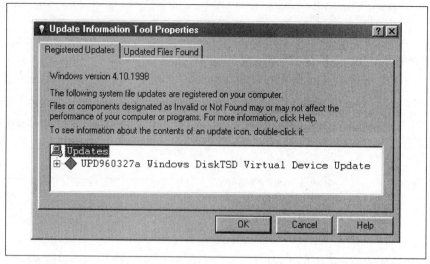

Figure 6-76: Win 98 Update Information Tool: Registered Updates tab (qfecheck. exe)

This opens the Explorer to the directory where the file is stored and highlights the actual file.

- You can find out the version for almost any *.dll* or *.exe* file by using the Version tab in the file's property sheet.

Version Conflict Manager   *\Windows\vcmui.exe*

Lets you view and restore versions of files replaced during Windows 98 installation.

To Launch

    Address → **vcmui**
    Start → Run → **vcmui**
    Start → Programs → Accessories → System Tools → System Information →
        Tools menu → Version Conflict Manager

Description

If you install (or reinstall) Windows 98 over a previous version of Windows, setup often finds that files of a more recent version than the ones it is attempting to install already exist on your drive. This is often the case when applications replace files originally created by the previous version of Windows. Win 98 setup automatically overwrites these files during installation, but backs the originals up in *\Windows\VCM*. Version Conflict Manager (*vcmui.exe*) lets you view a list of files replaced by Win 98 setup. It displays the filename, the date the file was backed up, the backed-up version, and the current version. You can replace any files by selecting them and clicking "Restore Selected Files."

Volume Control

Control volume and balance of the system's sound devices.

To Launch

    Address → sndvol32
    Start → Run → sndvol32
    Start → Programs → Accessories → Entertainment → Volume Control
    System Tray → Volume Control (if enabled via Control Panel)
    CDplayer → View → Volume Control

Description

sndvol32 pops up the Volume Control applet, which displays a series of sliders for controlling volume and balance of the system's sound devices, including speakers, microphones, the *.wav* file driver, and MIDI devices (see Figure 6-77). Volume Control offers sliders for both balance and volume. For mono devices (such as a simple built-in speaker), the balance control should be left in the middle.

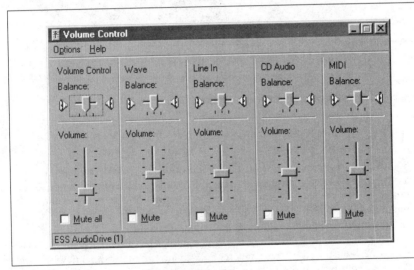

Figure 6-77: Volume Control (sndvol32.exe)

To set which controls are displayed, go to Options → Properties and check off the controls you want (see Figure 6-78). Options include:

Volume Control
    This is the master volume control and is the same control that pops up when you single-click the volume icon in the System Tray.

PC Speaker
    Control for the system's built-in speaker. This control does not override the hardware volume dial (if present), but interacts with it. For example, if the hardware volume control is turned all the way down, the Volume Control applet won't have any effect. However, if it's turned all the way up, you can

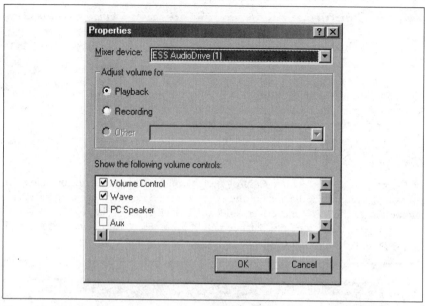

Figure 6-78: Selecting volume controls (sndvol32.exe)

turn the volume down using the software control. If the hardware control is in the middle, you can go in either direction.

Line In

Control for recording volume for a direct line in from another device.

Wave

Sound going to or coming from a *.wav* file on disk. This control also displays a visual readout of frequencies much like that on many high-end audio devices. Use *sndrec32* (Sound Recorder) or one of the many commercial multimedia devices to create or play *.wav* files. Note that adjusting the volume for *.wav* file playback here adjusts the overall playback level for all *.wav* files. You can also adjust the volume for a single *.wav* file by opening it with *sndrec32*, adjusting the volume there, and saving the file with its new volume. So you really have three volume levels that are being mixed: the volume of the actual input (in this case, the *.wav* file), the software volume control (*sndvol32*), and the hardware volume knob.

Microphone

The system microphone. Note that if both the speaker (Volume Control) and Microphone volume are turned up all the way, you may get feedback.

CD

Control the volume of CDs played with programs such as *cdplayer*. Note that you can record from a CD into a *.wav* files using *cdplayer* and *sndrec32*, with *sndvol32* controlling the playback and recording levels of both.

Synth

Control the volume of an attached synthesizer or other MIDI device.

You can check off a different set of controls to be displayed for recording, playback, or other purposes (such as voice input). The interface is a bit awkward, but once you've set up the chosen controls for each purpose, you can switch between the various sets of controls by going back to Options → Properties and choosing the radio button for recording, playback, or other. When recording is chosen, the titlebar shows the name Recording Control.

Notes

- Check Control Panel → Multimedia → Show volume control on the Taskbar for quick access to the volume control. Double-click on the indicator to pop up a full Volume Control application, or single-click to pop up a single slider for controlling only the master volume or temporarily muting the sound.

- If you want to be able to control both recording and playback volume at the same time, launch two instances of Volume Control, and choose Options → Properties → Recording for one, and Options → Properties → Playback for the other. You can arrange them one above the other on the screen for a complete audio control console.

- Control Panel → Multimedia → Audio gives access to a subset of the available volume controls. Selecting the Playback volume control launches the *sndvol32* volume control applet, and selecting the Recording volume control launches the recording volume control applet.

- The relationship between the various volume controls can seem mysterious if you don't have all the appropriate devices connected, since all of the controls are active, but some of them appear to do nothing. A common problem when trying to record and not getting any sound is that the devices in the "recording" section aren't "selected."

- Control Panel → Multimedia → CD Music contains a CD volume control bar that affects audio coming from the CD-ROM device itself. This volume bar interacts with the CD control in *sndvol32* in the same way the Master Out control interacts with the hardware volume dial (see the earlier "Master out" section).

See Also

"CD Player" and "Sound Recorder"
"Multimedia" in Chapter 5

For links to freeware and shareware sound applications:

http://aclass.com/SOFT/sound.html

WaveTop Data Broadcasting \Program Files\WaveTop\wavetop.exe

Receive certain types of web page content over the Public Broadcasting System's (PBS) Vertical Blanking Interval.

To Install

Add/Remove Programs → Windows Setup → Web TV for Windows →
WaveTop Data Broadcasting

To Launch

        Start → Run → `C:\Program Files\wavetop\wavetop.exe`
        Start → Programs → Accessories → WaveTop
        System Tray → WaveTop icon → right-click → Start WaveTop

Description

WaveTop is a free service provided by WavePhore, Inc. that transmits Web-based content from certain providers over the Vertical Blanking Interval (VBI) signal accompanying PBS broadcasts. Content providers include such companies as *USA Today*, *Time*, and *The Wall Street Journal*.

Notes

- Content from WaveTop is pushed to your system every hour or so. This means you must leave WaveTop running in order to receive updates. It also means that the information you view is stored locally on your system and may not be as up-to-date as content you would find over the Internet.

- WaveTop requires the installation of Web TV. If Web TV is not already installed, you will be prompted to include it in the installation when you install WaveTop.

- Like Web TV, the version of WaveTop that ships with Win 98 was designed for use with ATI All-in-Wonder display cards. Other tuner cards will often come with a customized version of WaveTop that must be installed. If you have a tuner card that does not provide a version of WaveTop, you can always check *http://www.wavetop.net/* for a list of supported tuners.

Web Publishing Wizard   *\Program Files\Web Publish\wpwiz.exe*

Lets you publish files to a web server.

To Launch

        Address → `C:\Program Files\Web Publish\wpwiz.exe`
        Start → Run → `C:\Program Files\Web Publish\wpwiz.exe`
        Start → Programs → Internet Explorer → Web Publishing Wizard

Description

The Web Publishing Wizard can help you publish files to a supported web server. The wizard can publish to web servers that support FTP, UNC, HTTP Post, or Front Page. In addition, the wizard supports certain ISPs, such as CompuServe and AOL. Basically, all *wpwiz* does is copy files from your local system to a designated web server using one of the supported protocols. You can achieve much the same effect (and have a little more control) using a standard FTP client or something like the full version of FrontPage. However, *wpwiz* does provide a convenient way to get files onto a web server.

In order to upload files to a web server, you will need to know several things:

- The location of the files to upload

- The URL of the web server

- The username and password to access the web server

In addition to the items listed above, you may need to know the protocol used to upload the files if the wizard cannot automatically determine it.

Notes

- In Windows 98 Second Edition, the Start Menu shortcut is Start → Programs → Accessories → Internet Tools → Web Publishing Wizard.

- The Web Publishing Wizard automatically remembers information you enter and provides it as the default the next time you run the wizard.

- When you use Front Page Express to save directly to a URL, it launches the Web Publishing Wizard.

- Don't confuse the Web Publishing Wizard with the Publish Web function of Personal Web Server (which also calls itself a Web Publishing Wizard). The PWS wizard is used to publish files in their original format to your personal web server. You can, however, use *wpwiz* to publish a whole web (basically a directory of files) created with PWS to another web server.

Web TV for Windows   \Program Files\TV Viewer\tvx.exe

Watch TV on your computer.

To Install

> Add/Remove Programs → Windows Setup → Web TV for Windows → Web TV for Windows

To Launch

> Address → tvx
> Start → Programs → Accessories → Entertainment → Web TV for Windows
> Quick Launch Bar → Launch Web TV for Windows

Description

Web TV allows you to use a TV tuner card on your system to watch television. It also provides an electronic program guide that allows you to browse through and search local programming. Web TV can also take advantage of interactive elements provided by some channels and shows. These interactive elements may be as simple as a link provided in the closed-captioning space that launches an external web browser to interactive content delivered within the actual TV viewing area through the Vertical Blanking Interval (VBI) of a standard television broadcast. Right now, the technology is fairly limited. In the future, however, the promise of high-speed digital transports, such as digital satellite and cable broadcasts, may bring fully interactive television.

Notes

- Web TV is finicky. For starters, it only works with certain models of TV tuners. It was designed to work with the ATI All-in-Wonder line of combination video-adapters. Other manufacturers (such as Hauppauge and STB) have begun to ship new tuner cards with drivers built to support Web TV. Even these newly designed cards, however, can be tricky to get working. If you really want to use Web TV, we recommend sticking with the ATI cards.

- Make sure Web TV is installed before you install your TV tuner card. If you install Web TV later, you may have to reinstall your tuner card drivers to get Web TV to work.

- While you're running Web TV, move your mouse to the top of the screen and hold it there for a moment to pop up a taskbar with a limited remote function and some settings. Hold your mouse over the main screen for 5 seconds or so to make the taskbar go away.

Windows Explorer

\Windows\explorer.exe

The 32-bit user interface shell that allows you to view files and directories in a tree-like structure.

To Launch

> Address → `explorer`
> Start → Run → `explorer`
> Right-click on the Start button or any folder → Explore
> Start → Programs → Windows Explorer

Description

The Explorer is the default Windows shell. It creates the Desktop and all of the standard icons, folders, and menus (including the Taskbar and the Start menu) the first time it is run. Running it thereafter will create a two-paned window in which you can navigate through all of the files, folders, and other resources on your computer. See "Windows Explorer" in Chapter 4 for a description of the user interface. In Windows 98, Explorer now has *.cab* file viewing and extracting functionality. See Chapter 4 for details.

Notes

- Using IE 4.0, it is possible to browse your local hard drive to view files and directories and even launch files in a way similar to using Explorer. With a little customization you can even configure Explorer to behave similarly to IE 4.0. See Chapter 9, *Web Integration*, for details.

- You can use the command-line switches for the Windows Explorer in shortcut links (see Figure 6-79) or batch files; for example, you can run the Explorer with a specified file selected.

- The Target line accepts all of the command options mentioned. Note that the "Start in:" line can be used instead of the `/root,object` option.

- After changing the shell= line in *system.ini*, loading a new shell requires only a logoff/logon; a full reboot is not necessary.

See Also

> "Internet Explorer"

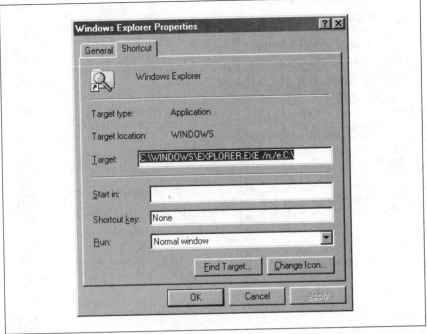

Figure 6-79: The standard Explorer configuration as seen in an Explorer shortcut

---

Windows Help and Windows HTML Help Viewer   \Windows\
winhlp32.exe; \Windows\hh.exe

WinHelp and HTML Help viewer.

To Launch

Select Help from the Start Menu, choose Help from any application, or double-click any *.hlp* or *.chm* file.

Description

Although some applications in Windows 98 still use WinHelp files, the majority of them use HTML Help to display tips and explanations about a given feature or product.

When you choose Help in many Win 98 applications, you are launching an HTML Help engine (accesses *.chm* files) and it is displaying the Help files (see Figure 6-80). When you choose Help in those programs that use WinHelp to access *.hlp* files, you are launching *winhlp32*, the WinHelp engine and viewer (see Figure 6-81). Regardless of the engine used, the Help dialog provides a consistent starting point and features three tabs: Contents, Index, and Search (this tab is named Find in any *.hlp* files using *winhlp32*). They are designed to help users locate information in three different ways:

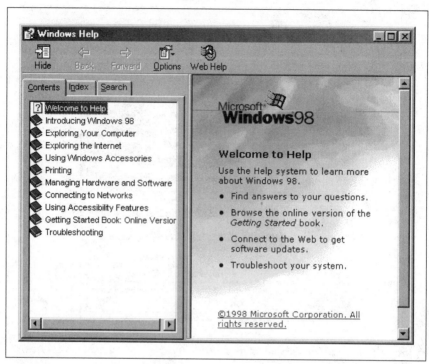

Figure 6-80: A Help dialog using HTML Help

Contents

The outline that appears under the Contents tab is defined in a *.cnt* file, and is located in the same directory as the application's *.hlp* file.

Index

This is identical to any book index, and contains keywords listed alphabetically, with second-level entries indented. The Index can encompass multiple help files.

Search

The Search tab can perform a full text search in HTML Help on the entire *.chm* file. A Find tab can be found when using WinHelp, and it allows a full text search on the entire *.hlp* file. The first time you click the Find tab, the Find Setup Wizard appears and prepares to generate a database of searchable text as an *.fts* (full text search) file, giving you the following options: Minimize Database Size (produces the smallest word list), Maximize Search Capabilities, or Customize Search Capabilities (allows you to select the topics). None of this is necessary when using HTML Help.

Notes

- If there is no *.cnt* file, *winhlp32* goes to a defined contents page which is the entry point to the help, bypassing the contents/index/find tabs. This is common for small help files.

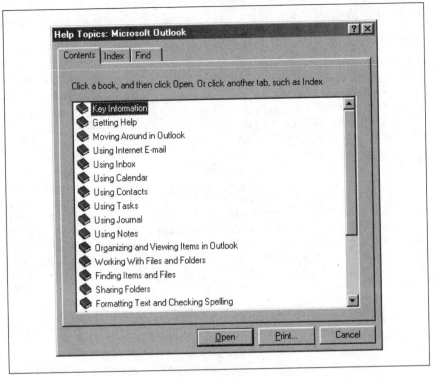

Figure 6-81: A Help dialog using winhlp32.exe

- The current version of HTML Help doesn't provide the annotating and book-marking features you may be used to in WinHelp, but future versions will have these capabilities.

- You'll find most of the *.hlp* and *.chm* files in the *\Windows\Help* directory; however, some applications store Help files in their own program directory.

- Since the WinHelp engine is run on over 100 million PCs running Win3.1, Win95, NT 3.51, and NT4.0, it will continue to be used along with HTML Help for many years.

- It is possible to save the URL to an HTML page and view it in a browser (of course the HTML links in the page won't work in your browser). To do this, right-click in the HTML help page and select properties. Select and copy everything in the address (URL) line, select the New → Shortcut option from the desktop context menu, paste the URL into the Command Line window, and press enter. The URL syntax for this is:

```
mk:@MSITStore: .chm file location ::/.htm page name
```

See Also

For more information about HTML Help:

http://msdn.microsoft.com/workshop/author/htmlhelp/

Windows Report Tool

\Windows\winrep.exe

Submit system information to a support provider over the Internet.

To Launch

> Address → `winrep`
> Start → Run → `winrep`
> Start → Programs → Accessories → System Tools → System Information →
>   Tools menu → Windows Report Tool
> Visit a support page in IE4 or IE5

Description

Windows Report Tool (*winrep.exe*) lets you submit a problem report to a support provider (such as Microsoft) over the Internet. It is also used for submitting bug reports during the Windows beta testing process. When submitting a problem, you must first browse to a submission support web page in IE4, where an ActiveX control will automatically launch *winrep* for you. You can enter a description of your problem, what you expect to happen, and steps needed to reproduce the problem. This information, along with collected information about your system and your user information, will be sent to the support provider.

You can change the user information sent using Options → User Information. You can also change the system information sent using Options → Collected Information. By default, only your basic system settings (Windows version, CPU type, etc.) are sent (see Figure 6-82). You can also elect to send copies of important system files, such as *autoexec.bat, win.ini*, and *system.ini*, along with the report, but you should really only do so if your support provider requests it. Use the Add button to include files not on the list, such as reports from *msinfo32*.

Notes

• By default, *winrep* makes an Internet connection using the settings specified for IE4 (Control Panel → Internet → Connections). You can specify an alternate proxy server using Options → User Information.

• *winrep* can also be used as a standalone app for collecting your system information and saving it to a *.cab* file. If you launch *winrep* manually on your system, you will be prompted to save your report instead of submitting it.

• Even if you are submitting a report, you can also save it using File → Save or Options → Autosave on Submit.

WinPopup

\Windows\winpopup.exe

Send pop-up messages to other Win 98 computers on your network.

To Launch

> Address → `winpopup`
> Start → Run → `winpopup`

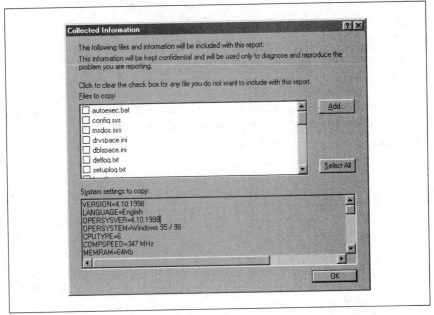

Figure 6-82: Default system settings in Windows Report Tool (winrep.exe)

Description

In order to successfully send a *winpopup* message to another Win 98 machine on your network, that machine must also be running *winpopup* (see Figure 6-83).

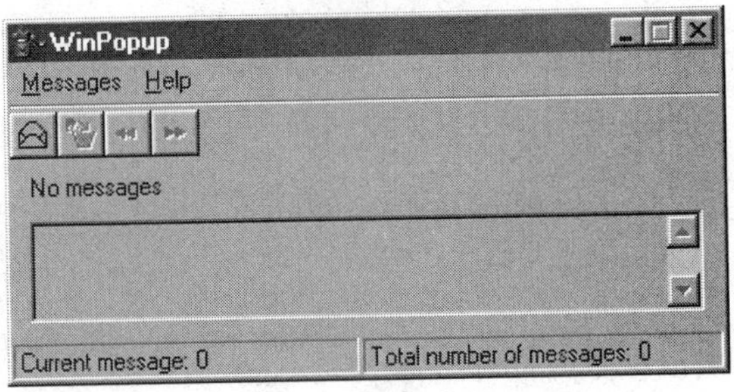

Figure 6-83: winpopup.exe

To send a message to an individual, click Messages → Send, or click the Send button on the toolbar. The "User of Computer" radio button is selected by default, so type in the network name (a UNC path to the computer—e.g., \\charles), tab to the Message field, type your message, and click OK.

To send a message to everyone in your workgroup, click Workgroup and type in the workgroup name. Type your message and click OK.

Notes

- *winpopup* messages can't be saved.

- *winpopup* will say "Message successfully sent" even if *winpopup* is not running on the target machine. The message just disappears into the ether.

- If you plan on using *winpopup* on a regular basis, place a shortcut to the program in the startup directory (\ *Windows\Start Menu\Programs\StartUp*) so that it's always running. The reason for this is that if *winpopup* isn't running, you won't be able to receive any *winpopup* messages from anyone.

- You can configure *winpopup* with the following options:

  - Play sound when a new message arrives

  - Enable "Always on top"

  - Pop up a dialog on message receipt

- Messages → Discard deletes the current message (navigate with Next and Previous menu items or buttons), and Messages → Clear All deletes all your received messages.

- For more sophisticated options and ways of delivering messages, you might consider Microsoft Chat or some type of email program such as Outlook Express or Windows Messaging.

See Also

"Outlook Express," "Microsoft Chat"
"Windows Messaging" in Chapter 8

WordPad   *Program Files\Accessories\wordpad.exe*

A simple word processor that comes with Windows 98.

To Launch

Address → `wordpad`
Start → Run → `wordpad`
Start → Programs → Accessories → WordPad

Description

Although *wordpad* lacks many of the features that come with Microsoft Word, it has many basic word-processing features. You can:

- Set word-wrap options: no wrap, wrap to window, or wrap to ruler

- Use Print Preview

- Apply 16 different colors to selected text

- Set the tab stop position and insert bullets

- Set the ruler to one of the following measurement units: Inches, Centimeters, Points, or Picas

- Automatically load the current WordPad document into Windows Messaging/ Exchange for sending through email

---

- Save or open any of the following types of files: *.doc*, *.rtf*, and *.txt*
- Undo multiple actions (`Ctrl-Z`), but there is no redo action
- Choose from a wide selection of different fonts and font sizes
- Insert objects of your choice

Notes

- Unlike Notepad, WordPad doesn't have a 57K limit; this is why Win 98 prompts you to open *.txt* files over 57K with *wordpad*.

- You can open Word 6.0 documents with WordPad, but you might lose some formatting. Before saving a Word 6.0 document, WordPad will display the following warning: "This document was created by Microsoft Word. WordPad does not support all of the features provided by Word; therefore, you may lose information by saving this file as a Word file with the same name." A similar thing applies to Word 97 documents, but WordPad will display the following warning: "WordPad cannot save documents created by Word 97. Would you like to save in a different format?" By saving a Word 6 or 97 file in WordPad, you still run the risk of losing some formatting.

- WordPad doesn't have spell-checking capabilities.

- WordPad's default font is Times New Roman, and there's no way for WordPad to open with any other default font. Once WordPad is running, you can select all or some of the text and change the font.

- Beware of the following when dragging a file onto WordPad: be sure to drop the file icon onto the WordPad icon (shortcut on Desktop) or onto the WordPad titlebar if you want to view it or edit it, and drop it onto the open WordPad window if you want to embed the icon as an object into a WordPad document.

- To prevent WordPad from overwriting your file extensions and adding its own when you save a file, place quotation marks around the name of the file you want to save (e.g., "read.me"), and click Save. Otherwise, you'll get *read. me.doc*

See Also

"Notepad"

You can download CWordPad, a freeware program similar to WordPad that *does* have spell-checker capabilities, from:

http://www.cetussoft.com/freeware.htm

CHAPTER 7

DOS and Other Command-Line Utilities

While you can run any of the Windows 98 GUI applications from the command line, the reverse is not true. There are many powerful commands, often known only to system adminstrators, that are only available from the command line or from within scripts or batch files. In this chapter we provide an alphabetical reference to these Windows 98 commands. This includes commands such as *copy* and *rename* that are built into the DOS command interpreter, as well as external DOS commands like *deltree* and *sort,* networking commands like *netstat, ping,* and *tracert,* and the command-line versions of utilities like *defrag, explorer,* or *regedit.*

Command Lines

Windows 98 provides several different command lines: the Run prompt (Start → Run), a DOS or "command" window, and an Address Toolbar (similar to the Run prompt but always visible on the Taskbar or Desktop once you have selected it from the Taskbar context menu). An easy way to open a DOS window is to use:

      Address → command

or:

      Start → Run → command

However, a DOS window is sufficiently useful that you may want to put a shortcut to \ *command.com* into \ *Windows\Start Menu\Programs\StartUp,* so that a DOS window will be opened up whenever you boot your machine. You can open multiple DOS windows at the same time.

There are a few significant differences between the Run prompt and Address Toolbar versus the DOS command line. The most important are:

- Some commands (such as *cd, dir, copy, rename,* and so forth) are internal to *command.com.* They can be invoked from the Run prompt or Address Bar only by a syntax too complex to be worthwhile. These internal commands are so noted in their reference entries.

- Each instance of the command interpreter runs in its own virtual machine, each with its own "environment." The environment includes such information as the current directory, the search path (the directories in which the command interpreter looks for the commands whose names you type), and the format of the prompt. Some commands, once issued, change the environment for subsequent commands. The most obvious example of this is when you type a sequence of related commands at the DOS prompt such as:

```
C:>cd \windows\desktop
C:\Windows\Desktop>notepad myfile.txt
```

This example illustrates one of the limitations of the Run prompt and Address Bar. Since they execute only one command at a time and then exit, concepts such as "the current directory" have little meaning for them. As a result, you must always specify complete pathnames for any filenames you want to edit.

Commands such as *cd, path, prompt, set*, and others whose principal function is to affect the command environment thus have no effect at the Run prompt or Address Bar.

- Both the Run prompt and the Address Toolbar keep a history of recent commands in a drop-down list. This makes commands easy to re-execute. (However, you can get an even more powerful command history function in a DOS window using the *doskey* command.)

In addition, the Run prompt and Address Toolbar allow you to type the pathname of a file to launch the associated application. Typing the name of a disk or folder will open a folder window to display its contents. Doing the same thing at a DOS prompt will earn you an error message. (However, you can run the application associated with a file even if you don't know the application, or even open a folder or drive window, using the *start* command at the DOS prompt.)

- The search path followed by the Run prompt and the Address Toolbar is:

  a. \ *Windows\Desktop*

  b. \ *Windows\System*

  c. \ *Windows*

  d. The contents of the environment variable PATH.

  e. The paths for applications installed in non-standard locations (i.e., not in \ *Windows*) may be defined in the Registry at HKEY_LOCAL_ MACHINE\Software\Microsoft\Windows\CurrentVersion\App Paths. (See Chapter 13, *The Registry*, for details.)

- You must enclose long filenames in quotes to use them in a DOS window, since the command interpreter uses spaces to separate command-line arguments.

What happens if a command is not found differs between the Run prompt and the Address Toolbar. The Run prompt will give an error message, while the Address Toolbar will interpret the command as a URL and launch the default browser. For example, if the Clipboard isn't installed, typing clpbrd will launch the browser, looking for the URL, *http://clpbrd/*, which the browser will eventually try as *http://www.clpbrd.com*.

For more information on the Run prompt, see Chapter 4, *The Windows 98 User Interface*; for more information on the DOS command interpreter, see the entries for *command* and *set* in this chapter, as well as Chapter 11, *The Batch Language*, which describes the Windows batch language.

Wildcards, Pipes, and Redirection

Special symbols that can be used on the DOS command line are listed in Table 7-1. These symbols cannot be used in the Address Toolbar or Run prompt command lines.

Table 7-1: Wildcards, Pipes, and Redirection Symbols

Symbol	Description
*	Refers to multiple characters in a file or directory name.
?	Refers to a single character in a file or directory name.
>	Redirects a command's output to a standard device or a file.
>>	Appends the output from a command to the specified file.
<	Directs input to a command from a nonstandard source, such as a file.
|	Redirects the output of a program or command to a second program or command. (This is called a "pipe.")

Examples

The following examples demonstrate some uses of wildcards, pipes, and redirection:

.
    All files with all extensions.

professor.*
    All files with "professor" anywhere in the name, with any extension.

bonelli.
    All files with names ending with "bonelli" (or "Bonelli"), with any extension.

chap?.doc
    All files named "chap" plus one character and with *doc* extensions (e.g., *chap1.doc*, but not *chap-1.doc* or *chap.doc*).

Keep in mind that not all commands handle wildcards in exactly the same way. For example, *dir ** and *dir *.** list the same thing, but *del ** will delete only files without an extension.

dir c:\windows /o/a > c:\data\windows.txt

List all files ordered alphabetically in the *Windows* directory, and create a file of this listing called *windows.txt*. If the file already exists, it will be overwritten.

Instead of directing to a file, you can direct to a device, such as NUL (an electronic void). This is useful if you want a command to run without sending output to the screen.

dir c:\windows\system /o/a >> c:\data\windows.txt

Add the directory listing of the files in the *C:\Windows\System* directory to the end of the file *windows.txt*.

If the specified file doesn't exist, one is created. If one does exist, the output from the command is added to it, unlike with the > key, where the original contents are overwritten.

sort /+12 < c:\nutshell\mylist.txt

To sort the lines in a text file (*c:\nutshell\mylist.txt*) on the twelfth character, the *sort* command is fed input from the file. The output is sent to the screen, not reordered in the file.

echo y | del *.*

If you try to delete all the files in a directory, *del* will prompt you for confirmation. Piping a "y" to the program using *echo* supplies the required answer automatically.

Commands and Their Syntax

In all of the command entries in this chapter (see Table 7-2), the "To Launch" section contains a description of the command-line syntax. For example:

```
ftp [options] [host] [-s: filename]
```

Command-line arguments shown in brackets are optional. If options must occur in a specific order, they are listed in that order on the syntax line. A vertical bar between two options means you can use one or the other, but not both.

For example:

```
[+|-]
```

means you can use a plus sign (+) *or* a minus sign (–).

If there are multiple option/argument combinations, or multiple names for a command, we list several syntax lines with the options and arguments that must be used together. Otherwise, we just use the dummy argument [options] and list the options later.

Unless specified otherwise, filename arguments can be any combination of drive letter, directory path, and filename. The directory path can be absolute (starting with \), relative to the current directory, or a UNC path (including the name of another host in the network). At the DOS prompt, or in batch files, the filename can include wildcards (* and ?).

Table 7-2: Complete List of Commands Covered, with Brief Descriptions

Command	Description
arp	Address Resolution Protocol utility
attrib	Set attributes for file and directory
cd	Change directory
cls	Clear DOS window
command	MS-DOS command interpreter
control	Open the Control Panel folder or one of its applets
copy	Copy files
date	Display date
debug	Debug MS-DOS files
defrag	Defragment disk
del	Delete files
deltree	Delete directories
dir	Display directory contents
diskcopy	Copy entire contents of a disk
doskey	Edit, recall, and create macros for DOS commands
drvspace	Compress a disk
edit	DOS-based ASCII file editor
exit	Exit MS-DOS
explorer	Windows Explorer
extract	Extract .cab files
fc	Compare the contents of two files
fdisk	Fixed disk configuration utility
find	Find file strings
for	Run commands in a loop, for some given number of arguments
format	Format disks
ftp	File Transfer Protocol utility
ipconfig	IP Configuration utility
jview	Java command line loader
label	Label disk volume
lfnfor	Disable/enable long filenames in for loops
md	Make directory
mem	Display memory usage
more	Display contents of a text file one screenful at a time
move	Move files and directories
nbtstat	Display NBT stats
net config	Run network configuration

Command	Description
net diag	Run network diagnostics
net help	Display network help
net init	Network initialization
net logoff	Logoff network
net logon	Logon network
net password	Set network password
net print	Display information about the print queue on a shared printer
net start	Start Win 98 networking services
net stop	Stop Win 98 networking services
net time	Synchronize a computer's clock with a shared clock on a server
net use	Connect or disconnect a computer from a shared resource
net ver	Display the type and version number of the workgroup redirector
net view	Display a list of computers in a specified workgroup
net	Contains all of the *net* commands above
netstat	Display protocol statistics and current TCP/IP network connections
path	Set or display the command search path
ping	Try to contact a remote internet host
prompt	Change the DOS command prompt
rd	Remove directory
regedit	Registry Editor
ren	Rename files and directories
route	Manipulate TCP/IP routing table
rundll32	Run Dynamic Link Library (*.dll*) files
scandskw	ScanDisk utility
set	Set environment variables
setup	Set up Windows 98
sort	Sort text input in alphanumeric order
start	Start Windows applications
sys	Copy system files and *command.com* to disk
telnet	Telnet utility
time	Display or set time
tracert	Traceroute utility
type	Type out contents of a text file
ver	Display Windows version
win	Win 98 bootstrap loader
xcopy32	Copy files and directories

arp

\Windows\arp.exe

Display or modify the IP-to-physical address translation tables.

To Launch

```
arp -s inet_addr eth_addr [if_addr]
arp -d inet_addr [if_addr]
arp -a [inet_addr] [-N if_addr]
```

Description

arp compares the destination IP address to a hardware address. If there is a matching entry, then the hardware address is retrieved from the cache. If not, *arp* broadcasts an ARP (Address Resolution Protocol) Request Packet onto the local subnet, requesting that the owner (machine) of the IP address in question reply with its address. When an *arp* reply is received, the *arp* cache is updated with the new information, and it is used to address the packet at the link layer. Entries in the *arp* cache may be viewed, added, and deleted using *arp.exe*.

arp accepts the following options:

-a Displays current *arp* entries by displaying the cache contents. If `inet_addr` is specified, the IP and physical addresses for only the specified computer are displayed. If more than one network interface uses *arp*, entries for each *arp* table are displayed.

-d Deletes the host specified by `inet_addr`.

`eth_addr`
   Specifies a physical address as six hexadecimal bytes separated by hyphens, such as 08-00-20-77-2B-87.

-g Same as -a.

`if_addr`
   If present, this specifies the Internet address of the interface whose address translation table should be modified. If not present, the first applicable interface will be used.

`inet_addr`
   Specifies an Internet address, such as 10.25.99.3.

-N `if_addr`
   Displays the *arp* entries for the network interface specified by `if_addr` (used with -a).

-s Adds the host and associates `inet_addr` with the `eth_addr`. The entry is permanent (i.e., across reboots, normal behavior is to lose cache as entries time out).

Examples

From the command line:

```
C:\>ping whitehouse.gov
C:\>arp -a
```

The host will return a reply from the Internet address, indicating that the address has been set and the communication is established. Output similar to the following is displayed:

```
Interface: 10.26.45.123
Internet Address        Physical Address        Type
198.137.241.30          20-53-52-43-00-00       dynamic
10.26.97.8              20-53-52-43-00-00       dynamic
10.26.97.50             20-53-52-43-00-00       dynamic
```

Notes

- *arp* tables don't normally require any manual intervention. They are built automatically. *arp* might be useful, for instance, if two systems were mistakenly set up to use the same IP address. You could use *arp* to discover the host that was misconfigured.

- Normally, cached entries will time out in a matter of minutes. Entries created with the −s option are always available.

- If you have an empty *arp* table (seen with **arp -a**), you must first *ping* an existing unit on your network (see previous example).

See Also

"ping"

TCP/IP Network Administration, by Craig Hunt (O'Reilly & Associates)

---

attrib   *Windows\Command\attrib.exe*

Display, set, or remove current file and directory attributes.

To Launch

```
attrib [+ | - attributes] [filename] [/s]
```

Description

Under DOS and Windows 98, each file has four attributes: read-only, archive, system, and hidden. These attributes are normally set and cleared by Windows or DOS applications, or on the property sheet for a file, but they can also be set or cleared manually with the *attrib* command. It is possible to set or clear attributes of multiple files in Explorer (see the note later in this section), but the *attrib* command may be preferable for those comfortable with using the command line.

attrib with no arguments displays the attributes of all files in the current directory (including hidden files). Specify a file path to see or set the attributes of the file. You can even use wildcards with *attrib* to help automate tasks (see examples).

attrib accepts the following arguments:

+   Sets an attribute.

−   Clears an attribute.

a   Archive file attributes set by applications whenever they create or modify a file, and cleared by backup programs such as *xcopy* when they make an archive copy of the file. This is merely a flag and doesn't affect operation of file.

h   Hidden file attribute. If set, the file will not show up in normal *dir* listing (use `dir /ah`). Windows Explorer can be set to show or not show hidden files. For this reason, hidden files are much less "secret" than they were in older versions of DOS and Windows.

r   Read-only file attribute. If set, the file can't be modified or deleted (without a warning).

s   System file attribute. If set, the file is used by DOS or Windows as part of its operation. The file should then not be deleted, moved, or renamed.

The following option, if specified, must follow the filename:

/s   Process files in all subdirectories in the specified path.

Examples

Set the file *readme.txt* to read-only:

```
C:\>attrib +r readme.txt
```

Note: Spacing is important.

Set the file *readme.txt* to read/write, and make it hidden:

```
C:\>attrib -r +h readme.txt
```

Make all files in the root directory (including *msdos.sys*, etc.) unhidden and writable:

```
C:\>attrib -s -h -r \*.*
```

If you just want to see these files, use `dir /a` or `dir /ah`.

Unmark archive attribute on all backup files created by applications before doing backup with *msbackup* or *xcopy* (first, change directory to the top of the directory hierarchy you plan to back up):

```
C:\>attrib -a *.bak /s
```

Notes

• Hidden files can still be opened by DOS programs; they just won't show up in *dir* listings. They will show up in the Explorer and in the open dialog box of Windows applications, as long as you select Explorer → View → Folder Options → View → Hidden files → Show all files.

• Multiple attributes can be set or cleared by combining options (separated by a space), but system and hidden attributes must be cleared before read-only and archive attributes can be cleared. For example:

```
C:\>attrib -s -h -r \msdos.sys
```

Old DOS hands will say that *attrib* is the only way to clear or set a from a group of files. But in fact, you can do this via the GUI, too. When you select a group of files, changes to Properties → Attributes will affect all selected files. This is particularly handy when combined with Start → Find → Files or Folders. Unfortunately, you are unable to clear or set the system attribute via the GUI, so you'll still need to use the *attrib* command to do this.

- Setting a file's system, hidden, or read-only attribute will prevent the file from being deleted or moved by the *del, erase,* or *move* commands, but it will not protect the file from the *deltree* or *format* commands.

- In the Explorer, you can view and change file/directory attributes in the File → Properties menu when a file/directory is selected.

- Hidden files and file attributes in detail view aren't shown by default in Explorer. Navigate to View → Folder Options → View to enable these options if you plan on frequently setting and clearing file attributes via the GUI. (You must restart a new instance of Explorer for these changes to take effect.)

- In the Explorer, an extra warning message is given when attempting to move or delete a directory or file with the read-only attribute set (see Figure 7-1).

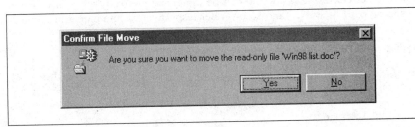

Figure 7-1: Warning when moving a read-only file

- Although you can process file attributes in subdirectories via the GUI in Explorer, it is easier to do this from the command line with the *attrib* command and the /s option.

- If you plan on working with attributes in Explorer, you may consider enabling the details view and dragging the Attributes heading (by default it is the last heading) next to the Name.

- You can also view file attribute settings with dir /v.

- In some instances, trying to change certain attributes without first clearing other attributes will fail. For example, the following won't work (assuming *filename* has +h and +s set):

```
attrib -h filename
attrib -s filename
```

But this does work:

```
attrib -s -h filename
```

"del or erase," "deltree," "dir," "explorer," "format," "move," "xcopy32"
"Backup" in Chapter 6, *Start Menu Programs and Other Graphical Applications*
To download Properties Plus, a utility that gives great control over attributes and files' dates: *http://www.ne.jp/asahi/cool/kish/*

---

cd or chdir

Internal to: \ *Windows\command.com*

Display the name of or change the current directory.

To Launch

```
cd [filename]
chdir [filename]
```

Description

With no arguments, *cd* displays the full pathname of the current directory. Given the pathname of another directory, it changes the current directory to the specified directory. Given only a drive letter, it changes to the same directory (if present) on the other drive.

Pathnames can be absolute (including the full path starting with the root) or relative to the current directory. A path can be optionally prefixed with a drive letter. The special paths .. and ... (and so on) refer respectively to the parent and grandparent of the current directory.

The *chdir* and *cd* commands are functionally identical.

Examples

If the current drive is *C:*, make *C:\temp\wild* the current directory:

```
C:\>cd \temp\wild
```

If the current directory is *C:\temp*, all that is necessary is:

```
C:\temp>cd wild
```

Change the current directory *C:\more\docs\misc* to the directory *C:\more*:

```
C:\more\docs\misc>cd ...
```

Move to the root directory of the current drive:

```
C:\Windows\Desktop\>cd \
C:\>
```

Notes

- The directory change affects only the DOS window and any programs subsequently launched from that window.

- To change to the current directory on a different drive, enter the drive letter followed by a colon (i.e., a:).

- The current directory is shown in the prompt (i.e., *C:\windows\desktop*).

---

cls

Internal to: \ *Windows\command.com*

Clear the DOS window, leaving only the command prompt and cursor.

Description

If you have information in your DOS box that you'd rather keep to yourself, just use the *cls* command and the window will be cleared instantly.

cls is also useful in complex batch files, for clearing the screen after one set of interactions or command output. The name *cls* (Clear Screen) refers to the old days when DOS owned the whole screen.

---

command

\ *Windows\command.com*

DOS 7.10 command interpreter.

To Launch

```
command [path] [device] [options]
```
Start → Programs → MS-DOS Prompt

Description

command starts a new copy of the Windows command interpreter, *command.com*. If entered from the Run prompt in the Start menu or the Address Bar, it also opens a new command interpreter window (i.e., DOS box).

The command interpreter allows you to perform many operations much more quickly than with the corresponding point-and-click programs.

The entire Windows 98 interface created by the Explorer runs in an invisible "system" DOS box that is created when the system boots. Each new instance of *command* inherits the environment created with that initial invocation of DOS. The *autoexec.bat* file (which DOS users will recognize as containing commands to be executed when DOS first starts up) is not reread for each new instance of *command* unless you use the /p option.

command accepts the following parameters and options:

/c *command*
> Executes the specified command and returns. This must be the last option on the command line. Note that the command doesn't normally wait for user input, so if you use this option from the Run prompt, the window will flash on the screen and disappear. Use /k if you want the window to stick around.

device
> Specifies the device to use for command input and output.

[*drive:*]*path*
> Specifies the directory containing *command.com*.

/e:*nnnnn*
> Sets the initial environment size to *nnnnn* bytes. The value of *nnnnn* should be between 256 and 32,768. See "set" for more information.

Command
Line Utilities

/f Forces a "Fail" response to the command interpreter's error handling routine query: "Abort, Retry, Fail?"

/k *command*
Executes the specified command and continues running. This must be the last option on the command line.

/l:*nnnn*
Specifies internal buffer length (requires the /p option). The value of *nnnn* should be between 128 and 1,024.

/low
Forces *command* to keep its resident data in low memory.

/msg
Stores all error messages in memory (requires the /p option).

/p Makes the new command interpreter permanent (can't use exit; will load *autoexec.bat*). You can still terminate the *command* window using the window's "Close" control or File → Close.

/u:*nnn*
Specifies the input buffer length (requires the /p option). The value of *nnn* should be between 128 and 255.

/y Steps through the batch program specified by /c or /k.

/z Causes the ERRORLEVEL number returned by external DOS commands to be displayed as follows: "Return code (ERRORLEVEL): *n*", where *n* is the ERROR-LEVEL returned by the last executed external command. If this option is used with a nonresident *command* (i.e., no /p), the following message is displayed: "WARNING: Reloaded COMMAND.COM transient."

Examples

Create a new instance of the DOS command interpreter from the Run prompt:

Start → Run → command

Start an instance of the command interpreter to give a single directory listing and then quit:

Start → Run → command /c dir c:\ /p

(The /p is necessary to display the listing long enough for you to read it.)

Run *command.com* and set the environment to 1024 bytes:

C:\>command /e:1024

Notes

- The *exit* command is used to quit any nonpermanent instances of *command*. In Windows 98, the "permanent" instances can actually be terminated with the close box, System Menu → Close (Alt-space C), or with a local reboot (Ctrl-Alt-Del).

- When a DOS window is opened from the Run prompt, the Start menu, or the Address Bar, a new instance of the command interpreter is run in a separate window; thus, several instances of *command.com* can be running independently at the same time. However, you may even want to run an instance of *command.com* from within another existing DOS window. This could be useful if, for example, you wanted to set special environment variables or other options for that instance of *command*. If you type `command` at the DOS prompt, the new instance of *command* overlays the previous one in the same window, rather than creating a new window.

- You can store a sequence of commands in any file with the *.bat* extension, and execute the file simply by typing its name. See Chapter 11 for details.

---

control

Display the Control Panel, which contains most of the configuration applets for Windows 98.

To Launch

```
control [filename.cpl] [applet_name] [,property_tab]
```

Description

As previously mentioned in Chapter 4 and Chapter 6, *control* launches the Control Panel folder, which contains many applets used to configure everything from Accessibility Options to Sounds. Chances are, if you need to configure something in Windows 98, this is the place to look. This section explains how to use *control* from the command line. This can be useful from the Run prompt or the Address Toolbar and can also be used to create shortcuts to individual tabs in some of the Control Panel applets.

control accepts the following parameters:

`applet_name`
> The name of the applet you want to launch. It must be spelled and capitalized exactly. Unless there's more than one applet within a *.cpl* file, you can omit the `applet_name`.

`filename.cpl`
> The filename of the applet in the Control Panel (found in *\Windows\System*) that you want to launch. If there's more than one control panel applet within the *.cpl* file, you also need to specify the `applet_name`. For example:

> *control sysdm.cpl*
>> Launches the System Properties dialog

> *control sysdm.cpl Add New Hardware*
>> Launches the Add New Hardware wizard

`,property_tab`
> The number (e.g., `, 0`—the comma is required) that launches an individual tab of a control panel applet. Not all tabbed control panel applets recognize the property tab arguments from the command line, since it's up to the applet to recognize this syntax, and not all do. For details on all the control panel applets, as well as the applicable `property_tabs`, see Chapter 5, *The Control Panel*.

Command
Line Utilities

Examples

Launch the Date/Time applet, with the Time Zone tab selected:

```
C:\>control timedate.cpl ,1
```

Launch the Add/Remove Program applet, with the Install/Uninstall tab selected:

```
C:\>control appwiz.cpl ,1
```

Notes

- Although some of the *control* command lines may seem a bit unwieldy, you can embed them in the Target lines in shortcuts on the Desktop or in the Start menu. This can be especially helpful if you have a certain tab in an applet that you acess frequently. For instance, if you add and remove Windows' components frequently, you might want a shortcut whose Target line (context menu → Properties → Shortcut → Target) would read:

```
C:\WINDOWS\CONTROL.EXE appwiz.cpl ,2
```

See Also

"rundll32"
Chapter 5

---

copy   Internal to: \ *Windows\command.com*

Copy one or more files to another location.

To Launch

```
copy source destination
copy [/a | /b] source [/a | /b] [+ source [/a | /b] [+ ...]]
[destination [/a | /b]] [/v] [/y | /-y]
```

Description

copy makes a complete copy of an existing file. If the destination filename already exists, you will be asked if you want to overwrite it.

It is also possible to use the *copy* command to concatenate (combine) files. To concatenate files, specify a single file for the destination, but multiple files for the source (using wildcards or *file1+file2+file3* format). You can specify a relative or absolute path (including disk names and/or UNC paths), or use a simple filename. When attempting to concatenate files, *copy* expects ASCII files by default, so in order to concatenate binary files, you need to use the /b option. The reason for this is that binary files typically contain one or more bytes outside the normal ASCII printable range (i.e., 32 through 127).

If the file (or files) to be copied is in a different directory or on a different disk, you can omit the destination filename. The resulting copy or copies will have the same name as the original.

You can use the special device name con (or con:) in place of either the source or destination filename to copy from the keyboard to a file, or from a file to the screen.

---

copy accepts the following parameters and options:

/a   Specifies that the file to copy is in ASCII format

/b   Specifies that the file to copy is a binary file

/v   Verifies that new files are written

/y   Suppresses prompting to confirm you want to overwrite an existing destination file

/-y Enables prompting to confirm you want to overwrite an existing destination file with the same name (default)

Examples

Copy the file *temp.txt* from *C:* to *D:\files* (both examples do the same thing):

```
C:\>copy c:\temp.txt d:\files\temp.txt
C:\>copy c:\temp.txt d:\files\
```

Copy all the files from the directory *D:\Cdsample\Images* to the current directory, giving the copies the same names as the originals:

```
C:\>copy d:\cdsample\images\*.*
```

Copy the file *words.txt* in the current directory to *D:\files*, renaming it to *morewords.txt*:

```
C:\>copy words.txt d:\files\morewords.txt
```

Create a text file by typing its contents directly, first enter:

```
C:\>copy con mystuff.txt
```

then type the text for the file followed by Ctrl-Z and Enter. The text typed from the keyboard in this example is saved as *mystuff.txt*.

Copy the contents of the file *mystuff.txt* to the screen:

```
C:\>copy mystuff.txt con
```

Concatenate *mon.txt*, *tue.txt*, and *wed.txt* into one file named *report.txt*:

```
C:\>copy mon.txt+tue.txt+wed.txt report.txt
```

Notes

- The *copy* command is internal and easy to use, but *xcopy* is more powerful and flexible.

- Binary file copy is assumed for normal copying, but the /b option should be used when appending one binary file to another, as in:

```
C:\>copy file1+file2 newfile /b
```

  By default, when concatenating, both source and destination files are assumed to be ASCII format, since binary files can seldom be usefully concatenated due to internal formatting.

- You can substitute a device (e.g., COM1) for either the source or the destination. The data is copied in ASCII by default.

- *copy* doesn't copy files that are 0 bytes long; use *xcopy* to copy these files.

Command
Line Utilities

- When concatenating, if no destination is specified, the combined files are saved under the name of the first specified file.

- *copy*, *move*, and *xcopy* normally prompt you before overwriting an existing file. To force these commands to overwrite in all cases without prompting you, set the copycmd environment variable to /y. To restore the default behavior, set copycmd to /-y.

See Also

"set," "xcopy32"

---

date

Internal to: \ *Windows\command.com*

Display or set the system date.

To Launch

    date [date]

Description

On most systems, a long-life battery retains the date information in memory, so the date doesn't need to be set every time the computer is started. If you type **date** on the command line without an option, the current date setting is displayed, and you are prompted for a new one. Press **Enter** to keep the same date.

date accepts the following options:

date
Specifies the date. Use *mm-dd-[yy]yy* format. Values for *yy* can be from 80 through 99; values for *yyyy* can be from 1980 through 2099. Separate month, day, and year with periods, hyphens, or slashes.

Notes

- The date format depends on the country setting you are using in your *config.sys* file. To display the date in other formats besides *mm-dd-yy*, add the country command to your *config.sys* file. You can change the date format to the European standard format (*dd-mm-yy*) or to the Scientific International (Metric) format (*yy-mm-dd*). You can also make these changes via Control Panel → Regional Settings (see Figure 7-2).

- MS-DOS records the current date for each file you create or change. This date is listed next to the filename in the directory listing.

See Also

"config.sys" in Chapter 12

---

debug

\ *Windows\Command\debug.exe*

Test and edit files and system memory in real-mode MS-DOS.

To Launch

    debug [filename] [testfile-parameters]

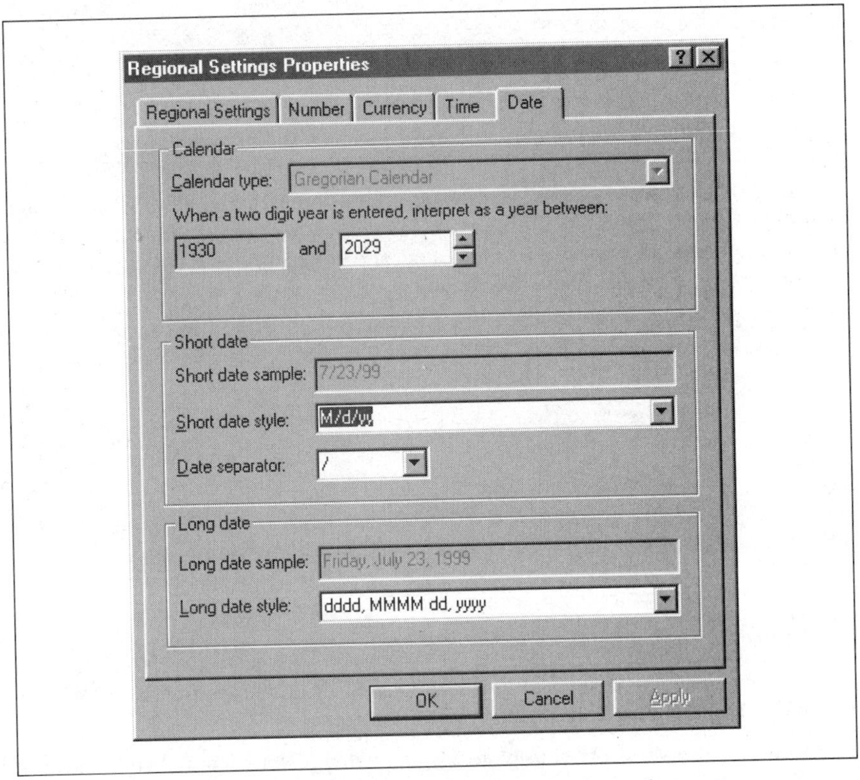

Figure 7-2: Setting the system date format via the Control Panel

Description

debug is limited to the first megabyte of memory, but it is useful for examining boot sectors and for determining the MS-DOS version on your system. Refer to an advanced-level book on MS-DOS programming for more information on how to use the *debug* commands.

The *debug* options are:

`filename`
   Specifies the file to test.

`testfile-parameters`
   Specifies the command-line information required by the file you want to test.

After *debug* starts, type ? to display the list of debugging commands.

Examples

Examine the boot sector (0) on drive C: (2), load data from the sector into address 100, then dump contents of memory at address 100:

```
C:\>debug

-L 100 2 0 1
```

```
-d 100 300
117A:0100 EB 3E 90 4D 53 57 49 4E-34 2E 30 00 02 20 01 00  > .MSWIN4.1.. ..
117A:0110 02 00 02 00 00 F8 C2 00-3F 00 20 00 3F 00 00 00  .....?. ?...
117A:0120 41 3D 18 00 80 00 29 E4-18 69 30 20 20 20 20 20  A=..)..i0
117A:0130 20 20 20 20 20 20 20 46 41-54 31 36 20 20 20 F1 7D  FAT16 .}
........
117A:02E0 53 59 53 4D 53 44 4F 53-20 20 20 53 59 53 80 01  SYSMSDOS SYS..
117A:02F0 00 57 49 4E 42 4F 4F 54-20 53 59 53 00 00 55 AA  WINBOOT SYS.U.
```

To check the MS-DOS version number by calling INT 21h Function 3306h, create the following script with a text editor such as *edit* or *notepad*. (In the example, we assume the script has already been created and saved in the file *dosver.dbg*. We use the *type* command to show the contents of the file.)

```
C:\>type dosver.dbg
a
mov ax,3306
int 21
ret

g 105
r bx

q
C:\>debug < dosver.dbg
....
BX 0A07
```

The number in BX at the end is the hexadecimal DOS version number: 0A07 for MS-DOS 7.10, 0007 for MS-DOS 7.0.

This example also shows how to write *debug* "scripts." Note that all blank lines are essential (for example, the first blank line exits from "A" mode).

You can also check the Windows version number with INT 2Fh function 160Ah: create a *winver.dbg* like *dosver.dbg* in the previous example, but change 3306 to 160A, and 21 to 2F. Windows 4.10 (Windows 98) is 040A, Windows 4.0 (Windows 95) is 0400.

See Also

For information on a genuine Windows debugger (Soft-Ice/Windows):

http://www.numega.com/

---

defrag
\Windows\defrag.exe

Reorganize the files on a disk to optimize disk performance.

To Launch

```
defrag [drive: | /all] [options] [/concise] [/detailed] [/f]
[/noprompt] [/q] [/u]
```

Description

If you use *defrag* from the command line, you can use options to control the behavior of the program without having to configure settings in the user interface.

If you type *defrag* at the command line without options, you will launch the *defrag* dialog described in Chapter 6, which contains the user interface for configuring settings.

defrag accepts the following options:

`/all`
    Defragment all local, nonremovable drives.

`/concise`
    Display the Hide Details view (default).

`/detailed`
    Display the Show Details view. The detailed view (accessible using the Show Details button (once *defrag* is running) gives a fascinating view of the state of your disk (see Figure 6-9).

    Click the Legend button for an explanation of what all the little colored boxes mean (see Figure 6-10).

`drive:`
    Drive letter of the disk to be optimized.

`/f` Defragment files and free space.

`/noprompt`
    Do not stop and display confirmation messages.

`/q` Defragment free space only.

`/u` Defragment files only.

Examples

Defragment files only (don't attempt to consolidate free space):

```
C:\>defrag c: /u
```

Defragment all non-removable drives (i.e., hard drives):

```
C:\>defrag /all
```

Defragment *E:* drive and show details:

```
C:\>defrag e: /detailed
```

Notes

- When you type `defrag` from the command line without parameters or options, *defrag* checks the drive for fragmentation, reports the amount of fragmentation (e.g., Drive C is 6% fragmented), and suggests whether you should defragment now (Start) or wait (Exit).

- Defragmentation is typically used with hard disk drives. *defrag* is unable to defragment a CD-ROM, a network drive, or a *subst*ed drive.

See Also

"Disk Defragmenter" in Chapter 6

del or erase

Delete one or more files.

To Launch

```
del filename [/p]
erase filename [/p]
```

Description

The *del* and *erase* commands are functionally identical; they can both delete one or more files from the command line.

The *del* options are:

filename
> Specifies the file(s) to delete. If you do not specify the drive or path, the file is assumed to be in the current directory. You can use standard * and ? wildcards to specify the files to delete.

/p Prompts for confirmation before deleting each file.

Examples

Delete the file *myfile.txt* in the *C:\files* directory:

```
C:\>del c:\files\myfile.txt
```

Delete all files with the pattern *myfile.** (*myfile.doc*, *myfile.txt*, etc.) in the current directory, but prompt for each deletion:

```
C:\>del c:\files\myfile.* /p
```

Notes

- Using the *del* command to delete a file does *not* move it to the Recycle Bin. In other words, you can't get a file back once you use the *del* command, unless you have disk recovery utilities to do so.

- Although *del* only accepts one parameter (**filename**), which specifies what is to be deleted, you can delete multiple files using wildcards (* and ?). For example: *del *.txt*. If more than one parameter is specified explicitly (e.g., *del c:\files.txt d:\myfile.doc*), the command aborts and an error message is displayed. Since *del* interprets long filenames with spaces as multiple options, you must enclose long filenames with spaces in quotes to delete the file.

- Files having read-only, hidden, and/or system attributes set can't be deleted with the *del* command. Use *deltree* or modify the file with *attrib* in order to delete these files.

- If you delete *.*, there is a prompt regardless of /p.

See Also

"attrib," "deltree"

deltree   \ *Windows\ Command\ deltree.exe*

Delete a directory and all the subdirectories and files in it.

To Launch

```
deltree [/y] directory
```

Description

deltree will delete a directory (and all its subdirectories), regardless of whether they are marked as hidden, system, or read-only. Like the *del* command, directories and/or files deleted by *deltree* will not be placed in the Recycle Bin.

The *deltree* options are:

directory
Specifies the name of the directory you want to delete.

/y Suppresses prompting to confirm that you want to delete any subdirectories.

Examples

Delete the *C:\ myfiles* directory and all subdirectories and files contained within it:

```
C:\>deltree c:\myfiles
```

Delete all the files and subdirectories but leave the directory itself:

```
C:\>deltree [/y] directory\*.*
```

Notes

- Use *deltree* with caution. To avoid mistakes, provide full and absolute paths when using the *deltree* command. This will help avoid deleting subdirectories you want to keep.

- Unlike the typical syntax order for most DOS commands, the /y option must *precede* the directory name.

- The *deltree* command supports wildcards, but if you specify a wildcard that matches both directory names and filenames, both will be deleted. Use the dir /a command to view files and directories you want to delete, to avoid deleting incorrect files or directories.

<hr>

dir   Internal to: \ *Windows\ command.com*

Display a list of files and subdirectories in a directory.

To Launch

```
dir filename [/p] [/w] [/a[[:]attributes]] [/o[[:]sortorder]] [/s] [/
b] [/l] [/v] [/4]
```

Description

Without any options, *dir* displays the disk's volume label and serial number, a list of all files and subdirectories (except hidden and system files) in the current directory in the order in which they are listed in the FAT, file/directory size, date/time of last modification, long filename, the total number of files listed, their cumulative size, and the free space (in bytes) remaining on the disk.

If you specify one or more file or directory names (optionally including drive and path, or full UNC path to a shared directory), information only for those files or directories will be listed.

Wildcards (* and ?) can be used to display a subset listing of files and subdirectories. * and *.* are equivalent.

dir accepts the following options:

/4 Display the listed years as four digits. By default, two-digit years are displayed. This option is ignored if used in conjunction with the /v option.

/a [*attributes*]
   Display only files with/without specified attributes (using – as a prefix specifies "not," and a colon between the option and attribute is optional). If no file with the specified attribute is found, you will get the message "File not found." That is, /a lists only files with the attribute. To see all files, including those with hidden attributes, use dir /a (without specifying any attributes). If you specify multiple attributes (separated by spaces), only those files with all of the specified attributes will be displayed. Attributes are:

   a   Files ready for archiving

   d   Directories

   h   Hidden files

   r   Read-only files

   s   System files

/b Use bare format (no heading information or summary). Use with /s to find a filename.

/c Display compression ratio of files on Dblspace or DrvSpace drives, assuming 16 sectors/cluster.

/ch Same as /c, but more accurate: uses actual sectors/clusters of host drive.

/l Use lowercase.

/o [*sortorder*]
   List files in sorted order (using – as a prefix reverses the order, and a colon between the option and attribute is optional):

   a   By last access date (earliest first)

   d   By date and time (earliest first)

   e   By extension (sorted alphabetically)

   g   Group directories first

   n   By name (sorted alphabetically)

   s   By size (smallest first)

/p Pause after each screenful of information. Press any key to continue.

/s Display files in specified directory and all subdirectories.

/v Verbose mode. Display attributes, date last accessed, and disk space allocated for each file in addition to the standard information.

/w Wide list format. File and directory names are listed in five columns.

Examples

Display all files in the current directory that end with *.txt* extension:

    C:\>dir *.txt

Display all files, listing years in four digits and pausing for each screenful:

    C:\>dir /4 /p

Display all files, sorted by date and time, latest first:

    C:\>dir /o-d

Display only directories:

    C:\>dir /ad

List all files on disk, sorted by size, and store output in the file *allfiles.txt*:

    C:\>dir \ /s /os > allfiles.txt

List the contents of the shared folder *cdrom* on machine *larryc*:

    C:\>dir \\larryc\cdrom

Notes

- You can preset *dir* parameters and switches by including the *set* command with the dircmd environment variable in your *autoexec.bat* file. For example:

      set dircmd= /p /o:gne

  presets *dir* to pause if the display gets too long to fit on a single screen, and to list subdirectories first, followed by files in alphabetical order, with files with the same name but different extensions alphabatized by extension.

---

dir filename /b /s acts as a kind of "find" command, looking in all subdirectories of the current directory. For example:

    C:\>dir telephon.ini /b /s

    C:\Windows\telephon.ini

    C:\Windows\Desktop\Win98\Misc\faq\telephon.ini

Unfortunately, you must specify an actual filename (not a wildcard) for this to work. For example, dir *.ini /b will not work.

- One of Windows Explorer's weaknesses is that it doesn't enable either of these very useful operations:

  - To print out a sorted directory listing of all files in the Windows directory:

    C:\>dir c:\windows /oa > lpt1

− To create a file containing the directory listing of the same directory:

`C:\>dir c:\windows /oa > c:\myfiles\windows.txt`

Actually, *dir* can be used to fix this weakness of the Explorer. See *Windows 98 Annoyances* for details on how to give the Explorer a Print-Dir facility.

- When using a redirection symbol (>) to send *dir* output to a file or a pipe (|) or to send *dir* output to another command, you may want to use /b to eliminate heading and summary information.

- If a directory is hidden but specified as an option, *dir* displays everything in the directory.

- The /s, /v, and /c options are not supported for UNC pathnames. In addition, when specifying a UNC path, you must specify the path to the actual shared folder. For example, even if folder *larryc**cdrom* is shared, typing *larryc* will give you the message: "The share name was not found. Be sure you typed it correctly."

See Also

"attrib," "set"

---

diskcopy
\ *Windows\Command\diskcopy.com*

Copy the contents (files and directories) of one floppy disk to another.

To Launch

```
diskcopy [source [destination]] [/1] [/v] [/m]
```

Description

When using *diskcopy* to copy contents of a floppy disk onto another disk, keep in mind that any data on the destination disk will be overwritten. Both *source* and *destination* must be valid floppy drive designations, such as *A:* and *B:*.

/1   Copies only the first side of the disk (seldom used).

/m   Force multipass copy using memory only.

/v   Verifies that the information is copied correctly.

Examples

Copy *A:* drive to *B:* drive:

`C:\>diskcopy a: b:`

Copy *A:* drive to another diskette using *A:* drive (*diskcopy* will prompt you to insert and remove the appropriate floppy):

`C:\>diskcopy a: a:`

Notes

- The two floppy disks must be the same type. That is, if the source drive is a 1.44MB floppy, the destination drive must be as well. If they are not, the error message "Drive and/or diskette types not compatible" is displayed.

- You may specify the same drive for source and destination. The system will prompt you to swap the diskettes as needed.

- *diskcopy* will not work with a hard disk or a network drive.

- Prompts to insert source and destination disks are displayed once *diskcopy* is running.

- The Explorer has a GUI diskcopy facility: right-click A drive → Copy Disk → Start.

---

doskey

Edit and recall command lines and create macros for DOS commands.

Syntax

```
doskey [options] [macroname=[text]]
```

Description

doskey is an essential aid for anyone using the DOS command line regularly; so much so that you should normally load it into memory from *autoexec.bat*. Once it is loaded, you can use the function keys on the keyboard to recall and edit previous commands before reissuing them. You can also define macros for commonly used commands.

doskey supports a number of command-line options. These options fall into two groups: those that affect the copy of *doskey* already running, and those that must be used the first time *doskey* is run. These are listed below as install options and runtime options. All options can be specified as a full word, or using only the first letter. To change an install option once *doskey* is running, use the /reinstall option.

doskey is a little unusual in that you issue the *doskey* command again, with any of the runtime options, to change its operation.

The install options are:

/bufsize:*size*
Sets the size of shortcut macro and command buffer (default is 512 bytes).

/keysize:*size*
Sets the size of keyboard type-ahead buffer (default is 15 bytes).

/line:*size*
Sets the maximum size of line edit buffer (default is 128).

The runtime options are:

/echo:on |off
Enables or disables echo of shortkey macro expansions (default is on).

/file:*file*
Specifies a file containing a list of shortcut macros. Each macro should be on a separate line and should be of the form:

macroname = text of macro

Macros can contain a number of special characters, as defined later in this section.

/history
> Displays all commands stored in memory.

/insert
> Inserts new characters into the line when typing. This makes it difficult to edit an existing command!

/macros
> Displays all *doskey* shortcut macros. Can be used with redirection to save existing macros to a file.

/overstrike
> Overwrites new characters onto line when typing (this is the default).

/reinstall
> Installs a new copy of *doskey*.

doskey Commands

The last command entered is referred to as the template. Function keys and other keyboard accelerators are used to recall a different command into the template, where it can be edited. Among the most useful keys are **F7**, which displays a numbered history of stored commands; **F9**, which lets you pick a numbered line from that history; and **F8**, which lets you pick a command beginning with a specified character or characters. The complete list of keyboard commands is as follows:

Left/Right arrow
> Moves the cursor back/forward one character.

Ctrl + L/R arrow
> Moves the cursor back/forward one word.

Home/End
> Moves the cursor to beginning/end of line.

Up/Down arrow
> Scroll up (and down) through the list of stored commands. Each press of the up arrow recalls the previous command and displays it on the command line.

Page Up/Down
> Recalls the oldest/most recent command in the buffer.

Insert
> Insert text at the cursor.

Delete
> Delete text at the cursor.

F1 Copies the next character from the template to the command line. This works with and without *doskey*.

F2 + *key*
> Copies text from the template up to (but not including) *key*.

F3 Copies the template from the present character position to the command line. This works with and without *doskey*.

F4 + *key*
> Deletes the characters from the present character position up to (but not including) *key*.

F5 Copies the current command to the template and clears the command line.

F6 Places an end-of-file character (^Z) at the current position on the command line.

F7 Displays a numbered list of the command history.

Alt-F7
> Deletes all commands stored in the buffer.

chars **+ F8**
> Entering one or more characters followed by F8 will display the most recent command beginning with *chars*. Pressing F8 again will display the next most recent command beginning with *chars*, and so on. If no characters are specified, F8 cycles through the existing commands in the buffer.

F9 + *command#*
> Displays the designated command on the command line.

Alt-F10
> Deletes all macro definitions.

doskey Macros

You can define macros on the *doskey* command line, but you will probably want to save them in a file to be reloaded using the /f option. Each macro should be on a separate line. Macros have the following form:

    macroname = text

The text of a macro can include spaces and tabs, and any of the following special codes:

$G Redirects output—equivalent to the redirection symbol >.

GG
> Appends output to the end of a file—equivalent to the append symbol >>.

$L Redirects input—equivalent to the symbol <.

$B Sends macro output to a command—equivalent to the pipe symbol |.

$T Separates commands when creating macros.

$$ Use for the $ sign.

$1 *to* **$9**
> Represents any command-line parameters that can be specified when the macro is run. Comparable with the %1 to %9 characters in batch programs.

$* Represents command-line information that can be specified when *macroname* is written. $* is similar to the replaceable parameters $1 through $9, except that everything typed on the command line after *macroname* is substituted for the $* in the macro.

Examples

Load *doskey* into memory:

    C:\>doskey

Create a *doskey* macro called *win98* to change to a frequently used directory:

    C:\>doskey win98 = cd "C:\Windows\Desktop\win98\tim's draft"

Play the macro:

    C:\>win98

Delete the macro:

    C:\>doskey win98=

Display all current *doskey* macros:

    C:\>doskey /macros

Notes

- To automatically run *doskey* in every DOS command window, you can either:

  - Open MS-DOS Prompt → Properties and enter \ *Windows*\ *Commands*\ *doskey.com* as the batch file.

  - Specify an actual batch file at that same location, including *doskey* as well as any other commands.

  - Run *doskey* from *autoexec.bat.* This uses extra memory and can increase boot time, but it means that you can have a global command memory no matter how many DOS prompts you open.

- Because macros are stored in the buffer, they are lost when a DOS session is ended or if *doskey* is reloaded with doskey /r. To save macros across sessions:

      C:\>doskey /m > macros.txt

  These macros can be retrieved in a later session by using:

      C:\>doskey /f:macros.txt

  Of course, you need to be in the same directory where you stored *macros.txt,* or provide the full path.

---

drvspace

\ *Windows*\ *drvspace.exe*

Compress and uncompress data on floppy disks or hard disk drives.

To Launch

```
drvspace /compress d: [/size=n| /reserve=n] [/new=e:]
drvspace /create d: [/size=n | /reserve=n] [/new=e:] [/cvf=nnn]
drvspace /delete d:\d??space.nnn
drvspace /format d:\d??space.nnn
drvspace /host=e: d:
drvspace [/info] d:
drvspace /mount [=nnn] d: | d:\d??space.nnn] [/new=e:]
```

---

324   Chapter 7 – DOS and Other Command-Line Utilities

```
drvspace /move d: /new=e:
drvspace /ratio[=n] d:
drvspace /settings
drvspace /size[=n| /reserve=n] d:
drvspace /uncompress d:
drvspace /unmount d:
```

Description

When you run *drvspace* without command-line arguments, the DriveSpace Manager appears, with menu commands for selecting the operations to perform.

drvspace creates a new uncompressed drive, called the host drive, where it stores the compressed volume file (*.cvf*). If the host drive contains any free space in addition to the *.cvf*, you can also use it to store files that must remain uncompressed.

drvspace accepts the following options:

/compress
> Compress a hard disk drive or floppy disk.

/create
> Create a new compressed drive in the free space on an existing drive.

/cvf=*nnn*
> Reports extension of the compressed volume file (*.cvf*) file.

d: The first drive.

d??space.*nnn*
> The filename of the hidden compressed volume file on the host drive, which can be either drvspace.*nnn* or dblspace.*nnn*, where *nnn* represents the actual filename extension.

/delete
> Delete a compressed drive.

e: The second drive.

/format
> Format a compressed drive.

/info
> Display information about a compressed drive.

/interactive
> Can be added to any command line to have DriveSpace ask for any missing parameters.

/mount
> Mount a compressed volume file (*.cvf*). When DriveSpace 3 mounts a *.cvf*, it assigns it a drive letter; you can then use the files that *.cvf* contains.

/new=e:
> Specifies the drive letter for the new compressed drive. The /new option is optional; if you omit it, DriveSpace assigns the next available drive letter to the new drive.

/noprompt

Can be added to any syntax except the /info option. The /noprompt option prevents any confirmation dialog boxes from appearing (except for error messages).

/ratio

Change estimated compression ratio of a compressed drive.

/reserve=n

Specifies how many megabytes of free space DriveSpace 3 should leave on the uncompressed drive. To make the compressed drive as large as possible, specify a size of 0.

/size

Change the size of a compressed drive.

/size=n

Specifies the total size, in megabytes, of the compressed volume file. (This is the amount of space on the uncompressed drive that you want to allocate to the compressed drive.) You can include either the /reserve switch or the /size switch, but not both.

/uncompress

Uncompress a compressed drive.

/unmount

Unmount a compressed drive.

Associated Files

drvspace.inf
drvspace.sys

Examples

Compress drive *E:*

    C:\>**drvspace /compress e:**

Create a new compressed drive that uses all available space on uncompressed drive *E:*

    C:\>**drvspace /create e: /reserve=0**

Delete the compressed volume for drive *C:*

    C:\>**drvspace /delete c:\dblspace.###**

Change the size of drive *C:* so that it is as large as possible:

    C:\>**drvspace /size /reserve=0 c:**

Notes

- You can include either the /reserve option or the /size option, but not both. If you omit both options, *drvspace* uses all but 2 MB of free space. The /reserve option can be abbreviated as /reser.

- To mount a compressed disk that wasn't present when you started your computer (for example, a floppy disk), you need to mount it. Use *drvspace* /mount from the command line or Advanced → Mount from the GUI. To delete a compressed drive, the /delete option must specify the complete pathname of the compressed volume file (e.g., *d:\drvspace.002*).

- For compression ratios of files, use *dir* /c and *dir* /ch.

See Also

"Drive Space 3" in Chapter 6

---

edit
Windows\Command\edit.com

A DOS-based full-screen ASCII text editor.

To Launch

```
edit [/b] [/h] [/r] [/s] [/<nnn>] [file(s)]
```

Description

edit is very useful when working with ASCII files (e.g., batch files) from the command line. It supports the standard cut, copy, and paste commands and their shortcuts, the Find, Repeat Last Find, and Replace commands, and it allows you to split the window and resize it (see Figure 7-3), and even to change the color settings for the program. Of course the standard File menu commands are also present (Save, Save As, Close, Print, and so forth).

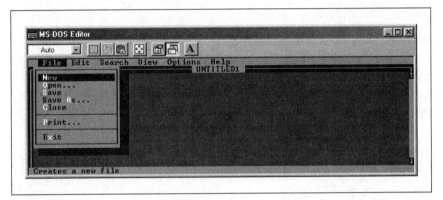

Figure 7-3: Using edit.com, the text editor

The *edit* options are:

/nnn
    Loads binary file(s), wrapping lines to *nnn* characters wide.

/b Forces monochrome mode.

file(s)
    Specifies the initial file(s) to edit. You may use wildcards and multiple filenames.

/h Displays the maximum number of lines possible for your hardware.

/r Loads file(s) in read-only mode.

/s Forces the use of short filenames.

Examples

View a binary file (for example, you can search for "MS-DOS Version 7", but be careful not to make any changes—do *not* save the file on exit):

```
C:\>edit /70 c:\Windows\notepad.exe
```

Edit *autoexec.bat* file:

```
C:\>edit c:\autoexec.bat
```

Edit all of the text files on your Desktop:

```
C:\Windows\Desktop>edit *.txt
```

Notes

- *edit.com* loads much faster than Notepad, WordPad, or Word.

- You can cut and paste between multiple files by switching windows. Edit's clipboard is not the same as Window's.

See Also

"Notepad" and "WordPad" in Chapter 6

---

exit
Internal to: \ *Windows**command.com*

Quit the *command.com* program.

Description

exit is used without parameters or options, and is also used to get back into Windows after you choose "Restart windows in MS-DOS mode" on startup.

Exit won't do anything if you are in a top-level instance of *command.com* (i.e., running in MS-DOS mode rather than under Windows 98).

---

explorer
\ *Windows**explorer.exe*

The 32-bit user interface shell that allows you to view files and directories in a tree-like structure.

To Launch

```
explorer [/n] [/e][,/root,object][[,/select],subobject]
```

Description

On the command line, *explorer* supports the following options (note that if you specify more than one option, including /e and /n, they must be separated by commas—this is different from most Windows 98 programs):

/e   Use the Windows Explorer view. The default is Open view (a one-pane folder) if you specify a folder or other object on the command line.

/n   Always open a new window when starting the Explorer (even if the specified folder is already open).

/root,object

Specify the object (directory) that will be used as the root of this Windows Explorer Folder. The default is to use the Desktop. The Explorer can go anywhere inside the root, but not outside or "above" it. The root can be a disk, UNC pathname, or folder name.

/select

Specifies that the parent folder is opened and the specified object is selected.

subobject

Specify the folder to receive the initial focus, unless /select is used. The default is the root.

Examples

Open a window rooted at *nut* so you can easily browse the whole server, but nothing else:

```
C:\>explorer /e,/root,\\nut
```

Open a folder window on *C:\Windows* (or make an open window active) and select *sol.exe*:

```
C:\>explorer /select,c:\windows\sol.exe
```

Notes

- You can use the command-line switches for the Windows Explorer in shortcut links or batch files; for example, you can run the Explorer with a specified file selected.

- The Target line accepts all of the command options mentioned. Note that the "Start in:" line can be used instead of the /root,*object* option.

- After changing the shell= line in *system.ini*, loading a new shell requires only a logoff/logon; a full reboot is not necessary.

- With Windows 98 it is now also possible to view *.cab* files and extract their contents using Windows Explorer (*explorer.exe*).

---

extract   *Windows\Command\extract.exe*

Extract files and lists from a Windows cabinet (*.cab*) file.

To Launch

```
extract [/y] [/a] [/d | /e] [/l dir] cabinet [filename ...]
extract [/y] source [newname]
extract [/y] /c source destination
```

Description

This utility lets you to extract one or more files from the cabinet archives on the Win 98 CD-ROM or on your actual hard drive. This is generally only done if it is suspected that an installed file was corrupted in some way. (To install optional pieces of Windows 98, it is best to use Control Panel → Add/Remove Programs → Windows Setup.) With Windows 98 it is now also possible to view *.cab* files and extract their contents using Windows Explorer (*explorer.exe*).

The Windows 98 CD-ROM contains several cabinet "sets," which are groups of .*cab* files arranged by function. The Win 98 files can be found in the set starting at *win98_22.cab* and ending at *win98_69.cab*. If you don't know the exact location of a file, use the /a option to "walk" the entire set, starting at *win98_22.cab*. Note, however, that there are several other sets containing various utility files:

precopy1.cab–precopy2.cab
    Setup and .*inf* files

catalog3.cab
    Catalog files for driver certification

base4.cab–base5.cab
    Boot files

net6.cab–net10.cab
    Network driver files (only during network installations)

driver11.cab–driver21.cab
    Win 98 drivers

chl99.cab
    Channel bar web pages

edb.cab
    Various utilities

mini.cab
    Mini Windows (only from MS-DOS setup)

There is a GUI equivalent of the *extract* command available in Windows 98 called the System File Checker (*sfc.exe*). In cases when you don't know the name of the .*cab* file, you can use *sfc* to "walk" through the .*cab* files on the Win 98 CD or on your own hard drive if you've stored them there. Of course you can do the same thing using the /a option with *extract*. The cabviewer feature now built into Windows Explorer automatically shows a .*cab* file's contents in the Explorer pane when you double-click a .*cab* file.

extract accepts the following options:

/a Process *all* cabinets. Follows cabinet chain starting in first cabinet mentioned.

/c Copy source file to destination (to copy from DMF disks).

cabinet
    Cabinet file (contains two or more files).

/d Display cabinet contents; do not extract files.

/e Extract (use instead of *.* to extract all files).

filename
    Name of the file to extract from the cabinet. Wildcards and multiple filenames (separated by blanks) may be used.

/l **dir**
    Location to place extracted files (default is current directory).

newname
> New filename to give the extracted file. If not supplied, the original name is used.

source
> Compressed file (a cabinet with only one file).

/y   Do not prompt before overwriting an existing file.

Examples

Display the contents of a *.cab* file called *win98_30.cab* in the current directory:

```
C:\>extract /d win98_30.cab
```

Extract the file *canyon.mid* from the entire set of Windows 98 *.cab* files; in the current directory, and place the extracted file in *C:\Windows*:

```
C:\>extract /a win98_22.cab /l c:\windows\ canyon.mid
```

---

fc   *\Windows\Command\fc.exe*

Compare two files (or sets of files) and display the differences between them.

Syntax

```
fc file1 file2
fc [/a] [/b] [/c] [/l] [/lbn] [/n] [/t] [/w] [/nnnn]
```

Description

fc is most useful if you can't quite remember the difference between two ASCII files that you'd like to run. For example, if you have two batch files named *foobar. bat* and *bar.bat*, you can run *fc* to see the differences quickly.

The *fc* options are:

/nnnn
> Specifies the number of consecutive lines that must match after a mismatch (default value of *nnnn*: 2).

/a   Display only first and last lines for each set of differences, as opposed to the default of every different line.

/b   Perform a binary comparison.

/c   Disregard the case of characters.

/l   Compare files as ASCII text.

/lbn
> Set the maximum consecutive mismatches to the specified number of lines (default value of *n*: 100).

/n   Display the line numbers on an ASCII comparison.

/t   Do not expand tabs to spaces. By default, tabs are treated as spaces with 1 tab = 8 spaces.

/w   Compress whitespace (tabs and spaces) to a single space for comparison.

Examples

Compare *autoexec.bat* with *autoexec.old*:

```
C:\>fc autoexec.bat autoexec.dos
```

Make a binary comparison of two files named *term.exe* and *year.exe*:

```
C:\>fc /b term.exe year.exe
```

Notes

If `filename1` includes a wildcard, all applicable files are compared to `filename2`. If `filename2` also includes a wildcard, each file is compared with the corresponding `filename1`.

---

fdisk

\Windows\Command\fdisk.exe

Configure a fixed disk for use with DOS or another operating system.

To Launch

```
C:\>fdisk
```

Description

fdisk is a menu-driven utility used to configure and/or display information about the partitions on a hard disk. You can control the operation of *fdisk* with command-line options, or from a menu that is displayed by typing *fdisk* without any options (see Figure 7-4).

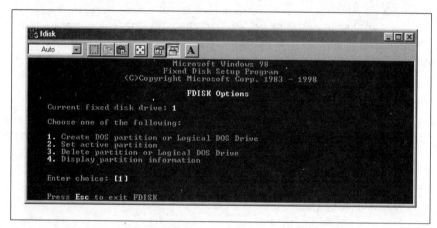

Figure 7-4: The fdisk menu (fdisk.exe)

The following tasks can be performed by *fdisk*:

- Creating a DOS partition or Logical DOS Drive
- Setting an active partition
- Deleting a partition or a Logical DOS Drive
- Displaying partition information

Using *fdisk* to create, modify, or delete partitions on a hard drive deletes all the data stored on that disk.

If you want to repartition a hard disk from multiple partitions into a single drive, you must first use *fdisk* to delete all existing partitions and logical drives, and then create a new primary partition and make it active.

fdisk accepts the following options:

/status
Displays partition information.

/x Ignores extended disk-access support. Use this switch if you receive disk access or stack overflow messages.

Examples

To display an overview of partition information, use the /status option:

```
C:\>fdisk /status
```

Notes

- If the /status option doesn't provide enough detail about your hard disk (such as the drive type of system), then start the *fdisk* program without the /status option and choose option 4 (Display partition information) from the GUI.

- By answering "yes" to enable large disk support, you will create a drive with FAT32, which supports drives over 2 GB. To change the size of a partition, it is necessary to delete the partition and create a new one of the required different size.

- If you convert your hard drive to FAT32 format using Drive Converter (*cvt1.exe*), you can't return to FAT16 unless you repartition and reformat the FAT32 drive. If you converted the drive Win 98 was installed on, you will need to reinstall Win 98 after repartitioning the drive.

- *fdisk* works only on hard disks physically installed on your computer. *fdisk* does not work on a drive formed by using the *subst* command, nor does it work on a network or an Interlink drive.

- *fdisk* doesn't display information about compressed drives, since they are hidden, read-only system files.

- *fdisk* won't run in Windows.

- For a better disk utility, try PowerQuest's Partition Magic:

  http://www.powerquest.com/

See Also

"Drive Converter" in Chapter 6

find

\Windows\Command\find.exe

Search one or more files for a specified text string.

To Launch

```
find [/v] [/c] [/n] [/i] "string" [filename[ ...]]
```

Description

After searching the specified files, *find* displays any lines of text that contain the string you've specified for your search. *find* is useful for searching for specific words (strings) in files, but don't get it confused with the Find → Files or Folders that is available in the Explorer (available from context menus, the Start menu, and elsewhere). Find → Files and Folders can search for text, files, directories, etc., and has many other capabilities that the *find* command doesn't have. See "Find Files and Folders" in Chapter 4.

The *find* options are:

/c Displays only the count of lines containing the string

/i Ignores the case of characters when searching for the string

/n Displays line numbers with the displayed lines

/v Displays all lines *not* containing the specified string

Examples

Search for "set" in *autoexec.bat*:

```
C:\>find "set" autoexec.bat
```

Search for "set" in *autoexec.bat* and *autoexec.dos*:

```
C:\>find "set" autoexec.bat, autoexec.dos
```

Count occurrences of "put" in *autoexec.bat*:

```
C:\>find /c "put" autoexec.bat
```

Search the current directory for the string "cls" in all *.bat* files and store the result in the file *cls.txt* (note that >> rather than > is necessary when redirecting the output of a *for* loop):

```
C:\>for %f in (*.bat) do find "cls" %f >> cls.txt
```

Notes

- You can search through multiple files by specifying each file to search on the command line, but unfortunately, wildcards (* and ?) are not accepted in the filename. To search for a string in a set of files, however, it's often possible to use the *find* command within a *for* loop structure. If redirecting *for* to a file, use >> rather than > (see the earlier example).

- If a filename is not specified, *find* searches the text input from the "standard" source (usually the keyboard), a pipe, or a redirected file.

  If you have a Unix background, you might be tempted to try something like:

```
dir c:\ /s /b | find "chap"
```

---

to search the contents of all files with "chap" in their names, but in fact, all you'd be doing is running *find* on the list of filenames, not on their contents.

- *find* won't recognize a string that has a carriage return embedded in it. For example, if "chapter" is at the end of the line, and "05" on the next, find won't report a match on "chapter 05."

---

for
Internal to: \Windows\command.com

Run a specified command for each instance in a list.

To Launch

```
for %variable in (set) do command [command-options] [%variable]
```

Description

A *for* loop is a programming construct that allows you to repeat a command for a list of items (such as filenames). You specify an arbitrary variable name and a set of values to be iterated through. For each value in the set, the command is repeated.

The values in the set are enclosed in parentheses, and should be separated by spaces. Wildcards can be used to supply a list of filenames.

Examples

Display the contents of all the files in the current directory that have the extension *.txt*:

```
C:\>for %f in (*.txt) do type %f
```

Redirect the output of the previous example to LPT1 (a printer port):

```
C:\>for %f in (*.txt) do type %f > lpt1:
```

Create a set of numbered directories (such as for chapters in a book):

```
C:\>for %x in (1 2 3 4 5) do md ch0%x
```

Notes

- in and do are not options, but a required part of the *for* command. If you omit either of these keywords, MS-DOS displays an error message.

- When redirecting the output of a *for* loop to a file, you must use >> (append to a file) rather than >, or else you will save only the last iteration of the loop. (The previous LPT1 reduction example is an exception, since LPT1 isn't a file, but a device, which will spool the output of each successive redirection in the loop.)

- When using the *for* command in a batch program, specify %%*variable* instead of %*variable*.

- You need not actually use the variable a second time as an argument to the command. You could, for instance, simply use the variable list to repeat a command some number of times.

See Also

"lfnfor"

format

\Windows\Command\format.com

Format a disk for use.

To Launch

right-click on Drive in Explorer → Format

```
format drive: [/v[:label]] [/q] [/f:size] [/b | /s] [/c]
format drive: [/v[:label]] [/q] [/t:tracks /n:sectors] [/b | /s] [/c]
format drive: [/v[:label]] [/q] [/1] [/4] [/b | /s] [/c]
format drive: [/q] [/1] [/4] [/8] [/b | /s] [/c]
```

Description

Before data can be stored on a disk, the disk must be formatted (most disks come pre-formatted). This process creates various low-level data structures on the disk, such as the File Allocation Table. It also tests the disk surface for errors and stores bad sectors in a table that will keep them from being used.

The *format* options are:

/b Allocates space on the formatted disk for system files.

/c Tests clusters that are currently marked "bad."

drive:
Specifies the drive that contains the disk to format.

/f:size
Specifies the size of the floppy disk to format (such as 160, 180, 320, 360, 720, 1.2, 1.44, 2.88).

/n:sectors
Specifies the number of sectors per track.

/q Performs a quick format, which means that the top-level filesystem information will be wiped out without actually erasing the data. After a quick format, data previously stored on the disk could possibly be recovered with an "unerase" or "unformat" utility.

/s Copies DOS system files to the formatted disk. This will be a DOS system disk only.

/t:tracks
Specifies the number of tracks per disk side.

/u Specifies an unconditional format, which saves floppy space by excluding the unnecessary "unformat" information that the Windows format includes.

/v[:label]
Specifies the volume label. This is an arbitrary title you give the disk. It can be up to 11 characters and can include spaces. The volume label will show up at the top of *dir* listings for the disk. See "label" for more information. If the /v option is omitted, or the label isn't specified, a prompt for a volume label is

displayed after the formatting is completed. If a label is specified with /v and more than one disk is formatted in a session, all of the disks will be given the same volume label.

/1   Formats a single side of a floppy disk.

/4   Formats a 5.25-inch 360K floppy disk in a high-density drive.

/8   Formats eight sectors per track.

Examples

Format floppy in drive *A:* using default settings:

    C:\>format a:

Format floppy in drive *A:* specifying 720K capacity:

    C:\>format a: /f:720

Format floppy in drive *A:* specifying a label:

    C:\>format a: /v:mydisk

Notes

- *format* size (specified with the /f option) must be equal to or less than the capacity of the disk drive containing the disk to be formatted. For example, a 1.44 MB capacity drive will format a 720K disk, but a 720K drive will not format a 1.44MB disk.

- *format* assumes that a floppy disk in a 3.5" drive will be formatted as 1.44MB, unless the /q option is used.

- A disk created with format /s won't boot into the Windows 98 GUI. To create a full boot disk, use the Startup Disk tab on the Add/Remove Programs applet, along with the following line in *autoexec.bat*:

    c:\windows\win.com

    See Chapter 5 for more details.

- By default, each sector on the disk is checked during formatting, so data can be sorted properly (unless /q is used). Bad sectors are marked and not used.

- *format* can't be used on network or *subst*ed drives.

- To format compressed disks, see "drvspace."

---

ftp   *\Windows\ftp.exe*

Transfer files between a host computer and a remote computer over the Internet (File Transfer Protocol).

To Launch

    ftp [-v] [-n] [-i] [-d] [-g] [host] [-s: filename]

Description

Like many Internet programs, *ftp* is a client-server application. Your local *ftp* client connects to a remote Internet server and issues commands to the server to upload or download files, display data, and so on. If you launch *ftp* from the Run prompt and get a file, it will be downloaded to your Desktop by default (unless you change the local working directory) since that's the default "current directory" for commands issued from the Run prompt. If you launch *ftp* from the Address Bar, there is no default current directory, so be sure you use the *lcd* command to change the local working directory to the desired location.

You must log in to the remote server; however, there are many public servers that allow anonymous ftp. Enter the login name *anonymous*, and enter your email address (or, frankly, any text) as the password. The complete list of commands you can issue once you are connected is documented later in this section.

You must specify the hostname or IP address of the remote computer. Most public ftp servers have a hostname beginning with "ftp," such as *ftp://ftp.uu.net*, but any remote host might be running an ftp server. Any files will be transferred to and from the current directory by default. Wildcards are supported for specifying the filenames in commands like *dir, ls, mget,* and *mput,* unless turned off with the *glob* command.

ftp options are:

-d Enables debugging, displaying all *ftp* commands passed between the client and server.

-g Disables filename globbing, which permits the use of wildcard characters in local file and path names. (See the *ftp* glob command.)

-i Turns off interactive prompting during multiple file transfers.

-n Suppresses autologon upon initial connection.

-s: *filename*
Specifies a text file containing *ftp* commands; the commands will automatically run after *ftp* starts. Use this option instead of redirection (>).

-v Suppresses display of remote server responses.

Figure 7-5 shows a sample *ftp* session.

FTP Commands

The following list shows the commands available once *ftp* is running. Not all commands may be effective for every server. For example, you may not be able to upload files to some servers, or delete files that are there. For most purposes, the most important commands to know are put, get, mput, mget, cd, lcd, and dir. If you are transferring binary files, be sure to use the binary command first, or the files will be damaged in transit.

! Runs the specified command (e.g., cd) on the local computer. ! allows you to issue local (DOS) commands. For example, you can use it to rename, copy, or delete files on the local disk, or to change the local working directory.

? [*command*]
Displays descriptions for *ftp* commands. Identical to help. ? by itself gives a list of available commands. ? command gives a brief description of each command.

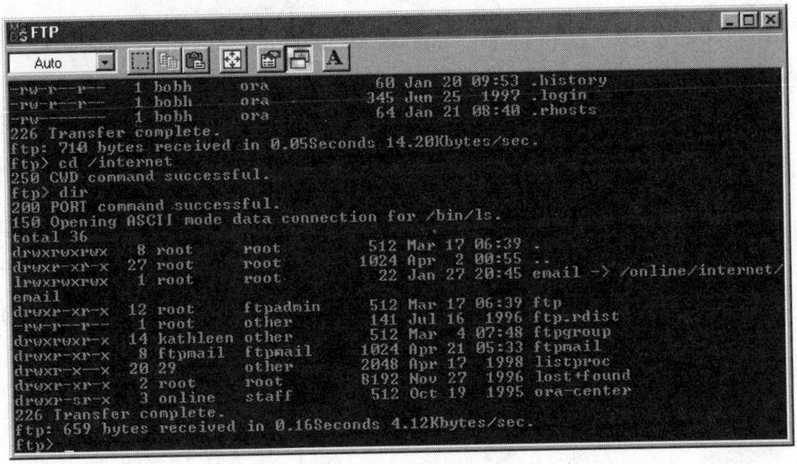

Figure 7-5: An ftp session

append
> Appends a local file to a file on the remote computer.

ASCII
> Sets the file transfer type to ASCII, the default.

bell
> Toggles a bell to ring after each file transfer command is completed. By default, the bell is off.

binary
> Sets the file transfer type to binary (crucial for *.zip*, *.gif*, and other binary file formats).

bye
> Ends the *ftp* session with the remote computer and exits *ftp*. Keep in mind that the standard DOS *exit* and *quit* commands won't work here.

cd [*directory*]
> Changes the working directory on the remote computer (to *cd* locally, use ! cd or lcd).

close
> Ends the *ftp* session with the remote server and returns to the *ftp* command interpreter. Use open to connect to a different *ftp* server.

debug
> Toggles debugging. When debugging is on, each command sent to the remote computer is printed, preceded by the string --->. By default, debugging is off.

delete *remote_file*
> Deletes a file on the remote computer. Only a single file can be deleted.

Command Line Utilities

`dir` Displays a list of a remote directory's files and subdirectories.

`disconnect`
Disconnects from the remote computer, retaining the *ftp* prompt.

`get remote_file [local_file]`
Copies a remote file to the local computer. If `local_file` is not specified, the copy will be given the same name as the original.

`glob`
Toggles filename "globbing." Globbing permits use of wildcard characters in local file or pathnames. By default, globbing is on.

`hash`
Toggles hash-mark (#) printing for each 2048-byte data block transferred. This is a crude status indicator. By default, hash-mark printing is off.

`help [command]`
Displays the description for each command (e.g., `help get`). For a list of the available commands, just type `help` or ? at the ftp prompt.

`lcd [directory]`
Changes the working directory on the local computer. By default, the current directory on the local computer is used.

`literal [command_line]`
Sends arguments, verbatim, to the remote *ftp* server. A single *ftp* reply code is expected in return. Allows you to send arbitrary command lines to the remote server. (Whether they can be executed depends on your login privileges at the remote server.) Spaces are allowed.

`ls` Displays an abbreviated list of a remote directory's files and subdirectories. This is useful when a directory contains a lot of files. Occasionally, anonymous users may not be able to use `ls`; in this case, you need to know the filename you're looking for. Typing `ls -1` will show the file details in the list.

`mdelete [files]`
Deletes multiple files on remote computers. Wildcards are supported.

`mdir [remote_files][local_file]`
Stores a directory listing of a remote directory's files and subdirectories, including file size and modification date. `remote_files` can be a list of file or directory names, and can include wildcards.

`mget [remote_files]`
Copies multiple remote files to the local computer using the current file transfer type. Wildcards (* and ?) can be used. You will be asked to confirm each transfer unless you turn off prompting with the **prompt** command. Local files will be given the same name as remote files.

`mkdir [directory]`
Creates a remote directory.

`mls [remote_dir][local_file]`
Stores a list of a remote directory's files and subdirectories in `local_file`.

mput [*local_files*]

Copies multiple local files to the remote computer, using the current file transfer type.

open [*hostname* or IP *address*]

Connects to the specified *ftp* server. If no host is specified, you will be prompted for one.

prompt

Toggles prompting. During multiple file transfers (**mget** and **mput**), *ftp* provides prompts to allow you to retrieve or store files selectively; **mget** and **mput** transfer all files if prompting is turned off. By default, prompting is on.

put [*local_file*] [*remote_file*]

Copies a local file to the remote computer, using the current file transfer type (ASCII or binary). If no local filename is specified, you will be prompted for one. If no remote filename is specified, the local filename will be used.

pwd Prints the current directory on the remote computer.

quit

Ends the *ftp* session with the remote computer and exits *ftp*.

quote [*command_line*]

Sends arguments, verbatim, to the remote *ftp* server. A single *ftp* reply code is expected in return. Identical to **literal**. Spaces are allowed.

recv [*remote_file*] [*local_file*]

Copies a remote file to the local computer. Identical to **get**.

remotehelp [*command*]

Displays help for remote commands supported by the server. This is probably similar to the commands available on the client, but may not be identical. As with **?** and **help**, supplying no arguments returns a list of command names. Use **remotehelp** *command* to get more info on each command. Figure 7-6 shows the output of **remotehelp**.

rename [*from_name*] [*to_name*]

Renames a remote file.

rmdir [*remote_directory*]

Deletes a remote directory.

send [*local_file*] [*remote_file*]

Copies a local file to the remote computer, using the current file transfer type. Identical to **put**.

status

Displays the current status of *ftp* connections and toggles.

trace

Toggles packet tracing; displays the route of each packet when running an *ftp* command.

type

Sets or displays the file transfer type.

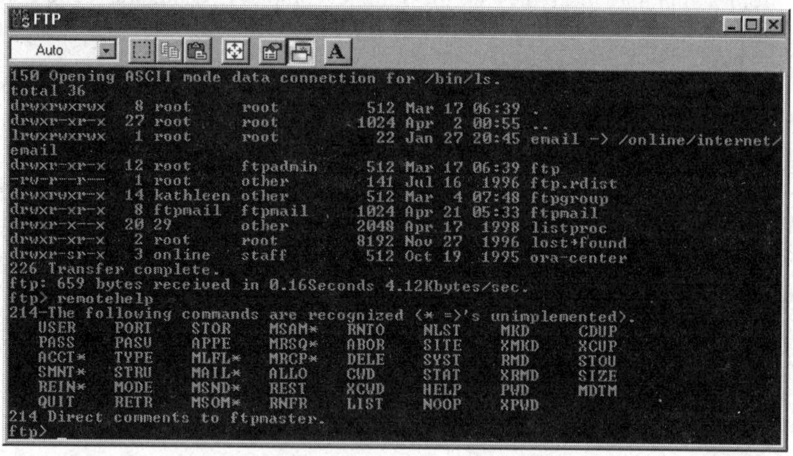

```
FTP                                                                    _ □ ×
┌─────────┐ ┌──┬──┬──┬──┬──┬──┬──┐
│ Auto    ▼│ │::│▣▣│▣▣│▣▣│▣▣│▣▣│ A │
└─────────┘ └──┴──┴──┴──┴──┴──┴──┘
150 Opening ASCII mode data connection for /bin/ls.
total 36
drwxrwxrwx   8 root     root         512 Mar 17 06:39 .
drwxr-xr-x  27 root     root        1024 Apr  2 00:55 ..
lrwxrwxrwx   1 root     root          22 Jan 27 20:45 email -> /online/internet/
email
drwxr-xr-x  12 root     ftpadmin     512 Mar 17 06:39 ftp
-rw-r--r--   1 root     other        141 Jul 16  1996 ftp.rdist
drwxrwxr-x  14 kathleen other        512 Mar  4 07:48 ftpgroup
drwxr-xr-x   8 ftpmail  ftpmail     1024 Apr 21 05:33 ftpmail
drwxr-xr-x  20 29       other       2048 Apr 17  1998 listproc
drwxr-xr-x   2 root     root        8192 Nov 27  1996 lost+found
drwxr-sr-x   3 online   staff        512 Oct 19  1995 ora-center
226 Transfer complete.
ftp: 659 bytes received in 0.16Seconds 4.12Kbytes/sec.
ftp> remotehelp
214-The following commands are recognized (* =>'s unimplemented).
   USER    PORT    STOR    MSAM*   RNTO    NLST    MKD     CDUP
   PASS    PASV    APPE    MRSQ*   ABOR    SITE    XMKD    XCUP
   ACCT*   TYPE    MLFL*   MRCP*   DELE    SYST    RMD     STOU
   SMNT*   STRU    MAIL*   ALLO    CWD     STAT    XRMD    SIZE
   REIN*   MODE    MSND*   REST    XCWD    HELP    PWD     MDTM
   QUIT    RETR    MSOM*   RNFR    LIST    NOOP    XPWD
214 Direct comments to ftpmaster.
ftp>
```

Figure 7-6: The output of remotehelp

user *username* [*password*]

> Specifies a user to the remote computer. If no password is specified, you will be prompted for one. If no username is specified, you'll be prompted for one of those, too. This is great for a second attempt at logging on to a machine that kicked you off for mistyping your password, without having to exit and start over.

verbose

> Toggles verbose mode. If on, all *ftp* responses are displayed; when a file transfer completes, statistics regarding the efficiency of the transfer are also displayed. By default, verbose is on.

Examples

To copy the file *preface.doc* from the directory */pub/nutshell* on a remote computer to *\temp\docs* on your local computer, once you're logged on to a server, you would perform the following from the DOS prompt (note that cd within *ftp* is for the remote computer):

```
C:\>cd \temp\docs
C:\temp\docs>ftp remote_computer
username
password
ftp>binary
ftp>cd /pub/nutshell
ftp>get preface.doc
```

Run a script containing *ftp* commands:

```
C:\>ftp -s:myfile.scr
```

This will load *ftp* and run *myfile.scr*, executing any *ftp* commands in the file.

Notes

- All *ftp* command names can be abbreviated to the first four letters; sometimes fewer.

- If arguments are omitted, you will be prompted for them.

- When using the get or mget commands, the files on the remote computer will be copied to whatever directory you launched *ftp* from, unless specifed otherwise with the lcd command. To switch from the local *C:* to the *A:* drive, for example, you would type:

  ```
  C:\>lcd a:/
  ```

- In *ftp* you must use the forward slash "/" instead of the backslash "\" in path-names; directory and filenames are case-sensitive in most instances, unless you log in to a computer running NT.

- *ftp* is a standard way to transfer files from computer to computer on the Internet, regardless of machine type. You can *ftp* any type of file from a Mac to a PC as easily as from one PC to another PC, or from a Unix workstation to a PC or Mac.

- Use remotehelp to get a command list from the remote server.

- Most web browsers support the *ftp://* protocol, which is equivalent to *ftp* get. See "Internet Explorer" in Chapter 6. You can also put files and log in with non-anonymous *ftp* (i.e., *ftp://username@host*) if you have login privileges on a given server.

- You must be connected to a network to use *ftp*.

- If you transfer a plain text file using ASCII mode, *ftp* does the right thing with the end-of-line characters. For example, if you *ftp* a text file from a Unix server to a Windows 98 machine using ASCII mode, the file will be converted using the MS-DOS end-of-line characters, but using binary mode will preserve the Unix end-of-line characters.

See Also

To download WS_FTP, a GUI *ftp* client for Windows 98, for qualified non-commercial use:

http://www.ipswitch.com/downloads/ws_ftp_LE.html

For a long list of alternative *ftp* utilities for Windows:

http://www.tsnsoftware.com/directories/internet-ftp/

---

ipconfig

Display the current TCP/IP settings on your computer.

To Launch

```
ipconfig [/all] [/batch [filename]] [/renew_all] [/release_all]
[/renew N] [/release N]
```

Description

ipconfig is similar to the Windows NT command and is the command-line equivalent of *winipcfg*. It displays TCP/IP configuration information from your computer and allows you to release or renew a dynamically allocated IP address and other information such as DNS servers, WINS servers, netmask, and the default gateway. The only difference between *ipconfig* and *winipcfg* is the way IP information is shown; the former on the command line and the latter in a GUI dialog. The command line options are the same for both *ipconfig* and *winipcfg*.

The *ipconfig* and *winipcfg* options are:

/all
  Display details

/batch *file*
  Write to *file*; if you do not specify a filename, it will write to *winipcfg.out* in the current directory

/renew_all
  Renew all adapters

/release_all
  Release all adapters

/renew *N*
  Renew adapter *N*

/release *N*
  Release adapter *N*

Examples

Launch *ipconfig*, renewing all adapters and sending all of the IP information to *iprenew.out* in the current directory:

```
C:\>ipconfig renew_all /batch iprenew.out
```

Notes

* *ipconfig* is useful if you have two different ways of connecting to a network. For example, you might have two different kinds of modems (e.g., one ISDN or cable) for connecting to two different kinds of networks, or you might dial in on your laptop, and then connect it directly at the office. After you've used one, you need to clear the cache of network information in order to use the other without rebooting Windows. This is done by doing the following:

```
C:\>ipconfig release_all
C:\>ipconfig renew_all
```

* For more information on IP configuration values, see "Network" in Chapter 5.

See Also

"IP Configuration" in Chapter 6

jview

Starts the Microsoft command-line loader for Java.

To Launch

```
jview [/a] [/cp <classpath>] [/cp:a <path>] [/cp:p <path>] [/d:<name>
=<value>] [/n <namespace>] [/p] [/v] <classname> [arguments]
```

Description

jview is used to run Java programs that aren't applets (Java programs run within a browser). *jview* uses Microsoft's version of the Java Virtual Machine (JVM), which is very fast, since it uses Just-In-Time compiler technology. *jview* supports the following options:

/a   Executes AppletViewer

arguments
   Command-line arguments to be passed on to the class file

classname
   .*class* file to be executed

/cp *<classpath>*
   Sets class path

/cp:a *<path>*
   Appends *path* to class path

/cp:p *<path>*
   Prepends *path* to class path

/d:*<name>*=*<value>*
   Defines system property

/n *<namespace>*
   Namespace in which to run

/p   Pauses before terminating if an error occurs

/v   Verifies all classes

/vst
   Prints verbose stack traces (requires debug classes)

Notes

- Typing *jview* in a command window will display the version of the currently installed JVM.

- Unfortunately, there is not an option or Registry setting for *jview* that enables Java logging. However, you can redirect the output when invoking an application, as in the following example:

  `C:\>jview main > javalog.txt`

- When you run a Java application using *jview* from within the Developer Studio IDE, the MS-DOS command prompt window closes immediately after the Java application terminates. To prevent the MS-DOS window from closing immediately, you can have an input statement as the last statement in your Java application. For example:

```
system.in.read();
```

A second option is to run your Java application externally (outside the Developer Studio environment).

For the Microsoft SDK containing the latest Java compiler and Virtual Machine for using Java with the WIN32 API only:

http://www.microsoft.com/java/download.htm

---

label
\ *Windows\ Command\ label.exe*

Create, change, or delete the volume label of a disk.

To Launch

```
label [drive:][label]
```

Description

The label appears at the top of the listing when you display a directory with the *dir* command or view the disk with the Explorer.

The *label* options are:

[drive:]
> Specifies the drive that contains the disk you wish to label. If you omit the drive option, the current drive is used by default.

[label]
> Specifies the label for the disk. If you omit the label, the system will prompt you to provide it. The label must be no more than 11 characters in length.

Examples

Create/change the label for the disk in drive *A*:

```
C:\>label a: newlabel
```

Notes

- To create, change, or delete the volume label of a disk with the GUI, do the following: select a disk drive in Explorer → right-click → Properties → General tab → type in the label box → OK.

- If label is not specified, the following prompt is displayed:

  Volume in drive A has no label

  Volume label (11 characters, ENTER for none)?

- A volume label can contain up to 11 characters and can include spaces, but not the following characters:

  * ? / \ | . , ; : + = [ ] ( ) & ^ < > "

- Volume labels are displayed in uppercase letters only.

- To display the current disk label, use the *dir* command.

See Also

"dir,"

---

lfnfor

Enable/disable long filenames when processing *for* commands.

To Launch

```
lfnfor [on | off]
```

Description

If you use the *lfnfor* command without any options, the current *lfnfor* setting (on or off) will be displayed.

The *lfnfor* options are:

off Disable long filenames

on Enable long filenames

Examples

Display in a batch file the contents of all the files in the current directory that have the *.txt* extension, and show the long filenames of these files:

```
C:\>lfnfor on
C:\>for %f in (*.txt) do type %f
```

See Also

"for"

---

md or mkdir

Create a new directory.

To Launch

```
md [drive:]path
mkdir [drive:]path
```

Description

Windows 98, like DOS and Windows 95, uses a hierarchical directory structure to organize its file system. On any physical disk, the file system begins with the root directory, signified by a backslash.

You can create additional directories (typically referred to as *folders* in any Windows 98 GUI application) via the New → Folder option in the Explorer File menu or on any context menu, or by using the DOS *mkdir* command. The *md* and *mkdir* commands are functionally identical.

md and *mkdir* accept the following option:

[drive:]path
    Specifies the directory to create

Examples

Create a new subdirectory called *newdir* under the *c:\olddir* directory:

```
C:\>md c:\olddir\newdir
```

Create a subdirectory named *BASIC*:

```
C:\>md basic
```

If you omit the backslash, *md* creates the new directory under the current directory.

Create a directory at the root called *this is a very long directory name*:

```
C:\>md "\this is a very long directory name"
```

Notes

- In order to create directories or subdirectories with long names including spaces, enclose the name in quotation marks.

- If you do not specify a drive, the current drive is assumed. If your path starts with a backslash (\), DOS starts its directory search with the root directory. If you omit the backslash, DOS uses the current directory.

- You may indicate an absolute or relative path for the path parameter. When absolute, the new directory is created as specified from the root directory. When relative, the directory is created in relation to the current directory.

- The maximum length of any path from the root directory to the new directory is 244 characters, including backslashes. See Chapter 1, *Using Windows 98*.

- When creating a series of directories and subdirectories, you must create them one at a time. For example, to create *\MyFiles\January*, you would need to issue two *md* commands:

```
C:\>md \MyFiles
C:\>md \MyFiles\January
```

---

mem

\Windows\Command\mem.exe

Display the amount of real-mode memory available on your system.

To Launch

```
mem [options]
```

Description

The PC was originally designed to store applications in the first 640K bytes of physical memory. This was an unfortunate design decision. With newer processors, larger amounts of memory could be addressed, but the system memory allocated above 640K created a barrier between the "conventional" memory and newer "extended" or "expanded" memory schemes. Most Windows 98 programs simply go right for the expanded memory above it, leaving low memory for any DOS programs that may be running.

While *mem* reports on the total amount of real-mode memory available (in the first megabyte), it provides the greatest amount of detail on the low memory area used by DOS programs. Using *mem* without options will display the available conventional, upper, reserved, and extended memory.

mem accepts the following options:

/a   Displays available memory in High Memory Area (HMA).

/c *(or* /classify*)*
    Classifies programs by memory usage. Lists the size of programs, provides a summary of memory in use, and lists largest memory block available.

/d *(or* /debug*)*
    Displays status of all modules in memory, internal drivers, and other information.

/f *(or* /free*)*
    Displays information about the amount of free memory left in both conventional and upper memory (but not expanded memory).

/m *(or* /module*)*
    Displays a detailed listing of a module's conventional memory use. This option must be followed by the name of a module, optionally separated from /m by a colon. A module is a DOS program, a device, or a TSR (Terminate and Stay Resident program).

/p *(or* /page*)*
    Pauses after each screenful of information.

Examples

Display the amount of conventional memory used by *doskey.com*:

    C:\>mem /m doskey

Display the status of the computer's used and free memory:

    C:\>mem

Notes

To display the status of the upper memory area, install a UMB provider such as *emm386* and include the command dos=umb in the *config.sys* file.

---

more   \ *Windows\Command\more.com*

Read one screen of text at a time.

To Launch

    more [*filename*]

Description

more displays one screen of text at a time. *more* is often used as a filter with other commands that may send a lot of output to the screen (i.e., to read standard input from a pipe or redirected file). Press any key to see the next screenful of output. Press Ctrl-C to end the output before it is done.

Examples

Display the contents of \ *Windows\system.ini* and pause for each screenful of text:

```
C:\>more \windows\system.ini
```

Keep the output of *net view* from scrolling off the screen before you can read it:

```
C:\>net view | more
```

Notes

Some commands (like *dir*) have a /p option that "pages" the output, but many do not. *dir* | more is the same as *dir* /p.

See Also

"type"

---

move   \ *Windows\Command\move.exe*

Move files and directories from one location to another.

To Launch

```
move [/y | /-y] [drive:][path]filename1[,...] destination
```

Description

To move several files in a directory, you can list the files as the *[drive:][path]filename1* option. In other words, you aren't limited to one filename. To move a directory full of files, use the directory name instead.

move can be used to rename directories (and files), but using the enhanced *rename* or *ren* command may be more intuitive.

The *move* options are:

[drive:][path]filename1
Specify the location and name of the file or files you want to move.

destination
Specify the new location of the file. The destination parameter can consist of a drive, a directory name, or a combination of the two. When moving one file, you may include a filename if you want to rename the file when you move it.

/y Suppress prompting to confirm creation of a directory or overwriting of the destination. This is the default when *move* is used in a batch file.

/-y Cause prompting to confirm creation of a directory or overwriting of the destination. This is the default when *move* is used from the command line.

Examples

Move *myfile.txt* from the current directory to *d:\files*:

```
C:\>move myfile.txt d:\files\
```

Same, but rename the file to *newfile.txt*:

```
C:\>move myfile.txt d:\files\newfile.txt
```

Change the name of the directory *d:\files* to *d:\myfiles*:

```
C:\>move d:\files myfiles
```

Notes

- *copy*, *move*, and *xcopy* normally prompt you before overwriting an existing file. To force these commands to overwrite in all cases without prompting you, set the copycmd environment variable to /y. To restore the default behavior, set copycmd to /-y.

- To override all defaults and the setting in the copycmd environment variable, use the /y option.

See Also

"ren or rename"

---

nbtstat

Display protocol statistics and current TCP/IP connections using NetBIOS over TCP/IP (NBT).

To Launch

```
nbtstat [-a RemoteName] [-A IP address] [-c] [-n] [-r] [-R] [-s] [-S]
[interval]
```

Description

nbtstat can display various statistics about current names, and can also delete names from the NetBIOS name cache. If you are having trouble reaching a remote computer, you can see if the remote computer name is in your name cache. If it is not listed, you can manually add it to the cache using the *lmhosts* file found in the \Windows directory.

Type the *nbtstat* command without options to display information about the command (same as nbtstat /?).

The *nbtstat* options are:

-a (Adapter status) Lists the remote machine's name table, given its name.

-A (Adapter status) Lists the remote machine's name table, given its IP address.

-c (Cache) Lists the remote name cache including the IP addresses (it's not "remote" unless you use –[aA]).

interval
    Redisplays selected statistics, pausing *interval* seconds between each display. Press Ctrl–C to stop redisplaying statistics.

IP address
    Dotted decimal representation of the IP address.

-n (Names) Lists local NetBIOS names.

Command
Line Utilities

-r   (Resolved) Lists names resolved by broadcast and via WINS.

-R   (Reload) Purges and reloads the remote cache name table (copying in entries from *lmhosts* with #PRE token).

remotename
    Remote host machine name.

-s   (Sessions) Lists sessions table converting destination IP addresses to host names via the *hosts* file.

-S   (Sessions) Lists sessions table with the destination IP addresses.

Examples

Display sessions using NetBIOS names:

```
C:\>nbtstat -s

NetBIOS Connection Table
Local Name State In/Out Remote Host Input Output
----------------------------------------------------
VECTRA2 <03> Listening
VECTRA2 <00> Connected Out ICA <20> 3KB 2KB
Display sessions using IP addresses:
NetBIOS Connection Table
Local Name State In/Out Remote Host Input Output
----------------------------------------------------
VECTRA2 <03> Listening
VECTRA2 <00> Connected Out 10.0.0.1 3KB 2KB
```

If you have an out-of-date or incorrect *lmhosts* file, you can edit it using *nbtstat*:

ping Host Address IP	*Make sure remote computer is reachable*
edit lmhosts	*Edit lmhosts file*
nbtstat -R	*Rebuild name cache*
nbtstat -c	*Display new cache*
**net view **computer name	*Try to view remote computer*

Notes

Notice the lower- and uppercase a, r, and s characters for the different options.

---

net   \ *Windows\net.exe*

Contains all of the *net* commands. The most useful for users are *net print, net use,* and *net view. net init, net logon, net logoff, net password,* and *net stop* can be used only from DOS before Windows is booted (e.g., from *autoexec.bat* or in Safe mode). These latter commands are largely obsolete, but may be useful in some circumstances, such as with a diskless Windows 98 system, or for testing networking before Windows is started. See Chapter 12, *Windows Startup.*

See Also

"net config," "net diag," "net help," "net init," "net logoff," "net logon," "net password," "net print," "net start," "net stop," "net time," "net use," "net ver," "net view"

---

net config

Internal to: \ *Windows* \ *net.exe*

Display your current workgroup settings.

To Launch

```
net config [/yes]
```

Description

Control Panel → Network → Identification is the GUI equivalent of *net config*.

net config accepts the following option:

/yes
> Carries out the *net config* command without first prompting you to provide information or confirm actions.

Examples

To display your computer's current workgroup settings:

```
C:\>net config

Computer name \\CHARLES
User name CHARLIE
Workgroup WORKGROUP
Workstation root directory C:\Windows
Software version 4.10.1998
Redirector version 4.00
The command was completed successfully.
```

net diag

Internal to: \ *Windows* \ *net.exe*

Run the Microsoft Network Diagnostics program.

To Launch

```
net diag [/names | /status]
```

Description

Use *net diag* to test the hardware connection between two computers and to display information about a single computer.

net diag can assist you in troubleshooting network connectivity problems by establishing a diagnostic server and then verifying that the local computer can connect to this server.

With no options, *net diag* looks for another computer that is already running *net diag* to act as the diagnostic server. If one is not found, it asks if *net diag* is currently running on any other computer. If you answer N, the current computer will act as the server. Go to the second computer, and run *net diag* there. If the *diag* server is found, the network is running correctly. The /status option gives more detail, and also does not require *net diag* to be already running on another computer.

Command
Line Utilities

The *net diag* options are:

/names

Specifies a custom diagnostic session name in order to avoid conflicts when *net diag* is used simultaneously by multiple users. This option works only when the network uses a NetBIOS API, which uses protocols such as TCP/IP, IPX/SPX, and NetBEUI. You will be prompted for the session name. You then have to use the same name on the other computer.

/status

Enables you to specify the computer you want more detailed network diagnostics information from. You will be prompted for the name of the remote computer you want to use to test network connectivity. Use the computer name without the \\ UNC prefix. For example, *troy* would be specified as *troy*. If you don't specify a name, the local computer's interface will be tested.

Examples

Check the status of a remote computer named *troy*:

```
C:\Windows\Desktop>net diag /status

Please enter the remote computer's NetBIOS name, or press ENTER to
examine a local adapter's status.

troy

Remote adapter status:

Permanent node name: 080009B10000

Adapter operational for 0 minutes.
64 free NCBs out of 64 with 64 the maximum.
0 sessions in use
0 sessions allocated
0 packets transmitted 0 packets received.
0 retransmissions 0 retries exhausted.
0 crc errors 0 alignment errors
0 collisions 0 interrupted transmissions.
name 1 TROY            status 04
name 2 WORK            status 84
name 3 TROY            status 04
name 4 WORK        -   status 84
name 5 TROY        _   status 04
The command was completed successfully.
```

net help   Internal to: *Windows**net.exe*

Display information about *net* commands and error messages.

To Launch

```
net help [command | errornum]
```

Description

If you type *net help* at the command line without any options, a brief description of all Microsoft *net* commands will be displayed. Specify a *net* command name for information about that command. Specify an error number for information about that error. This is rather bogus, since it simply repeats the text of the message.

By adding "/?" after an individual *net* command on the command line (e.g., **net diag /?**), the help information is displayed. This is the same information displayed by using the *net help* command (e.g., **net help diag**).

The *net help* options are:

command
> Specifies the *net* command you want information about. One of *config, diag, init, logoff, logon, password, print, start, stop, time, use, ver,* or *view.*

errornum
> Specifies the number of the error message that you want information about.

Examples

Since many of the help messages are longer than a single screen, you can pipe them through the *more* command (the message will pause at each screenful with `-- More --` displayed until you press a key):

```
C:\>net help stop | more
```

---

net init   Internal to: \ *Windows\net.exe*

Load protocol and network-adapter drivers without binding them to Protocol Manager. Cannot be used from within Windows.

To Launch
```
net init [/dynamic]
```

Description

net init may be required if you are using a third-party network adapter driver. You can then bind the drivers to Protocol Manager by typing:

```
C:\>net start netbind
```

net init accepts the following option:

/dynamic
> Loads the Protocol Manager dynamically. This is useful with some third-party networks, such as Banyan® VINES®, to resolve memory problems.

Examples

To set up VCSTS with Windows 98, make sure the following line exists in *autoexec.bat*:

```
net init /dynamic
```

---

net logoff

Break the network connection.

To Launch

```
net logoff [/yes]
```

Description

If you're using Microsoft Networking in MS-DOS mode, and have logged in with *net login,* you can use *net logoff* to break the network connection between your computer and the shared resources to which it is connected. This command can't be used from within Windows. If you are already logged on as another user, you may need to type *net logoff* to end your current session.

net logoff accepts the following option:

/yes

    Carries out the *net logoff* command without first prompting you to provide information or confirm actions.

See Also

    "net," "net init," "net logon," "net start"

---

net logon

Identify a computer as a member of a workgroup.

To Launch

```
net logon [user [password | ?]] [/domain:name] [/yes] [/savepw:no]
```

Description

Normally, if Microsoft Networking is enabled, you will log on to the network when starting Windows. (See "Logon" in Chapter 4.) If you're using the system in MS-DOS mode (perhaps because you're debugging a startup problem—see Chapter 12), and you want to use networking, you must log in with *net login.*

If you would rather be prompted to type your username and password instead of specifying them in the *net logon* command line, type *net logon* without options. *net logon* can be used only before Windows is started.

The *net logon* options are:

?   Specifies that you want to be prompted for your password.

/domain

    Specifies that you want to log on to a Microsoft Windows NT or LAN Manager domain.

---

name

Specifies the Windows NT or LAN Manager domain you want to log on to.

password

The unique string of characters that authorizes you to gain access to your password-list file. The password can contain up to 14 characters.

`/savepw:no`

Carries out the *net logon* command without prompting you to create a password-list file.

user

Specifies the name that identifies you in your workgroup. The name you specify can contain up to 20 characters.

`/yes`

Carries out the *net logon* command without first prompting you to provide information or confirm actions.

Examples

For a diskless computer that uses Client for Microsoft Networks, *autoexec.bat* might be set up like this:

```
net start basic
net logon /savepw:no /yes
net use x: \\server\share
```

See Also

"net start," "net use"

---

net password   Internal to: \ *Windows\net.exe*

Change your logon password.

To Launch

```
net password [oldpassword [newpassword]]
net password \\computer | /domain:name [user [oldpassword
[newpassword]]]
```

Description

The first syntax line is for changing the password for your password-list file. The second syntax line is for changing your password on a Windows NT or LAN Manager server or domain. *net password* can't be used from within Windows. Once Windows has been started, use Control Panel → Passwords → Change Windows Password to change passwords.

The *net password* options are:

computer

Specifies the Windows NT or LAN Manager server on which you want to change your password.

/domain

>Specifies that you want to change your password in a Windows NT or LAN Manager domain.

name

>Specifies the Windows NT or LAN Manager domain in which you want to change your password.

newpassword

>Specifies your new password. It can have as many as 14 characters.

oldpassword

>Specifies your current password.

user

>Specifies your Windows NT or LAN Manager username.

---

net print
Internal to: \ *Windows*\ *net.exe*

Display information about the print queue on a shared printer.

To Launch

```
net print \\computer[\printer] | port [/yes]
net print \\computer | port [job# [/pause | /resume | /delete]]
        [/yes]
```

Description

You can stop, suspend, or delete a print job on a network computer with *net print*, instead of using the GUI interface at Control Panel → Printers.

When you specify the name of a computer using the *net print* command, you receive information about the print queues on each of the shared printers connected to the computer.

The *net print* options are:

computer

>Specifies the name of the computer about whose print queue you want information.

job#

>Specifies the number assigned to a queued print job. You can specify the following options:

>/pause

>>Pauses a print job.

>/resume

>>Restarts a print job that has been paused.

>/delete

>>Cancels a print job.

>/yes

>>Carries out the *net print* command without first prompting you to provide information or confirm actions.

---

port
>Specifies the name of the parallel (LPT) port on your computer that is connected to the printer you want information about.

printer
>Specifies the name of the printer you want information about.

Examples

Examine the print queue DeskJet on a computer named ICA:

```
C:\>net print \\ica\DeskJet

Printers at \\ica
Name            Job #    Size    Status
DeskJet Queue   1 jobs           *Printer Active*
Administrator   5 1170041 Printing
```

---

net start

Internal to: \Windows\net.exe

Start Win 98 networking services.

To Launch

```
net start [basic | nwredir | workstation | netbind | netbeui |
nwlink] [/list] [/yes] [/verbose]
```

Description

To start the workgroup redirector you selected during setup, type net start without options (in most instances you won't need to use options). *net start* can only be run before Windows itself is started.

The *net start* options are:

basic
>Starts the basic redirector

/list
>Displays a list of the services that are running

netbeui
>Starts the NetBIOS interface

netbind
>Binds protocols and network-adapter drivers

nwlink
>Starts the IPX/SPX-compatible interface

nwredir
>Starts the Microsoft Novell®–compatible redirector

/verbose
>Displays information about device drivers and services as they are loaded

workstation
>Starts the default redirector

/yes

Carries out the *net start* command without first prompting you to provide information or confirm actions

---

net stop   Internal to: \ *Windows\net.exe*

Stop Win 98 networking services.

To Launch

```
net stop [basic | nwredir | workstation | netbeui | nwlink] [/yes]
```

Description

To stop the workgroup redirector, type net stop without options. This breaks all your connections to shared resources and removes the *net* commands from your computer's memory. *net stop* can only be run before Windows itself is started.

The *net stop* options are:

basic

Stops the basic redirector

netbeui

Stops the NetBIOS protocol

nwlink

Stops the IPX/SPX-compatible interface

nwredir

Stops the Microsoft Novell®–compatible redirector

workstation

Stops the default redirector

/yes

Carries out the *net stop* command without first prompting you to provide information or confirm actions

---

net time   Internal to: \ *Windows\net.exe*

Synchronize a computer's clock with a shared clock on a server.

To Launch

```
net time [\\computer | /workgroup:wgname] [/set] [/yes]
```

Description

net time displays the time from or synchronizes your computer's clock with the shared clock on a Microsoft Windows for Workgroups, Windows NT, Windows 98, Windows 95 or NetWare time server.

The *net time* options are:

computer

Specifies the name of the computer (time server) with whose time you want to check or synchronize your computer's clock.

/set

Synchronizes your computer's clock with the clock on the computer or workgroup you specify.

wgname

Specifies the name of the workgroup containing a computer with whose clock you want to check or synchronize your computer's clock. If there are multiple time servers in that workgroup, *net time* uses the first one it finds.

/workgroup

Specifies that you want to use the clock on a computer (time server) in another workgroup.

/yes

Carries out the *net time* command without first prompting you to provide information or confirm actions.

Notes

The /yes option is helpful when the *net time* command is used within a batch file.

---

net use   Internal to: \ *Windows*\ *net.exe*

Connect or disconnect a computer from a shared resource.

To Launch

```
net use [drive: | *] [\\computer\directory [password | ?]]
        [/savepw:no] [/yes] [/no]
net use [port:] [\\computer\printer [password | ?]] [/savepw:no]
        [/yes] [/no]
net use drive: | \\computer\directory /delete [/yes]
net use port: | \\computer\printer /delete [/yes]
net use * /delete [/yes]
net use drive: | * /home
```

Description

In addition to connecting or disconnecting your computer from a shared resource, *net use* also displays information about your connections.

With no options, *net use* prints a list of the computers with shared resources to which you have made connections, and the status of these connections.

The *net use* options are:

*   Specifies the next available drive letter. If used with /delete, closes all of your connections.

?   Specifies that you want to be prompted for the password of the shared resource. You don't need to use this option unless the password is optional.

computer

Specifies the name of the computer sharing the resource.

/delete

Breaks the specified connection to a shared resource.

directory
> Specifies the name of the shared directory.

drive
> Specifies the drive letter you have assigned to a shared directory.

/home
> Makes a connection to your home directory, if one is specified in your LAN Manager or Windows NT user account.

/no Carries out the *net use* command, responding with *no* automatically when you are prompted to confirm actions.

password
> Specifies the password for the shared resource, if any.

port
> Specifies the parallel (LPT) port name you assign to a shared printer.

printer
> Specifies the name of the shared printer.

/savepw:no
> Specifies that the password you type should not be saved in your password-list file. You must retype the password the next time you connect to this resource.

/yes
> Carries out the *net use* command without first prompting you to provide information or confirm actions.

Notes

- Be sure to use quotation marks for any computer name or share name that contains spaces.

- For the GUI equivalent of *net use*, see "Net Watcher" in Chapter 6.

Examples

Connect the shared printer named *hp* on machine *troy* to port LPT2:

```
net use lpt2: \\troy\hp
```

Connect the shared folder *budgets* on machine *sandy* as drive *F:* with password *secret*:

```
net use F: \\sandy\budgets secret
```

See Also

> Explorer → Tools → Map Network Drive
> "Net Watcher" in Chapter 6

---

net ver   Internal to: *Windows**net.exe*

Display the type and version number of the workgroup redirector.

To Launch

```
net ver
```

There are no options for this command.

Examples

```
C:\>net ver
Microsoft Client - Full Redirector. Version 4.00
Copyright (c) Microsoft Corp. 1993-1995. All rights reserved.
```

---

net view
Internal to: *Windows**net.exe*

Display a list of computers in a specified workgroup.

To Launch

```
net view [\\computer] [/yes]
net view [/workgroup:wgname] [/yes]
net view [/workgroup:wgname] [\\computer]
```

Description

net view displays the shared resources available on a specified computer (see Figure 7-7). This is often easier than clicking your way through the Network Neighborhood.

To display a list of computers in your workgroup that share resources, type *net view* without options.

The *net view* options are:

computer
> Specifies the name of the computer whose shared resources you want to see listed

wgname
> Specifies the name of the workgroup whose computer names you want to view

/workgroup
> Specifies that you want to view the names of the computers in another workgroup that share resources

/yes
> Carries out the *net view* command without first prompting you to provide information or confirm actions

Examples

net view \\troy, for example, produces the following output:

```
Shared resources at \\TROY

Sharename      Type        Comment
----------------------------------------
D              Disk
WIN98NUT       Disk
WINERROR       Disk
The command was completed successfully.
```

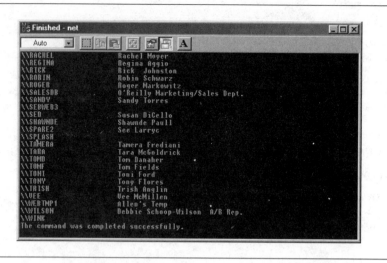

Figure 7-7: Shared resources display (net view)

netstat

Display protocol statistics and current TCP/IP network connections to and from the local computer.

To Launch

```
netstat [-a] [-e] [-n] [-s] [-p proto] [-r] [interval]
```

Description

netstat can be used to verify which TCP (Transmission Control Protocol) and UDP (User Datagram Protocol) services are being offered to other computers and who is currently using them.

Typing *netstat* without options will show all active TCP connections and their connection status.

The *netstat* options are:

-a Displays all connections and listening ports. (Server-side connections are normally not shown.)

-e Displays Ethernet statistics. This may be combined with the -s option.

interval

Redisplays selected statistics, pausing *interval* seconds between each display. Press Ctrl-C to stop redisplaying statistics.

-n Displays addresses and port numbers in numerical form (useful when DNS is not working or configured).

`-p` *proto*

Shows connections for the protocol specified by *proto*; *proto* may be `tcp` or `udp`. If used with the `-s` option to display per-protocol statistics, *proto* may be `tcp`, `udp`, or `ip`.

`-r`   Displays the contents of the routing table. This is the same as *route* `print`.

`-s`   Displays per-protocol statistics. By default, statistics are shown for TCP, UDP, and IP; the `-p` option may be used to specify a subset of the default.

Examples

Show active TCP connections and available UDP ports:

```
C:\>netstat -a

Active Connections
Proto Local Address Foreign Address State
TCP ray:1390 maple.work.net:80 CLOSE_WAIT
TCP ray:1391 maple.work.net:80 CLOSE_WAIT
TCP ray:1392 maple.work.net:80 CLOSE_WAIT
UDP ray:nbname *:*
UDP ray:nbdatagram *:*
UDP ray:nbname *:*
UDP ray:nbdatagram *:*
```

Display the addresses and port numbers in numerical form:

```
C:\>netstat -n

Active Connections
Proto Local Address Foreign Address State
TCP 10.0.0.1:1390 10.0.0.1:80 CLOSE_WAIT
TCP 10.0.0.1:1391 10.0.0.1:80 CLOSE_WAIT
TCP 10.0.0.1:1392 10.0.0.1:80 CLOSE_WAIT
```

Notes

- Table 7-3 lists the possible states *netstat* can return and their explanations.

- TCP sockets in the listening state aren't shown. This is a limitation of *netstat* in Microsoft's implementation.

- Before data transfer takes place in TCP, a connection must be established. TCP employs a three-way handshake. The *netstat* command can tell you what TCP connections are present between your computer and other computers. Only the TCP ports that are being used will be shown, but *netstat* does display the UDP ports your computer is listening on.

- It is normal to have a socket in the TIME_WAIT state for a long period of time.

Table 7-3: Possible States Returned by netstat

State	Explanation
SYN_SEND	Indicates active open.
SYN_RECEIVED	Server just received SYN from the client.

Table 7-3: Possible States Returned by netstat (continued)

State	Explanation
ESTABLISHED	Client received server's SYN and session is established.
LISTEN	Server is ready to accept connection.
FIN_WAIT_1	Indicates active close.
TIMED_WAIT	Client enters this state after active close.
CLOSE_WAIT	Indicates passive close. Server just received first FIN from a client.
FIN_WAIT_2	Client just received acknowledgment of its first FIN from the server.
LAST_ACK	Server is in this state when it sends its own FIN.
CLOSED	Server received ACK from client and connection is closed.
Ack flag	If on, indicates that the acknowledgment field is significant.
Syn flag	If on, indicates that the sequence numbers are to be synchronized. This flag is used when a connection is being established.
Fin flag	If on, indicates that the sender has no more data to send. This is the equivalent of an end-of-transmission marker.

path

Internal to: \ *Windows\command.com*

Set or display the command search path

To Launch

```
path = [drive:][directory]; ... [drive:][directory]
```

Description

By default, DOS searches for executable files in the current directory only. The *path* statement is used to define additional directories to be included while searching for files. It is intended to be used in the *autoexec.bat* file, but can be used anywhere.

The path consists of a series of absolute directory pathnames, separated by semicolons. No spaces should follow each semicolon. If no drive letter is specified, all pathnames are assumed to be on the boot drive. There should be no semicolon at the end of the statement.

When you type the name of a command, DOS looks first in the current directory, then in each successive directory specified in the path. Within each directory, it will look for executable files by their extension, in the following order: *.com, .exe, .bat*.

The order of directories in the search path is thus quite important. For example, you might run MKS Toolkit, a set of third-party tools that brings Unix functionality to Windows systems. MKS normally stores its files in \ *MKSNT.*

If you have the path set as follows:

```
path=C:\;C:\MKSNT;C:\Windows;C:\Windows\Command
```

you won't be able to run a DOS command like *find* without typing its full path-name, because the MKS *find* command will be found and executed first.

Run *path* without options to display the current path.

Examples

Specify the directories *C:*, *C:\DOS*, *C:\Windows*, and *C:\Programs* in the path:

```
C:\>path=c:\;c:\dos;c:\windows;c:\programs;
```

A typical *path* statement in *config.sys* might be:

```
path=c:\;c:\windows
```

or, in *autoexec.bat*:

```
set path=c:\;c:\windows;c:\windows\command
```

A useful batch file to add a directory to the front of the existing path is the one-line *addpath.bat*:

```
set path=%1;%path%
```

Or you can type something similar at the command line, putting the new directory at either the begining or end of the existing path:

```
C:\>set path =%path%; c:\newdir
```

Notes

- Type path ; to clear all search path settings and direct Windows to search only in the current directory.

- The *path=* statement is limited to 250 characters or less when set in *config.sys*. The *path=* statement is limited to 127 characters if set from a batch file (e.g., *autoexec.bat*) or from the command line.

- Use short names only (e.g., *C:\PROGRA~1* for *C:\Program Files*).

- When DOS or Windows 98 searches for a file, it first looks in the current directory, then in the directories listed in the *path* statement in the order in which they are listed.

- To fit more directories in the search path, you can either shorten your directory names or use the *subst* command to assign directories to logical drives (which shortens the entries on the *path* command line).

- You might think that you could simplify your search path by putting a short-cut file to a program in a directory that is already in your search path, but DOS isn't smart enough to follow shortcuts. You could, however, create a batch file containing only the complete pathname of the program, and place that in one of the directories in your path.

---

ping

\Windows\ping.exe

Verify connection to a remote TCP/IP host.

To Launch

```
ping [-t] [-a] [-n count] [-1 size] [-f] [-i TTL] [-v TOS] [-r count]
    [-s count] [[-j host-list] | [-k host-list]] [-w timeout]
    destination-list
```

Description

This diagnostic command verifies connections to one or more remote hosts. If you can *ping* another host, it proves that you can communicate with it, that TCP/IP is configured correctly, and that the remote host is operating.

For example, if you've just tried to connect to a web site with Internet Explorer and were unable to connect, you might want to *ping* the site to find out if it is really not responding, or if the problem is on your end of the connection.

Like *tracert*, *ping* is also useful for taking a look "under the hood" of an Internet connection.

ping accepts the following parameters and options:

-a   Specifies not to resolve addresses to hostnames.

destination-list
    Specifies the remote hosts to ping.

-f   Sends a Do Not Fragment flag in the packet. The packet will not be fragmented by gateways on the route.

-i ttl
    Sets the Time To Live field to the value specified by *ttl*.

-j host-list
    Routes packets by means of the list of hosts specified by *host-list*. Consecutive hosts may be separated by intermediate gateways (loose source routed). The maximum number allowed by IP is 9.

-k host-list
    Routes packets by means of the list of hosts specified by *host-list*. Consecutive hosts may not be separated by intermediate gateways (strict source routed). The maximum number allowed by IP is 9.

-1 length
    Sends echo packets containing the amount of data specified by length. The default is 64 bytes; the maximum is 8192.

-n count
    Sends the number of echo packets specified by count. The default is 4.

-r count
    Records the route of the outgoing packet and the returning packet in the Record Route field. A minimum of 1 to a maximum of 9 hosts must be specified by *count*.

-s count
    Specifies the timestamp for the number of hops specified by *count*.

-t   Pings the specified host until interrupted.

-v *tos*

Sets the Type Of Service field to the value specified by *tos*.

-w *timeout*

Specifies a time-out interval in milliseconds.

Examples

See how long it takes to reach Yahoo! (*tracert* tells you why):

```
C:\>ping yahoo.com

Pinging yahoo.com [204.71.177.35] with 32 bytes of data:

Reply from 204.71.177.35: bytes=32 time=162ms TTL=244
Reply from 204.71.177.35: bytes=32 time=160ms TTL=244
Reply from 204.71.177.35: bytes=32 time=158ms TTL=244
Reply from 204.71.177.35: bytes=32 time=159ms TTL=244
Reply from 204.71.177.35: bytes=32 time=157ms TTL=244
Reply from 204.71.177.35: bytes=32 time=147ms TTL=244

Ping statistics for 204.71.177.35:
    Packets: Sent = 6, Received = 6, Lost = 0 (0% loss),
Approximate round trip times in milli-seconds:
    Minimum = 147ms, Maximum =  162ms, Average =  157ms
```

Notes

- The *ping* command provides statistics for packets and approximate round trip time in milliseconds (see example earlier in this section).

- The *ping* command verifies connections to a remote host or hosts by sending Internet Control Message Protocol (ICMP) echo packets to the host and listening for echo reply packets. By default, four echo packets containing 64 bytes of data (a periodic uppercase sequence of alphabetic characters) are transmitted.

- You can use the *ping* command to test both the hostname and IP address of the host. If the IP address is verified but the hostname is not, you may have a name resolution problem. In this case, be sure that the hostname you are querying is in either the local *HOSTS* file or in the DNS database.

See Also

"tracert"

To use *ping* on the Web:

http://network-tools.com/

---

prompt

Internal to: \ *Windows\command.com*

Change the DOS command prompt.

To Launch

```
prompt [text]
```

Description

Run *prompt* without parameters to reset the prompt to the default setting: NG, current drive and the greater-than sign (>). A more useful setting is: PG, current drive and path, and >.

The $E code is typically used with *ansi.sys* escape sequences. See *prompt* /? for all $ codes.

The *prompt* options are:

text

Specifies a new command prompt. The prompt can contain normal characters and the following special codes:

$_ Carriage return and linefeed

$$ $ (dollar sign)

$b | (pipe)

$d Current date

$e Escape code (ASCII code 27)

$g > (greater-than sign)

$h Backspace (erases previous character)

$l < (less-than sign)

$n Current drive

$p Current drive and path

$q = (equal sign)

$t Current time

$v Windows version number

Examples

Specify the current drive and directory followed by the greater-than sign (>):

    C:\>**prompt pg**

Specify the drive and directory on one line, and the date followed by the greater-than sign (>) on another:

    C:\>**prompt p_dg**

Notes

By adding the line set winpmt=text to your *autoexec.bat* file immediately after the *prompt* line, you can display a message on the DOS prompt in Windows, which won't appear in real mode.

---

rd or rmdir   Internal to: *Windows**command.com*

Remove (delete) a directory.

To Launch

```
rd [drive:]path
rmdir [drive:]path
```

Description

The *rd* and *rmdir* commands are functionally identical. *rd* and *rmdir* will delete a directory containing no files or subdirectories only.

rmdir accepts the following options:

[drive:]path
> Specifies the directory to delete.

Examples

Delete the empty subdirectory *test* within the current directory called *Temp* (\ *Windows\Temp*):

```
C:\Windows\Temp>rd test
```

Delete the empty subdirectory called *newdir* located in the *C:\olddir* directory:

```
C:\>rd c:\olddir\newdir
```

Notes

- Attempting to delete a directory that is not empty will display the message:

  ```
  Invalid path, not directory
  or directory not empty
  ```

  If the directory appears empty, but still causes an error message, it may contain hidden files. Use the *dir* /ah command to view hidden files. To delete a directory or subdirectory containing files, either delete the files first with *del*, or use the *deltree* command (the files and the directory will be deleted). You can change the hidden attribute with the *attrib* command.

- In Windows 98, *rd* can remove the current directory.

See Also

"attrib," "deltree," "dir"

---

regedit

\ *Windows\regedit.exe*

View and modify the contents of the Registry.

To Launch

```
regedit [/c] [/e] [filename] [regpath]
```

Additional syntax (in MS-DOS only, before the Windows GUI starts):

```
regedit [/?] [/l:system] [/r:user]
```

Description

regedit allows you to view and modify the contents of the Registry, the master file that stores configuration settings for Windows 98 and many of the applications on your computer.

Command Line Utilities

regedit takes the following options:

/c `filename`
  Replace the entire Registry with the contents of *filename*

/e `filename [regpath]`
  Export a *.reg* file; if *regpath* omitted, exports entire Registry

`filename`
  Import or merge a *.reg* file

Additional options (only in MS-DOS mode, before GUI starts, not in Windows):

/? Display RegEdit command-line syntax

/l:*system*
  Path and filename of *system.dat*

/r:*user*
  Path and filename of *user.dat*

Examples

Export Registry settings into a *.reg* file, modify the *.reg* file, and merge the new settings back into the Registry:

```
C:\>regedit /e run.reg HKEY_LOCAL MACHINE\SOFTWARE\Microsoft\Windows\
CurrentVersion\Run
C:\>echo "Fooble"="c:\\testing\\fooble.exe" >> run.reg
C:\>regedit run.reg
```

Notes

- *.reg* files are straight ASCII text (with the signature "REGEDIT4" as their first line). They can be viewed and modified with any text editor or word processor that can read and save plain text files. If modifying a *.reg* file with Word-Pad or Word, remember to save it as plain text.

- By default, Windows 98 associates *.reg* files with *regedit*; double-clicking on a *.reg* file's icon in the Explore imports the *.reg* file's contents into the Registry. Since any modifications to the Registry can alter your system, a dialog box pops up when you double-click on a *.reg* file asking if you are sure you want to add this information to the Registry. If you proceed, another dialog box will pop up telling you whether or not the action was successful.

- If exporting a large chunk of the Registry, `regedit /e` will return before the file export completes; file writing takes place in the background. This can be important in batch files that process output from `regedit /e`. You can get around this by using `start /w` to wait for *regedit* to complete; for example:

```
start /w regedit /e \reg.reg
echo The \reg.reg file is now ready
```

See Also

"System Policy Editor" in Chapter 8, *Hidden Gems on the Windows 98 CD-ROM*
"Registry Editor" in Chapter 6
Chapter 13

ren or rename

Internal to: *Windows\command.com*

Rename a file or directory.

To Launch

```
rename [filename1] [filename2]
ren [filename1] [filename2]
```

Description

The *ren* and *rename* commands are functionally identical. You can't specify a new drive or path for your destination when using *ren* or *rename*, and the renamed file remains in the same drive and path as the file or directory you are changing.

The *ren* options are:

[filename1]
> The name of the current directory or file.

[filename2]
> The new name of the file. You can't move files to another directory with *ren*. You can rename a directory or files, but can't ren x*.* to y*.*. Use *move* instead.

Examples

Rename *myfile.txt* to *file.txt*:

```
C:\>rename myfile.txt file.txt
```

Rename *chap 5.doc* to *sect 5.doc*:

```
C:\>ren chap?5.doc sect?5.doc
```

Both *chap 5.doc* and *sect 5.doc* have spaces in the fifth character position, which are represented with the ? wildcard.

Change all filenames with *.txt* extensions in the current directory to *.rtf*:

```
C:\>ren *.txt *.rtf
```

Rename the files *chap1.doc*, *chap2.doc*, etc. to *revchap1.doc*, *revchap2.doc*, etc.:

```
C:\>ren chap*.doc revchap*.doc
```

Notes

- The file's creation date is not changed when using *ren*.
- Quotation marks are needed if the name of a directory or file contains a space. Or use ? as shown in the second example.
- Use wildcards (* and ?) to alter only part of a name in a series of files.

See Also

"move"

Command Line Utilities

ren or rename 373

route

Manipulate the TCP/IP routing table for the local computer.

To Launch

```
route [-f] [command [destination] [mask netmask] [gateway] [metric
    metric]
```

Description

The **route print** command is useful if you are having a problem (e.g., "Host Unreachable" or "Request timed out") with the routes on your computer, since it will display all the different fields in the active route (see the example).

command
> Specifies one of four commands:
>
> **print**
>> Prints a route (similar to **netstat -r**)
>
> **add** Adds a route
>
> **delete**
>> Deletes a route
>
> **change**
>> Modifies an existing route

destination
> The host or network that is reachable via *gateway*.

-f Clears the routing tables of all gateway entries. If this is used in conjunction with one of the commands, the tables are cleared prior to running the command.

gateway
> The gateway to be used for traffic going to *destination*. It is possible to use a hostname for the gateway, but it is safer to use an IP address, as a hostname may resolve to multiple IP addresses.

mask *netmask*
> Specifies the subnet mask for a *destination*. If not specified, a mask of 255.255.255.255 is used (i.e., a "host route" to a single host, not a network).

metric *metric*
> Specifies the **metric** or "hop count" for this route. The metric indicates which route is preferred when multiple routes to a **destination** exist, and signifies the number of hops or gateways between the local computer and the **gateway**. The route with the lowest metric is used unless it is unavailable, in which case the route with the next lowest metric takes over.

Examples

```
C:\>route print

Active Routes:
  Network Address        Netmask    Gateway Address      Interface Metric
        0.0.0.0          0.0.0.0      172.16.80.5    172.16.80.150      1
      127.0.0.0        255.0.0.0      127.0.0.1          127.0.0.1      1
   172.16.80.10   255.255.255.0   172.16.80.150      172.16.80.150      1
```

374   *Chapter 7 – DOS and Other Command-Line Utilities*

```
172.16.80.150    255.255.255.255      127.0.0.1      127.0.0.1    1
172.16.80.200    255.255.255.255   172.16.80.150  172.16.80.150    1
    224.0.0.0          224.0.0.0   172.16.80.150  172.16.80.150    1
255.255.255.255  255.255.255.255   172.16.80.150        0.0.0.0    1
```

Add a default gateway:

```
C:\>route add 0.0.0.0 10.0.0.200
```

Notes

- The fields in the previous example are as follows:

  Gateway Address
  The IP address of the gateway for the route. The gateway will know what to do with traffic for the specified network address.

  Interface
  The IP address of the network interface that the route is going to use when leaving the local computer.

  Metric
  The hop count or number of gateways between the local computer and the gateway.

  Netmask
  The mask to be applied to the network address. If all ones (255.255.255. 255), the route is a host route and refers to a single machine, not a network.

  Network Address
  Any network matched by this address should use this route. The default route is all zeros and is used if no other route is found.

- All symbolic names used for destination or gateway are looked up in the network and hostname database files *Windows**networks* and *Windows**hosts*, respectively.

- If the command is `print` or `delete`, wildcards may be used for the destination and gateway, or the gateway argument may be omitted.

---

rundll   *Windows**rundll.exe*

See "rundll32."

---

rundll32   *Windows**rundll32.exe*

Provides "string invocation," command-line–based runtime dynamic linking.

To Launch

```
rundll[32] dll_name, function_name [function arguments . . . ]
```

Description

rundll32 provides dynamic linking to functions exported from Dynamic Link Libraries (DLLs). *rundll* is for 16-bit (Win16) *dlls*, and *rundll32* is for 32-bit (Win32) *dlls*.

---

rundll32 is used throughout Windows 98. For example, almost all of the Control Panel applets invoke *rundll32*. Many GUI elements that appear to have no command-line equivalents actually employ *rundll32* behind the scenes. This means that these GUI elements can be semi-automated in a batch file.

The *rundll32* options are:

dll_name
> The filename of a Dynamic Link Library (DLL)

function arguments
> Case-sensitive string parameters to the function being called

function_name
> The case-sensitive name of a function exported from the DLL

Examples

Launch Dial-Up Networking from the command line or a batch file (the *type* command is used to show the contents of the batch file):

```
C:\>type dialup.bat
rundll32 \windows\system\rnaui.dll,RnaDial %1
C:\>dialup OReilly
```

Start the "Add New Hardware Wizard":

```
C:\>rundll32 shell32.dll,Control_RunDLL sysdm.cpl,Add New Hardware
```

Start the "OpenAs" dialog box for unknown file type *.xyz* without actually having a file of type *.xyz* handy:

```
C:\>type openas.bat
echo blah blah blah > foobar.%1
rundll32 shell32.dll,OpenAs_RunDLL foobar.%1
C:\>openas xyz
```

Notes

To locate many *rundll* and *rundll32* command lines, see the Registry:

```
C:\>regedit /e \reg.reg
```

(Wait while *regedit* command completes: it may take a few minutes!)

```
C:\>find /i "rundll" \reg.reg > rundll.log
```

---

scandskw   \Windows\Command\scandskw.exe

Check the disk surface for errors.

To Launch

```
scandskw [drive:] [/a] [/n] [/p] [dblspace.nnn] [drvspace.nnn]
```

Description

scandskw checks the disk surface, files, and folders of your computer for lost clusters (and other things), correcting them if they exist, thus freeing disk space by getting rid of unusable information.

Don't confuse running *scandskw* or *scandisk* from the Windows command line with running *scandisk* from the MS-DOS real-mode command line. *scandisk.exe* is a separate utility in the *Windows**Command* directory that can only be accessed in real-mode DOS. Typing *scandisk* from the Windows command line actually launches *scandskw*. There is a different set of options available for *scandisk* when run from the real-mode command line, which are described later in this section.

scandskw options are:

/a   Checks all your local, nonremovable hard disks

dblspace.*nnn* or drvspace.*nnn*
    Checks the specified unmounted DoubleSpace or DriveSpace compressed volume file, where *nnn* is the filename extension for the hidden host file

drive:
    Specifies one or more drives to be checked

/n *(or* /noninteractive*)*
    Starts and closes ScanDisk automatically

/p *(or* /preview*)*
    Runs ScanDisk in Preview mode; ScanDisk reports errors but does not write changes to the disk

Examples

Check all nonremovable hard disks, but prevent ScanDisk from correcting any errors it finds, with text in the Target box similar to the following:

```
C:\windows\scandskw.exe /a /p
```

Force a batch file to wait for *scandskw* to run *scandisk* on the *C:* drive, starting and closing *scandisk* automatically:

```
C:\>start /w scandskw c: /n
```

Run ScanDisk in the Preview mode from the command line, forcing ScanDisk to start and close automatically:

```
C:\>scandskw /n /p
```

Notes

When running ScanDisk in Preview mode (scandskw /p), it appears as though the program is fixing errors, but it isn't. To determine whether *scandisk* is running in Preview mode, look for the Preview tag in the caption of the main ScanDisk window.

The following syntax applies only to running ScanDisk in real-mode MS-DOS. You won't be able to use this syntax from MS-DOS once Windows is running. To execute real-mode MS-DOS, hold down the Ctrl key on startup once the hardware has loaded (holding the F8 key on startup will still work for some Windows 98 machines), then choose "Command Prompt Only." To launch the DOS version of ScanDisk:

```
scandisk [drive: | /all] [/checkonly | /autofix [/nosave]] [/surface]
scandisk drive:\drvspace.nnn [/checkonly | /autofix[/nosave]]
```

```
scandisk /fragment [drive:][path]filename
scandisk /undo [drive:] (specify the drive containing your undo disk)
```

The options for the DOS version of ScanDisk are:

`/all`
> Checks and repairs all local drives

`/autofix`
> Fixes damage without prompting

`/checkonly`
> Checks a drive, but does not repair any damage

`/custom`
> Configures and runs ScanDisk according to *scandisk.ini* settings

`/mono`
> Configures ScanDisk for use with a monochrome display

`/nosave`
> With `/autofix`, deletes lost clusters rather than saving as files

`/nosummary`
> With `/checkonly` or `/autofix`, prevents ScanDisk from stopping at summary screens

`/surface`
> Performs a surface scan after other checks

Examples

(These apply only to *scandisk* in real-mode MS-DOS.)

Run *scandisk* on drive *C*:

    `C:\>scandisk c:`

Run *scandisk* on all non-removable drives (e.g., hard disk drives):

    `C:\>scandisk /all`

Run *scandisk* according the settings in *scandisk.ini* (*\Windows\COMMAND*):

    `C:\>scandisk /custom`

Notes

- The DOS version of ScanDisk can also check unmounted drives compressed with DoubleSpace or DriveSpace, but it can't check for long filename integrity. As a rule, you should use the Windows version of ScanDisk first and then the MS-DOS version if you still need to correct other problems.

- You have the option to replace, append, or disable a log file that's created once ScanDisk has run. The name of the file is *scandisk.log*, stored in the root drive. *scandisk.log* will report all of the *scandisk* results.

See Also

"ScanDisk" in Chapter 6

Display, set, or remove MS-DOS environment variables.

To Launch

```
set [variable=[string]]
```

Description

The *set* command is primarily intended for use in the *autoexec.bat* file or other batch files, but it can be used at the command prompt.

Environment variables are a simple means of interapplication communication, as well as a mechanism for storing data used repeatedly in a batch file.

Run *set* without options to display the current environment variables.

The *set* options are:

string
> Specifies a series of characters to assign to the variable

variable
> Specifies the variable name

Standard *set* environment variables include:

COMSPEC
> The location of the DOS command interpreter, if not in *C:*.

COPYCMD
> Whether *copy*, *move*, and *xcopy* should prompt for confirmation before overwriting a file. The default value is /-y. To stop the warning messages, type set copycmd=/y.

DIRCMD
> Standard options for the *dir* command. For example, set dircmd=/p will cause *dir* to always pause after displaying a screenful of output.

PATH
> The sequence of directories in which the command interpreter will look for commands to be interpreted. Each additional directory in the path is separated by a semicolon. The path can also be set with the *path* command. See *path* for additional details.

PROMPT
> The format of the command-line prompt. This value can also be set with the *prompt* command. See *prompt* for details.

TMP, TEMP
> The location where many programs will store temporary files. *TMPDIR* is also sometimes used.

WINDIR
> The directory where Windows system files are found. Normally *C:\Windows*.

You can also display the value of any individual variable using the *echo* command, surrounding the variable name with percent signs. For example, echo %temp% will display the value of the temp variable. You can use the *%variable%* syntax to use environment variables in other ways as well:

```
C:\>set workdir="C:\Windows\Desktop\win98\tim's draft"
C:\>cd %workdir%
```

Here, the environment variable is used to store a long pathname, including spaces (which must be quoted), for quick navigation to a frequently used directory.

To clear the value of an environment variable, type set `variable=`, supplying no value.

Examples

Set the temporary files directory to *C:\temp*:

```
C:\>set temp=c:\temp
```

Set the *dir* command to display files in directories and subdirectories and sort by size with the largest first:

```
C:\>set dircmd= /s /o-s
```

A batch file to add directories to the front of the path:

```
C:\>set path=%1; %path%
```

Set the default DOS prompt to show the current time, followed by a right angle bracket:

```
C:\>set prompt=$t>
```

Notes

- The *set* command affects only the MS-DOS environment. To set master or global environment variables that will affect Windows, use *winset.*

- The total amount of memory allocated for environment variables is set with the /E switch to *command.com*. The default value is only 256 characters. If you use many environment variables, you may want to change this value. The maximum value is 32,768 bytes. You can set the environment in MS-DOS Prompt → Properties → Memory → Initial Environment, as shown in Figure 7-8. You can also set it in the shell= statement in *config.sys* (not to be confused with shell= in *system.ini*). For example:

```
shell=command.com /p /e:2048
```

See Also

"prompt," "path"
"Winset" in Chapter 8, *Hidden Gems on the Windows 98 CD-ROM*
"echo" in Chapter 11

---

setup

\ *Windows\Options\Cab\setup.exe*

Set options to customize and control a Win 98 installation.

To Launch

```
setup [options]
```

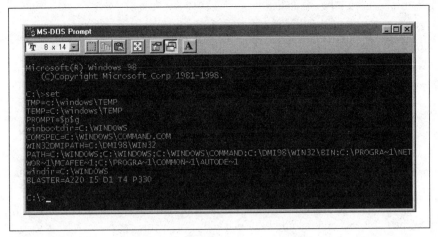

Figure 7-8: Setting MS-DOS prompt properties

Description

You can use *setup* to customize your Windows 98 installation from the Windows 95 user interface, the Windows 3.1x user interface, or from the MS-DOS command line.

The major *setup* options are:

/C Don't load the SmartDrive disk cache.

/D Bypass the existing Windows version in the early phases of Setup. Use this if you're having problems due to missing or damaged supporting files.

/DOMAIN: *domain_name*
Set the Windows NT Logon Validation domain used by Client for Microsoft Networks to *domain_name*.

/F Avoid looking in the local cache for filenames. Setup runs a little slower and saves a small amount of memory.

/IC Do a clean boot. If this is set and KeepRMDrivers=1 is not in the Registry, drivers are commented out from the *config.sys/autoexec.bat* file.

/ID Avoid checking for the minimum disk space required to install Win 98.

/IE Skip the Startup Disk screen.

/IF Do a "fast" setup.

/IH Run ScanDisk in the foreground to see the results. Use this if the system stalls during the ScanDisk check.

/IL Load the Logitech mouse driver. Use this if you have a Logitech Series C mouse.

/IM Skip the check for low conventional memory.

/IN Don't call the networking Setup software. Neither the networking software nor the Networking Wizard screens will be used.

/IQ Don't check for cross-linked files.

/IR Don't update the master boot record (MBR).

/IS Don't run ScanDisk.

/NOSTART

Copy a minimal installation of the required DLLs used by Windows 98 Setup, then exit to MS-DOS without installing Windows 98.

/NA#

Prevents notification of the following messages when Win 98 is running:

1   Don't display the warning message

2   Don't display the error message for running MS-DOS–based applications

3   Don't display either of the above messages

If you use the /NA option without specifying a number, Setup will default to the number 3 option and not display either of the messages.

/NF Don't prompt to remove the floppy disk from drive A at the end of step three in the Setup process. Use this when installing from a bootable compact disc.

/NR Skips the Registry check.

/PI Keep forced configured hardware settings. Some BIOSes require hardware to have a forced configuration to work. By default, Setup removes the forced configuration and some hardware doesn't work properly after this is done.

script_filename

Use settings in the specified script to install Win 98 automatically; for example, *setup msbatch.inf* specifies that Setup should use the settings in *msbatch.inf.* The script must have an 8.3 filename, not a long filename.

/SRCDIR

Specifies the source directory where the Win 98 Setup files are located.

/S filename

Load the specified *Setup.inf* file when starting setup.

/T:tempdir

Specifies the directory where Setup will copy its temporary files. This directory must already exist, but any existing files in the directory will be deleted.

/IV Don't display billboards.

/IW Don't display the License Agreement dialog box.

/IX Don't perform a character set check.

Examples

Start Windows 98 *setup* from MS-DOS:

1. If you're installing from the CD-ROM, put the CD in the drive and make that the active drive.

2. If you're installing from source files on a network server, connect to that server and switch to the shared network directory that contains the Win 98 source files.

3. At the command prompt, run *setup* and any options that you want configured, then press Enter.

Start Windows 98 Setup from a network computer using a setup script:

1. Log on to the network, running the existing network client.

2. Connect to the server that contains the Win 98 distribution files.

3. At the command prompt, type:

   `C:\>setup msbatch.inf`

   For example, type setup \\ntserver\win98\mybatch.inf to run *setup* using a setup script named *mybatch.inf* that is stored in the *win98* directory on a server named *ntserver.*

Notes

- If Win 98 is installed from a server, the location of that network directory is stored in the Registry. When you add a device or require additional support files to run Win 98, *setup* automatically attempts to retrieve the files from that same location on the server. This eliminates the need to maintain a permanent network connection on the computer and makes it easier to modify the configuration of a computer in a networked environment.

- You can use *batchs.exe* to create a setup script, or you can edit *msbatch.inf* with a text editor such as Notepad. See Chapter 9, *Web Integration*, for details on using *batchs.exe.*

See Also

"Notepad" in Chapter 6
"scandskw"

---

sort

\Windows\Command\sort.exe

Sort text input in alphanumeric order.

To Launch

    sort [/r] [/+n] [filenames]

Description

The *sort* command sorts text on a line-by-line basis. Each line of the input is ordered alphanumerically and output to the screen. By default, sorting starts with the character in the first column of each line, but this can be changed with the /+n option. *sort* is often used in conjunction with either pipes or output redirection. That is, you might want to sort the output of another command, and you will often want to redirect the output to a file so that it can be saved.

sort takes the following options:

command
    Specifies a command whose output is to be sorted

/+n Sorts the file according to characters in column *n*

/r Reverses the sort order; that is, sorts Z to A, then 9 to 0

Examples

Display an alphabetically sorted directory (similar to `dir /o`):

```
C:\>dir | sort
```

Sort the contents of a file starting with column 21:

```
C:\>sort /+21 txtfiles.log > txtfiles.srt
```

Notes

- The input to *sort* should be ASCII text, so that each line can be considered a record of data. For example, Notepad and *edit* produce text files, but Word-Pad and Word (by default) produce binary *.doc* files, not text.

- The lines (records) may be broken into fields, each beginning a fixed number of characters from the start of the line.

- *sort* is a real-mode program; it can handle files over 64K in size, but the maximum is about 640K. It may have problems with very long lines.

- Blank lines and leading spaces will be sorted. This can result in many blank lines at the top of the sorted output; you may need to scroll down in an editor to see non-blank lines.

- *sort*'s collating sequence is based on the country code and code-page settings. In particular, the sort order of characters greater than ASCII code 127 depends on the COUNTRY settings.

- If you do a lot of sorting, you may want to get a Windows version of the Unix *sort* utility, which is much more powerful. The Unix *sort* command lets you define and sort on fields within the line, ignore upper- and lowercase distinctions, and eliminate duplicate lines, among other things. See the MKS Toolkit:

  http://www.mks.com/solution/tk

  or the Hamilton C Shell:

  http://www.hamiltonlabs.com/cshell.htm

  If you have Unix access, you can also *ftp* your file to a Unix machine, use *telnet* to run the Unix *sort* command on it, and then *ftp* it back to your Windows machine.

See Also

"find"

---

start   \Windows\Command\start.exe

Start applications in a new window.

To Launch

```
start [/m][/max][/r][/w] program [arg...]
start [/m][/max][/r][/w] document.ext
start [/m][/max][/r][/w] url
```

Description

Normally, when you run a DOS program from the command prompt, the command runs in the same window. If you want to open a new window for the command to run in, use *start*. Opening in a new window is the default behavior for Windows programs, but even with Windows programs, *start* is handy, because it lets you specify whether the program is run maximized or minimized. You can also open a file with its associated application by typing start followed by the filename. The *start* command also makes it possible to open URLs from a DOS prompt or from a DOS batch file.

start accepts the following options:

arg Specifies the optional list of arguments for the program to run.

document.ext
> Specifies a document to open. Windows will launch or open the appropriate program based on the filename extension associated with that file type.

/m Runs the new program in a minimized window.

/max
> Runs the new program in a maximized window.

program
> Specifies the program to run. If the program is not in the current directory, a drive and/or path should be included.

/r Runs the new program restored (in the foreground). This is the default behavior.

url Specifies a URL (e.g., *http://www.oreilly.com/*) to open.

/w Specifies that control does not pass back to the window from which *start* was invoked until the new window is closed.

Examples

Run the Windows Notepad program, opening the window to full size:

    C:\>start /max notepad.exe

Run the DOS program *myprog.exe* in the *C:\DOS* directory, and wait until the window is manually closed:

    C:\>start /w c:\dos\myprog.exe

Run the Windows Notepad application to open the *readme.txt* file. (By default, any file with the extension *.txt* is opened by Notepad):

    C:\>start c:\windows\readme.txt

Open a URL with the default browser:

    C:\>start http://www.oreilly.com

Notes

- *start* will run executable programs with *.exe*, *.com*, and *.bat* extensions.

- Only one command, filename, or URL can be specified when using the *start* command. If more than one parameter is entered, it is ignored (no error message).

- To open folders quickly, use the *start* command followed by the folder's name at the MS-DOS Prompt. (Note that this works only if the folder is in the current path.) Windows will find the folder and open it on the Desktop.

 If you want to be able to run a command in the background (i.e., do its thing without putting up a window), use start /m.

Typing start . will open the current directory in a Desktop folder view; start .. will open the parent directory, and so on.

If you want to "preload" a set of URLs into your browser for quicker performance (e.g., if there are a group of news sites you like to check every morning), create a batch file containing one *start* command for each URL, then execute the batch file each morning while you go get your cup of coffee, or use Task Scheduler (*mstask.exe*) to schedule the batch file to run before you come in for work. Of course, this works best if you have a full-time Internet connection.

See Also

"command," mstask, "regedit"

---

sys
\Windows\Command\sys.com

Create a bootable MS-DOS disk.

To Launch

    sys [drive1:][path] drive2:

Description

sys is similar to format /s, except that *sys* works with already formatted disks, and *sys* lets you specify an optional location in which to find the system files.

Neither *sys* nor format /s do what's necessary to make Windows 98 bootable from a floppy: merely the MS-DOS 7.1 portion is booted. See the "Add/Remove Programs" section in Chapter 5 for details on how to do this.

The *sys* options are:

[drive1:][path]
Specifies the location of the system files

drive2:
Specifies the drive the system files are to be copied to

Examples

    C:\>sys a:

Notes

- Besides the boot record (containing a bootstrap loader for *io.sys*), the "system files" are *io.sys*, *drvspace.bin*, and *command.com*, and a small *msdos.sys* file is also created.

- Like *format*, the *sys* command doesn't work with *subst*ed or network drives.

- When *sys*ing a floppy, a new *msdos.sys* file is created. This means that if you then boot from the floppy, you won't be able to start Windows 98. The way around this is to copy the *msdos.sys* file from *C:* to the floppy after using *sys*.

See Also

"format"

---

telnet

Create an interactive session on a remote computer using TCP/IP.

To Launch

```
telnet [host [port]]
```

Description

telnet is a Windows Sockets–based application that simplifies TCP/IP terminal emulation with Windows 98.

telnet is useful for connecting with a Unix shell account. In addition, there are many useful library catalogs and other services provided via *telnet*.

telnet accepts the following options:

host

Specifies the hostname or IP address of the remote system to which you want to connect.

port

Specifies the remote name or number of the TCP port to connect to. The default value is specified by the *telnet* entry in the *services* file. If no entry exists in the *services* file, the default connection port value is decimal 23. The following port names are known by default in *telnet.exe*: *telnet, chargen, qotd, echo,* and *daytime.* (Each Internet server, such as *ftp, telnet,* or the Web (*http*) is assigned a standard port number, but it is also possible for alternative servers to be offered using other ports.)

Associated files

Windows\services

Examples

Connect to a library from the command line by typing:

```
C:\>telnet opac.sonoma.edu

Welcome to the Sonoma State University LIBAXP.
Username: OPAC
```

```
Welcome to OpenVMS AXP (TM) Operating System,
Version V6.2-1H3 on node LIBAXP
Last interactive login on Wednesday, 31-DEC-1997 10:52:39.10
Last non-interactive login on Tuesday, 30-DEC-1997 20:33:16.28
```

Notes

- The VT-100/ANSI setting will serve your purposes in most cases, unless the remote host instructs you differently when you log in.

- Adding "http 80/tcp" to the port number list in the \Windows\Services file enables you to type http instead of 80 as the port when connecting.

- Various *telnet* settings (i.e., WinPosTop, Machine1, Rows, etc.) are stored in the Registry at:

  `My Computer\HKEY_USERS\Default\Software\Microsoft\Telnet`

See Also

"Telnet" in Chapter 6

---

time   Internal to: *Windows\command.com*

Display or set the system time.

To Launch

`time [time]`

Description

Run *time* without options to display the current time setting and a prompt for a new one. Press **Enter** to keep the same time.

The *time* options are:

`time`

To set the system time without a prompt: *hh:mm:ss* [A|P]

hh Hours: valid values = 0–23

mm Minutes: valid values = 0–59

ss Seconds: valid values = 0–59

A|P A.M. or P.M. (for 12-hour format). If a valid 12-hour format is entered without an A or P, A is the default.

Notes

- *time* and *date* affect all of Windows, not just the DOS box in which they are run. These commands can be used instead of Control Panel → Date/Time.

- The time format can be changed in Control Panel → Regional Settings → Time, but this doesn't affect the output of the DOS *time* command even though it has an instant effect on the time displayed in the System Tray. The format of *time* is set with the COUNTRY= setting in *config.sys*. You have to reboot after making this change.

- *time* always prompts for new time. If you want a batch file to display the time without prompting for a new one, create a tiny file with just a return/linefeed character in it, and redirect this to *time*, as shown in the following example. Here, *x* is a file created with *copy con* that contains a single carriage return/linefeed:

```
C:\>type timex.bat
@echo off
time < x | find "Current"
echo.
C:\>timex
Current time is 9:56:54.33a
```

- Windows 98 has automatic changeover for daylight savings and a GUI interface for changing time zones (see Control Panel → Date/Time → Time Zone), so there is probably little reason to run *time* or *date*, except perhaps in a batch file to create a time or date stamp.

See Also

"date"

"Date/Time" in Chapter 5

---

tracert

\ *Windows\tracert.exe*

Internet traceroute utility.

To Launch

```
tracert [-d] [-h max_hops] [-j ip-list] [-w timeout] target
```

Description

tracert displays the route that IP packets take between the local system and a remote system. This is handy if you want to know why a connection is slow (since it shows the time associated with each hop). But it's also just a great look "under the hood" of the Internet. Doing a *tracert* to frequently visited Internet sites will give a useful perspective on how the Internet works. When you connect to the Internet, your data is forwarded from one system to another via a series of "hops." Depending on your Internet service provider, the route from any one system to another can be long or short. Understanding just how your data gets from here to there can help you understand Internet connection or performance problems.

tracert accepts the following options:

-d Do not resolve addresses to hostnames. This is helpful if there is also a problem with DNS.

-h *max_hops*

Maximum number (usually 30) of hops to search for target.

-j *ip-list*

Loose source route along *ip-list*; specifies a suggested route the packet should take.

target

Destination system whose connectivity you are checking. Can be either a TCP/IP hostname (such as *john.doe.com*) or an IP address (such as 10.0.0.1).

−w *timeout*

Number of milliseconds to wait for a reply before going onto the next hop.

Examples

```
C:\>tracert www.yahoo.com

Tracing route to www10.yahoo.com [204.71.200.75]
over a maximum of 30 hops:
  1    *       *       *       Request timed out.
  2  119 ms  118 ms   120 ms  e4-gw2.west.ora.com [192.168.50.5]
  3  122 ms  128 ms   125 ms  e3-gw.songline.com [10.0.0.1]
  4  124 ms  132 ms   120 ms  ans-gw.songline.com [172.16.30.4]
  5  165 ms  139 ms   134 ms  s2-5.cnss12.San-Francisco.t3.ans.net [192.103.60.61]
  6  137 ms  160 ms   133 ms  f2-1.t8-1.San-Francisco.t3.ans.net [140.222.8.222]
  7  144 ms  132 ms   136 ms  core5-fddi1-0.SanFrancisco.mci.net [206.157.77.1]
  8  148 ms  142 ms   145 ms  bordercore2.Bloomington.mci.net [166.48.176.1]
  9  149 ms  151 ms   155 ms  hssi1-0.br2.NUQ.globalcenter.net [166.48.177.254]
 10  148 ms  151 ms   148 ms  fe4-0.cr1.NUQ.globalcenter.net [206.251.1.1]
 11  171 ms  288 ms   231 ms  pos6-0.cr2.SNV.globalcenter.net [206.251.0.30]
 12  166 ms  229 ms   228 ms  www10.yahoo.com [204.71.200.75]
Trace complete.
```

Notes

- *tracert* is a version of the Unix *traceroute* command.

- The remote system does not have to be a computer; it can be a router or any type of system that implements ICMP (Internet Control Message Protocol).

- Sometimes *tracert* can hang for several minutes while trying to resolve each IP address to its TCP/IP name. This can happen if DNS is not working properly on the local computer or if there are IP addresses on the route without proper DNS records. If this happens, you can turn off DNS with the −d option.

See Also

There are many web-based versions of *tracert* that show the route taken between the web server and another machine. You can find an example here:

*http://dir.yahoo.com/Computers_and_Internet/Communications_and_
Networking/Software/Networking/Utilities/Traceroute/*

Another such program is Yahoo! traceroute:

http://net.yahoo.com/cgi-bin/trace.sh

---

type   Internal to: \ *Windows\command.com*

Display the contents of a text file.

To Launch

```
type filename
```

Description

The *type* command is useful if you need to quickly view the contents of any text file (especially short files). *type* is also useful for concatenating text files, using the >> operator.

Notes

• If the file is long and you'd like to quit displaying a file, press Ctrl-C to end the text display and return to the command prompt.

• To display binary (non-text) files (e.g., to search for strings), use *edit.com*.

See Also

"more"

---

ver   Internal to: \ *Windows\command.com*

Display the Windows 98 build number.

To Launch

```
ver [/r]
```

Description

ver shows the version of Windows 98 you're using. You can also find the Windows version at Control Panel → System → General, but it won't show you the revision number nor whether DOS is in high memory or not.

ver takes the following option:

/r This undocumented option also displays the revision number, and whether DOS is located in the high memory area (HMA; same as DOS=HIGH).

Examples

The following example unveils the Windows 98 Second Edition version number:

```
C:\>ver /r
Windows 98 [Version 4.10.2222]
Revision A
DOS is in HMA
```

Notes

• Windows 98 is really MS-DOS 7.10 + Windows 4.10.*xxxx*, where *xxxx* is the build/revision number.

• *ver* just shows the Windows 98 SE build number (2222), not the DOS or Windows version number. To get the DOS version number (7.10 for the version that supports FAT32), you can use *debug* to call the internal "Get DOS version" function:

```
C:\>copycon dosver.dbg
a
mov ax,3306
int 21
```

```
ret

g 105
r bx

q
ctrl z
enter
C:\>debug < dosver.dbg
....
BX 0007
```

(The number after BX at the end is the hexadecimal DOS version number: 0007 for MS-DOS 7.0, 0A07 for MS-DOS 7.10.)

- For more information on what Windows updates, patches, and fixes you might be running, use *qfecheck* (Update Information Tool).

See Also

"debug"
"Update Information Tool" in Chapter 6

---

win

\ *Windows\win.com*

Bootstrap loader for Windows 98.

To Launch

```
win [/d:[f][m][s][v][x]]
```

Description

win.com is the command that Windows 98 uses to start the Windows 98 GUI on top of MS-DOS 7.1. Normally it runs automatically after the processing of *autoexec.bat*. However, if you disable this default behavior (by placing BootGUI=0 in *msdos.sys*, for example, by booting Windows 98 from a floppy disk, or by pressing a function key during the boot process), you can then run *win* yourself from the DOS prompt. This is useful if you want to run some DOS commands before the Windows 98 GUI has started.

The *win* options are:

/d   Used for troubleshooting when Windows does not start correctly.

:f   Turns off 32-bit disk access. Equivalent to the *system.ini* file setting: 32BitDiskAccess=FALSE.

:m   Enables Safe mode. This is automatically enabled during a Safe start (function key F5).

:n   Enables Safe mode with networking. This is automatically enabled during a Safe start (function key F6).

:s   Specifies that Windows should not use ROM address space between F000:0000 and 1 MB for the V86BreakPoint. Equivalent to the *system.ini* file setting: SystemROMBreakPoint=FALSE.

:v   Specifies that the ROM routine will handle interrupts from the hard disk controller. Equivalent to the *system.ini* file setting: VirtualHDIRQ=FALSE.

:x   Excludes all of the adapter area from the range of memory that Windows scans to find unused space. Equivalent to the *system.ini* file setting: EMMExclude=A000-FFFF.

Notes

- If you try to run *win* when Windows 98 is already running, an error message will remind you that you are already running Windows.

- Windows 98's *win.com* will fail with an error message if the underlying DOS is not version 7.0 or higher. Some versions of *win.com* require DOS version 7. 10 or higher. *win.com* also requires that the underlying DOS loads (either implicitly or via DEVICE= in *config.sys*) appropriate versions of the XMS driver (*himem.sys*) and the Installable File System helper (*ifshlp.sys*).

- *win* is just a small bootstrap loader. Its main job is to run *vmm32.vxd*, which contains the Virtual Machine Manager (VMM) and virtual device driver (VxD) core of the Windows 98 operating system; *vmm32.vxd* in turn loads the Win16 and Win32 GUI.

See Also

"sys"

---

xcopy   \Windows\Command\xcopy.exe

Stub-loader for *xcopy32.mod*.

xcopy.exe and *xcopy32.exe* reside in the \Windows\Command directory and can be used interchangeably from the command line, since they both call *xcopy32. mod*.

See Also

"xcopy32"

---

xcopy32   \Windows\Command\xcopy32.mod

Copy files and directories, including subdirectories.

To Launch

```
xcopy source [destination] [/a | /m] [/d[:date]] [/p] [/s [/e]] [/w]
[/c] [/i] [/q] [/f] [/l] [/h] [/r] [/t] [/u] [/k] [/n]
```

Description

xcopy.exe and *xcopy32.exe* are both stub loaders (they aren't DOS programs, but are Win32 "Console" programs) that call *xcopy32.mod*. We refer in this section to "*xcopy32*," but keep in mind when typing *xcopy* or *xcopy32* from the command line that you are actually running *xcopy32.mod*.

xcopy32 provides more options and is often faster than *copy*.

The *xcopy32* options are:

/a Copies files with the archive attribute set, but doesn't change the attribute of the source file.

/c Continues copying even if errors occur.

/d:*date*
    Copies only files changed on or after the specified date. If no date is given, copies only those source files that are newer than existing destination files.

destination
    Specifies the location and/or name of new files. If omitted, files are copied to the current directory.

/e Copies directories and subdirectories, including empty ones. Same as /s /e. May be used to modify /t.

/f Displays full source and destination filenames while copying.

/h Copies hidden and system files also.

/i If a destination is not supplied and you are copying more than one file, assumes that the destination must be a directory. (By default, *xcopy* asks if the destination is a file or directory.)

/k Copies attributes. (By default, *xcopy* resets read-only attributes.)

/l Displays files that would be copied given other options, but does not actually copy the files.

/m Copies files with the archive attribute set, then turns off the archive attribute of the source file.

/n Copies files using short (8.3) file and directory names (for example, *PROGRA~1* instead of *Program Files*).

/p Prompts you before creating each destination file.

/q Does not display filenames while copying.

/r Overwrites read-only files.

/s Copies directories and subdirectories, except empty ones. (Probably the most useful *xcopy* option.)

source
    Specifies the file(s) to copy; must include either a drive or a path.

/t Creates directory structure, but does not copy files. Does not include empty directories (use /t /e to include empty directories).

/u Copies from source only files that exist on destination; used to update files.

/w Prompts you to press a key before copying.

/y Overwrites existing files without prompting.

/-y Prompts you before overwriting existing files. (This is the default; overrides opposite setting in COPYCMD= environment variable.) Only COPYCMD=/y and -/y have an effect on *xcopy32* (and *copy*).

Exit codes (can be tested in batch file with ERRORLEVEL):

0   All files were copied without errors.

1   No files were found to copy.

2   *xcopy* was terminated by Ctrl-C before copying was complete.

4   An initialization error occurred. Such an error would generally be caused by insufficient memory or disk space, or an invalid drive name or syntax.

5   A disk-write error occurred.

Examples

Copy all the files and subdirectories, including any empty subdirectories and hidden files, from *C:\foobar* to the disk in drive *A*:

```
C:\>xcopy \foobar a: /s /e /h
```

Notes

- *copy, move,* and *xcopy* normally prompt you before overwriting an existing file. To force these commands to overwrite in all cases without prompting you, set the copycmd environment variable to /y. To restore the default behavior, set copycmd to /-y.

- It has been reported that the /s and /e options have bugs when used in conjunction with /d and /u.

See Also

"copy," "diskcopy"

CHAPTER 8

Hidden Gems on the
Windows 98 CD-ROM

When you first install Windows 98, you are given a choice of three installations: standard, portable, and custom. If you choose custom, you are able to choose from a variety of optional packages via an interface similar to Control Panel → Add/Remove Programs. If Windows 98 is already installed, you can add all of the missing standard components using Add/Remove programs.

But even if you have a custom installation of Windows 98, or have checked every box in Add/Remove Programs, there are all sorts of goodies that have been left behind on the Win 98 CD-ROM. The majority of them can be installed quickly with one setup program on the CD. If, for instance, you are interested in faxing documents, customizing the system tray, limiting access to parts of Win 98, or even bringing back to life the pinball game from Win95 Plus!, then this is the chapter for you.

We've provided an alphabetical reference in this chapter to all of these hidden add-ons, and we show you how to set them up and put them to use. We also go into some detail about the new Windows Update feature and list some of the update items you can download, such as the Y2K update, the IE4 security patch, and IE5. You won't regret spending the small amount of time to install this stuff—the pay-off is big!

Note, however, that some of these utilities are intended for system administrators or knowledgeable users, so do proceed with caution if you think you might be getting in over your head.

Windows 98 Resource Kit Sampler

Many of the utilities listed in this chapter are part of the Windows 98 Resource Kit Sampler and you can install all of them in one step using Control Panel → Add/ Remove Programs → Windows Setup → Have Disk → \tools\reskit\setup on the Windows 98 CD-ROM.

Once you have installed the resource kit, you can access most of the tools using the Microsoft Management Console (see Figure 8-1). Launch the console using Start Menu → Programs → Windows 98 Resource Kit → Tools → Management Console. Throughout this chapter we leave off the Start → Programs → Windows 98 Resource Kit section of the path and just start with Tools → Management Console to avoid needless repetition. You'll notice it is much faster to just type in the application name from the command line anyway.

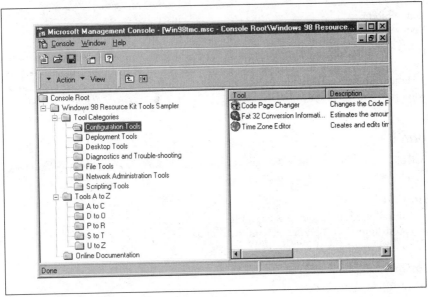

Figure 8-1: Microsoft Management Console

The left pane of the console, the scope pane, shows that there are two different ways of finding the tool you wish to use: by tool category or alphabetically. All available tools are represented in both views. The right pane shows the contents of anything selected in the left pane.

Once you have found the tool you are looking for, you can access it by double-clicking its icon. Many resource kit tools are executable files that you can run right from the Management Console or from the Win 98 command line. Others, such as TweakUI, must be installed and run outside the Management Console. The icon in the console for such tools opens a help file that gives you instructions on installation and use. We will also describe the installation and launch procedure for these tools in their individual entries later in this chapter.

The alphabetical reference entries are as follows:

Batch98
Check Links

SNMP Agent
System Policy Editor

Code Page Changer
Clip Tray
Drivers
Fat32 Conversion Information Tool
Fax Cover Page Editor
Inbox Repair Tool
Microsoft Fax
Minitel Font Emulation Files
MTS Utilties
Network Monitor
Quick Tray
Password List Editor
Remote Registry
Remote Procedure Call Print Provider

System Recovery
Text File Viewer
Time This
Time Zone Editor
TweakUI
USB Viewer
Wait For
Web-Based Enterprise Management
Where
Windiff
Windows 98 INF Installer
Windows Messaging
Winset
WSH Administrator's Guide

In the installation instructions for each program, you will often see two or more lines. "Install the full Resource Kit Sampler" means to follow the instructions in this section. The second line gives instructions for installing only the desired item, without using the Management Console.

Batch98
\Program Files\Win98RK\batch.exe

Batch98 lets you create information (*.inf*) files for automated installation of Windows 98 on other computers.

To Install

Install the full Resource Kit Sampler
Add/Remove Programs → Windows Setup → Have Disk → \tools\Reskit\ Batch\setup.exe on Win 98 CD

To Launch

Address → batch
Start → Run → batch
Management Console → Tool Categories → Deployment Tools → Batch98
Management Console → Tools A to Z → A to C → Batch98

Description

The installation of Windows 98 can be automated by using the command setup -s in combination with an *.inf* file that contains preconfigured system settings and user information. This feature allows an administrator to create a custom Windows 98 installation that can be repeated for multiple computers. Writing an *.inf* file used to be a tedious chore. Batch98 allows you to generate an *.inf* file automatically based on current registry settings using the Gather Now button or manually by selecting options yourself (see Figure 8-2).

You can configure options for the following:

398   *Chapter 8 – Hidden Gems on the Windows 98 CD-ROM*

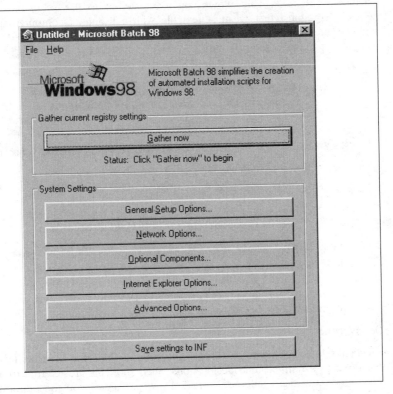

Figure 8-2: Batch98

General Setup
Includes basic information such as product ID, installation directory, user information, what items should appear on the desktop, printers, and user profiles.

Network
Includes protocols, services, clients, and access control as discussed in the "Network" section in Chapter 5, *The Control Panel.*

Optional
Allows you to select which components will be installed with Win 98.

Internet Explorer
Controls settings for IE, as discussed in the "Internet" section in Chapter 5.

Advanced
Allows you to add designated registry files and system policy files to Win 98 setup as well as specify a location for Windows Update, which is discussed later in this chapter.

Notes

If you are configuring an *.inf* file to automate the installation of multiple computers, save the *.inf* file you generate in Batch98 using File → Multiple

Machine-Name Save. This allows you to create up to 9,999 *.inf* files simultaneously. You must first create a text file with a listing of computer names on separate lines. Optionally, you can also provide IP addresses separated from the computer name by a comma.

See Also

"Windows Update" in Chapter 4, *The Windows 98 User Interface*
"setup" in Chapter 7, *DOS and Other Command-Line Utilities*

Check Links   *Program Files\Win98RK\checklinks.exe*

Scans your system for shortcuts that point to invalid file locations.

To Install

Install the full Resource Kit Sampler
Copy *checklinks.exe* from `Win 98 CD-ROM\`*tools\reskit\desktop*

To Launch

Address → checklinks
Start → Run → checklinks
Management Console → Tool Categories → Desktop Tools → Checklinks
Management Console → Tools A to Z → A to C → Checklinks

Description

Checklinks is actually a wizard that scans your C: drive for shortcuts (*.lnk* files) that point to a non-existent file locations. Such shortcuts are referred to as dead links. Once any dead links are found, the wizard gives you the opportunity to select those you want to remove from your system.

See Also

"Shortcuts" in Chapter 4

Code Page Changer   *Program Files\Win98RK\chdoscp.exe*

Lets you change the code page used for MS-DOS–based programs to match Windows 98 Regional Settings.

To Install

Install the full Resource Kit Sampler
Copy *chdoscp.exe* and *codepage* from `Win 98 CD-ROM\`*tools\reskit\config\chdoscp*

To Launch

Address → chdoscp
Start → Run → chdoscp
Management Console → Tool Categories → Configuration Tools → Code Page
    Changer
Management Console → Tools A to Z → A to C → Code Page Changer

---

Description

Your system interprets keys pressed on a keyboard as certain characters. What characters are mapped to what keys changes according to your locale (i.e., country or region) or your keyboard preference (i.e., QWERTY or DVORAK). In Windows 98, you change keyboard mappings using Control Panel → Regional Settings, as discussed in Chapter 5. In MS-DOS, however, these mappings are maintained via a code page. When you install Win 98, the MS-DOS code page used is automatically determined based on the regional settings you choose (or that setup chooses). However, if you later change your regional settings in Win 98, those changes are not reflected in the MS-DOS code page. *chdoscp.exe* lets you select an MS-DOS code page (based on country) to install.

Clip Tray   *\Program Files\Win98RK\cliptray.exe*

Lets you store and manage multiple clipboard text entries using an icon in the System Tray.

To Install

Install the full Resource Kit Sampler

To Launch

Address → `cliptray`
Start → Run → `cliptray`
Management Console → Tool Categories → Desktop Tools → Clip Tray
Management Console → Tools A to Z → A to C → Clip Tray

Description

Normally, the Win 98 clipboard can store one entry. Clip Tray is accessible through an icon on the System Tray and greatly extends the standard clipboard by allowing you to store and easily access up to 99 named entries. You can add an entry by right-clicking the Clip Tray icon and choosing Add from the context menu. Give the entry a name and enter any text you wish. Entries appear on the Clip Tray context menu and you can paste the entry into any document that has the focus by simply selecting the entry. Clip Tray is great for storing frequently entered text such as names and addresses (shown in Figure 8-3).

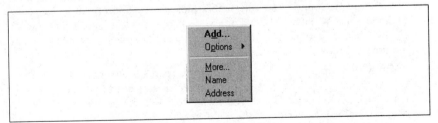

Figure 8-3: Entries on the Clip Tray menu

Notes

- You can edit existing entries using using ClipTray → right-click → Options → Edit. This opens the Clip Tray Editor, which lets you view and edit all entries in the currently loaded ClipTray file.

- When you activate the Preview Mode of Clip Tray (via a toggle on the context menu), a dialog appears showing you the text that will be pasted whenever you select an entry instead of immediately pasting it into the document.

- Your entries are stored by default in a text file called *ClipTray.txt* in *Program Files\Win98RK*. You can directly modify this text file instead of using Clip Tray, if you wish. Clip Tray can also use multiple text files, each holding a different set of entries. You can open new files using the context menu of the System Tray icon.

- If you find Clip Tray as handy as we do, you can put a shortcut to it in *\Windows\Startup* to have it automatically launch each time Win 98 starts.

See Also

"Clipboard Viewer" in Chapter 6, *Start Menu Programs and Other Graphical Applications*

Drivers

Win 98 CD-ROM\Drivers

Contains additional hardware drivers that are not part of the standard installation of Windows 98.

Description

The Drivers folder on the Win 98 CD-ROM contains hundreds of drivers categorized by hardware type, such as audio, display, modem, etc. The folder for each category contains an *index.txt* file listing the available drivers in that category. Folders for individual drivers usually have a file named *install.txt* that provides general installation instructions for that type of driver.

Notes

- If you are installing new hardware using Plug and Play or Control Panel → Add New Hardware, a wizard will prompt you to specify a location where drivers may be found. You can simply indicate the appropriate driver subfolder on the Win 98 CD-ROM for your hardware. The subfolders are all clearly labelled (e.g., Display, Modem, etc.), and the *Driver98.chm* help file in the drivers directory can be helpful.

- If you wish to upgrade the drivers for hardware that is already installed, go to Control Panel → System → Device Manager → **any_device** → Properties → Driver → Update Driver to launch a wizard that will let you specify where the new drivers may be found. It's a good idea to check with the manufacturer for a newer driver version before using this.

Fat32 Conversion Information Tool

\Program Files\Win98RK\
fat32win.exe

Estimates the amount of free space you may gain by converting a FAT drive to FAT32.

To Install

Install the full Resource Kit Sampler
Copy *fat32win.exe* from Win 98 CD-ROM\tools\reskit\config

To Launch

Address → fat32win
Start → Run → fat32win
Management Console → Tool Categories → Configuration Tools → FAT32 Conversion Information Tool
Management Console → Tools A to Z → D to O → FAT32 Conversion Information Tool

Description

FAT32 is a new version of the FAT file system. FAT32 is more robust and uses a smaller cluster size than FAT, so a drive formatted with FAT32 boasts more free space and is up to 50% faster than the same drive formatted with FAT. *Fat32win. exe* is a simple tool that scans a selected FAT drive and reports how much additional free space will be available should you convert the drive to FAT32 using Drive Converter (*cvt1.exe*).

See Also

"Drive Converter" in Chapter 6

Fax Cover Page Editor

\Windows\faxcover.exe

Add graphic elements to fax cover pages.

To Install

Install Microsoft Fax from the Windows 98 CD-ROM using \tools\oldwin95\ message\us\awfax.exe

To Launch

Address → faxcover
Start → Run → faxcover
Start → Programs → Accessories → Fax → Cover Page Editor

Description

You can add logos or other graphic elements to your fax cover pages using the application's built-in tools or by inserting bitmap (*.bmp*) files. If a desired graphic isn't in *.bmp* format, you can copy it to the Clipboard and then paste it in the cover page editor. When you have finished with a fax cover page, save it as a *.cpe* file so you can attach it when sending a Microsoft fax. See Figure 8-4.

Hidden Gems
on CD-ROM

Fax Cover Page Editor   403

Figure 8-4: Fax Cover Page Editor

Notes

- *faxcover.exe* stores several icons that can be assigned to fax cover pages, but you can easily add your own icons via Insert → Object. Once the icon has been inserted into the cover page, simply select it and drag it anywhere on the page.

- There are several *.cpe* files that act as fax cover page templates, which you can modify, or you can create your own *.cpe* files that contain customized cover pages. To modify an existing cover page (one of several *.cpe* files in *Windows*), right-click on a field (e.g., Urgent), and a context menu allows you to modify the font, color, text alignment, etc.

See Also

"Microsoft Fax"
"Windows Messaging"

Inbox Repair Tool

Program Files\Windows Messaging\scanpst.exe

The Inbox Repair Tool.

To Install

Install Windows Messaging from the Windows 98 CD-ROM using *tools\ oldwin95\message\us\wms.exe*

To Launch

Address → scanpst
Start → Run → scanpst
Start → Programs → Accessories → System Tools → Inbox Repair Tool

---

Description

If you use the Inbox, you might want to run *scanpst* periodically to prevent lockups and problems in the future. *scanpst* looks for errors in the *.pst* or *.ost* file, which stores all of your email messages if you use Windows Messaging. If you have a large number of messages stored in Windows Messaging, it will take *scanpst* longer to scan and repair them.

When the *scanpst* dialog box appears (see Figure 8-5), you must type the path of the personal folder file (*.pst*) or offline folder file (*.ost*) that you want to scan. Alternatively, you can use the Browse button to open the "Select File To Scan" dialog box, where you can locate the file you want to scan.

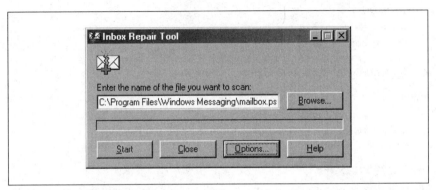

Figure 8-5: Inbox Repair Tool

Before starting the scan, you can select the Options button and choose one of three options for handling the log file that records errors in case they are found: Replace Log, Append to Log, or No Log.

If, after the scan is complete, no errors are found, just click the OK button (you're finished). If, however, errors are found, you have the option of checking the "Make Backup Of Scanned File Before Repairing" box. If you check this box, you must select the Browse button to specify the location where you'd like the backup file (e.g., *mailbox.pst*) to be placed.

scanpst places repaired messages into a special Lost & Found folder it creates. If errors are found, it is best to use Windows Messaging to create a new *.pst* or *.ost* file and move recovered messages there than to continue using the damaged *.pst* or *.ost* file.

Notes

- *scanpst* will perform eight different types of scans on the selected file. If errors are found during the scan and you decide to back up the file before having it repaired, you will need up to twice the available disk space of the *.pst* or *.ost* file size.

- If you're having problems finding your personal folder file, simply use Find and search for **.pst*.

Microsoft Fax
\Windows\System\awsnto32.exe

A Windows 98 fax server used with Windows Messaging (or another MAPI client) to send and receive faxes.

To Install

You must have Windows Messaging (or another MAPI client) installed before installing MS Fax.

> Add/Remove Programs → Install → Win 98 CD-ROM\tools\oldwin95\ message\us\awfax.exe

To Launch

> Address → awsnto32
> Start → Run → awsnto32
> Start → Programs → Accessories → Fax → Compose New Fax
> In Windows Messaging: Compose → New Fax

awsnto32 is also used to request a fax:

> Start → Run → awsnto32 -p
> Start → Programs → Accessories → Fax → Request a Fax
> In Windows Messaging: Tools → Microsoft Fax Tools → Request a Fax

Description

Microsoft Fax is a fax server that makes itself available as an information service to any MAPI-based messaging client. This includes Windows Messaging, Exchange Server Client, and Microsoft Outlook. If you have any of these installed, you can install MS Fax using \tools\oldwin95\message\us\awfax.exe on the Windows 98 CD-ROM. This section describes the use of awsnto32 from the command line and from within Windows Messaging.

You can send or request a fax by launching awsnto32 from the command line or from the Start menu, but you can also send or request a fax directly from within Windows Messaging. If you drag a shortcut of awsnto32 to your Desktop, you can simply drag a document you want to fax right onto the shortcut.

The following are the six steps (different dialogs use the Back and Next buttons to navigate between them) to sending a fax in Windows 98:

1. Dialing Properties (to access an outside line, tone dialing, and so on).

2. The recipient of the fax. (The Address Book button accesses your Personal Address Book if you have Windows Messaging installed, and retrieves the fax number, etc.)

3. Cover Page. (Choose a default one such as Generic, Urgent!, etc., or if you've created your own with faxcover, select it here.)

4. Choose a Subject and Note.

5. Add a file (select the Add File button and the Windows open dialog box appears).

6. Click the Finish button to send the fax.

Notes

- In Windows Messaging you can set passwords for your faxes (Tools →
  Microsoft Fax Tools → Advanced Security).

- You can access the fax properties (Tools → Microsoft Fax Tools → Options).
  This is the same dialog that is available from: Control Panel → Mail → Services → Microsoft Fax → Properties.

- You can view fax files (*.awd*) outside of Windows Messaging and the fax
  server with the *kodakimg* application.

- When you click the fax icon in the System Tray, you open the Microsoft Fax
  Status dialog box. From here you can click Answer Now to answer an incoming fax. Received faxes are placed in the Windows Messaging (or whatever
  client you use) Inbox. From the status dialog, you can also select Options →
  Modem Properties → Answer After to specify that MS Fax automatically
  answer incoming calls.

See Also

"Fax Cover Page Editor"
"Imaging" in Chapter 6

Minitel Font Emulation Files   *Program Files\Win98RK\minitel*

The Minitel font emulation files are used by Hyperterminal to emulate the look of
Minitel terminals.

To Install

Copy the font files from *Win 98 CD–ROM\tools\reskit\desktop\minitel* to
Windows\Fonts
Copy the font files from *Program Files\Win98RK\minitel* to *Windows\Fonts*
after installing the full resource kit

Description

HyperTerminal allows modem access to remote systems. The Minitel font emulation files allow HyperTerminal to emulate the display of terminals used to connect
to the French Minitel service.

See Also

"Fonts" in Chapter 5
"Hyper Terminal" in Chapter 6

MTS Utilities   *Win 98 CD–ROM\tools\mtsutil*

A collection of utilities from Microsoft Technical Support

To Launch

Double-click if the utility is an executable file (*.exe* or *.bat*)
`any utility` → right-click → Install if the utility is an *.INF* file

Description

Most of the utilities included in the \tools\mtsutil folder are used to achieve a single effect, such as changing an important registry entry. Some of the utilities are executable files (*.exe* or *.bat*), which you can launch with a simple double-click. Most are *.inf* files, which you can install by right-clicking and choosing Install from the context menu.

You can get a full description of each of these utilities and instructions for using them in the *mtsutil.txt* file in the \tools\mtsutil folder. Following are brief descriptions of a few of the more useful utilities:

Autolog.inf

A single registry entry governs whether or not you see a Network logon dialog box when you start Windows 98. You will not see the dialog box if at any time you logged on with a blank username. While this can be convenient for quicker starting of Windows, Win 98 will not allow you to save passwords (i.e., a dial-up networking password) unless you provide a user name at startup. Use *autolog.inf* to remove the autologon entry from the registry so that you will be shown the logon dialog when you start Win 98 and have the opportunity to enter a username and password.

Defrag.inf

You may have noticed that when you run *defrag.exe*, the defragmentation process will often have to restart several times and sometimes not finish at all. This is usually because programs running in the background write to the disk that is being defragmented. *Defrag.inf* adds an entry (`defrag.exe /all`) to the RunServiceOnce key in your registry, causing *defrag* to be run one time on each hard drive during the subsequent startup of Windows. This command actually happens before Win 98 itself loads in order to ensure that no background programs can cause interruption.

Pinball.inf

Many users of Windows 98 were disappointed to learn that they could no longer install files from the Windows 95 Plus! CD-ROM. Upon inserting the CD, an error message is displayed stating that your current version of Windows already includes the updated files you are attempting to install. This is not that important, because most of the utilities and enhancements from the Win95 Plus! package are included with Windows 98. One omission, however, is the pinball game. *Pinball.inf* initiates a setup routine that will install just the pinball game from the Windows 95 Plus! CD-ROM. Just right-click *pinball.inf* and choose Install from the context menu.

See Also

"Disk Defragmenter" in Chapter 6
Chapter 13, *The Registry*

Network Monitor Agent   Win 98 CD\tools\reskit\netadmin\netmon

The Network Monitor Agent allows network administrators to capture and examine packets of data transmitted or received by a Windows 98 system.

To Install

Control Panel → Network → Configuration → Add → Service → Have Disk →
Win 98 CD-ROM\tools\reskit\netadmin\netmon

Description

Network Monitor Agent runs as a Windows 98 service and allows the capture of data packets coming into or leaving the Windows 98 system by remote utilities such as Microsoft Network Monitor. Analysis of these packets allows administrators to gather network traffic statistics and troubleshoot networking problems.

Network Monitor Agent can also be used in combination with System Monitor to monitor the performance of remote systems on a network. Normally, System Monitor is used to monitor performance of the local system. To monitor remote systems, you will need to take four steps:

1. Install the Remote Registry service on both the system that will do the monitoring and the system(s) that will be monitored. Remote Registry is part of the Resource Kit sampler and is discussed later in this chapter.

2. Install the Network Monitor Agent on both the monitoring and monitored systems.

3. Enable user-level access on the systems to be monitored. You can do this using Control Panel → Network → Access Control → User-level access control.

4. Enable remote administration of the systems to be monitored using Control Panel → Password → Remote Adminitration → Enable remote administration.

Once you have completed these steps, you can launch System Monitor and connect to remote systems using File → Connect → *any_computer.*

Notes

- You can open multiple instances of System Monitor to monitor the performance of multiple remote systems simultaneously.

- If you don't want to use Network Monitor Agent as a networking service, you can also launch it by copying the *Win 98 CD-ROM\tools\reskit\netadmin\netmon* directory to your local hard drive and starting the *netmon.exe* program manually. This method also allows you to include *netmon.exe* in batch files.

Password List Editor

\Windows\pwledit.exe

Password List Editor lets you delete passwords from a stored password list.

To Install

Control Panel → Add/Remove Programs → Windows Setup → Have Disk →
Win 98 CD-ROM → *\tools\reskit\netadmin\pwledit*

To Launch

Address → pwledit
Start → Run → pwledit
Start → Programs → Accessories → System Tools → Password List Editor

Description

The Password List Editor allows you to view the resources listed in your password files (\ *Windows*\ *.pwl*). It doesn't let you view the actual passwords, but you can remove specific password entries. (If you forget a password, deleting it and starting over with a new one is normally the way to go.) You can remove passwords for remote sharing if you're logged on to the computer on which the password was defined. The easiest way to clear a password is just to delete the .*pwl* file.

Notes

pwledit only allows you to view password lists that are "unlocked," which means that the user associated with the list is actually logged on to Win 98.

Quiktray   *Program Files*\ *Win98RK*\ *quiktray.exe*

Quiktray lets you create shortcuts in your System Tray.

To Install

Install the full Resource Kit Sampler
Copy *quiktray.exe* from Win 98 CD-ROM*tools**reskit**desktop*

To Launch

Address → quicktray
Start → Run → quicktray
Management Console → Tool Categories → Desktop Tools → Quiktray
Management Console → Tools A to Z → P to R → Quiktray

Description

Quiktray lets you include shortcuts to programs, documents, and URLs as icons in your System Tray. This utility is really a holdover from the Windows 95 Resource Kit and what little value it ever had has been eclipsed by the much more versatile Quick Launch toolbar that is part of Window 98. When you run Quiktray, its icon is placed in the System Tray. Unfortunately, all of the icons currently in your System Tray disappear. Clicking the Quiktray icon opens a dialog that lets you add and remove shortcuts you wish included in the tray. These shortcuts are placed in the System Tray as icons whenever you run Quiktray and can be launched with a single click. Thus, Quiktray is really a way of replacing your System Tray with a limited kind of Quick Launch bar.

Notes

- The shortcuts controlled by Quiktray are not .*lnk* files, as are the normal type of shortcuts used by the Quick Launch toolbar. Quiktray shortcuts do not allow you to configure the running application in any way.

- Quiktray stores its shortcut information in a file named *Quiktray.dat* that is also located in the *Program Files*\ *Win98RK* folder.

Remote Registry

Remote Registry lets you modify the registry settings of another Windows 98 system on a network.

To Install

> Control Panel → Network → Configuration → Add → Service → Have Disk →
> *Win 98 CD-ROM\tools\reskit\netadmin\remotreg*

Description

The Remote Registry service allows you to modify the registry on a remote system. Before you can do this, you must do three things:

1. Install the Remote Registry service on both computers.

2. Enable Remote Administration on the computer whose registry you wish to modify using Control Panel → Password → Remote Adminitration → Enable remote administration.

3. Enable user-level access on the computer whose registry you wish to modify using Control Panel → Network → Access Control → User-level access control.

Once you have performed these three steps, you can modify a remote registry using either Regedit or System Policy Editor. In Regedit, use Registry → Connect Network Registry → *computer_name*. In System Policy Editor, use File → Connect → *computer_name*. Once you have connected with either tool, you can modify the remote registry using the tool just as you would to modify the local registry.

See Also

> "Registry Editor" in Chapter 6
> "regedit" in Chapter 7
> "System Policy Editor"
> Chapter 13

Remote Procedure Call Print Provider

RPC Print Provider provides enhanced network printing.

To Install

> Control Panel → Network → Configuration → Add → Service → Have Disk →
> *Win 98 CD-ROM\tools\reskit\netadmin\rpcpp*

Description

The RPC Print Provider service basically provides a set of APIs that allow a Windows 98 system to control certain processes for a shared printer on a Windows NT server. With RPCPP, a Win 98 user can pause, cancel, and get detailed information about any print jobs the user has sent to a Windows NT printer. In this way, a Win 98 user can attain the same kind of control over a remote printer that Start → Settings → Printers → Printer Properties gives over a local printer.

SNMP Agent

SNMP Agent lets SNMP management systems monitor computers running Windows 98.

To Install

Control Panel → Network → Configuration → Add → Service → Have Disk →
Win 98 CD-ROM\tools\reskit\netadmin\snmp

Description

Simple Network Management Protocol (SNMP) is a protocol that allows a piece of software called an SNMP management system to monitor and perform limited manipulation of any network device on which an SNMP Agent is installed. A system administrator, for example, could monitor various parts of a network, such as a Windows 98 computer or a router, from a central location. The Windows 98 SNMP Agent works with both the TCP/IP and IPX/SPX networking protocols.

Notes

Properties of the SNMP Agent, such as communities and permitted managers, are controlled directly by the Windows 98 Registry. To edit these properties, you must use *regedit* or System Policy Editor.

System Policy Editor   \ *Windows\poledit.exe*

System Policy Editor lets you create policies that govern the appearance and capability of a Windows 98 system.

To Install

Control Panel → Add/Remove Programs → Windows Setup → Have Disk →
Win 98 CD-ROM\reskit\netadmin\poledit

To Launch

Address → poledit
Start → Run → poledit
Start → Programs → Accessories → System Tools → System Policy Editor

Description

The System Policy Editor (see Figure 8-6) allows you to create or edit system policies to standardize the appearance and capabilities of Windows 98 for a single user, a group of users, or the entire network.

Once you've launched *poledit*, select File → Open Registry to customize settings on your computer. Two icons should be displayed: Local User (for user settings such as Control Panel and Desktop) and Local Computer (for system settings such as networking and sharing). Double-click each icon to view the profile listing of resources.

Each resource listed in the profiles has one of three possible settings:

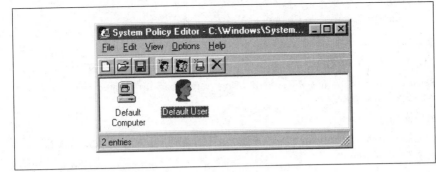

Figure 8-6: System Policy Editory (poledit.exe)

Off (white)
>When the button is white, the resource in question is available and/or ignored (whichever makes sense).

On (white with a checkmark)
>When a resource is checked, that resource is restricted from the user or computer in question.

Use Registry Setting (gray)
>When a resource box is gray, Windows 98 will use the default value for that resource as found in the Registry.

Examples

To disable the entire Display control panel, check off "Disable Display Control Panel." If you wish to disable individual pages found in Display properties, check off the appropriate page(s) listed under the "Disable Display Control Panel" option:

Local User → Control Panel → Display
>Check the "Restrict Display Control Panel" box

Select any of the settings you wish to restrict
>In a similar fashion, you can restrict the wallpaper used on the Desktop

Local User → Desktop Display
>Check the Wallpaper option and select the wallpaper from the drop-down list

If you've created wallpaper in the form of a *.bmp* file, type the location in the "Wallpaper Name:" box. If you plan to implement a custom wallpaper company-wide, be sure to copy the custom bitmap file into the Windows directory of each computer.

Notes

- Changes made in *poledit* alter the Registry, so be sure to back up the Registry on your machine before using the program. (*scanreg* does this on startup by default.)

- When configured correctly, *poledit* allows you to use the Connect option to access the Registries of other computers on the network.

Hidden Gems on CD-ROM

See Also

"Registry Checker" in Chapter 6

System Recovery

\Win 98 CD-ROM\tools\sysrec

Restores your Windows 98 system using a full backup created with Microsoft Backup (*backup.exe*).

To Launch

Start your system with a Win 98 startup disk and run *Win 98 CD-ROM\tools\ sysrec\pcrestor.bat*

Description

System Recovery can only be performed by starting your system using a Windows 98 startup disk with valid CD-ROM drivers. Once you start your system, switch to the \tools\sysrec\ folder on your Win 98 CD and run *pcrestor.bat*. This action begins a fully-automatic, minimal installation of Windows 98 on your *C:* drive. Once the installation is finished, a System Recovery Wizard launches that explains the recovery process to you and then in turn launches Microsoft Backup. You can then select the items you wish to restore from your backup. These include the entire registry, including any hardware settings, and any backed-up files.

Notes

- The primary reason you might want to use System Recovery instead of simply restoring your full backup the regular way is that you have the option of restoring your hardware and software settings in the Registry independently. This means that, should your system fail, you can run system recovery to reinstall Win 98 and your hardware and software settings without having to reinstall all of your existing applications.

- An additional advantage of using System Recovery over traditional restore methods is that *sysrec* operates within a protected mode environment, which means that the operation is usually considerably faster.

- In order to make reliable use of *sysrec*, it is important that you maintain a good startup disk and a current full system backup.

See Also

"Backup" in Chapter 6
"Add/Remove Programs" in Chapter 5

Text View

\Program Files\Win98RK\textview.exe

Text View lets you quickly find, display, and create text files.

To Install

Install the full Resource Kit Sampler
Copy *textview.exe* from *Win 98 CD-ROM\tools\reskit\file*

To Launch

Address → `textview`

Start → Run → `textview`

Management Console → Tool Categories → File Tools → Text View

Management Console → Tools A to Z → S to T → Text View

Description

Text View presents a familiar two-paned window (see Figure 8-7) that lets you browse for supported text files in the pane on the left and display them in the pane on the right. Once a file is displayed, you can edit and save it in the normal manner. Text View also lets you create new text files in the selected directory.

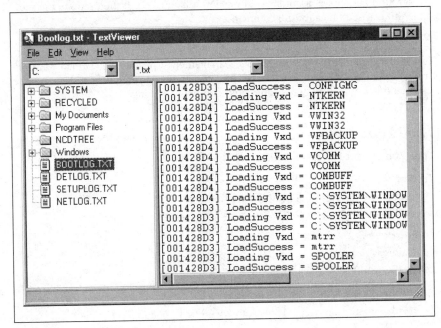

Figure 8-7: Text View (textview.exe)

Notes

- Text View is basically Notepad with a navigation pane attached. It suffers the same 57K file size limitation that Notepad does and can be used to view the same types of files as Notepad.

- Unlike Notepad, Text View does not let you search for text strings within a document or insert date/time stamps.

Time This

\Program Files\ Win98RK\ timethis.exe

Time This lets you time how long it takes your system to execute a command.

To Install

Install the full Resource Kit Sampler
Copy *timethis.exe* from `Win 98 CD-ROM`*tools**reskit**scripting*

To Launch

`timethis DIR [path]`

Description

Time This is a command-line utility that executes a specified command and reports the runtime in HH:MM:SS.TTT format, allowing you to time executions down to the thousandth of a second. Time This executes the *timethis* command in the background and closes it automatically when it is finished. It then reports the start, end, and elapsed times for the command.

Notes

Launching Time This from the Tools Management Console will launch MS-DOS and display the help contents for the command. Typing Time This at the command line will display the same help contents for *timethis*.

Time Zone Editor
Program Files\ *Win98RK**tzedit.exe*

Time Zone Editor lets you edit time zones.

To Install

Install the full Resource Kit Sampler
Copy *tzedit.exe* from `Win 98 CD-ROM`*tools**reskit**config*

To Launch

Address → `tzedit`
Start → Run → `tzedit`
Management Console → Tool Categories → Configuration Tools → Time Zone Editor
Management Console → Tools A to Z → S to T → Time Zone Editor

Description

The Time Zone Editor lets you create and edit time zone entries for the Date/Time applet in the Control Panel. *tzedit* has two main functions:

- To edit a time zone name or adjust the start and end dates for daylight savings time

- To create new time zone entries for the Date/Time tool

To edit a time zone:

1. Select a current time zone and click Edit.

2. Change the time zone name, abbreviation, or difference from Greenwich Mean Time.

3. If you want daylight savings time to be enabled automatically for the time zone, click the "Automatically Set Daylight Saving Time" box. Then, in the boxes underneath the option, fill in the start and stop days and times.

4. In the Daylight Bias box, select the amount of time to move forward or backward from the standard time for daylight savings time.

To create a new time zone:

1. Click New.

2. In the Time Zone Name box, type a name to be displayed in the Date/Time applet.

3. Time zone names should start with the general template GMT+\- 0x:00; they can't exceed 63 characters.

4. In the Abbreviation box, type a name for the standard time zone name abbreviation. The name can't exceed 31 characters.

5. In the "Offset From GMT" box, select the time difference from Greenwich Mean Time.

6. If you want daylight savings time to be enabled automatically for the time zone (if the area uses daylight savings time), click the "Automatically Set Daylight Saving Time" checkbox.

7. In the boxes underneath the option, fill in the start and stop days and times.

8. In the Daylight Bias box, select the amount of time to move forward or backward from the standard time for daylight savings time.

Notes

Changes made with *tzedit* affect the stored data for time zones in the Registry. If a time zone is already set on the computer, that data is saved in another location in the Registry. In order for the new information to be used, you must use the Date/Time applet in Control Panel and select or reselect the time zone.

TweakUI   \Windows\System\tweakui.cpl

TweakUI lets you configure hidden Windows 98 system settings.

To Install

> Program Files\Win98RK\PowerToy\Tweakui.inf → right-click → Install (if full reskit is installed first)
>
> Win 98 CD-ROM\tools\reskit\PowerToy\Tweakui.inf → right-click → Install

To Launch

> Control Panel → TweakUI
> Address → Start → Run → control tweakui.cpl

Description

TweakUI is a definite contender for the most useful Windows 98 utility around. TweakUI is available on the Win 98 CD-ROM and is a Control Panel applet that lets you configure many "hidden" Windows 98 system settings that you would otherwise have to configure using the Registry.

The TweakUI applet sports no fewer than thirteen tabs: Mouse, General, Explorer, IE4, Desktop, My Computer, Control Panel, Network, New, Add/Remove, Boot, Repair, and Paranoia. This applet can be a little confusing, as many functions that seem like they should be on one tab are really on another. You'll get used to it, though, as we're sure you'll be using this one a lot.

Mouse

Lets you control various settings related to mouse use (see Figure 8-8), including:

– How fast cascading menus appear when you hover your mouse over them

– How close together (in pixels) two clicks must be to be considered a double-click

– How far (in pixels) an object must move before Win 98 knows that it's being dragged

– How scrolling should work with your mouse wheel, if you have one

– Whether activation should follow your mouse. This setting causes the focus to follow your mouse pointer without having to click on a window to give it focus. Use this with the "X-Mouse Auto Raise" option and windows will not only be given the focus when your pointer over them, they will be brought to the foreground as well

General

Lets you control various visual effects on your system, such as window, menu, and list animations. The General tab also lets you specify where special Win 98 folders, such as desktop and favorites, should be kept. Be careful if you decide to change the locations of these folders, however. Many applications expect to find folders in specific places and may not function correctly if you move them.

Finally, the General tab lets you specify a web search engine that can be used in the Internet Explorer address bar by entering ? *keyword*. We're not sure why they decided not to include this one on the IE tab.

Explorer

Lets you control certain settings related to *explorer.exe* (see Figure 8-9). You can specify whether shortcuts display an arrow on their icon or not and even designate a customized overlay, if you wish. You can also disable the very annoying animated "Click here to begin" that appears on your Taskbar, and prevent Win 98 from showing you a tip of the day each time you boot.

The "Save Explorer window settings" option causes *explorer* to remember the display settings of any folder when you close it. When you reopen the folder, it will be displayed in the same way. When you shut down or restart Windows, *explorer* will remember which folders were open and reopen them for you.

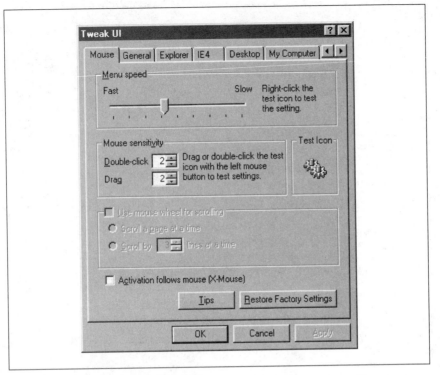

Figure 8-8: Mouse settings in TweakUI

IE4

Lets you control many of the IE4 features embedded in the Windows 98 UI. You can specify such things as whether special folders, such as Documents and Favorites, are shown on the Start menu; whether the Active Desktop is enabled and whether changes can be made to it; and whether the Logoff command is shown on the Start menu. You can also specify that the Documents folder and the history for the Run command be cleared when you exit Windows, an option that seems like it should be on the Paranoia tab.

Finally, you can also specify whether IE4 should be enabled at all. If you elect to disable the IE4 integration, the desktop will function in much the same way that it did under Windows 95.

Desktop

Lets you control which special items (such as My Computer, Internet Explorer, Network Neighborhood, and the Recycle Bin) appear on your desktop. These items are not inaccessible; they just don't show up as Desktop icons. You could, for example, still access Internet Explorer from the Start Menu or from a shortcut.

My Computer

Lets you control which disk drives (*A: – Z:*) are displayed in My Computer.

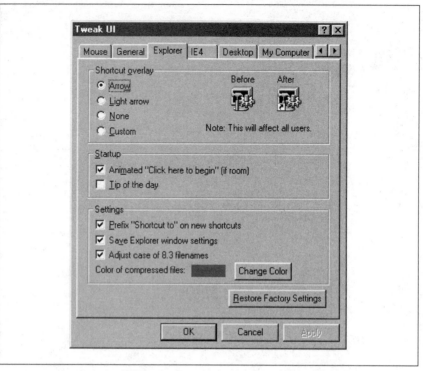

Figure 8-9: The Explorer tab of TweakUI

Control Panel

Lets you control which icons are displayed in Control Panel. Icons are listed by their command names and their common names.

Network

Lets you have Win 98 automatically enter username and password information and log you on at Windows startup. In order to use this function, the "Clear last user" option on the Paranoia tab must be disabled.

New

Lets you choose which document templates are displayed on the cascading File → New or *context_menu* → New menu of a folder. You can also use this tab to remove templates altogether. Be careful doing this, however, because you cannot use the tab to add the templates back.

Add/Remove

Most applications installed in Windows 98 retain information for uninstalling the applications. Whenever you install such an application, a reference to the uninstall information is placed in the list on Control Panel → Add/Remove Programs → Install/Uninstall. The Add/Remove tab of TweakUI lets you add, edit, or remove these references. If you choose to remove the reference to a program's uninstall information, you usually still uninstall the program using an uninstall executable in the program's main folder. This varies, however, depending on the program.

Boot

Lets you control what happens during the Windows 98 startup process (see Figure 8-10). Certain function keys issue special commands during startup. If you press F8 at the beginning of startup, for example, a boot menu appears that lets you start up in normal, safe, command-line, or interactive modes. F4 causes you to boot to a previous operating system (i.e., DOS), if one was installed. The "Function keys available" option lets you disable this feature.

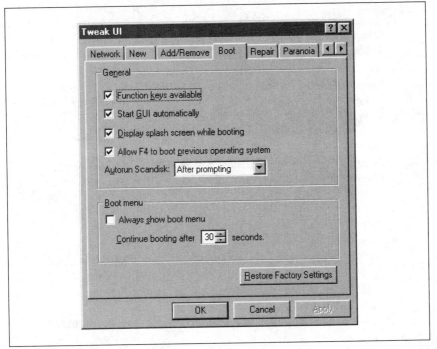

Figure 8-10: The Boot tab of TweakUI

If you disable "Start GUI automatically," then startup will end just before the Windows 98 graphic interface is loaded. This is basically the same as choosing a command-line startup. You can then start the GUI using the *win* command.

Scandisk, a program that checks the integrity of your disk file system, will by default run automatically on startup if Windows was not shut down properly. You can elect to have Scandisk automatically run after prompting you, without prompting you, or never.

Repair

Lets you attempt to repair certain settings for your system, including:

Icons

Sometimes, *explorer.exe* gets a little confused as to what icon goes with what item. Restarting Windows is one way of fixing the problem.

"Rebuild Icons" can help fix it without resorting to a restart. It also removes unused icons from memory.

Associations

This one is a little more powerful than the rebuild icons tool. Repair Associations actually restores all explorer icons to the default state. Even more important, it restores default associations for standard file types, like *.txt* and *.doc*. Be aware that, if you use this tool, some files may no longer be associated with the programs you want them to be and you may lose customized associations.

Font Folder

Sometimes, the Font folder (\ *Windows\fonts*) forgets that it's a Font folder and becomes a regular, garden-variety folder instead. "Repair Font Folder" restores the Font Folder's functionality (say that three times fast).

Regedit

"Repair Regedit" restores *regedit* to its original state, which can be useful if *regedit* is not showing all of the available columns for a view.

System Files

Many applications replace Win 98 system files with their own versions of the files during installation. If you are getting errors when starting programs, "Repair System Files" will check the files that are commonly overwritten and replace them, if necessary. However, Windows 98 now includes a great utility called System File Checker, which will check for corruption in all of your system files. You can read more about it in Chapter 6.

Temporary Internet Files

Like the Fonts folder, the Temporary Internet Files folder (\ *Windows\ Temporary Internet Files*) can sometimes lose its "magic." Use this command to restore its functionality.

URL History

Restores lost functionality of the URL History folder (\ *Windows\History*).

Paranoia.

Windows 98 remembers a lot of things for you, such as recently accessed documents, URLs, Run commands, find file and computer results, and even *telnet* history. If you'd like Windows not to remember these things, the Paranoia tab is for you. You can disable much of Win 98's "memory" using the "Covering Your Tracks" list. This tab also allows you to specify whether audio and data CDs are played automatically and that application errors be logged to a *faultlog.txt* file in your \ *Windows* folder.

Notes

- TweakUI has been left out of Windows 98 Second Edition, but it is still a very useful and functional utility that can be downloaded from *http://www. annoyances.org/win98/features/tweakui.html.*

- Sometimes, the Apply button on the TweakUI applet does not do what it should, which is to apply any changes but leave the applet open. Instead, it sometimes operates the same way as the OK button by applying changes and closing the applet.

- On the IE4 tab, the What's This tips you can get by right-clicking an item are all assigned to the wrong items. If you need a tip on any particular item, try getting tips for each item until you find the one you are looking for.

- Many of the settings in TweakUI control what a user can and can't see or have access to on a system. This makes it a pretty handy tool if you want to keep certain users (like your kids!) from messing around with your system. For example, you can make the hard drives, control panels, and desktop items completely invisible. If you make TweakUI invisible as well, then likely no one will figure out how to turn this stuff back on. You can always get back into TweakUI to change settings using the command line.

USB Viewer   \Program Files\Win98RK\usbview.exe

USB Viewer displays configuration information for USB devices on your system.

To Install

Install the full Resource Kit Sampler
Copy *usbview.exe* from *Win 98 CD-ROM\tools\reskit\diagnose*

To Launch

Address → usbview
Start → Run → usbview
Management Console → Tool Categories → Diagnostics and Trouble-shooting
→ USB Viewer
Management Console → Tools A to Z → U to Z → USB Viewer

Description

View information about your Universal Serial Bus (USB) ports and any devices attached to them. USB Viewer shows you the number of ports configured on your system, how your USB hub is powered (self or external), and connection information on any USB devices attached to those ports.

Wait For   \Program Files\Win98RK\waitfor.exe

Wait For causes your system to wait for a signal sent over the network.

To Install

Install the full Resource Kit Sampler
Copy *waitfor.exe* from *Win 98 CD-ROM\tools\reskit\scripting*

To Launch

Waitfor [-t <timeout>] [-s] <signal name>

Description

waitfor is a very useful scripting command that causes your system to wait for a specific signal from a remote computer on a network before continuing. The signal sent from the remote computer is also sent using the *waitfor* command. You could, for example, embed this command in a script on the waiting computer just before a command that was to launch a particular application. You could then embed the command in a script on the sending computer to send the signal. This would effectively let a script on one computer trigger a script on another computer.

waitfor.exe works with the following options:

-t <*timeout*>
> Causes *waitfor* to time out after a specified number of seconds.

-s Causes *waitfor* to send a signal.

<*signal name*>
> Is the signal you wish to send.

See Also

> Chapter 10, *The Windows Script Host*

Web-Based Enterprise Management

Allow systems administrators and support technicians to administer a Windows 98 system remotely.

To Install

> Add/Remove Programs → Windows Setup → Internet Tools → Web-Based Enterprise Mgmt

Description

Web-Based Enterprise Management (WBEM) is an industry-wide standard for accessing management information in an enterprise using many third-party HTML-based tools. Using this technology, developers and administrators can create management applications tailored to individual networks.

There's really nothing you can do from the Win 98 perspective with WBEM other than enable it on your system. Management software is usually run on an NT box somewhere else on the network. And chances are that if your network admins use WBEM, they will have already installed it on your system.

Where   *\Program Files\Win98RK\where.exe*

where.exe reports the location of a file on your system.

To Install

> Install the full Resource Kit Sampler
> Copy *where.exe* from *Win 98 CD-ROM\tools\reskit\file*

To Launch

> where [/r *dir*] [/qte] *pattern* ...

Description

where.exe is a command-line tool used to find a file on your system. You can search in a single directory, recurse along a current directory, and even search an entire drive for all instances of a single file name pattern. Wildcards (* and ?) are allowed. The syntax for *where.exe* is:

```
where [/r dir] [/qte] pattern ...
```

where.exe accepts the following options:

/r dir
>   Performs a recursive search beginning with directory *dir*

/q   Performs a "quiet" search, in which the results are not displayed

/t   Displays the size and modification times of files found in the search

/Q   Outputs results surrounded by double quotes

Examples

Find all files named *readme.txt* along the current path:

```
C:\Program Files\Win98RK>where readme.txt
```

Find all files named *readme.txt* along %windir% (the windows directory):

```
C:\Program Files\Win98RK>where $windir:readme.txt
```

Find all files named *readme.txt* on the current drive:

```
C:\Program Files\Win98RK>where /r \ readme.txt
```

Find all files named *readme.txt* recursing on the current directory:

```
C:\Program Files\Win98RK>where /r . readme.txt
```

Notes

where allows you to perform much the same functions as Start → Find → Files and Folders. Though *where* is a bit more cumbersome than the graphical Find Files and Folders tool, it can be very useful in combination with the Windows Scripting Host. Find out more about this in Chapter 10.

Windiff   *\Program Files\Win98RK\windiff.exe*

windiff compares the contents of two directories or files.

To Install

>   Install the full Resource Kit Sampler
>   Copy *windiff.exe* from *Win 98 CD-ROM\tools\reskit\infinst*

To Launch

>   Address → windiff
>   Start → Run → windiff
>   Management Console → Tool Categories → File Tools → Windiff
>   Management Console → Tools A to Z → U to Z → Windiff

Description

windiff.exe compares the contents of two directories or files and displays the results graphically. Figure 8-11 shows the results of a comparison between two simple, four-line text files: Document1 and Document2. The first three lines of both documents are identical and are shown with a white background. The line that reads "This is line 4" appears only in the left document (Document1) and is shown in red. The line that reads "This is line 5" appears only in the right document (Document2) and is shown in yellow. The graphic display to the left of the lines list allows you to move to specific places in the document by clicking on the appropriate color.

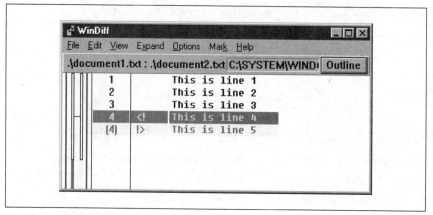

Figure 8-11: Comparing files with Windiff.exe

When you compare two directories with *windiff.exe*, you are presented a list of files in both directories. Each file is given one of four states:

- Appears only in left directory
- Appears only in right directory
- File is identical to both directories
- Filename is the same but content is different

Once the list of files is displayed, you can mark individual files to hide from the display. Expanding any selected file that exists in both directories gives you the same type of comparison display you see in Figure 8-11.

windiff can also be used from the command line using the syntax:

```
Windiff Path [Path2] [-D] [-O] [-N <name>] [-S [slrdx] <savefile>]
```

The following options can be used with *windiff.exe*:

-D Compares the current directory only, ignoring subdirectories

-O Forces *windiff* to stay in outline mode. The default is to expand single-file comparisons

-N <name>
    Does a NET SEND to <name> announcing the end of the comparison

```
-S [slrdx] <savefile>
```
    Saves the results of the comparison to *<savefile>*

s   Includes files that are the same in both directories

l   Includes files that are only in the left (first) directory

r   Includes files that are only in the right (second) directory

d   Includes files that are different in the two directories

x   Exits after the results have been saved

-?   Displays syntax and meaning of optional flags

Notes

fc.exe is a command-line alternative to *windiff* for comparing two files or sets of files. It is discussed in Chapter 7.

Windows 98 INF Installer   *\Program Files\Win98RK\infinst.exe*

Integrate *.inf* files from the Win 98 CD-ROM with Windows 98 setup.

To Install

    Install the full Resource Kit Sampler
    Copy *infinst.exe* and *infinst.chm* from *Win 98 CD-ROM\tools\reskit\infinst*

To Launch

    Address → infinst
    Start → Run → infinst
    Management Console → Tool Categories → Deployment Tools → Windows 98
        INF Installer
    Management Console → Tools A to Z → U to Z → Windows 98 INF Installer

Description

Windows 98 INF Installer (shown in Figure 8-12) can be used to add *.inf* (and related) files to the Windows 98 setup process.

The server-based setup for Windows 98 can't be used to add extra components, such as Resource Kit utilities or applications and services from the Win 98 CD. To add such components or any other software that uses Windows 98 *.inf* files, you must make sure the source files are installed correctly, the *.inf* files used by Windows 98 Setup are modified properly, and the correct entries are added to *msbatch.inf. infinst.exe* takes these actions automatically for any software that has a Windows 98 *.inf* file.

You can use the INF Installer to add external components, like the SNMP agent (in the *\tools\reskit\netadmin\snmp* folder on the Win 98 CD-ROM), to the setup of Win 98 and (optionally) force installation of the components using a batch script.

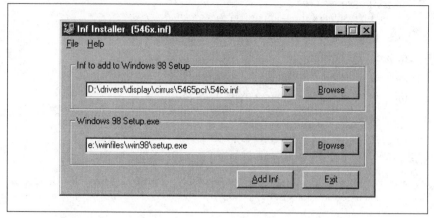

Figure 8-12: INF Installer (infinst.exe)

Windows Messaging   *\Program Files\Windows Messaging\exchng32.exe*

A MAPI-compliant Windows 98 messaging program that supports Internet mail, Microsoft Mail, and Microsoft Fax.

To Install

Add/Remove Programs → Install → *Win 98 CD-ROM\tools\oldwin95\ message\us\wms.exe*

To Launch

Address → exchng32
Start → Run → exchng32
Double-click the Inbox icon on the Desktop
Start → Programs → Windows Messaging

Description

Windows Messaging is a simple messaging client that can be used to access multiple information services simultaneously. Such services include Microsoft Mail, Exchange Server, Internet Mail, and Microsoft Fax. Since it would require a small book to explain Windows Messaging in detail, this section touches on some of the less obvious highlights that a user may find helpful when using the email program.

Outlook Express is a newer messaging program that is installed in Windows 98, but it doesn't support Microsoft Fax. You'll need to use Windows Messaging to fax in Win 98, unless you install a program like Outlook.

There are a couple of useful command-line options that can be used if Windows Messaging isn't running, with the following syntax:

exchng32 [/a] [/n]

Options include:

/a Opens the address book without launching *exchng32*.

/n Activates the New Message option without launching *exchng32*. The message won't be sent until *exchng32* is running.

Both of these command-line options can be used with a shortcut as well. Just point to the location of *exchng32* in the Target field under Properties, provide a space, and then list the option.

Figure 8-13 shows Windows Messaging running with the two-pane display, which can easily be toggled to one pane with the Show/Hide Folder List button.

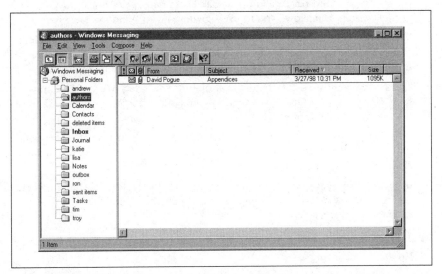

Figure 8-13: Windows Messaging, showing the folder list

Here is a short list of some non-obvious features:

Tools → Remote Mail
Lets you see mail headers without downloading the messages themselves. With this option, you can mark messages for download, delete messages without download, and so forth. It is very handy for reading mail from a dial-up connection.

Tools → Options → Services or Tools → Services
This is the same thing as Control Panel → Mail and Fax, where you configure server, connection, general, and other options.

Tools → Address Book
The Address Book is great for storing names and information for those people you send email to on a regular basis. You can create aliases, store phone numbers in the Business tab so they can be viewed from the Address Book list, and, when creating a new message, you can select the To, Cc, or Bc button to launch the Address Book.

View → Personal View

With this option, you can sort your mail in the Windows Messaging Folder list by From, Subject, or Conversation Topic. So, for instance, if you have a lot of email from several different people, you might want to sort by From, since this lists the names of the people only in the Inbox. Each name becomes a folder with all of the messages from that person nested within it.

Notes

- Windows Messaging can't use the signature feature available on most email programs. A third-party add-on located at *http://www.angrygraycat.com/goetter/widgets.htm* allows you to use signatures with Windows Messaging.

- You might want to run the Inbox Repair Tool (*scanpst.exe*) once in a while to prevent lockups and problems in Windows Messaging. If you have a large number of stored messages, it will take a while to scan and repair them.

- To preview your messages before you open them, select View → Columns → Item Text → Add → OK. This will give you a small portion of the first line of the message in the Inbox.

- You can quickly add an address to the Address Book in Exchange by right-clicking on the address in the From field and selecting Add to Personal Address Book on a message you've received.

- Installation of Microsoft Fax requires that a MAPI-compliant messaging client be installed. Windows Messaging is such a client, as are Outlook and the Exchange Server Client.

See Also

"Inbox Repair Tool"
"Microsoft Fax"
"Outlook Express" in Chapter 6

Winset   *\Program Files\Win98RK\winset.exe*

Set or remove global Windows environment variables.

To Install

Install the full Resource Kit Sampler
Copy *winset.exe* from `Win 98 CD-ROM`*tools**reskit**scrpting*

To Launch

```
winset [variable=[string]]
```

Description

winset.exe does not set an environment variable in a batch file's environment, only in the Windows global environment. In addition, variables set using *winset* only affect processes that start after the changes are made.

When an MS-DOS box starts, it gets a copy of the global environment owned by Windows, but then the connection is broken. Changes made in the copy don't

---

affect the global environment. They're not visible in other DOS boxes, and when the DOS box terminates, they're lost.

To view Windows' global environment variables, start an MS-DOS Prompt (duplicating the global environment variables), then use the *set* command without options.

The *winset* options are:

string
Specifies a series of characters to assign to the variable

variable
Specifies the environment variable name

Examples

Keep a batch file in sync with the global environment:

```
C:\>WINSET foo=bar
C:\>SET foo=bar
```

WSH Administrator's Guide   *Program Files\Win98RK\wshadmin.hlp*

Part of the resource kit, the Windows Scripting Host (WSH) Administrator's Guide is a Windows help file.

To Install

Install the full Resource Kit Sampler
Copy *wshadmin.hlp* from *Win 98 CD-ROM\tools\reskit\scrpting*

To Launch

Address → wshadmin.hlp
Start → Run → wshadmin.hlp
Management Console → Tool Categories → Scripting Tools → Windows Scripting Host Administrator's Guide
Management Console → Tools A to Z → U to Z → Windows Scripting Host Administrator's Guide

Description

Windows Script Host (WSH) is a scripting server that allows the execution of scripts on a Win 98 system. It is one of the optional components that you can install during setup of Win 98. Interestingly enough, *wshadmin.hlp* is the help file for WSH and is included with the resource kit sampler instead of being installed with WSH. *wshadmin.hlp* is a typical Windows help file, so you should have no problem using it. Chapter 10 is devoted primarily to using WSH.

See Also

Chapter 10

PART III

Under the Hood

CHAPTER 9

Web Integration

One of the most-advertised features of Windows 98 is its "web integration." We've seen signs of this integration throughout this book; this chapter talks about how to get under the hood and create customized web-aware regions on your desktop and in folders.

While the word "integration" suggests a seamless architecture, Windows 98 actually contains a hodgepodge of web-related features that reside in three main areas of the operating system: the browser (which can be Netscape Navigator instead of IE), the desktop, and folders. Just like in Windows 95, you can use the default browser to view the web and even create Uniform Resource Locator (URL) shortcuts in the desktop or in a folder. New to the Windows 98 desktop are the Address toolbar (to quickly launch URLs and commands) and the Active Desktop, which contains the Channel Bar, Active Desktop items and HTML wallpaper. Using new folder options, you can even web-enable standard folders, creating mini–web-like pages. This chapter provides you with the details to effectively use all of these web-integrated components.

The Browser

In order to understand web integration in Win 98, you must first realize that *iexplore.exe* does a lot more than just launch the Internet Explorer browser. The *iexplore.exe* file is actually more of a stub loader than a program, since it invokes various Dynamic Link Libraries (DLLs) that are also used by other programs such as Windows Explorer and the Active Desktop. This means that even if Netscape Navigator (or some other browser) is your default browser, you will be invoking these DLLs when using various aspects of web integration that we discuss in this chapter.

The default browser (Navigator, IE, etc.) is launched when you click an *.htm* or *.html* file or URL shortcut on the desktop or in a folder. It is also launched when you type a URL in the Address Toolbar (described in Chapter 4, *The Windows 98 User Interface*).

When you install Navigator or some other browser, you will be given the option to configure it as your default browser. If at any time you decide to switch your default browser, you can do so. Because of the war between Microsoft and Netscape, whichever browser was installed or upgraded last will try to make itself the default. What's more, if IE is not the default browser, it will ask you every time you use it whether or not to switch. To disable this behavior, go to Control Panel → Internet Options → Programs and turn off the "Internet Explorer should check to see whether it is the default browser" option. If you decide later you want to make IE the default again, simply enable this same option and select the "Yes" button when IE asks to be the default (when it is launched).

The Desktop

By default, Windows 98 starts with the Active Desktop enabled. This gives you a desktop with icons, a navy blue background and Win 98 logo, and the Channel Bar (see Figure 9-1). All of these features may appear like they are part of a single new interface, but in fact, you can pick and choose which of the elements you want to have available. Icons can be visible or not or changed to the web-like one-click behavior, the Desktop wallpaper (navy blue background and Win 98 logo) can be altered, and the Channel Bar can be customized or removed. You can also embed Active Desktop items, including ActiveX objects, web pages, and even local and remote folders.

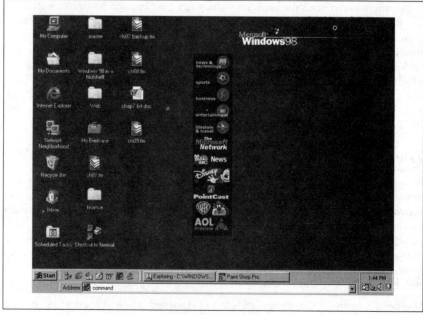

Figure 9-1: The first look at the Active Desktop

The Active Desktop is built from two separate layers: a transparent icon layer that exposes existing Desktop shortcuts (e.g., Recycle Bin, My Documents, etc.) and a background HTML layer that can contain Active Desktop items and wallpaper. This background HTML layer uses ActiveX to size and move Active Desktop items and stores information about the placement of the items on the Desktop.

The Active Desktop can be toggled on and off with one setting at: Desktop → right-click → Active Desktop → View as Web Page. As Figure 9-2 illustrates, when you select "Active Desktop" in the Desktop context menu, you also have the option to "Customize my desktop" and "Update now." The update command refreshes the Desktop, which you can also do by pressing the F5 key. The Customize option opens the Web tab in the Display Control Panel applet as shown in Figure 9-3. When modifying the Active Desktop, you will use the Web, Background, and Effects tabs in the Display Control Panel applet, which we explain later in the chapter.

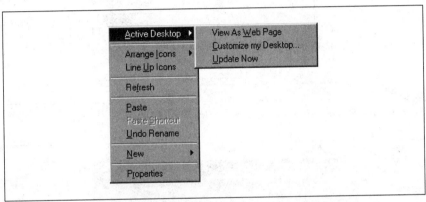

Figure 9-2: The Active Desktop options when right-clicking on the Desktop

Icons

You may be wondering why the Desktop icons in Figure 9-1 are still showing if the web page is covering the Desktop. This is due to a transparent icon layer in the Active Desktop. This effect can be toggled on and off by doing the following: Desktop → right-click → Properties → Effects → Hide icons when the desktop is viewed as a web page. (See Figure 9-4.) Whether you decide to show the icons on the desktop or not really depends on your style as a user. You can set the system to show no icons on the Active Desktop and then toggle the Active Desktop on and off to get at your Desktop icons.

But using icons and the Active Desktop as two layers in this way defeats the purpose. You could just as easily view your web content in the browser. Ideally, the goal of Active Desktop is to allow you to view both web content and the traditional icon view on the same desktop. If you don't fill up the desktop with icons, you can just create active content areas on your desktop (as is done by default with the Channel Bar), but there's also a neat trick we'll show you later (see Figure 9-11), where you can embed a view of the desktop folder as an Active Desktop item.

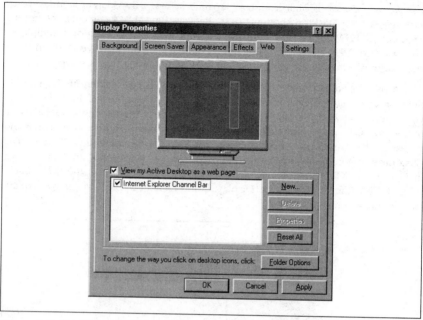

Figure 9-3: The Web tab in the Display Control Panel applet

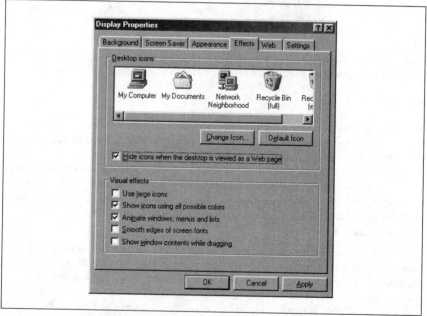

Figure 9-4: The Effects tab in the Display applet, to hide icons

Note that the "View as Web Page" option actually toggles the Active Desktop on and is in no way related to the View → "as web page" option available in a folder, which web-enables an individual folder. See the "Folders" section later in this chapter for more about the folder option.

Channel Bar

An Active Channel is a web site that delivers content automatically on a regular basis to your computer. To do this you must subscribe to an Active Channel by clicking a hyperlink to a Channel Definition Format (CDF) file. A copy of the CDF file is then downloaded to your \Windows\Temporary Internet Files directory, and a channel shortcut is added to your \Windows\Favorites\Channels folder. When you download the CDF file, you will be given the choice of using the predetermined subscription schedule or customizing it.

The Channel Bar contains default channels (e.g., Disney channel) that need to be activated if you plan to use them. By clicking on a channel, Internet Explorer is launched in the Channel view (see Figure 9-5). By clicking on a channel in the left pane, the channel page will be loaded in the right pane. The page will contain an Add Active Channel button, and by clicking on it a dialog will pop up (see Figure 9-6) giving you the option to subscribe to the channel or just keep it in the Channel Bar. If you choose to subscribe to the channel, the subscription wizard will walk you through the options. When you are finished, three tabs will be added to the property sheet of the file: subscription, receiving, and schedule (see Figure 9-7). You can access these tabs at any time to reconfigure your settings from the Properties sheet of the Active Desktop item (see the next section for details).

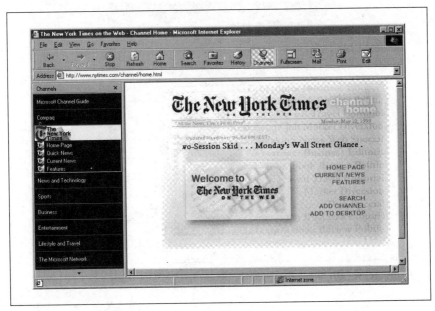

Figure 9-5: Internet Explorer in Channel View

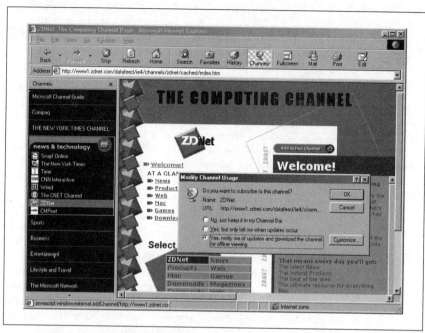

Figure 9-6: The Subscription Wizard when adding an active channel

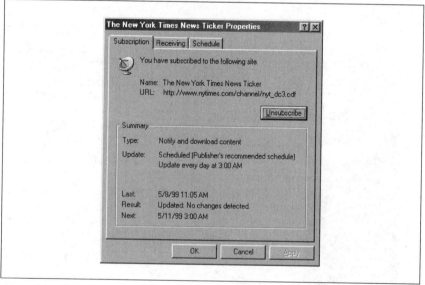

Figure 9-7: The CDF tabs: Subscription, Receiving, and Schedule

Active Desktop Items

There are plenty of useful items you may consider embedding into the Active Desktop. It's possible to embed a local or remote HTML file or folder or an ActiveX object. To embed an object, do the following:

Desktop → right-click → Active Desktop → Customize my desktop → New

When you select the New button, the dialog box shown in Figure 9-8 pops up and asks you if you want to navigate to the gallery. If you select Yes, Internet Explorer loads the gallery URL (*http://www.microsoft.com/ie/ie40/gallery/*), as shown in Figure 9-9. IE will automatically do this, even if Navigator is your default browser, since IE is the only browser that can display the gallery page. (Microsoft designed it this way.) If you decide you want to download an object from the gallery, just select the corresponding "Add to Active Desktop" button (see Figure 9-9). When you click this button, a copy of the CDF file is downloaded to the Active Desktop. This file contains a default schedule you can either accept or customize. Once the item is on the desktop, an outline of it can be seen in the Web tab of the Display Control Panel applet (see Figure 9-3). The outline shows where the object will be placed on the desktop. To move or size the item, you must click the OK button on the Web tab and make the changes to the item on the desktop (see below).

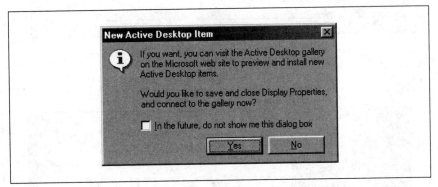

Figure 9-8: Microsoft Gallery dialog

In IE the fastest way to embed HTML is to right-drag any link from your browser and drop it on the Active Desktop. You will be asked to create a shortcut or an Active Desktop item. Figure 9-10 illustrates right-dragging a URL from a web site in IE to the Active Desktop.

Although Active Desktop items don't respond like typical windows, you can resize them and move them around. To do this, you must point the cursor to the top of the item so the navigational titlebar will pop up, as we've done in Figure 9-11. Notice the drop-down arrow in the left corner of the titlebar that contains options (e.g., Properties, Customize my Desktop, etc.), and an "x" in the right corner that closes the item.

The Active Desktop uses ActiveX to keep track of the size and placement of all items embedded in the desktop. Once you've sized and moved an item, it will stay there even when you close the item by clicking the "x" in the right corner of the

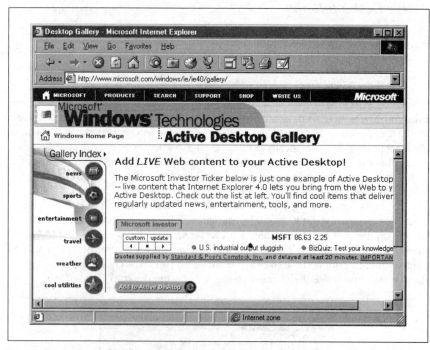

Figure 9-9: Microsoft Gallery in Internet Explorer

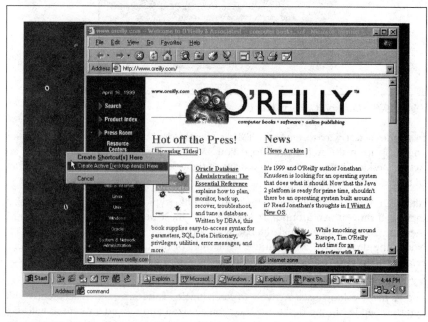

Figure 9-10: Right-dragging a link in IE to create an Active Desktop item

titlebar, which is the same thing as clearing its checkbox in the Web tab. Unless you delete the item from the Web tab (see Figure 9-3), it will show up in the same place with the same size when you enable it again by clicking the box on the Web tab.

> Regardless of which browser you use as your default browser, you can embed a local or remote folder into the Active Desktop. Select the New button from the Web tab of the Control Panel Display applet, click the No button (unless you've already clicked the option to disable the dialog from asking you about the gallery), and type the path. For example, to add the Desktop folder, you would type in: *C:\Windows\Desktop*. This embeds the folder in the Active Desktop and gives you access to all Desktop icons (except for virtual folders such as My Computer and Recycle Bin), even if you've hidden them using the option in the Effects tab of the Display Control Panel applet.

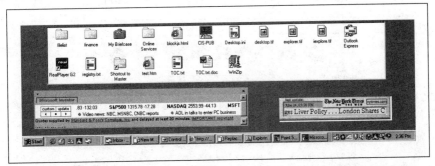

Figure 9-11: Embedded \Windows\Desktop folder with Active Desktop objects

If you've embedded a folder in the Active Desktop, you can also use any of the standard view options available in folders (e.g., Details, List, etc.). When you click a link in an object, it launches your default browser in a separate window and loads the page; if you click a file in a folder, it will be launched by its assigned program, and any folders you click on will be launched by Windows Explorer in a New Folder. Figure 9-11 shows an Active Desktop layout with the desktop embedded as a folder plus two ActiveX objects from the Microsoft gallery, each containing a continually updated news or stock ticker.

Wallpaper

We mentioned the navy blue background and Win 98 logo switched on by default when enabling the Active Desktop as a web page. This is actually a file called *windows98.htm* and is located in the *\Windows\Web\Wallpaper* folder. Its sole purpose is to display the navy blue background and the Win 98 *.gif* file. You can edit the HTML in *windows98.htm*, but it's easier to create your own HTML file or turn an interesting web page or graphic into wallpaper. You can set the wallpaper for the Active Desktop at:

Control Panel → Display → Background → Wallpaper

You can also reach the Background tab by doing the following:

Desktop → right-click → Active Desktop → Customize my Desktop → Background

Any *.htm* file you drop into the \ *Windows*\ *Web*\ *Wallpaper* folder will show up in the wallpaper selection list on the Background tab.

Figure 9-12 shows the Yahoo home page saved as HTML wallpaper. This only takes a few simple steps to create in your default browser:

1. After navigating to *http://www.yahoo.com/*, select File → Save As from your browser and save the file to \ *Windows*\ *Web*\ *Wallpaper*.

2. View the source of the file and make sure it has a <BASE HREF=url> tag in it (replace *url* with the URL of the page, in this case *http://www.yahoo.com/*).

3. In Win 98, go to the Background tab in the Display applet and select the named file from the wallpaper list, and click the OK button.

Figure 9-12: The Yahoo site saved as Active Desktop wallpaper

All the links will be active from your new Yahoo desktop, and you can use the search engine to initiate a search. The default browser will be launched to carry out these actions. This example makes the most sense if the icon layer in the

---

Active Desktop is turned off, or, as we mentioned earlier, you can embed the *\Windows\Desktop* directly as an Active Desktop item and still have access to all your Desktop icons (see Figure 9-11).

 The Active Desktop is unable to render framesets in HTML wallpaper. You can use frames when embedding objects or HTML pages, but not with wallpaper.

Folders

It's a stretch to come up with an Active Desktop that outperforms the regular icon-based Desktop for normal use. Perhaps more interesting is the ability to customize the HTML background of individual folders. This allows you to build special-purpose web applications in folders. For example, you could have one folder for all your stock market links (including the Active Desktop stock ticker), and another one for travel planning. Or, as we'll show later, you could integrate web links and local and remote files to create a multi-computer view of the files involved in a shared project.

There are two aspects to web handling of folders, both controlled by entries on the folder's View menu. Folder Options controls how items are displayed in the folder and whether they are activated by a single or double-click. This is pretty straightforward. The more interesting option, View as Web Page, produces a view that is not very, useful at first, but provides the basis for some useful customizations.

 The "View as Web Page" that can be selected by right-clicking on the Desktop and selecting Active Desktop is not the same thing as the View → "as web page" option available in a folder.

By default, Win 98 is installed with the View → "as web page" option activated. This option can potentially turn the look of any folder into a web page, but by default it simply adds a vertical pane in the folder containing information that can be obtained from the folder's property sheet (see Figure 9-13). It is easy to toggle the web view off and back on by selecting the View → "as web page" option in any folder.

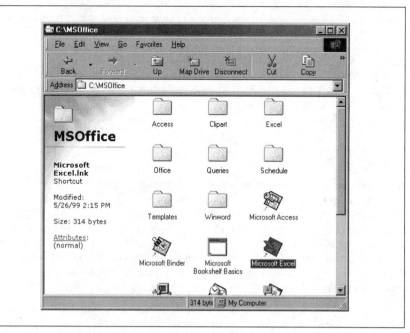

Figure 9-13: The MSOffice Folder in View → "as web page" view

 In order to get the most from this section, it is necessary to know a small amount of HTML, mainly hyperlinks and framesets (*HTML: The Definitive Guide* by Check Musciano and Bill Kennedy (O'Reilly & Associates) is an excellent resource). It's also possible, however, to use FrontPage Express to create pages without knowing all of the underlying code (see FrontPage Express in Chapter 6, *Start Menu Programs and Other Graphical Applications*).

The web page view is generated by Internet Explorer using HyperText Template (*.htt*) files. By default, standard folders get their web page view from the standard template file *folder.htt* located in the \ *Windows*\ *Web* directory when the View → "as web page" option is used. There are also several special *.htt* files used by folders such as the Control Panel that provide a unique view different from the standard one.

When you use the new "Customize this Folder" wizard to change the background of the folder, the standard template file *folder.htt* is copied to the target folder, and an editor is launched to let you modify the copy. The wizard also creates a file called *desktop.ini*, which contains some Windows arcana that you don't need to modify. Both of these files are hidden, so in order to view them you must have Windows Explorer configured to show all files. (You can do this by navigating in

Windows Explorer to: View → Folder Options → View and selecting the "Show all files" radio button.)

When you select View → Customize this Folder in any folder, the wizard gives you the following options:

Create or edit an HTML document
> Walks you through the wizard that opens a copy of *folder.htt*, lets you edit the file or just close it, creates *folder.htt* and *desktop.ini*, and then automatically initiates the Web view option in the folder.

Choose a background picture
> Allows you to select or browse any *.bmp*, *.gif*, or *.jpg* file on your system and display the image as the background for the folder.

Remove customization
> Deletes *folder.htt* and *desktop.ini*, returning your folder to the standard web view.

Note that you can run the customize wizard first to create the default *.htt* file, or you can create the file manually and then run the wizard to create the *desktop.ini* file that causes it to be recognized by the system.

The *folder.htt* file in the *Windows**Web* directory is actually an HTML file that contains a large amount of JavaScript, a language that is beyond the scope of this book. (A good reference is *JavaScript: The Definitive Guide* by David Flanagan, O'Reilly & Associates.) This code makes the HTML view seem nearly impossible to customize, but in fact, you can throw away everything but the FileList object (discussed later). Still, if you want to work within the confines of the Microsoft layout, there is one small section of the file that is easy to customize. Example 9-1 shows the section of the code where you can add some hypertext links or other HTML code, which will appear in the left pane of the folder, below the property info shown in Figure 9-13. It is certainly possible to drop in some URLs there. Be sure to alter only the *folder.htt* file for an individual folder using the "Customize this Folder" option. If you change the *folder.htt* file in *Windows**Web*, you will modify the web view for all your standard folders. So make sure you practice on a test folder!

Example 9-1: Segment in folder.htt Where You Can Add Your Own Links

```
<!-- HERE'S A GOOD PLACE TO ADD A FEW LINKS OF YOUR OWN -->
            <!-- (examples commented out)
        <p>
         <br>
        <a href="http://www.mylink1.com/">Custom Link 1</a>
        <p class=Links>
        <a href="http://www.mylink2.com/">Custom Link 2</a>
    -->
```

To add your own links, remove the <!-- (examples commented out) line and the --> line and then add valid URLs in the place of *www.mylink1.com* and *www.mylink2.com*. You then need to add real names to be shown in the folder, replacing Custom Link 1 and Custom Link 2 with whatever makes sense.

The FileList Object

All of the confusing JavaScript code in the default *folder.htt* file is used to print the property information for a selected file. The FileList object is what makes it possible to view the files in the folder. The FileList object is embedded in a box (whose size is determined in the <style> tag of the code, as shown in Example 9-2) in the Web page of the folder. You can define the size in pixels if you want the box fixed, but it's generally better to use percentages so the box can resize with the folder.

Despite the hundreds of lines in the default *.htt* file, the code in Example 9-2 is actually all you need to use to create a standard file listing area.

Example 9-2: FileList Object from the Unmodified folder.htt File

```
<style>
#FileList    {position: absolute; left: 30%; width 70%; height: 100%}
</style>
<object id=FileList border=0 tabindex=1
          classid="clsid:1820FED0-473E-11D0-A96C-00C04FD705A2">
</object>
```

The <object> and </object> tags define the FileList object. You will need to copy the exact contents from <object> to </object>, and paste it into your HTML file.

The <style> tag controls the placement of the object. In the example, the absolute left value of 30% is what creates the left web column (when you select View → "as web page" in a folder), and the other 70% is left to show the contents of the folder. (A 100% value for the height, and 100% for the width, would display the object in the entire folder area.) See *HTML: The Definitive Guide* for more help with the syntax of the <style> tag.

A FileList Example

Example 9-3 shows a custom *folder.htt* file we put together for managing access to files on three networked machines. This example requires you to create four HTML files. This example works even if you've chosen Netscape Navigator as your default browser, since Windows Explorer uses *iexplore.exe* DLLs to display the web content rather than the Internet Explorer browser itself.

Figure 9-14 illustrates the outcome, and you can see that clicking a link (which can be a URL, UNC pathname, or local file pathname) in the left "control pane" loads the file in the middle frame, but leaves the smaller third frame open to show the local folder's contents. This allows you to drag and drop (or cut and paste) the project files you are working with back and forth between machines from within a single folder as well as to view related web content. So, for example, you can click on "Updated Framemaker Files on Bob's Machine," grab a file from the middle frame (remote folder), and drop it into the third frame (local folder). You can then work on the file in the folder and place it back when you are finished with it.

Now let's walk through the four HTML files that make this possible. We start with creating a custom *folder.htt* file, which defines the three frames (*master_document.*

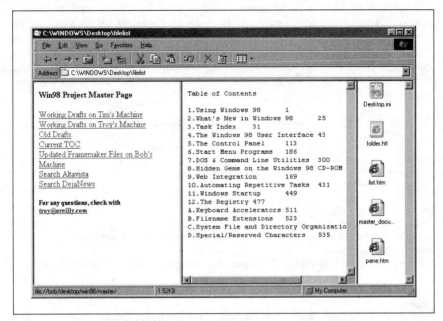

Figure 9-14: The Custom FileList example in a folder

htm, display_pane.htm, and *local_filelist.htm*) and points to the *.htm* files that fill the frames. The *folder.htt* file can be created with any editor, and then placed in the folder; we will later run the customize wizard in order to have it recognized by the system. Example 9-3 shows the HTML necessary for creating the *folder.htt* file.

Example 9-3: folder.htt Contains the Frames for the Example

```
<HTML>
<frameset cols="40%, 45%, *">
<frame src="master_document.htm">
<frame src="display_pane.htm" name="pane" scrolling="yes">
<frame src="local_filelist.htm" scrolling="yes" noresize>
</frameset>
</HTML>
```

The <frameset> tag defines three columns (defined as cols), and you'll notice we used percentages to define the area the frames will fill in the folder so they will automatically be resized with the folder. The 40% gives the first frame column that percentage of the total folder area, and the frame will be filled by *master_document.htm*. We have added name="pane" in the next line, which also specifies that *display_pane.htm* will fill the second frame, in a column filling 45% of the folder area. By naming this frame "pane", we will have the option in the *master_document.htm* file of targeting all content to display in this frame. The final frame is defined as *local_filelist.htm*, and it will fill a column in the third frame with the remaining amount of space available. Scrolling is enabled for both the second and third frames.

Example 9-4 shows the HTML used in the *master_document.htm* file. The tag `<base target="pane">` forces all the content displayed by clicking on the hypertext links in this file to be displayed in the second "pane" frame. The `<a href>` tags in this file contain UNC pathnames (e.g., Working Drafts on Tim's Machine), paths to local HTML files (e.g., Current TOC), and web links (e.g., Search AltaVista). All of the links pull together the various files needed for the sample Win 98 book project.

Example 9-4: master_document.htm Lists All the Links for the First Frame

```
<HTML>
<head>
<title>Windows 98 Project Master Page</title>
<base target="pane">
</head>
<body bgcolor="#FFFFFF">
<H4>Win98 Project Master Page</H4>
<a href="\\tim\desktop\win98\">Working Drafts on Tim's Machine</a>
<BR>
<a href="\\troy\desktop\win98\">Working Drafts on Troy's Machine</a>
<BR>
<a href="c:\windows\desktop\win98\drafts\">Old Drafts</a>
<BR>
<a href="c:\windows\desktop\win98\toc.htm">Current TOC</a>
<BR>
<a href="\\bob\desktop\win98\master\">Updated Framemaker Files on Bob's
Machine</a>
<BR>
<a href="http://www.altavista.com">Search Altavista</a>
<BR>
<a href="http://www.dejanews.com">Search DejaNews</a>
<BR>
<H5>For any questions, check with <a href="mailto:name@ora.com">name@ora.
com</H5></a>
</BODY>
</HTML>
```

The *display_pane.htm* file, displayed in Example 9-5, is really a bare-bones HTML file that is used to display the contents from links in the *master_document.htm* file. The "Viewing Area" heading text only shows when none of the links in the left pane have been clicked, which is why you don't see the text in Figure 9-14.

Example 9-5: display_pane.htm

```
<HTML>
<body bgcolor="#FFFFFF">
<H4>Viewing Area</H4>
</body>
</HTML>
```

In Example 9-6, you can see the FileList object defined by the `<object>` tag. As we mentioned earlier in this chapter, it allows files to be viewed in the folder when the View → "as web page" option is enabled in the folder. We set all margins at 0 in the <body> tag to avoid the ugly border that will otherwise form around the frame when it's veiwed in the folder. The width and height are set at 100% so the object will fill the entire frame.

Example 9-6: local_filelist.htm: the Frame Where the Folder's Contents Are Displayed

```
<HTML>
<BODY topmargin=0 leftmargin=0 bottommargin=0 name="list">
<object id="FileList" border=0 tabindex=1
classid="clsid:1820FED0-473E-11D0-A96C-00C04FD705A2"
style="position: relative; width: 100%; height:100%">
</object>
</BODY>
</HTML>
```

Once you have all four of these HTML files in a folder, there is one final step to take in order to get the view shown in Figure 9-14. To have the system recognize the custom *folder.htt* file we've created, select View → "Customize this folder." The wizard will be launched; select the "Create or Edit an HTML document" button and click the Next button. Click the Next button again and the existing *folder.htt* file will be opened (the one in Example 9-3). Close the file and then click the Finish button. The folder will automatically be started in the "as web page" view and you can use the modified folder view.

The Finance Example

In the FileList example, we showed you how to create a useful example blending HTML with the FileList object, which still allowed you to view the folder's contents. Example 9-7 uses HTML and an ActiveX ticker item to create a folder that acts as a custom web application devoted to finance.

Figure 9-15 shows the Finance example running in a folder on the Desktop. The ticker running on the bottom of the folder has been excerpted from the stock ticker that you can download from Microsoft's gallery as an Active Desktop item. The Quick Quote form has been added into the left frame using tables. Although the use of tables and forms necessary to adding the Quick Quote form and the stock ticker are beyond the level of this book (they require a certain level of HTML knowledge), we've added them to this example to show you what is possible.

Since the finance application is contained in a folder without a FileList object, you may be wondering what would happen to a file that you dropped into the folder. If you have the folder in View → "as web page" mode, you won't be able to view any files in the folder. If you toggle the "as web page" mode off, however, the entire contents of the folder will be in view and you will be able to access the file. As with the FileList example, this example works even if Netscape Navigator is your default browser. Normally, though, you wouldn't drag files into this folder.

In Example 9-7, you will notice that frames are being defined with absolute sizes rather than percentages. Three rows have been added: the first at 29 pixels (for the word Finances and the horizontal banner), the third at 41 pixels (for the stock ticker), and the second using the remainder of the space (for pages to be

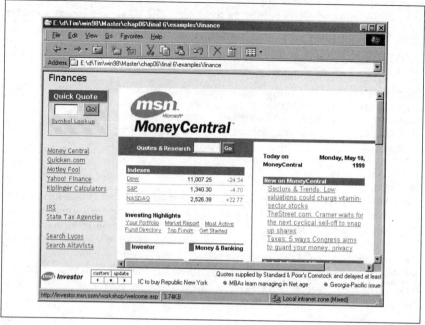

Figure 9-15: The Custom Finance example in a folder

displayed). Then two columns are added: the first at 151 pixels (for the column of links) and the second using the remainder of the space. Like the FileList example, you will notice the naming of the *banner.htm*, *navigation.htm*, *content.htm*, and *ticker.htm* files as frames and the defining of targets for placement in the folder. All of these *.htm* files are described below.

Example 9-7: The frameset File Holder, folder.htm, that Produces the Finances Page

```
<html>
<head>
<title>Finances</title>
</head>
<frameset framespacing="0" border="0" rows="29,*,41" frameborder="0">
  <frame name="top" scrolling="no" noresize target="contents"
src="banner.htm">
  <frameset cols="151,*">
    <frame name="contents" target="main" src="navigation.htm"
scrolling="no" noresize>
    <frame name="main" scrolling="auto" src="content.htm"        target="_
self">
  </frameset>
  <frame name="bottom" scrolling="no" noresize target="contents"
src="ticker.htm">
  </noframes>
</frameset>
</html>
```

The *banner.htm* file shown in Example 9-8 places the word Finances in the upper left corner of the folder, and also places the teal banner color in the frame.

Example 9-8: The banner.htm File

```
<html>
<head>
<title>Banner</title>
<base target="_self">
</head>
<body topmargin="0" bgcolor="teal">
<p><font face="Verdana" size="4">Finances</font></p>
</body>
</html>
```

The main file in this example is *navigation.htm*, and you can see the source in Example 9-9. A table has been created with the <table> tag to control the placement of the Quick Quote form. The hypertext links underneath the form are pretty basic and supply all of the links in the example. It is easy to add or delete these links to tailor this example to your preference.

Example 9-9: The navigation.htm File

```
<html>
<head>
<title>Navigation</title>
<base target="main">
</head>
<body bgcolor="teal" topmargin="5">
<table border="1" width="120" cellpadding="1" cellspacing="0"
bgcolor="#336666">
        <tr>
          <td>  <font  face="Verdana, Arial, Helvetica,
sans-serif" size="2" color="#ffffff"><b>Quick          Quote</b></
font></td>
        </tr>
        <tr>
          <td>
<form action="http://fast.quote.com/fq/quotecom/quote" method="get">
      <FONT size=2  face="Verdana, Arial, Helvetica, sans-serif">
          <input name="symbols" size="5">
               <font size=2><input type="SUBMIT" value="Go!">
      </font>
               <font size=1><nobr><a target="_top" href="http://
fast.quote.com/fq/quotecom/ticker">Symbol Lookup</a></nobr></font>
</form>
          </font>
        </td>
      </tr>
    </table>
<p><font size="2" face="Trebuchet MS"><a href="http://moneycentral.msn.
com">Money Central</a><br>
```

Example 9-9: The navigation.htm File (continued)

```
<a href="http://www.quicken.com">Quicken.com</a><br>
<a href="http://www.fool.com">Motley Fool</a> <br>
<a href="http://finance.yahoo.com">Yahoo! Finance <br>
</a><a href="http://www.kiplinger.com/calc/calchome.html">Kiplinger
Calculators</a></font></p>
<p><font size="2" face="Trebuchet MS"><a href="http://www.irs.ustreas.
gov/">IRS<br>
</a><a href="http://dir.yahoo.com/Government/U_S__Government/Taxes/State_
Tax_Agencies/">State
Tax Agencies</a></font></p>
<p><font size="2" face="Trebuchet MS"><a href="http://www.lycos.com">
Search Lycos</a> <br>
<a href="http://altavista.digital.com">Search AltaVista</a></font></p>
</body>
</html>
```

Like the *display_pane.htm* file in the FileList example, the only purpose of the *content.htm* file (see Example 9-10) is to display the pages generated by clicking on the links in the example generated by *nagivation.htm*.

Example 9-10: The content.htm File

```
<html>
<head>
<title>Content</title>
<base target="_self">
</head>
<body>
<p> </p>
</body>
</html>
```

If you download the stock ticker from Microsoft's gallery to your Active Desktop and then right-click in it to select the source, you'll notice that the HTML code is several times larger than what you see in Example 9-11. As we did with the FileList object from *folder.htt*, we simply extracted the ticker object and placed it in our own form, rather than using the entire downloaded file.

Example 9-11: The ticker.htm File

```
<html>
<head>
<title>Ticker</title>
<base target="main">
</head>
<body topmargin="0" leftmargin="0">
<form method="GET" name="Quote"  action="http://investor.msn.com/quotes/
quotes.asp">
  <p>
```

Example 9-11: The ticker.htm File (continued)

```
<OBJECT type="application/x-oleobject" classid="clsid:D3E12F51-0795-11d2-
91CC-00C04FA31C90" Codebase="http://fdl.msn.com/public/investor/v6//
ticker.cab#version=6,1998,1031,3" width=100% height=34></OBJECT></p>
</form>
<p>
 </p>
</body>
</html>
```

CHAPTER 10

The Windows Script Host

One of the features that distinguishes operating systems like Unix and Linux from Windows is that they make it relatively easy to write scripts that automate repetitive tasks. Since doing the same thing over and over again is one of the basic labor-saving benefits of a computer, the lack of robust scripting capabilities has always been one of the great weaknesses of Windows. Of course, scripting is difficult in an environment that is so heavily graphical.

Batch files (see Chapter 11, *The Batch Language*) have always provided some scripting capabilities for Microsoft operating systems, but batch files have little ability to interact with the graphical objects that make up so much of Windows. What's more, the programming language supported by batch files is remarkably weak.

Starting with Windows 98, a powerful scripting environment called Windows Script Host (WSH) is installed by default. (WSH is available for Windows 95 and Windows NT as a separate install.)

WSH provides a way to automate Windows-based graphical applications using powerful, full-featured scripting languages. WSH provides a set of objects that allow you to interact with the network, Registry, folders, and files—and with other applications—from scripting languages such as VBScript or Microsoft JScript, a JavaScript-like language. WSH has also been extended by third-party vendors to provide the same functionality in other scripting languages, such as Perl, Tcl, REXX, and Python.

WSH scripts can be used to create network login scripts that are more complex than those that are built in to Windows, and can be used to automate local desktop tasks. The resulting scripts can be run from the desktop, from the command line, or via the Explorer's Scheduled Tasks. WSH scripts can also be embedded in HTML files, which in turn can be used as part of the Active Desktop.

Unfortunately, while WSH is powerful, it is not for the faint-hearted. If you do not already know a scripting language such as VBScript, JavaScript, or Perl, you should get a good book on the language of your choice before starting out. *Learning VBScript*, by Paul Lomax; *JavaScript: The Definitive Guide*, by David Flanagan; and *Learning Perl on Win32 Systems*, by Randal Schwartz, Erik Olson, and Tom Christiansen are three useful books available from O'Reilly & Associates.

This chapter shows how to run WSH scripts, gives a brief introduction to VBscript programming, and describes the syntax of the objects provided by WSH. It also describes how to use the Object Browser to discover information about system and application objects, and concludes with some practical examples that illustrate the power of WSH scripts.

 The Windows Script Host is automatically installed during a typical Win 98 installation, but if it has been uninstalled for any reason, you can install the WSH engine using Control Panel → Add/Remove Programs → Windows Setup → Accessories → Windows Script Host.

What Is WSH?

So what is WSH? A language? As the name implies, WSH "hosts" a language, and provides a shell to run scripts in. Scripts can be created in the language of your choice (provided it's available).

By default, WSH provides Visual Basic Script (VBScript) and Jscript as available scripting languages. But other popular scripting languages, such as Perl, have been implemented in the WSH environment. (To obtain Perl, which many people regard as the most powerful and versatile scripting language available on any platform, visit *http://www.activestate.com/*.)

The capabilities provided in WSH, such as network and registry access, are provided by ActiveX Component Object Model (COM) objects.

A COM object is a component that performs one or more specific tasks. This may vary from something as simple as displaying a message to running large applications. All Office applications are COM objects and can be manipulated through WSH. Internet Explorer is also a COM object. WSH itself provides a number of COM objects, and there are also objects associated with some parts of the system, such as the file system.

The ability to use COM objects opens a whole world of possibilities that were once available only in dedicated programming environments such as C++ or Visual Basic.

Other functionality provided by COM objects includes file access, messaging (email), and database access.

Once an object is created, it exposes information and functionality to the programming environment (in this case WSH). Think of an object as a black box that performs specific operations. The box exposes information and functionality through a predefined set of commands.

Since WSH has implemented core functionality using COM objects, it doesn't rely on language-specific features; the concepts discussed in this chapter are applicable to any scripting language implemented through WSH.

Additional Resources

Table 10-1 lists additional resources available on the Internet.

Table 10-1: Additional Windows Script Host Resources

Link	Description
http://wsh.glazier.co.nz/frame.htm *http://cwashington.netreach.net/*	Excellent WSH resource web sites, including chat groups, scripts, and COM objects
http://msdn.microsoft.com/ scripting/	Microsoft's scripting site. Contains current versions of WSH, scripting engines, documentation, and tutorials
http://microsoft.public.scripting. wsh/	Microsoft scripting newsgroup

Executing Scripts

There are two programs supplied with Windows 98 that are used to run WSH scripts (whatever language they are written in). *wscript.exe* is used to run WSH scripts from the windows graphical environment, and *cscript.exe* is used to run them from the command line or from within batch files.

Using wscript.exe

Using *wscript.exe*, you can run scripts under Windows in the following ways:

- Double-click on script files or icons listed in My Computer, Windows Explorer, the Find window, the Start menu, or on the Desktop.

- Enter *wscript*, followed by a script name at the Run command on the Start Menu. You must enter the full name of the script you want to run, including the file extension and any necessary path information.

If you double-click a script file whose extension has not yet been associated with *wscript.exe*, an Open With dialog box appears asking which program you would like to use to open the file. See "File Types" in Chapter 4, *The Windows 98 User Interface*, if you need help.

After choosing WScript, if you check the "Always use this program to open this file" checkbox, WScript is registered as the default application for all files with the same extension as the one you double-clicked.

The *wscript.exe* application does not provide any command-line parameters. Instead, options related to running the script are provided in script property files. Properties are set in the usual way, but the properties are saved not in the Registry but in a text file with the *.wsh* extension. The file is created when you first set the properties of the script, but it can subsequently be edited with a text editor.

Figure 10-1 shows the Script tab of the properties for a script file. You can choose whether or not the script should time out, what the timeout for the script should be, and whether or not the script logo should be displayed when the script is run.

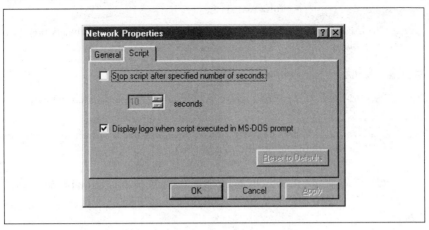

Figure 10-1: The Script tab in a .wsh property sheet

A *.wsh* file is created using the same name as the script file you right-clicked. The format is similar to the format of *.ini* files. A sample *.wsh* file might look like this:

```
[ScriptFile]
Path=C:\Scripts\MyScript.vbs
[Options]
Timeout=30
DisplayLogo=1
BatchMode=0
```

The Path setting in the [ScriptFile] section identifies the script file that this *.wsh* file is associated with. The keys in the [Options] section correspond to settings on the Script tab.

.wsh files are similar to the *.pif* files that were used to run older 16-bit applications. A *.wsh* file can be treated as if it were an executable or batch file. You can run a *.wsh* file directly by double-clicking on it, or by using it as the script name parameter with *wscript.exe* or *cscript.exe*.

.wsh files are very useful for administration purposes. Since you can run a *.wsh* file directly (rather than invoking the script itself), you can use a text editor to create multiple *.wsh* files for the same script, each containing different parameters but the same script name.

Using cscript.exe

Using *cscript.exe*, you can run WSH scripts at the command-line prompt. To use *cscript.exe*, open a command prompt window, and type a Cscript command line. *cscript.exe* uses the following syntax:

```
cscript [script name] [host options...] [script options]
```

script name is the name of the script file, complete with extension and any necessary path information.

host options enable or disable various Windows Script Host features. Host options are always preceded by two slashes (//).

script options are passed to the script. Script parameters are always preceded by only one slash (/).

Command-Line Host Options

The command-line host options supported by *cscript.exe* are detailed below:

`//I`

> Interactive Mode. Allows display of user prompts and script errors (this is the default, and the opposite of the `//B` option).

`//B`

> Batch Mode. Suppresses command-line display of user prompts and script errors.

`//T:`*nn*

> Enables a timeout. This is the maximum number of seconds the script can run. The default is no limit. This prevents excessive execution of scripts; it does this by setting a timer. When the timer is triggered, the script is terminated.

`//logo`

> Displays a banner. This is the default and the opposite of the `//nologo` parameter.

`//nologo`

> Prevents display of an execution banner at runtime.

`//H:Cscript` *or* `//H:WScript`

> Registers *cscript.exe* or *wscript.exe* as the default application for running scripts. If neither is specified, *wscript.exe* is assumed as the default.

`//S`

> Saves the current command-line options for this user.

`//?`

> Shows command usage.

Visual Basic Script

While WSH is language-independent, in this chapter we use Visual Basic Script (VBScript) for demonstrating its capabilities. This section provides a basic introduction to VBScript programming.

The concepts explained in this section, especially those related to the creation and manipulation of objects, apply to all scripting languages implemented in WSH. Even if you have worked with other languages such as Perl but have limited exposure to the concept of objects, you should have a read through it.

Scripting languages such as VBScript are interpreted. That is, the commands in a script are translated into low-level computer language and executed at the same time.

A script is composed of a number of elements. Variables are created to temporarily store values and object information. Commands, known as functions or methods, are executed to perform various predefined operations. Complex routines are built up with the aid of programming statements, such as conditional statements that are used to determine if a certain operation is to be executed based on a condition, and loops, which allow operations to be repeated a set number of times.

Creating a Script

Scripts are stored in an ASCII text format. Any text editor such as Notepad can create text files. If you choose a program such as Word or Wordpad to create scripts, you must save the file as a text file and not the native format.

There are no prerequisites in script file names except the file extension. The file extension relates to the language the script is created in. For VBScript scripts, this is *.vbs*, while for Jscript, it is *.js.*

Comments

It is important to add comments to your scripts, especially larger ones. Comments document the operation of the script. To add a comment in VBScript, add a single quote on a new line followed by text, which is the comment. You can add comments at the end of statements by adding the single quote followed by the comment. For example:

```
'this is a comment on its own line
strName="Fred" 'this comment is at the end of a statement
```

Continuation Character

If a statement is longer than one line, it can be continued onto another line by using an underscore as the last character on the line. For example:

```
Wscript.echo "This is a very long message" & _
             " to the user."
```

Variables

A variable is used to store information for use during the processing of the script. This might be text information such as a name, number, date, or an object.

A variable is identified with a name. A variable name can be any combination of letters or numbers, but cannot contain spaces. An example of a name could be startdate or employeewage.

Variable names do not have to be descriptive, but it's good practice to create human-readable names.

Scripting languages such as VBS are not "strongly typed" languages. This means that you do not have to identify what type of information a variable will store, which is required in languages like C++. While this doesn't limit the capability of VBScript, it is useful to be able to identify the data type of variables for debugging purposes.

The usual practice is to prefix variable names with a few characters to identify the type. There is no set standard you have to follow, but it's wise to keep it consistent and easy to read.

Table 10-2 lists the prefixes that are used throughout this chapter to identify data types.

Table 10-2: Variable Name Prefix Types and Examples

Prefix	Type	Example
str	String or text. This can be any combination of letters or numbers, including any character that can be entered from your keyboard	strName
date	Date	datStartDate
b	Boolean. A boolean variable is a switch or flag variable; its value is either True (−1[1]) or False (0)	bFlag
num	Number	numSalary
obj	Object	objMailMessage
int	Integer. Whole number, no decimals	intCounter
any	Any type. Can be any of the above mentioned data types	

[1] True is defined as −1, but any positive number will also be interpreted at True.

You do not have to explicitly declare variables in VBS. This means that when you create a script, you do not have to tell the script about the existence of a variable before using it. This is unlike other programming languages such as C++.

However, it is wise to declare variables before using them, again for debugging purposes. To declare a variable, use the Dim directive followed by the variable name:

```
Dim variablename
```

To force the explicit declaration of variables, add the statement Option Explicit at the beginning of your script.

To assign a value to a variable in VBScript, enter the variable name followed by an equals sign and the value you wish to assign:

```
variablename = value
```

Different types of data are assigned in different ways.

Text values, which are referred to as string values in programming jargon, need to be surrounded by quotes:

```
strEmpoyeename = "Fred Smith"
```

Numeric values don't need to be surrounded by anything, but should not include formatting characters such as commas:

```
intEmployeeage = 45
numEmployeesalary = 35000.50
```

Dates must be surrounded by hash symbols (#):

```
datBirth = #1/5/69# 'date format interpreted depending on system
                    'settings
datBirth = #January 5, 1999#
datBirth = #5-Jan-1999#
```

When assigning values to variables, you can perform calculations that involve other values or variables:

```
intAge = intAge +1 'increase the intAge variable by one
numTotal = intQuant * numPrice 'multiply quantity by price
```

You can combine strings using the ampersand operator:

```
strFirstName = "Fred"
strLastName = "Smith"
strFullName = strFirstName & " " & strLastName
```

The ampersand operator can also combine different types of data in one string:

```
'combine a string and a number
strNameAndAge = strFullName & " is " & intAge & " years old "
```

Object Variables

Objects are also stored in variables. Objects are assigned values just like other variable types, but you must use the Set statement when assigning an object a value:

```
Set objectA = objectB
```

As mentioned earlier, an object is similar to a black box. This black box exposes functions and information to the environment it was created in. When you create an object, it is referred to as an instance of the object. You can have multiple instances of any given object. Each object instance is independent of other instances of the same object.

For example, we have a mail message object. This object stores information and performs email-related operations. It would store information such as the message body, subject, and recipients. It would also contain the code to send the message.

Each instance of an object stores its own set of variables. These variables are known as object properties.

To access a property, use the object instance's name followed by a period, then the name of the property:

```
objMailmessage.subject= "Message subject" 'set the message subject
objMailmessage.text = "This is a message to fred" 'set message body
```

An object property might only allow you to read a value (read-only), write (write-only), or both. For example, the size of a mail message would be a read-only value.

```
intSize = objMailmessage.size 'show the size of the message
```

Object actions are performed using methods. A method performs a specific operation. When you execute or call a method, this is referred to as invoking the method. To invoke a method, enter the object name followed by a period and the method name.

```
objMailMessage.Send() ' invoke the send method
```

Before you can do any object-related operations, you must first create an instance of an object. Any scripting language implemented in the WSH environment automatically creates an instance of one object, the `Wscript` object. The `Wscript` object exposes a couple of basic methods, one of which is the `CreateObject` method.

The syntax for the `CreateObject` method is:

```
Set objInstance = Wscript.CreateObject(strObjectname)
'For example: create a network object instance
Set objMail = Wscript.CreateObject("Wscript.Network")
```

Another method the `Wscript` object exposes is the `Echo` method.

```
Wscript.Echo anyValue
```

The `Echo` method displays information specified in the `anyValue` parameter.

```
Wscript.Echo "Hello World"
```

The Wscript object model, its methods, and its properties will be covered in more detail later in the chapter.

Conditional Statements

When creating scripts, it is often necessary to check for a certain condition, and if it is met, perform specific operations; and if not, do something else or nothing at all.

A condition is the comparison of one or more expressions. The comparisons are made using standard mathematical operators: =, >, <, >=, >=, and <>. A condition evaluates to True if the condition is met; otherwise, it's False.

```
4>5 false
5>4 true
"Fred" = "Joe" false
10<=10 true
```

You might need to test more than one condition at a time. For example, in a personnel application, you might want to perform an operation only if the age is greater than 50 and the employee earned $40,000 or more dollars a year. To check multiple conditions, you would use the Boolean AND and/or OR operators (see

Tables 10-3 and 10-4). These operators combine two conditions, and the outcome of the operation returns either True or False.

Table 10-3: AND Operator Condition Examples and Results

Age	Salary	A>50	Salary>=40000	A>50 AND Salary>=40000
45	35000	False	False	False
52	39000	True	False	False
30	42000	False	True	False
56	43000	True	True	True

Table 10-4: OR Operator Condition Examples and Results

Age	Salary	A>50	Salary>=40000	A>50 OR Salary>=40000
45	35000	False	False	False
52	39000	True	False	True
30	42000	False	True	True
56	43000	True	True	True

You can combine multiple conditions.

The following set of conditions will return True if the age is greater than 40, the salary is greater than or equal to 50000, or the title is Manager.

```
Age>40 Or Salary>50000 Or Title ="Manager"
```

The following set of conditions will return True only if the age is greater than 40, the salary is greater than or equal to 50000, and the title is Manager.

```
Age>40 And Salary>50000 And Title="Manager"
```

You can also combine any number of AND and/or OR conditions. When combining AND and OR conditions, you have to be careful of the order in which you write the conditions. As in algebra, there is a precedence as to what operator is performed first. In the mathematical expression 1+2*3, the multiplication is performed before the addition and the result is 7. With Boolean operators, AND has precedence over the OR operator.

The following condition will return True if the salary is greater than 50000 and the title is Manager, or the age is greater than 40.

```
Age>40 Or  Salary>50000 And  Title ="Manager"
```

This is not quite what you'd expect. What if you wanted the condition to return True if the age is greater than 40 or the salary is greater than 50000, and the title had to be Manager? Going back to our math example, 1+2*3, what if we wanted the 1+2 to be executed before the 2*3? We would surround the 1+2 in parentheses: (1+2)*3=9. The same applies to conditional expressions. Any expressions surrounded in parentheses are executed first.

```
(Age>40 Or  Salary>50000) And  Title ="Manager"
```

To test a condition in a script, use the If Then Else statement.

```
If condition Then
  'do something if true
End If
```

If a condition is met, the code after the **Then** statement is executed. The following example would display a message if the value of the **intAge** variable is greater than 10:

```
intAge= 5
If intAge > 10 Then
Wscript.Echo "The person is older than 10 years old"
End If
```

If you wish to perform an operation if the statement is not true, include the **Else** statement after the **Then** and before the **End If** statements.

```
intAge= 5
numSalary = 65000
strTitle = "Manager"
If (Age>40 Or numSalary>50000) And strTitle ="Manager" > 10 Then
    Wscript.Echo "A Manager either over 40 or earns over 50000"
Else
    Wscript.Echo "Either Not a manager" & _
        " or less than 40 with lower salary"
End If
```

Functions and Subroutines

When creating scripts and with programming in general, it is important to break up larger programs into smaller parts and create reusable functions wherever possible. Large scripts can be unwieldy and difficult to read and debug.

To break up scripts into smaller parts, you can create subroutines and functions.

Subroutines allow smaller script elements to be created. To create a subroutine, enter the **Sub** statement, followed by a list of parameters (if required). Then add all of the statements to be executed within the subroutine, followed by an **End Sub**:

```
Sub subname([parameter1, parameterX])
statements...
End Sub
```

All of the code that belongs to the subroutine is contained between the **Sub** and **End Sub** routine statements.

```
Sub HelloWorld()
Wscript.Echo "Hello World"
End Sub
```

To execute a subroutine from somewhere else within the script, just type its name, like you would a built-in command. For example, to execute the **HelloWorld** routine above, add **HelloWorld** on its own line anywhere in your script.

Subroutines can also have parameters passed to them. Include all parameters within the parentheses on the subroutine declaration. Separate the parameters with commas:

```
Sub showhello(strMessage, strMessage2)
     Wscript.Echo strMessage & " " & strMessage2
End Sub
ShowMessage("Hello", "World")
```

A function is similar to a subroutine but returns a value. The value returned is based on a calculation of parameters passed to the function:

```
Function SquareRoot(numValue)
     SquareRoot = numValue * numValue
End Function
Wscript.Echo SquareRoot(5)
```

While you can create your own functions, VBScript has hundreds of built-in functions that perform certain operations, such as mathematical, string, and logic operations:

```
datToday= Date() 'return todays date
strName = Ucase(strName) ' convert string to upper case
```

For more information on VBScript's built-in functions, see the VBScript online reference, which can be downloaded from *http://msdn.microsoft.com/scripting/ vbscript/techinfo/vbsdocs.htm.*

Variable Scope

Both subroutines and functions can declare variables inside the routines. This is useful for larger routines where it is not practical to declare all variables in one spot, as well as for debugging purposes.

When you start declaring variables in different routines, you will encounter scope issues. These scope issues can cause problems if you are not careful how and where you declare your variables.

If you create a variable in a subroutine, you cannot access the variable outside of the subroutine. You can create duplicate variable names as long as they are separated by subroutine declarations.

```
Option Explicit 'force explicit declaration of variables
Dim strGlobal, strSameName

strGlobal = "I can see everywhere"
strSameName = "Global local"

Wscript.Echo strLocal 'this won't work - error will occur

Sub one
     Dim strLocal, strSameName
     strSameName = "Inside one "
     Wscript.Echo strGlobal 'this works
End Sub
```

Loops

Often a script needs to repeat an operation a set number of times. The For Next statement provides this ability. Its syntax is as follows.

```
For intVariable = start To end
    [Exit For]
Next
```

The code between the For and Next statements is executed the number of times specified between the start and end values:

```
For intCounter = 1 To 10
    intValue = intValue * 2 'multiply the variable intValue by two
Next
```

The Do While Loop provides the ability to repeat operations a set number of times based on a condition.

```
Do While condition
[Exit Do]
Loop
```

The code between the Do While and Loop statements is repeatedly executed while the condition is true.

```
Do While intCounter<100
    Wscript.Echo intCounter
    intCounter = intCounter + 1
Loop
```

Collections

An object exposes methods and properties to the programming environment. The properties can be of any data type, including an object. This can include a special type of an object known as a *collection*.

WSH objects, as well as any other COM objects, use collections to store lists of related information.

A collection is an object that contains a list of related objects. Table 10-5 lists a number of default properties that a collection object will always expose.

Table 10-5: Object Collection Properties

Property	Description
Count	Returns the number of items contained in the collection.
Length	Same as the Count property. Not all collections use this property.
Item	Returns a specified item from the collection.

We will use a fictitious Persons collection to demonstrate how to reference values from a collection. The Persons collection contains Person objects. The Persons object contains Name, Social Security, and PhoneNumber properties.

objPersons is an instance of a Persons collection object:

```
'list the number of Person objects in the Collection
Wscript.Echo objPersons.Count
```

To get an object stored in a collection, reference the Items property. The Items property returns the nth item in the collection:

```
objPerson =objPersons.Item(0) ' returns the first item
```

Many collections will return an item based on a key value used to identify objects within the collection:

```
anyValue =objCollection.Item(strKey)
```

For example, in the case of the **Persons** collection, we can reference **Person** objects based on the social security number, since it would uniquely identify the object within the collection. This method of referencing depends on how the object was implemented; not all collections will support this.

```
objPerson = objPersons("123-456-789")
For intCounter = 0 To objPersons.Count - 1
    Wscript.Echo objPersons(intCounter).Name
Next
```

VBScript has a special **For** statement sequence that can be used to iterate through a collection:

```
For Each objObject In objObjects Next
'list the name for all of the Person objects in the collection.
For Each objPerson In objPersons
    Wscript.Echo objPerson.Name
Next
```

Note that most collections start with a zero offset, so the first item is referenced as zero.

Error Handling

When you are executing a script, there is always the potential of running into errors. Errors may be due to bugs in your script as well as bugs in external objects or programs you reference.

When an error occurs in WSH, the script will terminate execution and display the error message. This may not be desirable, especially in scripts where you want to continue executing even if certain errors occur.

In order to implement error handling, we need to be able to have a script continue processing. This is done using the **On Error Resume Next** statement. Any errors encountered after this statement in a script are ignored.

Errors can be "trapped" by checking the **Err** object. The **Err** object returns a non-zero value if an error occurs. The **Err** object also exposes a **Description** property, which contains a description of the last error:

```
On Error Resume Next
intValue = 5
numDiv = intValue/0 'this will generate an error
If Err Then
    Wscript.Echo "Error# " & Err & " occurred. " _
        & "Description " & Err.Description
End If
```

Constants

When creating a script, you may want to store some values using symbolic names. These are called *constants*.

Constants are similar to variables, but you cannot modify a constant during the execution of the script. You can represent string and numeric values using constants.

It's often wise to define constant values using symbolic names at the start of your program. This way, if you later need to change the value, you only need to change it in one place, rather than searching through the program for multiple instances of the value.

To create a constant, enter the Const statement followed by the constant name and an assigned value:

```
Const Pi = 3.14
Const CompanyName = "Acme Inc"
Const StartDate = #1/1/99#
```

Constants are referred to in the same way as other variables:

```
Wscript.Echo "Company is " & CompanyName
```

Object Model

WSH includes a number of objects that provide access to Windows system-related operations. Table 10-6 lists the main objects and the operations they perform.

Table 10-6: WSH Objects and Their Functionality

Object	Functionality Provided
Wscript	Create new objects, output data, and process command-line arguments
WSHShell	Registry, shortcut, and environment variable manipulation, ability to execute external executables
WSHNetwork	Network directory and printer resource enumeration and manipulation
FileSystem	Text file manipulation and file maintenance operations such as creating, deleting, and moving files

The main objects expose additional objects. For example, the FileSystem object exposes a Drives collection object. These objects and their uses will be covered in the following section.

The object reference presented in this chapter covers the most important features of the objects listed in Table 10-6, but is not a complete reference. For more information, see the Windows Script Host programmer's reference at *http://msdn.microsoft.com/scripting/ windowshost/docs/reference/default.htm.*

Conventions

The next section provides a reference to the core WSH objects, describing their methods and properties.

The convention for the objects' methods is that any parameter surrounded by square brackets is optional. For example, in the syntax for the method `PrintName`:

```
PrintName strName, [strAddress]
```

the `strName` parameter is required, but the `strAddress` parameter is optional since it's surrounded with square brackets.

Wscript Object

The `Wscript` object is a built-in object. You do not have to create an instance of this object; it automatically exists. The `Wscript` object provides the ability to create new objects, output basic info, and exit a script.

Table 10-7 lists a number of properties the `Wscript` object exposes.

Table 10-7: Wscript Object Properties

Full Name	Name and Path of Executable
`Interactive`	Identifies if script is running in interactive (Wscript) or batch (Cscript) mode
`Name`	Name of the WSH (e.g., Windows Script Host)
`Path`	Path where WSH executables reside
`ScriptFullName`	Full name and path of script
`ScriptName`	Name of script
`Version`	Version of WSH

Echo Method

The `Echo` method outputs data to the screen. If you are running the script using *cscript.exe*, the information will be output to the DOS window from which the script was run, while *wscript.exe* will output the data as a Windows message box. Its syntax is:

```
Wscript.Echo [anyArg1, anyArg2...anyArgX]
```

CreateObject Method

The `CreateObject` method creates a new instance of a specified COM object. Once the object has been successfully created, you can access any properties or call any methods the object exposes. Its syntax is:

```
Set objObject = Wscript.CreateObject(strObjectId)
```

The `strObjectId` parameter identifies what component to create. This is unique for each type of COM object. The values will be provided in the documentation for each object.

Arguments Collection

The `Arguments` collection contains the parameters passed to the script. This is useful for scripts that perform operations based on information specified in command-line parameters.

You can access a specific argument by specifying the parameter number as it appears on the command line. The argument count starts at 0.

The following example lists all parameters passed to the script:

```
Wscript.Echo Wscript.Arguments(0) 'output the first parameter
For Each arg in Wscript.Arguments 'output all parameters
    Wscript.Echo arg
Next
```

The following example sets the file attribute on a file specified in the command line to `Hidden`:

```
Dim objFileSystem, objFile
'check if parameter count is a single parameter.
'If not, show the command syntax
If Wscript.Arguments.Count<>1 Then
    Wscript.Echo " Syntax: HideFile FileName " & vbCrLf & _
                " Filename: is valid path to file you wish to hide"
Else
    'create FileSystem object
    Set objFileSystem = CreateObject("Scripting.FileSystemObject")
    On Error Resume Next
    'get the file specified in command line
    Set objFile = objFileSystem.GetFile(Wscript.Arguments(0))
    'check if error occured - file not found
    If Err Then
        Wscript.Echo "File:'" & Wscript.Arguments(0) & "' not found"
    Else
        objFile.Attributes = 2
    End If
End IF
```

Quit

The `Quit` method forces the script to stop execution. Execution will terminate even if the script is in the middle of processing. Its syntax is:

```
Wscript.Quit([intExitValue])
```

The parameter `intExitValue` is the value returned to the calling program. This is useful if the script is being called from DOS batch files. Batch files can access the results using the `ErrorLevel` variable.

```
scriptname.vbs
If ErrorLevel 5 Goto ExitBatch
```

Shell Object

The WSH `Shell` object provides the ability to create Windows shortcuts, read environment variables, manipulate registry settings, and run external programs.

To create an instance of the WSH `Shell` object, pass the argument `Wscript.Shell` to the `Wscript.CreateObject` method:

```
Set objShell = Wscript.CreateObject("Wscript.Shell")
```

ExpandEnvironmentVariables Method

Environment variables are information stored by the Windows operating system. You can list the environment variables currently set by executing the DOS *Set* command from the command prompt. You can interpolate their values into your script using the `ExpandEnvironmentVariables` method of a `Shell` object. Its syntax is:

```
strValue = objShell.ExpandEnvironmentVariables(strString)
```

Any strings in the `strString` parameter that are enclosed with `%` symbols will be expanded using the corresponding environment variable value.

```
Set objShell = Wscript.CreateObject("Wscript.shell")
Wscript.Echo _
    objShell.ExpandEnvironmentStrings( _
    "Your temp directory is %TEMP%")
```

Run Method

The `Run` method executes an external program. This can be any Windows executable or command-line program. If you don't specify an explicit path to the application, the `Run` method will search the paths specified in the PATH environment variable.

The following example executes Notepad:

```
Set objShell = Wscript.CreateObject("Wscript.shell")
objShell.Run ("Notepad.exe")
```

SpecialFolders Collection

The `SpecialFolders` collection returns the path to a specified system folder:

```
strPath = objShell.SpecialFolders(strFolderName)
```

The strFolderName parameter can be any one of the following values: Desktop, Favorites, Fonts, MyDocuments, NetHood, PrintHood, Programs, Recent, SendTo, StartMenu, Startup, and Templates.

```
Set objShell = Wscript.CreateObject("Wscript.shell")
strDesktop = objShell.SpecialFolders("Desktop")
```

Registry Routines

The Shell object provides Windows Registry access through the RegRead, RegWrite, and RegDelete methods.

When accessing a registry key, you must specify the path. The path is built from the Registry hive name (the name of one of the major Registry branches described in Chapter 13, *The Registry*), followed by the path to the key separated by back-slash characters.

Table 10-8 lists the hive names.

Table 10-8: Registry Parameters

Short	Long
HKCU	HKEY_CURRENT_USER
HKLM	HKEY_LOCAL_MACHINE
HKCR	HKEY_CLASSES_ROOT
	HKEY_USERS
	HKEY_CURRENT_CONFIG
	HKEY_DYN_DATA

For example, the path to the Windows 98 version number would be represented as HKLM\Software\Microsoft\Windows\CurrentVersion\VersionNumber.

One way to easily get the path for registry values is to use the RegEdit application to search for Registry information and copy the key path to the clipboard using Edit → Copy Key Name. The Registry routines do not provide the ability to list any values under a particular key, so you need to know the path to any Registry values you wish to reference.

RegRead

RegRead reads the registry value from the specified Registry path:

```
strVal = objShell.RegRead(strKeyPath)
```

strKeyPath is a path to the Registry value you wish to read.

```
Set objShell = CreateObject("Wscript.Shell")
Wscript.Echo "Your Windows 98 Version Number is " _
    & objshell.RegRead _
  ( "HKLM\Software\Microsoft\Windows\CurrentVersion\VersionNumber")
```

RegWrite

`RegWrite` writes a value to a specified key value or creates a new key:

```
objShell.RegWrite strPath, anyValue [,strType]
```

The `strPath` parameter is the path to the key to write. If the Registry path ends with a backslash, then `RegWrite` attempts to create a new key.

Table 10-9 lists the possible values for the optional `strType` parameter.

Table 10-9: Registry Data Types

Registry Type Value	Description
REG_SZ	String value. This is the default value.
REG_EXPAND_SZ	Expandable string.
REG_DWORD	Integer value.

```
'change the default document directory for Word 97
Set objShell = CreateObject("Wscript.Shell")
objShell.RegWrite _
"HKCU\Software\Microsoft\Office\8.0\Word\Options\Doc-Path" _
, "H:\Data\Word"
'create new registry key
objShell.RegWrite _
"HKCU\Software\Microsoft\Office\8.0\Word\Options\NewPath\" _
, ""
```

`RegWrite` will create a Registry path if it does not already exist.

RegDelete

`RegDelete` deletes an existing Registry key or value:

```
objShell.RegDelete strPath
```

The `strPath` parameter is the path to the value or key you want to delete. If the Registry path ends with a backslash, then `RegDelete` will attempt to delete the specified key; otherwise, it assumes it's a value.

If you specify a key to delete, `RegDelete` will delete all child values and keys, so exercise caution when deleting keys.

```
'delete the Newpath key. This will delete the NewPath key and all
'values and keys under it
objShell.Delete _
"HKCU\Software\Microsoft\Office\8.0\Word\Options\NewPath\"
, ""
```

Shortcuts

The `Shell` object provides the ability to create shortcuts via the `CreateShortCut` method. This method returns a `WshShortCut` object:

```
objShortCut = objShell.CreateShortcut(strPath)
```

Once you have created a Shortcut object, you can set properties for it. This object provides the same settings that are available when creating shortcuts using Explorer.

Table 10-10 lists the properties that can be set for the shortcut.

Table 10-10: Shortcut Object Properties

Parameter	Type	Description
Description	String	Shortcut description.
Hotkey	String	Hotkey used to execute shortcut. The easiest way to get a hotkey is to use Windows Explorer to create a shortcut and copy the hotkey settings used by the shortcut.
IconLocation	String	Path to file containing icons to use in shortcut.
TargetPath	String	Path of the application or document to execute.
WindowStyle	Integer	Type of Window to display application in. 1 for normal, 2 for minimized, and 3 for maximized Window.
WorkingDirectory	String	Default working directory for application to use.

Once you have set the parameters for the shortcut, invoke the Save method to save and update the shortcut.

```
'create a shortcut on desktop linked to hello script
Set objShell = CreateObject("Wscript.Shell")
strDesktop = objShell.SpecialFolders("Desktop") 'get path to desktop
Set objShortcut = objShell.CreateShortcut(strDesktop & "\nlink.lnk")
objShortcut.TargetPath = "D:\heh.vbs" 'script to execute
objShortcut.Save 'save and update shortcut
```

Popup

The Popup method displays an interactive Windows popup message and returns a value depending on what button was selected (see Table 10-11):

```
intButton = object.Popup(strMessage, [numSecondsToWait], [strTitle],
           [intType])
```

Table 10-11: Popup Parameters

Parameter	Description
strMessage	Message to display.
numSecondsTo-Wait	Optional parameter. If specified, popup waits indicated number of seconds and then closes.
strTitle	Optional title for popup window.

Table 10-11: Popup Parameters (continued)

Parameter	Description
intType	Optional numeric value that determines the number of buttons and icons to show. This is determined by combining a value from Table 10-12 and Table 10-13. For example, the value of 65 would display an OK button and the Information icon.

Popup returns an integer value depending on what button was selected. Table 10-14 lists the return values.

```
'display a popup with yes/no buttons and question mark icon
Set objShell = CreateObject("Wscript.Shell")
intValue = objShell.Popup("Do you wish to continue?", _
    , , 36
'test if the Yes button was selected
If intValue = 6 Then
    'do something
End If
```

Table 10-12: Button Selection Values

Value	Buttons Shown
0	OK
1	OK and Cancel
2	Abort, Retry, and Ignore
3	Yes, No, and Cancel
4	Yes and No
5	Retry and Cancel

Table 10-13: Icon Types

Value	Icon to Show
16	Stop Mark
32	Question Mark
48	Exclamation Mark
64	Information

Table 10-14: Popup Return Values

Value	Description
1	OK button
2	Cancel button
3	Abort button
4	Retry button
5	Ignore button
6	Yes button
7	No button

Network Object

The Wscript Network object provides access to network resources and information. The ID for the object is `Wscript.Network`.

To create an instance of the Wscript Network object, pass the argument `Wscript.Network` to the `Wscript.CreateObject` method:

```
Set objNetwork = Wscript.CreateObject("Wscript.Network")
```

Table 10-15 lists the Network object properties.

Table 10-15: Network Object Properties

Property	Description
ComputerName	Name of computer
UserName	Name of user logged into the machine
UserDomain	Name of domain user is currently logged into

The following example displays the name of the user logged into the machine:

```
Set objNetwork = CreateObject("Wscript.Network")
Wscript.Echo "You are logged on as " & objNetwork.UserName
```

EnumNetworkDrives

EnumNetworkDrives returns a collection of the currently connected network drives. The collection that is returned is a special WSH collection; it doesn't operate the same way as other object collections.

For each connected drive, the collection contains an item for the drive letter and another item for the connected share name. If you have three connected network drives (K:, S:, and Y:), the collection would contain six elements, the first element being the K: drive, the second the share K: is connected to, etc.

```
Set objNetwork = Wscript.CreateObject("Wscript.Network")
Set objShares = objNetwork.EnumNetworkDrives()
Wscript.Echo "Drive " & objShares(0) & " is connected to " &
objShares(1)
```

The following example returns the next available network drive. If all drives are connected, it returns a blank string. It assumes your network drives start at F:.

```
Function ReturnNextDrive()
Dim nF, objNetwork, objShares, intNextDrive

Set objNetwork = Wscript.CreateObject("Wscript.Network")
Set objShares = objNetwork.EnumNetworkDrives()

intNextDrive = 0
For nF = 0 To objShares.Count - 1 Step 2
  If intNextDrive <> Asc(objShares(nF)) - 70 Then
    ReturnNextDrive = Chr(intNextDrive + 70) & ":"
    Exit Function
  End If
```

```
        intNextDrive = intNextDrive + 1
    Next

    ReturnNextDrive = ""
End Function
```

MapNetworkDrive

The `MapNetworkDrive` method connects a drive to a network share:

```
object.MapNetworkDrive strDrive, strRemoteShare, [bUpdateProfile],
        [strUser], [strPassword]
```

Table 10-16 lists the parameters for the `MapNetworkDrive` method.

Table 10-16: MapNetworkDrive Parameters

Parameter	Description
strDrive	The local drive letter to connect the network share to.
strRemoteShare	Name of remote share using UNC format. E.g., *server*\ *sharename.*
bUpdateProfile	Optional Boolean parameter that indicates if drive connection is remembered for next session.
strUser	Optional username to use when connecting to remote share.
StrPassword	Optional password to use when connecting to remote share. This is used with the strUser parameter.

If you attempt to connect to a drive that is already connected to a share, an error will occur. Therefore, the `On Error Resume Next` statement is required to ensure the script is completed.

Usually when users log on, they are connected to their home share. This is usually identified by their network user ID. The following example would connect the H: drive to the user's home share:

```
Set objNetwork = Wscript.CreateObject("Wscript.Network")
objWshNetwork.MapNetworkDrive "H:", _
"\\THOR\" & objWSHNetwork.UserName & "$" , True
```

RemoveNetworkDrive

The `RemoveNetworkDrive` method disconnects a specified network share:

```
object.RemoveNetworkDrive strName, [bForceDisconnect],
        [bUpdateProfile]
```

The `RemoveNetworkDrive` method has two optional parameters, the first being a Boolean `ForceDisconnect` flag. If set to True, it will forcefully disconnect the drive, even if it is currently in use. The second parameter specifies whether the user's profile is to be updated.

If there is a possibility of a drive being mapped to another network connection and you wish to connect it to a different network share, first delete the existing connection using the RemoveNetworkDrive method.

The following would (forcefully) remove the T: drive connection:

```
objWshNetwork.RemoveNetworkDrive "T:", True, True
objWshNetwork.MapNetworkDrive "P:", _
       "\\THOR\PublicArea", True
```

Network Printer-Related Functions

WSH provides access to connected network printers in a similar fashion to network drives. You can enumerate (list), add, and remove network printer connections. The network printers are connected to a specified printer port, such as LPT1.

 These connected printers are not the same as printers added using Control Panel settings, so they are not accessible to Windows applications and are therefore of limited use. The SetDefaultPrinter method uses the Control Panel printer settings. Future versions of WSH will support manipulation of Windows printers.

EnumPrinterConnections

The EnumPrinterConnections method returns a special WSH collection with a format similar to the one described for the EnumNetworkDrives method. It lists the printer port and connected network printer information.

```
Set objNetwork = CreateObject("Wscript.Network")
Set objPrinters = objNetwork.EnumPrinterConnections()
'loop through and display all connected printers
For nF = 0 To objPrinters.Count - 1 Step 2
    Debug.Print objPrinters(nF) & _
            " is connected to " & objPrinters(nF + 1)
Next
```

AddPrinterConnection

The AddPrinterConnection method connects a port to a specified shared network printer.

```
AddPrinterConnection(strPrinterPort,strRemoteName,[bUpdateProfile],
    [bUserName], [bPassword])
```

Table 10-17 lists the parameters for the `AddPrinterConnection` method.

Table 10-17: AddPrinterConnection Parameters

Parameter	Description
strPrinterPort	The local drive letter to connect the network share to; e.g., LTP1:.
strRemoteName	Name of remote shared printer in UNC format; e.g., \\ *server\printername.*
bUpdateProfile	Optional Boolean parameter that indicates if printer connection is remembered in future sessions.
strUser	Optional username to use when connecting to remote printer.
strPassword	Optional password to use when connecting to remote printer. This is used with the strUser parameter.

For example:

```
Set objNetwork = CreateObject("Wscript.Network")
objNetwork.AddPrinterConnection "LPT2", "\\training_06\laserjet"
```

SetDefaultPrinter

The `SetDefaultPrinter` method sets the default Windows printer. This method uses the printers specified under the Printers icon under Control Panel, not the printers connected using the `AddPrinterConnection` method. Its syntax is:

```
SetDefaultPrinter(strPrinterPort)
```

The `strPrinterPort` parameter specifies the UNC path of the printer you wish to make the default printer. This printer must be defined under Control Panel → Printers.

```
objNetwork.SetDefaultPrinter "\\thor\laserjet"
```

RemovePrinterConnection

The `RemovePrinterConnection` method disconnects connected network printers:

```
object.RemovePrinterConnection strName, [bForceDisconnect],
        [bUpdateProfile]
```

The `RemovePrinterConnection` method has two optional parameters, the first being a Boolean `bForceDisconnect` flag. If set to True, it will attempt to forcefully disconnect the printer. The `bUpdateProfile` parameter specifies whether the user's profile is to be updated.

FileSystem Object

The default WSH scripting languages (VBScript/Jscript) do not have any native file manipulation capabilities. This functionality is provided by the COM object `FileSystem`.

The `FileSystem` object (FSO) exposes a number of separate objects that provide the ability to perform file-related operations. Table 10-18 lists the objects exposed by the `FileSystem` component.

Table 10-18: FileSystem Objects

Object	Description
Folders	A collection that contains a list of folders for a specified folder
Folder	Exposes folder information such as size, attributes, and date information and methods to move, delete, and copy
Files	A collection that contains a list of files for a specified folder
File	Exposes file information such as size, attributes, and date information and methods to move, delete, and copy
Drives	Collection object that contains a list of available drives on the local machine
Drive	Exposes drive information, such as size and type
TextStream	Provides text file manipulation

The FSO exposes methods and properties that perform file manipulation operations. Before you can reference any of the objects listed in Table 10-18, you must create an instance of the FSO object:

```
'create an instance of an FSO object
Set objFSO = CreateObject("Scripting.FileSystemObject")
```

The FSO object exposes a number of file manipulation methods and properties. The following commands are a few of the most useful FSO-related methods and properties. See *http://msdn.microsoft.com/scripting/vbscript/techinfo/vbsdocs.htm.* An FSO function reference can be found at *http://msdn.microsoft.com/library/* under the VB6 documentation.

GetTempName Method

The `GetTempName` method returns a temporary filename.

```
strTempName = objFSO.GetTempName()
```

FileExists/FolderExists Methods

The `FileExists/FolderExists` methods return True if the specified path exists, False otherwise.

Drives Collection

The `Drives` collection contains a list of drives available to the local machine. This includes any drive visible to the system, including fixed hard, removable floppy, CD-ROM, or network drives. This collection is returned from the FSO object. The information for each object in the collection is exposed as a `Drive` object.

```
Set objFSO = CreateObject("Scripting.FileSystemObject")
Set objDrive = objFSO.Drives(0) 'get the first drive in collection
Set objDrive = objFSO.Drives("C") 'get a reference to the C drive
```

Table 10-19 contains `Drive` object properties. All properties are read-only unless otherwise specified.

Table 10-19: Drive Object Properties

Property	Description
AvailableSpace, FreeSpace	Free space on drive in bytes. These properties return the same operation
DriveLetter	Drive letter associated with drive
DriveType	Type of drive. Unknown=0, Removable=1, Fixed=2, Remote=3, CD-ROM=4, RamDisk=5
FileSystem	Files system drive utilities, e.g., FAT, NTFS, CDFS, etc.
IsReady	Returns True if drive is ready, False otherwise. Useful for removable media such as floppy and CD-ROM drives to determine if there is media in the drive
RootFolder	Returns root folder for drive
SerialNumber	Serial number uniquely identifying the drive
ShareName	Displays share name if network drive
TotalSize	Total size in bytes
VolumeName	Name of drive. This is read/write, so you can set a drive's volume name

The following example displays the percentage of space used by each drive:

```
Dim objFSO, objDrive
Set objFSO = Wscript.CreateObject("Scripting.FileSystemObject")
For Each objDrive In objFSO.Drives
    'check if drive is ready
    If objDrive.IsReady()
        Wscript.Echo objDrive.Name & " is " & _
        Fix(((objDrive.TotalSize - objDrive.FreeSpace) _
            / objDrive.TotalSize) * 100) & "% used"
    Else
        Wscript.Echo objDrive.Name & " is not ready"
    End If
Next
```

Folders Collection

The `Folders` collection contains list of a `Folder` objects for a specified folder. To get a reference to a `Folders` collection, use the FSO object's `GetFolder` method to return a `Folder` object, and then use the folder's `SubFolders` property to return the `Folders` collection. Its syntax is:

```
Set objFolder = objFSO.GetFolder(strFolderPath)
```

The `strFolderPath` parameter identifies which folder to reference.

Table 10-20 lists `Folder` object properties. Properties are read-only unless otherwise indicated.

Table 10-20: Folder Properties

Attributes	Attributes
Attributes	Directory attributes. Numeric value is comprised of one or more directory attribute types. The attribute values are added together to form the directory Attributes property. Read/Write property. Normal=0, Hidden=2, System=4, Volume=8, Archive=32, Compressed=2048
DateCreated/ DateLastAccessed/ DateLastModifed	Returns file created, last accessed, and modified date for file
Drive	Drive object folder resides on
Files	Files collection containing all files in folder
IsRootFolder	True if `Folder` object is folder directory root
Name	File name
ParentFolder	Folder object with folder's parent folder
Path	Full path to folder
ShortName/ ShortPath	DOS short name for folder and path, respectively
Size	Size of all files and folders in folder, including all subfolders
Type	Folder type, e.g., File or Subscription Folder

For example:

```
Dim objFSO, objFolder, objSub
Set objFSO = Wscript.CreateObject("Scripting.FileSystemObject")
Set objFolder = objFSO.GetFolder("C:\Windows")
For each objSub In objFolder.SubFolders()
    Wscript.Echo "Folder " & objSub.Name & " is " & objSub.Size _
    & " bytes"
Next
```

The folder object provides methods to copy, move, and delete a `Folder` object.

Copy/Move Methods

The `Copy` and `Move` methods copy or move the contents of the folder object, including all subfolders and their contents, to a specified destination folder:

```
objFolder.Copy strDestination, [bOverWriteFiles]
objFolder.Move strDestination
```

Both methods require a destination folder parameter. The `Copy` method has an optional `bOverWriteFiles` parameter. This parameter is set to True by default, but if it is set to False, the copy operation will generate an error if a file already exists in the destination folder.

```
Dim objFSO, objFolder, objSub
Set objFSO = Wscript.CreateObject("Scripting.FileSystemObject")
Set objFolder = objFSO.GetFolder("C:\LocalData")
'copy items from folder to network folder
objFolder.Copy("H:\Data")
```

Delete Method

The `Delete` method deletes the folder object and its contents. The folder does not have to be empty, and any subfolders and their contents will be deleted when the method is invoked:

```
objFolder.Delete [bForce]
```

The `Delete` method has an optional `bForce` parameter that will attempt to delete the folder and its contents if there is a situation such as a locked file that prevents it from being deleted normally. However, there are situations even when using the `bForce` parameter where the folder and its contents will not be deleted.

Files Collection

The `Files` collection contains a list of `File` objects for a specified folder:

```
Set objFSO = Wscript.CreateObject("Scripting.FileSystemObject")
Set objFolder = objFSO.GetFolder("C:\Windows")
Set objFiles = objFolder.Files
```

Once you have a `Files` collection, you can enumerate the individual `File` objects in the collection. Table 10-21 lists `File` object properties. The properties are read-only unless otherwise indicated.

Table 10-21: File Object Properties

Attributes	Description
Attributes	File attributes. Numeric value comprised of one or more file attribute types. The attribute values are added together to form the directory Attributes property. Read/Write property. Normal=0, Hidden=2, System=4, Volume=8, Archive=32, Compressed=2048
DateCreated/ DateLastAccessed /DateLastModifed	Returns file created, last accessed, and modified date for file
Drive	Drive object file resides on
Name	File name
ParentFolder	Folder object containing file's parent folder
Path	Full path to file
ShortName/ ShortPath	DOS short name for folder and path, respectively
Size	Size of all files and folders in folder, including all subfolders
Type	File type description, e.g., Text Document

The `File` object for an individual file can be referenced using the FSO object's `GetFile` method:

```
For each objFile In objFolder.Files()
    Wscript.Echo objFile.Name & " is " & objFile.Size _
    & " bytes"
Next
```

Copy/Move Methods

The `Copy` and `Move` methods copy or move the file to a specified destination folder. (This is the same method described above for copying or moving folders; it is described here a second time in the context of manipulating files instead of folders.) These methods use the following syntax:

```
objFolder.Copy strDestination, [bOverWriteFiles]
objFolder.Move strDestination
```

Both methods require a destination folder parameter. The `Copy` method has an optional `bOverWriteFiles` parameter. This parameter is set to True by default, but if it is set to False, the copy operation will generate an error if a file already exists in the destination folder.

```
Dim objFSO, objFolder, objSub
Set objFSO = Wscript.CreateObject("Scripting.FileSystemObject")
Set objFolder = objFSO.GetFolder("C:\LocalData")
'copy items from folder to network folder
objFolder.Copy("H:\Data")
```

Delete Method

The `Delete` method deletes a file:

```
objFolder.Delete [bForce]
```

The `Delete` method has an optional `bForce` parameter that will attempt to force a delete of the file if there is a situation such as a locked file that prevents it from being deleted normally. Using `bForce` does not guarantee that a locked file will be deleted.

TextStream Object

The `TextStream` object provides powerful text file creation and manipulation abilities. To create a new `TextStream` object, invoke the FSO object's `CreateTextFile` method:

```
Set objText = objFSO.CreateTextFile(strFileName,
    [bOverwrite],[bUnicode])
```

The `strFileName` parameter identifies the new filename. The optional `bOverwrite` parameter will overwrite any existing files with same name if True. The default value is True. The optional `bUnicode` parameter will create a Unicode file if True. The default is False.

The following example creates a new text file:

```
Set objFSO = Wscript.CreateObject("Scripting.FileSystemObject")
Set objTextFile = objFSO.CreateTextFile("C:\Data\data.txt")
```

Once you have created a `TextStream` object, you are ready to write data to it. The `Write` or `WriteLine` method will write data to the file:

```
objTextStream.Write|WriteLine(strText)
```

The `strText` parameter is the text that will be written to the file. The difference between the `Write` and `WriteLine` methods is that the `WriteLine` method writes an end of line character at the end of the line.

Whenever you are done performing operations on a `TextStream` object, invoke the `Close` method. The `Close` method closes the object and flushes any updates to the file.

```
Dim objFSO, objTextFile

Set objFSO = CreateObject("Scripting.FileSystemObject")
Set objTextFile = objFSO.CreateTextFile("D:\data.txt")

objTextFile.WriteLine "Write a line with end of line character"
objTextFile.Write "Write string without new line character"

objTextFile.Close
```

To open an existing text file, invoke the FSO object's `OpenTextFile` method:

```
Set objText = objFSO.OpenTextFile(strFileName, intIOMode, bCreate,
intTrisState)
```

Table 10-22 lists the `OpenTextFile` method parameters.

Table 10-22: OpenTextFile Parameters

Parameter	Description
strFileName	Filename to open
intIOMode	Optional. Specifies whether file is to be opened for Reading=1 or Appending=2. Default is reading
bCreate	Optional. If set to True, a new text file will be created if it is not found. Default is False
TriState	Optional. If -2, then open using file system settings; if -1, then use Unicode; and if 0, use ASCII. Default is 0, ASCII file

If you have opened the file for read access, you can read in parts or the whole file.

There are three methods for reading data. The `ReadAll` method returns the whole text file as a string. `ReadLine` reads the line up to the end of line character sequence. The `Read` method reads a specified number of characters.

```
strData = objTextFile.ReadLine() 'read a single line
strData = objTextFile.Read(10) 'read 10 characters
strData = objTextFile.ReadAll() 'read the whole file
```

If you are reading the file either character by character using the Read method or line by line using the ReadLine method, you need to be able to determine when you hit the end of the file.

The following example opens the *data.txt* file and lists the contents of it:

```
Set objFSO = CreateObject("Scripting.FileSystemObject")
Set objTextFile = objFSO.OpenTextFile("D:\data.txt")

Do While Not objTextFile.AtEndOfStream
    strData = strData & objTextFile.ReadLine & vbCrLf
Loop

objTextFile.Close
```

Object Browser

It is easy to be overwhelmed by the number of objects and what they do. It's equally overwhelming when you realize the number of objects that might be available to your machine without your being aware of it.

Office 97 and 2000 provide a powerful programming environment based on the Visual Basic for Applications language (similar to VBScript). Within this environment, there is an object browser, which allows you to browse objects installed on your system and investigate the methods and properties associated with them. You do not actually have to write any code to take advantage of the Object Browser.

 If you aren't familiar with the Visual Basic Environment, the Object Browser can be a little intimidating. See *Learning Word Programming* or *Writing Excel Macros*, both by Steve Roman (O'Reilly & Associates) for an introduction.

From either Microsoft Word or Excel:

1. Select Tools → Macro → Visual Basic Editor

   This will start the VBA environment.

2. Select Tools → References

   The dialog box shown in Figure 10-2 will appear.

Select the library references you wish to use. The reference name for the WSH Wscript object is Microsoft Windows Script Host Object Model, and the FileSystem object is Microsoft Scripting Runtime.

Once you have selected the libraries you wish to reference, select the Ok button.

Now press the F2 key. This will display the object browser window.

Select the object you wish to browse from the drop-down list in the upper left-hand corner. The Classes window on the left lists all objects related to the compo-

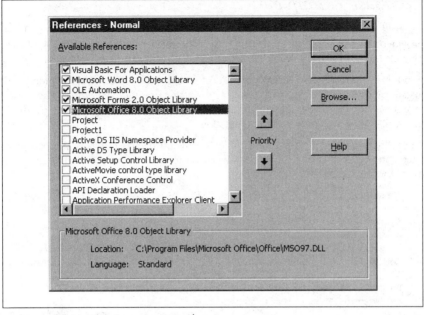

Figure 10-2: Object references dialog box

nent, while the right window lists all methods and properties related to the selected object. Figure 10-3 shows the Object Browser viewing the FileSystem object.

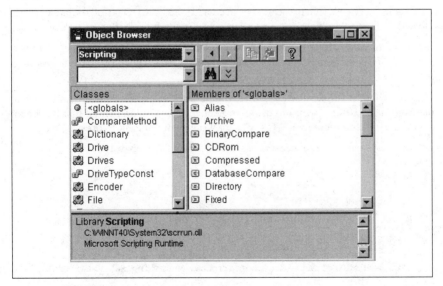

Figure 10-3: Object browser

Database Example

VBScript does not provide native database access. As with other functions provided in the WSH environment, this is implemented using a COM object. ActiveX Data Objects (ADO) is a COM object that provides database access.

Windows 98 and IE4 use ADO version 1.5 for data access. You can download and install a more recent version from *http://www.microsoft.com/data/*. The more recent versions provide additional capabilities and include up-to-date database interfaces. They also provide documentation.

The following example uses the sample Northwind database that is shipped with Microsoft Access. This sample assumes that an ODBC entry called Northwind exists for the database.

```
Const adCmdText = 1
Dim objRst, objConn
Set objConn = CreateObject("ADODB.Connection")
objConn.Open "Northwind"
'execute the query against the provider
Set objRst = objConn.Execute("Select * From Customers",, adCmdText)

Do While Not objRst.Rst
    Wscript.Echo objRst("CompanyName")
Loop
objRst.Close
objConn.Close
```

Messaging

Messaging services (email) can be accessed using CDO (Collaborative Data Objects). This COM object contains a large and powerful selection of objects.

CDO is a powerful but complex object model. The web site, CDO Live, at *http://www.cdolive.com/start.htm* is an excellent resource to get you started working with CDO.

The following example will log on to your default messaging profile and send a message. This assumes you are using an Exchange or Outlook client that has been set up to send Internet email. This will not work with Outlook Express.

```
Dim objSession, objMessage, WshShell, sPrf, objRecipient

Set WshShell = CreateObject("WScript.Shell")

'create a MAPI session
Set objSession = CreateObject("MAPI.Session")

'check if the OS string contains NT
'set the profile string. This will read your default setting
sPrf = "HKCU\Software\Microsoft\Windows Messaging Subsystem\Profiles"

'log on using the default profile name
objSession.Logon WshShell.RegRead(sPrf)
```

```
'create a new message, setting the subject to Hello There
Set objMessage = _
        objSession.Outbox.Messages.Add("Hello There")

objMessage.Text = "This is the body of the message"

'send to Joe Blow
Set objRecipient = objMessage.Recipients.Add("Joe Blow", _
        "SMTP:joeb@abc.com")
objRecipient.Resolve 'resolve the address

'send the message
objMessage.Send

objSession.Logoff
```

CHAPTER 11

The Batch Language

Most Windows 98 books treat batch files as if they were some kind of skeleton in the closet, or a crazy aunt you wouldn't want anyone to meet. While it's true that batch files are much less important than they were in DOS, they still crop up throughout the system. If you are in the unfortunate position of needing to write or understand one, you need documentation—perhaps even more than you need it for parts of the system that you use more often. What's more, even in the world of graphical user interfaces, scripting has an important place. The principal complaint about batch files should not be that they are obsolete, but that Windows 98 has done too little to integrate scripting into its interface. Fortunately, the Windows Script Host (WSH), discussed in Chapter 10, *The Windows Script Host*, makes it easier to use much more advanced scripting languages such as Visual Basic, Perl, PerlScript, JavaScript, or Python. But even with WSH, batch files are not completely obsolete.

A batch file is an ASCII text file containing a series of commands, each on its own line, which will be executed one line at a time. A batch file can't have the same name as a DOS internal command (such as *dir*, *copy*, or *cd*), and it must have a *.bat* extension.

Although any commands you can type at the command line can be used in a batch file, there are several additional commands that can be used only in a batch file. These commands are used for loops, conditionals, and other programming functions within the batch file and are explained in detail later in this chapter.

Creating Batch Files

You can create batch files with any text editor or word processor that can save plain ASCII text files, such as notepad or edit.

When naming a batch file, make sure you don't use a name that is already used by a DOS internal command or by a *.com* or *.exe* file in your search path. The reason for this is that when DOS executes programs, it first looks for the *.com* extension, then the *.exe* extension, before finally executing a file with the *.bat* extension. So, for instance, if you have a file called *work.exe*, and you create *work.bat* in the same directory, your batch file will not execute unless you type the full name, including the extension.

 You can create and execute batch files from the current directory or any directory in your search path, or by specifying their complete pathname, just as with any other command. But if you're going to use batch files a lot, it makes sense to keep them all in one place. Create a directory called *Batch* and add it to your search path. (See the *path* command in Chapter 8, *Hidden Gems on the Windows 98 CD-ROM*, and *autoexec.bat* in Chapter 12, *Windows Startup*.)

Some Rules of the Road

Here are the basics of batch file programming:

- Each command in a batch file must be on a separate line. The last command line in the file should end with a carriage return.

- You can use wildcards, pipes, and redirection inside a batch file, but you can't redirect or pipe the output of a batch file. If you type something like:

  `myfile.bat > savefile`

  the batch file will execute, but the redirection will be ignored. Put the redirection (using >> if there's output from multiple commands) on the command lines inside the batch file.

- A batch file can take arguments such as filenames or options. Up to nine arguments are stored in the variables %1 through %9. So, for example, the following line in a batch file:

  `copy %1 %2`

  would mean that the batch file would copy the filename specified in the first argument to the name specified in the second argument.

- The name of the batch file itself is stored in the variable %0. This allows you to do things like have a temporary batch file that deletes itself when done. The name is stored as it was typed at the command line, so if you had typed `myfile.bat`, %0 would be *myfile.bat*, but if you had typed `C:\batch\myfile`, %0 would be *C:\batch\myfile*.

- A batch file run from the command prompt or by double-clicking on its icon will open a DOS window while it is executing. (A batch file run from an existing DOS window will run inside that window, unless it contains an explicit command such as **start** that opens another window.) If you don't want this behavior, use the batch file's Properties → Program → Run to specify that the batch file should be run minimized rather than in a normal window. The property sheet lets you specify a working directory for the batch file, although you can also change the directory with a *cd* command within the batch file. If necessary, the property sheet also lets you specify that Windows exit before running the batch file and restart when finished. (See "Shortcut Properties of DOS Programs" under the entry "Shortcuts" in Chapter 4, *The Windows 98 User Interface*, for details.)

- You can stop a running batch file by pressing Ctrl-Break or Ctrl-C; the following message will appear in its DOS window: "Terminate batch job (Y/ N)?" Press Y to abort or N to continue running the batch file.

- By default, each command in a batch file is echoed to its DOS window. To execute a command silently, precede it with an @ symbol. Alternatively, you can turn command echo off with the command @echo off.

- A batch file can contain any command that you can type at the command prompt (i.e., anything described in Chapter 5, 6, 7, or 8, plus any third-party applications). However, keep in mind that each line in the batch file is executed sequentially, so there are a couple of gotchas, especially when the batch file runs programs that pop up a separate window. When you run a Windows program and it pops up its own window, control returns immediately to the batch file and the next line is executed. But what if you don't want that next command to run until the user is finished with the application in the popup window? In this case, you can make the batch file wait for completion of the Windows program by using start /w. But there's also the opposite problem, where you don't want the batch file to wait. Use start (without the /w) for that case. The call command performs the same function as start /w for DOS programs—i.e., it calls another command and waits for it to complete before continuing. A batch file can even call itself. (See call later in this chapter for an example.)

The following commands, described in Chapter 7, *DOS and Other Command-Line Utilities*, are particularly helpful in writing batch files:

cd   Change directory

cls   Clear the screen

exit Exit from a command or batch file

for   Repeat a command for a set of variables

set   Set or clear the value of a variable

start
> Start a command in a separate window, continuing execution in the current batch file

The following commands are normally used only in batch files, and are documented later in this chapter:

call
> Invoke another batch file or external command and wait for it to finish before continuing

choice
> Prompt the user for input

---

echo [on | off]

Turn on or off printing of batch file commands to the screen as they are executed; also, echo messages to the screen

errorlevel

Test return value of a command in an `if` statement

goto

Branch to another part of the batch file

if Test a condition and act accordingly

pause

Wait before continuing

rem

What follows is a comment (remark), not a command to be executed

shift

Read and discard a command-line argument, shifting over the remaining arguments

You can store temporary data in your batch file using environment variables created with the *set* command. To use the value of any variable, surround its name with % symbols. There is a limit on the size of the environment, which you can change in *config.sys*. See the discussion of *config.sys* in Chapter 12.

Looping constructs in batch files are extremely weak. There is no *while* or *until* loop, and the *for* loop and *if* conditional let you run only one command. There's no *else*. As a result, the only way to iterate is with a complex set of kludges too ugly to demonstrate. Users of Unix shells or AppleScript are likely to be really disgusted.

- A debugging environment can be created to test batch files by starting a new instance of *command.com*:

```
command /y /z /c batchfile.bat [arguments]
```

- /y will show each line of *batchfile* with % variable substitutions completed, followed by the prompt:

```
[Enter=Y,Esc=N]?
```

Enter or Y will execute the *.bat* file line. Esc or N will skip the *.bat* file line.

When to Use Batch Files

This section gives a few examples of when you might want to use batch files.

First, while Windows 98 no longer requires the use of an *autoexec.bat* file, if present, this file is executed whenever the system is booted before Windows itself is launched. Any commands you want to have executed automatically can be run from there. This is a batch file like any other, and the features described in this chapter can be used there. See Chapter 12 for more information on *autoexec.bat*.

Second, if you still use older DOS programs on your machine, they sometimes require what is called MS-DOS mode, in which all Windows programs are shut down before the DOS program is run. (See "Shortcuts" in Chapter 4.) When a program requires a switch to MS-DOS mode, the file *dosstart.bat* is executed (if found), and the file *winstart.bat* is executed when returning to Windows mode. These batch files let you run commands to customize your DOS environment and restore your Windows environment.

Third, if you look at Properties → Program for any DOS program, you'll see that you can specify the name of a batch file to be run whenever the shortcut is executed. This allows you to do things like set environment variables required by the program, change to a particular directory when the program is run, and so on.

But there's more to batch files than backwards compatibility with legacy DOS programs. Let's make a little digression about shortcuts. Since any shortcut, even a shortcut to a Windows program, actually specifies a command line as part of its properties, you can think of a shortcut as performing the same function as a one-line batch file. Typically, users simply create shortcuts that point to some program, and leave it at that. However, if the program supports any command-line options, you can specify them on the shortcut's command line as well. For example, when you run the Direct Cable Connection (*directcc*), you are prompted to specify whether the computer acts as the host or the guest. Embedding the command line:

    directcc connect

in the shortcut on the guest computer avoids the prompt and simplifies life all around.

As described in Chapter 5, *The Control Panel*, knowing the command line to complex dialogs such as control panel applets lets you build shortcuts directly to a specific tab in a dialog. A shortcut or batch file containing the following command line could replace the following five mouse clicks: Start → Settings → Control Panel → System → Device Manager:

    control sysdm.cpl ,1

But sometimes a single line of stored commands is not enough. Let's say you occasionally play *mshearts* with a friend. *mshearts* requires *netdde* to be running before you can use it over the network. The conventional advice is to put *netdde* in your *Windows**Start Menu**Programs**StartUp* folder, so it is always running. But if you use this program only occasionally, why have *netdde* running all the time? It might be better to create a batch file that always starts up *netdde* before running *mshearts*:

    rem myhearts.bat
    netdde
    mshearts

 One problem with a batch file like this is that it creates a DOS window, which by default will remain open even when the batch file completes. To make this window go away automatically, go to Properties → Program for the batch file, and click "Close on exit." (You should probably also select "Run minimized" from the drop-down box.)

Or suppose you are a big fan of the playlist feature of *cdplayer.exe*, so much so that you can't keep all of your playlists in *cdplayer.ini* due to its size limitations (see "CD Player" in Chapter 6, *Start Menu Programs and Other Graphical Applications*). You might want to organize your playlists into a series of *.ini* files, one per artist, for instance, or by music category. Then you might well want to run *cdplayer* from a batch file like this one, called *play.bat*:

```
@echo off
rem syntax:  play playlist, where playlist is rock,
rem country or classical
rem save the default cdplayer.ini file
rename \windows\cdplayer.ini \windows\cdplayer.save
rem replace cdplayer.ini with a custom playlist before
rem starting cdplayer
copy \myplaylists\%1.ini \windows\cdplayer.ini
start /w cdplayer.exe
rem save the ini file that's just been used, in case there
rem are changes
copy \windows\cdplayer.ini \myplaylists\%1.ini
rem restore the original cdplayer.ini
rename \windows\cdplayer.save \windows\cdplayer.ini
```

Batch files are particularly powerful for creating and moving files and directories. For example, when starting a new project, an author might always want to create the same directory structure and put some basic files into each directory. Here's the kind of batch file you might create for this kind of housekeeping:

```
@echo off
if "%1"=="" goto skip
mkdir %1\figures
mkdir %1\sources
mkdir %1\old
copy c:\templates\mainfile.doc %1
copy c:\templates\other.doc %1
copy c:\templates\image.tif %1\figures
:skip
```

Create a new folder in the Explorer, and then drag and drop it onto this batch file (or add the batch file to the SendTo menu). Subdirectories called *figures*, *sources*, and *old* will be created inside, and three template files are copied into the new directories. Voilà—you just saved about a minute of clicking and dragging.

The construct:

```
if "%1"=="" go to skip
```

is a useful error-checking technique. You can use an *if* statement to test for null arguments (or other similar conditions), and if encountered, either issue an error message or simply quit. (This example will exit after jumping to the :skip label, since there are no further commands to be executed.)

You can also use batch files to work around some of the limits of Windows 98. For example, the Explorer doesn't let you print out a hardcopy listing of the contents of a folder. You can do this simply from the command line by typing:

```
dir > lpt1:
```

But the following batch file does even better—you can drag and drop a folder icon onto it to get a printed directory listing:

```
@echo off
if "%1"=="" goto skip
dir %1 > lpt1:
:skip
```

You could, of course, replace `lpt1:` with something like `c:\windows\desktop\dir-list.txt` to output the directory listing to a text file instead, or construct a loop so that the batch file could repeat itself automatically for multiple directory name arguments.

Alphabetical Reference

The following list contains descriptions of the commands that are used principally within batch files.

---

call   Internal to: *Windows\command.com*

Invoke a batch file from within another batch file, returning control to the original when the called file completes.

Syntax

```
call [filename] [arguments]
```

Description

The *call* command lets you invoke a batch file from within another batch file and wait for it to finish before continuing. Once the called file has completed its execution, the control returns to the original batch file. *call* will also recognize executable programs, which can be useful if you've designed a batch file to launch a program (e.g., *regedit.exe*) and then continue with other DOS commands in the batch file.

call options can be passed on to the secondary batch file either as variables generated by the primary file or as replaceable variables holding data entered on the command line.

 If you run another batch file from within a batch file without using *call*, the control will never be returned to the parent batch file when the child process is finished. The whole thing just quits. Of course, this fact can be put to use; for example, it helps to avoid recursion when a batch file calls itself.

The options for *call* are as follows:

arguments
Specifies any command-line information required by the batch program, such as replaceable parameters.

---

filename

This can be a batch name or the name of any other executable program.

Examples

The following *sample.bat* calls *sample2.bat*, and then returns the control back to itself:

```
@echo off
rem this is a call test
call sample2.bat
cls
cd \windows\desktop
```

sample2.bat:

```
command /c
cd "c:\win98 nutshell\current\chap06"
start chap06.doc
cls
```

sample.bat launches *sample2.bat*, which opens *chap06.doc* after navigating to the proper directory. *sample2.bat* then returns to *sample.bat*, the DOS screen is cleared, and the directory is changed to \ *Windows\Desktop*.

The batch file *loop.bat* runs itself again and again, using *call* to start whatever external program and arguments are passed to it. (The following implementation is limited to a program name plus no more than eight arguments.)

```
@echo off
if (%1) == () goto usage
%1 %2 %3 %4 %5 %6 %7 %8 %9
loop call %1 %2 %3 %4 %5 %6 %7 %8 %9
:usage
echo Usage: loop [program] [args...]
```

---

choice

\ *Windows\Command\choice.com*

Ask for user input in a batch program.

Syntax

```
choice [options]
```

Description

choice provides a prompt string that waits for the user to choose one of a set of choices. The exit value of the command is used to decide which response was chosen.

If no alternate choices are specified with /c, the default choices are Y and N, and the prompt to the user will be "[Y,N]?". You can specify only single characters as choices; if you use /n to suppress the normal choice prompt and supply a longer prompt, you should be careful to supply a corresponding list of choices using /c.

choice recognizes the following options:

`/c[:]choices`
> Specify allowable keys (default is YN).

`/n` Do not display choices and ? at end of prompt string.

`/s` Treat choice keys as case-sensitive. By default they are not.

`/t[:]c,nn`
> Default choice to c after nn seconds (c must exist; nn must be in the range 0 to 99).

`text`
> Prompt string to display.

Examples

If you'd like to have the option of running *defrag* on drive *C:* before logging in to Windows, the following lines could be added to *autoexec.bat*:

```
@echo off
choice run defrag /ty,10
if errorlevel 2 goto skipdefrag
defrag c:
:skipdefrag
```

If you press N within 10 seconds, *defrag* won't be launched and *choice* returns an errorlevel value of 2. If you don't press N within 10 seconds, or if you choose Y, *defrag* runs on drive *C.*

The following errorlevel values are used by the *choice* command:

0   *choice* was terminated by Ctrl-C before a choice was entered.

1   The key corresponding to the first choice was pressed.

n   The key corresponding to the *n*th choice was pressed.

255 An error occurred.

See Also

> "errorlevel," "goto," "if"

---

echo   Internal to: *Windows\\command.com*

Displays messages, turns command echoing on or off, or forces a blank line in a batch file.

Syntax

```
echo [on | off] [message]
```

Description

By default, each command in a batch file is echoed to the screen as it is executed. You can turn this behavior on and off with *echo.*

To display the current *echo* setting, type echo without any options. The following options can be used with *echo:*

on | off
>   Toggles the *echo* command on or off

message
>   Types the message you'd like displayed

To turn *echo* off without displaying the *echo* command itself, use @echo off. The @ symbol in front of any command in a batch file prevents the line from being displayed.

To force a blank line, use one of the following:

```
echo.
echo,
echo"
```

Note the absence of the space between the *echo* command and the punctuation. (You can also use a colon, semicolon, square brackets, backslash, or forward slash.)

Examples

Announce the success or failure of a condition tested in a batch file:

```
if exist *.rpt echo The report has arrived.
```

It's a good idea to give the user usage or error information in the event that they don't supply proper arguments to a batch file. You can do that as follows:

```
@echo off
if (%1) == () goto usage
. . .
:usage
echo You must supply a filename.
```

One handy use of *echo* is to answer y to a confirmation prompt such as the one *del* issues when asked to delete all the files in a directory. For example, if you wanted to clear out the contents of the *temp* directory every time you booted your machine, you could use the following command in *autoexec.bat*:

```
echo y | del c:\temp\*.*
```

or even:

```
echo y | if exists c:\temp\*.* del c:\temp\*.*
```

This construct works because the pipe character takes the output of the first command and inserts it as the input to the second.

---

errorlevel

Although not a command, *errorlevel* is used with the *if* statement, since most batch files make decisions based on the *errorlevel* value returned from a program.

Description

When a program exits, it returns an integer value to the operating system that can be used by *errorlevel*. In a batch line, *errorlevel* is followed by a return code (number). If the return code from the application is greater than or equal to this number, then the condition is considered true and any action in the *if* statement is then taken (which is why you want to start with the highest number first when using *errorlevel* in a batch file). Normally, a return code of 0 indicates that the command was successful, with various errors receiving higher error codes. It's up to the program to define what error codes it uses.

If you're curious about the *errorlevel* number in any of the external DOS commands, just run *command.com* with the /z option. The *errorlevel* number will be displayed as follows once the command has been executed:

```
Return code (ERRORLEVEL): n
```

n is the *errorlevel* returned by the last executed external command.

Examples

The following batch file illustrates the use of *errorlevel* with the *find* command:

```
@echo off
find /i "98" c:\windows\desktop\win98.txt
if errorlevel 2 goto error
if errorlevel 1 goto nomatch
if errorlevel 0 goto match

:match
echo a match was found!
goto end

:nomatch
echo sorry, but a match wasn't found.
goto end

:error
echo sorry, but an error has occurred!

:end
pause
```

In this example, *find* searches for 98 in *win98.txt*, then, depending on the return code, displays the proper message before pausing at the end.

While the *errorlevel* varies from program to program, you don't necessarily have to use all the information provided. It's often enough simply to test:

```
if errorlevel 1  ...
```

after running a program (like *scandisk*), since if the program finds any errors, it will return a nonzero errorlevel.

See Also

"choice," "goto," "if"
"find" in Chapter 7

Run a specified command for each instance in a list.

Syntax

```
for %%variable in (set) do command [options] %%variable
```

in and do are not options, but a required part of the *for* command. If you omit either of these keywords, MS-DOS displays an error message.

Description

Use this command to create loops in a batch file. A *for* loop is a programming construct that allows you to repeat a command for a list of items (such as file-names). You specify an arbitrary variable name and a set of values to be iterated through. For each value in the set, the command is repeated.

The syntax for using *for* in a batch file is different from that used on the command line. You must specify %%*variable* instead of %*variable*.

When redirecting the output of a *for* loop to a file, you must use >> (append to a file) rather than >, or you will save only the last iteration of the loop. The values in the set are enclosed in parentheses, and should be separated by spaces. Wild-cards can be used to supply a list of filenames.

Examples

Create a set of numbered directories (such as for chapters in a book):

```
@echo off
C:\>for %%n in (1 2 3 4 5) do md ch0%%n
```

Since the *for* loop works only for a single command (and it doesn't work well with *goto*), you need to do something like this to run multiple commands with *for*:

```
for %%f in (1 2 3 4 5) do call loop1.bat %%f
echo done!
```

loop1.bat might then look like this:

```
if not exist file%1 goto skip
copy file%1 c:\backup
copy file%1 lpt1
del file%1
:skip
```

Or you could get really clever, and put it all in one batch file, creating the loop file dynamically with *echo* and then removing it before you exit:

```
echo if not exist file%1 goto skip > loop1.bat
echo copy file%1 c:\backup >> loop1.bat
echo copy file%1 lpt1 >> loop1.bat
echo del file%1 >> loop1.bat
echo skip >>loop1.bat
for %%f in (1 2 3 4 5) do call loop1.bat %%f
del loop1.bat
echo done!
```

goto

Branches to a labeled line in a batch program.

Syntax

```
goto label
...
:label
```

Description

goto is typically used with an *if* or *choice* statement to branch to a particular part of a batch file depending on the result of the condition or the user response.

A label marks the beginning of a subroutine, letting the batch file know where to begin processing after it encounters a *goto* command.

The label value you specify on the *goto* command line must match a label in the batch program. The second instance of the label (at the location where execution should resume after the *goto* is executed) must be preceded with a colon.

The *goto* command uses only the first eight characters of a label. Therefore, the labels `mylabel01` and `mylabel02` are both equivalent to `mylabel0`. The label cannot include separators such as spaces, semicolons, or equals signs.

If your batch program doesn't contain the label you specify, the batch program stops and MS-DOS displays the message "Label not found."

Examples

Format a floppy disk in drive *A:* and display an appropriate message of success or failure:

```
@echo off
format a:
if not errorlevel 1 goto end
echo an error occurred during formatting.
:end
echo successfully formatted the disk in drive a.
```

See Also

"if"

---

if

Performs conditional branching in batch programs.

Syntax

```
if [not] errorlevel number command
if [not] string1==string2 command
if [not] exist filename command
```

Description

Conditional branching lets your batch file test to see whether a condition is true, and if it is, forces the batch file to execute a subroutine. By using the [not] option, you can force a batch file to execute a subroutine if the condition is false.

The following options can be used with the *if* command in batch files:

command
> Specifies the command to be carried out if the condition is met.

not Specifies that Windows should carry out the command only if the condition is false.

errorlevel *number*
> Specifies a true condition if the last program returned an exit code equal to or greater than the number specified. See "errorlevel" earlier in this chapter.

exist *filename*
> Specifies a true condition if the specified filename exists. If the condition is true, the specified command is executed. The not exist condition is useful if you'd like a specified command to execute if the condition is false.

string1==string2
> Specifies a true condition if the specified text strings match. To test for an empty string (for example, the presence or absence of a command-line argument), use quotes or parentheses:

```
if "%1"==""
```

or:

```
if (%1)==()
```

Examples

The following batch file checks the current directory for the file *form.bat*. If it finds it, the message "It exists!" is displayed, and if it doesn't, "The file doesn't exist" is displayed:

```
@echo off
if exist form.bat goto jump
goto stop

:jump
echo It exists!
pause
goto end

:stop
echo The file doesn't exist.
pause
goto end

:end
cls
```

See Also

"goto"

---

pause

Internal to: \ *Windows\command.com*

Suspends processing of a batch program and displays a prompt in the DOS box to press any key to continue.

Description

The *pause* command causes the execution of the batch program to stop and display a message, prompting the user to press a key to continue. This allows users sufficient time to read menu options or displayed text.

The message "Press any key to continue..." is automatically displayed whenever the *pause* command is used. The comment line will not appear if *echo* is off.

At a *pause* point, a batch file may be terminated by pressing Ctrl-C or Ctrl-Break, at which point MS-DOS displays the following message:

```
Terminate batch job (Y/N)?
```

If you press Y (for yes) in response to this message, the batch program ends and control returns to the operating system. Therefore, you can insert the *pause* command before a section of the batch file you may not want to process.

Examples

Prompt the user to change disks in one of the drives in a batch program:

```
echo Insert next disk in drive A
pause
```

When this *pause* command is executed, the following message will appear:

```
Insert next disk in drive A
Press any key to continue ...
```

Something like this is also common:

```
Echo Press Ctrl-C to cancel, or
pause
```

---

rem

Internal to: \ *Windows\command.com*

Insert comments ("remarks") into a batch file. Lines beginning with *rem* will be ignored when the batch file is executed.

Syntax

```
rem [comment]
```

The comment can say whatever you want. It's a good idea to put comments in your batch file so that others (including you in the distant future) can figure out how it works.

The *rem* command is also useful for disabling commands. Just add *rem* right before the command to disable it.

Unlike other DOS commands, *rem* also works in the *config.sys* file.

Examples

A batch file that uses remarks for explanations and to disable a command:

```
@echo off
rem This batch program may one day change a directory.
rem But not until I remove the rem before the cd command.
rem It is called mydir.bat.
rem cd \batch\ch2
```

See Also

"echo"

---

shift   Internal to: \ *Windows\command.com*

Deletes the variable that holds the first command-line argument (%1) and shifts over the remaining arguments. %2 becomes %1, %3 becomes %2, and so on. This is particularly useful when processing loops.

Examples

In the following batch file, *shift* is used so that each of the (unknown number of) command-line options becomes option #1 (%1) for processing within the loop:

```
@echo off
rem MTYPE.BAT
rem example: mtype foo.txt bar.txt *.bat
:loop
if (%1)==() goto done
for %%f in (%1) do type %%f
shift
pause
goto loop
:done
echo.
```

The *if* statement tests for an empty argument, and if it finds it, ends the loop. Otherwise, it repeats as many times as needed to use up all the arguments.

 If you use a wildcard on the command line, it is passed to the batch file as a single argument (e.g., *.*), which can be used as-is. It isn't expanded first, as by Unix shells, so you can't pick it apart in the script and use each matched filename separately.

CHAPTER 12

Windows Startup

The process of starting up a computer is called *bootstrapping*, because it's analogous to the proverbial "pulling yourself up by your own bootstraps"—only in this case, that's really what happens. A very small piece of code is loaded, which then loads the next piece, which loads the next, and so on, until the entire system is up and running. The Windows 98 boot process involves the loading of literally hundreds of files. At the risk of gross over-simplification, though, we can say that it consists of six major phases:

1. Hardware startup. The BIOS (Basic Input-Output System) stored in ROM runs a hardware self-test (sometimes called the POST, or Power On Self Test), and then loads the software it finds in the boot sector on the startup disk drive. If the BIOS can't find system software in the boot sector (for example, because you've left a non-system disk in the floppy drive), you'll get a message such as "Invalid System Disk." Pressing F1 during this stage will normally enter the BIOS's setup mode. In modern systems, with larger ROM chips, this can be a fairly substantial environment, in which you can make detailed system configuration decisions. Most users need never enter this setup mode.

2. MS-DOS 7.x is loaded. The *io.sys* file contains the Real mode operating system. *io.sys* in turn loads a number of other programs and configuration files, including *msdos.sys*, *logo.sys* (the screen that says "Starting Windows"), *drv-space.bin* or *dblspace.bin* (if present), the system portion of the Registry (*system.dat*), *config.sys*, and *autoexec.bat*. In so-called "Safe mode" (accessible via startup function keys, as described later in this chapter), *config.sys* and *autoexec.bat* are bypassed. It is also at this point that any hardware profiles defined in Windows 98 are applied. The name of each hardware profile matches a menu item in a multiconfigured *config.sys* file that is run automatically based on the detected profile (such as when a notebook is docked or undocked).

3. The Windows VxD layer is loaded. This starts with *win.com*, which under Windows 98 is just a stub loader for the VxDs that follow, rather than the

Windows Desktop environment that it contained in Windows 3.1. The real work at this stage is done by \Windows\System\vmm32.vxd, the Virtual Machine Manager.

4. The DLLs that provide the raw material for the GUI are loaded, starting with \Windows\System\krnl386.exe, which loads the Win16 environment. It is at this stage that the user portion of the Registry (\user.dat) is first loaded. If present, the file winstart.bat is executed. Then \Windows\System\kernel32.dll loads the Win32 environment. It is at this point that keyboard, mouse, and display drivers are loaded, as well as many system fonts. The \Windows\System.ini file is first consulted at this stage. While most of what used to be stored in the system.ini file has been moved to the Registry, there is a minimal set of device settings that are required, and the shell= line (described in step 6) specifies which command interpreter is to be provided as the overall system shell.

5. If multiple users or networking passwords are configured, the login screen is shown. The user actually logs in. The user's password file (\Windows\username.pwl) is consulted. If user profiles are enabled, the user portion of the Registry is reloaded, this time from the file \Windows\Profiles\username\user.dat.

6. The Explorer (or other shell specified by the shell= line in system.ini) is loaded. The Explorer uses the user Registry data to build the Desktop and other remembered states.

Portions of this sequence are recorded in the file bootlog.txt the first time Windows is started. Thereafter, a new bootlog file will be created only if you specifically ask for it during a manual startup, using the option keys described in the next section.

While you probably don't want to look at every detail of the boot sequence—it really is quite remarkable just how many files are loaded—it's definitely useful to have a rough idea of what happens at each stage, because it makes sense of some of your available options. Especially if you are familiar with DOS or Windows 3.1, you may have to throw some of your preconceptions out the window. For example, in DOS you may be used to having autoexec.bat executed each time you log in. So when you select "Close all programs and login as a different user" you might think that autoexec.bat will be executed again. But it is read only at the initial loading of DOS. If you make changes there and want them recognized, you must do a full reboot.

Each of the following options for the Shut Down command on the Start menu simply restarts the process at one of the stages in the boot process:

Shut down the computer?
Any software loaded in steps 3–6 is removed from memory, and the "It is now safe to turn off your computer" screen is shown. On systems with Advanced Power Management enabled, the system will simply shut down without the final warning screen.

Restart the computer?
Any software loaded in steps 3–6 is removed from memory, and the process starts over with step 2. However, if you hold down the Shift key when selecting this option, only the software loaded in steps 4–6 is removed from

memory, and you start over at step 4. This isn't a real reboot; it saves time, but is sometimes insufficient to clear any problems or instigate some changes.

Restart the Computer in MS-DOS Mode?
Any software loaded in steps 4–6 is removed from memory, and an MS-DOS prompt is displayed. Note, however, that the step 3 Windows/VxD bootstrap layer remains in memory, so that when you type exit, Windows restarts.

Cold Boot Versus Warm Boot

A *cold boot* is what happens when you turn off the computer, wait at least 10 seconds, and then turn the computer back on. A cold boot is required to change any hardware settings.

A *warm boot* is what happens when you hit the reset button on the computer (if there is one), or when you select Restart from the Shut Down dialog box. The only difference is that invoking Restart from the Shut Down screen closes Windows 98 gracefully, and pressing the hardware Reset button does not. Ctrl-Alt-Del entered twice is also a warm boot.

If you choose the Log Off command from the Start menu, only the software loaded in steps 5 and 6 is unloaded from memory; you start over again at step 5. Logging back in as the same user is thus a way to do a "local reboot" of the Explorer without going all the way back to the beginning and restarting all of Windows 98.

For further details on various configuration files used in the boot process, see the alphabetical reference later in this chapter. The next section focuses on the ways you can intervene in the boot process.

Startup Option Keys

The following keys may be pressed during Windows startup (when the "Starting Windows" message appears) to invoke special startup options:

Ctrl
> In some systems, you will need to use the Ctrl key rather than the F8 key to display the Windows startup menu

Esc Disables logo (the logo is not shown; the screen displays the progress of startup).

F4 Starts previous version of MS-DOS (if available). BootMulti=1 must be specified in *msdos.sys*.

F5 Initiates Safe mode startup, without networking support.

F6 Initiates Safe mode startup, with networking support.

F8 Displays Windows Startup menu. See "Windows Startup Menu" for more information.

The Win 98 documentation states that safe mode with networking is no longer supported in Win 98. This is untrue. Although the safe mode with networking option is not available from the startup menu, you can still launch this mode using the F6 key during Windows startup.

Windows Startup Menu

In normal operation, Windows 98 loads and runs automatically. However, additional load-time options are available. Many of these options are useful when troubleshooting Windows startup malfunctions.

To initiate the load-time options menu, press F8 or Ctrl at any time after the various hardware BIOSes have loaded (a good time is when you see the "Starting Windows" message). A menu will then be displayed, giving you several options as follows:

Normal
Normal start.

Logged
System starts, creates *bootlog.txt* file.

Safe mode
Starts Windows, bypassing startup files and using only basic system drivers. No network support. Same as pressing F5 or typing win /d:m at the command prompt. See "Safe Mode Startup" later in this chapter for more information.

Step-by-step confirmation
Starts Windows, confirming startup files line by line. Same as pressing F8 or Ctrl when the Startup menu is displayed. For more information, see "Step-by-Step Confirmation" later in this chapter.

Command prompt only
Starts the operating system with startup files and Registry, displaying only the command prompt. You may lose CD and other peripheral support. Allows for starting Windows using *win.com* command-line switches. See "win.com Startup Switches" for more information.

Safe mode command prompt only
Starts the operating system in Safe mode and displays only the command prompt, bypassing startup files. Same as pressing Shift+F5. See "win.com Startup Switches" for more information.

Previous version of MS-DOS
Starts the operating system that was installed on your computer before you installed Windows 98. Same as pressing F4 during startup. This option is available only if the line BootMulti=1 is in *msdos.sys*.

Step-by-Step Confirmation

Step-by-step confirmation allows you to accept or skip one or more startup options, and is useful when troubleshooting startup errors. You will be given the following options (press Enter to confirm; Esc to skip):

1. Load DoubleSpace (or DriveSpace) driver (if files are present)?

2. Process the system Registry?

3. Create a startup log file (*bootlog.txt*)?

4. Process your startup device drivers (*config.sys*)?

   config.sys options will be displayed (Enter=Yes; Esc=No; Tab to accept all options).

5. Process your startup command file (*autoexec.bat*)?

   autoexec.bat options will be displayed (Enter=Yes; Esc=No; Tab to accept all options).

6. Run *win.com* to start Windows 98 (if BootGUI=1 in *msdos.sys*)?

7. Load all Windows drivers?

Answering Yes (or pressing Enter) to each prompt results in the same operating environment as starting Windows 98 normally, except that the logo does not appear.

Answering No to "Load All Windows Drivers?" runs Windows 98 in Safe mode.

Safe Mode Startup

Safe mode startup provides an alternative boot process for Windows should normal startup fail. Normal startup may fail for any of a number of reasons, including:

- One or more drivers are incompatible with Windows or the system.
- The Registry is corrupted.
- An application requests Safe mode startup (which may occur if you prematurely quit Windows before it has completely started).

Safe startup loads only the minimal drivers necessary for using the Windows GUI. These drivers include:

- Mouse
- Keyboard
- Standard VGA
- Device Manager drivers

You may start Windows in Safe mode in any of the following ways:

- Press F8 or Ctrl during system startup to display the Windows Startup menu. Choose Safe mode or Safe mode with network support.
- Press F5 when the "Starting Windows" message appears during system startup for Safe mode startup without network support.

There are actually three variations of Safe mode invoked by F5, Ctrl-F5, and Shift-F5, respectively. The differences are shown in Table 12-1.

Table 12-1: Safe Mode Options

Function	F5	Ctrl-F5	Shift-F5
Process *config.sys* and *autoexec.bat*	N	N	N
Load networking drives	N	N	N
Load *himem.sys* and *ifshlp.sys*	Y	N	N
Process Registry information	N	Y	N
Load *command.com*	N	Y	Y
Load DoubleSpace or DriveSpace if present	Y	N	Y
Start Windows 98 GUI (run *win.com*)	Y	N	N

win.com Startup Switches

The Windows 98 GUI can be started using switches (options) from the command prompt. This is useful if you need to troubleshoot a balky system (if options in *msdos.sys* are correct; i.e., not from the startup diskette).

To run *win.com* manually using these switches, press F8 or Ctrl at startup and choose either command prompt only, or Safe mode command prompt only.

Syntax

```
win [/b] [/d:[options]
```

Options

/B   Creates a *bootlog.txt* file that records operating-system messages generated during system startup.

/D: Used for troubleshooting when Windows 98 does not start correctly. Combine this switch with one or more of the following options (most of these are for legacy support, except the M option):

F   Turns off 32-bit disk access. Equivalent to setting 32BitDiskAccess=FALSE in *system.ini*.

M   Starts Windows 98 in Safe mode. Same as pressing F5.

S   Specifies that Windows 98 should not use the ROM address space between F000:0000 and 1 MB for a break point. Equivalent to setting SystemROMBreakPoint= FALSE in *system.ini*.

V   Specifies that the ROM routine will handle interrupts from the hard disk controller. Equivalent to setting Virtual-HDIRQ=FALSE in *system.ini*.

X   Excludes all of the adapter area from the range of memory that Windows 98 scans to find unused space. Equivalent to setting EMMExclude=A000-FFFF in *system.ini*.

Examples

Start Windows in Safe mode:

```
C:\>win /d:m
```

System Configuration Utility

Fortunately for those of us who do a lot of startup configuration, Windows 98 includes a handy new utility called the System Configuration Utility (*Windows\ System\msconfig.exe*). *msconfig* (shown in Figure 12-1) collects all of the Win 98 startup configuration elements into a tabbed dialog box that lets you select and deselect individual startup parameters using checkboxes. *msconfig* thus provides three advantages. First, it collects all of this information in a single place, meaning you don't have to go scouring through your system looking for the right parameters in the right system file. Second, the use of checkboxes to select and deselect startup parameters means you don't run the risk of mistyping some of those cryptic commands. Finally, *msconfig* lets you do a few things that you really can't do anywhere else, unless you really want to dive into the Registry.

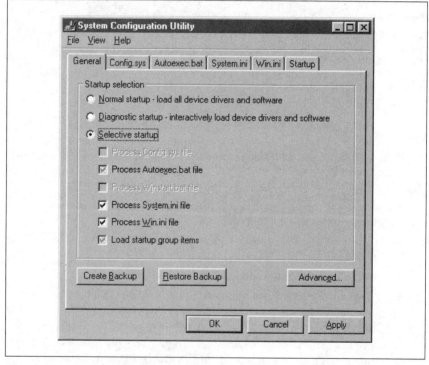

Figure 12-1: System Configuration Utility (msconfig.exe)

The *msconfig* dialog box contains six tabs: General, Config.sys, Autoexec.bat, System.ini, Win.ini, and Startup.

General

The General tab is used for diagnosing startup problems (refer to Figure 12-1). The startup selection section lets you choose between three types of startups to perform: normal, diagnostic (in which you choose what loads during startup), and selective (in which you choose what loads on this screen). When performing a selective startup, simply check the items you wish to load. A grayed-out selection (such as *config.sys* in Figure 12-1) means the file is empty. A dimmed check (such as startup group items in Figure 12-1) means that only some of the items are selected to run. You will select which components using the other five tabs of the dialog.

We like to think of this tab as letting you make broad strokes in the trouble-shooting process. For example, prevent your startup items from loading by clearing the "Load startup group items" box (this clears all items in the Startup tab). If that solves a startup problem for you, you can then go to the Startup tab to enable individual items.

"Create Backup" backs up all of the system configuration files that you can alter with the *msconfig* utility—a good idea before you start monkeying around. "Restore Backup" is how you return to your backed-up files. When you create the backups, the original files are renamed with a *.pss* extension in the same directory as the originals.

The Advanced button opens a dialog (shown in Figure 12-2) that lets you enable or disable certain other things that occur at Windows startup. Most of these have to do with your system hardware and are unlikely to cause startup problems in Windows. In general, we recommend that, when troubleshooting, you only disable one feature at a time to test your startup.

Config.sys and Autoexec.bat

The Config.sys and Autoexec.bat tabs let you selectively enable and disable items from your *config.sys* and *autoexec.bat* files (see Figure 12-3). Whenever you disable (uncheck) an item, *msconfig* actually just remarks it out (adds rem to the front of the line) in the actual file. You can also use this tab to move lines up and down and to create and edit lines.

System.ini and Win.ini

The System.ini and Win.ini tabs let you selectively enable and disable items from your *system.ini* and *win.ini* files (see Figure 12-4). Lines from these files are conveniently grouped into Explorer-like hierarchies, often making it much easier to browse for entries than when using Notepad. One thing Notepad has over *msconfig*, though, is that Notepad lets you search for keywords.

Startup

The Startup tab lets you enable and disable items from the \ *Windows*\ *Start Menu*\ *Programs*\ *Startup* directory, the Registry's RUN and RUNSERVICE keys, and the *win.ini* RUN= and LOAD= entries (see Figure 12-5). These locations are used by most applications that need some component to load at Windows startup. If your

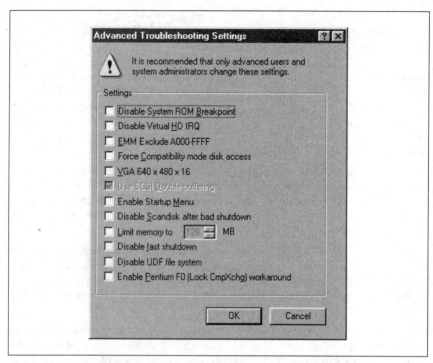

Figure 12-2: Advanced troubleshooting settings dialog in msconfig

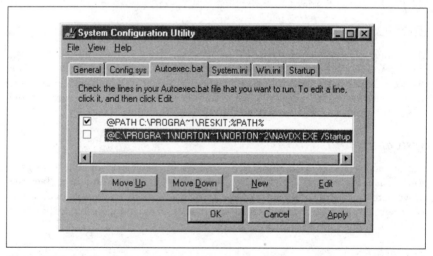

Figure 12-3: Editing the path in the autoexec.bat tab of msconfig

startup problems started after installing a particular application, this is probably the first place you'll want to look. This is also the place to come if you just want to get

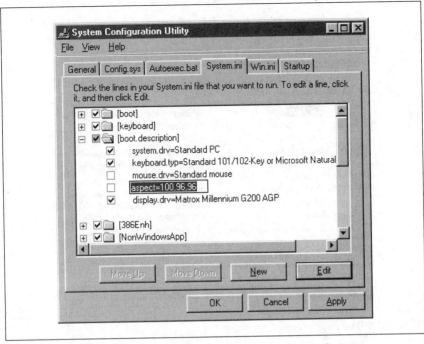

Figure 12-4: Editing boot options in the system.ini tab of msconfig

rid of some of the clutter surrounding Windows startup (such as when AOL 4.0 decides it has to load that icon into your System Tray).

The Msconfig View menu provides a convenient shortcut for launching other Windows applications, such as Control Panel, Device Manager, Printers Folder, Display Settings, Multimedia Settings, and Fonts Folder, that may be useful in troubleshooting startup problems.

System Configuration Files and Commands

This section describes the contents of various system configuration files, especially those used during the startup process. (See Appendix C, *System File and Directory Organization*, for a list of other important files whose contents we don't document in detail.) The files are listed in alphabetical order for easy reference, but it is wise to understand just where they are consulted in the boot process. Since there is some overlap in the settings that can be stored in some of the files, a setting in a later file can override one stored earlier. See Chapter 13, *The Registry*, for information about the Registry (*system.dat* and *user.dat*).

Files are used in the following order:

> *io.sys*
> *msdos.sys*

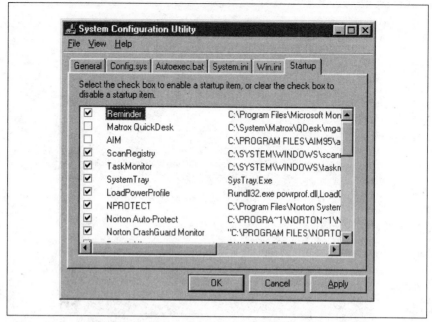

Figure 12-5: The startup tab of msconfig

> *logo.sys*
> *system.dat* (Registry)
> *config.sys*
> *autoexec.bat*
> *user.dat* (Registry)
> *system.ini*
> *user.dat* (Registry) (again)
> *winstart.bat*
> *win.ini*
> *system.ini* (again)
> *Password file (<username>.pwl)*
> *user.dat* (again)
> *system.dat* (again)
> *system.ini* (again)

This alphabetical reference section also lists the following commands, which can be invoked only from system startup files:

> *emm386*
> *loadhigh*
> *setver*

autoexec.bat

Windows 98 does not require the *autoexec.bat* startup batch file. *autoexec.bat* is supported for backward compatibility, and as a means to run DOS-based programs at startup.

autoexec.bat is not read each time you create a new DOS window, unless you create the window with `command /p` (permanent). Neither is *dosstart.bat* (for "MS-DOS Mode"; see MS-DOS → Properties → Program → Advanced). Each new DOS window inherits its environment and other settings from the *autoexec.bat* file run at startup, but it is not rerun. If you have a batch file that you want to run for each new DOS window, specify it in MS-DOS Prompt → Properties → Program → Batch File.

IO.SYS Equivalent Commands

The *io.sys* file is a binary file, but it contains various settings that can be overridden in *autoexec.bat*. Table 12-2 lists variables you can set in *autoexec.bat* to override the defaults in *io.sys*. The examples in the table show the format of each possible entry, but actually just reset the default value in *io.sys*.

Table 12-2: io.sys Environment Variables That Can Be Overridden in autoexec.bat

Entry	Description	Example Showing Default Setting
tmp	Path for temporary files	set tmp=c:\windows\temp
temp	Path for temporary files	set temp=c:\windows\temp
prompt	Command prompt	prompt=pg
path	Search path for executable files	path=c:\windows;c:\windows\command
comspec	Name and location of command-line interpreter	set comspec=c:\windows\command.com

Network Settings

Windows 98 runs the following network command, which may be overridden in the *autoexec.bat* file:

`net start`
Binds the real-mode network components and validates the binding

Notes

Observe the following rules when editing the *autoexec.bat* file:

- The path statement in your *autoexec.bat* file should not include folders of versions of Windows that may be on the system.
- The path= statement line should begin with the following: *C:\Windows;C:\Windows\Command* (use the actual paths for Windows 98 on your hard disk), although Windows should automatically include this path.
- Use the "Reconnect at Logon" option from Windows Explorer to connect to a network server upon startup rather than putting networking commands into

autoexec.bat. If necessary, you may use a batch file in \ *Windows\Start Menu\Programs\StartUp* to accomplish this as well.

- Remove unnecessary statement lines from *autoexec.bat*. When possible, specify initializing parameters for applications in the System Properties sheet in the System Control Panel.

- Do not use long filenames. *autoexec.bat* is processed before *vmm32.vxd* is loaded, so long filenames are not yet supported.

- If present, *autoexec.bat* is executed just before *win.com* is loaded. Windows 98 effectively acts as though *win.com* were the last line of *autoexec.bat*, so if you put the *pause* command as the last line of *autoexec.bat*, the boot process will pause before loading the GUI portion of Windows 98. Press Enter to continue the boot, or press Ctrl-C to cancel the GUI boot, leaving you at the DOS 7 C:\> prompt.

---

config.sys   *config.sys*

The *config.sys* file may contain drivers and configuration information needed by certain hardware or software installed on the computer. Windows 98 does not require the *config.sys* file. *config.sys* is supported as a means for backward compatibility with MS-DOS applications, as well as for computers that require special drivers, or that require special setup (such as double-buffering for SCSI drives).

Windows 98 provides default values for most configuration settings that can be specified in the *config.sys* file (see *io.sys* for more details on these default values). However, you may override any of these default values by inserting a new value in the *config.sys* file. The *config.sys* file may also contain application- or driver-specific information, as required. Examples include drivers for special memory or network managers.

You can add DOS application–specific commands using the Properties → Program → Advanced dialog box for the DOS application in question. (Navigate to the program using the Explorer, then right-click on the program icon for access to the Properties sheet.) This works for DOS programs only.

Notes

- Under Windows 98, the *config.sys* file should *not* contain the following:
  - Command line for loading the *smartdrv* driver. Windows 98 includes built-in disk-caching.
  - "DOS=High" command.
  - Command line for loading a mouse driver or drivers for other pointing devices. Windows 98 includes built-in mouse support.

- Many of the commands that require some allocation of memory have two forms (e.g., *buffers* and *buffershigh*). The "high" form of each command stores its information in high memory. The limit on high memory is 64K, so depending on the amount of memory required, you may not be able to get all the data structures into high memory.

Commands Used in config.sys Files

The following commands are allowed in *config.sys* files under Windows 98. Note, though, that even though they are allowed, they may affect only DOS applications.

`accdate=drive1+|- [drive2+|-]`

For each drive, specifies whether to keep track of the last access date for all files (+) or not (–). Last access dates are turned off for all files when in Safe mode, and are off by default for floppy drives. They are on by default for hard disks.

`break`

Sets or clears extended `Ctrl-C` checking. Normally, DOS checks for `Ctrl-C` only when reading from the keyboard or writing to the screen (or a printer). With extended checking, it checks for `Ctrl-C` during disk read and write operations as well.

`buffers=n[,m]` and `buffershigh=n[,m]`

Allocates memory for a specified number of disk buffers when the computer starts. *n* must be from 1 to 99 (default is 30). An optional second value (*m*) specifies the number of buffers in the secondary cache, and must be from 0 to 8 (default is 0).

`country=xxx [[, yyy] [, path]]`

Enables the operating system to use country-specific conventions for displaying dates, times, and currency; for determining the order by which characters are sorted; and for determining which characters can be used in filenames. *xxx* specifies the country code and *yyy* (optionally) the character set. *path* specifies the drive and path of the file containing country information. The following is an example:

`country=049,437,c:\windows\command\country.sys`

Country codes are usually the same as international telephone dialing prefix (e.g., 44 for UK). See *http://www.memoware.com/country.txt*. The character set value 850 applies to most countries.

`device=driver [options]` *and* `devicehigh=driver [options]`

Loads the device driver you specify into memory. `options` specifies any parameters required by the device driver command line. See *Windows\config.txt* for a description of additional options for `devicehigh`.

The following device drivers can be loaded in *config.sys* using a device= statement:

display.sys

Displays international character sets on EGA, VGA, and LCD monitors.

driver.sys

Creates a logical drive that you can use to refer to a physical floppy disk drive.

emm386.exe

Provides support for loading real-mode device drivers in the UMBs (dos=high) if both *emm386.exe* and *himem.sys* are loaded with device= commands in *config.sys*. See *emm386* later in this chapter for details.

himem.sys

Loads *himem.sys*, an extended memory manager. This command line must come before any commands that start applications or device drivers that use extended memory.

keyboard.sys

Enables the operating system to use a keyboard other than the standard U.S. QWERTY keyboard layout.

mscdex.exe

Provides DOS access to CD-ROM drives.

 The file *Windows\\ios.ini* is a text file that contains a list of drivers known to be safe or unsafe for use in *config.sys*. Drivers that are listed in the "unsafe" portion of this file will cause Windows 98 to use a 16-bit MS-DOS compatibility mode for file access and virtual memory. Check Control Panel → System → Performance to make sure you are in 32-bit mode. If you are in 16-bit mode, and your driver is simply not listed in *ios.ini*, try adding it to the safe list and see if Windows 98 still runs normally. Don't try this with disk compression utilities, DOS disk caching utilities, or VESA and PCI disk drivers.

The following device drivers should not be used under Windows 98, either because of incompatibility reasons, or because the device drivers are not included in Windows 98:

ansi.sys
ega.sys
printer.sys
ramdrive.sys
romdrive.sys

dos=[high|low] [, umb|noumb] [, auto|noauto]

Specifies that the operating system should maintain a link to the upper memory area (UMA), load part of itself into the high memory area (HMA), or both.

high

Loads part of DOS into high memory

low Keeps all of DOS in conventional memory (default)

umb Manages upper memory blocks created by a program like *emm386.exe*, if they exist

noumb

Does not manage upper memory blocks (default)

auto

Loads *himem.sys*, *ifshelp.sys*, *dblbuff.sys*, and *setver.sys*, and automatically uses *buffershigh*, *fileshigh*, *fcbshigh*, *lastdrivehigh*, and *stackshigh* (default)

noauto
>   Does not do all of the things listed under auto automatically

drivparm=*options*
>   Defines parameters for devices (e.g., disk and tape drives) when the operating system starts. Options include:

/D:*n*
>   Specifies the physical drive number. Values for *n* must be in the range 0 through 255 (for example, drive number 0 = drive A, 1 = drive B, 2 = drive C, and so on). This parameter is required, since it specifies which drive the following parameters refer to.

/C   The drive can detect whether the drive door is closed.

/F:*n*
>   Specifies the drive type ("factor"). The default value for *n* is 2. Values include:

>   *0*   160K/180K or 320K/360K

>   *1*   1.2 MB

>   *2*   720K (3.5-inch disk)

>   *5*   Hard disk

>   *6*   Tape

>   *7*   1.44 MB (3.5-inch disk)

>   *8*   Read/write optical disk

>   *9*   2.88 MB (3.5-inch disk)

/H:*heads*
>   Specifies the maximum number of heads. Values for heads must be in the range 1 through 99. The default value depends on the value you specify for /F.

/I   Specifies an electronically compatible 3.5-inch floppy disk drive. (Electronically compatible drives are installed on your computer and use your existing floppy disk drive controller.)

/N   Specifies a nonremovable block device.

/S:*sectors*
>   Specifies the number of sectors per track that the block device supports. Values for sectors must be in the range 1 through 99. The default value depends on the value you specify for /F.

/T:*tracks*
>   Specifies the number of tracks per side that the block device supports. The default value depends on the value you specify for /F.

fcbs=*n and* fcbshigh=*n*
>   Specifies the number of file control blocks that the operating system can have open at the same time. *n* must be between 1 and 255 (default is 4).

`files=n` *and* `fileshigh=n`

> Specifies the number of files that the operating system can access at one time. *n* must be between 8 and 255 (default is 8).

`install progname [options]`

> Loads a memory-resident program into memory. This works only for programs that have no user interface, such as *keyb.com.*

`Lastdrive=x` *and* `Lastdrivehigh=x`

> Specifies the maximum number of drives you can access. *x* must be a letter between A and Z (default is Z).

`Numlock=[on|off]`

> Specifies whether the Numlock setting on the numeric keypad is on or off.

`rem` Comments out a line and prevents it from executing.

`set var=[string]`

> Sets an environment variable (see set in Chapter 7, *DOS and Other Command-Line Utilities,* for details).

`shell=command [options]`

> Specifies the name and location of the command interpreter for use with Windows 98. Most often used to specify additional options for *command.com,* such as /e (to increase the size of the environment). For example:
>
> `shell=/command.com /e:1024`

`stacks=n, s` *and* `stackshigh=n, s`

> Supports the dynamic use of data stacks to handle hardware interrupts. *n* is the number of stacks, and can be 0 or a value from 8 to 64. *s* is the size in bytes of each stack, and can be 0 or a value from 32 through 512.

`switches`

> Specifies special startup options for DOS. See the file \ *Windows\config.txt* for available options.

---

dosstart.bat

\ *Windows\dosstart.bat*

This is an optional DOS batch file that, if present, runs when you exit Windows 98 into real-mode "MS-DOS Mode." (You can enter MS-DOS mode via Start → Shutdown → Restart in MS-DOS mode, or by running an MS-DOS program with the setting Properties → Program → Advanced → MS-DOS Mode.) The file *winstart.bat* is executed when you re-enter Windows GUI mode.

Normally, you might use *dosstart.bat* to run *mscdex.exe* for CD-ROM access from DOS and a mouse driver for mouse support. The default *dosstart.bat* contains only a set of comments describing its intended use.

---

emm386

\ *Windows\emm386.exe*

Used to display the current status of *emm386.exe* expanded memory support and to turn the device driver on or off.

Description

The *emm386.exe* device driver is different from the *emm386* command used from the command line. In order to use the *emm386* command from the command line, you must have an 80386 or higher processor, and you must have the *emm386.exe* device driver installed in the *config.sys* file by using the *device* command. The device driver is loaded by the execution of *config.sys*; without it, the *emm386* command is inoperable. The *emm386* command, issued at the command-line prompt, enables or disables support for expanded memory services. Expanded memory allows compatible DOS programs to run in expanded (1 MB and beyond) memory.

emm386.exe has the folllowing syntax:

```
emm386 [on|off|auto] [w=on|w=off]
```

The *emm386.exe* options are:

on   Turns the *emm386* device driver on. This is the default setting.

off Turns the *emm386* device driver off.

auto
    Enables expanded memory support only when a program calls for it.

w=on
    Enables support for the Weitek co-processor.

w=off
    Disables support for the Weitek co-coprocessor. This is the default setting.

Notes

- To display the current status of *emm386* expanded memory support, type emm386 at the command prompt.

- In order to use the *emm386* command, you must load the *emm386.exe* device driver from within the *config.sys* file, using the syntax:

    ```
    device=x:\path\emm386.exe
    ```

    where *x:\path* is the drive and path to the directory containing the *emm386.exe* program.

---

io.sys   /Windows/io.sys

The *io.sys* file contains the real-mode MS-DOS 7.x operating system. This is a binary file; it is no longer an editable text file. The Windows 98 *io.sys* file is renamed to *winboot.sys* when you start the computer using the previous version of MS-DOS.

io.sys loads several system drivers by default, if they are found:

himem.sys
ifshlp.sys
setver.exe
dblspace.bin or *drvspace.bin*

---

io.sys does not load *emm386.exe*. If any of your applications require expanded memory or load data into high memory, you should run *emm386.exe* in *config.sys*.

autoexec.bat and config.sys Defaults

io.sys contains default values of setup switches and command parameters that can be overridden in *config.sys* and *autoexec.bat* (see the entries for those files for additional details):

himem.sys
> Enables access to the high memory area. Loads and runs the real-mode Memory Manager, typically *himem.sys*. (The Windows GUI won't load without it.) Compatibility: used by Windows 98; loaded by default.

ifshlp.sys
> Loads the Installable File System Helper, which allows the system to make file system calls. Only the minimal file system from *io.sys* is used if this driver is not loaded. (The Windows GUI won't load without it.) Compatibility: used by Windows 98; loaded by default.

setver.exe
> Loads optional TSR-type program for compatibility with older MS-DOS–based applications that require a specific version of MS-DOS to be running. When queried by an application, *setver.exe* responds with the appropriate version number for that application. Compatibility: used by Windows 98; loaded by default.

dos Loads MS-DOS into the high memory area. *umb* setting is used only if *emm386.exe* is loaded in *config.sys*. Default value: dos=high,umb. Compatibility: used by Windows 98; loaded by default.

files
> Specifies the number of filehandle buffers to create under MS-DOS. Default value: files=60. Compatibility: not required by Windows 98; included for compatibility with MS-DOS applications.

lastdrive
> Specifies the last drive letter available for assignment. Default value: lastdrive=z. Compatibility: not required by Windows 98; included for compatibility with MS-DOS applications.

buffers
> Specifies the number of file buffers to create. Default value: buffers=30. Compatibility: not required by Windows 98; included for compatibility with MS-DOS applications.

stacks
> Specifies the number and size of stack frames. Default value: stacks=9,256. Compatibility: not required by Windows 98; included for compatibility with MS-DOS applications.

shell

Indicates the command process to use. (The /p switch indicates that the command process is permanent and should not be unloaded; when /p is not specified, the command process can be unloaded when exiting the system.) Default value: shell=command.com /p. Compatibility: not required by Windows 98; included for compatibility with MS-DOS applications.

fcbs

Specifies the number of file control blocks to be created. Default value: fcbs=4. Compatibility: not required by Windows 98; included for compatibility with MS-DOS applications.

You may override the default values in *io.sys* by inserting an entry in *config.sys*. Override values for files, buffers, and stacks must be equal to or greater than the default values specified in the previous list.

---

loadhigh or lh   Internal to: \ *Windows\command.com*

The *loadhigh* command loads a program into the upper memory area. The command can be used in the *config.sys* file or the *autoexec.bat* file to load programs when the computer starts. The *lh* command is a shortcut name for *loadhigh*.

loadhigh has the following syntax:

```
loadhigh [filename] [options]
loadhigh [/L:region1[,minsize1][;region2[,minsize2]...] [/S]]
filename [options]
```

Options

filename
Specifies the location and name of the program you wish to load.

/l:region1[,minsize1] [;region2[,minsize2]]
Specifies the region(s) of memory into which to load the program. You can specify as many regions as you want.

region1
Specifies the number of the first memory region.

minsize1
Specifies the minimum size, if any, for *region1*.

region2
Specifies the number of the second memory region, if any.

minsize2
Specifies the minimum size, if any, for *region2*.

/s   Shrinks a UMB (Upper Memory Block) to its minimum size while the program is loading.

Associated Files

config.sys
autoexec.bat

Examples

In *config.sys*:

```
C:\device=c:\windows\himem.sys
C:\device=c:\windows\emm386.exe
DOS=high,umb
fileshigh=16
buffershigh=50
devicehigh=mscdex.exe
```

In *autoexec.bat*:

```
lh c:\windows\command\doskey
lh mscdex.exe
```

Notes

- Using Upper Memory Blocks (UMBs) is a way to free conventional memory for use by MS-DOS–based applications and thus improve performance. In conventional memory, UMBs are the unused part of upper memory from 640K to 1 MB (the old system area, in earlier versions of DOS), where information can be mapped to free memory below 640K.

- Before you can load a program into the upper memory area, you must install an upper memory area manager. You can use *emm386.exe*, which manages the upper memory area for computers with an 80386 or higher processor. To install *emm386*, add a *device* command to your *config.sys* file.

---

logo.sys, logos.sys, and logow.sys

\logo.sys,
\Windows\logos.sys,
\Windows\logow.sys

\logo.sys contains the startup image with the Microsoft Windows logo. If not present, *io.sys* uses a built-in logo. *\Windows\logow.sys* and *\Windows\logos.sys* contain the shutdown screens that read "Please wait while your computer shuts down" (*logow.sys*) and "It is now safe to turn off your computer" (*logos.sys*), respectively. These files are just bitmaps, so you can substitute other bitmap files if you like, provided that you get the aspect ratio and number of colors right. The files must be 256-color (8-bit) Windows bitmaps, 320 × 400 pixels in size. You should make copies of the existing files before replacing them. See *Windows 98 Annoyances*, by David A. Karp (O'Reilly & Associates), for a detailed description of how to replace these files.

---

msdos.sys

\msdos.sys

Startup information for Windows 98. This file, located in the root directory of the computer's boot drive, may be edited to alter the boot or runtime behavior of Windows. In DOS 6 and earlier, *msdos.sys* was a binary file, part of the MS-DOS kernel. The entire DOS kernel is now stored in *io.sys* (with the installation version on the Windows 98 CD-ROM called *winboot.sys*). *msdos.sys* is now a text file containing configuration settings.

On machines with compressed hard disks, the entire version of *msdos.sys* is stored on the non-compressed (host) drive.

The *msdos.sys* file is editable; however, in normal use, the file is hidden and read-only. These attributes should be changed prior to editing.

Use the following command at the command line to make the *msdos.sys* file editable:

```
C:\>attrib -s -h -r \msdos.sys
```

After the desired changes have been made, use the following command to restore *msdos.sys* to its normal attributes:

```
C:\>attrib +s +h +r \msdos.sys
```

Restart Windows to have your changes take effect.

Important note: for compatibility with MS-DOS and some older applications, *msdos.sys* must be at least 1024 bytes in length. The file may contain the following remarked lines, which should not be removed:

```
;The following lines are required for compatibility with other
;programs.
;Do not remove them (MSDOS.SYS needs to be >1024 bytes).
;xxxxxxxxxxxxxxxxxxxxxxxxxxxxxxxxxxxxxxxxxxxxxxxxxxxxxxxxxxxxxxxxxxxxx
xa
;xxxxxxxxxxxxxxxxxxxxxxxxxxxxxxxxxxxxxxxxxxxxxxxxxxxxxxxxxxxxxxxxxxxxx
xb
;xxxxxxxxxxxxxxxxxxxxxxxxxxxxxxxxxxxxxxxxxxxxxxxxxxxxxxxxxxxxxxxxxxxxx
xc
...
```

Among the information stored in *msdos.sys* is the path to critical Windows files. The *msdos.sys* file contains two sections, [Paths] and [Options], and one or more keys defined under each section. Following is a description of the sections and keys found in the *msdos.sys* file.

[Paths] Section

HostWinBootDrv=*path*
    Points to the boot disk (optional). Default: HostWinBootDrv=C.

UninstallDir=*path*
    Points to the directory that will be used for Uninstall (optional). Default: UninstallDir=C:\.

WinDir=*path*
    Points to the main Windows directory, as specified during Windows Setup (required). Default: WinDir=C:\Windows.

WinBootDir=*path*
    Points to the main Windows directory, specifically for files needed to start Windows (optional). Default: WinBootDir=C:\Windows.

[Options] Section

AutoScan=*n*

Specifies whether *scandisk* should be run automatically after improper shutdown. Values for *n* include:

0   No scanning

1   Prompt the user, but scan automatically if no response within 60 seconds (default)

2   Scan automatically without prompting

Example:

```
Autoscan=0.
```

You can also change this setting using Control Panel → TweakUI → Boot → Autorun Scandisk.

BootDelay=*r*

Sets initial startup delay to the number of seconds; the default is 2 seconds. Examples:

```
Set to 1 second delay: BootDelay=1
Set to no delay: BootDelay=0
```

BootFailSafe=*n*

Enables/disables Safe mode startup. Examples: .

```
Disable: BootFailSafe=0
Enable (default): BootFailSafe=1
```

BootGUI=*n*

Enables/disables automatic graphical startup. If BootGUI=0, the system boots only to the DOS 7 prompt. Type **win** at the DOS prompt to start the Windows 98 layer. If Windows 98 is started manually in this way and then shut down, typing **MODE CO80** followed by the **Enter** key when the "It is now safe to turn off your computer" screen is displayed will return you to the MS-DOS prompt. Examples:

```
Disable: BootGUI=0
Enable (default): BootGUI=1
```

BootKeys=*n*

Allows/prevents special option keys (e.g., **F5**, **F6**, and **F8**) from functioning during Windows startup. Note that if Bootkeys=0 is set, BootDelay will be ignored. (That is, the system will assume BootDelay=0.) Examples:

```
Prevent: BootKeys=0
Allow (default): BootKeys=1
```

Bootmenu=*n*

Displays/skips Windows startup menu. By default, you must press **F8** within the time specified by BootDelay to see the startup menu. Set Bootmenu=1 to always display the menu. Examples:

```
Displays: Bootmenu=1
Skips (default): Bootmenu=1
```

BootMenuDefault=n

Sets the default menu item on the Windows startup menu. The default is normally 1, but is changed to 4 if the system hung on the last reboot. Example:

```
Set default to item 3: BootMenuDefault=3
```

BootMenuDelay=n

Specifies number of seconds to display the Windows startup menu before running the default menu item. Examples:

```
Delay for three seconds: BootMenuDelay=3
No delay (default): BootMenuDelay=0
```

BootMulti=n

Enables/disables dual-boot capabilities. This allows you to boot multiple operating systems, such as Windows 98 and Linux, or Windows 98 and Windows NT, from separate partitions on the same boot disk. If BootMulti=1, the *boot. ini* file gives additional boot instructions. Examples:

```
Disable (default): BootMulti=0
Enable: BootMulti=1
```

BootWarn=n

Enables/disables Safe Start warning and menu. Examples:

```
Disable: BootWarn=0
Enable (default): BootWarn=1
```

BootWin=n

Enables/disables Windows 98 as the default operating system (used when another operating system is also available on the computer).

Note: pressing **F4** inverts the default if BootMulti=1. (For example, pressing the **F4** key when BootWin=0 forces Windows 98 to load.) Examples:

```
Disables: BootWin=0
Enables (default): BootWin=1
```

DblSpace=n

Prevents/allows automatic loading of *dblspace.bin*. Examples:

```
Prevent: DblSpace=0
Allow (default): DblSpace=1
```

DoubleBuffer=n

Enables/disables double-buffering for SCSI controller. A value of 1 enables double buffering for controllers that need it (such as SCSI controllers). A value of 2 enables double buffering regardless of whether the controller needs it. Examples:

```
Disables: DoubleBuffer=0
Enables (default): DoubleBuffer=1
```

DrvSpace=n

Prevents/allows automatic loading of *drvspace.bin*. Examples:

```
Prevent: DrvSpace=0
Allow (default): DrvSpace=1
```

LoadTop=n

Enables/disables loading of *command.com* and/or *drvspace.bin* at the top of 640K memory. If you are having problems with software that makes assumptions about the available memory, try setting this to 0. Examples:

```
Disable: LoadTop=0
Enable (default): LoadTop=1
```

Logo=n

Hide/show the animated Windows logo (during logo display, Windows loads interrupt drivers that can cause incompatibility with some memory managers; hiding the logo prevents the loading of these drivers). Examples:

```
Disable: Logo=0
Enable (default): Logo=1
```

Network=n

Safe Mode with Networking is no longer supported in Windows 98. The Network value should be set to 0 or left blank to disable the feature.

SystemReg=n

Load/don't load Registry. Examples:

```
Load registry (default): SystemReg=1
Don't load registry: SystemReg=0
```

Registry

\system.dat, \user.dat,
\Windows\Profiles\username\user.dat

The Registry provides Windows 98 and applications with a hierarchically-organized database of settings and configuration information. While initialization files such as *config.sys*, *system.ini*, and *win.ini* remain important in Windows 98, the Registry holds a lot of the information that previous versions of Windows kept in separate *.ini* files.

For more information on the Registry, see Chapter 13.

---

setver

\Windows\setver.exe

Lie about the MS-DOS version number on a program-by-program basis.

Description

Some Windows and DOS programs (including ones written by Microsoft) check the DOS version number incorrectly: for example, the program will actually run properly in any DOS version greater or equal to 5.0, but it instead checks to see whether the DOS version is *exactly* 5.0. To allow such programs to be run under Windows 98 (which includes MS-DOS 7.00 or 7.10), *setver* can be used to fake the DOS version number that Windows 98 reports to that program. For example, *winword.exe* apparently has to be told that it's running under DOS version 4.10.

setver has the following syntax:

```
setver [drive:path] filename n.nn
setver [drive:path] filename /delete [/quiet]
```

By using *setver* without any options, the current version table is displayed. The *setver* options are:

[drive:path]
> Specifies location of the *setver.exe* file (*not* of the program for which you want to change the DOS version number).

filename
> The filename of the program. No drive or path can be specified.

n.nn
> Specifies the MS-DOS version to be reported to the program.

/delete *or* /d
> Deletes the version-table entry for the specified program.

/quiet *or* /q
> Hides the message typically displayed during deletion of version-table entry.

Examples

Tell Win 98 to report DOS version 5.0 to *myprog.exe*:

```
C:\>setver myprog.exe 5.00
```

Delete *myprog.exe* from the version table:

```
C:\>setver myprog.exe /d
```

Notes

- Changes to the *setver* table don't take effect until the system is restarted.
- *setver* displays a dire-sounding warning message when a change is made to the version table.
- drive:path in the *setver* syntax specifies the location of *setver.exe* itself, *not* the location of the program for which the DOS version number is being set. The drive:path of *setver* itself can be specified because the version table is stored within the *setver.exe* executable file. Drives and paths cannot be specified for the program to be given a fake DOS version number; thus, setting the version number for *foobar.exe* sets it for *any foobar.exe* on any drive or directory.
- To load the version table stored in *setver.exe*, the Windows 98 boot process performs a device=setver.exe, whether or not *config.sys* actually contains an explicit statement.

---

system.ini

\ *Windows\system.ini*

Most configuration information that used to be stored in the *system.ini* file has been moved to the Registry or is no longer valid. However, the file is still required, and there is a minimal set of essential entries, perhaps most importantly shell=, which specifies the overall operating system shell (not to be confused with the shell= command in *config.sys*, which specifies the DOS command-line interpreter). This is normally specified as *explorer.exe*, but could be changed to *taskman.exe*, *command.com*, or a standalone application for kiosk or demo use.

While *system.ini* is a text file and can be edited with any text editor, large parts of its format are poorly documented, so tread with caution. You may find the System Configuration Utitility that we described earlier in this chapter safer, since it backs up any entries that are modified.

The continuing use of *system.ini* and other *.ini* files as a data storage area for system programs indicates once again that Windows 98 is not an integrated system so much as a collection of independent applications, some of which have been updated to take advantage of newer system services, and some of which have not.

---

win.ini \ *Windows*\ *win.ini*

As with *system.ini*, many of the functions that were formerly performed by *win.ini* have migrated to the Registry. Still, a surprising amount of data is stored there. For example, Desktop settings from Control Panel → Desktop, such as the colors of various user interface items and the pathname and tiling options of Desktop wallpaper, can be found in the [Colors] and [Desktop] sections, respectively. Regional settings are also stored here, in the [Intl] section. While you can change these values with a text editor, you're far better off using the GUI Control Panel interfaces.

win.ini is also used for storing font substitution information (i.e., which Microsoft fonts correspond to various PostScript fonts), as well as information about ports and printers.

Additional information about other Control Panel settings is stored in the file \ *Windows*\ *control.ini*.

Probably the most useful statements in *win.ini* are load= and run=. These statements can be used to specify programs that will be run automatically upon system startup. Specify the complete pathname of any program(s) to be run, separated by spaces. (Programs specified with load= are run first, then run=.)

Generally, though, it's easier to run programs automatically by putting shortcuts into \ *Windows*\ *Start Menu*\ *Programs*\ *StartUp*, especially since there are limits on the length of the run= and load= statements. These statements can each contain only 128 characters. By the time you specify a set of program pathnames (especially if they are in out-of-the-way places), you can fill up these statements pretty quickly. Note that if you exceed 128 characters, any programs specified beyond that limit will be silently ignored. What's more, there are documented cases of programs run with load= and run= statements not running properly, or having unintended side effects. (You can also specify programs to be run automatically at startup in the Registry at the key HKLM\SOFTWARE\Microsoft\Windows\ CurrentVersion\Run and the corresponding keys RunOnce, RunServices, and RunServicesOnce.)

---

winstart.bat \ *Windows*\ *winstart.bat*

This is a regular DOS batch file that the DOSMGR VxD (inside *vmm32.vxd*) runs (if present) when starting up the System Virtual Machine in which all Win16 and

Win32 apps run. In other words, the System VM is really a DOS box in which you can start DOS TSRs, etc., just before the GUI appears.

winstart.bat also runs when you exit from MS-DOS mode to normal Windows 98. (See "dosstart.bat.")

CHAPTER 13

The Registry

The Registry provides Windows 98 and applications with a hierarchically organized database of settings and configuration information. While initialization files from earlier versions of Windows such as *config.sys*, *system.ini*, and *win.ini* do remain important in Windows 98, the Registry holds a lot of the information that previous versions of Windows kept in separate *.ini* files.

An amazing amount of what you assume is "hardwired" into Windows—the location of key directories, the names of objects such as the Recycle Bin, even the version number of Windows 98 reported on Control Panel → System—is actually the product of data stored in the Registry. Change the Registry data and key parts of your system can be affected. For this reason, Microsoft provides only minimal user documentation on *regedit*, the Registry Editor, preferring to leave such things in the hands of experienced system administrators and programmers.

 Despite the enormous potential for harm, the Registry is fairly robust, and for every entry that you can wreak havoc by changing, there are hundreds that you can change with impunity. Nonetheless, you should back up the Registry files before making significant changes with *regedit*. See "Backing Up the Registry" later in this chapter for details.

The Registry is normally consulted silently by the programs (such as the Explorer) that build the Windows 98 user interface, as well as by most applications. Programs also write data to the Registry when they are installed, when you make changes to configuration settings, or just when they are run. For example, a game like Freecell keeps statistics in the Registry on how many games you've won and lost. Every time you play the game, those statistics are updated. For that matter, every time you move an icon on your Desktop, the position is recorded in the Registry.

You can view and modify the contents of the Registry with *regedit*. This program is not visible on the Start Menu. To run it, you either need to navigate to \ *Windows*\ *regedit.exe* in the Explorer, or (more practically), type the command name at the Address, Run, or Command prompt. When you first start the program, you'll see the display shown in Figure 13-1.

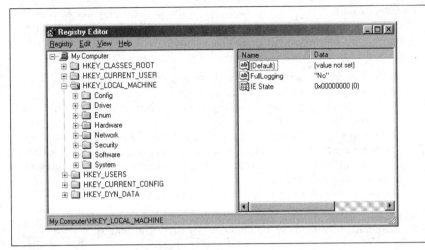

Figure 13-1: The Registry Editor dialog box

This interface looks familiar, even if the "folders" shown have strange names. (In the Registry, these folders are referred to as *keys*.) As in the Explorer, you have a two-pane view. Click on any item in the left pane to navigate, and click on the tiny plus signs or double-click on the folders to expand and collapse branches. View the results on the right. Given the familiar interface, you might hope just to start clicking away and see something familiar, like you do in the Explorer. Unfortunately, you can soon find yourself lost in a bewildering morass of tantalizing but ultimately meaningless data. You need to arm yourself with a few basic concepts, and then back up a few steps and start over with the big picture. That's what we'll do in the next two sections.

What's in the Registry

The Registry contains keys (represented in *regedit* by folder icons, even though they are nothing of the sort) and values. Keys can contain other keys and/or values. That keys can in turn contain other keys establishes a hierarchy; a key with all its subkeys and values is often called a *branch*.

For example, information about the current user's configuration is kept in the key HKEY_CURRENT_USER. This key includes many subkeys, including one called Software, which includes keys for each vendor whose software is installed on the machine. In turn, each vendor will probably have a further key for each individual product, and then additional keys for whatever amount of data they want to store for the application. This can be a single value or an entire hierarchy of additional keys. What the authors of any program store in the Registry is entirely up to them.

Backslashes are used to represent the key/subkey hierarchy (i.e., path), much as they are used to represent the directory/subdirectory hierarchy in the file system.

For example, Microsoft Word keeps information in the Registry about where to find the Startup Folder in the key HKEY_CURRENT_USER\Software\Microsoft\Office\8.0\Word\Options (shown in the status bar).

The contents of this key are shown in Figure 13-2.

 It's easy to get confused about keys and values. You might be tempted to refer to a value name (e.g., "Startup-Path" in Figure 13-2) as a key, and think of its associated data as the value, but in fact, the final item in any path is referred to as a value, whether or not it contains any data. It has two components: the value name and the value data. Anything that appears in *regedit*'s left pane is considered a key, while anything that appears in the right pane is considered a value.

Every key contains the value whose name shows up as (Default). If there is no default value for the key, you'll see the value data (value not set), as in Figure 13-2. You'll also see this in the right pane whenever you open a key that contains one or more subkeys with no values. But in other cases, you'll see the

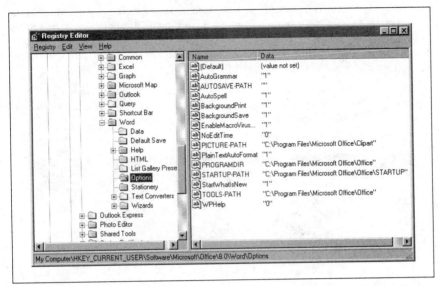

Figure 13-2: The Registry Editor illustrating values of Microsoft Word Options key

value name (Default) with an actual data value. See the discussion of HKEY_ CLASSES_ROOT later in this chapter for an example.

With the exception of (Default), all of the value data shown in Figure 13-2 is in string format—text enclosed in quotes. To change a value, simply double-click on it or select it and choose Modify from the Edit menu. An edit dialog box will be displayed. For example, if I wanted to change the location of my Word Startup Folder, I could double-click on Startup-Path to see the edit dialog box shown in Figure 13-3. The current value is highlighted in the dialog box; simply replace the entire value by typing over it, or click to move to a particular point in the value to edit it.

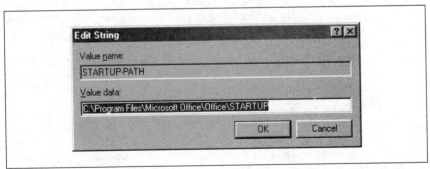

Figure 13-3: Editing a string value to change Microsoft Word Startup directory

There are two other formats commonly found in the Registry—binary and DWORD (32-bit unsigned integer)—as well as three other internal formats that can't be modified by *regedit* and so are not discussed here.

Note that "string" values might be real text strings (such as pathnames, text messages, and so forth) or numeric values. It's up to the program that stored them to interpret them correctly. So-called binary values are actually stored as hexadecimal numbers, shown as four pairs of digits. As these are hex values, the digits range from 0 to F rather than from 0 to 9.

For example, the FreeCell game keeps its statistics in the Registry in binary format. Figure 13-4 shows the FreeCell statistics, plus a new value that was added to the FreeCell key in order to show how a Dword value is represented.

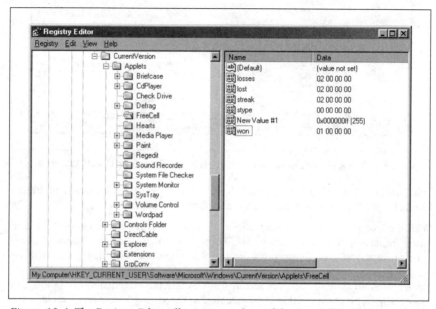

Figure 13-4: The Registry Editor illustrating values of the FreeCell key

In general, if a value is stored in binary or DWORD format, you can guess that it was either programmatically generated or the program's author wished to make the value a little more obscure and difficult to edit. However, if you know what you are doing, you can edit binary or DWORD values almost as easily as you can string values. For example, if I want to lie to my friends to tell them I've won 435 games of FreeCell rather than just one, I simply need to double-click on "won" and edit the value as shown in Figure 13-5.

Even if you're not a programmer, you can figure out hexadecimal values pretty easily with *calc* (see Chapter 6). Just enter the number you want to convert and click the Hex radio button to see the hexadecimal equivalent: 435 is 1B3. Note, however, that the hex values stored in a binary Registry value are in a somewhat unexpected format. The two low-order digits appear in a pair on the left, followed by the next two digits, and so on. The hex value 1B3 thus needs to be entered as B3 01.

If you want to convert a binary value shown in *regedit* to decimal, you have to reverse this notation. For example, if I wanted to find the decimal equivalent to a

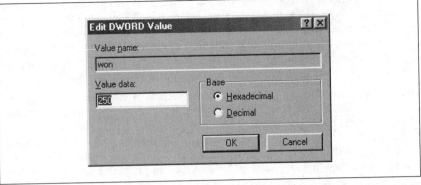

Figure 13-5: Editing a DWORD value to alter the number of games won in FreeCell

value shown as 47 00 65 6e, I'd set *calc* to hexadecimal mode, enter the digits 6e650047, and then switch to decimal mode to find out that the equivalent decimal number is 1,852,112,967. Of course, if the numbers get that big, it's likely that they have a meaning you might not want to muck with. If the purpose was simply to encode a value to make it harder to edit, you'll probably see smaller numbers, using only the leftmost pairs of digits, as in the FreeCell example.

If you aren't sure about the meaning of a specific Registry value, don't be afraid to experiment. Experimenting might include editing a value with *regedit*, but it might be easier or safer to work from the other end: open the application whose data is stored there (e.g., a Control Panel applet), change a setting, and watch how the Registry data changes. In this way, you can get a sense of the meaning of many binary-encoded values. Note that the Registry data may change immediately, but in order to update the view in *regedit*, you need to press F5 (Refresh).

It's a good idea, though, to make a backup copy of a Registry key before making any changes. See "Editing the Registry" and "Exporting and Importing Registry Keys" later in this chapter for details.

Figure 13-4 showed an additional value, called New Value #1, which I entered into the FreeCell key using `regedit` → Edit → New → DWORD Value. This example makes two points:

1. The DWORD format is also a hexadecimal number, but this time in a more conventional representation. The leading 0x is a standard programmer's notation for a hex value, and the number can be safely read from left to right. The equivalent decimal value is shown in parentheses following the hex value. What's more, when you edit a DWORD value, the edit dialog box gives you a choice of entering the new value in decimal or hex notation.

2. A Registry entry is meaningless unless a program actually reads it. You can enter new keys or values all you like, with the only consequence being that

you've bloated your Registry. The chief danger is in deleting or modifying existing entries. (Note that there are sometimes undocumented Registry values that are meaningful to a program but that are not normally present. Adding them to the Registry can make useful changes; see *Windows 98 Annoyances* by David Karp (O'Reilly & Associates) for several examples. However, the chance of hitting upon such a value at random is vanishingly small!)

This last point is critical. You can use a tool such as *regedit* to add, rename, and delete values and keys (except for the very top-level keys such as HKEY_CURRENT_USER or HKEY_LOCAL_MACHINE, which cannot be deleted, supplemented, or renamed). If you modify the FreeCell statistics in *regedit* to say so, FreeCell will dutifully report that you've won 1,000 games and lost none. On the other hand, if you add some new Registry keys and values that no program ever looks for, then these new keys and values will have no effect. Conversely, if you change some Registry setting without understanding how the system relies on the setting, this change can have a disastrous, unintended effect. It's worth noting that in some cases, the mere presence or absence of a key (without any value) may have meaning to some program.

A final note: don't confuse *regedit* with the Registry itself. *regedit* is just one program that displays and modifies the Registry. (In fact, almost all Windows 98 programs rely on and modify the Registry in some way). The Registry itself is typically loaded from two files, *Windows\system.dat* and *Windows\user.dat*, which Windows 98 loads into memory when it boots up. While Windows 98 is running, it modifies this in-memory version; whenever the system is idle, and when you shut down, it automatically writes the Registry back out to *system.dat* and *user.dat*, saving the previous version in the files *Windows\system.da0* and *Windows\user.da0*. These backups are used in the event that the Registry gets corrupted. If user profiles are enabled, a separate *user.dat* file for each profile is typically stored in *Windows\Profiles\username\user.dat*. Regardless, there is always only one *system.dat*.

A third file, *policy.pol*, is used to hold system policy values created with System Policy Editor (*poledit.exe*—see Chapter 8, *Hidden Gems on the Windows 98 CD-ROM*, for more details). Values in *policy.pol* are designed to override any settings contained in the other two registry files. Unlike *system.dat* and *user.dat*, *policy.pol* is not a required component of Windows 98. It will only be present if system policies are enforced.

The fact that Registry changes are applied immediately is one reason why editing the Registry is considered dangerous. There's no "save" and no "undo" in *regedit*. Any changes you make are applied immediately. (If you've saved Registry patches as described later in this chapter, you can apply them for a limited form of undo.)

Organization of the Registry

The Registry is enormous and complex; a full Registry might easily contain 15,000 keys and 35,000 values. Entire books have been written about it, and we can't do it justice here. Our purpose in this section is to arm you with a basic understanding of how the Registry is organized, not to document individual values in detail or suggest changes you might want to make with *regedit*.

Speeding Up Registry Navigation

As in the Explorer, it's wise to train yourself to use the keyboard rather than the mouse. Typing the first letter of a Registry key is a quicker way to navigate to it than scrolling and clicking with the mouse.

When the focus is in the left (navigation) pane, you can also use the Backspace key and the arrow keys to navigate through the Registry hierarchy. Backspace will pop you up to the top of the next level in the key hierarchy (parent) but will not collapse any expanded keys. The left arrow will actually collapse the branch while moving back a level. The right arrow will expand the current key if it's collapsed. The up and down arrows will simply move vertically through any expanded keys. This is harder to explain precisely than it is to do; experiment, and you'll quickly get a feel for how it works.

Other useful navigation tools are Edit → Find (Ctrl-F) and Find Next (F3). You can search for a particular key, value, or value data, or can look in all three. One thing that's a bit confusing, though, is that Find starts its search from the currently highlighted Registry key and doesn't wrap around to the beginning. So if you want to search the entire Registry, be sure to start by highlighting the My Computer icon at the top of the Registry tree. Alt-Home will take you right there, as long as the focus is in the left pane.

Conversely, if you want to speed up your searches, first move down the navigation tree closer to where you think the target may be.

David A. Karp's book *Windows 98 Annoyances* provides many tips and tricks that rely on the Windows 98 Registry. Ron Petrusha's book *Inside the Windows 95 Registry*, while it is aimed primarily at software developers and covers Windows 95, contains several chapters aimed at experienced users. In particular, see Chapters 1 to 3, which give a good overview of the Registry and a detailed description of how to use *regedit*, and Chapter 8.

http://142.104.153.201/www/Registry.html also contains a number of useful Registry tips.

As was shown in Figure 13-1, the top level of the Registry is organized into six main branches, or hives. By convention, the built-in top-level keys are always shown in all caps, even though the Registry itself is case-insensitive. (For example, HKEY_CURRENT_USER\SOFTWARE\MICROSOFT\Windows is identical to HKEY_CURRENT_USER\Software\Microsoft\Windows.) For convenience in referring to them in documentation (though not in the actual software), the names of the top-level keys are often abbreviated as shown in Table 13-1.

Table 13-1: Registry Key Abbreviations

Key	Abbreviated Name
HKEY_CLASSES_ROOT	HKCR
HKEY_CURRENT_USER	HKCU
HKEY_LOCAL_MACHINE	HKLM
HKEY_USERS	HKU
HKEY_CURRENT_CONFIG	HKCC
HKEY_DYN_DATA	HKDD

The function of each of these branches is briefly summarized in the following list. Subsequent sections go into their contents in more detail.

HKEY_CLASSES_ROOT (HKCR)

Contains file types, filename extensions, URL protocol prefixes, and OLE and DDE information. This information is the "glue" that ties Windows 98 together. It is critical to drag-and-drop operations, context menus, double-clicking, and many other familiar user interface semantics. The actions defined here tell Windows 98 how to react to every file type available on the system.

This entire branch is a mirror of HKLM\SOFTWARE\Classes, provided purely for convenience. Because the information here is accessed so frequently, it is made available at the top level.

HKEY_CURRENT_USER (HKCU)

Contains user-specific settings for the currently logged-in user. This entire branch is a mirror of HKEY_USERS\login-name, or, if profiles aren't enabled, of HKEY_USERS\.Default. An application that keeps information on a per-user basis should store its data in HKCU\Software, and put information that applies to all users of the application in HKLM\SOFTWARE.

However, it is somewhat arbitrary what Windows applications seem to consider user-specific, and what is for all users on the machine. Like many aspects of Windows 98, the Registry provides a mechanism for applications to store configuration data, but does little to enforce any policies about how and where it will actually be stored.

HKEY_LOCAL_MACHINE (HKLM)

Contains information about hardware and software on the machine, not specific to the current user. The values in this branch are loaded from \Windows\system.dat.

HKEY_USERS (HKU)

Stores underlying user data from which HKEY_CURRENT_USER is drawn. The values in this branch are loaded from \Windows\user.dat or, if present, \Windows\Profiles\login-name\user.dat.

HKEY_CURRENT_CONFIG (HKCC)

Much as Windows 98 can handle multiple users on a single machine, and therefore preserves individual users' settings within the Registry, so too it supports multiple hardware configurations, which are also preserved within the Registry, under the HKEY_CURRENT_CONFIG branch.

This key is loaded from HKLM\Config*xxxx*, where *xxxx* is a subkey representing the numeric value of the hardware configuration currently being used by Windows 98. On a system with only a single hardware configuration, its value is 0001. The name of the configuration that is current—and therefore the subkey of HKLM\Config to which this key points—is stored in the CurrentConfig value entry of the HKLM\System\CurrentControlSet\control\IDConfig key.

HKEY_DYN_DATA (HKDD)

This branch contains dynamic data, only in-memory, not associated with *system.dat* or *user.dat*. Used in Plug and Play (Configuration Manager); also for performance monitoring statistics.

As noted above, HKEY_CLASSES_ROOT is identical to HKEY_LOCAL_MACHINE\Software\Classes, HKEY_CURRENT_USER is identical to HKEY_USERS\.Default and HKEY_USERS*xxxx* (where *xxxx* represents the currently logged-in user), and HKEY_CURRENT_CONFIG is identical to HKEY_LOCAL_MACHINE\Config*xxxx* (where *xxxx* represents the current hardware configuration).

HKEY_CLASSES_ROOT (HKCR)

On the surface, Windows 98 seems very object-oriented. Files, folders, and devices are represented by icons that respond differently to various actions such as single or double clicks, right clicks, and left clicks. But in a true object-oriented system, the object itself contains the knowledge of how to respond to events such as mouse clicks.

By contrast, Windows 98 performs much like the Wizard of Oz, not with true object-oriented magic, but with a complex machinery hidden behind a screen. The knowledge of how the Explorer should treat each object is stored in the Registry, in a complex chain of interrelated keys.

Much of the system's behavior depends on file extensions. It's quite important that file extensions (almost always the old DOS-style three-letter extension) accurately reflect the file type. There is nothing in the system that enforces this relied-upon connection between file extensions and file contents. It's purely a convention, but one that much of Win 98's behavior depends upon. That's why it's so stupid that the Explorer hides extensions by default.

When you open HKCR, the first thing you'll see is a very long list of file extensions known to the system, from *.acp* (Office Actor Preview) to *.zip* (WinZip or other similar compressed "zip" archive file). The subkeys and values associated with each extension vary. In some cases, the application that opens a file with the specified extension is named directly, but in others, there's just a pointer to another key elsewhere in the list.

Following the list of extensions, you'll see a set of keys that are sometimes referred to as *class definition keys* or *document type keys*. These keys provide a level of indirection that lets one extension point to one of several possible applications.

For example, should a file with the *.doc* extension be opened by Word 6 or Word 8? When you upgrade from Word 6 to Word 8, the installation program simply needs to change the key that describes the *.doc* file extension so that it points to *Word.Document.8* instead of *Word.Document.6*.

Should a file with the *.htm* extension be opened by Netscape Navigator or Microsoft Internet Explorer? If you use Navigator, the *.htm* key will have the value name (`Default`) with the data "NetscapeMarkup." If you use Internet Explorer, the value name (`Default`) will have the value data "htmlfile." If you then look at either of those two class definition keys (NetscapeMarkup or htmlfile), you'll see a different chain of subkeys. While both Navigator and Internet Explorer know how to handle HTML files, they use a different set of internal instructions for figuring out how to display or edit the files, what icon to display for the file, and so on.

The detailed subkeys and values that appear under the class definition and document type keys start to get really confusing. Because each program may record and retrieve different keys, it's very hard to generalize about them. The best we can do is to mention some of the kinds of keys you might see associated with a particular file extension subkey or class definition subkey. Here are some of the most common:

CLSID

Class Identifier for OLE (Object Linking and Embedding) services. This is a randomly generated 16-byte number in the following format: {aaaaaaaa-bbbb-cccc-dddd-ffffffffffff}, where each letter represents a hexadecimal digit. (That's a sequence of eight, four, four, four, and twelve hex digits, with a hyphen between each group of digits and the whole thing enclosed in curly braces.)

CLSID appears both as a subkey of many class definition keys and as a class definition key in its own right. That is, the key HKCR\NetscapeMarkup might have a subkey CLSID with the data value {61D8DE20-CA9A-11CE-9EA5-0080C82BE3B6}, but there's also a key called HKCR\CLSID with the subkey {61D8DE20-CA9A-11CE-9EA5-0080C82BE3B6}, which in turn has the data value "Netscape Hypertext Document." The first entry is simply a pointer to the second, which contains the actual class data. You must always be on the lookout for this kind of indirection.

There are some CLSID keys that don't correspond to any particular extension. The CLSID itself represents the file type. This is the case for various system objects such as the Recycle Bin, Control Panel, and so forth. This is the source of the tips you will frequently encounter on the Net telling you how to rename or relocate these system objects by typing the new name followed by the long and seemingly incomprehensible CLSID as an extension.

Content Type

This is the MIME (Multipurpose Internet Mail Extension) type corresponding to this file type. This key will typically exist for Internet-related file types such as GIF and JPEG. Email programs that support attachments and web browsers such as Netscape Navigator use MIME Content Types as well as or instead of extensions to recognize the format of a file.

DefaultIcon

The location (usually a pathname and an optional "icon index" within the file) of the file containing the default icon to be used for this file type. If you see the value data "%1", that means that the file will act as its own icon.

Note that there may be more than one default icon for a given file type. A good example is the Recycle Bin, which shows a different icon when it is empty and when it is full. In cases like this, what happens is that the program knows to copy its icon for the appropriate state to the DefaultIcon (Default) value. In other cases, though, a DefaultIcon may be specified in more than one place (e.g., under a document type key and under an associated CLSID key).

Shell

Contains subkeys that define actions (open, edit, print, play, and so forth) that may be available for the object. These are some of the items that will appear on the context menu for the associated file type. The shell keys under file extension keys sometimes seem to be empty. Look under the file class definition key for more information (e.g., look under HKCR\NetscapeMarkup\Shell, not HKCR\.htm\Shell).

Note that you might find a subkey sequence like Shell\Open\Command, where the value for Command is the command that will be used to open the file, or the command line including options to perform other operations. As in batch files, the syntax %1 represents the first argument to the program (typically the filename).

You might also find something like Shell\Open\ddeexec, where the value is the DDE (Dynamic Data Exchange) subroutine call for performing the specified operation. (For example, Windows might send a DDE message to an application to tell it to print a file after opening it.) DDE is supposedly obsolete, supplanted in Microsoft's toolkit by ActiveX (the API formerly known as OLE), but you wouldn't know it from the number of ddeexec keys in the Registry.

You'll see the same split between command-line options and DDE using the Explorer interface to file associations, via the View → Options → File Types menu on any folder. Some actions will list a command line; others will use DDE. If you're not a programmer with access to the DDE documentation for a particular application, you may find this difficult to follow at times.

What's often a little perplexing is why a given file type's subkeys don't seem to show a particular action, even though you know that action is supported for the file type. There's such a maze of indirection that the key you expect to find in one place just isn't there. It's somewhere else in the chain of associations.

ShellEx

Shell Extensions. These keys, usually via subkeys called Context-MenuHandlers, define actions that are added only in specific contexts. For example, files and folders have an "Update" action on their context

Registry

menu only when they are within a Briefcase. As often as not, `Context-MenuHandlers` involve some further redirection, usually involving a `CLSID`. There is also sometimes a `PropertySheetHandlers` subkey under `ShellEx`, which defines cases where a file type has a special property sheet associated with it. This is how applications add their own specific tabs to the property windows for a given file type.

`ShellNew`

Defines whether the file type will appear on the context menu → New menu. The value name may be Command, Filename, NullFile, or Data. In most cases, this key will be empty, if it exists at all. (Contrast the enormous number of file types defined in the Registry with the much smaller number that appear on the New menu.)

Command contains a command line to create the new file. (This is used only for the *.bfc* and *.lnk* extensions.)

Filename contains the name of a file "template" to be copied to the new location. Its value data may contain a complete pathname, but if it's just a filename (e.g., *netscape.html*, *winword.doc*, or *winword8.doc*), it will be found in the directory \ *Windows\ShellNew*.

Some file types (such as *.bmp* files, which may contain data in any one of a number of related formats, as specified by binary header data within the file itself) are described by the value NullFile. NullFile has the empty string (`""`) as its value data. An application that opens a new file of this type will write out any necessary format data only when the file is first saved.

Data contains binary data that needs to be written to the new file. This might, for example, be some kind of binary header data.

Before leaving HKCR, two other keys are worthy of note.

`HKCR\*` contains information that will be applied to all files, regardless of their extension.

`HKCR\Unknown` describes, via its `Shell\OpenAs\Command` subkey, just what will happen to a file whose type is unknown. As we know from Chapter 4, *The Windows 98 User Interface*, it will pop up the Open With dialog box. It is here that the *rundll32* command line to bring up that dialog box can be found. (It's amazing just how many system behaviors that don't seem to have a command line associated with them actually do. Quite often, you'll find a magical incantation starting with *rundll32* somewhere behind the scenes.)

HKEY_CURRENT_USER (HKCU)

The Registry separates user settings from global machine settings. In the FreeCell example earlier in this chapter, each user of the machine can have his or her own separate won/lost statistics because the program keeps these statistics in the HKCU branch of the Registry. If it instead used HKEY_LOCAL_MACHINE, all users would share the same statistics.

Information for all users is kept in HKEY_USERS (HKU), and the information for the current user is mirrored to HKCU. If there is only one user of the machine, the mirror is from HKU\.Default. If profiles are enabled, the mirror is from HKU\ *login_name*. (The preceding statement is a bit of an oversimplification. See the discussion of HKU later in this chapter for the full story.)

There are seven top-level subkeys: AppEvents, ControlPanel, Install-LocationsMRU, keyboard layout, Network, RemoteAccess, and Software. Note the inconsistent capitalization, which illustrates once again how the Registry is not a monolithic structure managed by one program or individual, but rather an inconsistent repository for whatever data the author of a particular program or subsystem chose to put there.

HKCU\AppEvents

This is where the associations between events and system sounds are kept. (See "Sounds" in Chapter 5, *The Control Panel*.) There are two branches here: EventLabels and Schemes. EventLabels contains the labels that will be used for the sounds; Schemes contains the pointers to the actual sounds.

Schemes has two main subkeys: Apps and Names.

Applications that use sounds can create their own subkey under Schemes\ Apps, or they can add sounds into the default list, which is kept in the subkey Apps\.Default. If they add their own subkey, the sounds will show up in a separate section of the sounds list in Control Panel → Sounds. So you might see a subkey such as Mplayer or Office97, since these applications add some of their own sound events in addition to the default sounds.

Schemes\Names is used to list named sound schemes like Jungle, Musica and so forth. When you change the sound scheme using the drop-down Scheme list on Control Panel → Sounds, the appropriate scheme is copied into .Default. (That's why, if you've made changes to your system sounds, you must save them as a new scheme before switching to another scheme.)

HKCU\ControlPanel

This is where data from several of the Control Panel applets is stored, particularly Accessibility and some (but not all) of the Display settings. (Additional Display settings are still stored in *.ini* files.) The names don't match up cleanly to the names used in the Control Panel, but you can usually figure out what's what by going back and forth between *regedit* and the target Control Panel applet. For example, HKCU\ControlPanel\Accessibility maps directly to Control Panel → Accessibility, but HKCU\ControlPanel\Cursors maps to Control Panel → Mouse → Pointers.

As is typical in the convoluted world of the Registry, some entries point somewhere else entirely. For example, HKCU\ControlPanel\International simply defines a Locale value, such as "00000409," which is the standard code for what the Control Panel calls "English (United States)." If you use *regedit*'s Find function to trace this value, you'll eventually find the scattered locations of many of the individual values that Control Panel → Regional Settings brings together in one place.

This example illustrates a key point: there's little reason to poke around in the Registry for values that have a convenient user interface in the application. The point is to understand the overall structure of the Registry so that you can find and manipulate entries for which the application developer has provided no user interface.

HKCU\InstallLocationsMRU

This key lists the last five locations from which software has been installed. MRU stands for "MostRecentlyUsed"; whenever you see a drop-down list showing recent commands or actions, there's likely a *something*MRU key somewhere behind it. The five entries in this MRU list are stored in values named a, b, c, d, and e, with their order in the list specified by the value MRUList (e.g., "dceba"). It's usually safe to erase this type of list.

HKCU\keyboard layout

This key is used only if you have installed more than one keyboard layout via Control Panel → Keyboard → Language. A Preload subkey lists a separate subkey for each installed language, with subkey 1 specifying the default language.

HKCU\Network

This key lists Network connections you've made. Persistent lists the UNC paths for connections for which you've mapped a local drive letter (using Explorer → Tools → Map Network Drive) and checked Reconnect at logon. Recent lists network connections you've made recently, regardless of whether they've been made persistent.

The format of the names shown in Recent seems a little odd. While Persistent uses UNC paths, Recent changes the leading \\ to ././ when representing the network name, and inserts a . before every additional / in the path. What's more, it truncates any name to 12 characters.

HKCU\RemoteAccess

This key lists various types of information used by Dial-Up Networking, including the default connection to be used by Internet applications. The Implicit subkey lists the UNC path of any shared folders or printers that are accessed over a particular Dial-Up Networking connection. The Profile subkey stores information specific to each connection, such as the saved login name that will be supplied automatically when you make the connection.

HKCU\Software

This key contains subkeys for each vendor whose software is loaded onto the machine, and, within each vendor's area, subkeys for each product. The keys stored here contain only user-specific settings for each software application. Other settings, which are common to all users of software on the machine, are stored in HKLM\SOFTWARE. (Note the difference in capitalization between HKCU\Software and HKLM\SOFTWARE. Even though a search of the Registry and other Registry operations are case-insensitive, case can be used like this to make references to similarly-named keys a little more distinguishable.)

The structure of these interrelated Registry branches (and particularly of the Microsoft\Windows\CurrentVersion branch under both) is described later in this chapter, in the section "HKCU\Software and HKLM\SOFTWARE."

HKEY_LOCAL_MACHINE (HKLM)

HKLM describes the configuration of your machine. It has nine top-level subkeys: Config, DesktopManagement, Drivers, Enum, hardware, Network, Security, SOFTWARE, and System. (DesktopManagement will not be present on all systems.)

HKLM\Config

Hardware profiles (Control Panel → System → Hardware Profiles) are stored in this branch. If hardware profiles are enabled, each profile will be stored in a key with a four-digit name starting with 0001. If hardware profiles are not enabled, only the key 0001 will appear. The current profile is mirrored to HKEY_CURRENT_CONFIG (HKCC); the details will be discussed there.

HKLM\DesktopManagement

This branch provides information used by Microsoft's Desktop Management Interface (DMI).

HKLM\Drivers

This branch is designed to provide configuration data used by hardware drivers, but that type of data is mostly stored in HKLM\Config.

HKLM\Enum

This branch "enumerates" every device known to the system. It is the heart of the Plug-and-Play (PnP) system. It contains an entry ("node") for each device or bus controller (SCSI, etc.). From this list, the Windows 98 Configuration Manager (a set of core routines in the Ring 0 portion of the operating system) builds the list of currently active device nodes in HKEY_DYN_DATA\Config Manager\Enum.

Plug and Play is a set of architecture specifications that allow a PC, its operating system, and any add-in hardware devices and associated device drivers to work automatically without user intervention. PnP enumeration happens whenever the system is booted, as well as when Windows 98 is notified that you've changed the hardware (e.g., by swapping out a PCMCIA card, or by docking or undocking a laptop that supports so-called "hot docking" rather than requiring a reboot). Drivers are automatically loaded or unloaded from memory; a static set of drivers does not need to be loaded at boot time. (At least that's the theory.)

PnP is not something that Windows 98 can implement perfectly by itself, since it requires that not only the operating system but also the underlying PC BIOS and any add-in devices support the PnP specification.

PnP devices include PCMCIA cards and devices that attach to PCI or ISAPNP buses. Advanced Power Management (APM) is also a Plug-and-Play feature. If you have a Control Panel → Power applet, or a Suspend item on your Start menu, APM is installed.

In cases where Windows 98 is running on legacy (pre-PnP) hardware or with legacy devices, it goes through a process called hardware detection. This process is initiated from Control Panel → Add New Hardware, rather than being carried out automatically during the boot process. The Add New Hardware wizard creates a log file called *detlog.txt*, which can be helpful for debugging purposes.

The Plug-and-Play BIOS specification is available at *http://www.microsoft.com/hwdev/*.

Walking through the Enum key in detail would require covering more hardware concepts than we have space for in this book. What's more, much of the information in this branch may be irrelevant to you, since it lists all devices known to your system, rather than what's currently installed. To see what devices are actually active in your system, go to HKEY_CURRENT_CONFIG. However, since this is where you'll see the complete list of available entries, we'll list some of the top-level subkeys you may find here.

Basically, the devices are listed by the buses they are attached to, much as they are in Control Panel → System → Device Manager when you select View devices by connection. Each device node is identified by a branch made up of three subkeys, effectively giving each device a three-level name. The first subkey is the enumerator—the portion of the Configuration Manager that tracks this type of device—the second subkey is the device-id, and the third subkey is the instance of the device (in case there is more than one). The format of the last two subkeys depends on the enumerator. The instance is usually a sequence number, the position on a bus (PCI), or the combined enumerator, device-id, and instance of the parent device concatenated and separated by &.

Example names are:

```
BIOS\*PNP0C04\00
ESDI\GENERIC_IDE__DISK_TYPE<7_\BIOS&*PNP0600&0800
PCI\VEN_8086&DEV_1234\BUS_00&DEV_01&FUNC_00
```

If you're not a hardware jockey, this stuff can get pretty stiff. Even Device Manager (which is a lot friendlier than looking at this stuff in *regedit*) can be tough to follow if you don't really know much about hardware.

BIOS

A key found on systems with a Plug-and-Play BIOS (Basic Input/Output System) for devices found on the motherboard. On systems without a PnP BIOS, many of the same entries will be found in the Root key.

ESDI

Lists Enhanced System Device Interface devices. This is a hard disk device type. A CurrentDriveLetterAssignment value name contains the drive letter assigned to the drive. If a disk is partitioned, there may be more than one drive letter shown.

FLOP

Lists information about your floppy drive controller and attached floppy drives. There is one subkey below this one for each installed floppy drive.

HTREE

Stands for "Hardware Tree." We're not sure what this one does, although it seems to be referred to by a number of the other keys. We suspect it has something to do with the generation of the dynamic hardware tree in HKDD.

LPTENUM

Appears if a Plug-and-Play printer is configured for a parallel port.

MF

Stands for Multifunction PCI devices. The parent device is elsewhere in the tree, and the individual child devices appear separately here. An example might be the OSI Trumpcard, which combines a modem and Ethernet controller on a single PCMCIA card.

Monitor

Lists available monitors. The `Default_Monitor` subkey doesn't always indicate which monitor is currently in use. Instead, look at `HKDD\Config Manager\Enum\Monitor`.

Network

Specifies some parameters related to any network hardware. It doesn't list the actual hardware.

PCI

Stands for Peripheral Component Interconnect, Intel's 1992 local bus standard. The naming convention for keys here is pretty funky. You'll see names like `PCI\VEN_8086&DEV_1234\BUS_00&DEV_01&FUNC_00`.

Each vendor, device, bus, and function has a unique identifier. If you get to the end of the branch, you'll find some identifying data. But the Device Manager is a lot easier to use.

PCMCIA

Stands for Personal Computer Memory Card International Association. These days, PCMCIA cards are often called PC cards.

Root

Lists any non-PnP devices. For example, printer drivers may be listed here. Bindings will list protocols bound to a network adapter. (See "Network" in Chapter 5.)

SCSI

Stands for Small Computer System Interface.

Serenum

Lists any devices installed on a serial port.

HKLM\hardware

According to the Microsoft Windows 98 Resource Kit, the `devicemap\ serialcomm` key is used by HyperTerminal. It lists values for COM1 and COM2 on my system. The `System\CentralProcessor` and `System\ FloatingPointProcessor` branches tell me that my CPU is "GenuineIntel." I hope the thought police aren't checking this key.

HKLM\Network

The Logon subkey tracks information for Dial-Up Networking, such as your username and whether to process a login script. The username is the name of the user who last successfully logged in. So, for example, if you logged in by pressing Esc at the initial Network logon prompt, this key will show the name of the last person who logged on with a valid name.

HKLM\Security

If remote administration is enabled, this subkey apparently contains information about the computer that will be used for administration. The format is obscure.

HKLM\SOFTWARE

This is the big one. It lists all of the software installed on your system. HKEY_ CLASSES_ROOT is mirrored from the Classes subkey. As noted earlier, there is a subkey for each vendor. The Microsoft branch is discussed later in this chapter, in the section "HKCU/Software and HKLM/SOFTWARE."

HKLM\System

This branch contains a subkey called CurrentControlSet, which in turn has the two subkeys Control and Services.

The Control key contains a CurrentUser value as well as numerous subkeys. The CurrentUser value is the same as HKLM\Network\Logon\username. It will exist only on a networked system. However, if the username was bypassed for the current login (by pressing Esc at the initial login prompt), this branch will not exist.

HKLM\System\Control

Some of the interesting subkeys in the Control branch include:

ComputerName
Stores the name you give your system in Control Panel → Network → Identification.

InstalledFiles
Seems to include a list of *.exe* and *.dll* files relating to networking that are installed on your system.

Keyboard Layouts
Lists all of the available keyboard layouts, with pointers to the associated *.kbd* file.

Media Resources
Lists multimedia drivers.

NLS
Defines the code page values that are used to associate languages with keyboard layouts and other regional settings.

Perfstats
Stores information about performance data that is kept in HKDD.

Print

Lists keys for each of the printers in your *Printers* folder and pointers to the associated drivers. Also lists keys for the `FAX:` and `PUB:` virtual print devices.

SecurityProviders\SCHANNEL

Lists certification authorities known to your system, as well as Ciphers, Hashes, and KeyExchangeAlgorithms (if any). Also lists the security protocols known to your system, such as SSL 2.0 or SSL 3.0.

SessionManager

Contains lots of tantalizing but obscure subkeys with names like `AppPatches`, `CheckBadApps`, `CheckVerDLLs`, `Known16DLLs`, and `Warn-VerDLLs`. They are presumably of use to software developers who want to check what DLLs and application patches are installed in your system, and for Windows 98 to patch applications dynamically, but there may be some meat for browsing power users in here as well.

TimeZoneInformation

Stores the data set as a result of Control Panel → Date/Time → Time Zone.

VMM32Files

Lists all the *.vxd* files that have been incorporated into *Windows\ System\VMM32.vxd.*

HKLM\System\Services

The **Services** branch gets into a miscellany of hardware- and system-related services, including:

Arbitrators

Subkeys here store reserved system addresses for legacy hardware with fixed hardware address, DMA addresses, I/O port addresses, and IRQ assignments. This is the information that shows up in Control Panel → System → View Resources.

Class

Subkeys here provide information on current devices. The information here is at a much higher level than that provided in `HKLM\Enum`. For example, the `Modem` key might list the Hayes commands to be used for each class of modem command. The `Display` key might include subkeys for available resolutions and the currently selected resolution.

RemoteAccess

Includes some information used by Dial-Up Networking.

VxD

Lists the installed Virtual Device Drivers.

HKCU\Software and HKLM\SOFTWARE

As noted earlier, both `HKEY_CURRENT_USER` and `HKEY_LOCAL_MACHINE` include a similarly structured Software branch (although in the first case, it is spelled with only an initial capital, where in the latter it is in all caps). Each has a branch for each vendor who has software installed on the system.

In theory, the HKCU branch should include information that is configurable on a per-user basis (which would be the case, for instance, with a software package with a per-user license, or per-user customization). The HKLM branch should include software that is standard for all users. In practice, though, it doesn't seem to be as consistent as that. The information that is stored in each branch sometimes overlaps (or doesn't overlap) in unexpected ways. So if you're looking for something, look in both branches. In the discussion that follows, we will try to compare and contrast what you will find in each branch.

Because this is a book about Windows 98, and not about the third-party applications that might be installed in it, the primary focus of this discussion is on the Microsoft\Windows\CurrentVersion branch. Except for the first entry, all the entries are relative to that key.

Microsoft\Windows\CurrentVersion

HKCU shows no data for this key at the top level. HKLM is where the goodies are: lots of information about the system configuration, including the registered owner of the software and his or her organization, and the version and sub-version of Windows 98. And obviously, since this is just an editable Registry entry, be wary of what you find. The *ver* command is a safer way to find out your system version.

Application Paths

HKLM only

This branch lists a path for many applications that are installed in nonstandard locations (i.e., not in \, *Windows*, or *Windows\Command*). It is the reason why you can successfully type a command name like **excel** or **winword** at the Run prompt, but not at the command prompt, unless you add *Program Files\Microsoft Office\Office* to your search path. They have listed their path individually under this key.

Note that in contrast to many of the keys in HKLM/SOFTWARE/Windows/CurrentVersion, this branch includes references for non-Microsoft applications. The reason is that it's an information area to be used by a Microsoft application (to wit, the Explorer's Run prompt) to find other applications. Some, but not all, applications install a path here.

 If you have an application that installs a shortcut on the Start menu, but doesn't let you type its name at the Run prompt, add a key for it here. It's fairly easy to duplicate the format of the existing keys. For example, I added a *PSP.EXE* key, with the values:

```
(Default) "C:\Program Files\Paint Shop Pro\PSP.EXE"

Path      "C:\Program Files\Paint Shop Pro"
```

Now I can type **psp** at the Run prompt when I want to start up Paint Shop Pro (see *http://www.jasc.com/*) to make a new screen capture for this book. This is similar to *autoexec.bat*'s path statement.

Applets

HKCU stores settings here for Backup, Briefcase, Check Drive, FreeCell, Hearts, Media Player, Paint, RegEdit, Sound Recorder, System Monitor, SysTray, Volume Control, and WordPad. Most of the values are encoded binary or DWORD values that you probably don't want to mess with, but there are some values that may prove of interest. For example, both Paint and WordPad keep a `Recent File List` key here.

HKLM includes subkeys for `Backup`, `Check Drive`, and `Popup`. The values stored for `Backup` and `Check Drive` do not overlap.

Explorer

This is where you hit pay dirt. There are many MRU lists, paths to system folders, and so forth. Here are some of the interesting subkeys in HKCU:

`DeskView`
> Contains the state of the Desktop as an encoded binary value. `ExpView` does the same for other Explorer states.

`Doc Find Spec MRU`
> Contains the last ten names you searched for using Find → Files and Folders. These are the items that appear in the drop-down list in the Find dialog box. While this may seem somewhat useless, you can imagine, for instance, writing a Registry editing script that would preload the Find drop-down list with a set of long names you wanted to search for repeatedly.
>
> As with all MRU lists, the value names are a series of letters; there is also a value called `MRUList` that specifies the order in which the entries should be displayed. That is, if you've just typed in the filenames *.dll* and then *.exe* into the Find dialog box, they might appear as items h and i in the list. But then, if you picked *.dll* again from the list, the `MRUList` would show "ijabc-defgh." The list is updated only when you actually execute a find, not when you type in a new filename to search for or pick an item from the drop-down list. In addition, when you quit Find, value j, which always contains an empty string, rotates to the front of the list.

`FindComputerMRU`
> Contains the MRU list for Find → Computer. It operates just like the previous example and most MRU lists in the Registry.

`RecentDocs`
> Contains an encoded version of the contents of *Windows**Recent*, the list of the twenty most recently opened files. The values are in binary format. The function of this data is unclear, since if you delete all the shortcuts in *Windows**Recent*, the Start → Documents list will indeed be empty, but the Registry entry will be unchanged.

`RunMRU`
> Stores the last 26 commands you issued at the Run prompt. The 26-command limit comes stems from MRU's use of lowercase letters of the alphabet as value names for each command.

`ShellFolders`

Specifies the location of many of the standard Windows system folders, including Desktop, NetHood, Programs, Send To, Start Menu, Startup, and Templates (see the discussion of ShellNew earlier in this chapter in "HKEY_CLASSES_ROOT (HKCR)").

This branch really brings home the extent of Win 98's mutability. Even the directory names that the Explorer relies on, such as \ *Windows\Desktop*—even these are not hard-wired. So the Explorer doesn't know anything about *C:\ Windows\Desktop*. All it knows is that it can get the name of the folder it's supposed to use as the Desktop from the Registry. Most of these values probably shouldn't be changed.

`User Shell Folders`

Supposedly stores the location of application-specific folders that are personal to each user. For example, you'll see Microsoft Office's Personal again here, as well as IE's Favorites. Note, however, that both of these also appear in the Shell Folders key. It's not immediately clear if this is a belt-and-suspenders kind of thing, or just an oversight. If you want to make changes, either change both or experiment to see which setting takes precedence. Whenever a key seems to be duplicated in more than one place, it's good practice to make changes in both places.

The `Explorer` branch in `HKLM` contains very different information. Here are some of its subkeys:

`Desktop\NameSpace`

Contains keys named with the CLSID of system folders that appear on the Desktop such as the Recycle Bin, Inbox, and Microsoft Network. Anything involving CLSIDs in the Registry is usually a maze of indirection.

`LastBackup`

Contains a value for each disk drive letter, with the data being the number of days since the last backup of that drive. The data is binary encoded; there's probably more than just the number of days in there, but that's what you see when you go to the *drive* → Properties → Tools tab. Similar keys exist for LastCheck (length of time since the last *scandisk*) and LastOptimize (length of time since the last *defrag*).

`mycomputer\NameSpace`

Contains a key named with the CLSID of Dial-Up Networking.

HKEY_USERS (HKU)

If there is only one user of a machine, `HKU` will contain only a branch labeled `.Default`. (Note the leading period.) If Profiles are enabled, there will be a second branch named after the currently logged-in user.

If it exists, the branch named after the currently logged-in user is mirrored to `HKEY_CURRENT_USER`; if not, the `.Default` branch is mirrored there.

Why is it that there are never more than two profiles contained here, even if there are multiple users? Basically, when you create a second username on the machine, the current contents of the Registry are written to a *user.dat* file in the directory

Windows\Profiles\username. That file contains as its `.Default` branch the user data as of the time the profile was created. This is copied verbatim to the second branch, named after that user. As the new user makes configuration changes, the two branches gradually diverge. The `.Default` branch remains an unchanged copy of the settings that were in effect when the user's profile was first created.

During system idle time, and when the user logs out, any changes are written back to the *Windows\Profiles\username\user.dat* file.

This process is repeated for each user who logs in to the machine. When they log back in, only their own *user.dat* file is loaded, which is why multiple users don't show up in the active Registry.

This design prevents one user from easily viewing or changing another user's settings.

HKEY_CURRENT_CONFIG (HKCC)

As noted earlier, HKCC is mirrored from the `HKLM\Config\`*000x* key, where *000x* is the name of the current hardware profile. If hardware profiles are not enabled, the source will be `HKLM\Config\0001`.

HKEY_DYN_DATA (HKDD)

HKDD contains two main branches: `Config Manager` and `PerfStats`.

`Config Manager\Enum` reflects the hardware devices for which drivers are actually loaded in memory. The HardWareKey value points to the corresponding path for each entry in `HKLM\enum`.

`PerfStats` contains pointers to the routines that gather the source data for the statistics displayed by the System Monitor (`sysmon`).

Backing Up the Registry

In Windows 95, the Registry was backed up each time you started your computer by simply copying the existing *.dat* files and renaming the copies with the extension *.da0*. Windows 98 has done away with all that.

Windows 98 includes a new utility named Registry Checker (*scanregw.exe*—see "Registry Checker" in Chapter 6 for details on using it as a stand-alone utility), which scans the Registry for inconsistencies and can restore the Registry from a known good backup. Should the restore attempt fail (or should a backup be unavailable), *scanregw* can also attempt to repair the Registry.

scanregw runs automatically each time Windows 98 starts. If no problem is found on the first time it runs during a given day, a backup of the Registry is made. These backups actually include the *User.dat* and *System.dat* files, as well as the *Win.ini* and *System.ini* configuration files. Backups are stored as *.cab* files in the *Windows\sysbckup* folder. Backups are given the name *Rbxxx.cab*, where *xxx* is a unique number assigned by *scanreg*. Five good backups are maintained at any given time. When a sixth backup is formed, the earliest existing backup is deleted.

If you are thinking of messing around with the Registry, you can use Registry Checker yourself to back up the system files using Start → Run → scanregw. Even if the Registry has already been scanned and backed up that day, you will be given the chance to back it up again.

Here's the procedure to follow if you think you've screwed up your Registry and want to get back to the last known good version:

1. Click Start → Shut Down

2. Click Restart in MS-DOS mode → Yes

3. Type the following at the DOS prompt:

    C:\>scanreg /restore Rbxxx.cab

4. Restart your computer

Of course, this procedure assumes that you haven't already restarted your computer since you made the damaging changes to your Registry.

In addition, the file \System.1st contains the contents of HKLM immediately after your system was first installed. It's not much of a backup, since it is probably fairly out of date. But it may be better than nothing if you have lost everything.

If you're planning to do any serious Registry hacking, you may want to create additional backups. Simply copy the appropriate .cab files before making any major changes.

You can also export the branch of the Registry you're working on (see "Exporting and Importing Registry Keys" later in this chapter for details), and reimport it, overwriting your changes if you don't like what you've done. This is probably the simplest form of backup if you are making only small changes.

Editing the Registry

As we've suggested earlier, editing the Registry with *regedit* is fairly simple.

To create a new key or value, use Edit → New. The key or value is created within the currently selected key. A new string value will have the null string as its value; a new binary value will show the following message in parentheses: (zero length binary value). A new DWORD value will show up as zero: 0x00000000 (0). You can then edit that value (see following description) to change it.

To delete a key or value, select it and click Edit → Delete, or simply press the Del key. But be warned, there's no undelete, so you might want to first write out the branch containing the key you're about to delete as a .reg file (see following instructions). Or you can simply use Edit → Rename to rename the key. This disables it while preserving its data. (A key in the Registry that no program looks for does take up space, but otherwise has no effect.)

To edit a value, select it by clicking on the icon beside its name, and then choose Edit → Modify. Or just double-click on the icon. Enter the new value. Within the edit dialog box, you can select data, copy and paste in the normal way, dragging the cursor over data to select it, and using the Ctrl-C, Ctrl-X, and Ctrl-V keyboard accelerators to copy, cut, and paste.

These selection and copying techniques don't work for key names or other information on the left (navigation) pane in *regedit*. However, there's a Copy Key Name
command on the Edit menu. This simply copies the full path to the key to the
Clipboard. It doesn't copy the contents of the key. It's useful mainly for documentation purposes, since you can paste the key name into an external text file. (You
can also paste it into *regedit*'s Find dialog box using Ctrl-V, even though there
isn't a Paste command on the Edit menu. Of course, if you're already at the key,
why search for it? I suppose you could edit down the path to the terminal component, and then look for other keys with the same name. This is handy if you're
looking for other instances of a complex name like a CLSID key.)

If you want to copy an existing value, double-click on it and select all of the data
in the edit window, as shown in Figure 13-6.

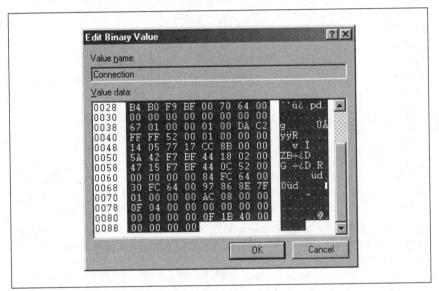

Figure 13-6: Copying an existing Registry value

Ctrl-C will copy the data to the clipboard. Then create a new value, being sure
to match the type (string, binary, or DWORD) of the original value. Double-click
on the new value to edit it. Use Ctrl-V to paste the copied data into the edit
window.

This is a handy thing to do not only when using an existing value as a template
for a new value, but also whenever you're going to make changes to an existing
value. You can make little "inline backups" by creating a new value (*whatever.
bak*, for instance) and pasting in the old value data before you change it. This
might seem a little tedious, but it might prevent future headaches if you're about
to change a complex value whose format you aren't completely sure you
understand.

To copy a value name to the Clipboard, you can use a similar workaround. Ctrl-C won't work in the normal *regedit* window, but if you select Edit → Rename (or press F2), you can copy the name from there.

Unfortunately, there's no easy way to copy a key and all of its contents within *regedit*. If you want to copy an entire key and all its values, you'll have to do it one value at a time. It's usually much easier to export the key, edit the resulting file with a text editor, and then import the edited file. (See "Exporting and Importing Registry Keys" later in this chapter.)

In addition to the Edit menu, you may find it handy to use *regedit*'s context menus. Right-clicking on a key in the left pane gives a context menu with Expand or Collapse, New, Find, Delete, Rename, and Copy Key Name. (Expand opens a Registry key with subkeys. It will be grayed out if there are no subkeys below the selected key. If the branch is already expanded, the first item on the menu will be Collapse instead of Expand.)

Right-clicking with a value selected in the right pane gives a context menu with Modify, Delete, and Rename. Right-clicking in the right pane with no value selected gives a context menu with New (to create a new string, binary or DWORD value). You can also get to the New menu by pressing Shift-F10.

Exporting and Importing Registry Keys

You can export an ASCII copy of the entire Registry or any branch. Highlight the key you want to export and select Registry → Export. You'll get the standard Save As box. The selected key, any subkeys, and all their data will be saved in a file with the *.reg* extension. You probably don't want to select My Computer to export the entire Registry, since HKDD is huge and can't be reimported in any case.

Exporting Registry files is a great idea. They are saved in text format, and they are generally easier to search, examine, and edit with your favorite text editor (especially if you have a powerful one) than with *regedit*.

 Before making any changes to a Registry key, do a quick backup by exporting the key. Depending on what changes you've made, the Registry might not be identical after reimporting the key (see later explanation), but at least you'll have a record of what the key looked like before the changes.

Importing *.reg* files is more dangerous. The contents are merged into the Registry, overwriting the current contents. Especially if you've gone at the exported file with a text editor, which does less to ensure data integrity than *regedit*, you could potentially cause major harm. Note that the imported file is merged into the current Registry, not copied over it. This means that modified keys and values replace their equivalents, and new keys and values are added, but old keys that don't have a corresponding value in the saved *.reg* file are not deleted.

So, for example, if you export a branch, delete a few keys from the *.reg* file, and then import the file, the Registry will be unchanged. (Your deletions will not be imported.) On the other hand, if you delete keys in *regedit*, then change your mind and import a *.reg* file you created before the deletions, the original keys will be restored.

Stop! Do Not Double-Click on This File!

The default value for double-clicking on a *.reg* file is not to edit the file, as you might expect, but to merge it into the Registry. One welcome change in Win 98 is that when you double-click a *.reg* file, a warning pops up asking if you're sure you want to merge the file into the Registry. In Windows 95, it was automatically and silently imported. Nonetheless, even in Windows 98 this is a dangerous association, and one you should consider changing if you plan to work with *.reg* files. Before you do your first export, go to any folder's View → Options → File Types dialog box as described in Chapter 4, and edit the association for Registration Entries. Highlight the Edit verb and click Set Default, so that Edit rather than Merge will be the default action for files with the *.reg* extension. If you have a favorite text editor, you might want to edit the Edit verb as well, so that it points to your text editor rather than to Notepad.

You can also import and export Registry branches from the command line using the command-line options to *regedit* documented in Chapter 7, *DOS and Other Command-Line Utilities*.

The format of data values in *.reg* files is nothing like the way they are shown in *regedit*. The key name is printed first, enclosed in brackets. This is followed by a list of values for that key.

If set, the (`Default`) value shows up as `@="somevalue"`; if not set, it is omitted. Binary values are shown prefixed with the keyword `hex:`, and backslashes (for filenames in data values) are doubled to distinguish them from the backslashes in key names. In addition, the file opens with the string `REGEDIT4`, followed by two carriage-return/linefeed pairs. This header must be preserved if you want to re-import the *.reg* file.

Here are the contents of a sample key from a Win 98 system:

```
REGEDIT4

[HKEY_LOCAL_MACHINE\SOFTWARE\Microsoft\Windows\CurrentVersion]
"InstallType"=hex:03,00
"SetupFlags"=hex:04,01,00,00
"DevicePath"="C:\\WINDOWS\\INF"
"ProductType"="9"
"LicensingInfo"=""
"SubVersionNumber"=" B"
"InventoryPath"="C:\\WINDOWS\\SYSTEM\\PRODINV.DLL"
"ProgramFilesDir"="C:\\Program Files"
"CommonFilesDir"="C:\\Program Files\\Common Files"
```

```
"MediaPath"="C:\\WINDOWS\\media"
"ConfigPath"="C:\\WINDOWS\\config"
"SystemRoot"="C:\\WINDOWS"
"OldWinDir"="C:\\WINDOWS"
"ProductName"="Microsoft Windows 98"
"FirstInstallDateTime"=hex:e1,73,4a,22
"Version"="Windows 98"
"VersionNumber"="4.00.1111"
"PiFirstTimeOnly"="1"
"AuditMode"=hex:00,00,00,00
"OtherDevicePath"="C:\\WINDOWS\\INF\\OTHER"
"BootCount"="3"
"RegisteredOwner"="user"
"RegisteredOrganization"=""
"ProductId"="11197-OEM-0021533-28231"
```

Ten Cool Things You Can Do in Your Registry

Armed with your new understanding of the Windows 98 Registry, you're no doubt ready to get in there and start exploring. Hopefully, this chapter has provided the "lay of the land" you need to get and keep your bearings in the often-confusing wilderness of the Registry. While we don't have the kind of room in this book it takes to make you an expert, we would like to send you on your way by pointing out some interesting landmarks—ten cool changes you can make in your own Registry.

1. Making IE's AutoComplete more efficient.

   In IE4, you can enter an incomplete URL (i.e., *oreilly* instead of *www.oreilly. com*) and IE will attempt to complete the address itself. However, IE only searches using the *.com*, *.edu*, and *.org* top-level domains by default. To add new domains, go to:

   `HKLM\SOFTWARE\Microsoft\Internet Explorer\Main\UrlTemplate`

   You find two entries for each of the registered domains. For *.com*, for example, one entry takes the form `www.%s.com` and the other `%s.com`. Just add two entries using this format for any top-level domain (such as *.net*) that you'd like to add.

2. Change your default search engine.

   When you launch Start → Find → On the Internet or click the Search button in IE, you are taken to *http://home.microsoft.com/access/allinone.asp* as your default search page. You can change this using:

   `HKCU\Software\Microsoft\Internet Explorer\Main key`

   Edit the SearchPage value to include the URL of the search engine you want.

3. Get rid of Start → Documents.

   Start → Documents contains a list of your most recently run documents. Control Panel → TweakUI → Paranoia lets you set Win 98 to automatically clear the Documents folder each time you start Windows, but you can easily get rid of it altogether using the Registry. Just go to:

   `HKCU\Software\Microsoft\Windows\CurrentVersion\Policies\Explorer`

Choose Edit → New → Binary Value. For the value name, enter NoRecentDocsHistory. For the value data, enter 01000000. Follow this same procedure to add a NoRecentDocsHistory value. Once you restart Windows, no more Documents menu! To reverse the procedure, just remove the values or change their data to 00000000.

4. Get rid of Start → Favorites.

Windows 98 adds your Favorites folder to the Start menu. If you'd rather it wasn't there, just go to:

HKCU\Software\Microsoft\Windows\CurrentVersion\Policies\Explorer

Add a new Binary value named NoFavoritesMenu with the data 01000000. Restart Windows and the Favorites menu will be gone. To reverse it, just remove the entry or change the data to 00000000.

5. Disable the Shut Down command.

If you're running a kiosk or demo system (or if you just don't want people shutting down your machine), you can disable the ShutDown command by going to:

HKCU\Software\Microsoft\Windows\CurrentVersion\Policies\Explorer

Modify the NoClose value data to 1. If the entry isn't there, add it as a new string value. The Shut Down command will still be visible; it just won't work.

6. Change the size of your desktop icons.

Control Panel → Display → Effects lets you switch between using large and normal size icons, but that's all the control it gives you. You can take a little more control using the Registry. Just go to:

HKCU\Control Panel\Desktop\WindowMetrics

Note that the Shell Icon Size value defaults to 32 (pixels). Change the value's data to your desired pixel size. You may need to refresh your desktop to see a change. If the Shell Icon Size value isn't there, just create it as a new string value. You can change the icon size between the range of 16 to 72 pixels by selecting the icon item in the Display → Appearance tab.

7. Change the registered user and company names for Win 98.

When Win 98 is installed, a user and company name are entered. Unfortunately, there is no convenient way to change this information after installation. However, you can do so in the Registry. Just go to:

HKLM\Software\Microsoft\Windows\CurrentVersion

The values you are looking for are RegisteredOrganization and RegisteredOwner. Change them to whatever you'd like.

8. Change your default installation path.

When you install Windows 98, the path to your installation files is set in the Registry. Unfortunately, it is not updated if you point it to a different file source or when drive letters change. To change the default setup path, go to:

HKLM\Software\Microsoft\Windows\CurrentVersion\Setup

Change the SourcePath value to the new path.

9. Try something new with My Computer.

Would you believe you can actually make the My Computer icon do something different when you double-click it? You can if you're willing to delve into the Registry a bit. This example causes My Computer to launch Windows Explorer instead of just opening the My Computer folder. First, go to:

`HKCR\CLSID\{20D04FE0-3AEA-1069-A2D8-08002B30309D}`

Right-click on the shell subkey and create a new key named open. Inside the new open key, create a new key named command. For the default value of that new command key, change the data for the Default value to "*explorer. exe*" (or the path of anything else you'd like to run). Close *regedit*, refresh the desktop, and try it out.

10. Permanently remove some of the System Tray icons.

In Chapter 12, *Windows Startup*, we mention how to disable System Tray icons using *msconfig.exe*. These are usually created from third-party programs, since many of the Win 98 icons can be toggled on and off from Control Panel applets. If you are interested in preventing the services that create the icons from automatically launching on startup, go to:

`HKLM\Software\Microsoft\Windows\CurrentVersion\RunServices`

Select the appropriate value and delete it. Note: this disables the entire service, not just the tray icon.

PART IV

Appendixes

APPENDIX A

Keyboard Accelerators

This appendix lists many useful keyboard accelerators. The listings are organized both by type (alphabetically within groups such as function key, Alt-key combination, and so forth) and then by function or context (during startup, in the Recycle Bin, for managing windows, and so forth). The first section lists the key, and then the function. The second section lists the desired function, and then the required key(s).

Note that in addition to the standard keyboard accelerators, you can define additional accelerators of your own. For example, you can define a Ctrl-Alt combination to invoke any shortcut, whether it's on the Desktop, in the Start menu, or in any other folder. On the property sheet for any shortcut, go to the Shortcut tab, and in the Shortcut key field, hold down Ctrl, Alt, or both Ctrl and Alt, and then enter the additional key you'd like to have invoke this shortcut. You can use any key except Esc, Enter, Tab, the spacebar, PrintScreen, BackSpace, or Delete. If it conflicts with an accelerator used by any existing application, the accelerator you've just defined will override the existing accelerator. To clear an existing shortcut's accelerator, just go to the field on the property page and press Ctrl or Alt again, with no following key.

Keyboard Accelerators Listed by Key

Function keys have special meanings while Windows 98 is starting up. See Table A-1 later in this appendix for details. In addition, there may be hardware-specific functions, often activated on laptops by pressing the Fn key plus a numbered function key. For example, on most laptops, pressing Fn-F7 will toggle between the built-in screen and an external monitor. Note that the following accelerators work in the Explorer and most of the applets that come with Windows. However, some applications don't always follow the rules.

In addition, Alt can be used to generate non-ASCII characters in fonts such as Wingdings. Open the Character Map (*charmap.exe*) and select any cell to see its

Alt-key combination down in the status bar. While you can then simply select a non-keyboard character to be pasted into another application, it's quicker to hold Alt and type the four-digit ASCII code with the numeric keypad; example: Alt-0169 for the copyright symbol. This will of course produce the requisite character only in applications that have the ability to display different fonts, such as Notepad.

Table A-1: Function Keys

Key	Action
F1	Start Help.
F2	Rename selected item.
F3	Find files or folders.
F4	Open a drop-down list.
F5	Refresh Desktop, explorer, or folder view.
F6	Move focus between panes in Explorer.
F10	Select first item on menubar.

Table A-2: Miscellaneous Keys

Key	Action
Arrow keys	Move through a drop-down menu, extend selection, and so on.
Backspace	Move up one level in folder hierarchy.
Delete	Delete selected item(s) or selected text.
End	Go to end of line (in Word, Notepad, etc.), or end of file list.
Enter	Activate highlighted choice in menu or dialog box.
Esc	Close dialog box or menu without activating any choice, goes up one level in menus.
Home	Go to beginning of line (in Word, Notepad, etc.), or beginning of file list.
Page Down	Scroll down one screen.
Page Up	Scroll up one screen.
PrintScrn	Copy entire display as a bitmap to Clipboard.
Spacebar	Toggle a choice that is selected in a dialog box, or activate a command button.
Tab	Move focus to next control in a dialog box or window.

Table A-3: Alt Keys

Key(s)	Action
Alt	Select first item on menubar of current window. Press again to deselect.
Alt-*x*	Activate menu or menu item where letter *x* is underlined. Some of the more interesting combinations are summarized later in this appendix.

Table A-3: Alt Keys (continued)

Key(s)	Action
Alt-double-click (on icon)	Display Properties sheet.
Alt-down arrow	Drop down a drop-down list.
Alt-Enter	Display Properties sheet for selected icon. Switch DOS application between window and full screen.
Alt-Esc	Drop active window to bottom of pile, which, in effect, activates next open window.
Alt-F4	Close current window; if Taskbar or Desktop has the focus, exit Windows.
Alt-hyphen	Pull down document's system control menu in an MDI application.
Alt-PrintScrn	Copy active window as a bitmap to Clipboard.
Alt-Shift-Tab	Same as Alt-Tab, but in the opposite direction.
Alt-spacebar	Pull down system control menu for a window.
Alt-Tab{+Tab}	Switch to next running application via Task Manager—hold Shift while pressing Tab to cycle through running apps.
Alt-M	When focus is on taskbar or desktop, minimizes all windows and moves focus to desktop.
Alt-S	Bring up Start menu (if focus is on the Desktop).

Table A-4: Ctrl Keys

Keys	Action
Ctrl-A	Select All.
Ctrl-Alt-x	User-defined accelerator for a shortcut, where x is any key.
Ctrl-Alt-Del	Close a wedged program, or reboot from DOS mode.
Ctrl-arrow key	Scroll without moving selection.
Ctrl-C	Copy to Clipboard. Interrupt a DOS program.
Ctrl-click	Used to select non-contiguous items.
Ctrl-drag	Copy a file.
Ctrl-End	Move to end of a document (in Word, Notepad, etc.). Skip to the end of an auto-completed URL in IE.
Ctrl-Esc	Bring up Start menu. If Explorer is not running, bring up Task Manager.
Ctrl-Esc Esc Tab	Move focus to Taskbar.
Ctrl-Esc Esc Tab Tab	Move focus to Desktop.
Ctrl-F4	Close a document window in an MDI application.
Ctrl-F6	Same as Ctrl-Tab.
Ctrl-G	In Explorer, Go To.
Ctrl-Home	Move to start of document (in Word, Notepad, etc.).

Table A-4: Ctrl Keys (continued)

Keys	Action
Ctrl-Shift-drag	Display right-drag context menu without having to use right mouse button.
Ctrl-Tab	Tab through dialog pages or multiple document windows in same application. In Word, you must use Ctrl-F6 instead.
Ctrl-Shift-Tab	Same as Ctrl-Tab, but in reverse.
Ctrl-V	Paste contents of Clipboard.
Ctrl-X	Cut to Clipboard.
Ctrl-Z	Undo text just entered, or undo last file operation in Explorer. Insert an End of File when using *copy con* in DOS.

Table A-5: Shift Keys

Key(s)	Action
Shift	While inserting CD, hold to disable autoplay.
Shift-click	Select all items between first selected item and item on which you're clicking.
Shift-click on Close	Close current folder and all parent folders.
Shift-Del	Delete a file without putting in Recycle Bin.
Shift-double-click	Open folder in two-pane Explorer view.
Shift-Tab	Same as Tab, but in reverse order.

Table A-6: Logo Key (WIN) on Win95 Keyboards

Key(s)	Action
WIN	Display Start Menu.
WIN-F1	Start Windows Help.
WIN-Tab	Cycle through taskbar buttons.
WIN-E	Start Windows Explorer.
WIN-F	Find Files or Folders.
WIN-CTRL-F	Find Computer.
WIN-M	Minimize all windows and move focus to desktop.
Shift-WIN-M	Undo minimize all.
WIN-R	Display Run dialog.
WIN-Break	Display System Properties dialog.

Startup Mode Keys

Table A-7 lists special key combinations that work while Windows is booting—while the message "Starting Windows 98" is displayed, but before the splash screen is shown.

Table A-7: Startup Mode Keys

Key(s)	Action
F4	Boot into DOS instead of Windows 98.
F5	Start Windows 98 in Safe mode. Bypass *autoexec.bat* and *config.sys*, use VGA driver only for the screen, and do not load networking software.
Ctrl-F5	Start DOS without compressed drives.
Shift-F5	Start DOS in Real mode (loaded in conventional memory), without executing *autoexec.bat* or *config.sys*.
F8	Open startup menu (see Chapter 12, *Windows Startup*).
Shift-F8	Go through *config.sys* and *autoexec.bat* one line at a time, with confirmation before executing each command.

Doskey Accelerators

Table A-8 lists keystrokes that work when *doskey.exe* has been enabled in a DOS window.

Table A-8: Doskey Accelerators

Key(s)	Action
Left/Right arrow	Move cursor back/forward one character.
Ctrl + Left/Right arrow	Move cursor back/forward one word.
Home/End	Move cursor to beginning/end of line.
Up/Down arrow	Scroll up (and back) through list of stored commands. Each press of the "up" key recalls the previous command and displays it on the command line.
Page Up/Down	Recall oldest/most recent command in buffer.
Insert	Insert text at cursor.
Delete	Delete text at cursor.
F1	Copy next character from template to command line. This works with/without *doskey*.
F2 + *key*	Copy text from template up to (but not including) *key*.
F3	Copy template from present character position to command line. This works with/without *doskey*.
F4 + *key*	Delete characters from present position up to (but not including) *key*.
F5	Copy current command to template and clear command line.
F6	Place an end-of-file character (^Z) at current position of command line.

Key(s)	Action
F7	Display a numbered list of command history.
Alt-F7	Delete all commands stored in buffer.
chars + F8	Entering one or more characters *chars* followed by F8 will display the most recent command beginning with *chars*. Pressing F8 again will display the next most recent command beginning with *chars*, and so on. If no characters are specified, F8 simply cycles through existing commands in buffer.
F9 + *command#*	Display designated command on command line.
Alt-F10	Delete all macro definitions.

Keyboard Accelerators Listed by Function

The following keys operate in most contexts—i.e., on the Desktop, in the Explorer, and within most applications and dialogs. Functions are listed alphabetically, except where a logical order might make more sense.

Note also that many of the keystroke commands listed here are really just selections from the context menu or various window menus and dialog boxes, with navigation via keystrokes. The list is far from complete. For instance, Ctrl-Esc will bring up the Start menu, and Alt will take you to the menubar of the currently active window; thereafter, you can choose any item by typing a character sequence. And so Ctrl-Esc+S+C+R is really just another way of saying Start → Settings → Control Panel → Regional Settings, and Alt+F+O is another way of saying File → Open. Similarly, once you right-click on an item to get its context menu, you can pick from that menu by typing the underlined character. (Note that this is not always the first character of the menu item name.) So right-click+R is another way of saying context menu → Properties.

Table A-9: Miscellaneous

Action	Key(s)
Get help on selected item	F1
Bypass CD or CD-ROM autoplay	Shift while inserting disc
Cut selected item	Ctrl-X
Copy selected item	Ctrl-C
Jump to a Desktop, Explorer, or menu item	Type initial characters
Paste copied or cut item	Ctrl-V
Undo last command	Ctrl-Z

Table A-10: File Management

Action	Key(s)
Copy a file	Right-click drag file+C or hold Ctrl key with left-click drag
Create a shortcut	Ctrl-Shift drag file+S

Table A-10: File Management (continued)

Action	Key(s)
Create a shortcut	Right-click-drag an item+S
Delete an item to Recycle Bin	Drag to Recycle Bin, or press Del, or right-click+D
Delete an item with no undelete	Shift-Del, or Shift-right-click+D, or Shift-drag item to Recycle Bin
Find a file or folder	F3
Rename an item	F2
Undo any file operation	Right-click on Desktop+U
View an item's Properties sheet	Alt-Enter
View an item's Properties sheet	Alt-double-click

Table A-11: Menus

Action	Key(s)
Display menu for selected item	Shift-F10, or context menu key on Win 98 keyboard
Display Start menu	Ctrl-Esc, or Windows logo key on Win 98 keyboard
Display current window's system menu	Alt-spacebar
Display current document's system menu	Alt-hyphen
Select first item on menubar	F10 or Alt
Move through menu headings	Left arrow, right arrow
Activate menu item where letter x is underlined	Alt-x if menu doesn't have focus, x by itself if menu has focus
Drop down selected menu	Alt-down arrow or F4
Move through menu items	Up arrow, down arrow
Go up a level in menu	Esc
Cancel current selection on menu bar	Alt or F10

Table A-12: Dialog Box Navigation

Action	Key(s)
Move focus forward through dialog box options	Tab
Move focus backward through dialog box options	Shift-Tab
Move forward between tabbed pages	Ctrl-Tab
Move backward between tabbed pages	Ctrl-Shift-Tab
Activate an option with the letter x underlined	Alt-x

Table A-12: Dialog Box Navigation (continued)

Action	Key(s)
Open a drop-down list box	Alt-down arrow
Go to top of a list box	Home
Go to bottom of a list box	End
Move to item in list box starting with letter *x*	x
Select or deselect items in a checkbox or list box	Space
Select or deselect one item at a time in a list box	Space while navigating with Ctrl-up arrow or Ctrl-down arrow
Make noncontiguous selections from list box	Ctrl-left-click
Open Look In list (Open dialog box)	F4
Open Save In list (Save as dialog box)	F4
Go to parent folder	Backspace
Create a new folder	Right-click+W+F

Table A-13: Windows, Icons and Desktop Layout

Action	Key(s)
Turn on/off Toolbar in Explorer and some Windows applets	Alt-V+T
Cascade all windows	Right-click on Taskbar+S
Close current application window	Alt-F4
Close current document window	Ctrl-F4
Close parent folders	Shift-click on Close button
Close a taskbar	Right-click on taskbar+C
Cycle through open applications	Alt-Tab (hold Alt while pressing Tab)
Line up icons	Right-click on empty area of Desktop or Explorer +E
Minimize all windows	Right-click on Taskbar+M Windows logo key+M
Quit a program	Alt-F4
Switch to last window used	Alt-Tab or Ctrl-Esc
Switch to next document window	Ctrl-F6 or Ctrl-Tab
Tile all windows horizontally	Right-click on Taskbar+H
Tile all windows vertically	Right-click on Taskbar+V
Toggle maximized and windowed displays	Alt-spacebar, or right-click on titlebar
Turn on (or turn off) icon autoarrange	Right-click on empty area of Desktop or Explorer+I+A

Table A-14: Taskbar and Win 98 Toolbars

Action	Keys
Turn on or off Taskbar autohide	`Ctrl-Esc`, `Alt-Enter`, U, `Enter`
Remove clock from System Tray	`Ctrl-Esc`, `Alt-Enter`,+R+C, `Enter`
Auto hide taskbar	`Ctrl-Esc`, `Alt-Enter`, U, `Enter`
Reduce size of icons in Start menu	Ctrl-Esc, Alt-Enter,+R+S, Enter
Clear contents of Documents menu	Ctrl-Esc, Alt-Enter,+R, Ctrl-Tab+C, Enter
Add item to Start menu	Ctrl-Esc, Alt-Enter,+R, Ctrl-Tab+A+Alt-B, Enter
Make taskbar always on top	Ctrl-Esc, Alt-Enter, T, Enter
Show toolbar title	Right-click on toolbar, W
Show text for toolbar buttons	Right-click on toolbar, X

Table A-15: Start Menu

Action	Keys
Activate Start menu	`Ctrl-Esc`, Win95 logo key
Activate Start menu from Desktop	Alt-S
Add item to Start menu	Ctrl-Esc, Alt-Enter, Ctrl-Tab+A+ Alt-R
Remove item from Start menu	Right-click on Start menu+ O+P+`Enter`
Reduce size of icons in Start menu	Ctrl-Esc, Alt-Enter+S
Clear contents of Documents menu	Ctrl-Esc, Alt-Enter, Ctrl-Tab+C
Bring up Find utility	Right-click on Start button+F

Table A-16: Recycle Bin

Action	Keys
Empty Recycle Bin	Right-click+B
Cancel delete confirmation dialog box	Right-click+R+D
Reinstate delete confirmation dialog box	Right-click+R+D
Cancel undelete option for every deletion	Right-click+R+R

Table A-17: Explorer

Action	Key(s)
Open Explorer	Right-click on Start menu, My Computer, or any folder icon+E; Win95 logo key+E
Refresh a window	F5
Jump to a folder (two-pane explorer only)	Tab or F6 to activate tree, type its initial character(s)

Table A-17: Explorer (continued)

Action	Key(s)
Jump to a file	Tab or F6 to activate file list, type its initial character(s)
Undo	Ctrl-Z
Select all (file list only)	Ctrl-A
Move to parent folder (one level up)	Backspace
Close selected folder and its parents (folder windows only)	Shift-click on Close button
Rename selected item	F2
Find a file or folder	F3
Cut selected item	Ctrl-X
Copy selected item	Ctrl-C
Paste copied or cut item	Ctrl-V
Cancel copy/cut operation	Esc
Delete an item to Recycle Bin	Del, or right-click+D
Delete an item with no undelete	Shift-Del or Shift-right-click+D
View an item's Properties sheet	Alt-Enter, or Alt-double-click
Copy a file	Ctrl-drag file
Create a shortcut	Ctrl-shift-drag file, select "Create Shortcut here"
Switch between left and right panes	F6 or Tab
Expand current folder's subfolders	Tab or F6 to activate tree, * on numeric keypad
Expand selected folder	Tab or F6 to activate tree, + on numeric keypad
Collapse selected folder	Tab or F6 to activate tree, − on numeric keypad
Expand current selection	Right Arrow
Select first subfolder (if expanded)	Right Arrow
Collapse current selection	Left Arrow
Select parent folder (if collapsed)	Left Arrow
Change icon size to small	Alt-V+M, or right-click on empty area of file list+V+M
Change icon size to large	Alt-V+G, or right-click on empty area of file list +V+G
Change icon view to a list	Alt-V+L, or right-click on empty area of file list +V+L
Change icon view to a detailed list	Alt-V+D, or right-click on empty area of file list +V+D
Arrange icons in alphabetical order	Alt-V+I+N, or right-click on empty area of file list +I+N
Arrange icons by size	Alt-V+I+S, or right-click on empty area of file list +I+S

Table A-17: Explorer (continued)

Action	Key(s)
Arrange icons by type	Alt-V+I+T, or right-click on empty area of file list +I+T
Arrange icons by modification date	Alt-V+I+D, or right-click on empty area of file list +I+D
Line up icons	Alt-V+I+A, or right-click on empty area of file list +I+A
Add Toolbar to any Windows applet or folder	Alt-V+T
Activate Toolbar's List box	Tab or F4

APPENDIX B

Filename Extensions

This appendix lists many of the most common filename extensions that you'll find on your system or that you might download or have sent to you over the Internet.

Extensions were universally used on DOS and Windows 3.1 files, but Microsoft has gone to some difficulty to hide them in Windows 98. This is unfortunate, since they play a major role in the way Windows 98 decides what application will be used to open a file, as well as which files will be visible when opening files in a given application. While direct associations are made between some files without extensions and the applications needed to open them, in most cases, the association is between an extension and a Registry setting that tells the system what application to use.

If you double-click on an unknown file type, the Open With dialog box (see Chapter 4, *The Windows 98 User Interface*) appears, allowing you to make a new association. However, to change an association once it has been made, you need to go to View → Options → File Types on any folder.

We've tried to list the most common system extensions, but there are literally thousands of file formats used by third party applications. With the expansion of the Web, you may even find yourself trying to open files in formats native to other operating systems.

Some of these file types can be opened only if you have the appropriate application. However, especially with the growth of the Web, there are often viewers available that allow you to at least view the contents of the file, even if you can't change them. A good collection of viewers can be found at *http://www.winfiles. com/apps/98/graph-view.html*. The viewer download links are not always up to date, but you can often figure out an alternative by modifying the download address that shows up in the status bar of your browser. A good technique is to back up each element of the URL path until you find something recognizable. (For example, change *http://www.fineware.com/peeper32.zip* to *http://www.fineware. com.*) If the address is given as an *ftp* address, you can also change it into an equivalent *www* address and see what happens. (For example, change *ftp.jasc. com/somepath* into *www.jasc.com,* and start browsing till you find what you need.)

For more details on dealing with downloads and file formats found on the Net, see *Internet in a Nutshell,* by Valerie Quercia. For details on the internals of many graphics file formats, see *The Encyclopedia of Graphics File Formats* by James Murray and Bill van Ryper.

Note that file types can be registered with QuickView as well, and if so, a Quick View option will appear on the file's context menu.

Extension	Description
.386	Windows Virtual Device Driver.
.3gr	Screen grabber for MS-DOS applications.
.aam	MacroMedia Shockwave.
.acm	Audio Compression Manager Driver.
.adf	Admin config files.
.arc	Archive file (obsolete). Open with PKZip or WinZip, available from *http://www.winzip.com.*
.avi	Video clip. Open with *mplayer,* IE, or Navigator with plugin.
.bak	Backup file; used by many applications.
.bas	Visual Basic code module.
.bat	Batch File. Run with double-click, or type filename and optional arguments at command line. Edit with Notepad.
.bfc	Briefcase file. Left off of most system-created Briefcases (never visible).
.bmp	Windows bitmap. Open with MS Paint or many third-party graphics programs.
.c	C compiler source file.
.cab	Cabinet file. A compressed format used to store Windows files on the Win 98 CD in \ *Windows\Options,* and in \ *Windows\Sysbckup.*
.cdb	Clipboard file.
.cdf	Channel Definition Format file, used for dynamically updated regions of Active Desktop.
.cfg	Configuration file.
.chk	ScanDisk file.
.chm	Compiled HTML Help file.
.cis	CompuServe mail file.
.clp	Clipboard file.
.cls	Visual Basic class module.
.cnt	Help system table of contents file.
.com	MS-DOS command file. Run with double-click, or type filename and arguments.
.cpi	International Code Page information.

Extension	Description
.cpl	Control Panel applet. Normally stored in *Windows**System*. Double-click to open applet, or use *rundll32* command line. (See Chapter 5, *The Control Panel*, for details.)
.cpp	C++ compiler source file.
.cpx	Control Panel control file. Internal.
.csv	Comma-delimited text file.
.cur	Windows cursor file. Open with icon or cursor editor.
.dat	Data file. Used by several applications and system functions, notably the Registry (loaded from *system.dat* and *user.dat*). Not to be opened directly.
.dbf	dBase/FoxPro database file.
.dcr	MacroMedia Shockwave.
.dcx	FaxView document.
.dll	Dynamic Link Library. Internal, but can run with *rundll32*.
.doc	MS Word document.
.dos	MS-DOS file. May contain text. DOS versions of system files are important when setting up a dual boot with WinNT.
.dot	Microsoft Word template.
.drv	Device driver.
.dwg	AutoCad file.
.dxb	AutoCad database file.
.dxf	AutoCad drawing interchange file.
.eps	Encapsulated Postscript. Printable, or open with postscript viewer or publishing program.
.exe	Executable file. Run with double-click or type filename and arguments.
.faq	Frequently Asked Questions. Almost always a text file.
.fon	Bitmapped font file. Used by many applications, but viable with *fontview* or *charmap*. Normally stored in *Windows**System**Fonts*.
.fot	Font metric for TrueType font.
.fpx	Kodak FlashPix.
.frm	Visual Basic form file, Adobe FrameMaker document.
.fts	A full text search file. The find wizard prepares this database of searchable text on setup when using the Find tab in a Help file.
.fxd	Winfax file. Also *.fxr* and *.fxs*.
.g3	Group 3 fax file.
.gif	Graphics Interchange Format. A common image format, especially on the Web. Open with IE, Netscape Navigator, other web browser, or most graphics editing programs.
.gr3	Windows 3.0 screen grabber.
.gz	Gzip file.
.h	C programming header file.
.hlp	Help data file. Double-click or open with *winhlp32 filename*.

Extension	Description
.htm	Same as .html.
.html	HyperText Markup Language file, the base format of the World Wide Web. Open with IE, Netscape Navigator, or other web browser. Editable with any text editor.
.hqx	BinHex archive format (Macintosh).
.ico	Windows icon. Open with icon editor.
.inf	Setup information file. Edit with text editor. Sometimes used by right-clicking and selecting Install to set up drivers or shell extensions.
.ini	Configuration settings file. Edit with any text editor.
.jpg	Same as .jpeg (.jpg is more common).
.jpeg	Joint Photographics Expert Group format, an image file format widely used for high-resolution images. View with web browser or image editing program.
.kbd	Keyboard layout data.
.lgo	Windows logo driver.
.lib	Static-link library file.
.lnk	A Desktop shortcut. Double-click to open linked application or file, or type filename at command line. This extension can be viewed in the Properties sheet of a shortcut or in a DOS box.
.log	A log file. Created by many applications. Typically readable with any text editor.
.lst	Audio playlist, sometimes text file.
.lzh	LHArc compressed file (use WinZip).
.mak	C/C++ make file.
.mdb	Microsoft Access database.
.mid	MIDI Sequence.
.mif	MIDI Instrument File.
.mov	QuickTime movie. View with Apple QuickTime player, IE (with QuickTime ActiveX control), or Netscape with QuickTime plug-in.
.mpg	Motion Picture Experts Group video format (MPEG). Open with MPEG player or in IE/Netscape with plug-in.
.msc	Microsoft compressed archive.
.msg	CompuServe message file.
.msp	Microsoft Paint (obsolete).
.ocx	ActiveX Control (32-bit version of .vbx).
.nls	Natural Language Services driver.
.pcd	Kodak PhotoCD file. Open with most image editors.
.pcx	PC Paintbrush. Open with most graphics programs.
.pdf	Portable Document Format. A PostScript derivative viewable with Adobe Acrobat. Download viewer from http://www.adobe.com/prodindex/acrobat/readstep.html.
.pdx	Paradox database.

Filename Extensions

Extension	Description
.pif	PIF file. Shortcut to MS-DOS program; used to provide Windows context information for character-mode applications. Edit with Properties sheet of associated application. Extension invisible in Win 98.
.pj	HP PaintJet file.
.pot	PowerPoint template.
.ppd	PostScript Printer Description file.
.ppt	PowerPoint Presentation file.
.ps	PostScript output file. Printable. Edit with vector graphics program.
.pwl	Password list. Can clear data with *pwledit*.
.qt	QuickTime movie. Viewable by *mplayer*, Apple QuickTime player, web browser with QuickTime plug-in.
.ra	Real Audio data file. Read automatically when corresponding .*ram* file is launched.
.ram	Real Audio file. Can be listened to via web browser with Real Audio plug-in. *http://www.realaudio.com/*
.reg	Exported Registry patch file. Double-click to import data into the Registry, or type *regedit filename*. Can be viewed and edited with any text editor. Create with *regedit /e* or *regedit* → Registry → Export menu item.
.rle	Picture file, Run Length Encoded (compressed) format (obsolete).
.rtf	Rich Text Format file, exported by Microsoft Word. Load with *winword.exe /n*.
.scp	Dial-Up Networking script.
.scr	Screen Saver file. Run automatically if set up in Control Panel → Display; double-click on filename to run, or type *filename /s*. (Typing filename without */s* will open Control Panel applet.)
.shs	Scrap object.
.sig	Signature file. Appended to outgoing mail messages by many email programs. Usually editable with text editor.
.sit	Stuffit archive (Macintosh).
.spd	PostScript Printer Description file.
.spl	Shockwave Splash file. Also used as extension for temporary printer spool files in Win 98.
.swp	Swap file, used for virtual memory storage—no need to open or edit.
.sys	System configuration file.
.tar	A Unix archive format. Open with WinZip.
.tif	Tagged Image File Format. Open with graphics editing program. Also .*tiff*.
.tmp	Temporary file. Could be used by any program. Usually found in \ *Windows\Temp*.
.tsp	Windows Telephony Service Provider.

Extension	Description
.ttf	TrueType Font. Used by many applications. View with *fontview* or *charmap*.
.txt	Text file. Typically opened by default with Notepad by double clicking, or typing *notepad filename.txt* at command line. Can be imported into word processors and edited with any text editor.
.url	Internet shortcut (Universal Resource Locator). Edit with Properties sheet or in text editor.
.uu	UUencoded file. Open with WinZip.
.vbx	Visual Basic Custom Control (16-bit) File.
.vxd	Virtual device driver.
.wav	Waveform file. Contains sound data, including system sounds stored in *\Windows\System\Media*. Open with double-click or *sndrec32* filename.
.wdb	Microsoft Works database.
.wks	Lotus 1-2-3 worksheet. Also *.wk1* through *.wk4*.
.wlg	Dr. Watson log file.
.wll	Microsoft Word add-in.
.wmf	Windows MetaFile.
.wp	WordPerfect file. *.wp4*, *.wp5*, *.wp6* refer to WordPerfect versions.
.wpg	WordPerfect bitmap.
.wps	Microsoft Works text file.
.wpt	WordPerfect template.
.wri	WordPad file.
.xbm	X Window System bitmap (Unix). View with web browser.
.xlm	Excel macro file.
.xls	Excel worksheet.
.xlt	Excel template.
.xlw	Excel workspace.
.xwd	X Window System dump (Unix).
.z	Compressed Unix file. Open with WinZip.
.zip	Compressed archive file. Open with WinZip.

Filename
Extensions

APPENDIX C

System File and Directory Organization

The following directories and files play a significant role in Windows. The lists are not complete, but may be helpful in understanding where certain types of information are stored.

Note that the locations are generally accurate, but represent only the default values. For example, it is possible for Windows 98 to be installed in a directory other than \ *Windows*, and many of the locations are defined in the Registry. If you change a single Registry setting, Windows programs won't know where to look for these directories.

Dragging and dropping certain Windows folders in the Explorer will cause Windows to update automatically its location in the Registry. For example, if you drag *Desktop* from *C:\Windows* to *C:\Windows\Start Menu*, it will still work. Your Desktop items will also be accessible from the Start menu.

Also, these folders don't all need to be on the same disk—for example, your setup might include *D:\Windows* and *E:\Program Files*.

System Directories

Directory	Description
\	Root directory of the file system on any disk
\My Documents	A standard place for applications (especially MS Office) to save and open documents
\Program Files	Default installation directory for third-party and Microsoft applications
\Recycled	The Recycle Bin
\Windows	Core Windows 98 files and directories, .ini files, screen savers, and some components, such as Notepad

Directory	Description
\Windows\All Users	Desktop and start menu items visible to all users on a multi-user system
\Windows\Applications Data	User data saved by various applications, such as Outlook Express and Address Book
\Windows\Command	DOS command executables
\Windows\Config	general.idf, the MIDI instrument definition, is stored here
\Windows\Cookies	Temporary files placed on your hard disk by web sites you visit, so they can identify you on future visits (only if IE is installed)
\Windows\Cursors	Standard and optional mouse cursors
\Windows\Downloaded Programs	ActiveX Controls and Java applets downloaded by IE
\Windows\Desktop	Whatever files and folders appear on the Desktop
\Windows\Favorites	Internet Explorer sites you've asked to remember; applications such as Word use it to remember documents
\Windows\Fonts	System and application font files
\Windows\Help	System and application Help files
\Windows\History	Shortcuts to web pages you've recently visited
\Windows\Inf	Device driver installation and setup files
\Windows\Java	The Win32 Java Virtual Machine
\Windows\Media	Sound and video files; used by Control Panel → Sounds (can safely be deleted)
\Windows\Nethood	Pointers to systems in the Network Neighborhood
\Windows\Options	The .cab files from the Windows 98 CD-ROM. Allows Control Panel → Add/Remove Programs → Windows Setup to be run without a physical CD-ROM. (This is subject to OEM installation.)
\Windows\Samples\WSH	Sample scripts for Windows Script Host
\Windows\Recent	Shortcuts to recently opened files; this is the list that appears on Start → Documents
\Windows\Sendto	Shortcuts and folders here appear on the SendTo menu
\Windows\Shellnew	Templates for the Explorer to use when creating new files with Context Menu → New
\Windows\Spool\Fax	Storage area for temporary fax files (only when Exchange and Windows Fax Services are installed)
\Windows\Spool\Printers	Storage area for temporary printer files
\Windows\Start Menu	Shortcuts and folders here appear on the Start menu
\Windows\Start Menu\Programs	Shortcuts to programs that will appear in the Programs section of the Start menu

System Files & Directories

Directory	Description
\Windows\ Subscriptions	Links to web sites you have subscribed to
\Windows\Start Menu\Programs\ Startup	Shortcuts, programs, and batch files stored here will be run automatically every time Win 98 boots
\Windows\Sysbackup	Backup versions of system drivers and DLLs (hidden by default)—Windows will use these to replace important files that get overwritten
\Windows\System	Drivers, DLLs, OCXs, VxDs, CPL files, and other system files
\Windows\System\ Viewers	QuickView viewers (if installed)
\Windows\System\ Vmm32 and \Windows\System\ iosubsys	VxDs added after installation
\Windows\System\ Shellext	Any installed Shell Extensions
\Windows\Tasks	Tasks configured using Task Scheduler
\Windows\Temp	Scratch file area for Windows system and applications
\Windows\ Temporary Internet Files	IE cache files
\Windows\Web	Active Desktop configuration files

System Files

Chapter 12, *Windows Startup*, gives a degree of detail on some of the most important system configuration files. The following files may also be of interest.

File	Description
\command.com	The DOS command-line shell.
\io.sys	Essential system file for starting DOS and loading Windows (hidden).
\msdos.sys	Settings for loading Windows (hidden).
\autoexec.bat and \config.sys	Startup files for legacy support.
\Windows\win386.swp or \win386.swp or 386spart.par	The swap file, used for storing virtual memory data on disk. Make sure your swap file is on a partition with enough space to grow as needed, or performance will suffer (hidden).

Log Files

The following log files are found in the root directory of whatever disk is used to start up the system.

File	Description
\bootlog.txt	Log of Win 98 startup process
\detlog.txt	Hardware detection log
\scandisk.log	Log from the last time Scandisk was run
\setuplog.txt	Log of the setup process

Setup Files

File	Description
\Windows\msbatch.inf	Master setup information file (only seen sometimes when the system was set up by OEM).
\Windows\control.ini	Initialization file for control panel.
\Windows\hosts	Mapping of IP addresses to host names. Not required if DNS is running but can help with quick lookup. A sample file showing the format is found in \Windows\Hosts.sam.
\Windows\lmhosts	Mapping of IP addresses to NetBIOS host names. A sample file can be found in \Windows\LMhosts.sam.
\Windows\protocol.ini	Initialization file for some networking protocols.
\Windows\system.ini	Initialization file for Windows. Largely but not entirely superseded by the Registry.
\Windows\telephon.ini	Initialization information for modem dialing.
\Windows\win.ini	Initialization file for Windows. Largely but not entirely superseded by the Registry.

Registry

File	Description
\Windows\system.dat	System portion of Registry
\Windows\system.da0	Current backup of system portion of Registry
\system.1st	System portion of Registry first created by setup
\Windows\user.dat	User portion of Registry. May exist in \Windows\Profiles\<username>
\Windows\user.da0	Current backup of user portion of Registry. May exist in \Windows\Profiles\<username>
\Windows\user.man	If present, user cannot change Registry settings (rename to user.dat to make changeable again)

Other Files Worth Knowing

File	Description
\Windows\programs.txt	Release notes for third-party apps under Windows 98

File	Description
\Windows\readme.txt	Master *readme* file pointing to many subsidiary *readme* (release notes) files
\Windows\System*.cpl	Control Panel applets
\Windows*.scr and \Windows\System*.scr	Screen saver files

APPENDIX D

Special/Reserved Characters

The characters listed here have special meaning to the system (in certain contexts).

Character	Use
$	*prompt* command; *doskey* macros; also used internally (DOS device names, NetDDE shares)
%	Batch files; *for* command; shell command lines in Registry
>	DOS command-line output redirection; use >> rather than > to append to a file
<	DOS command-line input redirection
|	DOS pipe symbol
*	Used as a wildcard to represent any number of characters in a file-name
.	Separates a filename from its extension; can also be used as a directory name to indicate the current directory, parent directory, grand-parent, greatgrandparent (., .., ..., etc.) in *cd*, *md*, and *rd* commands and at the Run prompt
\	Directory paths; Registry key hierarchy; \\UNC names; also used as escape sequence in the Registry (e.g., \" for quotes and \\ for backslashes)
/	Command-line switches (options); a few programs use –
"	On command line to hold together long filenames (LFNs) containing spaces; used in *regedit* to surround string values
~	In 8.3 aliases for LFNs, but not a reserved character
:	Separates drive letter from path; also batch file label (target for *goto*)
?	As a wildcard to represent a single character
=	Set environment variables in *config.sys* settings
;	Separate parts of *path*; also as comment in *config.sys* and **.ini* files

Index

SessionManager key (HKLM\System
  \Control), 555
set command, 379
Set statement (VBScript), 463
set var= statement (config.sys), 524
SetDefaultPrinter method (Network),
  481
settings (see configuring/customizing)
Settings dialog box (Mouse), 117
Settings tab
  Disk Cleanup, 191
  Display control panel, 128–130
  Scheduled Tasks, 86
setup.exe, 380
setver.exe driver, 526, 532
sfc.exe, 274–276
ShareName property (Drive), 483
shares (network), 478–481
sharing
  directories, viewing users, 236
  folders across network, 74
  Internet connections, 142–146
  memory over network (netdde.exe),
    496
  printers (see printers/printing,
    sharing printers)
  programs with NetMeeting, 232
  server clocks, 360
sharing Internet connections, 31
Shell keys (HKCR), 547
Shell object (WSH), 473–477
shell= statement (config.sys), 524
ShellEx keys (HKCR), 547
ShellFolders key (Software\Explorer),
  558
ShellNew keys (HKCR), 548
shift command, 507
Shift key
  accelerators, 572
  clicking and, 6, 7
  Shift-Tab to move focus, 13
  when booting, 98
short filenames, 22–23
Shortcut key (shortcut property), 90
Shortcut object (WSH), 476
shortcuts, 8, 88–94
  adding to Start menu, 96, 101
  creating with WSH Shell object, 475
  invalid, checking for, 400

keyboard (see keyboard accelerators)
  to programs, 89
  properties of, 78, 89–91
  recently opening files, 97
  running batch files from, 496
  as System Tray icons, 410
ShortName property (File), 485
ShortName property (Folder), 484
ShortPath property (File), 485
ShortPath property (Folder), 484
Show Clock (Taskbar property), 101
Show Multiple Schedules option, 86
ShowSounds utility, 116
shutting down, 25, 95, 509
Signature Checking feature, 270
Signature Verification Tool, 270
signatures, email, 252
sigverif.exe, 270
size
  Active Desktop items, 441
  file size, finding files by, 68
  filename length, 22–23
  folder contents icons, 17
  Taskbar buttons, 100
Size property (File), 485
Size property (Folder), 484
sliders, 11
sndrec32.exe, 166, 272, 284
sndvol32.exe, 283–285
SNMP Agent, 412
Socket Status tab (PCMCIA), 160
Software Environment category
  (msinfo32), 277
Software key (HKCU), 550, 555–558
SOFTWARE key (HKLM), 554–558
software vendor information, 550
sol.exe game (Solitaire), 270
solitaire card games
  freecell.exe (Freecell), 199
  mshearts.exe (Hearts), 208
  sol.exe (Solitaire), 270
sorting email messages, 246
sorting text input (sort.exe), 383
Sound Recorder (sndrec32.exe), 166,
  272, 284
Sounds control panel, 165–167
Sounds tab (Accessibility Options), 116
SoundSentry utility, 116
speaker control, 283

About the Authors

Tim O'Reilly is founder and president of O'Reilly & Associates. In addition to running the company, he has written numerous books on computer topics, most notably *UNIX Text Processing* (with Dale Dougherty; Howard Sams, 1987), *Managing UUCP and USENET* (with Grace Todino), *The X Window System Users' Guide* (with Valerie Quercia), and *The X Toolkit Intrinsics Programming Manual* (with Adrian Nye). As an editor, he has also had a hand in the development of many of the company's other titles. Tim also conceived the award-winning series of travel books published by O'Reilly affiliate Travelers' Tales. Tim graduated from Harvard College in 1975 with a B.A. cum laude in classics. His honors thesis explored the tension between mysticism and logic in Plato's dialogues.

Troy Mott is Managing Editor for O'Reilly & Associates. He coauthored *Windows 95 in a Nutshell* and is currently developing a line of books for intermediate to advanced users. He has B.A in English from California Polytechnic University and an M.A. from Sonoma State University. In his spare time he enjoys writing fiction and is an avid moviegoer.

Walter Glenn is a freelance consultant, writer, and editor in Huntsville, Alabama. He has been working in the computer industry for 14 years and provides solutions for small- to medium-sized businesses. Walter is a Microsoft Certified Systems Engineer and Trainer and specializes in Internet and networking technologies. He also holds bachelor's degrees in literature and biology from the University of Alabama in Huntsville.

Colophon

Our look is the result of reader comments, our own experimentation, and feedback from distribution channels. Distinctive covers complement our distinctive approach to technical topics, breathing personality and life into potentially dry subjects.

The animal appearing on the cover of *Windows 98 in a Nutshell* is a Reinwardt's gliding frog (order *Salientia*). There are more than 2600 species of frog and toad, all easily distinguishable as members of this order. Frogs differ generally from toads in that they jump (toads tend to walk), are more dependent on access to water, and are slimy (as opposed to dry and warty).

Frogs range in size from less than half an inch to almost a foot in length (plus leg length). Despite their dependence on environmental conditions, frogs live in many different surroundings, including water, semi-deserts, and mountains. The only conditions in which they cannot exist are salt water and the iciest and driest frontiers. Frogs undergo a metamorphosis from swimming tadpole larvae to adult form; tadpoles are more subject to predation than are adults. Adult frogs rely on various methods of defense, including flight, poison, and many patterns and colors of camouflage.

Frogs breathe and absorb water through their skin, which is periodically shed. Most are nocturnal or twilight animals, and rely more on their sense of vision and smell than hearing. Many species hibernate through the winter months. Almost all male frogs produce a noise amplified by vocal sacs on the floor of the mouth. Females are frequently somewhat larger than the male, but have a more limited and quieter repertoire of calls. Despite fairy tale claims, it has not yet been proven that frog-kissing produces princes.

A group of frogs is called an *army*. The worldwide frog population has for some years been declining at unprecedented rates, causing speculation about the overall health of the biosystems from which they are disappearing.

Ellie Fountain Maden was the production editor and copyeditor for *Windows 98 in a Nutshell*; Sheryl Avruch was the production manager; John Files proofread the book, and Nancy Kotary, Abby Myers, and Jane Ellin provided quality control. Mike Sierra provided FrameMaker technical support. Seth Maislin wrote the index.

Edie Freedman designed the cover of this book, using a 19th-century engraving from the Dover Pictorial Archive. The cover layout was produced by Kathleen Wilson with Quark XPress 3.32 using the ITC Garamond font.

The inside layout was designed by Alicia Cech, based on a series design by Nancy Priest, and implemented in FrameMaker 5.0 by Mike Sierra. The text and heading fonts are ITC Garamond Light and Garamond Book. The illustrations that appear in the book were produced by Robert Romano and Rhon Porter using Macromedia FreeHand 8 and Adobe Photoshop 5. This colophon was written by Nancy Kotary.

Eliminating Annoyances

Windows Annoyances

By David A. Karp
1st Edition June 1997
300 pages, ISBN 1-56592-266-2

Windows Annoyances is a comprehensive, detailed resource for all intermediate to advanced users of Windows 95 and NT version 4.0. This book shows step-by-step how to customize the Win95/NT operating systems through an extensive collection of tips, tricks, and workarounds. Covers **Registry**, **Plug and Play**, networking, security, multiple-user settings, and third-party software.

Word 97 Annoyances

By Woody Leonhard, Lee Hudspeth & T.J. Lee
1st Edition August 1997
356 pages, ISBN 1-56592-308-1

Word 97 contains hundreds of annoying idiosyncrasies that can be either eliminated or worked around. *Word 97 Annoyances* takes an in-depth look at what makes Word 97 tick and shows you how to transform this software into a powerful, customized tool.

Outlook Annoyances

By Woody Leonhard, Lee Hudspeth & T. J. Lee
1st Edition June 1998
400 pages, ISBN 1-56592-384-7

Like the other Microsoft Office-related titles in the Annoyances series, this book points out and conquers the annoying features of Microsoft Outlook, the personal information management software included with Office. It is the definitive guide for those who want to take full advantage of Outlook and transform it into the useful tool that it was intended to be.

Excel 97 Annoyances

By Woody Leonhard, Lee Hudspeth & T.J. Lee
1st Edition September 1997
336 pages, ISBN 1-56592-309-X

Excel 97 Annoyances uncovers Excel 97's hard-to-find features and tells how to eliminate the annoyances of data analysis. It shows how to easily retrieve data from the Web, details step-by-step construction of a perfect toolbar, includes tips for working around the most annoying gotchas of auditing, and shows how to use VBA to control Excel in powerful ways.

Office 97 Annoyances

By Woody Leonhard, Lee Hudspeth & T.J. Lee
1st Edition October 1997
396 pages, ISBN 1-56592-310-3

Office 97 Annoyances illustrates step-by-step how to get control over the chaotic settings of Office 97 and shows how to turn the vast array of applications into a simplified list of customized tools. It focuses on the major components of Office 97, examines their integration or lack of it, and shows how to use this new Office suite in the most efficient way.

O'REILLY®

TO ORDER: **800-998-9938** • **order@oreilly.com** • **http://www.oreilly.com/**
OUR PRODUCTS ARE AVAILABLE AT A BOOKSTORE OR SOFTWARE STORE NEAR YOU.
FOR INFORMATION: **800-998-9938** • **707-829-0515** • **info@oreilly.com**

Hand-held Computers

PalmPilot: The Ultimate Guide

By David Pogue
1st Edition June 1998
520 pages, Includes CD-ROM
ISBN 1-56592-420-7

This PalmPilot "bible" covers the PalmPilot, PalmPilot Professional, and the new software and features of the 1998 PalmPilot model, the Palm III, as well as OEM models such as the IBM Workpad. Dense with undocumented information, it contains hundreds of timesaving tips and surprising tricks to help both intermediate and advanced users master this exciting new device. Includes CD-ROM containing 900 PalmPilot programs.

Palm Programming: The Developer's Guide

By Neil Rhodes & Julie McKeehan
1st Edition December 1998
482 pages, Includes CD-ROM
ISBN 1-56592-525-4

Emerging as the bestselling hand-held computers of all time, PalmPilots have spawned intense developer activity and a fanatical following. *Palm Programming*, endorsed by Palm as their official developer's guide, is a tutorial-style book eagerly awaited by developers and experienced C programmers. Includes a CD-ROM with source code and third-party developer tools.

How to stay in touch with O'Reilly

1. Visit Our Award-Winning Site

http://www.oreilly.com/

★ "Top 100 Sites on the Web" —*PC Magazine*
★ "Top 5% Web sites" —*Point Communications*
★ "3-Star site" —*The McKinley Group*

Our web site contains a library of comprehensive product information (including book excerpts and tables of contents), downloadable software, background articles, interviews with technology leaders, links to relevant sites, book cover art, and more. File us in your Bookmarks or Hotlist!

2. Join Our Email Mailing Lists

New Product Releases

To receive automatic email with brief descriptions of all new O'Reilly products as they are released, send email to:
listproc@online.oreilly.com
Put the following information in the first line of your message (*not* in the Subject field):
subscribe oreilly-news

O'Reilly Events

If you'd also like us to send information about trade show events, special promotions, and other O'Reilly events, send email to:
listproc@online.oreilly.com
Put the following information in the first line of your message (*not* in the Subject field):
subscribe oreilly-events

3. Get Examples from Our Books via FTP

There are two ways to access an archive of example files from our books:

Regular FTP
- ftp to:
  ftp.oreilly.com
  (login: anonymous
  password: your email address)
- Point your web browser to:
  ftp://ftp.oreilly.com/

FTPMAIL
- Send an email message to:
  ftpmail@online.oreilly.com
  (Write "help" in the message body)

4. Contact Us via Email

order@oreilly.com
To place a book or software order online. Good for North American and international customers.

subscriptions@oreilly.com
To place an order for any of our newsletters or periodicals.

books@oreilly.com
General questions about any of our books.

software@oreilly.com
For general questions and product information about our software. Check out O'Reilly Software Online at **http://software.oreilly.com/** for software and technical support information. Registered O'Reilly software users send your questions to:
website-support@oreilly.com

cs@oreilly.com
For answers to problems regarding your order or our products.

booktech@oreilly.com
For book content technical questions or corrections.

proposals@oreilly.com
To submit new book or software proposals to our editors and product managers.

international@oreilly.com
For information about our international distributors or translation queries. For a list of our distributors outside of North America check out:
http://www.oreilly.com/www/order/country.html

O'Reilly & Associates, Inc.
101 Morris Street, Sebastopol, CA 95472 USA
TEL   707-829-0515 or 800-998-9938
          (6am to 5pm PST)
FAX   707-829-0104

O'REILLY®

Titles from O'Reilly

WEB

Advanced Perl Programming
Apache: The Definitive Guide, 2nd Ed.
ASP in a Nutshell
Building Your Own Web Conferences
Building Your Own Website™
CGI Programming with Perl
Designing with JavaScript
Dynamic HTML: The Definitive Reference
Frontier: The Definitive Guide
HTML: The Definitive Guide, 3rd Ed.
Information Architecture for the World Wide Web
JavaScript Pocket Reference
JavaScript: The Definitive Guide, 3rd Ed.
Learning VB Script
Photoshop for the Web
WebMaster in a Nutshell
WebMaster in a Nutshell, Deluxe Ed.
Web Design in a Nutshell
Web Navigation: Designing the User Experience
Web Performance Tuning
Web Security & Commerce
Writing Apache Modules

PERL

Learning Perl, 2nd Ed.
Learning Perl for Win32 Systems
Learning Perl/TK
Mastering Algorithms with Perl
Mastering Regular Expressions
Perl5 Pocket Reference, 2nd Ed.
Perl Cookbook
Perl in a Nutshell
Perl Resource Kit—UNIX Ed.
Perl Resource Kit—Win32 Ed.
Perl/TK Pocket Reference
Programming Perl, 2nd Ed.
Web Client Programming with Perl

GRAPHICS & MULTIMEDIA

Director in a Nutshell
Encyclopedia of Graphics File Formats, 2nd Ed.
Lingo in a Nutshell
Photoshop in a Nutshell
QuarkXPress in a Nutshell

USING THE INTERNET

AOL in a Nutshell
Internet in a Nutshell
Smileys
The Whole Internet for Windows95
The Whole Internet: The Next Generation
The Whole Internet User's Guide & Catalog

JAVA SERIES

Database Programming with JDBC and Java
Developing Java Beans
Exploring Java, 2nd Ed.
Java AWT Reference
Java Cryptography
Java Distributed Computing
Java Examples in a Nutshell
Java Foundation Classes in a Nutshell
Java Fundamental Classes Reference
Java in a Nutshell, 2nd Ed.
Java in a Nutshell, Deluxe Ed.
Java I/O
Java Language Reference, 2nd Ed.
Java Media Players
Java Native Methods
Java Network Programming
Java Security
Java Servlet Programming
Java Swing
Java Threads
Java Virtual Machine

UNIX

Exploring Expect
GNU Emacs Pocket Reference
Learning GNU Emacs, 2nd Ed.
Learning the bash Shell, 2nd Ed.
Learning the Korn Shell
Learning the UNIX Operating System, 4th Ed.
Learning the vi Editor, 6th Ed.
Linux in a Nutshell
Linux Multimedia Guide
Running Linux, 2nd Ed.
SCO UNIX in a Nutshell
sed & awk, 2nd Ed.
Tcl/Tk in a Nutshell
Tcl/Tk Pocket Reference
Tcl/Tk Tools
The UNIX CD Bookshelf
UNIX in a Nutshell, System V Ed.
UNIX Power Tools, 2nd Ed.
Using csh & tsch
Using Samba
vi Editor Pocket Reference
What You Need To Know: When You Can't Find Your UNIX System Administrator
Writing GNU Emacs Extensions

SONGLINE GUIDES

NetLaw   NetResearch
NetLearning   NetSuccess
NetLessons   NetTravel

SOFTWARE

Building Your Own WebSite™
Building Your Own Web Conference
WebBoard™ 3.0
WebSite Professional™ 2.0
PolyForm™

SYSTEM ADMINISTRATION

Building Internet Firewalls
Computer Security Basics
Cracking DES
DNS and BIND, 3rd Ed.
DNS on WindowsNT
Essential System Administration
Essential WindowsNT System Administration
Getting Connected: The Internet at 56K and Up
Linux Network Administrator's Guide
Managing IP Networks with Cisco Routers
Managing Mailing Lists
Managing NFS and NIS
Managing the WindowsNT Registry
Managing Usenet
MCSE: The Core Exams in a Nutshell
MCSE: The Electives in a Nutshell
Networking Personal Computers with TCP/IP
Oracle Performance Tuning, 2nd Ed.
Practical UNIX & Internet Security, 2nd Ed.
PGP: Pretty Good Privacy
Protecting Networks with SATAN
sendmail, 2nd Ed.
sendmail Desktop Reference
System Performance Tuning
TCP/IP Network Administration, 2nd Ed.
termcap & terminfo
The Networking CD Bookshelf
Using & Managing PPP
Virtual Private Networks
WindowsNT Backup & Restore
WindowsNT Desktop Reference
WindowsNT Event Logging
WindowsNT in a Nutshell
WindowsNT Server 4.0 for Netware Administrators
WindowsNT SNMP
WindowsNT TCP/IP Administration
WindowsNT User Administration
Zero Administration for Windows

X WINDOW

Vol. 1: Xlib Programming Manual
Vol. 2: Xlib Reference Manual
Vol. 3M: X Window System User's Guide, Motif Ed.
Vol. 4M: X Toolkit Intrinsics Programming Manual, Motif Ed.
Vol. 5: X Toolkit Intrinsics Reference Manual
Vol. 6A: Motif Programming Manual
Vol. 6B: Motif Reference Manual
Vol. 8 : X Window System Administrator's Guide

PROGRAMMING

Access Database Design and Programming
Advanced Oracle PL/SQL Programming with Packages
Applying RCS and SCCS
BE Developer's Guide
BE Advanced Topics
C++: The Core Language
Checking C Programs with lint
Developing Windows Error Messages
Developing Visual Basic Add-ins
Guide to Writing DCE Applications
High Performance Computing, 2nd Ed.
Inside the Windows 95 File System
Inside the Windows 95 Registry
lex & yacc, 2nd Ed.
Linux Device Drivers
Managing Projects with make
Oracle8 Design Tips
Oracle Built-in Packages
Oracle Design
Oracle PL/SQL Programming, 2nd Ed.
Oracle Scripts
Oracle Security
Palm Programming: The Developer's Guide
Porting UNIX Software
POSIX Programmer's Guide
POSIX.4: Programming for the Real World
Power Programming with RPC
Practical C Programming, 3rd Ed.
Practical C++ Programming
Programming Python
Programming with curses
Programming with GNU Software
Pthreads Programming
Python Pocket Reference
Software Portability with imake, 2nd Ed.
UML in a Nutshell
Understanding DCE
UNIX Systems Programming for SVR4
VB/VBA in a Nutshell: The Languages
Win32 Multithreaded Programming
Windows NT File System Internals
Year 2000 in a Nutshell

USING WINDOWS

Excel97 Annoyances
Office97 Annoyances
Outlook Annoyances
Windows Annoyances
Windows98 Annoyances
Windows95 in a Nutshell
Windows98 in a Nutshell
Word97 Annoyances

OTHER TITLES

PalmPilot: The Ultimate Guide
Palm Programming: The Developer's Guide

O'REILLY®

TO ORDER: **800-998-9938** • **order@oreilly.com** • **http://www.oreilly.com/**
OUR PRODUCTS ARE AVAILABLE AT A BOOKSTORE OR SOFTWARE STORE NEAR YOU.
FOR INFORMATION: **800-998-9938** • **707-829-0515** • **info@oreilly.com**

International Distributors

UK, EUROPE, MIDDLE EAST AND AFRICA (EXCEPT FRANCE, GERMANY, AUSTRIA, SWITZERLAND, LUXEMBOURG, LIECHTENSTEIN, AND EASTERN EUROPE)

INQUIRIES
O'Reilly UK Limited
4 Castle Street
Farnham
Surrey, GU9 7HS
United Kingdom
Telephone: 44-1252-711776
Fax: 44-1252-734211
Email: josette@oreilly.com

ORDERS
Wiley Distribution Services Ltd.
1 Oldlands Way
Bognor Regis
West Sussex PO22 9SA
United Kingdom
Telephone: 44-1243-779777
Fax: 44-1243-820250
Email: cs-books@wiley.co.uk

FRANCE

ORDERS
GEODIF
61, Bd Saint-Germain
75240 Paris Cedex 05, France
Tel: 33-1-44-41-46-16 (French books)
Tel: 33-1-44-41-11-87 (English books)
Fax: 33-1-44-41-11-44
Email: distribution@eyrolles.com

INQUIRIES
Éditions O'Reilly
18 rue Séguier
75006 Paris, France
Tel: 33-1-40-51-52-30
Fax: 33-1-40-51-52-31
Email: france@editions-oreilly.fr

GERMANY, SWITZERLAND, AUSTRIA, EASTERN EUROPE, LUXEMBOURG, AND LIECHTENSTEIN

INQUIRIES & ORDERS
O'Reilly Verlag
Balthasarstr. 81
D-50670 Köln
Germany
Telephone: 49-221-973160-91
Fax: 49-221-973160-8
Email: anfragen@oreilly.de (inquiries)
Email: order@oreilly.de (orders)

CANADA (FRENCH LANGUAGE BOOKS)
Les Éditions Flammarion ltée
375, Avenue Laurier Ouest
Montréal (Québec) H2V 2K3
Tel: 00-1-514-277-8807
Fax: 00-1-514-278-2085
Email: info@flammarion.qc.ca

HONG KONG
City Discount Subscription Service, Ltd.
Unit D, 3rd Floor, Yan's Tower
27 Wong Chuk Hang Road
Aberdeen, Hong Kong
Tel: 852-2580-3539
Fax: 852-2580-6463
Email: citydis@ppn.com.hk

KOREA
Hanbit Media, Inc.
Sonyoung Bldg. 202
Yeksam-dong 736-36
Kangnam-ku
Seoul, Korea
Tel: 822-554-9610
Fax: 822-556-0363
Email: hant93@chollian.dacom.co.kr

PHILIPPINES
Mutual Books, Inc.
429-D Shaw Boulevard
Mandaluyong City, Metro
Manila, Philippines
Tel: 632-725-7538
Fax: 632-721-3056
Email: mbikikog@mnl.sequel.net

TAIWAN
O'Reilly Taiwan
No. 3, Lane 131
Hang-Chow South Road
Section 1, Taipei, Taiwan
Tel: 886-2-23968990
Fax: 886-2-23968916
Email: benh@oreilly.com

CHINA
O'Reilly Beijing
Room 2410
160, FuXingMenNeiDaJie
XiCheng District
Beijing
China PR 100031
Tel: 86-10-86631006
Fax: 86-10-86631007
Email: frederic@oreilly.com

INDIA
Computer Bookshop (India) Pvt. Ltd.
190 Dr. D.N. Road, Fort
Bombay 400 001 India
Tel: 91-22-207-0989
Fax: 91-22-262-3551
Email: cbsbom@giasbm01.vsnl.net.in

JAPAN
O'Reilly Japan, Inc.
Kiyoshige Building 2F
12-Bancho, Sanei-cho
Shinjuku-ku
Tokyo 160-0008 Japan
Tel: 81-3-3356-5227
Fax: 81-3-3356-5261
Email: japan@oreilly.com

ALL OTHER ASIAN COUNTRIES
O'Reilly & Associates, Inc.
101 Morris Street
Sebastopol, CA 95472 USA
Tel: 707-829-0515
Fax: 707-829-0104
Email: order@oreilly.com

AUSTRALIA
WoodsLane Pty., Ltd.
7/5 Vuko Place
Warriewood NSW 2102
Australia
Tel: 61-2-9970-5111
Fax: 61-2-9970-5002
Email: info@woodslane.com.au

NEW ZEALAND
Woodslane New Zealand, Ltd.
21 Cooks Street (P.O. Box 575)
Waganui, New Zealand
Tel: 64-6-347-6543
Fax: 64-6-345-4840
Email: info@woodslane.com.au

LATIN AMERICA
McGraw-Hill Interamericana
Editores, S.A. de C.V.
Cedro No. 512
Col. Atlampa
06450, Mexico, D.F.
Tel: 52-5-547-6777
Fax: 52-5-547-3336
Email: mcgraw-hill@infosel.net.mx

O'REILLY®